Historical Dictionary of the Third French Republic, 1870–1940

Historical Dictionaries of French History

This five-volume series covers French history from the Revolution through the Third Republic. It provides comprehensive coverage of each era, including not only political and military history but also social, economic, and art history.

Historical Dictionary of the French Revolution, 1789–1799
Samuel F. Scott and Barry Rothaus, editors

Historical Dictionary of Napoleonic France, 1799–1815
Owen Connelly, editor

Historical Dictionary of France from the 1815 Restoration to the Second Empire
Edgar Leon Newman, editor

Historical Dictionary of the French Second Empire, 1852–1870
William E. Echard, editor

Historical Dictionary of the Third French Republic, 1870–1940
Patrick H. Hutton, editor-in-chief

Historical Dictionary of the Third French Republic, 1870–1940

A-L

PATRICK H. HUTTON,
Editor-in-Chief

AMANDA S. BOURQUE *and*
AMY J. STAPLES,
Assistant Editors

Greenwood Press
New York • Westport, Connecticut

Library of Congress Cataloging in Publication Data
Main entry under title:

Historical dictionary of the Third French Republic,
    1870–1940.

  Bibliography: p.
  Includes index.
  1. France—History—Third Republic, 1870-1940—
Dictionaries. I. Hutton, Patrick H. II. Bourque,
Amanda S. III. Staples, Amy J.
DC337.H57   1986   944.081′03′21   84-15737
ISBN 0-313-22080-8 (lib. bdg.)
ISBN 0-313-25551-2 (lib. bdg. : v.1)
ISBN 0-313-25552-0 (lib. bdg. : v.2)

Library of Congress Catalog Card Number: 84-15737
ISBN: 0-313-22080-8 (set)
ISBN 0-313-25551-2 (v.1)
ISBN 0-313-25552-0 (v.2)

First published in 1986

Greenwood Press, Inc.
88 Post Road West
Westport, Connecticut 06881

Printed in the United States of America

The paper used in this book complies with the
Permanent Paper Standard issued by the National
Information Standards Organization (Z39.48-1984).

10 9 8 7 6 5 4 3 2 1

Contents

Contributors

Robert Aldrich, Department of History, University of Sydney (Australia)
Jane P. Ambrose, Department of Music, University of Vermont
Kathryn E. Amdur, Department of History, Emory University
Julian P. W. Archer, Department of History, Drake University
Oscar L. Arnal, Department of Religion and Culture, Wilfred Laurier University
Susan A. Ashley, Department of History, Colorado College
Philip C. F. Bankwitz, Department of History, Trinity College
William R. Beer, Department of Sociology, Brooklyn College
Michael Berkvam, Department of French, Indiana University
Patrick K. Bidelman, Department of History, Purdue University
Carol L. Bird, West Virginia Wesleyan College
Joel Blatt, Department of History, University of Connecticut at Stamford
Jeanette D. Bragger, Department of French, Pennsylvania State University
John R. Braun, Department of History, University of Waterloo
James B. Briscoe, Department of History, University of Arkansas
Marvin L. Brown, Jr., Department of History, North Carolina State University
Michael Burns, Department of History, Mount Holyoke College
Frederick Busi, Department of French, University of Massachusetts
Stuart L. Campbell, Department of History, Alfred University
Philippe Carrard, Department of Romance Languages, University of Vermont
Larry Ceplair, Los Angeles, California
Myrna Chase, Mount Morris, New York
Lisa C. Chewning, West Virginia Wesleyan College
Petra ten-Doesschate Chu, Department of Art, Seton Hall University
Linda L. Clark, Department of History, Millersville State College
Lynn H. Cline, University of Vermont
William B. Cohen, Department of History, Indiana University
Barbara T. Cooper, Department of Romance Languages, University of New Hampshire

Wallace L. Cooper, Exeter Area High School, Exeter, New Hampshire
Grant Crichfield, Department of Romance Languages, University of Vermont
Gary S. Cross, Department of History, Pennsylvania State University
Charles R. Day, Department of History, Simon Fraser University
Leslie Derfler, Department of History, Florida Atlantic University
C. Stewart Doty, Department of History, University of Maine
Allen Douglas, Department of History, University of Southern Mississippi
John E. Dreifort, Department of History, Wichita State University
Donald E. English, Department of History, Stanford University
Marjorie M. Farrar, Chestnut Hill, Massachusetts
Janis Kilduff Franklin, Department of Art History, Virginia Commonwealth
  University
Charles E. Freedeman, Department of History, State University of New York
  at Binghamton
James Friguglietti, Department of History, Eastern Montana College
Rachel G. Fuchs, Department of History, University of Arizona at Tempe
Daniel W. Gade, Department of Geography, University of Vermont
Emily W. Galvin, University of Vermont
David E. Gardinier, Department of History, Marquette University
Reed G. Geiger, Department of History, University of Delaware
Thomas H. Geno, Department of Romance Languages, University of Vermont
Charlotte F. Gerrard, Department of French and Italian, Indiana University
Mary Jean Green, Department of French and Italian, Dartmouth College
Louis M. Greenberg, Department of History, University of Maryland
Alan C. Grubb, Department of History, Clemson University
Jeffery A. Gunsburg, Department of History, Virginia Military Institute
Joy H. Hall, Department of History, Troy State University
Paul G. Halpern, Department of History, Florida State University
Carolyn J. Hamm, Department of History, University of Vermont
Michael Hanagan, Department of History, Columbia University
Patrick J. Harrigan, Department of History, University of Waterloo
C. James Haug, Department of History, Mississippi State University
Steven C. Hause, Department of History, University of Missouri at St. Louis
Claire D. Hebert, University of Vermont
Alf Andrew Heggoy, Department of History, University of Georgia
John W. Hellman, Department of History, McGill University
Paul M. Hohenberg, Department of Economics, Rensselaer Polytechnic Institute
William A. Hoisington, Jr., Department of History, University of Illinois at
  Chicago Circle
Jolyon Howorth, School of Modern Languages, University of Bath (England)
Patrick H. Hutton, Department of History, University of Vermont
John K. Hyde, Department of French and Italian, Indiana University
Georg G. Iggers, Department of History, State University of New York at Buffalo
William D. Irvine, Department of History, York University

Joel Isaacson, Department of Art History, University of Michigan
Jean T. Joughin, Department of History, American University
Roy G. Julow, Department of Romance Languages, University of Vermont
William R. Keylor, Department of History, Boston University
Thomas A. Kselman, Department of History, University of Notre Dame
Richard F. Kuisel, Department of History, State University of New York at Stony Brook
James M. Laux, Department of History, University of Cincinnati
Laurie LeClair, University of Vermont
John E. Lesch, Department of History, University of California at Berkeley
Miriam R. Levin, Amherst, Massachusetts
William H. Logue, Department of History, Northern Illinois University
Leo A. Loubère, Department of History, State University of New York at Buffalo
Miriam D. Maayan, Institute for Historical Research, New York, New York
Linda C. Maley, University of Vermont
Theresa McBride, Department of History, College of the Holy Cross
Mary Lee McIsaac, University of Vermont
Sally Marks, Department of History, Rhode Island College
Benjamin F. Martin, Department of History, Louisiana State University
Michael R. Marrus, Department of History, University of Toronto
David J. Martz, Jr., University of Toledo
Judson I. Mather, Department of Humanities, Michigan State University
Paul Mazgaj, Department of History, University of North Carolina at Greensboro
John Merriman, Department of History, Yale University
Peter V. Meyers, Department of History, North Carolina Agricultural and Technical State University
Martin L. Mickelsen, Rome, Georgia
Allan Mitchell, Department of History, University of California at San Diego
Paul Monaco, Department of History, University of Texas at Dallas
Thomas Moodie, Department of History, Lake Forest College
Bernard H. Moss, Department of History, The University of Auckland (New Zealand)
J. Kim Munholland, Department of History, University of Minnesota
Reverend Francis J. Murphy, Department of History, Boston College
David S. Newhall, Department of History, Centre College of Kentucky
Philip G. Nord, Department of History, Princeton University
Mary Jo Nye, Department of History, University of Oklahoma
Robert A. Nye, Department of History, University of Oklahoma
Patricia A. O'Brien, Department of History, University of California at Irvine
J. Dean O'Donnell, Department of History, Virginia Polytechnic Institute and State University
Karen M. Offen, Center for Research on Women, Stanford University
Robert F. O'Reilly, Department of French, Syracuse University
Jane C. Overton, Boston College

Nicholas Papayanis, Department of History, Brooklyn College
Allan H. Pasco, Department of French, Purdue University
Henry D. Peiter, Center for Western European Studies, University of Michigan
David B. Ralston, Department of Humanities, Massachusetts Institute of Technology
Charles W. Rearick, Department of History, University of Massachusetts
Jack E. Reece, Department of History, University of Pennsylvania
J. Merle Rife, Jr., Department of History, Indiana University of Pennsylvania
John Rothney, Department of History, Ohio State University
Peter M. Rutkoff, Department of History, Kenyon College
Roy E. Sandstrom, Department of History, University of Northern Iowa
David L. Schalk, Department of History, Vassar College
Wolfe W. Schmokel, Department of History, University of Vermont
Frederic H. Seager, Department of History, University of Montreal
Alexander Sedgwick, Department of History, University of Virginia
Michael L. Seidman, Department of History, Rutgers University
Josefina Z. Sevilla-Gardinier, Milwaukee, Wisconsin
Gary Shanafelt, Department of History, McMurry College
Theda Shapiro, Department of Languages and Literature, University of California at Riverside
George J. Sheridan, Department of History, University of Oregon
John M. Sherwood, Department of History, Queens University
William I. Shorrock, Department of History, Cleveland State University
Martin Siegel, Department of History, Kean College of New Jersey
Bonnie G. Smith, Department of History, University of Rochester
Michael S. Smith, Department of History, University of South Carolina
Robert J. Smith, Department of History, State University of New York at Brockport
David A. Stafford, Department of History, Victoria University
Amy J. Staples, University of Vermont
Henry J. Steffens, Department of History, University of Vermont
Judith F. Stone, Department of History, Reed College
Jacques Szaluta, Department of History, U.S. Merchant Marine Academy
Robert W. Thurston, Department of History, University of Texas at El Paso
David G. Troyansky, Department of History, Brandeis University
Marjorie Field Trusler, Department of French, West Virginia Wesleyan College
Irwin M. Wall, Department of History, University of California at Riverside
Patricia A. Ward, Department of French, Pennsylvania State University
Gabriel P. Weisberg, Department of Fine Arts, University of Pittsburgh
Lee Shai Weissbach, Department of History, University of Louisville
George Weisz, Department of Humanities and Social Studies in Medicine, McGill University
Susan M. Whitebook, Department of Romance Languages, University of Vermont
John K. Whiting, University of Vermont
Roger L. Williams, Department of History, University of Wyoming

Rosalind H. Williams, Department of the Humanities, Massachusetts Institute of Technology

Judith Wishnia, Interdisciplinary Program in the Social Sciences, State University of New York at Stony Brook

David Wright, Department of History, University of Wisconsin

Preface

The *Historical Dictionary of the Third French Republic* is the first comprehensive work of reference in its field, in either French or English. Containing over 750 entries written largely by American scholars, the volume scans all aspects of French civilization between 1870 and 1940. That it has become possible to compile such a volume is a measure of the maturity that the study of modern French history has achieved in the United States. Long in the shadow of the more popular topic of the French Revolution, historical writing about the Third Republic in this country effectively dates from the era of reconstruction after World War II when American students of French history, looking beyond the humiliation of the Vichy regime, sought to evaluate the prospects for the Fourth Republic by examining the strength and depth of the French commitment to liberal democracy in the Third. French political democracy, while in many ways unique, sprang from the same eighteenth-century intellectual sources as our own political tradition, and its development, especially as made manifest in the Third Republic, provides important parallels with the political experience of our own country. Since then, the rapid growth and diversification of historical writing about the Third Republic has continued to reflect the changing meanings American scholars have sought to derive from the French experience—from their inquiries in the 1950s into the dynamics of French parliamentary politics, to their interest in the 1960s in popular movements and radical ideologies, to their studies in the 1970s of social structure, everyday life, and popular culture. Each of these approaches has produced studies of intrinsic interest, yet each casts light on the intellectual and political preoccupations of succeeding generations of American historians. In the process, a historiographical tradition has been elaborated. The *Dictionary* is a useful way of gathering up these accumulating interests.

Political topics are important elements of this volume, but social, economic, and cultural issues also receive detailed attention. For this reason, the *Dictionary* will be a valuable resource not only for students of French history but also for those in literature, art, and the social sciences. The volume contains biographies of nearly all of the leading personalities in politics, the arts, and intellectual life, and it includes as well a wide range of topical entries dealing with institutions, movements, organizations, and ideas. In addition, it contains twenty-four long, interpretive essays that provide an overview of major areas of human endeavor. The broad rubrics with which the *Dictionary* has been composed—delineated by entry in Appendix I—include:

1. Politics: Politicians, journalists, governmental institutions, ideologies, parties and movements, major events, foreign affairs, overseas empire, military topics

2. Society: Social stratification, social mores and attitudes

3. Economics: Industry and commerce, the labor movement

4. Culture: Writers, savants, artists, and musicians; artistic, intellectual, and scientific movements; media; education; religion; geography

The *Dictionary* will be of particular value to students seeking acquaintance for the first time with French civilization during the Third Republic. Each of the entries provides clear definitions and essential facts and presupposes no prior knowledge of the topics discussed. But it will also be useful to mature scholars already familiar with this field because it identifies recent scholarship and unifies so many specialized areas of learning. To group so many diverse topics in a single volume, moreover, is bound to reveal unsuspected relationships among them. In this sense, the *Dictionary* marks the boundaries of current scholarly interest in this field. It is my hope that it will provide not only a handbook of practical knowledge about the Third Republic but a resource for stimulating new lines of research as well. Some of the entries, while of necessity brief, outline and interpret topics not treated directly or comprehensively before.

The entries vary in length (from biographies of 150 words to interpretive topical essays of 3,000), but all follow a common format, whose essential elements are as follows:

1. Topics are listed alphabetically, according to their common names or the labels by which they are most easily identified. For biographies, the French tendency to list a lengthy string of given names has been discarded in favor of mentioning only the one ordinarily used. Those individuals known primarily by pseudonyms have been so listed. Birth and death dates follow all biographical topic identifications. Dates for the other entries are given only if they do not correspond to the entire Third Republic (1870–1940).

2. The first phrase identifies the topic concisely so that the reader will recognize the nature of the entry at a glance.

3. The body of each entry provides essential facts about the topic under discussion. The focus is on the experience of the Third Republic, but in instances in which the subject

matter predates and/or extends beyond that era, enough data are included to be sure the topic is coherently presented.

4. The full names of organizations and the first names of persons are given on first mention in each entry. Abbreviations or acronyms are employed only when they have already been spelled out previously in the same entry. The dates of important events in most cases accompany their first citation in following parentheses. Appendix III, a chronology of major events of the Third Republic, will provide a helpful supplementary reference.

5. The concluding sentence or paragraph usually offers some evaluation of the meaning or significance of the topic.

6. The text of each entry is followed by a brief bibliography. Of necessity, these are selective, but the works cited are standard or recent studies or those particularly valuable for their more extensive bibliographies. They will be valuable as points of departure for further research.

7. Most entries conclude with a list of related entries, which will provide a context or additional information on the subject discussed. Readers will also find Appendix I, which groups entries by topics, useful in this respect.

The *Dictionary* has been very much a cooperative venture. One hundred fifty-three scholars have contributed, most of them American but with a sizable contingent of Canadians, and I have been gratified by their enthusiasm for this project. In my search for contributors, I became acquainted with a fair number of the North American scholars currently working in Third Republic studies. I have been impressed with the breadth of their interests and the high standards of scholarship they have set for their research and writing. I thank especially those who had the vision (and courage) to draft the interpretive and thematic entries. Among colleagues who were willing to prepare multiple entries, I owe special thanks to Theda Shapiro, who helped me formulate the scheme for entries dealing with art and who then proceeded to write most of these entries herself. I am also grateful to David Newhall, who, steeped in knowledge of the Third Republic through his work on Georges Clemenceau, volunteered for and composed with skill a number of entries long in search of an author. Many of my colleagues at the University of Vermont participated in the project; in this venture as in so many others they have my admiration and respect. I also had the pleasure of permitting a few of my most able students in French history to prepare entries under my supervision.

I wish to thank Susan Baker and Cynthia Harris, editors at Greenwood Press, for their advice, encouragement, and patience at all stages of my work. I am also most appreciative for the support of the Graduate College of the University of Vermont for a grant to defray the clerical expenses of this project. In the end, the foundation of a work of reference is the detail of preparation. Reams of correspondence have circulated in and out of the History Department for the past four years, and there have been unending chores of recording and typing. For these services, I am in awe of the loyalty of a number of talented and underpaid secretaries and study assistants, among them Kimberly Parsons, Carolyn Perry, Susan Lacy, Lee McIsaac, Matthew Hutton, Sean Hutton, and Susan Tobler. Without the moral encouragement and material help of my assistant editors (and former students) Amanda S. Bourque, who did all of the recording and supervised most of the correspondence in the early stages of the project, and Amy J. Staples, who wrote more entries than any other contributor, I could not have persevered with this project. Prepared with my students in mind, this *Dictionary* is dedicated to them. May their excursions into this rich field of history be easier for its existence.

P. H. H.

The Dictionary

A

ACTION FRANCAISE (1898-1944), a militantly nationalist and royalist movement that, from its inception at the time of the Dreyfus affair until it was superseded by the facist leagues of the 1930s, was the cutting edge of the radical Right in France. Founded in 1898, the Action française was hardly more than a nationalist study circle until Charles Maurras, young and virtually unknown, came to the movement and gave it a doctrinal basis in royalism and antirepublicanism. Singlehandedly Maurras not only converted the existing membership to royalism but won over some of the most talented anti-Dreyfusards from the older nationalist leagues, most notably Léon Daudet, with whom Maurras launched the daily *Action française* in 1908. The newspaper, which became the focal point of Action française operations, blended tightly and often exquisitely reasoned political commentary with verbal violence toward individuals, races, and nations rarely equaled even in the gutter press.

In the decade before 1914, years of growth for the Action française, the neoroyalists distinguished themselves by their persistent efforts to put together a new coalition in support of monarchism. Predictably, they had some appeal among the older rightist clienteles, battered in the wake of their defeat in the Dreyfus affair—conservative Catholics, the army and nobility, and the rank and file of the nationalist leagues of the 1890s. Yet the neoroyalists attempted more than a resurrection for the nineteenth-century Right and worked to fuse a reactionary and elitist traditionalism with a radical and populist nationalism. Armed with this new amalgam, they assiduously courted two new groups. To the conservatively inclined but activist prewar youth cohort, they offered the Camelots du roi, an organization that, foreshadowing interwar paramilitary groups, became famous for its street brawling and periodic disruptions of public order. To agitated workers, taken up with revolutionary syndicalism and involved in bloody confrontations with the Republic, they sent public expressions of solidarity and made private overtures for a joint offensive against the republican status quo. Despite the modesty of their practical success along these lines, especially with the labor movement, the neoroyalists did breathe some new life into the French radical Right, managing not only to lend it an avant-garde allure but also to infuse it with many of the features of interwar fascism.

The height of the movement's influence came during and just after World War I when both its intransigent nationalism and its anti-Communism were well received in France. This newly found influence, however, was purchased at the price of throttling its antirepublicanism; not only did the Action française support the wartime *union sacrée*, but it also involved itself in electoral politics, forbidden fruit before the war. This latter venture not only infuriated some of the more radical militants, who complained of domestication, but yielded mediocre results. Although neoroyalist influence was more widespread than ever among the elite, it did not translate into extensive mass support. The Action française never managed to bridge the gap between an immensely influential pressure group and a viable mass movement.

The mid-1920s saw the beginning of a long but steady decline of the movement's prestige and influence, even among an elite. First came condemnation from the Vatican in 1926. Over a period of years, this condemnation cut deeply into neoroyalist membership and into the sympathies of fellow-traveling Catholic intellectuals. Even more serious was the increased competition from the newer fascist leagues to which the Action française lost some of its most talented younger recruits. By the 1930s, the Action française was beginning to be an anachronism on a radical Right that now wore uniforms, had dynamic young leaders, and no longer talked of restoring kings. The decline of the neoroyalists was hastened by their failure to find a realistic policy toward Nazi Germany. This last failure—not uncommon on the French Right in the 1930s—had its origin in the refusal to pay the price for an all-out effort against Hitler. The neoroyalists balked at the idea of allying externally with the Soviet Union and internally with the antifascist Left, including, most unpalatably for them, Communists and Jews. The tide of decline was temporarily halted with the advent of the Vichy regime in 1940 (which ironically realized much of the neoroyalist program) but proceeded apace after 1942. When the Vichy regime went down amid recrimination and ignominy in 1944, the Action française shared its fate.

P. Mazgaj, *The Action Française and Revolutionary Syndicalism* (Chapel Hill, N.C., 1979); C. C. Peter, *Charles Maurras et l'idéologie d'Action française* (Paris, 1972); E. R. Tannenbaum, *The Action Française* (New York, 1962); E. Weber, *Action Française* (Stanford, Calif., 1962).

P. Mazgaj

Related entries: CAMELOTS DU ROI; CONSERVATISM; DAUDET, L.; DREYFUS AFFAIR; FASCISM; MAURRAS.

ACTION LIBERALE POPULAIRE, the first modern political party of the conservatives, active between 1899 and 1914. The Action libérale populaire had its origin in a legislative faction formed in 1899 by Albert de Mun and Jacques Piou to group the Ralliés, Progressists, and Independents of the Chamber of

Deputies. In June 1901, de Mun and Piou transformed it into an organized political party of the Center-Right with a wide popular base to oppose the left-wing republican coalition led first by René Waldeck-Rousseau and later by Emile Combes. Between 1901 and 1914, the party never managed to elect more than seventy-eight deputies in any single election (1902), despite establishing a nationwide press and propaganda network and attracting large monetary contributions, some of which were illegal and were laundered through a London bank. Nevertheless, the Action libérale populaire did establish an organization— 1,200 local election committees and 200,000 dues-paying members (1906)— that no other political party was able to equal before World War I.

B. F. Martin, "The Creation of the Action Libérale Populaire," *French Historical Studies* 9 (1976); P. T. Moon, *The Labor Problem and the Social Catholic Movement in France* (New York, 1921).

B. F. Martin

Related entries: COMBES; MUN; PIOU; PROGRESSISTS; RADICAL AND RADICAL-SOCIALIST PARTY; WALDECK-ROUSSEAU.

ADAM, JULIETTE (1836-1936), conservative feminist and influential *revancharde*. Known simply as Madame Adam after her marriage to the future Senator Edmond Adam in 1868, the former Juliette Lamber twice intervened on behalf of women's rights. Her first intervention came in 1858 when, provoked by Pierre-Joseph Proudhon's attacks on women in general and her friends George Sand and Daniel Stern in particular, she wrote *Idées antiproudhoniennes sur l'amour, la femme et le mariage*. A major contribution to the literary foundation on which others subsequently organized the feminist movement, Adam's treatise lauded motherhood in the name of gender equivalence but juxtaposed to Proudhon's option of *ménagère ou courtisane* a vision of women endowed with full civil rights and equal employment opportunities.

Adam's second intervention came in 1893 when she joined Jeanne Schmahl's conservative group, l'Avant courrière. Of the group's two demands, Adam especially felt the need for the right of wives to control their own income (enacted in 1907), the absence of which had plagued her throughout a stormy first marriage. She was also drawn to the group's eclectic composition, which included the former Boulangist and Roman Catholic Duchesse Marie-Clémentine d'Uzès. She parted company with Schmahl and d'Uzès, however, when they helped to found in 1909 the Union française pour le suffrage des femmes. In Adam's opinion, women's suffrage would compound the disaster that manhood suffrage had already inflicted on France by further subverting the likelihood of meritocratic government.

Adam's sharp rejection of universal suffrage coincided with a conservative shift in her political outlook. During the late Second Empire and throughout the first decade of the Third Republic, her salon served as one of the most influential centers of anticlerical republicanism in Paris, and, according to the Orléanist Duc Albert de Broglie, Adam herself emerged as the soul of the republican opposition during the 1877 *seize mai* crisis. By then too she had helped to project

Léon Gambetta into the first rank of French politicians. Yet when Gambetta proved willing to use diplomacy to seek redress from Bismarckian Germany, Adam broke with him and began a lifelong drift to the Right. Never able to overcome the chagrin of France's defeat in the war of 1870–71, she created *La Nouvelle Revue* in 1879, through which, in addition to promoting young writers such as Paul Bourget and Pierre Loti, she personally trumpeted *revanche* for the next twenty years. *Revanche* in turn required closer ties to Russia, she argued, but even the 1894 Franco-Russian alliance failed to stem her rightward drift. Consequently, by the time that she enlisted in the Croisade des femmes françaises to help maintain women's morale during World War I, Adam had become virtually an inversion of her former self, an inversion presaged in anti-Dreyfusardism and fully consummated in a wartime return to religious faith.

J. Adam, *Mes souvenirs*, 6 vols. (Paris, 1902–10); Dossier Madam Adam (Paris, Bibliothèque Marguerite Durand); J. O. Baylen, "Mme. Juliette Adam, Gambetta, and the Idea of a Franco-Russian Alliance," *Social Studies No. 4* (20 May 1960); P. Bidelman, *Pariahs Stand Up!* (Westport, Conn., 1982); C. Moses, *French Feminism in the Nineteenth Century* (Albany, 1984); W. Stephens, *Madam Adam* (New York, 1917).

P. K. Bidelman

Related entries: BROGLIE; DREYFUS AFFAIR; FEMINISM; GAMBETTA; SCHMAHL; *SEIZE MAI* CRISIS; UZES; WOMEN: MOVEMENT FOR CIVIL RIGHTS.

ADAM, PAUL (1882–1920), novelist, journalist, and essayist of some renown during the Third Republic. Of modest means, Adam sought to make a living as a writer from an early age. Despite some initial difficulties (prosecution for the explicit eroticism of his first novel, *Chair molle*, 1886), he soon established his reputation as an author. In the course of his career, he published some sixty books, mostly novels but also collections of travel memoirs and essays in literary criticism.

As a young man, he flirted briefly with politics. In 1889, he accompanied Maurice Barrès to Nancy, where they organized the Boulangist electoral campaign. If his own candidacy for the Chamber of Deputies (Nancy, Second district) failed, the campaign provided him with material for one of his most successful novels, *Le Mystère des foules* (1895), closely modeled on his own experiences.

Thenceforth Adam devoted himself exclusively to his literary endeavor. He was a highly eclectic novelist in terms of both style and subject matter. In his early work, he sought to identify himself with the most innovative literary trends of the late nineteenth century, notably with naturalism and symbolism. He possessed a special fascination with the occult, exotic cultures, and the irrational sources of group psychology. Adam's travels, like his imagination, took him to faraway places, which served as the settings for many of his novels. But his historical novels of early nineteenth-century France (a tetralogy beginning with *La Force*, 1899) have received the higher critical acclaim. While Adam's early novels were self-conscious attempts to explore the possibilities of this genre as an art form, his later writings became increasingly didactic as he sought to reaffirm the idealism of the Enlightenment in an age that was beginning to doubt its efficacy. The specific causes that Adam championed, however, never embodied the transcendent idealism he extolled. If his political attitudes were liberal, they were also elitist and chauvinistic. Fearing the mediocrity of mass society and the protean irrationality of crowds, he advocated a political meritocracy in which only the educated (the *bacheliers*) would be eligible to vote or to hold public office. A partisan of revenge against Germany for the loss of Alsace-Lorraine in the Franco-Prussian War (1870–1871), he preached a xenophobic nationalism with growing fervor until the end of the First World War (1918).

Today Adam is largely forgotten. Although he was a talented and versatile author, his ideas and his style were too bound up in the transient interests of his own day to have an enduring appeal. He is to be remembered, nonetheless, as a rare yet easily identifiable intellectual type in the Third Republic: the savant for whom literature was less a career than a vocation.

J. Balteau, ed., *Dictionnaire de biographie française* (Paris, 1933), vol. 1; A. Beaunier, "Paul Adam," *Revue des deux mondes* 55 (1920); J. A. Duncan, "The Early Novels of Paul Adam, "*Modern Language Review* 69 (1974); G. Richard, "Le Boulangisme à Nancy," *Pays lorrain* (1962).

P. H. Hutton

Related entries: BARRES; BOULANGER AFFAIR; LITERATURE; SYMBOLISM.

AFFAIRE DES FICHES (1904), an epilogue to the Dreyfus affair involving the exposure of a private espionage network used to spy on army officers in an effort to republicanize the army. This system was used by the René Waldeck-Rousseau (1899–1902) and Emile Combes (1902–5) regimes in the hope of purging army officers identified with the traditional (conservative, royalist, and Catholic) background of the army officer corps. It was carried out by the Masonic lodges, which transmitted information on the religious devotions of army officers to their headquarters (Grand Orient) in Paris. The information was then relayed to General Louis André, minister of war (1901–4) and a confirmed anticlerical. This information was used to reward the agnostic officers and to punish those who attended religious observances. Over 3,000 small slips of paper, or *fiches*, were discovered, divided into two groups: Corinthe (the officers to advance) and Carthage (officers who would not be promoted). The affair ended in a violent interpellation in the Chamber of Deputies on 28 October 1904 by the nationalist deputy, Guyot de Villeneuve. After unconvincingly defending himself in front of the Chamber, General André resigned his post. This scandal prompted the downfall of the entire Combes cabinet on 18 January 1905.

R. D. Anderson, *France, 1870–1914: Politics and Society* (London, 1977); J. Balteau, *Dictionnaire de biographie française* (Paris, 1933); J. Chastenet, *Histoire de la Troisième*

République (Paris, 1955); J. B. Duroselle, *La France et les français, 1900–1914* (Paris, 1972); J. Paul-Boncour, *Recollections of the Third Republic* (New York, 1957).

A. J. Staples

Related entries: COMBES; DREYFUS AFFAIR; ROMAN CATHOLICISM: CHURCH-STATE RELATIONS.

AGING. France was the first nation to experience the aging of populations that has been associated with modernization. As a result of its falling fertility rate, the population of France had been growing old since the start of the nineteenth century and continued to age throughout the Third Republic, when demographic trends were frequently noted with much alarm. France consistently had the most mature population in the world. In 1800 7 percent of the population was aged sixty or over. By mid-century the figure reached 10 percent, by 1900 12 percent, and by 1940 15 percent. In the same century and a half, women comprised an increasing majority of the aged. As they bore fewer children and obstetrical care improved, they succumbed less often to birth-related maladies. While they outlived men, however, they remarried less frequently.

Aging varied in its intensity from region to region. Normandy and much of the southwest had aged earlier than other regions, but by the end of the nineteenth century some northern and eastern areas had caught up. On the whole, the generational split occurred along urban-rural lines. As the city was becoming the focus of the French economy and the countryside was being abandoned by those of working age, much of rural France became dominated by the elderly. Aged villagers were joined by new retirees, sometimes natives of the village, returning from careers in the city.

Until World War I, displacement in old age was common among the working classes, particularly working-class widows who could no longer afford to live in the city. Retirement to the country became a middle-class phenomenon only after World War II. Between the world wars, though, working-class retirement to the country declined, and the urban old stayed put. Center city neighborhoods whose small apartments were suited for people living alone attracted the elderly widowed as well as the young unmarried. As certain French industries declined, their workers aged around them.

The cause of demographic aging was the falling birthrate, exacerbated somewhat by an unevenly declining mortality rate at birth. Contemporaries failed to identify falling natality as the prime reason for aging—aging from below—and placed more emphasis on longer life expectancy—aging from above. This view was corrected through studies by Alfred Sauvy and other demographers in the 1940s.

Falling natality, however, had not gone unnoticed during the Third Republic. It was remarked upon by alarmists of all political persuasions who viewed depopulation as the great enemy of French power and prestige. Indeed, net rates of reproduction remained below replacement level in every decade from the 1890s through the 1930s. Depopulation was blamed for military defeat at the hands of the Prussians and French failure to compete with other national economies of Europe. The First World War was seen as a test between populous Germany and depopulated France, and the loss of a generation of Frenchmen in that war compounded the problem. Historians of the Third Republic have seen a relationship between demographic troubles and political and economic stagnation and have characterized the Republic and the subsequent Vichy regime as a period of gerontocracy.

Clearly the solution to demographic aging and depopulation was to raise the birthrate, but it was not until the late 1940s that pronatalist policies succeeded in reversing the aging trend. Moreover, a solution to demographic aging would have had no effect on the plight of the aged themselves, who were considered more a symbol of a demographic problem than a problem in their own right. French culture has been accused of traditional prejudice against the aged, and the nineteenth century saw little progress in old age assistance. But some doctors and politicians began to address the growing problem of *le troisième âge* (as old age came to be called).

The aged inmates of the large Parisian hospitals of Bicêtre (for men) and the Salpêtrière (for women) proved useful subjects for medical study. Important geriatric research by Drs. Jean-Martin Charcot, Joseph Reveillé-Parise, and Maxime Durand-Fardel in the 1850s and 1860s was furthered by such Third Republic doctors as Georges Rauzier, Boy-Teissier, and Otto Josué. But some of the work—for example, the experiments in rejuvenation by Charles-Edouard Brown-Séquard—was simply fanciful. Geriatric medicine had no effect on longevity; life expectancy at age sixty remained constant throughout the nineteenth century. Medical research on the aged fell into decline after the First World War.

Beginning in the 1890s old age was taken up as a social question. The vast majority of France's aged lived either alone or among relatives. An amendment of 9 March 1891 reaffirmed the Civil Code's requirement that support of parents and other ascendants in need be provided by children. But family assistance was insufficient to support the growing numbers of the aged.

Savings provided some insurance for old age. An old-age pension fund was created in 1850 and modified in 1886 but failed to attract working-class depositors. Mutual aid societies saw some success in the early years of the Third Republic; however, old age assistance was not the unique purpose of such societies, nor were hospices designed solely for the aged, who were housed with orphans, incurables, and the insane. Deplorable conditions in a hospice in the Parisian suburb of Nanterre in the period between the world wars were described in Léon Bonneff's novel *Aubervilliers*.

A law of 14 July 1905 recognized the aged as a group requiring specialized care. But until the acts of 1910 and 1911 (Retraites ouvrières et paysannes), pensions were obligatory only for seamen, railroad workers, and miners, the last consistently forced by poor health to retire earlier than other members of French society. In 1910 pensions were accorded retirees at sixty-five, in 1911 at sixty. But in a system of capitalization, several years were needed for funds to accumulate.

Moreover, the coming of war, which would occasion its own pensions, disrupted the system, and financial instability in the interwar period reduced the value of savings and pensions. Unions came late to the pension question; until the 1920s they concentrated on more immediate issues. Only under the 1936 Matignon Agreements did workers gain representation in pension administration. A successful social security system was achieved only after the Second World War.

S. de Beauvoir, *The Coming of Age* (New York, 1972); L. Bonneff, *Aubervilliers* (Paris, 1949); J. Bourgeois-Pichat, "La deuxième conférence démographique européenne de Strasbourg. Le vieillissement des populations," *Population* 27 (1972); J. Daric, "Vieillissement démographique et prolongation de la vie active," *Population* 1 (1946); C. Dyer, *Population and Society in Twentieth-Century France* (New York, 1978); H. Le Bras and J.-C. Chesnais, "Cycle de l'habitat et âge des habitants," *Population* 31 (1976); P. Paillat, *Sociologie de la vieillesse* (Paris, 1963); A. Sauvy, *Richesse et population* (Paris, 1944); J. J. Spengler, *France Faces Depopulation* (Durham, 1979); P. N. Stearns, *Old Age in European Society: The Case of France* (New York, 1976); P. Strauss, *Assistance sociale* (Paris, 1901); J. C. Toutain, *La population de la France de 1700 à 1959* (Paris, 1963); United Nations, *The Aging of Populations and Its Economic and Social Implications* (New York); H. de Villeneuve et al., *L'assistance aux vieillards aux infirmes et aux incurables* (Paris, 1911); P. Vincent, "Vieillissement de la population, retraites et immigrations," *Population* 1 (1946); T. Zeldin, *France 1848–1945* (Oxford, 1977), vol. 2.

D. G. Troyansky

Related entries: LABOR MOVEMENT; MATIGNON AGREEMENTS; MEDICINE: DEVELOPMENTS IN; POPULATION TRENDS; RURAL SOCIETY, LIFE IN; SOCIAL REFORM: GOVERNMENTAL POLICIES AND ACTS; URBANIZATION AND THE GROWTH OF CITIES.

AIR FORCE: ORGANIZATION. Air power was a key component of France's military power during the later years of the Third Republic and a gauge of the Republic's interest in and support of technological innovation. The success of the Republic in creating air power played a major role in the triumph of 1918; the inability to match German air power was a critical cause of the decline of French diplomacy in the late 1930s and of the fall of France in 1940.

The Third Republic used air power from its inception: besieged Paris communicated by balloon in 1870–71. In 1877 the Republic created a military observation balloon service, out of which came the first dirigible—*La France*—in 1884. In that year balloons saw combat duty in Indochina. Lighter-than-air observation units played a role throughout the life of the Third Republic, especially during the First World War.

In 1892 the Republic sponsored the research of the aviation pioneer Clément Ader, although he failed to construct an airplane that could fly. But succeeding governments and the public too took interest in the new aeronautical technology. In 1909 France bought its first Wright brothers biplane, and as war approached, the heavier-than-air service developed rapidly, both technically and tactically.

In 1912 the minister of war created an *Aéronautique militaire* as a principal arm of the French Army; that year French planes saw combat in Morocco.

At the beginning of the First World War, France had some 150 reconnaissance and observation planes in service, and plans were prepared for bombing and fighting aircraft. The air forces expanded at a frenetic pace both technically and numerically, although hindered by conflicting demands of the inspector general attached to the Ministry of War in the rear and the tactical commander at General Headquarters near the front. The work of Commandant (later General) Joseph Barès in the latter position was important for the addition of bomber and fighter components to the service and for the massing of air strength that helped save Verdun in 1916. Colonel (later General) Victor Duval expanded the service and concentrated the day bomber strength with fighters into the powerful Air Division, which played a crucial role in the war of movement in 1918. French air forces conducted reconnaissance, spotted for ground troops, attacked enemy targets on and behind the battlefield (including strategic targets like factories and railroads), and defended French troops and citizens of Paris and other towns from similar treatment. Best known to the public, however, were the aces, the high-scoring fighter pilots whose meteoric careers in single combat lent this war the only touch of romanticism it was to find. By 1918 the French air industry had some 200,000 workers and had produced by war's end some 50,000 planes and 90,000 motors; the French air service mustered some 4,500 planes in frontline service, including some 1,300 bombers and 1,000 fighters.

By 1923, however, there were only 160 day bombers and 230 fighters in frontline service, and the air industry shrank to 10,000 workers. Although these were powerful air forces by the standard of the day, the Republic replaced aircraft only as they wore out and added new planes in small numbers. Thus the air industry stagnated, most of the companies remaining at the artisanal level of production. But the French military was convinced of the effectiveness of air power, and the air forces operated, albeit on a shoestring, throughout the French overseas empire. The 1920s and 1930s saw the popularization of strategic air war—air attack against enemy economic and population centers—in the media. The image of bombers dropping gas and incendiary weapons onto helpless civilians was terrifying, and (unsuccessful) efforts were made at the League of Nations disarmament conferences to ban the bomber. One consequence was the creation of the French Air Ministry in 1928. A struggle ensued between the partisans of strategic air war and those who favored combining air operations with those of the older services. The issue was settled by compromise under the Air Ministries of Pierre Cot in 1933 and General Victor Denain (sometimes called the father of the *Armée de l'air*) in 1934.

Denain sought to fulfill both missions by building slow and heavy multimission aircraft; Denain's Plan I, funded in 1934, proposed the reequipping of the air force with some 1,000 new aircraft. But in 1935 Germany began to rearm openly, and France could not match German manpower or industrial production. Cot returned to the Air Ministry in 1936 and nationalized much of the air industry, increasing its capacity, but this was a slow process. By late 1937 the Luftwaffe had far more aircraft and these of new models superior to those of Plan I. In early 1938 General Joseph Vuillemin took command of the *Armée de l'air*. His Plan V called for a force of some 2,600 new aircraft (comparable to those of the Luftwaffe) in frontline service by the spring of 1941. Vuillemin favored building more attack aircraft to work with the army but had to concentrate on fighters to offset German numerical superiority. By the time of the Munich crisis (Sept. 1938), none of the new French machines was in frontline service; Vuillemin's warning of weakness and the danger of terror attacks on French cities played a large part in Edouard Daladier's decision to abandon Czechoslovakia.

In 1939 the Republic for the first time put most of its arms budget into air power, expanding the air industry from 35,000 workers in spring 1938 to 80,000 in early 1939 (171,000 in early 1940) and increasing warplane production from some 40 per month to 320 in September 1939. This was the limit of the capacity of the air forces to train crews to fly them. By September 1939 Vuillemin felt that he had enough fighters to risk war, although his force was weak in observation and modern bomber aircraft.

By May 1940 the Third Republic had some 600 modern fighters and 100 modern bombers in the frontline against approximately 1,050 to 1,650 fighters and 1,450 bombers of the Luftwaffe. Britain contributed only a small proportion of the Royal Air Force (RAF) to the Continent: some 450 planes, including only 160 fighters. Moreover, the RAF refused to use most of its bombers against any but strategic targets. When the invasion came, the crews of the *Armée de l'air* and the French naval air service fought to the limit of their capability, but they were unable to prevent the Luftwaffe from seizing control of the air over critical battlefields. French losses were very heavy—some 750 aircraft—although production nearly replaced them. In revenge, French pilots, better trained than their opponents, claimed nearly 1,000 enemy planes shot down. Facing a larger and more industrialized enemy, unable to obtain enough support from their allies, the French air forces could not halt the Blitzkrieg.

"L'Aviation militaire française 1919–1939," *Revue historique des armées* 2 (1977); "Histoire des forces aériennes françaises: Tomes I et II et III," *Icare: Revue de l'aviation française*, 91, 92, 97 (Winter 1979–1980, Spring 1980, Summer 1981).

J. A. Gunsburg

Related entries: ARMY: ORGANIZATION; COT; DALADIER; FALL OF FRANCE, 1940; VERDUN, BATTLE OF; VUILLEMIN; WORLD WAR I, FRANCE'S ROLE IN.

ALAIN (pseudonym of EMILE AUGUSTE CHARTIER) (1868–1951), journalist, lycée professor, political theorist. Alain was one of the most prolific and widely read of the journalists who exercised influence on the politics of the Third Republic. He became famous in the decade before World War I for his column ("Propos d'Alain"), which appeared in *La Dépêche de Rouen*. After the war, his essays appeared in *Les Libres propos* of Nîmes, a newspaper that bore the subtitle, "Journal d'Alain." Simultaneously, he influenced two generations of the French elite as a professor at the Lycée Henri IV in Paris.

Alain's observations (*propos*) made him one of the leading theoreticians of radicalism, and his influence endured through the Fourth Republic. Unlike advocates of Radical solidarism, Alain stressed individualism and sought to defend the citizen against the state. He distrusted all forms of power—military, clerical, economic. Against these forces he exalted "the little"—small farmers, small shopkeepers, small towns, the little man. Alain idealized life in the country and was so suspicious of Paris that he advocated shifting the capital to Tours or Orléans. Paris meant the centralized state, against which he urged Radicals to build "a little barricade" every day.

Alain, *Les Propos d'Alain* (Paris, 1920), *Eléments d'une doctrine radicale* (Paris, 1925), *Le Citoyen contre les pouvoirs* (Paris, 1925), *Propos de politique* (Paris, 1934), *Histoire de mes pensées* (Paris, 1936), *Politique*(Paris, 1952), *Propos d'un normand, 1906–14*, 2 vols. (Paris, 1952–55).

S. C. Hause

Related entries: SCHOOLS, SECONDARY: *LYCEES*; NEWSPAPERS, ROLE OF; RADICAL AND RADICAL-SOCIALIST PARTY; SOLIDARISM.

ALAIN-FOURNIER, HENRI (pseudonym of HENRI-ALBAN FOURNIER) (1886–1914), novelist. Born 3 October in La Chapelle d'Angillon of peasant stock, Alain-Fournier was educated in the primary school of the village, where his father was a teacher. At age twelve he was sent to a collège in Paris, and at fifteen he passed an unhappy year in Brest at the naval training school with the idea of becoming an officer. He returned to Paris in 1903 to enroll at the Lycée Lakanal to prepare for the Ecole normale supérieure. There he began literary experiments in prose poems and free verse. He also formed a lifelong friendship with Jacques Rivière; their correspondence is one of the longest and most revealing in modern French literature. In June 1905, in the Saint-Germain quarter of Paris, Alain-Fournier met Yvonne de Quièvrecourt. Although he spent only an innocent hour's walk with her, she became his platonic passion. Knowing her to be an aristocrat whom he could not aspire to marry, he sought to escape his feelings by studying for several months in London. Returning to Paris at the end of 1905, he failed his examinations for the Ecole normale. Two more fruitless years of study brought him to the age of compulsory military service, during which he was commissioned.

By 1909, he had come to feel that in Paris he had betrayed the innocence he had known in his peasant village. A series of unhappy love affairs, culminating in 1912 with a liaison with the actress Mme. Simone (Pauline Benda, wife of Claude Casimir-Périer) made this sentiment keener. A second meeting, in April 1913, with the now-married Yvonne de Quièvrecourt, caused his life to be almost unbearable. Alain-Fournier resolved these feelings through the novel for which he is remembered, *Le Grand Meaulnes* (1913). It depicts the growing awareness of loss as a function of passing time and the tragic agony caused by a failure to rationalize the intensity of adolescent feelings. At the beginning of 1914, he sketched the beginnings of a second novel, *Colombe Blanchet*, but in August he joined his unit on the Western Front at the outbreak of the First World War. Alain-Fournier died leading his troops at Hauts-de-Meuse on 22 September 1914.

J. Loize, *Alain-Fournier, sa vie et le Grand Meaulnes* (Paris, 1968); J. Rivière and H. Alain-Fournier, *Correspondance, 1905–1914*, 4 vols. (Paris, 1926–28).

B. F. Martin and C. L. Bird

Related entry: LITERATURE.

ALGECIRAS CONFERENCE (1906), a three-month international meeting held in Algeciras, Spain, to settle the dispute between France and Germany over control of Morocco. It culminated in a reaffirmation of French privileges there as originally defined in the Entente Cordiale (1904).

The conflict between France and Germany known as the Moroccan crisis arose out of French efforts to extend its economic influence and political control over Morocco. Threatened by these attempts, Wilhelm II, emperor of Germany, traveled to Tangiers, ostensibly to champion Moroccan independence (31 March 1905). In actuality, German motives were selfish. The kaiser wanted to sow seeds of discord between France and England, and he hoped to oust France from its pre-dominant place in Morocco in order to pursue trade there himself. In the face of rising Franco-German tension, the sultan of Morocco, Abd el Aziz, called for the conference.

Those present at the conference were France, Britain, Spain, Italy, Germany, Austria, and Morocco. The participants argued from January to April 1906 before concluding with l'Acte d'Algeciras. The significant provisions of this pact included a Franco-Spanish police force and a Moroccan state bank dominated by France (Banque de Paris et de Pays-Bas). France's privileged status in Morocco was reaffirmed, but France was not allowed to annex this country.

This victory for France not only defeated the already weak sultan but also damaged German prestige. Germany had expected the other powers to support it against France. Instead the conference aroused suspicions about German imperialist objectives and drew France and Britain closer together.

D. Porch, *The Conquest of Morocco* (New York, 1983).

L. LeClair

Related entries: FOREIGN POLICY; GERMANY, RELATIONS WITH (1871–1914); MOROCCAN CRISES; OVERSEAS EMPIRE: MOROCCO.

ALLAIN-TARGE, FRANCOIS (1832–1902), republican deputy and minister, journalist, and intimate of Léon Gambetta. His republican militancy under the Empire carried him from law to journalism and politics and established lasting friendships, particularly in Gambetta's circle. After the Commune he collaborated in founding and operating Gambetta's paper, *La République française*, and served in the Chamber of Deputies for Paris from 1876 through 1889.

In a political migration typical of early republican militants, he sat first with the extreme Left in the Chamber and then with the progressive Left as a member of Gambetta's Union républicaine and later of the Gauche radicale. He supported full amnesty for the Communards (1876) and campaigned actively for government management of the railroads (1877). Gambetta drew on Allain-Targé's financial expertise and made him finance minister in his cabinet (1881).

In 1885, he joined Henri Brisson's cabinet at the Interior and enforced government neutrality in the legislative elections. In 1889 he retired from politics and wrote occasionally for the provincial press.

F.-H.-R. Allain-Targé, *La République sous l'Empire* (Paris, 1939); J. Reinach, *Le Ministère Gambetta* (Paris, 1884).

S. A. Ashley

Related entries: BRISSON; GAMBETTA; NEWSPAPERS, ROLE OF; OPPORTUNISTS; RAILROADS.

ALLEMANE, JEAN (1843–1935), communard, working-class militant, and founder of the Parti ouvrier socialiste révolutionnaire (POSR). Born in Bouconen-Sauveterre (Haute-Garonne), Allemane became a printer in Paris and helped organize the Chambre syndicale des typographes in the 1860s. He was an active militant in the Fifth Arrondissement during the Paris Commune, for which he was sentenced to forced labor for life in New Caledonia. Amnestied in 1880, he returned to France and joined the Parti ouvrier. Then, in company with Paul Brousse, he broke with the Marxists and helped found the Fédération des travailleurs socialistes (Possibilists). In 1888 he established the newspaper *Le Parti ouvrier* to counter the Boulangist threat and then assumed the leadership of dissident elements within the Fédération. He and his supporters were expelled in 1890, and in 1891 he founded the Parti ouvrier socialiste révolutionnaire (Allemanists). This was subsequently merged in the Socialist party (SFIO), for which Allemane sat as a deputy from 1906 to 1910.

Allemane has often been described as the only major socialist party leader in the Third Republic who was a workingman. A self-educated activist with strong syndicalist and antimilitarist sympathies, he was deeply mistrustful of politicians, careerists, and bourgeois party intellectuals. While he took a prominent role in cooperating with radicals in the cause of republican defense at the time of the Boulanger affair (1886-89), he was quick to seek an end to it once the crisis was past. It was largely Brousse's emphasis on electoral politics and his desire to extend the radical alliance that led to Allemane's opposition and the foundation of the POSR.

J. Maitron, ed., *Dictionnaire biographique du mouvement ouvrier*, vol. 4 (Paris, 1967); M. Charnay, *Les Allemanistes* (Paris 1912); G. Lefranc, *Le Mouvement socialiste sous la Troisième République (1875–1940)* (Paris, 1963); M. Winock, "La Scission de Châtellerault et la naissance du parti 'allemaniste' (1890–1891)," *Le Mouvement social 75*

(1971), and "Jean Allemane, une fidelité critique," *1871: Jalons pour une histoire de la Commune*, ed. J. Rougerie (Paris, 1973).

D. A. Stafford

Related entries: ALLEMANISTS; BOULANGER AFFAIR; BROUSSE; POSSIBILISTS; SOCIALIST PARTY.

ALLEMANISTS, socialist grouping associated with Jean Allemane that formed the Parti ouvrier socialiste révolutionnaire (POSR) in 1891. After being expelled from the Fédération des travailleurs socialistes françaises (Possibilists) at the Châtellerault Congress of 1890, the Allemanists founded the POSR in 1891. This continued in existence until the formation of the Socialist party (SFIO) in 1905. The Allemanists represented the more militant and working-class elements of the Possibilist party and in many ways were the forerunners of syndicalism.

In 1888 party activists had forced leading members of the Possibilist party, including Jean Allemane himself, to withdraw from the Société des droits de l'homme, a joint radical-socialist organization formed to defend the Republic against the Boulangist threat. This withdrawal testified to a strong distrust among Parisian militants for bourgeois politicians, a legacy of the repression of the Commune, and it underlay a growing division within the party over the next two years. The final split was provoked in the summer of 1890 over the issue of party control over its elected members, some of whom favored a continuation of electoral arrangements with the radicals. The dissidents, now headed by Allemane and his newspaper *Le Parti ouvrier*, were expelled from the party, although it is probable that within Paris they enjoyed majority support. In June 1891, they constituted themselves as the POSR.

The new party's statutes emphasized the need for strict party control over all elected members, who were excluded from its central secretariat and required to hand over their salaries to the party. Electoral alliances with other parties in the second round of elections were forbidden. Programmatically, the party continued to embrace many Possibilist objectives, such as the importance of municipal action and the creation of municipal industries and public services. It also stressed the purely propaganda value of municipal action, declared that the working class would be the sole instrument of its emancipation, and embraced the general strike as the most direct mechanism for transforming society. Hence, the party placed great stress on trade union activity and made trade union membership obligatory for its members. This antipolitical and strongly pro-syndicalist bias characterized the party throughout the 1890s, and its members took a major part in the formation of the Fédération nationalè des bourses du travail (1892) and the Confédération générale du travail (1895).

After 1895, the party began to decline. Many of its most militant members defected to the syndicalist movement, its resistance to political action led it to be overshadowed by other socialist movements as the decade progressed, and it was never strong in the provinces. Eventually Allemane and most of his followers joined the Parti socialiste français formed by Jean Jaurès in 1902, and the POSR ceased to exist with the formation of the united socialist party in 1905.

M. Charnay, *Les Allemanistes* (Paris, 1912); G. Lefranc, *Le Mouvement Socialiste sous la Troisième République (1875–1940)* (Paris, 1963); B. Moss, *The Origins of the French Labor Movement, 1830–1914* (Berkeley, 1976); F. F. Ridley, *Revolutionary Syndicalism in France* (Cambridge, England, 1970); M. Winock, "La Scission de Châtellerault et la naissance du parti 'allemaniste' (1890–1891), *Le Mouvement social* 75 (1971).

D. A. Stafford

Related entries: ALLEMANE; BOURSE DU TRAVAIL; CONFEDERATION GENERALE DU TRAVAIL; LABOR MOVEMENT; POSSIBILISTS; SOCIALISM, 1870–1914; STRIKE, GENERAL.

ALSACE. While race, language, and customs link the Alsatians with the Swiss and Baden Germans, their political culture derives from the French Revolution in its original sense: that of a great federation that came together on the Champs de Mars in Paris on 14 July 1790. Alsace was ceded to the new German Empire by the Treaty of Frankfurt in May 1871. For the first French generation after the Franco-Prussian War, Alsace was the lost province, whose recovery—epitomized in the slogan *la revanche*—was of paramount importance in foreign affairs and in public opinion. As the years passed, however, this goal lost its significance as an objective of French foreign policy, despite lingering traces of sentimental concern for the province, kept alive by novelists like Maurice Barrès and by the mordant caricatures of Hansi (Jean-Jacques Waltz) and Henri Zislin.

The most important political move made in Alsace by the Germans was the granting of partial autonomy under the Constitution of 1911. As the war of 1914–18 drew to an end, the last imperial chancellor gave Alsace full autonomy, but this fulfillment of the chief aim of the long-standing home rule movement was lost in the joyous enthusiasm expressed throughout the province when French soldiers returned to the Rhine following the armistice of 11 November. As President Raymond Poincaré announced to cheering crowds from the Hôtel de Ville balcony in Strasbourg on 9 December 1918, "le plébescite est fait!"

But the Third Republic of 1918 was no longer the France of 1870 in which the church maintained its influence and the notables cultivated a limited but vigorous regionalism. The Separation Law of Church and State (1905) had been passed and applied with success, and political power was centralized in Paris. The institutions of 1911 were dismantled, and control was transferred to the capital. The prevailing official opinion was, "Germany is a federal state while France is one and indivisible."

Under the circumstances, it is not surprising that a movement for autonomy, the major political phenomenon of the interwar years of French control in Alsace, appeared. From the beginning, autonomism was divided into three parts, each with different goals. First and foremost was the Union populaire républicaine (UPR), the Alsatian French version of the Old German Catholic Zentrum, solidly implanted in Haut-Rhin; its goal was to maintain the pre-1870 French religious settlement. Second was the secular Parti progressiste, centered in Bas-Rhin; it desired the preservation of the dialect and of Alsatian culture. Third were the Landespartei and the Communist Workers' and Peasants' party, both based in the Lutheran Germanophone communes along the Palatinate border and in the Strasbourg industrial suburbs; their aim was legislative autonomy and even separatism.

A clash with the central government in Paris was inevitable. It first appeared with Edouard Herriot's attempt in 1924 to apply both an assimilationist policy to Alsace and to enforce the standing French anticlerical legislation. The Alsatian reply (issued long after the Conseil d'état had declared Herriot's program to be unconstitutional), was a solemn manifesto of a temporarily unified autonomist front, the Heimatbund, calling for full administrative and limited legislative autonomy.

Three months after the publication of this manifesto in 1926, the major Alsatian irredentist in Germany, Robert Ernst, met with an autonomist delegate near Zurich to give him money for three prominent anti-French Alsatian journals. The funds came from private industrial German sources. Since the summer of 1924, Catholic autonomists had been meeting near Basel with Abbé Emile Scherer, secretary of the large and rich Verein der deutscher Katholiken im Ausland, and had received money from him. Finally, the secret funds of the German Foreign Ministry paid over 1 million marks for Alsatian autonomist activities between 1925 and 1929, despite Gustav Stresemann's agreement at Locarno that Germany's boundaries with France would remain those defined by the Treaty of Versailles.

Paris suspected German involvement in the flourishing autonomist movement in Alsace and brought twenty-four of its leaders to trial in Colmar in May 1928. But the French made the fundamental mistake of accusing them of high treason when nothing but rumors of German connections existed, the actual facts being kept secret by prior agreement among those concerned. The accused denied their German contacts, claiming that theirs was a cultural autonomism strictly within the French legal framework. Five autonomists were found guilty; of these, two had been triumphantly reelected to their seats in the Chamber of Deputies during their incarceration. When parliament invalidated their mandates—with 416 abstentions—two other autonomists were chosen as replacements by the Alsatian voters.

During the remainder of the interwar period, the autonomist movement only infrequently united against threats from Paris. The three autonomist factions were too divided on their essential aims to constitute a potent, unified front. Most Alsatians were regionalists, not separatists, and were pushed into autonomism by the systematic lack of comprehension in Paris. The only group to show any sympathy for Alsatian grievances was Charles Maurras' Action Française, whose extremism placed it outside the boundaries of regular parliamentary life, although repeated royalist projects for limited autonomy in Alsace showed relevancy and practicality. Whether the Third Republic, plagued by instability, could have granted any of the autonomists' demands without collapsing is an open question. Certainly the conditions of total mobilization in both France and Adolf Hitler's Germany in the 1930s precluded a bilateral solution of the Alsatian problem. Whatever chances remained for negotiation were overturned by another roundup of autonomist leaders during the first ten days of the war in September 1939. The autonomists, incarcerated at Nancy, were interrogated on charges of high treason during the winter of 1939–40, and one of them, Karl Roos, was convicted and shot. The rest, when liberated from French custody in July 1940, surrendered under German duress all of their cherished autonomist goals in favor of immediate incorporation into the Reich. They were under the illusion that a secret clause in the armistice of 22 June 1940 at Rethondes had transferred Alsace from French control to German.

The Third Republic's political failure in Alsace should be measured against a certain degree of economic success and a flourishing cultural revival. High-quality wine, potash, oil, and industrial production increased. The names of René Schikelé, Albert Schweitzer, Charles Munch, Marcel Haedrich, Jean Arp, and Charles Spindler testify to the brilliance of Alsatian literature, art, music, and handicrafts. The nightmare of the Nazi occupation of Alsace from 1940 to 1944 taught the Alsatians the pricelessness of the political freedom for which the Third Republic, whatever its faults, had stood. Alsace today has finally emerged as the connecting link between two great cultures within a common European framework.

Annuaire statistique de la France (Paris, 1878–); P. C. F. Bankwitz, *Alsatian Autonomist Leaders, 1919–1947* (Lawrence, Kans., 1978); M.-J. Bopp, *L'Alsace sous l'occupation allemande, 1940–1945* (Le Puy, 1945); F. G. Dreyfus, *La Vie politique en Alsace, 1919–1936* (Paris, 1969); F. L'Huillier, "L'Alsace contemporaine: un destin exceptionnel," in *Histoire de l'Alsace*, ed. Philippe Dollinger (Toulouse, 1970); D. P. Silverman, *Reluctant Union: Alsace-Lorraine and Imperial Germany, 1871–1918* (University Park, Penn., 1972); M. Schlenker, *Die wirtschaftliche Entwicklung Elsass-Lothringens, 1871 bis 1918* (Frankfurt-am-Main, 1931); *Statistisches Jahrbuch für das deutsche Reich* (Berlin, 1871–1918).

                                                                    P. C. F. Bankwitz

Related entries: AUTONOMIST AND SEPARATIST MOVEMENTS; GERMANY, RELATIONS WITH.

AMIENS, CHARTER OF (1906), a resolution passed by the Confédération générale du travail (CGT) declaring that organization's independence of all political parties. The charter stated that the CGT would prepare for the revolt against capitalism on the economic plane alone. That revolt included both the struggle for immediate remedies for the workers' condition and also that for the eventual overthrow of the capitalist system through a strategy based on the general strike.

The resolution was drafted by Emile Pouget, Victor Griffuelhes, Niel and André Morizet, and Paul Delesalle. Despite some opposition by moderates

(Auguste Keufer and Victor Renard), the resolution passed the CGT congress almost unanimously (830 votes for, 8 against, 1 abstention).

E. Dolléans, *Histoire du movement ouvrier*, 3 vols. (Paris, 1936–53); G. Lefranc, *Le Mouvement syndical sous la Troisième République* (Paris, 1967).

N. Papayanis

Related entries: CONFEDERATION GENERALE DU TRAVAIL; GRIF-FUELHES; LABOR MOVEMENT; POUGET; STRIKE, GENERAL; SYND-ICALISM; TRADE UNION MOVEMENT.

ANARCHISM. In France as elsewhere, anarchism has been characterized more by a diversity of conceptions and tendencies than by a consistent philosophy or political program. In general terms, anarchists espouse the elimination or minimization of the state in society, to be replaced by the spontaneous cooperation of free individuals. Like the classical liberals, anarchists stress the essential goodness of human nature and conclude that restrictive laws or institutions are unnecessary and even dangerous. But they carry the libertarian idea to its logical conclusion by questioning all rules of authority and the very idea of rule itself, as implied by the Greek word *anarchos* ("without a ruler") from which the doctrine's name is derived.

The Greek derivation also implies the term's inherent ambiguity. Does it stand for unruliness or disorder or for simply the absence of rules arbitrarily imposed? This ambiguity is heightened by the popular image of anarchists as bomb-throwing terrorists or assassins, bent on destroying the present but with no clear vision of the future. Not all anarchists favor violence, however, as the means of social change, and few are simple nihilists, even if their constructive aims are often vague. Most anarchists stress decentralization or federalism as the basis for some form of noncoercive association, however difficult to balance with the ideal of individual liberty. They also recognize the dilemma of ends and means, as apparent in their rejection of a transitional revolutionary dictatorship as the prelude to an ultimate withering away of the state.

Although anarchist ideas circulated in France as early as the French Revolution, their first systematic philosophical exposition in France was Pierre-Joseph Proudhon's *What Is Property?* (1840), which gave the notorious reply, "Property is theft." Proudhon's writings, which have continued to influence the syndicalist and other left-wing movements, called for a federalist or decentralized plan of authority, based on workers' association in self-governing workshops. Proudhon's ideas also promoted the interests of small craftsmen and peasant farmers against the mechanization and concentration of modern industrialism. As a result, Marxists have condemned the movement as a reactionary quest for an idealized past rather than a progressive course toward a utopian future. Anarchists and Marxists also conflicted, within the First International, on the role of politics in revolutionary action and on the control of the economy by a centralized state. Despite Marxism's eventual victory in the international socialist movement, Proudhon's influence is one reason for Marxism's slower and weaker development in France.

After reaching a peak during the Paris Commune of 1871, anarchism (and most other leftist movements) waned during the early Third Republic as a result of the imprisonment or exile of leading militants. Still, exiles in Switzerland took part in secret societies in southeastern France, near the Swiss frontier, which remained a center of anarchist influence throughout the years of the Third Republic. Anarchists also helped to form the early socialist parties of Jules Guesde, Jean Allemane, and Paul Brousse, as well as the nascent syndicalist movement. In the midst of this organizational and doctrinal fluidity, a distinct anarchist current emerged in France by the early 1880s, with an estimated fifty regional groups, three thousand active members, and several thousand more sympathizers, as measured by the readership of the anarchist press. (A main title was *Le Libertaire*, founded in 1895 and published continuously, except for wartime interruptions, through the mid-1950s.)

As they separated from the socialist mainstream, anarchists faced the familiar dilemmas of individualism versus collectivism and of local autonomy versus larger regional, national, or international ties. Their first active national organization in France was the Fédération communiste révoluntionnaire anarchiste (FCRA), formed in 1913. Most anarchist theorists, including Jean Grave and Sébastien Faure, instead stressed individual action and propaganda, and the movement won more aesthetic appeal among *fin-de-siècle* artists and intellectuals than political impact or numerical support. In extreme form, this individualist ethos contributed to the era's sensational acts of terrorism, known by the term *propaganda of the deed*. This phase peaked during the years 1892–94, marked by eleven dynamite explosions in Paris, which killed nine people, and by the assassination of French President Sadi Carnot.

After this climax and a renewal of governmental repression, French anarchism entered a new phase, which culminated in the movement known as anarchosyndicalism and in the libertarian orientation of the early Confédération générale du travail (CGT). Despite their presumed distaste for collective organization, anarchosyndicalists joined the trade unions both to gain access to the mass of workers and to convert them from reformism to a revoluntionary ideology. To these syndicalists, the unions represented not only the vehicle of revolution but the form of postrevolutionary society, as productive organs much like Proudhon's mutualist workshops. The syndicalists also retained the anarchists' federalism and their contempt for parliamentary politics. Instead all social change must come from direct action, including industrial sabotage and the revolutionary general strike. These ideas were expressed most notably by Georges Sorel in his *Reflections on Violence* (1908). But the movement predated and surpassed Sorel's own influence; it stemmed from workers' deeper distrust in a socialist movement deemed too bourgeois and reformist and in a political system deemed incapable of true social change.

Although pure anarchists continued to resist trade unionism, most shared the syndicalists' commitment to such ideas as anti-militarism and revolutionary pacifism. Like most other leftists in France or elsewhere, however, anarchists failed to take action against the outbreak of war in August 1914. Although some individuals fled to escape conscription or even planned acts of military sabotage, most obeyed their military orders or managed to secure safe industrial jobs in the rear. Still, anarchism contributed to the eventual rise of wartime pacifist agitation in France and to the postwar wave of labor strikes in 1919–20, as well as to the birth of the French Communist party and the left-wing trade union confederation, the CGTU ("Unitaire"), in 1920–21. Many anarchists, in fact, initially hailed the Russian Revolution as the triumph of revolutionary spontaneity and social justice and likened the early *soviets* to their own ideas of autonomous worker organization. But they were quickly disenchanted by Lenin's postrevolutionary dictatorship and by the consolidation of Soviet militarism and totalitarianism during Stalin's rule.

Disillusioned by both communism and the CGT's increasing reformism, anarchists turned to ever more fragmented alternatives, such as the tiny CGTSR (Syndicaliste révolutionnaire), founded in 1926 and linked to the new Anarchist International at Berlin. The French movement was also divided between a collectivist wing, organized in a Union anarchiste communiste (UAC), heir to the prewar FCRA, and the more individualist Association des fédéralistes anarchistes (AFA) led by Faure. These currents reunited in 1934 on a platform of autonomy as against organizational discipline, but dissident factions persisted on both individualist and collectivist extremes. Due in part to this fragmentation, anarchism has never attained a mass following in France or achieved a lasting political impact, but it has continued to influence literary, labor, and political circles, most notably in the *gauchiste* fringe groups that rose to prominence in 1968.

These latent anarchist tendencies in France are sometimes explained by the ambivalence toward authority in a highly authoritarian and centralized political culture or by the taste for extremism and violence commonly attributed to the Latin or Mediterranean personality. Economic considerations may be more to the point, however; anarchism has arisen especially in areas of uneven industrial development, where workers are caught in the transition from an artisanal economy and disinclined to organize in large-scale unions or parties to defend their interests as a class. These factors help to explain the movement's appeal to printers, shoemakers, and other skilled craftsmen, as well as to romantic or antimodernist artists and thinkers. Indeed the nostalgia for an idealized past may account for the movement's continued appeal in France today among those who prefer a simpler life-style to the rigidity and alienation perceived in the modern world.

Le Libertaire, Paris (1895–1914, 1919–39, 1944–56); J. Maitron, *Le mouvement anarchiste en France*, 2 vols. (Paris, 1964); F. F. Ridley, *Revolutionary Syndicalism in France* (Cambridge, England, 1970); G. Woodcock, *Anarchism*(Cleveland and New York, 1962).

K. E. Amdur

Related entries: ANTIMILITARISM; COLLECTIVISM; COMMUNIST PARTY; CONFEDERATION GENERALE DU TRAVAIL; FAURE, S.; INTERNATIONAL, FIRST WORKINGMEN'S; MARXISM; MUTUALISM; RECLUS; SOCIALISM, 1870–1914; SOREL; SYNDICALISM; TRADE UNION MOVEMENT.

ANTICLERICALISM, a political ideology that condemned the influence of the Catholic clergy in French political and social life. Fear and resentment of the Catholic clergy are rooted in the power and wealth of the medieval church. There were numerous attacks on the French clergy during the French Revolution when priests were suspected of being royalist sympathizers and were accused of using superstitions and fear of divine retribution to maintain their power. During the nineteenth century anticlericalism became a political issue on several occasions: in the late 1820s when opponents accused Charles X of being subservient to the Jesuits and in 1845 when the Jesuits were expelled from France. Anticlericalism was based on a conviction that the Catholic clergy, an order of men self-consciously separated from the majority of Frenchmen by education, dress, and loyalty to the church, desired to dominate the political and social institutions of France. This fear of clerical influence was fed by the philosophy of positivism, which claimed that a religious explanation of the world should be replaced by one based on the findings of science.

Anticlericalism in the Third Republic was initially a response of republicans to clerical support for a restoration of the monarchy in the early 1870s. Republican leaders like Léon Gambetta and Jules Ferry argued that the return of the comte de Chambord, who was known to be influenced by the ultramontane bishop of Poitiers, Monsignor Louis Pie, would lead France into a war with Italy for the sake of restoring the Papal States to Pius IX. The clergy were also held responsible for the loss to Prussia. According to the anticlericals, students educated by the clergy had been trained to rely on the will of God and to denigrate the use of human reason. The competition between religious and secular secondary schools created *deux jeunesses* ("two youths") in France and was a major source of the division and weakness of the nation in 1870.

Political anticlericalism was able to draw on long-standing social resentments of the clergy derived from their involvement in the lives of French families. The fees charged for baptisms, marriages, and funerals, the influence of the clergy over women (exercised in confession), and the frequent clerical condemnation of dances and cafés created tension between priests and people. The novels of Anatole France and Emile Zola both expressed and contributed to the popular resentment of clerical attempts to control the manners and morals of Frenchmen.

Anticlericalism remained a major issue in the 1880s when it inspired a series of laws designed to restrict clerical influence in education and the army. After declining in intensity during the *ralliement* of the 1890s anticlericalism resurfaced with the Dreyfus affair, when the clergy were accused of aligning themselves with the army in opposing a revision of Dreyfus' conviction. Following the separation of church and state in 1905, anticlericalism again declined in significance. Some radicals, however, persisted in seeing a clerical threat. During World War I anticlericals accused priests of shirking duty at the front, and Pope Benedict XV was criticized for being sympathetic to the Germans. There was a final resurgence of anticlericalism in the electoral campaign of 1924, when the Cartel des gauches argued for a rigorous application of the laic laws, which had been suspended during World War I. A statement of the French bishops condemning the laic laws in 1925 refueled the old fears of clerical influence in education. But while journals like *Le Canard enchaîné* continued to snipe at the clergy, anticlericalism no longer excited the mass enthusiasm that had made it a critical political force in the pre–World War I period.

The political significance of anticlericalism resided in its ability to draw together moderate republicans, radicals, and socialists who disagreed on the need for structural changes in French society. Anticlericalism provided republicans with a common ideology in support of a secular republic that was an important element in the political consensus that was the basis of the Third Republic.

L. Capéran, *Histoire contemporaine de la laïcité française*, 3 vols. (Paris, 1957–61); J. N. Moody, *The Church as Enemy—Anticlericalism in Nineteenth-Century French Literature* (Washington, D.C., 1968); R. Rémond, *L'Anticléricalisme en France de 1815 à nos jours* (Paris, 1976).

T. A. Kselman

Related entries: ASSOCIATIONS, LAW OF; BERT; BERTHELOT; CLERI-CALISM; FERRY; FRANCE; FREE THOUGHT MOVEMENT; GAMBETTA; POSITIVISM; ROMAN CATHOLICISM: CHURCH-STATE RELATIONS; SCHOOLS, ROMAN CATHOLIC; SEPARATION OF CHURCH AND STATE, LAW OF.

ANTIMILITARISM, cultural, intellectual, and political current or doctrine. Antimilitarism is an eclectic, heterogeneous phenomenon whose existence has always been more cultural and intellectual than political or practical. It is not to be confused with pacifism (restricted to religious, moral, or mystical refusal to bear arms) or internationalism (which does not necessarily involve a critique of military culture).

Antimilitarism in the Third Republic has a number of discrete levels, roots, and themes, which became more interconnected and sophisticated over the years. At the most elemental cultural level, human aversion for war is expressed in the anguish and despair of the hapless peasant who draws the wrong number and is marched away from the village to certain death on a foreign field (as expressed in the anonymous poem, dating from the Napoleonic era, "Conscrit du Languedoc"). As warfare became more gratuitous under the Second Empire, this instinctive cultural revolt acquired a more political dimension. The *Appeals* of the First Workingmen's International against the Austro-Italo-Prussian War (1866) and against the Franco-Prussian War (1870–71) first raised the prospect of a "popular strike against war," which pacifists and disarmers have returned to ever since.

As military service became more and more generalized in the late nineteenth century, a second level of antimilitarism grafted itself onto the first: a critique of the brutal regimen obtaining in the barracks. This was a cause espoused most eloquently by writers and novelists in the 1880s. The trial in 1889 (for "insults to the army") of Lucien Descaves and the publishers of his *Les Sous-Offs* became a cause célèbre and increased the readership of other, similar works (Rémy de

Gourmont's *Le JouJou patriotisme* and, especially, Georges Darien's *Biribi, armée d'Afrique*), which drew widespread attention to the unnecessarily harsh and degrading conditions of life in the barracks. These themes were also disseminated at a more popular level by the *chansonniers*, especially Montéhus (Gaston Brunswick). Rarely, however, did this type of critique involve wholesale questioning of military institutions. When the surrealists (Louis Aragon, Georges Sadoul, and André Breton) took up the refrain in the 1920s, the intensity of their verbal violence ("je crache sur les trois couleurs") merely highlighted the absence of any theory or doctrine of antimilitarism at this level.

A third level, which did attempt to generate a doctrine, was constituted by the pre-1914 socialists. The socialists, heirs to Jacobinism, never questioned the need for armies and for national defense. Their approach was stimulated by the events of June 1848 and May 1871 when the merciless suppression of popular revolt underscored the divorce between the army and the nation, symbolized by the peasant soldier or the permanent army massacring the urban insurrectionary of the social revolution. Eugène Pottier, in a famous line from the "Internationale," called on the soldiers to use their bullets on their own generals, but the pre-1914 French Socialist party (SFIO) never went that far. Instead an attempt was made to bridge the gap between the permanent officer corps and the republican masses, between military power and civil authority, which was so poignantly illustrated by the Dreyfus affair. Urbain Gohier's *L'Armée contre la nation* (1898) was the logical prelude to Jean Jaurès's monumental *L'Armée nouvelle* (1911), which remains to this day the most complete exposé of the socialist case for citizens' militias. While the SFIO announced its willingness to strike against French military aggression in Europe, it stated with equal conviction its determination to take up arms to defend *la patrie* against attack.

It was syndicalists who took antimilitarism to a fourth level, albeit a largely rhetorical one. With the gradual convergence between the anarchists and the labor movement in the 1890s, the cerebral revolt of the *littérateurs* found a ready echo among workers who, on the strike field, were increasingly being confronted (and occasionally killed) by their fellow proletarians in conscript uniform. While organizations like the Ligue des antipatriotes (1886) and above all the Ligue antimilitariste, founded by Georges Yvetot in 1902, never attracted more than a few thousand members, the Confédération générale du travail (CGT) succeeded in sensitizing generations of workers to the antimilitarist cause. The *Manuel du soldat* (an antimilitarist handbook distributed by the Bourses du travail to departing conscripts) sought to remind workers of their class duty not to fire on their civilian brothers, but it neglected to offer any more far-reaching solution to the problem of war and peace. The *sou du soldat* (a five cent levy on CGT members for a fund serving to distribute antimilitarist propaganda by the Bourses to serving soldiers) performed the same function as the *Manuel*.

This activity had its moments of triumph. On 21 June 1907, the soldiers of the Seventeenth Regiment, locally recruited, refused an order to fire on the crowd of demonstrators in Béziers and fraternized with them instead (immortalized in the most popular antimilitarist song of all "Gloire au 17e"). But at Montceau les Mines, at Narbonne, at Raon l'Etape, at Draveil and above all at Villeneuve St. Georges, the terrorized recruits did not hesitate to continue a tradition inaugurated at Fourmies on May Day 1891 to shoot down striking fellow workers.

The antimilitarism of the pre-1914 CGT was too exclusively oriented to the question of the-army-as-strikebreaker, while its antipatriotic rhetoric, propagated by writers such as Emile Pouget in *Le Père Peinard* or the socialist maverick Gustave Hervé in *La Guerre sociale*, was too abstract and cerebral. Thus, despite a dramatic increase in the numbers of deserters (6,000 in 1902, 77,000 in 1911) and despite the intensity of the protests against the 1913 three-year service bill, August 1914 saw the French workers march off to the front with scarcely a murmur.

The war eventually led to two further types of antimilitarism, typified by the Communist and Socialist parties in the interwar years. Although 1914 effectively silenced antimilitarist activity in France, 1917 saw not only revolution in Russia but mutiny in the trenches (involving up to 40,000 troops). Although the mutinies were due to physical rather than political revolt, the seeds of the latter were already germinating. When France sent an intervention fleet to the Crimea in 1919, the sailors, led by André Marty and Charles Tillon, threatened to hand the ships over to the Bolsheviks if they were not withdrawn. Admiral Amet decided to put an end to French intervention in the Russian civil war, and Marty and Tillon became heroes of the Comintern. It was the Comintern that presided over the birth of a structured theory and practice in French antimilitarism.

Under condition number 4 for membership in the Third International, it became the duty of communists to engage in antimilitarist propaganda within the armed forces of capitalist countries, to form cells within the army, and to carry out such illegal activity as may have been necessary to undermine the effectiveness of the nation's defenses. During the occupation of the Ruhr (1924) and the Rif rebellion (1925), French communists systematically agitated for fraternization with the "enemy" and military disobedience. The Young Communists claimed to have infiltrated over seventy-five regiments, but despite great personal sacrifice, their overall impact was limited. But the discipline of collective struggle, combined with the Comintern's eradication of the remnants of pacifism in pre-1914 antimilitarism and the propagation of the virtues of armed struggle and revolutionary resistance, transformed the French Communist party (PCF) into a fighting force, equally capable of sapping the vitality of the regular army and of forming the backbone of national resistance to the German occupier. Since 1944, the PCF has solidly upheld the spirit and the structures of French national defense.

The socialists, on the other hand, were totally confused by the interwar world. Traumatized by the bloodletting of World War I, the post-Tours party was no longer convinced of the merits of national defense. After a long internal wrangle throughout the 1920s, the SFIO eventually passed into the hands of a pacifist majority synthesizing two quite different antimilitarist traditions. The first, epitomized by the party's general secretary, Paul Faure, regarded war as the ultimate evil, to be avoided at all cost—even at the cost of national defeat (as his later involvement with Vichy implied). Rejecting as potentially dangerous the Jaurèsian notion of a national defensive military capacity, this faction put all its faith in international negotiations for collective security and sought salvation in the League of Nations. Their spiritual descendants, the Atlanticists of the post-1945 SFIO, conscious that appeasement had not worked, looked for a similar solution in the North Atlantic Treaty Organization.

As for the other wing of the SFIO, which might be labeled revolutionary internationalist, these people espoused a class-based ideology close to the PCF and roundly condemned any talk of national defense under a bourgeois government. After the rise of Adolf Hitler, one faction, under Jean Zyromski, rallied the communist project of marrying national defense with the international struggle against fascism, while the other, inspired by Marceau Pivert, continued to reject as class collaborationist any defense preparations prior to the revolution. It was this faction, combined with the defeatist group around Faure, that effectively prevented the SFIO from adopting any viable defense policy in the prewar years, and that memory also assisted in the development of a militarist tendency in the SFIO after the war.

Antimilitarism in France has always suffered from an irreconcilable tension within the Left between the Jacobin heritage and the class ideology.

M. Bilis, *Socialistes et pacifistes* (Paris, 1979); A. Brossat and Y. Potel, *Antimilitarisme et révolution*, 2 vols. (Paris, 1976); R. Gombin, *Les Socialistes et la guerre* (Paris, 1970); J. Howorth and P. Chilton, eds., *Defence and Dissent in Contemporary France* (London, 1983); J. Rabaut, *L'antimilitarisme en France, faits et documents* (Paris, 1976).

J. Howorth

Related entries: COMMUNIST PARTY; FAURE, P.; HERVE; JAURES; MARTY; MUTINIES OF 1917; PIVERT; POUGET; SOCIALIST PARTY; YVETOT; ZYROMSKI, J.

ANTISEMITIC LEAGUE (1889–1906), the most important of a cluster of sects and splinter parties dedicated to attacking the status, property, and person of Jews during the prewar Third Republic. Originating in the Boulangist campaign (1889–90), the activities of the league culminated in the Dreyfus affair (1897–99). The league established the themes of discourse, the modes of propaganda, and the organizational structure of anti-Semitism in modern France. In this it prepared the way for the fascist groups of the interwar years (1920–40) and for the Vichy regime (1940–44).

The league in fact had two incarnations. The first of these, the Ligue national antisémitique de France, was founded in September 1889, just as the Boulangist movement was beginning to disintegrate. The animating figure in its formation was the marquis de Morès, an ex-army officer and aristocratic adventurer, who endeavored to make anti-Semitism the central theme of one of the Boulangist movement's last electoral campaigns: that in behalf of Francis Laur, a Boulangist running for the Chamber of Deputies in Neuilly in January 1890. While anti-Semitism had been only one of many themes of hatred and exclusion voiced during earlier Boulangist electoral campaigns (and not one to which General Georges Boulanger himself subscribed), Morès believed it the most provocative for pandering to a popular need for a simple explanation of all of France's troubles. Although the league's specific critique decried the overweening power of the Jewish financier, the term *Jew* served symbolically as the archetypal alien, a convenient label for the foreign worker, the Protestant, the great entrepreneur, and other foreigners criticized severally during Boulanger's campaign. Morès' Antisemitic League was erected on the precedent of the League of Patriots as a new kind of political organization: fraternal, highly disciplined, demonstrative, and focused on a single cause. Aspiring to capitalize on the grievances roused by the Boulangist movement, the league instead shared in its downfall in 1890. While Laur was elected, league candidates for local elections in Paris failed to win popular endorsement as the various Boulangist factions fell to quarreling with one another.

What survived into the 1890s was a skeletal remnant of the league's inner circle, renamed Morès et ses amis, these being some fifty butchers from the La Villette quarter of northeastern Paris. A maverick given to theatrical gesture, Morès outfitted his militants in purple shirts and sombreros, a souvenir of his days as a rancher in the Dakotas but also a harbinger of the distinctive garb of fascist groups in the twentieth century. Morès' following was too sectarian to exercise much political influence. It disappeared after Morès' departure for Tunisia, where he died on an expedition into the desert in 1896. During the early 1890s, anti-Semitic politics were sustained largely through the writings of Edouard Drumont. In a series of books and his newspaper, *La Libre Parole*, he became anti-Semitism's most notorious spokesman, but he lacked the charismatic qualities needed of a leader of an organization of streetfighters. Caught up in nostalgic fantasies about old Paris and traditional France, he preferred to propagate a more abstract, even respectable image of anti-Semitism for France's social elite rather than the more revolutionary, plebeian brand identified with the league.

The Antisemitic League's second incarnation was the Ligue antisémitique de France. Building on the structure and style of Morès' earlier organizations, it was founded in 1897 by Jules Guérin. An unsuccessful oil dealer, twice bankrupted and prosecuted for fraud and theft, Guérin was more successful in transforming the league from a sect into a substantial political movement. By 1898 the league possessed a membership of at least 11,000, divided into 130 sections in 52 departments and some overseas territories. The league was an urban movement, building its cadres in the same constituencies where Boulangism had been popular a decade before. Rank-and-file militants included artisans and shopkeepers but also large numbers of unskilled workers. Leaders of the league, mostly erstwhile radicals turned nationalists, tried to give the league a socialist image by championing measures designed to protect French workers against the competition of foreign labor. But the league also enjoyed the tacit support of many conservative

Catholics and received important subsidies from the royalist pretender, Philippe d'Orléans. Such subsidies, together with membership fees, enabled Guérin to outfit a townhouse, renamed le Grand Occident, on the rue de Chabrol in central Paris as his headquarters, complete with lavish accommodations and a staff of fifty. In this combination of populist activism and secret royalist financing, the configuration of forces sustaining the league was reminiscent of the political alliance that had animated the Boulangist movement.

Taking advantage of anti-Dreyfusard sentiment, Guérin and his league sought to move beyond the theoretical critique of the role of Jews to political action against them. League leaders called not only for divesting Jews of their property but also of their right to public office and to French citizenship. With the aid of its newspaper, *L'Antijuif* (circulation about 40,000), the league campaigned in behalf of official anti-Semitic candidates for the legislative elections of 1899. Twenty-two anti-Semitic deputies were elected, of whom nine were members of the league. Its forte was street action, which included not only public demonstrations but attacks on Jewish property and persons. These culminated in the anti-Semitic riots of 1897 and 1898, which erupted in many of the major cities in France. In this respect, special mention must be made of the role of the league in Algeria, where a number of anti-Semitic candidates were elected to municipal and legislative offices and where reprisals against Jews were particularly violent.

The riots incited by the league's agitation from 1897 to 1899 enabled the pro-Dreyfusard ministry of René Waldeck-Rousseau to prosecute its leaders in 1899. Attempts to arrest Guérin produced the Fort-Chabrol affair (1901), a much-publicized drama in which Guérin and his elite guard held out in their citadel under forty days of siege by the police. Guérin and other league leaders were prosecuted and imprisoned, and the league disintegrated once more into a scattering of splinter parties, most of which had disappeared by 1906.

As the political arm of anti-Semitism, the league was important both as a sustaining institution of the radical right wing during the Dreyfus affair and as a precedent for the anti-Semitic politics of Vichy.

R. F. Byrnes, *Antisemitism in Modern France* (1950; reprint, New York, 1969); Z. Sternhell, *La Droite révolutionnaire, 1885–1914* (Paris, 1978); G. Terrail (Mermeix, pseud.), *Les Antisémites en France* (Paris, 1892); S. Wilson, *Ideology and Experience* (Rutherford, N.J., 1982).

P. H. Hutton

Related entries: ANTI-SEMITISM; BOULANGER AFFAIR; DREYFUS AFFAIR; DRUMONT; FASCISM; GUERIN; LAUR; LEAGUE OF PATRIOTS; NATIONALISM; RIGHT, THE; WALDECK-ROUSSEAU.

ANTI-SEMITISM, dislike of and hatred for Semitic peoples and culture. In a European context, the word denotes anti-Jewish sentiment. Traditionally associated with religious differences and ethnic discord, anti-Semitism became politicized during the early years of the Third Republic. Of great significance for the future of the regime, this development arose from diverse sources on both sides of the political spectrum. For example, since the time of the Second Empire, socialists, and in particular Blanquists and Fourierists, had portrayed Jews as agents of high finance and capitalism. On the Right, members of the clergy produced a torrent of anti-Semitic literature that attributed the church's difficulties to a historical conspiracy dating from 1789 and perpetrated by Jews, Protestants, and Freemasons. In addition, a diffuse and populist anti-Semitism associated Jews with usury and plutocratic manipulations—orchestrated by the Rothschilds and their cohorts—of France's economic and political life.

With the political struggles of the 1880s and 1890s, anti-Semitism came to be identified with a general disenchantment with the Republic. During the Boulanger episode, politicians and publicists such as Maurice Barrès, Edouard Drumont, Henri Rochefort, and the marquis de Morès employed anti-Semitism's protean appeal to launch a coalition joining Left and Right. What began as one of several features of Boulangism became a dominant characteristic of the nationalist Right during the Dreyfus affair, when anti-Semitism provided limited but popular support for an attack on the liberal Republic. This ploy, pursued with seriousness of purpose by Charles Maurras and the Action française, ultimately failed because the leadership of the socialist Left joined with moderate republicans to defend the regime. Because of the affair, anti-Semitism thereafter remained primarily and properly understood as an ideological device meant to garner popular support for a nationalist politics of anti-Republicanism.

French anti-Semitism's politicization seems to have resulted from the close identification of the Jewish community in France with the Republic. That identification developed because native Jews throughout the nineteenth century eagerly followed a path of assimilation. Still, French Jews maintained a limited sense of group identification and therefore needed a political and civil context characterized by a certain degree of pluralism and tolerance. This is precisely what the Republic, with its parliamentary politics, provided and by the end of the century Jews perceived the regime as more than just symbolic of their general condition. Founded on the principles of the emancipating Revolution, the Republic had become for Jews an important agent of their integration into the larger community while at the same time allowing them to retain some sense of solidarity.

The identification of Jew and Republic was shared by both the Jewish and non-Jewish communities. For non-Jews hostile to the regime in the name of a nationalist politics, the Jew became a natural and convenient target. Indeed the exclusiveness of a conservatively inspired nationalism emphasizing purported traditional values easily portrayed the Jew as an internal alien opposed to national mores. Further, anti-Semitism brought under attack, and provided an excuse for attacking, the Republic's limited pluralism necessary for the Jewish community's continued existence. To make matters worse, the regime was weak and easily became a tool of special interests, all of which raised additional questions about the Republic and its Jews. Finally, the traumas associated with the Union générale bank, the Panama scandal, and the Dreyfus affair lent credence to the allegations of anti-Semitic publicists.

The virulence of political attacks against the Jews diminished during the early years of the twentieth century. The difficulties of the interwar period, however, brought a resurgence in a radical Right, which expressed alarm over the growing influx of Jews from Central and Eastern Europe and accused French Jews of trying to provoke a war to further the interests of European Jewry. When the Republic collapsed in 1940, to be replaced by a rightist regime committed to traditional and national values supposedly thwarted by the liberal Republic, control of France's political life fell into the hands of those dedicated to a politics of anti-Semitism.

H. Arendt, *The Origins of Totalitarianism*, 2d ed. (Cleveland, 1958); R. Byrnes, *Antisemitism in Modern France* (New Brunswick, 1950); P. Hyman, *From Dreyfus to Vichy* (New York, 1979); M. R. Marrus, *The Politics of Assimilation* (Oxford, 1971); P. Sorlin, *La Croix et les juifs* (Paris, 1967); Z. Sternhell, *La Droite révolutionnaire* (Paris, 1978); N. Wilson, *Bernard Lazare* (New York, 1978).

S. L. Campbell

Related entries: ACTION FRANCAISE; ANTISEMITIC LEAGUE; BARRES; BLANQUISTS; BOULANGER; DREYFUS AFFAIR; DRUMONT; FREE-MASONS; MAURRAS; NATIONALISM; PANAMA SCANDAL; PROTES-TANTISM; ROCHEFORT; UNION GENERALE.

APOLLINAIRE, GUILLAUME (1880–1918), poet, critic, journalist, publisher, playwright, avant-gardist. Guillaume Apollinaire was the official pen name of one of the most versatile and daring avant-gardists of the early twentieth century. He also published several times under the feminine nom de plume Louise Lalanne.

Apollinaire was born illegitimately in Rome and was given his mother's surname, Kostrowitsky. Attempts by researchers to determine who his father was have proved inconclusive. He spent most of his school years in Monaco, living with his mother and her lover and attending Catholic colleges on the Riviera. He moved to Paris in his late adolescence.

During the first decade of the twentieth century, Apollinaire established a reputation as critic of the arts, writing in both *L'Intransigeant* and *Le Mercure de Paris*. As a sideline he published licentious novels, including several works by the marquis de Sade. In 1904 he became friends with Pablo Picasso. After that he was an integral figure in the circle of artists and savants that dominated the Parisian avant-garde. He noticed the cinema, which hardly any other serious thinkers did, and from 1908 on he wrote several essays speculating on the dreamlike and poetic qualities of motion pictures. He delighted in flaunting convention, a fact that may have led to his imprisonment in 1911 for six days on suspicion of being involved in the theft of the *Mona Lisa* from the Louvre. His greatest contribution to letters was his poetry, in which symbolist influences are evident. His two best-known volumes of poetry are *Le Bestiaire ou Cortège d'Orphée* (1911, illustrated by Raoul Dufy) and *Alcools* (1913).

Although not a French citizen, Apollinaire joined the nation's army in 1914. He was seriously wounded in 1916 and returned to Paris to convalesce. He recovered from his wounds and early in 1918 completed a play, *Couleurs du temps*. He fell victim to the influenza epidemic that swept Europe that year and died on 9 November 1918.

K. Cornell, *The Post-Symbolist Period: French Poetic Currents, 1900–1920* (New Haven, 1958); M. Deacaudin, ed., *Oeuvres complètes de Guillaume Apollinaire*, 4 vols. (Paris, 1964–65); R. Little, *Guillaume Apollinaire* (London, 1976); R. Shattuck, *The Banquet Years: Origins of the Avant-Garde in France, 1885–World War One* (New York, 1961).

P. Monaco

Related entries: LITERATURE; SYMBOLISM.

ARAGO, EMMANUEL (1812–1896), lawyer by profession, scholar by avocation, republican politician by reputation. He was born in Paris, the son of the distinguished astronomer, François. As a young man he wrote poetry and light theatrical comedy before turning to the study of law. Admitted to the bar in 1836, he established a successful practice and acquired a certain renown for his defense of republican rebels, such as Armand Barbès and Martin Bernard, against the July Monarchy. In 1848 he himself became actively involved in the republican revolution and served as a delegate to the Constituent Assembly (1848) and to the Legislative Assembly (1849), in both instances representing the department of the Pyrénées-Orientales. He retired from politics for the better part of the Second Empire, returning to political office only after that regime liberalized its governing institutions in 1869. He was then elected to the Legislative Body as a delegate from Paris.

At the founding of the Third Republic (4 September 1870), Arago was named a member of the Government of National Defense, which was responsible for prosecuting the war with Prussia. Following the armistice (28 January 1871), he served briefly as minister of the interior. He was to become a prominent figure in the politics of the Third Republic, conspicuous especially for his opposition to the policies of the Orleanist leaders of the government, Albert de Broglie and Maurice de MacMahon. A leading spokesman for the moderate republicans, he was elected to the National Assembly (1871–75) and to three successive terms in the Senate (1876–96), in all instances as a representative of the department of the Pyrénées-Orientales. He closed his long career by serving as ambassador to Switzerland from 1891 to 1894. His stature as one of the leading republican politicians of nineteenth-century France was confirmed in 1895 when he was encouraged to present himself as a candidate for the presidency of the Republic, an honor which he declined. He died in Paris the following year.

J. Balteau, ed., *Dictionnaire de biographie française*, vol. 3 (Paris, 1939); J. Jolly, ed., *Dictionnaire des parlementaires français*, vol. 1 (Paris, 1960); G. Vapereau, ed., *Dictionnaire universel des contemporains* (Paris, 1893).

P. H. Hutton and L. LeClair

Related entries: FRANCO-PRUSSIAN WAR; SEPTEMBER 4, 1870; SWITZERLAND, RELATIONS WITH.

ARAGON, LOUIS (1897–), poet, novelist, and essayist, one of the founders of the surrealist movement and since 1932 a writer committed to the cause of communism. Aragon's premedical training led him to be dispatched in 1917 as an auxiliary doctor trainee to Val de Grâce, where he met André Breton and Philippe Soupault, two young men with whom he founded in 1919 the avant-garde review *Littérature*. In 1920, the group joined dada and participated in its activities until the movement disintegrated in 1922. By then Aragon and other avant-garde writers and artists had begun experimenting with automatic techniques, an activity he described in his "Une Vague de rêves" (*Commerce*, 1924) and which was to become a hallmark of surrealism. During that period he produced other works that echoed the intellectual ferment of the postwar years: *Anicet ou le panorama, roman* (1921), which contains transparent portraits of avant-garde companions, and *Les Aventures de Télémaque* (1922), which incorporates many of his dadaist texts as well as descriptions of dada scandals.

In 1924, Aragon cosigned Breton's *Manifeste du surréalisme* and until 1932 functioned as a leading member of the surrealist movement, contributing to its major activities and theoretical formulations and creating works that illustrate its techniques and philosophy. *Le Paysan de Paris* (1926) brings to light the surreal quality of ordinary Parisian sights; *Traité du style* (1928) vigorously condemns the prevalent intellectual modes and cult of established works; and *La Peinture au défi* (1930), in addition to discussing collage, a pictorial technique meant to upset the habitual perception of things, suggests that the *merveilleux* results not only from the rejection of commonplace reality but also from the development of a new reality that this rejection has made possible.

In 1927, together with Breton and other surrealists, Aragon joined the Communist party. Three years later, he participated in the Congress of Revolutionary Writers at Kharkov where he signed a letter criticizing some aspects of the surrealist doctrine. In spite of his subsequent "Le Surréalisme et le devenir révolutionnaire," which tried to reconcile his new communist militancy with his old surrealist allegiance, Aragon had to break with his former associates. The rupture came in 1932 when the publication of his *Front rouge*, a propagandistic poem attacking the French government, led to his prosecution. The surrealist group undertook his defense by launching a petition that objected to the use of the literal content of a poem as evidence for legal action. Since this argument implied that Aragon declined responsibility for the political message of his work, the Communist party pressed him to disavow the surrealist position; this he promptly did in a note published in *L'Humanité* of March 1932. From then on, he unequivocally put his pen in the service of the party. His *Les Cloches de Bâle* (1934), the first in a series significantly entitled "Le Monde réel," illustrates the conflicting class interests in prewar France by demonstrating the impossibility of love between people of different social backgrounds. *Les Beaux Quartiers* (1936) and the remaining two works in the series (*Les Voyageurs de l'impériale*, 1942, and *Aurélien*, 1944) concentrate on the struggle of the bourgeoisie to maintain its privileges. In addition, through numerous articles and essays, Aragon actively defended the party's positions, including its views on the duty of committed intellectuals to practice a socialist realist art (*Pour un réalisme socialiste*, 1935).

Aragon spent most of the war years in the Resistance, emerging after the liberation as a leader of French communist intellectuals.

R. Daix, *Aragon* (Paris, 1975); R. Garaudy, *L'Itinéraire d'Aragon* (Paris, 1961); Y. Gindine, *Aragon* (Geneva, 1966); J. L. Rabeux, *Aragon* (Paris, 1977).

M. D. Maayan

Related entries: BRETON; COMMUNIST PARTY; DADAISM; SURREALISM.

ARCHITECTURE AND URBAN PLANNING. The history of architecture and urban planning—of both thought and practice in both fields—during the Third Republic in France is beset with paradox. The prestigious official institution for architectural training, the Paris Ecole des beaux-arts, greatly influenced architectural practice from Saigon to San Francisco as well as in France during the period but was just then also losing its influence over modern architects, many of whom it had trained. During the nineteenth century, its professors had pioneered new structural techniques and materials made possible by the Industrial Revolution but had insistently embedded the new frameworks in traditional classically or eclectically decorated structures. Against this the modernists, beginning in the 1890s with the art nouveau movement, opposed a more explicit use of structural elements and a more rational aesthetic inspired by natural or industrial models. The modernists became world famous for their projects, writings, and private buildings, but, particularly after 1900, only a few of them received commissions from the governments of the Third Republic, which proved conservative in taste though liberal in fostering considerable artistic freedom. Thus a great deal of advanced architecture was formulated and some was constructed in France between 1870 and 1940 but relatively little with official support (in contrast to Weimar Germany, for instance); and the majority of buildings constructed in French cities during this period adhere to nineteenth-century traditions (such as the use of stone, eclectic decoration, and orthogonal symmetry) more than they add anything new beyond superficial decorative modes. Moreover, a sharp drop in the rate of new housing construction during the interwar period, due to rigid rent controls that made rental units unprofitable, considerably slowed the development of applied modern architecture in France.

The public architecture of the last three decades of the nineteenth century in France was largely based on developments in the use of iron and was influenced jointly by the Ecole des beaux-arts and the rationalist, neomedieval architect Eugène Viollet-le-Duc (1814–79). Beaux-arts architects increasingly had used iron for structural elements throughout the century, and they freely used iron and glass for utilitarian buildings (markets, railroad stations, exhibition halls) while insisting on the traditional stone facades for more elevated uses (churches, government buildings, theaters, and so on). During the first decades of the Third Republic, iron architecture reached the peak of its development in France with the engineer Gustave Eiffel's several railway viaducts in the Massif Central (1869–84) and with two structures built for the 1889 Paris World's Fair: Eiffel's 300 meter high tower and the 420 meter long Galerie des machines, by the architect Ferdinand Dutert (1845–1906) and the engineer Victor Contamin (1840–98). These structures proved the ability of iron to span huge spaces, rise to extraordinary heights, and offer great wind resistance and thus led to the skyscrapers and immense bridges of the twentieth century, built mostly outside France.

Most architecture in late-nineteenth-century France, however, had a more traditional look, despite the partial use of modern materials. The Grand Palais, faced with stone beneath its magnificent iron and glass roof, and the nearby Pont Alexandre III, both built for the 1900 Paris World's Fair, display a marriage of modern engineering with the lavish, eclectic decoration characteristic of the Beaux-arts manner. The major churches built after 1870, including Sacré Coeur in Paris and Notre Dame de Fourvière in Lyons, adhere to the Beaux-arts tradition, while adopting previously little-used models such as Byzantine, Romanesque, and Near Eastern architecture.

In the course of the nineteenth century, the thinking of the professors at the Beaux-arts had broadened, under the influence of historicism, to an acceptance of all historical architectural styles, beyond the classical one previously uniquely approved. French architectural teaching in the late nineteenth century, particularly by the theoreticians Julien Guadet (1834–1908) and Auguste Choisy (1841–1909), stressed symmetrical composition and conceived of the building as a sum of various separately designed parts and elements, while expecting young architects to chose their styles of ornament from among the many models provided by the past. Most future modernist architects, with the notable exception of Le Corbusier, received this influence as students at the Beaux-arts, though few remained at the school long enough to graduate and only Tony Garnier won the prestigious Prix de Rome. Modernists were also strongly influenced by Viollet-le-Duc, an adversary of the school who stressed a rational and structural approach to building in which the major determinants of style were to be the technical necessities and historical or regional realities of a given time and place. Viollet-le-Duc's influence emerged strongly in the work of the major French contributors to Art Nouveau (c. 1895–1905) in which rustic and refined materials were juxtaposed in buildings conceived as organic wholes, with sinuous asymmetrical iron structures breaking down the angularity of walls in favor of natural curves taken from flowers and plants. While short lived because of its eccentricity, the Art Nouveau movement destroyed architects' attachment to historical stylistic motifs and contributed to the thinking in volumes rather than in accretions of elements, which characterizes much of twentieth-century architecture.

After 1900 the major structural emphasis in French modern architecture was on the development of reinforced concrete rather than iron. While iron continued to be widely used elsewhere, the abundance and relative cheapness of cement in France, and the power of the cement lobby, imposed a predilection for concrete construction. The French had been prominent in the development of concrete since the eighteenth century. The patenting by François Hennebique (1842–1921) in 1892 of a method of joining reinforced concrete parts made possible the use of concrete for structural framing and brought about huge savings in building costs. Buildings could now be supported on very slender columns embedded with iron, and concrete provided a plastic medium through which nonbearing walls could be given any desired shape or texture. A pioneering building, though constructed with a pre-Hennebique method of reinforcement, is the Paris church of Saint Jean-de-Montmartre (1897–1904) by Anatole de Baudot (1834–1915); another, using the Hennebique system, is Auguste Perret's 1903 apartment house on the rue Franklin in Paris, in which thin supports and walls made possible the efficient use of a very small lot. Both buildings were faced with elegant materials— brick and ceramic tiles—but it soon became possible to cut costs further by exposing the concrete, and totally bare or white-painted concrete facades became a hallmark of the modernist architecture of Perret, Robert Mallet-Stevens, Le Corbusier, and others. Later prestressed concrete, developed by the engineer Eugène Freyssinet, made possible the prefabrication of structural building parts, thereby greatly decreasing the cost of the wooden forms that shape the concrete.

Modern architecture, in France as elsewhere, is characterized by the use of industrial materials in free-form compositions with sparing decoration. France had no unified modern architectural movement between 1900 and 1940 but rather a variety of approaches: the conservative, classicizing buildings of Perret and the young Tony Garnier, both influenced by the Beaux-arts tradition; Henri Sauvage's socialist-inspired apartment buildings, featuring terraces, communal services, and ceramic tile facing; Mallet-Stevens' and Le Corbusier's ultrasimplified, cubist-influenced concrete villas; Pierre Chareau's townhouse of iron, glass brick and industrial rubber. Only Le Corbusier participated in the international architectural movement, as its major theoretician and a founding member of the International Congress of Modern Architecture in 1928. The most impressive modernist buildings constructed in France during the early twentieth century are, with the exception of one church (Perret's Notre Dame du Raincy of 1922–23), residential structures: Sauvage's tiled apartment buildings (1912–25), Le Corbusier's Villa Savoie (1929–31), Mallet-Stevens' villas in Auteuil (1926–27), Chareau's townhouse for Dr. Dalsace in Paris (1930).

In the field of urban planning, France produced two bold theoreticians during the Third Republic, Garnier (1869–1948) and Le Corbusier (1887–1965), who were influential internationally. But actual planning in French cities up to 1940 was largely based on an earlier model, Georges-Eugène Haussmann's rebuilding of Paris during the Second Empire. In Paris, Haussmann's work of wide, tree-lined boulevards and up-to-date public works was completed and extended by the succeeding generation, particularly under public architect Eugène Hénard, and the government continued to legislate mandatory limits on heights and building profiles, albeit allowing somewhat more leeway for invention than before. In Marseilles, Lyons, and other French cities, Haussmannization had begun before

1870 and continued afterward. In Paris, as the metropolis continued to grow in population and suburbs multiplied at an alarming rate, modest attempts at long-range planning were begun by the late 1920s. The peculiar administrative arrangement, whereby Paris was governed nationally while suburban towns had their own local governments, made planning for the entire region especially difficult. In 1932, Henri Prost, chief architect for the French government, was charged with recommending planning measures for the Paris suburbs but was not allowed to include the City of Paris in his study. On the whole, the region grew haphazardly and not always in a salubrious manner. Even the previously fortified zone, originally destined for green space and recreational uses, was in reality largely parceled out piecemeal for development. In the historic Paris neighborhoods, little was done beyond some demolition to rid the city of seventeen *ilôts insalubres*, densely congested areas in which tuberculosis and other diseases were especially prevalent.

The theoreticians of the modern city in France, Garnier and Le Corbusier, were both steeped in the utopian socialist thinking of Henri de Saint-Simon and Charles Fourier and were followers to some extent of the attempts to build ideal industrial cities since the late eighteenth century, such as Claude-Nicholas Ledoux's half-completed saltworks at Arc-et-Senans (1770s), the industrialist Jean-Baptiste Godin's *familistère* in Guise (1859–77), and the chocolate magnate Emile Menier's factory village in Noisiel-sur-Marne (1864). A basic idea animating both twentieth-century planners was the task of providing decent, healthy, aesthetically pleasing dwellings for all social groups while accepting the presence of industry and the exigencies of urban living. For them, zoning and the separation of sources of pollution from residential areas and of potentially dangerous traffic paths from recreational green space assumed great importance. Their plans remained utopias, however, during the Third Republic; very little got built.

Garnier was given considerable support by his native city, Lyons, under Mayor Edouard Herriot; nevertheless, Garnier was able to build only isolated elements of his industrial city (a dairy, a slaughterhouse, a hospital), and even the one entire neighborhood he built, the Cité des Etats-Unis, was so severely limited in space that most green areas had to be eliminated. Le Corbusier, whose plans for Paris (insistently reworked and republished at intervals) involved the razing of historic neighborhoods, was violently opposed by the Parisians, and he received no major public commissions in France until after World War II.

F. Borsi and E. Godoli, *Paris 1900* (New York, 1977); P. Chemetov and B. Marrey, *Architectures. Paris, 1848–1914* (Paris, 1980); P. Collins, *Concrete: The Vision of a New Architecture* (London, 1959); A. Drexler, ed., *The Architecture of the Ecole des Beaux-Arts* (New York, 1977); M. Emery, *Un Siècle d'architecture moderne, 1850–1950* (N. p., 1971); N. Evenson, *Paris: A Century of Change, 1878–1978* (New Haven, 1979); L. Hautecoeur, *Histoire de l'architecture classique en France*, vol. 7 (Paris, 1957); P. Lavedan, *Histoire de l'urbanisme à Paris* (Paris, 1975); R. Middleton, ed., *The Beaux-Arts and Nineteenth-Century French Architecture* (London, 1982); M. Ragon, *Histoire mondiale de l'architecture et de l'urbanisme modernes* (Paris, 1972); A. Sutcliffe, *The Autumn of Central Paris: The Defeat of Town Planning, 1850–1970* (London, 1970).

T. Shapiro

Related entries: ART DECO; ART NOUVEAU; CHAREAU; EIFFEL; FREYS-SINET; GARNIER; GUIMARD; JOURDAIN; LE CORBUSIER; MALLET-STEVENS; PARIS; PERRET; SAUVAGE; URBANIZATION AND THE GROWTH OF CITIES.

ARISTOCRACY, descendants of the privileged elite of the Old Regime. This class not only lost much of its power through the loss of land during the French Revolution but was undermined by the rise of the bourgeoisie during the nineteenth century. At the outset of the Third Republic, it appeared to be regaining something of its former political position since so many of the delegates elected to the National Assembly were aristocrats or sympathetic to them. But the long-range trend was toward their elimination from public life. In the face of the democratizing policies of Jules Ferry and especially Emile Combes, few opportunities for public service remained for the old aristocracy, except in the army or the foreign service. In the aftermath of the Dreyfus affair (1894–99), the officer corps of the army was increasingly republicanized. Jesuit-trained country gentlemen, however, remained a characteristic type in the army at the outbreak of World War I.

Those aristocrats who had been unable to regain their place in the countryside frequently took up residence in Paris' faubourg St. Germain, where they were a visible anachronism well into the twentieth century. Intermarriage with other classes inevitably eroded their status. Nevertheless, their titles retained some ceremonial importance throughout the Third Republic.

R. R. Locke, *French Legitimists and the Politics of Moral Order in the Early Third Republic* (Princeton, N.J., 1974).

M. L. Brown, Jr.

Related entries: LEGITIMISM; NOTABLES; ORLEANISM; RIGHT, THE.

ARMISTICE OF 1918, ending of hostilities in the First World War pending signing of treaties of peace. Four armistices were granted: to Bulgaria (Salonika, 29 September), Turkey (Mudros, 30 October), Austria-Hungary (Padua, 3 November), and Germany (Compiègne/Rethondes, 11 November). General Louis Franchet d'Espèrey and Marshal Ferdinand Foch were chiefly responsible for drafting the Bulgarian and German armistices, respectively. The Turkish armistice was negotiated by a British admiral, Sir Somerset Gough-Calthorpe, who did not allow his French counterpart to participate and thereby fueled disagreements between Georges Clemenceau and Lloyd George about Near Eastern questions. France played a secondary role to Italy in the Austro-Hungarian armistice.

Final negotiation (8–11 November) of the German armistice and its signature (5:10 A.M., effective 11 A.M.) took place between delegations headed by Foch and Minister of State Matthias Erzberger in a converted dining car on Foch's train parked at a siding in the forest of Compiègne (Oise) near the hamlet of

Rethondes. The terms had been prepared by Foch and approved by the Interallied Conference in Paris (31 October–4 November) to which President Woodrow Wilson had submitted general conditions agreed to by Germany (27 October) following diplomatic exchanges initiated by Germany on 4 October. They included, significantly, an evacuation by Germany from all occupied territories, withdrawal behind the Rhine, and establishment of a demilitarized zone and three Allied bridgeheads on the Rhine's east bank. At this conference the Allies for the first time officially accepted Wilson's Fourteen Points as the basis of a peace, but when Great Britain entered a reservation on freedom of the seas, Clemenceau entered a commentary on restoration of invaded territories, which reserved a right to claim compensation for damage to civilians and their property. The reservations and the Rhineland occupation opened the door to later peace terms that Germany would regard as violations of the pre-armistice understanding on the Fourteen Points.

Some French authorities, among them President Raymond Poincaré and General Philippe Pétain, doubted the wisdom of granting an armistice without invading Germany and inflicting a catastrophic defeat in the field, which they anticipated might result from an offensive into Lorraine set for 14 November. But Foch, observing that "war is only a means to a result," judged that Germany was resigned to accepting terms that would render it militarily helpless, a result that would make further bloodshed pointless. Clemenceau, despite some misgivings, never seriously challenged Foch's conclusion.

J.-J.-H. Mordacq, *L'Armistice du 11 novembre 1918* (Paris, 1937); P. Renouvin, *L'Armistice de Rethondes, 11 novembre 1918* (Paris, 1968); H. R. Rudin, *Armistice 1918* (New Haven, 1944); C. Vilain, *Les quatre armistices de 1918* (Paris, 1968).

D. S. Newhall

Related entries: CLEMENCEAU; FOCH; GERMANY, RELATIONS WITH (1914-1940); GREAT BRITAIN, RELATIONS WITH; PARIS PEACE CONFERENCE; PETAIN; POINCARE, R.; UNITED STATES, RELATIONS WITH; WORLD WAR I, FRANCE'S ROLE IN.

ARMISTICE OF 1940, armistice between France and the Axis (25 June 1940) that divided France into a zone of occupation and a free zone, originally permitted the French fleet to be disarmed under Axis supervision, required that political refugees be surrendered, and disarmed and reduced French military forces (later set at 100,000 soldiers and 60,000 sailors). Differences concerning the need to seek an armistice emerged by May 1940. Believing that the war was already lost when he assumed command of the army, the commander in chief, General Maxime Weygand, wished to spare France needless destruction, save the army's honor, and preserve the army so it might maintain internal order. Weygand's pleas to stop the fighting became more strident with each passing day. Reminding the general that the Anglo-French Accords of 28 March 1940 prohibited the conclusion of a separate armistice, Premier Paul Reynaud instead instructed Weygand to defend France from a stronghold in Brittany and to make preparations for a stand in French North Africa. Weygand refused; he considered the stronghold idea a fantasy and felt he lacked the resources to prolong the struggle elsewhere. *Capitulards*, led by prestigious Marshal Philippe Pétain and Weygand and supported by members of Reynaud's personal staff and cabinet, gained ground as Reynaud's government fled from Paris to Bordeaux. They also became increasingly unsure of Britain's support. Britain had refused to commit its airplanes to the battle and had furnished insufficient aid to France. French interests therefore had to come before any accord with Britain. The dispute between Weygand-Pétain and Reynaud intensified on 14 June when Weygand refused to order a cease-fire or leave with the government for North Africa. The impasse was broken by Vice-Premier Camille Chautemps who proposed they simply ask for conditions without asking for an armistice. If the German conditions were dishonorable, the war could continue. Reynaud countered that the British must agree first, thinking they would refuse. Instead the British gave limited approval to Chautemps' proposal on condition that the French fleet be sent first to British ports. The British government's approval was then abruptly cancelled in favor of an offer of union between the two governments and countries. This proposal was rejected by Reynaud's cabinet. A broken Reynaud resigned in favor of Pétain, who requested German terms. Finding that these terms were harsh but not dishonorable, Pétain's government accepted them on 22 June and less severe Italian terms on 24 June.

F. Avantaggiato Puppo, *Gli Armistizi francesi del 1940* (Milan, 1963); H. Böhme, *Entstehung und Grundlagen des Waffenstillstandes von 1940* (Stuttgart, 1966); A. Goutard, "Comment fut demandé l'armistice?" *Le Monde* (1963); A. Kammerer, *La Vérité sur l'armistice* (Paris, 1945); L. Martin, "Autour de l'armistice du juin 1940," *Revue d'histoire de la deuxième guerre mondiale* 3 (1951).

M. L. Mickelsen

Related entries: CHAUTEMPS; DARLAN; FALL OF FRANCE, 1940; GAMELIN; GAULLE; GEORGES; GERMANY, RELATIONS WITH (1914–1940); HERRIOT; ITALY, RELATIONS WITH; LAVAL; LEBRUN; NOGUES; PETAIN; REYNAUD; VUILLEMIN; WEYGAND.

ARMY: ORGANIZATION. The disastrous Franco-Prussian War (1870–71) led to fundamental army reorganization. Rather than continue with a restricted, mostly professional force or opt for a Swiss-model militia, the Republic in effect combined them: a mass of conscripts serving two to four years actively and twenty or more in reserves plus a large cadre of professionals to train them, conduct small (usually colonial) operations, and in case of war flesh out the covering force (*couverture*), mainly trained conscripts, until the reserves were mobilized. The only departure came between 1928 and 1935 when conscription fell to a year and the active army was defined as solely a training force. The system was reinstated, however, to meet the Hitler menace.

Parliament seldom cut army budget requests, but these typically were tailored to what the traffic would bear, not to the real needs, which were greater. France's officers and noncommissioned officers (NCOs) were nearly the worst paid in Europe. Compared with Germany (and to some extent Great Britain), where officers and even NCOs formed something like self-renewing castes with unimpeachable social respectability, French officers comprised an underpaid occupational group of rather diverse origins and imprecise, insecure standing. Until 1890 and again in the 1920s, up to two-thirds had risen from the ranks, a tradition since the French Revolution. Saint-Cyr and Ecole polytechnique graduates predominated in time, but training centers like Saint-Maixent (infantry) and Saumur (cavalry) continued to commission rankers, thus skimming the cream from the chronically undermanned NCO corps while undermining the officer corps' social standing. The latter body tended to be kept overmanned; more promotion slots would help retention rates. But the practice undermined arguments for better pay, a vicious circle. The result too often was stagnation in mind and morale while one waited for promotion. Pensions were so small as to make keeping one's respectability even more of a struggle, hardly an aid to recruitment.

The Soult law (1832) governed promotion: to major, two-thirds by seniority, the rest by selection; above major, half and half. Decentralized boards selected. This wisely left judgment to those superiors most familiar with an officer's work but did allow some intrusion of personal relations and club spirit. Imaginative, unconventional types hence often drifted to the Colonial Army. Following the Dreyfus affair anticlericals viewed the boards as infected by Catholic and antirepublican biases. General Louis André (minister of war, 1900–1904) centralized promotions in the ministry and encouraged notation of religious and political attitudes. He resigned owing to a scandal (the *affaire des fiches*) involving use of the Freemasons to furnish notes, but political reports continued until 1912. Centralized promotion decisions spawned political favoritism and seriously affected standards and morale.

Reforms and the prospect of renewed war kept officers' morale firm until about 1890, but thereafter it languished until about 1912. The 1889 and 1905 laws inducted masses of conscripts. Efforts were needed to soften a traditional harshness in discipline and convert officers into teachers, but this social role confused many, who worried about the army's fighting fitness. Also they deeply resented frequent use of the army as police in religious and labor disorders (1902–10). Not surprisingly, most welcomed the so-called nationalist revival (1911–14) and a return to three-year conscription (1913) as needed preparation for a now-looming war.

Professional education advanced dramatically before 1914, training rather less. Schools were founded or improved, notably the Ecole supérieure de guerre (1876) for staff officers. It trained promising junior officers in the nuts and bolts of administration, however, more than in the science of war. The Centre des hautes études militaires (1911) sought to remedy this but did not become fully operational until after the war. Staff performance in 1914–18, especially in logistics, vastly surpassed 1870–71, however, and probably averted defeat in the opening weeks. Field training still left much to be desired, basically due to lack of funds. The same applied to organization and training of reserves, although some improvement occurred after 1908. The Long memories of poor National Guard performances in 1870–71 colored attitudes among the professionals, who often regarded all but the most recently released conscripts as unfit for serious fighting. The Germans thought otherwise. Their use of reserves in frontline units at the start of the war led to strategic miscalculations by the French, who soon learned that their own reserves, after some early panics due to poor training and morale, could be forged into solid, all-purpose soldiers. But the anvil exacted a terrible price.

The Republic made certain the high command would answer to civilian authority, but in pursuit of this admirable objective it dispersed leadership to the point that before 1911 the army was all but acephalous. It permitted no rank above *général de division* (major general). (Marshal of France, revived during the war, was in effect an honorary grade.) Commands rotated frequently. The General Staff, unlike its German counterpart (an autonomous organ with permanent personnel, answering only to the kaiser), was simply an agency in the Ministry of War whose personnel rotated between staff and command postings. In wartime its chief was also designated the major general, and served as chief of staff to the commander of the principal group of armies in the Eastern Theater. In peacetime leadership was assumed by the Generalissimo, who was ordinarily the vice-president of the Conseil supérieur de la guerre (1872), a consultative body chaired by the minister of war and staffed by several senior generals presumably ticketed for major field commands in wartime. Long-range planning suffered as a result of these and many more complexities. Finally, peacetime and wartime staff and command functions were combined when Chief of the General Staff Joseph Joffre was made generalissimo designate in 1911. The army now had its own head and with more authority in it than in anyone since Bonaparte.

When the war came, the post of chief of the general staff (CSG) lapsed, but it reappeared, subordinated to the field commander in chief, when Joffre was relieved (December 1916). After the war the pre-1911 scheme returned: the vice-president of the CSG, titled now inspector general of the armies, again was generalissimo designate, while the chief of the general staff, the major general designate, answered to the minister of war. Between 1935 and 1940, however, General Maurice Gamelin held both posts, the Joffre solution. Planning did not suffer as it had before 1911. The war had proved the need for it and interservice coordination. The prestige of Marshal Philippe Pétain (inspector general, 1920–31) and Generals Maxime Weygand (1931–35) and Gamelin helped ensure direction, as did a permanent secretariat for the Counseil supérieur de la défense nationale (1906). Inactive before the war, this policymaking council of those ministers most involved in defense was expanded (1921) and added the service chiefs as advisers. It was seconded for more purely military questions by the Haut comité militaire (1932–36) and the Comité permanent de la défense nationale (1936–39). An interservice Ministry of National Defense was briefly tried in 1932; after 1936 Edouard Daladier, minister of war, held the title minister of national defense, a coordinating post. And in 1938 Gamelin was named chief of staff of national defense but with an authority over the army, navy, and air force (independent since 1934), which remained ill defined to the end in 1940.

Regarding field organization, the 1870–71 war proved the need to make peacetime and wartime units correspond. The regiment heretofore had been the largest peacetime unit. After 1873, following Germany's example, permanent divisions and corps were formed, with only armies and army groups left to wartime improvisation. France was divided into eighteen corps areas, plus one in North Africa and a twentieth (1897) based at Nancy. In 1914 a corps (40,000 men) comprised two infantry divisions, one cavalry regiment, four reserve infantry battalions, twelve corps artillery batteries, and three engineer companies; a division (16,000) comprised two brigades of two infantry regiments each, one squadron of cavalry, nine batteries, and one engineer company; an infantry regiment (3,400) comprised three battalions (1,100) of four companies (240) each. The importance of automatic weapons and artillery in World War I, the introduction of the tank, and the decline of horse cavalry brought variations in type and composition of divisions. In the mid-1930s infantry divisions (15,000, wartime 18,000) contained three regiments plus two artillery regiments and sundry service units. New corps included by 1940 some three heavy armored, four light mechanized (a misnomer—they were as powerful as German panzers), three light cavalry (light tanks), seven motorized infantry (including light tracked and half-tracked vehicles), and fourteen fortress (Maginot Line) divisions.

Finance and conscription laws affected overall levels. Until the 1890s France and Germany kept about 400,000 men in active service. Numbers rose, Germany's more rapidly, making alliances all the more important for France. By 1911 France kept about 500,000 in arms and Germany about 635,000. The Three Years Law (1913) and German increases raised these to about 800,000 apiece in 1914. France mobilized about 3.58 million and Germany about 3.75 million in August 1914. During the war about 7.842 million plus 587,450 colonial natives served; 1.383 million died (including 66,000 natives). After the war authorized levels fell (523,769 in 1928), with about 450,000 actually serving (1933), but figures rose somewhat before World War II. By the eve of the 1940 invasion, France had mobilized 4 million men in some 115 divisions.

The post-1918 figures reveal how important North African and other colonials had become. Of the 523,769 cited above, colonials comprised 177,762 (113,723 volunteers and 64,039 conscripts), substantial numbers of them stationed in France. Before 1914 the autonomous Colonial Army, until 1900 under the Ministry of Marine, only served abroad and contained no conscripts from France unless they volunteered for it. (The Foreign Legion plus Regular units as needed for operations also served in North Africa, among them the notorious Bataillons d'Afrique, penal units.) Its size mounted with colonial conquests from about 16,600 (1880) to about 70,200 (1900); in 1914 it numbered 61,241. Its independent ways and promise of action attracted and shaped some of the Republic's most renowned officers—Joffre, Joseph Gallieni, Hubert Lyautey, Charles Mangin, Louis Franchet d'Esperey, Henri Gouraud.

In equipment, the army of 1914 was built around the modified Lebel rifle (1884) and 75mm gun (1893–97), the latter, boasting a twenty rounds per minute rate, unquestionably the world's best light artillery piece. Compared with Germany, France was notably deficient in heavy artillery, trench mortars, and electrical communications, though not (contrary to legend) in machine guns, which both countries were slow to adopt. Until mid-1916 France's lack of heavy artillery was cruelly felt. In 1914 its only modern pieces were 104 Rimailho 155mm guns (1904). Germany's lead in heavy artillery dated from about 1905 and caused protracted debates in the army and Parliament, much less about the need for heavy pieces as about competing designs and their proper battlefield role. All heavy guns in use in 1918 were of prewar design. By November 1918 the field army contained about as many men as in 1914 (about 2.7 million), but its armament was prodigiously greater: machine guns, 60,576 versus 5,100; automatic rifles, 120,099 versus none; trench mortars (*crapouillots*), 18,000 versus a few hundred; 75s, 4,986 versus 3,840; heavy guns, 5,128 versus 308; tanks 2,297 versus none; airplanes, 2,470 versus 120. (Also, nearly all artillery, tanks, and planes used by U.S. forces were French.)

Although designing of weapons went forward between the wars, production lagged until after the 1936 program went into effect. The Maginot Line, constructed (1927–36) between Longwy and the Swiss border to supersede a curtain of fortresses built in the late nineteenth century by General Raymond Séré de Rivières, absorbed huge sums. By the invasion of 1940, the French army was a well-equipped force, compared with Germany deficient mainly in assault rifles, anti-aircraft artillery, and anti-tank mines, superior in artillery and anti-tank guns, and in tanks equal if not superior in quality and quantity: in the northeast on 10 May 1940, 3,254 to 2,574. The tank question has been much debated. Generally French tanks were superior in armor and firepower and inferior (with two exceptions) in speed, range, and communications. Their design served their intended use, which was basically support for infantry. Tank divisions as such, however, could operate more independently. German doctrine concentrated on the latter mission, grouping the divisions and looking to speed.

Strategic planning between 1871 and 1940 assumed that France would first have to contain invading forces before launching a winning offensive. War plans were at bottom plans of deployment, not operation. The enemy's opening operations would create the situation to which one would then respond. Fortifications in the east would tend to attract the Germans toward the northeastern invasion routes, probably into part of Belgium. Before 1914 it was assumed a war would be short. Hence little serious thought was given to industrial planning and stockpiling—a critical concern by early 1915 due to desperate shortages of artillery shells—despite the vogue of doctrines derived from Karl von Clausewitz and Napoleon emphasizing masses of men and materiel. After 1905, however, fears that Germany's growing strength might lead to a swift attack that would destroy French concentration led to plans for counterattacking an invasion speedily and with great force rather than with a progressively engaged battle in which the morale needed for attacking—needed all the more by underdogs—would be sapped. Tragically, these ideas, promoted by General Ferdinand Foch and, above all, after 1911, by Colonel François Loyseau de Grandmaison, filtered down to divisional and regimental commanders as an admonition to attack no matter what. The result was a slaughter of hasty, unsupported infantry assaults in the first months of the war. German doctrine emphasized attack scarcely less than the French but with careful fire preparation, use of terrain, and variations in methods, such as night approaches, infiltration, and envelopment. As the war ground on, the French army learned to coordinate arms, absorb attacks with elastic defenses, prepare the ground, adjust artillery to the advance (not the stopwatch), attack in combat groups with automatic weapons rather than in rigid lines of riflemen, and disintegrate the enemy's front with rapid, successive blows around a perimeter rather than try to pierce it in a headlong rush.

World War I taught the French Army the importance of firepower, materiel, and manpower (especially the worth of reserves) and, above all, defensive tactics. France had survived because it had been able to defend itself long enough to permit its allies to add their resources to its and thus force Germany out of its plan of rapid attack into a war of attrition. Unless France adopted a strategy of a preemptive strike without allies against a Germany not yet fully armed—a gamble flatly defying public opinion at home and abroad—its only course was to defend itself—at best in Belgium, at worst at the border (for nearly 80 percent of its natural and industrial resources for a war of attrition lay in the invasion routes)—and hang on until the wherewithal was available to mount a decisive offensive. Powerful fortifications could deny entry in the east. From the Ardennes northward the terrain was mostly unsuited for deep fortification save at prohibitive cost. The field army hence would concentrate there, with forces holding a continuous front that could not be outflanked, while a general reserve, spearheaded by mechanized and heavy armored divisions, would stand ready to smash any breakthrough. When Belgium dropped its defensive alliance with France in 1936, however, the problem became more acute: French forces could be posted to the best defensive line, the Meuse River, only after the Germans had already invaded.

In the light of these considerations, rejection of proposals by Colonel Charles de Gaulle, supported by Paul Reynaud, to organize a large, elite, armored strike force to break through and operate behind enemy lines was predictable. It gambled too much on the offensive; its failure could lead the enemy back through the gap; for the present (1936) it would siphon too many tanks from the rest of the army; and its elite character and independence would be a standing denial of the role of a united nation in arms that the army saw itself as embodying.

The army of the late 1920s and 1930s was basically a training body that could conduct no important operations without mobilizing huge numbers of reserves, a step fraught with grave political and diplomatic consequences. After full mobilization in 1939–40, it was a truly formidable force. Hitler gambled heavily when he ordered his reluctant High Command only to feint in the north while driving heavy armored divisions through the Ardennes, which both sides had thought unsuitable ground for them. The French commanders could not adjust their thinking quickly enough to grasp the new dimensions of speed and distance revealed by armored attack and to perceive the main threat in time to crush it. Coordination with the allies was defeated by clumsy command structures and a snowballing desire on the Allies' part to escape. A dangerous penetration of the continuous front thus became enough to set off an avalanche into the abyss.

R. Challener, *The French Theory of The Nation in Arms, 1866–1939* (New York, 1955); H. Contamine, *La Revanche* (Paris, 1957); R. Couret, ed., *Guide bibliographique sommaire d'histoire militaire et coloniale française* (Paris, 1969); S. Davis, *The French War Machine* (London, 1937); R. Girardet, *La Société militaire dans la France contemporaine, 1815–1939* (Paris, 1953); J. Gunsburg, *Divided and Conquered* (Westport, Conn., 1979); J. Hughes, *To the Maginot Line* (Cambridge, Mass. 1971); P. de La Gorce, *The French Army* (London, 1963); D. Porch, *The March to the Marne* (Cambridge, 1981); D. Ralston, *The Army of the Republic* (Cambridge, Mass., 1967); J. Revol, *Histoire de l'armée française* (Paris, 1929); R. Stolfi, "Equipment for Victory in France in 1940," *History* 55 (1970); R. Young, *In Command of France* (Cambridge, Mass., 1978).

D. S. Newhall

Related entries: AFFAIRE DES FICHES; ANTICLERICALISM; ANTIMILITARISM; ARMY, POLITICAL ROLE; BELGIUM, RELATIONS WITH; BOULANGER; CONSCRIPTION, MILITARY; DALADIER; DREYFUS AFFAIR; FALLEN SOLDIER, CULT OF THE; FOCH; FOREIGN LEGION; FRANCO-PRUSSIAN WAR; FREYCINET; GALLIFFET; GAMELIN; GAULLE; GERMANY, RELATIONS WITH; GREAT BRITAIN, RELATIONS WITH; JOFFRE; LYAUTEY; MAGINOT LINE; MARNE, BATTLE OF THE; MILLERAND; MUTINIES OF 1917; OVERSEAS EMPIRE: FRENCH IMPERIALISM; PAINLEVE; PETAIN; POPULATION TRENDS; REYNAUD; RIF REBELLION; RUHR OCCUPATION; RUSSIA, RELATIONS WITH; SCHOOLS, MILITARY; SOMME, BATTLE OF THE; VERDUN, BATTLE OF; WORLD WAR I, FRANCE'S ROLE IN.

ARMY: POLITICAL ROLE. The army had no defined or overt political role under the Third Republic, although it was a significant institution within both the state and French society. The Third Republic was a liberal, parliamentary regime, increasingly democratic in its form and spirit. The French army, on the other hand, was a highly authoritarian institution, organized in accordance with rigid hierarchical principles. Many army officers harbored feelings of antipathy toward the republican regime since it claimed to embody and champion ideals different from the ones to which they were dedicated. Nevertheless, as long as the Republic lasted, the professional soldiers as a group did not seek to influence the political evolution of the country or to intervene in its governance.

With respect to the Republic, the military maintained the same disciplined detachment they had learned to display toward preceding regimes in the nineteenth century. Given the chronic political instability of the era, the soldiers came to the conclusion that only by guarding their distance from the political arena could they keep the divisive ideological quarrels characteristic of French public life from entering the military milieu. The solidarity and moral cohesion of the army would thus be protected. A necessary corollary to the nonpolitical stance of the soldiers was the presumption that they obey without question all orders and directives. In short, the political role desired by the military under the Third Republic was that of *la grande muette* (the silence on political issues enjoined upon army personnel because of their military status).

For their part, republican politicians were always somewhat wary of the army. Well aware of the fragility of their mandate, especially during the early decades of the Republic, and conscious of the persistent strength of antirepublican sentiment in the country, they might also remember the behavior of a few ambitious soldiers in the coups d'états that terminated France's two prior experiments in republican government, first in 1799 and then in 1851. Military men were also involved either tangentially or directly in several of the crises that periodically threatened the stability of the Republic. But none of them—the *seize mai* crisis, the Boulangist episode, the Dreyfus affair, or such conspiratorial undertakings as the Corvignolles network of the 1930s—represented an attempt by the military as a corporate body to play a political role. It was not until after the defeat of 1940, once the Republic had effectively voted its own demise, that military and naval officers in significant numbers took positions of responsibility under the Vichy regime. At that point, perhaps, the army may be seen as entering actively into the political life of France.

In order to perform its traditional role as the repository of organized force in civil society, the army was of necessity constituted in accordance with its own particular canons. Because their way of life and their peculiar professional concerns were alien to the normal existence of the French people, soldiers were deprived of the right to vote and placed under a special legal code. For these reasons and also as a natural complement to their avowed disinterest in politics, they assumed that the civilian elements in the state would not interfere in internal military affairs. Republican politicians were generally willing to admit their incompetence here, with the result that the army came to occupy a place apart. Although in theory completely subordinated to the responsible political authorities, the army had become by the last quarter of the nineteenth century an autonomous body within the state. Between the army and the Republic there was in effect an entente, as between two independent, self-governing entities. By the terms of this entente, each party respected the rights and prerogatives of the other in its own accepted sphere of competence.

The pragmatic accommodation between the army and the Republic worked well enough during most of the seven-decade history of the regime. Those military issues requiring legislative or executive action by the political authorities were generally settled on their ostensible merits, with the politicians doing little more than providing an official imprimatur to measures initiated at the behest of the army. In those few areas, such as conscription, where political factors impinged on military necessity as it was understood and defined by the soldiers, the latter accepted the consequences of republican lawmaking, though with misgivings. The organization of an effective high command was about the only question possessing potential political ramifications serious enough that it resisted easy solutions. The Republic eventually accepted a system whereby the power and authority of the chief of staff was increased at the expense of the prerogatives of the minister of war, his superior and the constitutional head of the army. The quasi-independent situation of the army regarding the state was thereby accentuated.

The delineation of spheres of competence and the distribution of functions between the politicians and the soldiers worked well enough in time of peace, but it faltered during World War I, a consequence of the unforeseen hyperbolic growth in the scale of the war. No one had made the constitutional or legal provisions for a conflict that disrupted the life of the nation through the mobilization of almost all of its available resources, both human and material. In order to exploit most effectively the massive means placed at its disposal by the government for the defeat of the enemy, the high command found itself issuing directions and assuming responsibilities that ordinarily were within the purview of the civil authorities. Nevertheless, the so-called dictatorship of Joseph Joffre, lasting through the first two years of the war, was instituted with the tacit consent of the politicians. Only when the staggering losses in men and material did not lead to a rapid victory were the politicians ready to reassert control over the conduct of the war. It should also be noted that the military was happy to return to a more circumscribed role within the state once the war was over.

The military may have aspired to no overt peacetime political role under the Third Republic. Even so, the army exerted a considerable influence on the workings of state and society by its very existence. Its upkeep demanded a sizable portion of the national revenues, of itself reason for the politicians to be constantly aware of it, while there also passed through its ranks an increasing percentage of the young men of the country. Soldiers also were the focus of periodic surges of patriotic emotion, associated first with the Left but later and more frequently with the Right. The army, then, had a role, albeit tacit and passive, within the French body politic whether the soldiers welcomed it or not.

P. Bankwitz, *Maxime Weygand and Civil-Military Relations in Modern France* (Cambridge, Mass., 1967); R. D. Challener, *The French Theory of the Nation in Arms, 1866–1939* (New York, 1955); R. Girardet, *La société militaire dans la France contemporaine, 1815–1939* (Paris, 1953); J. C. King, *Generals and Politicians* (Berkeley and Los Angeles, 1951); P. M. de La Gorce, *The French Army* (New York, 1963); D. B. Ralston, *The Army of the Republic* (Cambridge, Mass., 1967); J. D. Tanenbaum, *General Maurice Sarrail* (Chapel Hill, N.C., 1974).

D. B. Ralston

Related entries: ARMY: ORGANIZATION; CONSCRIPTION, MILITARY; NAVY: GOVERNMENTAL POLICY ON NAVAL WARFARE.

ARP, JEAN (1886–1966), painter, poet, and collagist of the dadaist and surrealist schools in the 1910s who evolved an abstract yet biomorphic expression in relief and free-standing sculpture beginning in the 1930s and throughout the later years of his career. He was born in Strasbourg (Alsace) under German occupation and was educated at German art schools. His initial instruction at the Strasbourg School of Arts and Crafts was supplemented by private painting lessons with Georges Ritleng, with whom he shared a lifelong interest in poetry. Arp was introduced to the Sturmer group consisting of René Schickele, Otto Flake, and Ernst Stadler, and was inspired by the tradition of German romantic poetry.

Arp continued his formal training in painting at the Weiman art school and did not come into contact with contemporary French painting until 1907. In 1908 he moved to Paris for a year and studied at the Académie Julian and then at Weggis, Switzerland, where he began experimenting with abstraction. In 1910–11 he founded the Moderne Bund of experimental art with several Swiss artists. He began a pattern of making frequent sojourns to Paris where he came into contact with cubism and also was stylistically influenced by the experiments in orphism undertaken by his friend Robert Delauney. From 1911 to 1913 he was in Munich where he exhibited with Vasily Kandinsky's Blaue Reiter group in a strongly expressive and vibrantly colored mode. He then returned to Paris until the outbreak of World War I, when he retreated to Switzerland. In the late 1910s he illustrated numerous publications of the Zurich dadaist group and some of Tristan Tzara's work; collaborated with his lifelong friend Max Ernst on a series of paintings titled "Fatagaga" in Cologne; and devised collages of layers of wood veneer in amoeba-like forms.

In the 1920s he empathized, on the one hand, with the Dutch DeStijl and the related Russian constructivist movement, which favored abstract planar and spatial relationships and more geometrical forms. On the other, he continued in a fantasy-based biomorphic mode, appreciated by André Breton's surrealist circle. He contributed to that group's first show and then resettled in Paris in 1926 with his wife, the artist Sophie Tauber. Tauber had artistic influence on him, collaborating with him on collages and translating his idiom of abstract shapes reminiscent of plant and animal forms into the medium of tapestry until her death in 1943.

Beginning in the1930s, Arp added the medium of sculpture in the round to his existing vocabulary of wood veneer, cardboard, paint, and string. By 1931 Arp joined the Abstraction Creation group, utilizing empty space as a positive visual expression and designing amoeba-like forms seemingly prototypical of the human form. Arp's work in sculpture became visually antithetical to the hard-edged or geometricized abstractions of the constructivist and DeStijl schools where planar separation of form predominated. His sensuous organic images are fetal-like with growing meshings of solids, which he aptly named "human concretion." They seem far removed from the destructive fragmentation of early dada images. He returned to Switzerland permanently at the onset of World War II.

Arp was a prolific artist, succeeding in a number of dissimilar media. His painting is said to have influenced Joan Miró's work in the use of similar fantastic shapes teeming with life on free color fields; his sculpture to have influenced Henry Moore's in its sensuous, gestational massing. The first comprehensive monograph on his work in all media, including poetry, edited by the American artist Robert Motherwell with a text by Arp himself, was published in 1948, a year before his first trip to the United States. In 1950, the architectural master Walter Gropius invited Arp to create a wall relief for the Harvard University Graduate Center. This marked the beginning of a decade and a half of worldwide recognition replete with retrospective shows and lecture tours before his death on 7 June 1966.

J. Arp, *Arp on Arp*, ed. Marcel Jean (New York, 1972), and *On My Way* (New York, 1948); J. Cathelin, *Jean Arp* (New York, 1959); R. Last, *German Dadaist Literature* (New York, 1973); H. Read, *The Art of Jean Arp* (New York, 1968); J. Soby, ed., *Arp* (New York, 1958); H. Watts, ed., *Three Painter-Poets: Arp, Schwitters, Klee* (Baltimore, 1974).

C. J. Hamm

Related entries: BRETON; DADAISM; MONDRIAN; SURREALISM.

ART: MAJOR STYLES AND MOVEMENTS. The Third Republic was a period of extraordinary creativity in the fine arts in France. It witnessed an unprecedented proliferation of new styles and movements and was the culmination of France's world leadership in the plastic arts since the eighteenth century. Throughout the nineteenth century, aspiring artists came from all Western countries to study at the Paris Ecole des beaux-arts, the most prestigious of academic art institutions. After 1870, many came to study painting and sculpture outside the academic system as well, at the source of an array of modernist styles elaborated in rapid succession from the 1850s to the 1930s: realism (1848–70), impressionism (1860s–80s), symbolism (1860s–c. 1900), postimpressionism (1885–1900), neoimpressionism (1880s–90s), fauvism (1895–1906), cubism (1910–25), orphism (1910–14), dada (1915–23), purism (1918–25), surrealism (1925–39), abstraction (1929–39). A major characteristic of French modernism is its cosmopolitanism: its fusion of the insights of generations of foreign artists living in Paris with the national tradition (classicism, romanticism, realism, impressionism).

While the coexistence and rapid succession of distinct artistic styles during the Third Republic makes any overall generalization difficult, it might nevertheless be said that after impressionism, a realist mode that nevertheless made a technical breakthrough toward abstraction, the modernist art of the period in France falls into two basic innovative types: one that exalts emotion, religious awe, the unconscious, in order to express the nonrational aspects of experience, whether religious, mystical, sensuous, or psychological (postimpressionism,symbolism, expressionism, surrealism); and one that abstracts radically from visual reality in an attempt at rational analysis of light, space, form, color (neoimpressionism, cubism, orphism, purism, abstraction). Overall in both tendencies is a rejection of both surface realism and idealizing classicism in favor of fragmentary and highly personal modes that seemed to the artists better to express individual experience, rapidly changing modern life, or the new scientific understanding of the universe (Einstein) and of the human psyche (Freud).

In the course of the nineteenth century, as the academic system (institutionalized in the Académie des beaux-arts, in its educational organ, the Ecole des beaux-arts, and in the annual government-sponsored Salon) proved unable to accommodate the growing number of artists and diversity of outlooks, artists increasingly rejected its idealist philosophy. By the early Third Republic it was only marginally relevant to the thriving artistic life in France. New organizations—most notably the Société des artistes indépendants, founded in 1884, and the Salon d'automne, founded in 1903— provided more liberal exhibition opportunities. Art schools and open studios proliferated, and increasing numbers of commercial art galleries provided further exposure. This fragmentation of every aspect of style, production, exhibition, and sale of art characterizes the period.

Predominant in French art between 1870 and 1900 were impressionism and symbolism, with the transformation and some blending of the two into several different styles by the 1880s and the 1890s. Impressionism, at its height in the 1870s, was the more unified of the two as a movement, though it nevertheless encompassed several distinct outlooks. Impressionism's main characteristic is its portrayal of incidental aspects of modern French life, primarily the most attractive ones: the look of the countryside, the bustle of towns, the middle class at its habitual amusements, occasionally the poor at their chores. The oblique perspective and asymmetrical composition of the Japanese woodblock prints then flooding Europe provided a means of isolating a slice of life.

Most impressionists (particularly Claude Monet, Pierre-Auguste Renoir, Alfred Sisley, Camille Pissarro, and Mary Cassatt) were out-of-door painters who captured fleeting scenes under the effects of sun and clouds. To achieve the desired luminosity they used purer colors in larger, more separated strokes than anyone before them, counting on optical fusion of the strokes to create an effect of mottled light and shade. Other impressionists, notably Edgar Degas and to some extent Edouard Manet, kept to a more traditional type of studio painting, nevertheless emphasizing the everyday subject, depicted informally and with little or no social commentary. The impressionists held eight group exhibitions in various private galleries between 1874 and 1886.

Symbolism was the antithesis of impressionism, embodying a rejection of surface reality and of modern life in pursuit of mysticism, aestheticism, and the fantasies and dreams of the unconscious. Represented most notably by the painters Gustave Moreau, Rodolphe Bresdin, Pierre Puvis de Chavannes, Odilon Redon, Eugène Carrière, and the illustrator Gustave Doré, symbolism was never a coherent movement. While some symbolists painted in a traditional academic manner (Moreau, Puvis) and others with a palette influenced by impressionism (Redon), all had in common the search to express a higher spiritual or emotional reality behind the visual objects in their works.

After 1885 both movements continued (impressionism, for instance, lasting until the deaths of Renoir and Monet, in 1919 and 1926, respectively) but in dialectical interaction with newer modes. Primitive and non-Western art, including medieval stained glass, Japanese woodblock prints (already a major influence on the impressionists), Egyptian, Oceanian, and, later, African art, in this age of imperialism and developing ethnology, had a great impact on the evolution of French art. The neoimpressionists or pointillists (Georges Seurat, Paul Signac, Henri-Edmond Cross, Maximilien Luce, and others), under the influence of the scientific optical and color theories of Michel-Eugène Chevreul (1786–1889), Charles Henry (1859–1926), and others, developed a hard-edged divisionism of dots of pure color in an attempt at rational analysis of light rendition in rigorously composed paintings of the typical impressionist subjects. The postimpressionists (a term coined to classify the unclassifiable) had in common little more than a criticism of impressionism as being superficial. Paul Cézanne concentrated on perspective and spatial relationships, turning his back on light and color studies. Henri de Toulouse-Lautrec further developed Degas' technique in pastels and oils to create luminous, melancholy images of the pleasure spots and lowlife of Montmartre. Vincent Van Gogh heightened the impressionist brushstroke into an expressive and symbolic medium for a sympathetic depiction of the southern French landscape and people and an anguished personal struggle with madness. Paul Gauguin turned to a flattened, decorative mode in which brilliant color depicted the emotional world of religious faith (in Brittany) and of primitive life, beliefs, and fears (in Tahiti). The Nabis (Hebrew for "prophets"), followers of Gauguin (including Maurice Denis, Paul Sérusier, and Félix Vallotton), some of them Rosicrucians, linked brilliant color and symbolism in an attempt to recapture the original bond between art and religion. In iconic images of symbolic and mystical intent, they tried to break down the barriers between decorative and fine art. Pierre Bonnard, Edouard Vuillard, and Ker Xavier Roussel, remotely connected to the Nabis but more worldly and more tolerant of impressionism, heightened the impressionist color while retaining its brushstroke and composition in depicting landscape, middle-class Parisian interiors, and the street life of the metropolis.

Between the late 1890s and 1906, a new movement, again merely a collection of remotely related approaches, arose and was pejoratively dubbed fauvism, the painting of wild beasts. Its unifying characteristic was color: pure, unrestrained color straight from the tube, applied in an expressionist manner derived from Van Gogh, or in the flat, decorative way of Gauguin, or the more restrained divisionism characteristic of neoimpressionism. A last phase in the exploration of color, brushstroke, and the everyday event begun by the impressionists thirty years earlier, fauvism briefly brought together many of the young painters who would soon develop individual styles and become great twentieth-century innovators: Henri Matisse, Georges Braque, André Derain, Maurice Vlaminck, Kees van Dongen, Raoul Dufy, Albert Marquet, Georges Rouault, and others. The fauvist works are expressionalist emotionalizations of landscape (as with the Chatou painters Vlaminck and Derain) or of the daily scenes (Rouault, Dufy, van Dongen); sensuous exaltations of sinuous shapes and vibrant colors (Matisse); flattened abstractions of landscape rendered in enlarged, emotionalized divisionist dots (Derain, Braque). Matisse, in particular, continued throughout his long career to build on the study of color and sensation begun during the fauvist period. Other fauves, however, soon turned to a more cerebral approach.

From about 1906 until 1914, many French avant-garde artists focused on spatial rendition, culminating in a radical break with post-Renaissance perspective and in a growing abstraction. The chief architects of the new spatial system were the Spaniard Pablo Picasso and the ex-fauve Georges Braque, under the influence of African sculpture and of the postimpressionist Cézanne, whose works came into prominence through a posthumous retrospective at the 1907 Salon d'automne. Between 1906 and 1910, Picasso, Braque, and to some extent Derain developed cubism through an attempt to restore volume and a heightened sense of structure to painting while rejecting the traditional system of perspective and chiaroscuro predominant in the West since 1500. Their analytic cubism of 1910–12 featured a fragmentation of objects through the juxtaposition of varied perspectives, rendered almost without color—a complete revision of perspectival representation remotely influenced by Einstein's special theory of relativity (1905) and by Johann Sebastian Bach's counterpoint. Color was reintroduced in the collages that began in 1912—assemblages of bits of newspaper, wallpaper, and advertising into cubist studies of café tabletops: the first artworks made by selection and positioning of prefabricated industrial materials. In synthetic cubism (1913–25), the fragmented images became more legible, and color was reintroduced to define separate planes in a highly arbitrary way not dependent on the actual color of things.

By 1912 many other artists had come under cubist influence, resulting in a proliferation of cubist styles and derivatives. Closest to Picasso and Braque were Juan Gris, Louis Marcoussis, and Jacques Villon, and later the sculptors Raymond Duchamp-Villon, Henri Laurens, and Jacques Lipchitz. Another group, led by Albert Gleizes and Jean Metzinger, the theoreticians of the movement, practiced a more conservative, Cézannian variation of the style. It was their works, displayed in room 41 at the 1911 Salon des indépendants, that caused a public scandal; those of Braque and Picasso were exhibited only privately in galleries. An offshoot of cubism was the Italian futurist movement, proclaimed from Paris in 1910, which sought to revise the cubist spatial analysis in order to represent the dynamism and movement of modern life. Influenced by both futurism and cubism, various artists in Paris, lumped together arbitrarily by the poet-art critic Guillaume Apollinaire as orphists (colorists, or searchers after a pure art, in various readings of the term), developed individual styles between 1912 and 1914. Fernand Léger applied cubism to strongly colored, abstract mechanical forms. Marcel Duchamp rendered moving objects as series of juxtaposed stills before deserting painting for mechanism and dadaism. Francis Picabia eliminated the object entirely in pursuit of cubist-inspired fantasies. The Czech Frank Kupka developed a nonobjective style composed of highly colored, rhythmical forms. Robert and Sonia Delaunay, the most deserving of the name of orphists, experimented with highly colored cubist representations of the city and modern life, culminating in an abstract mode in which space is expressed entirely through color contrasts. A group exhibiting between 1912 and 1925 as the Section d'or (Gleizes, Gris, Villon, Duchamp-Villon), sought to codify a rational system of abstract representation by applying classical systems of proportion to cubism.

The First World War interrupted and greatly changed the course of French art; many artists were drafted, others emigrated, a few were killed or seriously wounded, and the system of exhibition and sale was disrupted until the early 1920s. Two different artistic responses to the war shaped the major styles of the 1920s and 1930s: the nihilism and irrationalism of dada and its more lasting offspring, surrealism, and a return to classical values and a retreat from modernism, which has been called a return to order. Alongside these new manifestations, prewar modernism continued, though with a more classical cast, in the synthetic cubism of Picasso, Braque, and Gris, the sensuous expressionism of Matisse, and a purified, geometrical abstraction that became a major movement by the 1930s.

Dada, and later surrealism, were revolutionary protests against the complacent bourgeois spirit of the *belle époque* and the unthinking conformism and untrammeled capitalism that were deemed responsible for the war. The nihilist dada spirit was spread by groups of antimilitarist artist-refugees in New York and in Zurich, but it had its origin just before the war in Duchamp's ready-mades, manufactured objects signed and thus sanctified as art by the artist, and in Francis Picabia's irreverent paintings of fanciful, erotic machines. Duchamp and Picabia were reunited in New York in 1915, and in exhibitions and reviews they mocked the pretensions of artists and the art public. In Zurich, meanwhile, an international group of artist-exiles held riotous soirées in which they denounced all artistic, political, and social philosophies, annihilated language by composing nonsense verses, and declared psychic automatism as the only valid creative method. When dadaism reached Paris in the early 1920s, with the arrival of Duchamp and Man Ray from New York, of Picabia, Tristan Tzara, Jean Arp, and Max Ernst from Zurich and Germany, and the adherence of a group of younger French poets (André Breton, Louis Aragon, Philippe Soupault, Robert Desnos), it quickly split into two factions. One, led by Tzara, continued for a while to keep alive the original spirit of mockery, but other French poets and artists insisted on finding a constructive style and developed surrealism by the mid-1920s. Based on Freud's view of the primacy of the unconscious, surrealism proposed artistic and social liberation through the unleashing of the human imagination in cre-ativity. To the surrealists, only the images welling up from the unconscious in the form of dreams or fantasies are genuine. To liberate the imagination was to destroy the efficacy of social constraints; while this philosophy, in recognizing only the individual, is properly anarchist, various surrealists were optimistically drawn to communism until the triumph of socialist realism in the Soviet Union in the early 1930s. The surrealist painters—Max Ernst, Joan Miró, André Masson, Yves Tanguy, René Magritte, and, at a distance, Picasso, Duchamp, and Balthus—remained aloof from these political squabbles. Surrealist painting, influenced by the prewar dream images by Giorgio de Chirico of empty streets and ominous buildings but also by the playfulness of Duchamp's ready-mades, his verbal and artistic puns, and his erotic machine images, is extremely varied. The inevitably irrational imagery is depicted sometimes in a totally spontaneous way (Masson's sand paintings, Ernst's *frottages*) but often in a painstakingly realist, academic style (Dali, Tanguy, Balthus, Magritte). It can be abstract, or nearly so, as in the work of Joan Miró, since the unconscious can conjure up abstract as well as naturalistic images; it is often frankly erotic or sadistic.

Among other artists, both prewar innovators and newcomers, the war and the dislocation of the avant-garde art market produced a reaction in favor of figurative art and more traditional subject matter, relearned from models as diverse as the Italian quattrocento and northern primitive painting, the Dutch seventeenth century, Jean-Auguste Ingres, and Camille Corot. While Picasso, Braque, Matisse, Léger and other leaders sought to demonstrate, without any return to academicism, the compatibility of modernism and traditional values in art, other artists adopted frankly realist modes of representation and subject matter (Derain, Roger de La Fresnaye, de Chirico and Gino Severini), while others sought to adapt academicism to new subjects (Picabia, Balthus, the young Giacometti), and still others turned to a worldly mixture of fauvism, cubism, and tradition that was commercially successful (Dufy, Vlaminck, Van Dongen, Tamara De Lempicka). Nevertheless, Matisse's and Léger's classically inspired odalisques and Braque's canephores exist in a fully post-cubist space; Picasso produced cubist and proto-surrealist works in alternation with works of great classical purity and others of mythological inspiration; and others, including Léger, the Delaunays, and Kupka, continued the evolution toward abstraction started during the last years before the war. The purists, Amédée Ozenfant and Charles Edouard Jeanneret (the future Le Corbusier), briefly seconded by Léger, called in their review *L'Esprit nouveau* (1920–25) for a clean, emotionless abstraction of real-life objects that would have the precision and beauty of machinery. The Paris Exposition des arts décoratifs of 1925 displayed the modernists' continued worship of the machine age and of trim, highly simplified cubic images in painting, sculpture, and architecture, as well as a more popular ornamental style (Art Deco) consisting of pristinely stylized flowers and geometric motifs. Virtually all French artists stopped short of total abstraction, however, until the 1930s when Paris became a center for abstract art due to the presence of the Dutch painter Piet Mondrian, the Dutch architect Theo Van Doesburg, and after the Hitlerian takeover in Germany, the lyrical abstractionist Wassily Kandinsky. Known at various times as Cercle et carré, Art concret, Abstraction-création, the French abstractionist movement of the 1930s brought together as many as 400 exhibitors, mostly practicing a highly geometric art totally devoid of figuration.

Amid the economic crisis of the 1930s, which hit artists especially hard, and the gathering storm clouds of war, the Popular Front offered a broad spectrum of artists a last opportunity, during the Third Republic, to exhibit and produce large decorative projects for the Exposition universelle held in Paris in 1937. The dominant artistic tone of the exposition, manifested in its major buildings, the Palais de Chaillot, the Palais de Tokyo, and the German and Soviet pavilions, was the search for heroic grandeur through a return to classicism. But the modernist movement, and particularly the pristine abstract style of the 1930s, was also well represented, demonstrating its continued vitality in huge murals celebrating modern technology in aviation, electricity, and rail transport by the Delaunays, Dufy, Léger, Gleizes, and others. In addition, Picasso was able to exhibit *Guernica*, his fierce outcry against modern warfare, in the pavilion of the Spanish Republic.

The impending world war, and in particular the German occupation, would sweep away France's leadership in the arts, as many artists would emigrate, others retreat into the silence of private life, and as the Right (whether in Paris or Vichy) would enforce a return to traditional values in the arts.

D. Ades et al., *Dada and Surrealism Reviewed* (London, 1978); *L'Art dans les années 30 en France* (Saint Etienne, 1979); D. Cooper, *The Cubist Epoch* (London, 1971); J. Golding, *Cubism: A History and an Analysis, 1907–14* (Boston, 1968); D. E. Gordon, *Modern Art Exhibitions, 1900–1916* (Munich, 1974); W. Hofmann, *Turning Points in Twentieth-Century Art, 1890–1917* (New York, n.d.); R. Huyghe and J. Rudel, *L'Art et le monde moderne* (Paris, 1969–70); *Le Livre des expositions universelles* (Paris, 1983); *Paris-Berlin* (Paris, 1978); *Paris-Moscou* (Paris, 1979); *Paris-New York* (Paris, 1977); *Paris-Paris, 1937-1957* (Paris, 1981); *Petit Larousse de la peinture* (Paris, 1979); G. Picon, *Journal du surréalisme, 1919–1939* (Geneva, 1976); *Les Réalismes, 1919–1939* (Paris, 1980); J. Rewald, *The History of Impressionism* (New York, 1973); J. Rewald, *Postimpressionism* (New York, 1962); R. Rosenblum, *Cubism and Twentieth Century Art* (New York, 1966); M. Seuphor, *L'Art abstrait* (N.p., 1971–73); T. Shapiro, *Painters and Politics: The European Avant-garde and Society, 1900–1925* (New York, 1976); V. Spate, *Orphism* (Oxford, 1979). *Le symbolisme en Europe* (Paris, 1976); D. Vallier, *Repères* (N.p., 1976).

T. Shapiro

Related entries: ARCHITECTURE AND URBAN PLANNING; ART: OFFI-CIAL; ART DECO; CUBISM; DADAISM; EXPRESSIONISM; FAUVISM; IMPRESSIONISM; NABIS, THE; NEOIMPRESSIONISM; POSTIMPRES-SIONISM; SURREALISM; SYMBOLISM.

ART: OFFICIAL, a term denoting the role of the state in sponsoring art exhibitions and in providing commissions and purchases for selected artists. Although the state had surrendered its control of the Salon by 1882 to meet the vocal demands of numerous artists for a liberalized exhibition system, it tenaciously sought to retain influence in the art world through the periodic organization of large-scale exhibitions. In the international exhibitions of 1879, 1889, and 1900, the state presented serious retrospective sections of French creativity. Other state-sponsored exhibitions, such as the Exhibition nationale (1883), seemed motivated by the notion that high quality in art could be sustained only by the interactions of jurors representing governmental standards and tastes. The state, with its sanction of official art, was closely involved with the training and education of individual artists. By this means it could ensure the continued fulfillment of its priority: a promotion of art for the masses, or, more precisely, the middle classes.

Thus, in 1883, at the very moment that the Salon was being liberalized, the state went into competition by its organization of the Exhibition nationale. For this, a jury, composed of governmental representatives and such conservative artists as Jules Breton, Jean Jacques Henner, Jules Lefebvre, Puvis de Chavannes, and Gustave Moreau, screened all submitted works, previously shown or not. Many independent painters refused to submit anything to the jury and were not represented. Since few, if any, of the exhibited works were for sale (one major difference from the annual Salon), the Exhibition nationale became an event reflecting official taste, in which the public could browse without distraction over the most successful exhibits of earlier, governmentally sponsored Salons. In this way, the government mustered support for its system of awards and purchases. Many artists, including Jules Bastien-Lepage, participated, presumably to bask in the air of rarefied and contrived official prestige.

Curiously, however, it was not the avant-garde artists who severely chastised the government for this self-indulgent attitude. Rather it was the members of the less radical Société des Artistes Français (originally formed to help liberalize the Salon) who denounced the establishment of state-sponsored exhibitions as a deliberate attempt to compete with the Salon. It was apparent that such official retrospectives threatened the Salon's very existence since it represented a state power of veto over new talent. Some of the artists participating in the 1883 Exhibition nationale took stock of this dilemma; they petitioned the government to change the opening date of the show. But even though this was conceded, mainly through the advocacy of Jules Breton, the Exhibition nationale gave rise to many uneasy feelings concerning the extent of state dominance in art.

Similar policies were adopted by the government with regard to the large retrospective sections of the Paris World Fairs of 1878, 1889, and 1900. Again, it was official decree that differentiated good and bad creativity, and again a furor in the art world ensued. The experimentation revealed in the various pavilions of art seemed at odds with the shortsighted attempt to standardize all exhibited works by showing them in accepted categories. Although the opportunity existed for a given painter to have a miniretrospective of his work, he had to submit to censure all relatively innovative examples. Often the works that were eventually exhibited proved to be quite dated, so that well-established painters found themselves represented by some of their less-challenging works. Such was the case with Jules Breton at the 1878 Paris fair. Here he was represented by earlier Salon-medal-winning paintings, which in the meantime had been purchased by the government for the official state museum (Musée du Luxembourg). Such a paucity of new work was galling to many art critics, who questioned the necessity of such an elaborate show merely to underscore old policies.

By 1900, however, the state had recognized the relevance of the decorative arts. Under the sponsorship of the Union centrale des arts décoratifs, many innovative works were brought forward to demonstrate the growing interrelations between art and industry (an area of some interest to the state since it increased the market viability of art).

Information is difficult to obtain about commissions and governmental purchases. Many of the works that were purchased from the different Salons have disappeared from view, and we have only photographs to remind us of their former popularity. Subsidizing artists by purchasing individual works was a practice the state had initiated during the early Second Empire. It was unfortunate that the familiar consequence of patronage—works intended to satisfy the patron—had the effect of filling the public galleries with an art that was anachronistic and misrepresentative: late romantic narrative painting, pastoral scenes, sentimental genre scenes, and heroic sculpture. Only on occasion, as in the case of a large-scale canvas by P. A. J. Dagnan-Bouveret, *The Horses at the Watering Trough* (Musée de Chambéry), from the 1885 Salon, were new stylistic tendencies considered in state purchases.

If a few works were destined for the sophisticated critics at the Musée du Luxembourg, the majority of purchases conformed to didactic themes that could be easily comprehended by unskilled observers. Some paintings were eventually situated in provincial museums, public places, and town halls and used in a manner intended to instill the message of the Third Republic in its people. When an official commission was given to an artist, such as in the case of Auguste Rodin for the doors of the new Museum of the Decorative Arts, money was allocated for materials and work; however, the work had to be assessed by governmental critics at various stages of its evolution. With regard to the fiercely independent Rodin, this meant that the Gates of Hell was never to be finished to the artist's satisfaction. His personal vision fell victim to extraneously imposed constraints.

In summary, state sponsorship of the arts had the adverse effect of hampering the development of independent creativity. This gave rise to exceptional acrimony between the state, which craved to uphold the morality of the status quo, and numerous secessionist movements, which attacked the biased policies dominating patronage. Eventually this resulted in the creation of new exhibition sites: in cafés, newspaper offices, private galleries and new salons, so in effect the forces of restraint accentuated the artist's sense of independence.

A. Boime, *The Academy and French Painting in the Nineteenth Century* (London, 1971); G. P. Weisberg, *The Realist Tradition, French Painting and Drawing, 1830–1900* (Cleveland, 1980); P. Vaisse, "La Troisième République et les peintres, recherches sur les rapports des pouvoirs publics et de la peinture en France de 1870 à 1914" (Doctoral thesis, University of Paris, 1980).

G. P. Weisberg

Related entries: ART: MAJOR STYLES AND MOVEMENTS; ART DECO; DECORATIVE ARTS; RODIN; SALON, ROLE OF THE.

ART DECO (1925–1939), also labeled *art moderne*, a dominant design trend in Western Europe and North America during the decades between the world wars. Its stylistic hallmarks of geometricized representational motifs appeared in all modes of ornamentation: architecture, interior design, stage sets, print lettering, decorative arts, clothing, and jewelry. In its superficial rejection of the classical Western artistic tradition, it is linked to the earlier Art Nouveau design movement. In contrast to the Art Nouveau style prevalent on the Continent at the turn of the century, the characteristics of which were sinuous lines, organic massing, sensuously curved profiles, and floral motifs of an abstracted naturalism, Art Deco featured fractured lines, jagged or zig-zagging profiles, more machine-made forms, and hard-edged images of power such as lightning bolts. Whereas some Art Nouveau work revitalized the handicraft tradition, the image Art Deco created was one of futuristic, machine-based power. Nevertheless, the *moderne* image was conveyed through a traditional idiom, that of surface ornamentation remotely based on historic design precedents such as the strong geometric patterns of primitive African, ancient Mayan, and Egyptian art.

The name *Art Deco* comes from L'Exposition des arts decoratifs, an international design fair planned before the war but not actually held in Paris until 1925. Germany was not invited to participate, and the pavilions built for the Paris exhibition extolled French artistic values. These pavilions were symmetrically composed white blocks, enlivened inside and out with an abundance of surface ornamentation that looked machine made, nontraditional, and powerfully kinetic because of the fractured lines and zig-zagged profiles used. It was thus new and forward looking, as befitted a postwar exhibition in the second decade of the twentieth-century machine age. It was, at the same time, derived from the French tradition of rich ornamentation and emphatically not German. Art Deco ornamentation was on one level a retort to the spare designs of contemporary avant-garde German architects at the Bauhaus artistic-educational enclave in Dessau.

The 1925 exposition, dedicated to the glorification of the beautiful and utilitarian, was cataloged at the time as showing by its ornamentation souvenirs of old French traditions, allusions of contemporary life, and (at least superficial awareness of) issues of the paradoxical geometry of the cubist movement in French painting. Classical ornaments such as fluted columns were stripped down to look more machined, and paired scrolls were given zig-zag edges and a futuristic gloss, because according to contemporary reviews, the 1925 exposition architecture was also meant to show that the French cultural tradition was not only still alive but also ready to reestablish its ascendancy in the new age. The introduction to the official guide to the pavilion architecture stated that, at the very least, the exposition proved to the world the vitality of France, mutilated by the war but intact in its pacifying genius and ready to collaborate on the rebuilding of the world.

The Art Deco style had overtones of high culture. Its fractured lines create superficial visual linkages to experiments in painting (such as cubism and de Stijl) and in architecture (such as Russian constructivism), all involving ideational constructs of perceptions about spatial relationships of volumes interpenetrating. High art interest by Pablo Picasso and other avant-garde painters had arisen in the primitive art of Polynesia and Africa and ethnological museums had opened by the second decade of the century. Archaeologists and the public were in a fervor over discovery of Tutankhamen's tomb in Egypt in 1922. Simplistic references in color, line, and form to other artistic interests of the time appear in Art Deco and were readily translated to a commercial idiom. Reproducible by machine, Art Deco motifs appear in linoleum floors, refrigerator door fronts, earrings, cigarette cases, and floor lamps to be sold at exclusive shops or dime stores.

Decorative art and architectural journals transmitted the style displayed at the 1925 Paris exposition to the rest of Europe and the United States. By the time of the Century of Progress fair in Chicago in 1933, the style had become streamlined. There was less ornamentation, less business in the lines of decoration; the preferred machine image became the sleeker aerodynamism of advanced aircraft of the time. The move to sparer, less ornamented treatment in Art Deco architecture in the 1930s coincided with the international economic recession. Streamlined *moderne* became the preferred style for the great prototypical skyscraper office buildings in the United States, the Chrysler Building and the Empire State Building in New York City.

Vestiges of the stylized geometry of Art Deco were to live on in Europe and the United States into the late 1940s predominantly in the decorative arts. In domestic architecture in Europe and in commercial architecture in Europe and the Americas, the International style (nonornamented buildings of the Bauhaus architects Walter Gropius and Ludwig Mies Van der Rohe, and the parallel theories and, for the most part, paper designs of Le Corbusier) was to become ascendant from 1945 through the late 1970s. Only in the late 1960s and 1970s did Art Deco receive any widespread popular approval again or become the subject of serious scholarly analysis. By then, its importance was recognized as being *le dernier cri* of the French decorative arts tradition and as being simultaneously the last decorated architectural style until the postmodernist rebellion of the late 1970s in image and engineering.

R. Banham, *Theory and Design in the First Machine Age* (London, 1960); M. Battersby, *The Decorative Thirties* (New York, 1971), and *The Decorative Twenties* (London, 1969); L. Deshairs, ed., *L'Art decoratif français* (Paris, 1925); D. Gebhard and H. Von Breton, *The Moderne in Southern California* (Santa Barbara, 1969); B. Hillier, *Art Deco of the Twenties and Thirties* (London, 1968); K. J. Sembach, *Style 1930* (New York, 1971); G. Veronesi, *Style and Design, 1909–1929* (New York, 1968).

                                                                              C. J. Hamm

Related entries: ARCHITECTURE AND URBAN PLANNING; ART: MAJOR STYLES AND MOVEMENTS; ART NOUVEAU; DECORATIVE ARTS.

ART NOUVEAU (1890–1910), a style in the decorative arts popular around 1900. Also known as the modern style and the style of 1900, Art Nouveau was virtually synonymous with the *belle époque*. First emerging from the handcrafted glassware and furniture produced in Nancy, Art Nouveau was brought to Paris by a dealer in oriental art, Samuel Bing, in the 1890s.

Art Nouveau represented a revolution against the banality of mass-produced furniture and decorative pieces. It was primarily a decorative style affecting the production of wallpapers, fabrics, glass, upholstery, and furniture. The style was characterized by continuous, dynamic lines, rich detailing, biomorphic forms, and abstract naturalism. Colorful, sinuous, luxurious, sensual, Art Nouveau interiors gave a strikingly coherent and unique impression. The often bizarre animal or plant-like forms were fanciful, exotic, and even frightening.

Like the arts and crafts movement in England by which it was partially inspired, Art Nouveau provoked a revival of some of the traditional crafts. The decline of apprenticeship in crafts like cabinetmaking and the continuing popularity of eighteenth-century furniture styles had inhibited the achievement of a distinctive late nineteenth-century style until the emergence of Art Nouveau.

Art Nouveau was not for everyone; it was expensive fancy work for the leisured classes. It expressed an aesthetic that disdained industrial society and represented a retreat by the aristocracy of taste from mass culture. An overwhelming triumph at the World's Fair of 1900 held in Paris, the style lost its popularity before World War I and gave way in the 1920s to the spare, geometric style of Art Deco. A few remnants of the style, created by Hector Guimard in 1900, still decorate some Parisian Métro stations.

Issues of *L'Art décoratif, Art et Décoration,* and *Revue des Arts décoratifs,* 1900–1910. S. Bing, *Artistic America, Tiffany Glass, and Art Nouveau,* ed. Robert Koch (Cambridge, Mass., 1970); R. Guerrand, *L'Art nouveau en Europe* (Paris, 1965); Ministère du Commerce, *Rapports du Jury International, Exposition universelle internationale de 1900 à Paris* (Paris, 1902).

T. M. McBride

Related entries: ART: MAJOR STYLES AND MOVEMENTS; ART DECO; *BELLE EPOQUE, LA*; BING; DECORATIVE ARTS.

ARTAUD, ANTONIN (1896–1948), writer, actor, director, and theoretician of the Theater of Cruelty, whose ideas, largely unaccepted during his lifetime, have triumphed in the contemporary theater. In 1923 Artaud submitted a group of poems for publication to Jacques Rivière, editor of *La Nouvelle revue française* (*NRF*), who rejected them but invited Artaud to converse with him. In the resulting correspondence, Artaud explained his difficulty in finding words to translate his emotions and then raised the momentous question whether a work growing out a of painful struggle for expression and whose language was awkward deserved less recognition than a formally more accomplished but facile work. Rivière found Artaud's self-analysis so convincing that he published the *Correspondence* in the *NRF* in September 1924 and encouraged him to persevere in his efforts. But having come across surrealist automatic techniques (spontaneous, personal expressions interjected into the text), Artaud decided to abandon conventional literary standards and to join the surrealist group. Although short-lived (until 1926), his participation in the group's activities was particularly intense. He directed the Centrale surréaliste, edited the third issue of *La Révolution surréaliste* (to which he contributed a series of forceful open letters), and produced the collection of essays, *L'Ombilic des limbes* and *Le Pèsenerfs* (both 1925), that evinced a sustained preoccupation with expressing the depths of his being. From his surrealist collaboration, Artaud retained an unshakable belief in the liberating power of the subconscious, a belief that inspired his ideas on the Theater of Cruelty.

As formulated in *Le Théâtre et son double* (1938), the Theater of Cruelty was to function as a force of redemption for individual and society. Borrowing Saint Augustine's analogy between the plague and the theater, Artaud contended that the two were alike in their cathartic effects. The plague brought all that was noxious and hidden to the surface and left the bodily organs purified, while the theater, by causing actor and audience to experience in a collective setting the passions lurking in the subconscious, cleansed the mind. That is why the theater had to be cruel, for only by confronting the spectator with the worst that can happen could it exorcise his fears. That is also why it had to communicate directly to the senses, through gestures, colors, rhythms, or sounds, bypassing discursive language, an exclusively intellectual means of exchange.

Artaud had few opportunities to implement his conceptions. He entered the theatrical field in 1921, playing various parts on stage and in film. In 1927 he founded with Roger Vitrac the Théâtre Alfred Jarry, which succeeded in giving four performances before closing in 1929 for lack of funds. In 1935 he opened the Théâtre de la Cruauté where he produced his own *Les Cenci* but again failed to create a positive impact. His ideas came of age only in the 1950s and 1960s when they emerged in the plays of Samuel Beckett and Jean Genet and inspired productions that emphasized stage imagery at the expense of dialogue.

In 1937, after a series of extravagant acts, Artaud was arrested, sent to an asylum, and diagnosed a schizophrenic. From then until 1946 he was held in various institutions, sometimes undergoing electric shock therapy. Because his writings teemed with revolt against conventional standards of morality, art, literature, and social behavior, he became a symbol of the individual branded insane by a society whose rules he refused to accept. Accordingly, while his ideas influenced contemporary playwrights and directors, his fate inspired such books as Michel Foucault's *Histoire de la folie* (1961) and made him a hero for the 1968 student *revoltés*.

A. Artaud, *Oeuvres complètes* (Paris, 1956–78); A. Bermel, *Artaud's Theater of Cruelty* (New York, 1977); M. Esslin, *Artaud* (New York, 1976); A. Virmaux, *Antonin Artaud et le théâtre* (Paris, 1970).

M. D. Maayan

Related entries: BRETON; CINEMA; SURREALISM; THEATER.

ASSOCIATIONS, LAW OF (1901), republican and anticlerical measure designed to control the activity of religious orders in France. These religious orders were regarded with suspicion by the French state throughout much of the nineteenth century. Republicans feared that the many schools and hospitals run by the orders were a source of division in France because of their advocacy of royalism and ultramontanism. In 1880 the government of Jules Ferry had made an attempt to enforce legislation that required all religious congregations to be authorized officially by the state. This attempt by the Opportunists stopped far short of eliminating the orders. In 1899 they had over 1,500 establishments in France, which housed over 37,000 priests and brothers and 120,000 nuns. Over half of these orders were not authorized.

The Dreyfus affair provided an opportunity for anticlerical politicians to expel the orders from France. The anti-Semitism of the Assumptionists in their daily *La Croix* antagonized public opinion and made a general attack on the orders likely to succeed. The government of René Waldeck-Rousseau introduced legislation in November of 1899 that would grant greater freedom of association for laic organizations such as labor unions and learned societies while restricting the rights of associations with headquarters outside France whose rules implied a renunciation of the Declaration of the Rights of Man, provisions clearly directed at religious congregations. By the time the legislation was passed in July 1901, radical deputies in the Chamber of Deputies, led by Georges Trouillot, had rewritten the bill to make it a more extreme measure. In its final version the bill prohibited any member of an unauthorized congregation from teaching, even if he demonstrated that he was no longer affiliated with the order. Furthermore, the Chamber transferred the right to authorize associations from the administration to the legislature, which intended to use this power to eliminate rather than control the congregations.

Confusion about the provisions of the law led to a delay in its application until after the elections of May 1902. The Radicals won a clear majority and, led by the new government of the anticlerical Emile Combes, rigorously enforced the Law of Associations. Thousands of schools were closed, the property of the orders was confiscated and sold by the state, and those members of orders who wished to continue as religious had to leave France. Protests by the secular clergy against the measure led to the suspension of salaries and to administrative action designed to curtail contacts between Rome and the French church. The conflict over the Law of Associations formed the background for the separation of church and state that took place in 1905.

M. Larkin, *Church and State after the Dreyfus Affair* (New York, 1974); M. A. Partin, *Waldeck-Rousseau, Combes and the Church: The Politics of Anticlericalism, 1899–1905* (Durham, N.C., 1969).

T. A. Kselman

Related entries: ANTICLERICALISM; COMBES; ROMAN CATHOLICISM: CHURCH-STATE RELATIONS; ROMAN CATHOLICISM: CLERGY; SEPARATION OF CHURCH AND STATE, LAW OF; WALDECK-ROUSSEAU.

AUCLERT, HUBERTINE (1848–1914), founder and principal leader of the French women's suffrage movement during the first half of the Third Republic. Orphaned young but possessed of a modest inheritance, she began her feminist career in the early 1870s as a young recruit to the campaign for women's civil

rights directed by Léon Richer and Maria Deraismes. Firmly convinced that
women had first to win the right to vote in order to secure their civil rights,
however, Auclert broke with Richer and Deraismes when they forbade her to
raise the issue of women's suffrage at the first French Congrès international du
droit des femmes of 1878. Thereafter, as the founder and general secretary of
the Société le droit des femmes, established in 1876 and renamed the Société
le suffrage des femmes in 1883, and as the director of *La Citoyenne* (1881–91),
as well as a contributor to *Le Radical* and numerous other journals, Auclert
sought to win over the general public and to convince moderate feminists that
women's emancipation required a suffrage-first orientation backed by public
confrontations with the authorities, a strategical and tactical stance known as the
politique de l'assaut. Only during a brief marriage to her long-time friend and
lawyer Antonin Lévrier, which lasted from 1888 until his death in 1892, did she
partially withdraw from feminist activism. Even then, while in Algeria where
Lévrier served as a justice of the peace, Auclert wrote a series of articles that
later appeared in book form as *Les Femmes arabes en Algérie* (1900).

Auclert conducted her assault along a wide front. She personally secured a
sweeping endorsement of women's civil and political rights from the French Left
at the Marseilles socialist congress of 1879, while from the French Right she
later gained access to and the tentative support of Edouard Drumont's *La Libre
Parole*. Through a protracted tax strike, a call for a census boycott, and repeated
attempts to register to vote and to run for office, Auclert not only provoked
additional publicity for her cause but helped as well to clarify the inadequacy
of existing legal and administrative remedies for women's grievances. Within
her lifetime, she played an instrumental role in winning passage of the 1900 seat
law that required employers to provide chairs for sales personnel, in pioneering
propaganda techniques such as suffrage postal cards and letter stamps, and in
pushing, through opposition as much as cooperation, the French feminist movement
to accord priority to women's suffrage shortly after the turn of the century.
Although living to see neither the Senate's close defeat of women's suffrage at
the end of the First World War nor its passage in the final days of the Second
World War, Auclert continued to influence the course of events through the
example of her activism, which even her detractors grudgingly admired, and her
exhaustive liberal-republican defense of women's right to vote, the essence of
which appeared in two book-length works: *Le Vote des femmes* (1908) and *Les
Femmes au gouvernail* (1923).

J. Maitron, ed., *Dictionnaire biographique du mouvement ouvrier français*, vol. 10
(Paris, 1973); *Dictionnaire de biographie française*, Vol. 4 (Paris, 1947); *Larousse du
XXe siècle* (Paris, 1933); introduction by Auclert's sister Marie Chaumont to Auclert,
Les Femmes au gouvernail (Paris, 1923); P. Bidelman, *Pariahs Stand Up!* (Westport,
Conn., 1982); E. Taieb, *Hubertine Auclert* (Paris, 1982); C. Moses, *French Feminism
in the Nineteenth Century* (Albany, 1984); J. Rabaut, *Histoire des féminismes français*
(Paris, 1978).

P. K. Bidelman

Related entries: DERAISMES; FEMINISM; RICHER; WOMEN: MOVE-
MENT FOR POLITICAL RIGHTS.

AULARD, ALPHONSE (1849–1928), historian, teacher, and journalist specializing in the history of the Revolution and Napoleon. He was born in Montbron (Charente), the son of a professor of philosophy and secondary school inspector. The young Aulard received his primary education at Tours and Lons-le-Saunier. He continued his studies at the Collège Sainte Barbe and the Ecole normale supérieure, where during his three-year stay (1867–70) he displayed strong republican and anticlerical feelings. The outbreak of the Franco-Prussian War led him to join the mobile National Guard of the Seine, in which he served during the siege of Paris and at the Battle of Buzenval. Resuming his education after the conflict, he became an *agrégé de lettres* in 1871, and then taught at various provincial lycées. He was promoted, first to the lycée Janson de Sailly in Paris and then in 1886 to a position as the first professor of the history of the French Revolution at the University of Paris. Five years later, he received an endowed chair and held it until he retired in 1922.

Originally a literary historian, Aulard received the doctorate for a dissertation on the Italian poet Giacomo Leopardi (1877). His interest in rhetoric encouraged him to study the orators of the Revolution and to produce his *Eloquence parlementaire pendant la Révolution française* (3 vols., 1882–86). Influenced by Léon Gambetta, Aulard became an admirer of Danton, whom he sought to rescue from charges of corruption and immorality and to elevate as the greatest figure in the Revolution. From the 1880s Aulard devoted himself almost exclusively to the study of the Revolutionary and Napoleonic periods and contributed to *La Révolution française*, serving as its editor from 1887 to his death. With state subsidies and unacknowledged assistance from a team of copyists, Aulard produced numerous volumes of documents: *Recueil des Actes du Comité de Salut Public* (26 vols., 1889–1923); *La Société des Jacobins* (6 vols., 1889–97); *Paris pendant la Réaction thermidorienne et sous le Directoire* (5 vols., 1898–1902); *Paris sous le Consulat* (4 vols., 1903–19); and *Paris sous le Premier Empire* (2 vols., 1912–14). His other works include *Le Culte de la Raison et le Culte de l'Etre Suprême* (1893), a study of Revolutionary religions; *Histoire politique de la Révolution française, 1789–1804* (1901), his synthesis of the political and religious history of the period, based on his lectures at the Sorbonne; *La Révolution française et les Congrégations* (1903), a study of religious orders and their abolition; *Taine, historien de la Révolution française* (1907), a polemical work attacking the history of the Revolution written by Hippolyte Taine; *La Révolution française et le régime féodal* (1919), an account of the end of feudalism; and *Le Christianisme et la Révolution française* (1925), a general study of religion during the revolutionary period. Many of his articles were collected in his *Etudes et leçons sur la Révolution française* (9 vols., 1898–1924). In addition to purely historical writings, Aulard contributed columns on political, religious, and educational questions to a variety of Radical-Socialist newspapers and reviews, notably *La Dépêche de Toulouse, La Justice, L'Aurore, Progrès civique*, and *Ere nouvelle*. Hostile to organized religion, he fought strongly for a secular school system and the separation of church and state. During World War I, Aulard was a patriotic nationalist, but he became a strong supporter of the League of Nations after the conflict. He was active in the Ligue des droits de l'homme from its founding in 1898, serving as its vice-president from 1921 to 1928.

Archives Nationales, F17 22600 (personal file); A. Aulard, lecture notes, Houghton Library, Harvard University, MS Fr 46; G. Belloni, *Aulard, historien de la Révolution française* (Paris, 1949).

J. Friguglietti

Related entries: FRANCO-PRUSSIAN WAR; GAMBETTA; TAINE.

AUMALE, HENRI-EUGENE-PHILIPPE, DUC D' (1822–97), Orleanist politician. Born in Paris, the fourth son of Louis Philippe, he left the lycée Henri IV for the army at the age of seventeen. Serving under Thomas Robert Bugeaud in Algeria, he gained fame at an early age by defeating Abd-el-Kader in 1843. He became governor of French Africa in 1847. The Revolution of 1848 interrupted his career. He was also a man of literary and cultural accomplishments and published a book on the princes of Condé.

His election to the National Assembly in 1871 gave him new opportunity for public service. He took his seat with the Center-Left and displayed special interest in the problems of agriculture. In 1872 he was appointed general of division and in 1873 presided over the tribunal that tried Marshal François Bazaine. Among the Orleanist princes, he was the least sympathetic to a compromise with the legitimist pretender, the comte de Chambord.

The duc d'Aumale was the Orleanist counterpart to Prince Napoléon-Jérôme (''Plon-Plon'') in the Bonapartist camp. Sporting and intellectual, he had ambitions to be president, perhaps even lieutenant general of the realm. With the decline of the Orleanist cause, his role in cultural matters became relatively more important. Elected to the Académie française in 1871, he was also chosen for the Académie des beaux-arts in 1880, and in 1889 the Académie des sciences morales.

In General Georges Boulanger's purge of Orleanists from the army in 1886, he lost his rank. His gift of Chantilly to the Institut de France became a bond between him and the nation. He died in Zucco, Sicily, in 1897.

M. Barrière, *Les Princes d'Orléans* (Paris, 1933); R. Burnand, *Le Duc d'Aumale et son temps* (Paris, 1948); E. Daudet, *Le Duc d'Aumale* (Paris, 1898).

M. L. Brown, Jr.

Related entry: ORLEANISM.

AURIOL, VINCENT (1884–1966), lawyer, socialist deputy. Born in Revel (Haute-Garonne) on 25 August 1884 into a family of well-to-do farmers, Auriol studied law in Toulouse, where he received his doctorate in law and his *licence* in philosophy. Interested above all in the theories of Jules Guesde and Jean Jaurès, he became active in the socialist movement at a young age. As a member of the Socialist party (SFIO) in 1905, he contributed to the newspaper *La Cité* and in 1909 became editor in chief of *Le Midi socialiste*. During this time, he divided his efforts among newspaper work, his law practice, and politics. At the Tours Congress in 1920, he sided with Léon Blum and the Socialist party against the Communist party.

Auriol served continuously in the Chamber of Deputies from 1914 to 1942. In 1919, he began sixteen years as general secretary of the socialist delegation in parliament. He served in many official posts, including Finance Committee president (1924), accompanied Edouard Herriot to London for Dawes plan negotiations (1925), and went to Washington, D.C., with Joseph Caillaux to help negotiate the settlement of war debts. Auriol later served as finance minister under ·Blum (1936–37), a post in which he was forced to devaluate the franc. He served as minister of justice under Camille Chautemps (1937) and again held a ministerial post under his close friend Blum in 1938. He was known as a man of compromise and conciliation.

Following the French defeat in 1940, he was one of the eighty legislators who voted against the granting of full powers to Marshal Philippe Pétain. He fled to London where he joined General Charles de Gaulle's Free French government in exile and later accompanied de Gaulle to Algiers. After serving as the first president of the Fourth Republic (1947–54), he died in Paris on 1 January 1966.

L. Derfler, *President and Parliament* (Boca Raton, 1983); J. Jolly, ed., *Dictionnaire des parlementaires français* (Paris, 1960); J. Maitron, ed., *Dictionnaire biographique du mouvement ouvrier français (1914–39)* (Paris, 1982); A. Rothe, ed., *Current Biography* (New York, 1948).

A. J. Staples

Related entries: BLUM; GUESDE; JAURES; SOCIALISM (1914–40); SO-CIALIST PARTY.

AUSTRIA-HUNGARY, RELATIONS WITH. France had few common interests or conflicts with either Austria-Hungary or, after 1918, the successor states of Austria and Hungary. Its policies toward them were determined largely by the demands of its policies toward Germany.

Before the Franco-Prussian War (1870–71), French policy treated Austria-Hungary as a counterweight to the growing power of Prussia-Germany. In the following years, however, Austria-Hungary was closely associated with Germany; the connection became a formal alliance in 1879. Two currents of thought influenced French policy toward the dual monarchy after this date. Most French statesmen considered any loosening of Vienna's ties with Berlin to be a practical impossibility and came to view the monarchy either with indifference or as a passive German satellite. The Franco-Russian alliance strengthened this tendency. Although directed against Germany, the alliance also discouraged closer French relations with the dual monarchy because of the ongoing Austro-Russian conflict of interest over the Balkans. This line of policy reached its logical conclusion during World War I when France and Great Britain used the promise of large areas of Austro-Hungarian territory to recruit allies against Germany and viewed dismemberment of the monarchy as an important means of destroying German power in Eastern Europe. The second current of thought believed that Vienna could indeed be separated from Berlin and hoped by so doing to revive the earlier policy of maintaining an independent Austria-Hungary as a counterweight to Germany. It culminated in the secret Austro-French peace feelers of 1917, but never received more than sporadic support in either France or Austria-Hungary. The idea persisted in modified form after the war in the abortive hope of constructing a Danubian federation that would unite into a single political or economic entity all the successor states of the dissolved dual monarchy.

After 1918 France sought to prevent a resurgence of German power by constructing a system of alliances with those new states of Eastern Europe most interested in preserving the status quo of the peace treaties (Poland, Little Entente of Czechoslovakia, Rumania, and Yugoslavia). Austria and Hungary, however, wished to alter the peace settlement; French support of the postwar status quo therefore meant that French relations with both of these states would remain minimal. Austria was prohibited by treaty from becoming part of Germany as many Austrians wished, and French financial pressure was instrumental in blocking an Austro-German customs union project in 1931. Hungary was more opposed to the postwar settlement than any other state in Eastern Europe; it maintained territorial claims on all the states of the French-supported Little Entente. France thus could offer it little. In the 1930s, Austria and Hungary gravitated first toward revisionist Italy and then Germany. The French proved powerless to block German annexation of Austria in 1938 or to prevent Hungary from becoming a German ally in World War II.

C. Andrew, *Theophile Delcassé* (London, 1968); C. A. Macartney and A. Palmer, *Independent Eastern Europe* (London, 1962); R. Poincaré, *Au service de la France* (Paris, 1926–33); A. Wolfers, *Britain and France between Two Wars* (New York, 1940).

G. Shanafelt

Related entries: CZECHOSLOVAKIA, ALLIANCE WITH; GERMANY, RELATIONS WITH; POLAND, RELATIONS WITH; RUSSIA, RELATIONS WITH.

AUTONOMIST AND SEPARATIST MOVEMENTS. Groups favoring many varieties of autonomy, independence, regionalism, and cultural preservation appeared in Alsace, Brittany, French Catalonia, Corsica, Flanders and Occitania.

Alsace. In the 1920s the Edouard Herriot government tried to impose the Law of Separation of Church and State and suppress use of regional dialect in Alsace. Great animosity was aroused by these measures, and three small parties, the Elsassische Fortschritts-partei (leftist), the Landespartei (regionalist), and the Elsass-Lothringischer Heimatbund (nationalist), were founded. In 1928 twenty-two autonomists were indicted and tried for sedition at Colmar. Four were found guilty but released because of the public outcry. Autonomist activity subsequently declined as the power of the Nazis in Germany increased.

Brittany. The royalist Association bretonne was reconstituted in 1873, an association of landowning aristocrats. The moderate, cultural, and regionalist Union régionaliste bretonne (URB) was established in 1898 and the Gorsedd, an association of druids, at about the same time. The Catholic cultural group Bleun-Brug ("heath flower") was established in 1905. The separatist Strollad Broadel Breiz (Breton Nationalist party) was established by dissidents from the URB in 1911, whose periodical was *Breiz Dishual (Free Brittany)*. Dissidents from the Breton Nationalist party in turn broke away, the Breton speakers to establish the periodical *Brittia* in 1912 under Yves le Diberder and the socialists to establish the periodical *Brug* under Emile Masson. World War I spelled a hiatus in these activities. In 1918 the Groupe régionaliste breton was set up by, among others, Olier Mordrel and Fanch Debeauvais. This group began publishing *Breiz Atao (Brittany Forever)* in the next year; its Breton language supplement, *Gwalarn (Northwest)*, appeared in 1925. In response to the events in Alsace, the Parti autonomiste breton (PAB) was set up by this circle of people in 1927. Many splits plagued the PAB. Catholic conservative separatists broke away in 1931 to establish the Parti nationaliste intégrale breton, represented in the periodical *Breiz Da Zont (Brittany Tomorrow)*; the same year on the extreme Left *War Zao (Stand Up)* appeared; extreme Right Nationalistes bretons-chrétiens broke away in 1932, publishing *Breiz digabestr (Brittany without Shackles)*.

In 1932 a terrorist cell that had developed in the PAB and led by Celestin Lainé, Kentoc'h Mervel ("sooner death"), started a bombing campaign under the name Gwenn Ha Du ("black and white," Brittany's national colors). Soon after the PAB was taken over decisively by nationalists Mordrel and Debeauvais, and the group, renamed the Parti nationaliste breton (PNB), became increasingly fascistic. The Front breton, a non-PNB coalition formed to oppose the Front populaire, won 30 percent of the vote in the districts where their candidates ran in the first round of the 1936 elections and 43 percent in the second round. The government was increasingly concerned by the pro-Nazi drift of the PNB; the establishment of a Breton storm trooper unit, Kadervenn ("trench"), by Celestin Lainé led to the law of 23 May 1938 against "whosoever undertakes, in whatever fashion, to undermine the integrity of the national territory or to subtract from the authority of France a part of territory where this authority is exercised," which is still in effect and in use against separatist groups. The leaders of the Kadervenn were arrested and convicted under this law.

In August 1939 *Breiz Atao* was suppressed, and Mordrel and Debeauvais fled to Germany. They returned to France with the invading Wehrmacht.

French Catalonia. The Société d'études catalanes, a nostalgic cultural society, was established in 1906. In the 1920s some Catalan literary magazines began publication. A more politically oriented review, *Nostra Terra*, appeared in 1937.

Corsica. In 1920 the Rocca brothers established the separatist A Muvra and in 1922 set up the Partitu Corsu d'Azzione (Corsican Action party). It became increasingly separatist and pro-fascist and in 1927 was renamed the Partitu Corsu Autonomistu (Corsican Autonomist party); it was secretly supported by Benito Mussolini. In 1934 an Estates General of Corsica was held, which attracted 600 people. These activities ceased with the onset of World War II.

Flanders. A cultural society that had been in existence since 1852, the Comité flamand de France, attracted a right-wing clerical following after the enactment of the Law of Separation of Church and State. These same elements established the Vlaamse Verbond van Frankrijk (the French Flemish Union), led by the Abbé Jean-Marie Gantois in 1924. This group moved to the right during the interwar period. Gantois and his group collaborated with the Germans during the Occupation.

Occitania. During the early days of the Third Republic, the Félibrige, a romantic literary movement oriented toward the culture of Provence, led by the poet Frédéric Mistral, became associated with right-wing clerical politics; one of its members was Charles Maurras. In 1906 occurred the so-called red Félibrige, an outbreak of protests by vintners led by Ernest Ferroul, the mayor of Narbonne, who identified the strikers as heirs of Occitan culture persecuted by the French.

W. R. Beer

Related entries: ALSACE; BRITTANY; LANGUAGES OF FRANCE; MISTRAL.

AVENEL, GEORGES, VICOMTE D' (1855–1939), social theorist. D'Avenel's work demonstrates an unusually fertile interaction between his roles as historian and social critic. After a brief period in government administration, he decided to devote his life to historical scholarship. His early work (published from 1878 to 1890) dealt with monarchy, administrations, high church officials, and nobles at the time of Richelieu. In composing these studies, however, d'Avenel, himself a wealthy aristocrat, became convinced that such eminent public figures bore little relevance to the lives of most people. He came to believe that there were two Frances—the public and the private—and that the private was the more significant of the two. He turned away from conventional political history and instead began to study the gradual evolution of material life, in particular of household budgets, noting that these data had not yet been treated seriously. The result of these studies was his monumental work *Histoire économique de la propriété, des salaires, des denrées, et de tous les prix en générale, depuis l'an 1200 jusqu'en l'an 1800* (1894–98), based on a statistical compilation of private incomes and expenditures over seven centuries. D'Avenel's ultimate purpose in writing this book was to reveal the mental life of people in the past. From his research he concluded that economic life is not based on a logical, objective assessment of money, but rather on a wide variety of psychic, subjective pleasures.

As a social critic, D'Avenel stressed that economic life is, above all, a matter of imagination, by which he meant that the objective measuring of income is far less significant than subjectively assessed factors. D'Avenel's more important contribution is not his theory, however, but his elevation of familiar, everyday activities from the level of unconscious, unrecorded routine to the level of conscious historical study. By viewing contemporary events in the light of history and history in the light of contemporary events, he defined consumption habits and psychology as an area for historical and social inquiry.

E. Seillière, "Georges d'Avenel, historien et moraliste," *Revue des deux mondes*, 15 (September 1939); R. H. Williams, *Dream Worlds* (Berkeley, 1982).

R. H. Williams

AYME, MARCEL (1902–67), novelist and playwright. Born in Joigny (Yonne), the last of six children and orphaned by his mother at the age of six, Aymé was raised by his maternal grandmother and then by aunts in rural and village atmospheres. After a brief career as a soldier, he supported himself as a reporter, and wrote as an avocation until the great and somewhat scandalous success of *La Jument verte* (1933) established his career as a novelist. This work reveals admirably Aymé's unsentimental appreciation of peasant and village life and his disdain for clericalism, bourgeois sensitivity, hypocrisy, and foolishness of every stripe. A rich verbal humor combines with acuity of human observation in this family saga, narrated in part by the green mare. The collection of animal fables, *Les Contes du chat perché* (1934) shows a deftness of touch and gentle satire of human vice that makes it a favorite of children as well as of adults. The title story of Aymé's celebrated collection of short stories, *Le Passe-muraille* (1943), is a classic of Gallic whimsy, subtlety, and amoralism. In a lucid and objective style, he satirizes the pretensions and mediocrities of modern life in such novels as *Les Jumeaux du diable* (1929), *La Table aux crevés* (1929), *Le Vaurien* (1931), *Le Boeuf clandestin* (1939), *Le Chemin des écoliers* (1946), and nine others. The same themes appear in his collection of essays, *Silhouette du scandale* (1938) and *Le Confort intellectuel* (1949). Less blessed as a playwright, he nonetheless wrote the very successful *Clérembard* (1950) and *La Tête des autres* (1952). He published five additional collections of stories, among them *La Traversée de Paris* (1947).

Famous personally for his taciturn nature and his wooden countenance as well as his disdain for politics, Aymé died in Paris in 1967.

J. Cathelin, *Marcel Aymé ou Le Paysan de Paris* (Paris, 1958); P. Vandomme, *Marcel Aymé*, (Paris, 1960).

S. M. Whitebook

Related entry: LITERATURE.

B

BACHELARD, GASTON (1884–1962), philosopher of science and literary critic. Born 27 June 1884 in Bar-sur-Aube in the Champagne, Bachelard wrote nostalgically of his early childhood in the country. In 1907 he became a postal worker in Paris while simultaneously preparing a *licence* in mathematics, which he obtained in 1912. He married in July 1914 and was mobilized for World War I a month later. He served until 1919, when he began a career as a teacher of physics and chemistry. Shortly after he undertook formal studies in philosophy and obtained the doctorate from the University of Paris in 1927. Three years later he was named professor of science and director of the Institut d'histoire des sciences et des techniques. He received the Légion d'honneur in 1951 and retired officially in 1954. The following year he was elected to the Académie des sciences morales et politiques and in 1961 was awarded the Grand Prix national des lettres. He died on 16 October 1962.

Bachelard's varied professional career indicates the broad intellectual interests that allowed him to make significant contributions to scientific theory, psychoanalysis, philosophy, and literary criticism. His earliest writings predominantly concerned scientific thought and reveal the influence of the philosopher Henri Bergson. In his *Essai sur la connaissance approchée* (1928), based on his doctoral dissertation, he presented an epistemology which attacked positivism, especially the idea that scientific discoveries grow out of necessary preconditions; he argued for what he called "approximationalism," which emphasizes the importance of speculative ideas rather than precise analysis that stifles creativity.

Bachelard pursued his work in the philosophy of science with publications that include *Le Nouvel esprit scientifique* (1938) and *La Philosophie du non* (1940). His interest in the relationship between scientific thought and reality led him to the study of the history of science. He became particularly intrigued by the psychological influence of mythic imagination on scientific thought. With *La Psychanalyse du feu* (1938), he joined his interests in scientific history, creative imagination, and Freudian psychology in order to analyze how certain mental predispositions, or "complexes," falsify the perception of fire. This study led to the publication of several other books that utilize mythic elements as keys to the understanding of poetic images. In his later works, Bachelard rejected a predominantly Freudian interpretation of literature in favor of a phenomenological approach.

G. Canguilhem, *Etudes d'histoire et de philosophie des sciences* (Paris, 1968); F. Dagognet, *Gaston Bachelard* (Paris, 1965); P. Quillet, *Bachelard* (Paris, 1964).

M. F. Trusler

Related entries: BERGSON; LITERARY CRITICS AND CRITICISM; POSITIVISM; SCIENCE AND TECHNOLOGY; THOUGHT AND INTELLECTUAL LIFE.

BAINVILLE, JACQUES (1879–1936), one of the most prolific and widely read historians in modern France. At the turn of the century he became a charter member of the royalist organization, L'Action française, which subjected the democratic political institutions of the Third Republic to a continual barrage of criticism and promoted the cause of a royalist restoration. Bainville's historical writing represented a very effective weapon in the intellectual arsenal of the Action française. Although a devotee of the royalist cause to the end of his life, Bainville presented his historical arguments against democracy and in favor of monarchy in such a rational, moderate tone that he acquired considerable popularity among readers who were not otherwise sympathetic to the extreme right-wing movement to which he belonged. Eschewing the provocative, even violent, approach that characterized much of the writing of the two other leading spokesmen of the Action française, Charles Maurras and Léon Daudet, Bainville served as a bridge between the royalist movement and the more respectable circles of French conservatism.

The principal theme that underlay all of Bainville's historical writings was the incompatibility of France's democratic political institutions and its aspiration to the status of a world power. Since the Revolution of 1789, he alleged, the patient work of France's forty kings in forging national unity and establishing French hegemony in Europe had been undone by the proponents of democracy. The destructive political revolutions and military invasions that France had experienced in the nineteenth century were the unhappy results of the French people's ungrateful abandonment of the monarchical principal. Only by resurrecting the institution of absolute monarchy, Bainville asserted, could France regain the domestic stability and international power that it had enjoyed during the centuries of royal rule.

Variations on this simple message were presented not only in Bainville's forty-odd works of history but also in the thousands of articles that he contributed to a number of right-wing newspapers. As foreign affairs specialist for the *Action française* daily newspaper, he applied the lessons of history to affairs of the present. Often astonishingly accurate, his trenchant analyses of world events were read attentively by diplomats and statesmen of all political persuasions. Particularly after the First World War, his criticism of the Versailles Treaty and his predictions of future calamities earned for him the reputation of the clairvoyant Cassandra of French journalism. Elected to the Académie française in 1935, he continued to warn his countrymen of the menace posed by a resurgent Germany until his premature death in February 1936. Subsequent events seemed, at least in the eyes of his admirers, to confirm many of his observations about the decadence of democracy and his prognostications of a military rematch with Germany.

H. Massis, ed., *Le Souvenir de Jacques Bainville* (Paris, 1936); R. Joseph, *Qui est Jacques Bainville?* (Orléans, 1962); W. R. Keylor, *Jacques Bainville and the Renaissance of Royalist History in Twentieth-Century France* (Baton Rouge, 1979).

W. R. Keylor

Related entries: ACTION FRANCAISE; CONSERVATISM; DAUDET; MAURRAS.

BANKS AND BANKING. The banking system of France in 1870 was a multitiered structure that underwent significant changes during the Third Republic. At the apex stood the Bank of France, created in 1800, which, though privately owned, was the government's banker and the sole bank of issue. The Bank of France functioned as a central bank, discounting short-term paper bearing two signatures for a limited clientele of banks and large companies. The bank was governed by a Council of Regents elected by the 200 largest stockholders until 1936. In that year the elective council was abolished by the Popular Front government because of the bank's reluctance to cooperate with left-wing governments, notably the Cartel des gauches of 1924. In leftist parlance, the council constituted a *mur d'argent*, which prevented social reforms from being carried out. In the interwar years, the public banking sector expanded with the creation of numerous specialized banks to provide credit for postwar reconstruction,agriculture, exports, hotels, and for other areas that were inadequately served by the private sector or were deemed worthy of special encouragement.

During the Third Republic the banking system came to resemble that of England with a separation of functions between deposit banks (*banques de dépôts*), offering only short-term credit, and investment banks (*banques d'affaires*), which provided medium and long-term credit. These institutions differed from the so-called continental model of mixed banks, which the Crédit mobilier of the Pereire brothers had popularized during the Second Empire and of which Germany became the leading exemplar.

Among investment banks, the most important were the Banque de Paris et de Pays-Bas, founded in 1872, the Banque d' Indochine, founded in 1875, whose activities were focused on the Far East, the Banque de l'union parisienne, founded in 1904, and the Banque française pour le commerce et l'industrie from its founding in 1901 until its merger with another bank in 1922. These banks played an important role in financing a large number of industrial and commercial enterprises in France, its colonies and in foreign countries.

Four giant banks dominated deposit banking: the Crédit lyonnais, the Société générale, the Comptoir d'escompte de Paris and the Crédit industriel et commercial, all founded between 1848 and 1864 and all headquartered in Paris (the Crédit lyonnais officially moved its seat from Lyons to Paris in 1881). These banks grew rapidly between 1870 and 1914, covering all of France with numerous branches (the Crédit lyonnais expanded from three branches in 1870 to 240 by 1914). They were designed to mobilize the savings of the entire country. Unlike the others, the Crédit industriel et commercial limited its branches to the Paris area but was closely allied with a number of large regional banks. Except for the Crédit industriel et commercial, these banks originally functioned as mixed banks, but following the lead of Henri Germain, president of the Crédit lyonnais for forty years, they gradually reduced their long-term credit operations to a relatively small proportion of their operations by 1914. The divorce of deposit and investment banking in France, however, was never as complete as in England. The sudden demise in 1889 of the Comptoir d'escompte, which was involved in an ill-fated scheme to corner the world's copper market, and its reorganization as the Comptoir national d'escompte the same year, appeared to confirm the wisdom of Germain's example.

Although these banks progressively abandoned employing their own resources for other than safe short-term operations, they did participate in the highly profitable flotation of securities—foreign government bonds and the stocks and bonds of domestic and foreign corporations—using their branch offices as sales outlets. These banks were the target of much criticism after 1900 for channeling a large part of the country's savings into foreign securities, to the alleged detriment of domestic industry, and for the role their branches played in destroying independent regional and local banks.

The once-dominant role of the twenty or so private banking firms in Paris known as the *haute banque* continued to decline in importance relative to banks employing the corporate form of business organization, though these banking families, such as Rothschild, Lazard, Mirabaud, and Neuflize, still remained a powerful force, either directly through their own activities or indirectly as regents of the Bank of France (until 1936) and as directors of major investment banks.

Outside the Paris area, the numerous local and regional banks suffered after 1870 from the invasion of their territory by branches of the giant Parisian deposit banks. Many succumbed, but others, such as the Banque Renauld of Nancy and the Banque Charpenay of Grenoble, prospered by supporting local commerce and industry with long-term credit, which was not available from the conservatively run branches of Paris banks. A few, such as the Crédit du Nord, established regional networks of branches in imitation of the Parisian banks. The depression of the 1930s took an immense toll of local and regional banks.

Overall there were four major developments for the period 1870–1940: (1) growing concentration with the rise to dominance of a few giant banks or groups of banks, (2) the separation of deposit and investment functions, (3) the appearance of specialized banks serving particular industries, and (4) the increasing role of the state in banking, particularly after the First World War.

E. Baldy, *Les Banques d'affaires en France depuis 1900* (Paris, 1922); J. Bouvier, *Un Siècle de banque française* (Paris, 1973); E. Kaufmann, *La Banque en France* (Paris, 1914).

C. E. Freedeman

Related entry: COMMERCE: FOREIGN.

BARBUSSE, HENRI (1873-1935), novelist, essayist, militant communist. Barbusse was instrumental in opening a dialogue between French and Soviet intellectuals in the 1920s and 1930s, and his *Clarté* movement was a leading advocate of leftist ideology and of pacificism. Barbusse's early career in journalism with the *Petit Parisien* and the *Echo de Paris* gave little indication of the leftist orientation his career would take. A collection of poems, *Pleureuses* (1895), was critically acclaimed, especially by Catulle Mendès whose youngest daughter Barbusse married. His first novels, *Les Suppliants* (1903) and *L'Enfer* (1908), showed a clear and incisive prose with a profound social message.

Despite his declared pacifism and internationalism, Barbusse at age forty-one joined the army at the outbreak of World War I as an infantry soldier. He related his experiences in one of France's greatest war novels, *Le Feu* (1916), in which he tried to give a true picture of combat in order to counteract the optimistic statements of those who were far from the front. A second war novel, *Clarté* (1919), and Barbusse's letters to his wife not only attacked war but also social injustice and illustrated the writer's growing socialist militancy and his hope that war might transform humanity for the better.

After the war, Barbusse founded several associations for veterans from all countries, including France's former enemies, and he set up the journal *Clarté*. Increasingly fascinated by the ideas of Lenin and the Third International, Barbusse joined the French Communist party in 1923. In 1927 he traveled to the Soviet Union for the first time and participated in the organization of the International Union of Revolutionary Writers. In spite of his failing health, Barbusse participated in numerous international meetings throughout Europe and the United States, and after 1933 he spoke with renewed vigor against the crimes of fascism and nazism. Barbusse died in Moscow in 1935 where he was attending a meeting of Soviet writers and the proceedings of an international congress. Among his other major works are: *Nous autres* (1914), *La Lueur dans l'abîme* (1920), *Paroles d'un combattant* (1921), *Les Enchaînements* (1925), *Les Judas de Jésus* (1927), *Zola* (1932), and *Staline* (1935). Barbusse will be remembered for his great novel *Le Feu* and his role in establishing communications between the French Communist party and the Soviet Union.

V. Brett, *Barbusse, sa marche vers la clarté, son mouvement "Clarté"* (Prague, 1963); J. Duclos and J. Fréville, *Henri Barbusse* (Paris, 1946); F. Field, *Three French Writers in the Great War: Barbusse, Drieu la Rochelle, Bernanos* (Cambridge, 1975); G. Normand, "Henri Barbusse and his *Monde*: Precursors to the *Littérature engagée* Movement," *Kentucky Review Quarterly* 24 (1977).

M. Berkvam

Related entries: COMMUNIST PARTY; LEFT, THE; LITERATURE, PROLETARIAN; MARXISM; NOVEL, POLITICS AND THE.

BARRERE, CAMILLE (1851–1940), French Ambassador to Italy, 1897–1924. A communard and an exile, he entered the diplomatic service in 1880. He received the patronage of Léon Gambetta and Jules Ferry. Barrère was a French patriot who opposed Germany and socialism. As ambassador to Italy beginning in 1897, he worked to secure an alliance with that country against Germany. From 1898 to 1914 Barrère wooed Italian leaders away from the Triple Alliance, a policy that succeeded in 1914 when Italy declared neutrality. During the First World War, which Italy entered in May 1915 after signing the Treaty of London, the ambassador smoothed over discord between the two allies. Barrère opposed the German Armistice in November 1918 and advocated harsher peace terms for Germany in 1919. At the Paris Peace Conference, he sought a compromise with Italy over the status of Fiume. Fearing that his labors from 1897 to 1914 would be undone when Georges Clemenceau followed Woodrow Wilson's lead in rejecting Italian demands at Paris, he disagreed bitterly with the premier. From 1919 to 1924 Barrère sought to repair the damage to Franco-Italian relations.

From 1920 to 1924 the ambassador sympathized with the rise of Italian fascism, partly because of his hostility to communism, socialism, and the segment of Italian liberalism led by Francesco Nitti and partly because he thought that Benito Mussolini would be anti-German. From October 1922, when Mussolini took power, until 1924, when the electoral victory of the Cartel des gauches in France led the ambassador to resign, Barrère's embassy conciliated the Italian regime but without sacrificing major French territorial interests. In June 1924 the murder of Giacomo Matteotti, a moderate Italian socialist leader, by Mussolini's closest aides gave Barrère and his colleagues pause, but they feared the succession if the Duce lost power. In Rome the ambassador was assisted by a number of collaborators who later became important French diplomats, notably Jules Laroche and François Charles-Roux.

Barrère died in 1940 in occupied Paris. His reputation rests primarily on his persistent courtship of Italian support against Germany.

F. Charles-Roux, *Souvenirs diplomatiques: Rome-Quirinal, février 1916–février 1919* (Paris, 1958), and *Une Grande Ambassade à Rome, 1919–1925* (Paris, 1961); G. Dethan, "Barrère et Sonnino en 1914–1918, deux 'compagnons d'armes'," in *La France et l'Italie pendant la première guerre mondiale*, ed. P. Guillen (Grenoble, 1976); J. Laroche, *Quinze ans à Rome avec Camille Barrère (1898-1913)* (Paris, 1948); L. Noël, *Camille Barrère* (Paris, 1948); E. Serra, *Camille Barrère e l'intesa italo-francese* (Milan, 1950).

J. Blatt

Related entries: DELCASSE; ITALY, RELATIONS WITH; ITALY, SECRET TREATY WITH.

BARRES, MAURICE (1862-1923), major novelist and nationalist politician. Fame came to Barrès early with the first of a three-novel cycle, "Le culte du moi." In the first novel, *Sous l'oeil des barbares* (1888), the *porte-parole* of Barrès discovered that the old value system was bankrupt and brought only decadence because it could not nourish individual fulfillment. In the second novel, *Un Homme libre* (1889), unsuccessful cultivation of one's selfhood with systematic study and discipline led to the discovery that action was needed. By linking up with instinctual masses in the action of an electoral campaign in the third novel, *Le Jardin de Bérénice* (1891), Barrès and his *porte-parole* at last energized their selfhoods, formerly beaten down by the "barbarians."

The need for political action to spur his quest for self-fulfillment took Barrès, like the character in his novel, into one political movement after another. Under the aegis of Boulangism, whose "barbarian" enemies appeared similar to his own, Barrès won election to the Chamber of Deputies in his native Nancy (1889). His working-class constituency quite by accident led him leftward into socialism. It provided a theme for a new novel, *L'Ennemi des lois* (1892), which preferred Charles Fourier, Joseph Proudhon, and Ludwig II over Karl Marx. Proudhonist socialism and federalism served as the rationale for his Paris daily newspaper, *La Cocarde* (1894–95). Socialism's increasing internationalism and refusal to support his three unsuccessful electoral campaigns in Neuilly (1893–96) turned him to a new political ideology, nationalism. Socialism's rational analysis was also inconsistent with Barrès's fascination with instinct and sensibility.

Nationalism informed Barrès's next trilogy, "the novel of national energy," actually a rewriting of "*Le Culte du moi*" to provide a nationalistic and antiparliamentary morality tale for the France of the Dreyfus affair. The young Lorrainers seeking Parisian careers in *Les Déracinés* (1897) found that only the common blood and soil of Lorraine sustained them in a France *déracinée, dissociée, et décérébrée*. The other novels of the cycle, *L'Appel au soldat* (1900) and *Leurs figures* (1902), were fictionalized, didactic rewritings of Boulangism and the Panama scandal, respectively. *Leurs figures* sought to demonstrate that the Republic was so corrupt that a mere change of ministries was not a remedy. Boulangism, rather than being Barrès' path into socialism, had been a missed opportunity for overthrowing the corrupt Republic, missed because it had no doctrine.

With the Dreyfus affair providing a new opportunity for ending the Republic, Barrès now offered the necessary doctrine in two books of essays, *Scènes et doctrines du nationalisme* (1902) and *De Hegel aux cantines du Nord* (1904). The doctrine called for antiparlimentarianism, authority at the top, decentralization, an "armed, glorious, and organized" Republic, and a new spirit rooted in France's soil and dead and hostile to Freemasons, Jews, foreigners, socialists, and German idealists. Try though he did, Barrès failed to win the anti-Dreyfusard nationalist leagues to his doctrine, even though he was a key figure in the League of Patriots, the League of the Patrie française, and the League of the Action française. He was equally unsuccessful in winning the voters to his doctrine in parliamentary campaigns at Nancy in 1898 and in Paris's Fourth Arrondissement in 1903.

With these failures he abandoned this doctrine in favor of conservative nationalism by the time of his 1906 parliamentary victory in the First Arrondissement, which he represented to the end of his life. In that same year, he was elected to the Académie française. From then on he limited himself to fostering French awareness of the Alsace-Lorraine question in his two "Bastions de l'est" novels, *Au service de l'Allemagne* (1905) and *Colette Baudoche* (1909); supporting the church and Catholicism in *La Colline inspirée* (1913) and *La Grande Pitié des églises de France* (1913); propagandizing the home front in daily newspaper columns collected into fourteen volumes of *La Chronique de la grande guerre* (1920–24) and *Les Diverses Familles de la France* (1917); and urging a postwar autonomy for the Rhineland in *Le Génie du Rhin* (1921) and *Les Grands Problèmes du Rhin* (1930). In those years he shed his antiparlimentarianism and came to support the prewar ministries of Aristide Briand and Raymond Poincaré and the postwar Bloc national.

In spite of this later career of conservatism, he remains best known for "Le Culte du moi" and his novels and nationalist doctrine of the era of the Dreyfus affair. Surely most lycéens passed through a Barrèsian stage between the era of Boulangism and World War I.

C. S. Doty, *From Cultural Rebellion to Counterrevolution* (Athens, Ohio, 1976); R. Soucy, *Fascism in France* (Berkeley, 1972); Z. Sternhell, *Maurice Barrès et le nationalisme français* (Paris, 1972).

C. S. Doty

Related entries: ACTION FRANCAISE; ALSACE; ANTI-SEMITISM; BLOC NATIONAL; BOULANGER; BOULANGER AFFAIR; DEROULEDE; DREYFUS AFFAIR; LEAGUE OF PATRIOTS; LITERATURE; MAURRAS; NATIONALISM; SYMBOLISM; THOUGHT AND INTELLECTUAL LIFE.

BARTHOU, LOUIS (1862–1934), moderate republican politician, author, and diplomat. He was born at Oloron Sainte-Marie (Basses-Pyrénées) on 23 August 1862, the son of an ironmonger. He studied at the lycée in Pau, received his *licence* in letters from the University of Bordeaux in 1883, and then studied law in Paris, where he was admitted to the bar in 1886. The following year, he returned to Pau, where he practiced law and edited the newspaper, *l'Indépendant des Basses-Pyrénées*.

He then embarked on a long and distinguished political career. He represented Oloron in the Chamber of Deputies from 1889 to 1922 and the Basses-Pyrénées in the Senate from 1922 until 1934. During that time he simultaneously served in a number of ministries and was premier in 1913. A man of exceptional vitality, he quickly established a reputation among his parliamentary colleagues as an eloquent orator and skillful debater. He possessed a photographic memory, which enabled him to overwhelm his opponents with his erudition, and he could be cutting with his sarcastic wit. He was also a prodigious worker and was willing to serve on a variety of commissions. In the course of his career, he played a role in drafting legislation concerning electoral procedures, military service, labor reform, and public works. A moderate republican, he was identified especially with the Progressists, the dominant parliamentary faction in the 1890s. Over the years, he worked in close alliance with Aristide Briand and Raymond Poincaré.

Following World War I, Barthou devoted himself increasingly to problems of foreign affairs. He served as chairman of the League of Nations' Reparations Commission during the 1920s, and in 1934 was called to serve as foreign minister to deal with the growing threat of German aggression. As foreign minister, he traveled to Eastern Europe to bolster France's ties with Poland and the Little Entente. Adamant in his opposition to German expansionism, he hoped to preserve Austrian independence and favored a Franco-Soviet pact.

Barthou was assassinated, together with King Alexander of Yugoslavia, by a Croatian terrorist while they were traveling en route from Marseilles to Paris on 9 October 1934 to sign a mutual assistance treaty. At the time of his death, he was despondent over mounting Franco-German tensions and presaged the coming of war and France's defeat for lack of preparation.

Barthou enjoyed a certain reputation as a man of letters and authored a number of books on historical and literary topics, among them *Mirabeau* (1913), *Lamartine orateur* (1918), *Danton* (1932), and *Victor Hugo* (1935). He was elected to the Académie française in 1918.

L. Barthou, *Impressions et essais* (Paris, 1913), and *La Politique* (Paris, 1923); J. Jolly, ed., *Dictionnaire des parlamentaires français*, Vol. 2 (Paris, 1962).

J. M. Rife, Jr.

Related entries: CONSCRIPTION, MILITARY; FOREIGN POLICY; GER-MANY, RELATIONS WITH (1914-40); LITTLE ENTENTE; PROGRESSISTS.

BASLY, EMILE JOSEPH (1854–1928), miner, trade union leader, socialist deputy. Basly was born in Valenciennes (Nord) on 29 March 1854, the son of a cooper and a pit girl. Orphaned in 1864, he worked in the mines until 1883 when he was fired for organizing the local mineworkers' union of which he became general secretary and later president. Basly was one of the architects of the Anzin coal strike of 1884, immortalized by Emile Zola in *Germinal*.

Elected deputy for the Seine department in 1885, he became labor and employment spokesman for the small socialist parliamentary caucus. After losing his seat in 1889, he was reelected as an independent socialist for the constituency of Béthune-Lens-Carvin (Pas-de-Calais) in February 1891. He retained this seat for the rest of his life.

Basly initiated several important laws on mineworkers' conditions, including the 1900 law on the eight-hour day, but his political activity increasingly concentrated on his local role as mayor of Lens (1900–28) and as general councillor for the Pas-de-Calais. Both as politician and trade unionist, Basly represented a moderate, reformist approach to socialism and appears never once to have uttered the word *revolution*. He was instrumental in keeping the miners out of the

Confédération générale du travail until 1908 and in combating Guesdism in the north of France. Worshipped in his own area as the unchallenged leader of the labor movement, he was recognized nationally as a living symbol of social republicanism.

J. Maitron, *Dictionnaire biographique du mouvement ouvrier français*, vol. 10 (Paris, 1973).

J. Howorth

Related entries: CONFEDERATION GENERALE DU TRAVAIL; INDUS-TRY: COAL; LABOR MOVEMENT; SOCIALISM, 1870–1914; STRIKES; SYNDICALISM; TRADE UNION MOVEMENT.

BEAUVOIR, SIMONE DE (1908–), novelist, essayist, existential philosopher, and intellectual. At the end of the 1920s, while completing her studies in philosophy at the Sorbonne and the Ecole normale supérieure, Simone de Beauvoir joined the circle of young Parisian intellectuals around her fellow student Jean-Paul Sartre. Receiving the *agrégation de philosophie* in 1929, de Beauvoir taught in provincial and Parisian lycées until 1943. Beginning in the 1930s she was a member of that philosophical, literary, and political group characterized as existentialists after the Second World War. De Beauvoir's collaborators, friends, and acquaintances of the 1930s also included Paul Nizan and Maurice Merleau-Ponty, Alberto Giacometti, and Pablo Picasso. During the 1930s de Beauvoir began to plan her own literary projects. Her first novel, *L'Invitée*, was published in 1943. After 1945 there followed an uninterrupted series of novels, philosophical treatises, sociohistorical essays, and autobiography. Among these postwar publications is the most seminal modern study of women's situations and feminist theory, *Le Deuxième Sexe* (1949). By the late 1950s and 1960s she had attained considerable recognition as a writer (winning the Prix Goncourt in 1954), an independent leftist, a feminist, and an existentialist.

Although de Beauvoir reached maturity during the Third Republic, her major intellectual contributions and impact have occurred in the post–World War II period. The experience of war, defeat, occupation, and liberation has significantly marked her thought and writing. Nonetheless, several of her publications provide insight into aspects of the Third Republic based on her personal recollections. In *Mémoires d'une jeune fille rangée* (1958) she examines her family's Catholic, conventional, bourgeois environment during the first three decades of the twentieth century. The exuberance of intellectual, artistic, and political Left Bank Paris of the 1930s contrasts with the austerity, seriousness, and new realism of the occupation in her *La Force de l'âge* (1960). De Beauvoir offers a rich portrait and critique of Parisian intellectuals in the final years of the Third Republic.

S. de Beauvoir, *Le Deuxième Sexe* (Paris, 1949), *La Force de l'âge* (Paris, 1960), *L'Invitée* (Paris, 1943), *Mémoires d'une jeune fille rangée* (Paris, 1958), *Pour une morale de l'ambiguïté* (Paris, 1947), and *Le Sang des autres* (Paris, 1946); G. Gennari, *Simone de Beauvoir* (Paris, 1958).

J. F. Stone

Related entries: EXISTENTIALISM; FEMINISM; NIZAN; SARTRE.

BECQUEREL, HENRI (1852–1908), physicist. Becquerel was born in Paris into a family of physicists; both his father and grandfather were professors of physics and members of the Academy of Sciences. Becquerel studied at the Lycée Louis-le-Grand, the Ecole polytechnique (1872–74), and the Ecole des ponts et chaussées (1874–77). He later became ingénieur en chef with the National Administration of Bridges and Highways. He also held several positions as professor of physics and was elected a member of the Academy of Sciences.

Becquerel's early scientific interests concentrated on the characteristicsof polarized light and on the process of phosphorescence in crystals. In 1896 he heard of the discovery of X rays by Wilhelm Röntgen. He knew that the X rays emanated from a fluorescent spot on the wall of a cathode ray tube, where the cathode rays struck the glass. He wondered if other fluorescent substances might produce such rays and set about investigating various luminescent crystals. He quickly discovered that crystals of a uranium compound produced rays that would expose a photographic plate, even when both were kept in the dark. Only crystals with uranium produced the rays. He then tested a sample of pure uranium and discovered that it was responsible for the production of rays. Marie Curie would soon call this property radioactivity. He shared the Nobel Prize in physics with Marie and Pierre Curie in 1903 for the discovery of radioactivity.

Becquerel's continued experiments from 1896 to 1903 placed him at the center of the most exciting work in physics. He investigated the rays that were given off by uranium and determined in 1900 that they had similar properties to those of the electrically charged particles that J. J. Thomson discovered in 1897. "Electrons" were part of the process of radioactivity. His work with various compounds of uranium allowed him to realize that radiation was associated with atomic transformation. By chemically separating uranium compounds, he realized that uranium compounds, which seemed to lose their radioactive properties after chemical separation, soon regained that property. His experiments interested Ernest Rutherford and Frederick Soddy who were working on thorium compounds. They soon proposed the theory of atomic disintegration and natural transmutation to account for the experimental results for both thorium and uranium.

O. Lodge, "Becquerel Memorial Lecture," *Journal of the Chemical Society* 101 (1912); L. Badash, "Chance Favors the Prepared Mind: Henri Becquerel and the Discovery of Radioactivity," *Archives internationales d'histoire des sciences* 18 (1965); A. Romer, "Becquerel, (Antoine-) Henri," *Dictionary of Scientific Biography*, vol. 1 (New York, 1970).

H. J. Steffens

Related entries: CURIE, M.; CURIE, P.

BELGIUM, RELATIONS WITH. From 1871 to 1914 Franco-Belgian relations rested on mutual, partially justified distrust. Belgians, especially Flemings, feared French domination while France doubted Belgian willingness and ability to defend itself. France never forgot that Belgium constituted Germany's best invasion route into France's industrial heartland.

After 1870 Belgium rejoiced at the reduction of France's power but remained distrustful. Before 1900 Franco-Belgian relations were conducted in a minor key as France clashed with Léopold II over the Congo but rarely with Belgium. France deplored Belgian political divisions, military weakness, and economic success, both at Antwerp and overseas. Belgians complained of French protectionism and the tax levied on goods entering France by non-French ports. After 1900 France feared German economic domination of Belgium as well as invasion, while Belgium feared that the Entente Cordiale of 1904 would remove the British brake on French domination or render German attack more probable.

Belgium's wholehearted resistance in August 1914 earned French gratitude and lavish promises based on the assumption that postwar Belgium would become a French satellite. As wartime negotiations revealed Belgium's commitment to independence, the promises evaporated. At the peace conference, France supported Belgian claims furthering or not conflicting with French aims, otherwise remaining inflexible. Deadlock over Luxembourg dissolved in 1920 after Belgian consent to a limited Franco-Belgian military accord in return for French acceptance of Belgo-Luxembourgeois economic union. As rising Flemish consciousness exacerbated distrust of France, Belgium sought a counterbalancing British tie, gaining only the inoperable Locarno guarantee.

Belgium's hope of balancing between Britain and France against Germany was frustrated by British indifference. In postwar reparations diplomacy, Belgium mediated Anglo-French disputes to avoid choosing sides, devising pro-British compromises with face-saving features for France. Forced to choose in 1923, Belgium followed France into the Ruhr occupation, complaining first of Raymond Poincaré's timidity and then of his intransigence. When German passive resistance ended, Belgium reverted to a middle position, contributing to France's defeat in 1924. Thereafter as the Versailles Treaty unraveled, Belgium's role diminished and Franco-Belgian relations became less intimate, although Belgium shared in the Rhineland occupation until 1930.

By 1931, the largely inoperative Franco-Belgian military accord had become a political embarrassment in Belgium. Despite French insistence on its continuation, domestic division dictated its abrogation in March 1936 and subsequent Belgian reversion to guaranteed neutrality. This policy was dictated partly by fear of entanglements arising from France's eastern alliances but primarily by the need for domestic pacification as a prerequisite to rearmament. Nonetheless, it rendered effective French aid difficult.

During the 1939–40 phony war, Belgium remained neutral, refusing Anglo-French preventive occupation lest it provoke German attack. Again French hopes of defending itself on Belgian soil were dashed. In the ensuing debâcle of May 1940, there was ample blame for all, but both French and Belgian politicians found a scapegoat in Léopold III.

B. Bond, *France and Belgium, 1939–1940* (London, 1975); J. E. Helmreich, *Belgium and Europe* (The Hague, 1976); D. O. Kieft, *Belgium's Return to Neutrality* (Oxford,

1972); S. Marks, *Innocent Abroad* (Chapel Hill, 1981), *Les Relations franco-belges de 1830 à 1934* (Metz, 1975), and *Les Relations militaires franco-belges* (Paris, 1968).

S. Marks

Related entries: ENTENTE CORDIALE; FALL OF FRANCE, 1940; GERMANY, RELATIONS WITH; GREAT BRITAIN, RELATIONS WITH; POINCARE, R.; RUHR OCCUPATION; WORLD WAR I, FRANCE'S ROLE IN.

BELLE EPOQUE, LA, an expression used to characterize the stability, prosperity, and serenity of French middle-class life in the years before the First World War, roughly the period 1890 through 1914. For the most part, it reflected the retrospective nostalgia of the postwar generation for the quality of life it believed had been lost with the war. The expression connoted a number of interrelated images: the enjoyment of economic prosperity, the benefits of technological achievement and scientific advance, the satisfaction with a Republic that provided a blend of democracy, moderation, and commitment to secular progress. Underpinning all of these images was the self-assurance of the middle class, confident in the enduring vitality of its well-ordered society. Visual images of *la belle époque* are primarily derived from the genre paintings of the impressionists and other avant-garde artists who depicted the middle class at leisure on the wide boulevards of Paris or in the pleasant landscapes of the surrounding countryside. The accent was on the openness and tranquility of life in the modern age. Critics point out that the expression projects an image of the society as a whole, whereas only an elite enjoyed such a life-style. The middle class before the war was often oblivious to the dour existence of the lower classes and was as yet unshaken by the critique of the superficial proprieties and materialism of the middle-class life-style presented by a new generation of writers (Maurice Barrès, André Gide, Marcel Proust).

R. Shattuck, *The Banquet Years* (New York, 1955).

P. H. Hutton

Related entry: IMPRESSIONISM.

BENDA, JULIEN (1867–1956), critic, essayist, novelist, and philosophical writer; a defender of reason and an advocate of the intellectual's detachment from political passions. The development of his ideas and character from childhood until the last years of the Third Republic are lucidly analyzed in his autobiographical *La Jeunesse d'un clerc* (1936) and *Un Régulier dans le siècle* (1938). Born in Paris and educated at the Lycée Charlemagne and the Sorbonne, Benda developed a strong attachment to the Greco-Roman tradition and to French classicism. This explains his unflagging allegiance to the rational ideal and his rejection of all sentimental, mystical, or intuitive interpretations of life and literature. His earliest writings, articles on the Dreyfus affair in *La Revue blanche* (1898), inveighed not only against those who attacked Alfred Dreyfus but also against those who defended him out of sentiment rather than reason. His first novel, *L'Ordination*

(1912), centered on the conflict between feelings and intellect, trying to make a case for the necessity of reason to control the passions.

Benda published *Le Bergsonisme ou une philosophie de la mobilité* in 1912, which was followed by *Une Philosophie pathétique* (1913) and *Sur le succès du Bergsonisme* (1914), all three part of a massive attack on the philosophy of Henri Bergson. Benda criticized Bergson's work for its glorification of mobility, for its praise of intuition, and for its irrationalism. He even implied, maliciously, that the success of Bergson's philosophy was derived from his pandering to the public's wish that sentiment be labeled science and mystical speculation philosophy. In *Belphégor* (1918), Benda turned against the aesthetic temper of his time, deploring that writers and readers had lost the capacity of enjoying intellectual pleasures and so found delight only in the emotions and sensations. This idea resurfaced with added vigor in *La France byzantine* (1945), a strong criticism of the French literature of the interwar years.

Benda's most famous work, *La Trahison des clercs*, appeared in 1927. It vehemently condemned the intellectuals (*clercs*) who had allowed themselves to be swayed by national, social, or political passions and thus had betrayed their responsibility to interpret their times impartially from the vantage point of reason, truth, or justice. The *clercs*, Benda argued, had forgotten that their "kingdom was not of this world" and had succumbed to the desire to demonstrate that their principles had meaning and validity in the practical realms of life.

In spite of his indictment of intellectuals who involve themselves in politics, Benda often took political sides. During World War I he wrote ardently patriotic articles for *Le Figaro*. In the 1930s he condemned the growing fascist menace, supported the Popular Front, and in general, sided with the Left against nazism and the extreme Right. In his view, these positions did not represent betrayal for they were based on reason, truth, and justice.

Because he unwaveringly defended the rationalist ideal and rejected irrationalism under all its forms, Benda remains in the history of French thought as the intellectual who put reason and intelligence above all other considerations.

J. Benda, *Dialogues à Byzance* (Paris, 1900) and *La Fin de l'éternel* (Paris, 1928); R. Nichols, *Treason, Tradition and the Intellectual* (Lawrence, Kans., 1978); R. Niess, *Julien Benda* (Ann Arbor, Mich., 1956).

M. D. Maayan

Related entries: BERGSON; DREYFUS AFFAIR; THOUGHT AND INTEL-LECTUAL LIFE.

BERGERY, GASTON (1892–1974), dynamic lawyer and politician, in turn leader of the Radical party, founder of the Parti frontiste, and Vichy ambassador to Russia and Turkey. As befits a man who always broke the moral codes of the Third Republic effortlessly, Bergery was born illegitimately in Paris. His studies for a doctorate in law were interrupted by World War I, during which he rose through the ranks to become a lieutenant. A liaison officer with the British Army for the last two years of the war, he was named assistant secretary-general of the Reparations Commission on demobilization, a post he held until 1924. His anonymous articles attacking Raymond Poincaré's reparations policy during his last year at this post came to the attention of Edouard Herriot, who hired Bergery as his *chef du cabinet* at the Foreign Ministry during the first government of the Cartel des gauches. Pilloried as a French Rasputin by the rightist press, Bergery added to his notoriety the following year by marrying the daughter of Leonid Krassin, the Soviet ambassador to France. In 1926 he was admitted to the bar in Paris as a specialist in international law and maintained an active practice for the rest of his life, with Ford Europe as his most publicized interwar client.

Elected as a deputy for Mantes (Seine-et-Oise) in 1928, he quickly became the leader of the left wing of the Radical party and a constant thorn in Herriot's side. His appeal for the younger generation of leftist intellectuals such as Emmanuel Berl, Pierre Drieu La Rochelle, and Bertrand de Jouvenel lay less in the originality of his thought than in the forceful, business-like way he presented old leftist notions. His life-style added to the appeal; the Bugatti, the American cord tie, and the elegant society he frequented gave the impression of a thoroughly modern man of action, a force that could break through the encrusted conser-vatism of the regime.

The inaction of the Radicals and, above all, their inability to risk reforms in delicate political situations led to his resignation from the party in 1933. He immediately began organizing the Popular Front, intended as an umbrella organization of the parties of the Left, from Radicals to Communists, for the struggle against both fascism and the threat of war. That aim was not accomplished, though the effort did provide a clear conception for the Popular Front, and Bergery had to content himself with forming an independent political party, which took the name *Parti frontiste* in 1936. He had resigned his seat in the Chamber of Deputies in February 1934 to protest the formation of the Gaston Doumergue government, only to lose the resultant by-election. Until he regained Mantes in 1936, his energies went largely into building his party. To supplement *Mantes-Républicain*, his local weekly since 1928, Bergery founded another, *La Flèche*, to serve as the party organ. To fill its columns, he was able to attract a number of prominent intellectuals, including the Troisième force group that had split from *Esprit* in 1933.

Bergery's main themes in the late 1930s were the need to muzzle the trusts that ruled France and the imperative to preserve international peace. When the Communists showed a willingness to gamble a war in support of Loyalist Spain, *La Flèche* became violently anti-Communist. Bergery's uncompromising pacifism was demonstrated not only by his support for the Munich accords but even more by his solitary vote against military credits in September 1939. Opposed to the war even while it was being fought, he was an active supporter of the armistice in June 1940 and loyally seconded Philippe Pétain and Pierre Laval in their dismantling of the Third Republic. Although his hopes that Vichy would accomplish through an authoritarian reformism what democracy could not were disappointed, he was rewarded with the post of ambassador to Moscow and then to Ankara.

P. Larmour, *The French Radical Party in the 1930's* (Stanford, 1964); G. Rossi-Landi, *La Drôle de guerre* (Paris, 1971); S. A. Schuker, *The End of French Predominance in Europe* (Chapel Hill, 1976).

J. R. Braun

Related entries: BERL; FEBRUARY RIOTS; HERRIOT; JOUVENEL; MOUNIER; POINCARE, R.; POPULAR FRONT; RADICAL AND RADICAL-SOCIALIST PARTY.

BERGSON, HENRI (1859–1941), the most famous French philosopher during the Third Republic. His ideas challenged the assumptions of materialism and scientific positivism by their stress on individual creativity and intuition. Jewish, one of seven children of the Polish-Parisian composer Michel Bergson and his English wife, nine-year-old Henri was left behind as a scholarship student in Paris when the family moved to England. He fully assimilated to traditional French culture. His early life was distinguished by numerous academic triumphs while at the Lycée Condorcet and the Ecole normale supérieure where he rivaled Jean Jaurès for class (1878) honors. During this period he came under the personal influence of Jules Lachelier and Félix Ravaisson, although he claimed that he was then less susceptible to their spiritualist ideas than to the materialistic philosophy of Herbert Spencer. Aside from classical studies, he had displayed a gift for mathematics and always took pride in the methodical care with which he approached philosophical problems. But the revelation, while teaching at a lycée in Clermont-Ferrand, that Spencer, Hippolyte Taine, and positive science in general had a flawed view of time that ignored the psychological dimension of real movement and duration (*la durée*) provided the theme for Bergson's principal doctoral thesis, "Essai sur les données immédiates de la conscience" (1889). By now he had returned to Paris to teach philosophy at the Collège Rollin and subsequently at the Lycée Henri IV.

In spite of his brilliance, Bergson remained in secondary education for sixteen years. His next book, *Matière et memoire* (1896), enjoyed only a modest immediate success, and the Sorbonne, dominated by neo-Kantians and positivists, repeatedly refused his candidacy. He nevertheless received an appointment to lecture at the Ecole normale supérieure in 1898, and two years later the Collège de France unanimously elected him professor of philosophy.

The enormously successful lectures that Bergson gave at the Collège between 1900 and his retirement from teaching in 1914 allowed him to expound his philosophy. Aside from the popularity of his eloquence among patrons of Parisian high society, the success of his lectures indicated a revival of idealism throughout Europe, especially welcomed by a younger generation whose optimism rebelled against the mechanistic doctrines of their teachers, the heirs of Taine and Ernest Renan, of Immanuel Kant and Auguste Comte. With the appearance of *L'Evolution créatrice* (1907), Bergson's critical philosophy had evolved into a metaphysical statement in which the drive of a single spiritual force, the *élan vital*, created a reality that could only be fully comprehended by an intuition that supplemented rational intelligence.

Lacking a formal school of disciples but exercising a pervasive cultural influence, the quiet and introspective Bergson, elected a member of the Academy in 1914, enjoyed a worldwide reputation that led to diplomatic missions abroad during World War I and to his selection after the war to the presidency of the Commission for Intellectual Cooperation, sponsored by the League of Nations. Although honors continued, culminating in the Nobel Prize for Literature in 1927, the onset of crippling arthritis in 1925 curtailed the philosopher's productivity during the last fifteen years of his life. His last important work, *Les Deux sources de la morale et de la religion* (1932), praised the morality of free and open societies responsive to the insights of saints and heroes. While his philosophy had encouraged the Catholic modernists, it was not the church's institutional constraints that Bergson favored, and if he came close to a public conversion to Catholicism, he refused because of the Nazis's anti-Semitic persecutions. Bergson declined the exemption from the Jewish laws offered by Vichyite friends and died in Nazi-occupied Paris on 4 January 1941 under a new order whose exaltation of the irrational had little place for freedom, creativity, or the individual.

M. Barthélemy-Madaule, *Bergson* (Paris, 1967); H. Bergson, *Ecrits et paroles* (Paris, 1957–59), *Oeuvres* (Paris, 1971), and *Mélanges*(Paris, 1972); P. A. Y. Gunter, *Henri Bergson: A Bibliography* (Bowling Green, Ohio, 1974); R.-M. Mossé-Bastide, *Bergson éducateur* (Paris, 1955).

L. M. Greenberg

Related entries: BENDA; PEGUY; POSITIVISM; PROUST; SOREL; THOUGHT AND INTELLECTUAL LIFE.

BERL, EMMANUEL (1892–1976), gifted essayist and journalist. Born in Le Vésinet (Seine-et-Oise), Berl was raised in the cultured milieu of the Jewish bourgeoisie. He attended the Lycées Carnot and Condorcet and studied briefly at the Ecole des sciences politiques and at the Sorbonne before spending a year at the University of Fribourg (1913–14). After serving with distinction in the First World War, he took up the life of a man of letters. A cousin of Henri Bergson and a friend of Marcel Proust, he had known many among the Jewish intelligentsia from childhood. He now befriended many of the political and literary leaders of interwar France and published a long succession of essays on love, politics, and, most often, the intellectual bankruptcy of the bourgeoisie.

His pursuit of active journalism began in 1927 when, with his closest friend, Pierre Drieu La Rochelle, he founded the short-lived *Les Derniers Jours*. In 1930 he was briefly editor of Henri Barbusse's *Monde*, and in 1932 he became the director of Editions Gallimard's prestigious literary weekly *Marianne*. His leftism proved too genteel for the new owners in 1937, but his pacifism grew ever sharper as war approached and found expression in a weekly review he wrote entirely by himself, *Pavés de Paris* (1938–40). As a Jewish supporter of the Munich pact, he was much fêted by the pacifist Right and not surprisingly asked at Bordeaux on the eve of the armistice to rework a speech for Philippe Pétain.

His masterful literary abilities are most apparent in the four remarkable volumes of memoirs written after the war: *Sylvia* (Paris, 1952), *Présence des morts* (Paris, 1956), *Rachel et autres graces* (Paris, 1965), and *A contretemps* (Paris, 1969). His other writings include: *Méditation sur un amour défunt* (Paris, 1925), *La route numéro 10* (Paris, 1927), *Mort de la pensée bourgeoise* (Paris, 1929), *Mort de la morale bourgeoise* (Paris, 1930), *Le bourgeois et l'amour* (Paris, 1931), *La politique et les partis* (Paris, 1932), *Lignes de chance* (Paris, 1935), *Le fameux Rouleau compressor* (Paris, 1937), *Frères bourgeois, mourrez-vous?* (Paris, 1938), *Histoire de l'Europe* (Paris, 1946–47), and *La Fin de la IIIe République* (Paris, 1968).

P. Andreu and F. Grover, *Drieu La Rochelle* (Paris, 1979); C. Estier, *La Gauche hebdomadaire* (Paris, 1962); P. Modiano, *Emmanuel Berl: Interrogatoire* (Paris, 1976).

                                                                                             J. R. Braun

Related entries: BARBUSSE; BERGSON; DRIEU LA ROCHELLE; PROUST; THOUGHT AND INTELLECTUAL LIFE.

BERNANOS, GEORGES (1888–1948), prominent novelist, moralist, and social critic. Bernanos was born in Paris to a pugnacious, extroverted businessman father and an extremely sensitive and devout mother, who felt close to her family's peasant origins. As a particularly solitary child, Bernanos was free to wander about the countryside and develop the idea that stayed with him throughout life: that only children and saints have the spontaneous relationship with God that the rest of humanity seeks. On his deathbed Bernanos maintained that he had been saved from despair by recalling the Grace of his First Communion. Thus Bernanos, a violent, vigorous, proud, tormented, and passionate man, depicted meek, sensitive, devout, self-effacing losers as the heroes of his novels. In this way Bernanos' novels expressed the vision of prophets like Edouard Drumont and Léon Bloy that the Nietzschean and egotistical values of the modern world would be overturned by the Jesus of the poor.

In contrast to the vast majority of French religious novelists, neither Bernanos nor his major characters were troubled by a lack of belief or by the conflict between flesh and spirit but rather by the conflict between good and evil in the universe. His first major novel, *Sous le soleil de Satan* (1926), owed much to the story of the remarkable "living saint" of mid-nineteenth-century France, the curé d'Ars. It was a work of extraordinary intensity and hallucinatory power, which presented a nightmarish world in which a few characters had hope while many more were in despair. Bernanos' artistry was highly praised, and his peculiar genius for depicting spiritual problems was compared to that of Dostoevsky. Ten years later he had another success comparable to that of *Satan* with his *Journal d'un curé de campagne* (1936). This classic work presented another humble, ascetic curé as the hero of a cosmological drama in which good and evil met, once again, in an obscure French village. The teachings of Jesus are depicted as representing the transvaluation of all values of the modern world, as a radical rejection of middle-class values, the business world, and the whole range of materialistic passions that Bernanos believed were poisoning the West.

Bernanos' political and social thought was marked by his conviction about the incompatibility of Christianity and capitalism. His biography of Edouard Drumont, *La Grande Peur des bien-pensants* (1931), sympathized with Drumont's detestation of Jews as symbols of the capitalist economic system and particularly with his apocalyptic juxtaposition of the Christ of the poor to the greedy, self-centered bourgeoisie who were using Catholicism to defend their property. Drumont, according to Bernanos, was one of the few men who had seen the need for a new Right in France that would abandon its alliance with the bourgeoisie and appeal to the common people to join in a relentless battle to preserve the traditions of an older France against the dehumanizing power of money.

Bernanos was living in Majorca in 1936 when the Spanish Civil War broke out. He had been sympathetic to José Antonio and the Falange and at first was sympathetic to Francisco Franco and the rebel forces. Once again the Spanish people were demonstrating their contempt for the materialistic values of the modern world, he believed, and "after all it is better to fight and die for one's altar, and one's gods, than for one's national trade." But first-hand observation of Franco's forces on Majorca caused him to reverse his views radically.

By 1937 Bernanos' disgust with the brutality, cynicism, and hyprocrisy of Franco's forces resulted in his *Les Grands Cimitières sous la lune*, which was quickly recognized as one of the greatest antifascist polemics of the decade. Bernanos came to join the Franco, Adolf Hitler, and Joseph Stalin dictatorships as similar phenomena; like Benito Mussolini they were simply clever enough to utilize the most generous instincts of humanity to pursue their perverted ends. After the Majorca experience, Bernanos, whom some had seen as a potential Nazi, became one of the most effective literary adversaries of all kinds of fascism, including Hitlerism. Although on the eve of the war he moved to Brazil, he continued to be passionately concerned with the fate of Europe whose affliction with "the deficiency disease of the democracies . . . the unemployment of the heart" had led it into a death threat from the fascisms and Stalinism. He was one of the few French Catholic intellectuals whose opting for the Resistance was clear from the late 1930s.

F. Field, *Three French Writers and the Great War* (Cambridge, England, 1978); Thomas Molnar, *Bernanos: His Political Thought and Prophecy* (New York, 1960); C. C. O'Brien, *Maria Cross, Imaginative Patterns in a Group of Catholic Writers* (London, 1964); H. U. von Balthasar, *Le Chrétien Bernanos* (Paris, 1956).

J. W. Hellman

Related entries: CATHOLIC LITERARY RENAISSANCE; DRUMONT.

BERNARD, CLAUDE (1813–1878), premier physiologist of the nineteenth century, leading advocate of experimentalism in medicine and biology, and spokesman for science. The son of vineyard workers, Bernard was born in St.-Julien (Côte d'Or), and received his early education in local religious schools. Literary ambitions brought him to Paris in 1834. On the advice of the critic Saint-Marc Girardin he decided to acquire a profession, however, and entered the Paris Faculté de médecine in the same year. In 1839 he began an internship in the Paris hospitals, where his mentors included Pierre Rayer at the Charité and François Magendie at the Hôtel-Dieu. By 1841 he had become Magendie's assistant and collaborator in the latter's course on experimental physiology at the Collège de France. Magendie's leadership and example turned him decisively toward science. Although he completed the M.D. in 1843, Bernard never practiced medicine. Instead he devoted himself with great energy and perseverance to physiological research on a range of topics, including nutrition and digestion, the nervous system, animal heat, and poisons.

In the decade 1843–53 Bernard either made or took the first steps toward his most important discoveries: the role of the pancreas in digestion, the glycogenic function of the liver, the existence of vasomotor nerves, and the mechanisms of poisoning by carbon monoxide and curare. Moral support for Bernard's scientific endeavors and a forum for the presentation and discussion of his findings were provided by the Paris Société de biologie. Founded in 1848 with Bernard serving as one of the first vice-presidents, the Société gave expression to the scientific interests and activity of a segment of the Paris medical community and to its desire to give substance to Auguste Comte's call for a science of biology not subordinated to practical medicine. Specialized positions for physiologists did not exist in the France of the 1840s, however, and apart from service as substitute lecturer for Magendie at the Collège de France, Bernard was long without an official research or teaching post.

Recognition—and a major step toward the institutionalization of his science—came in 1854 when the government created for Bernard the first chair of general physiology at the Sorbonne. In 1854 he was elected to membership in the Paris Académie des sciences, and on Magendie's death in 1855 Bernard succeeded his teacher in the chair of medicine at the Collège de France.

His career established, Bernard turned to the consolidation and extension of his major discoveries and to their systematic exposition in teaching. At the same time he began the elaboration of the fundamental physiological concepts and methodological principles that were characteristic of his later work and to which he owed much of his fame outside of specialized physiological circles.

As Magendie's student Bernard was heir to the experimental physiology that had been taking form in France since the early years of the century. Physiologists studied higher vertebrate function through direct intervention in the living organism (vivisection) aided by normal, pathological, and comparative anatomy, chemistry, and physics. Brilliant and resourceful in the design and execution of experiments, especially those involving surgical, manipulative skills, Bernard extended and deepened this tradition in the research that led to his major discoveries. In his later career he began to move beyond the preoccupation with human and mammalian function carried over by physiology from its medical origins and to seek laws governing the phenomena common to all living things. In so doing Bernard took an important step toward the extension of the experimental ideal to general biology, a movement that was to take on great importance in the decades around 1900.

In the essay for which he is best known, *Introduction à l'étude de la médecine expérimentale* (1865), Bernard gave powerful expression to his view that neither medicine nor the natural history disciplines could base themselves solely on observation, description, and classification. The functioning of the organism could be understood, and rational, effective therapies could be evolved, only through the experimental control of life processes. The possibility of control was based in turn on two ideas that—in their effective formulation and application—were original with Bernard. The principle of experimental determinism ensured that the same physiological phenomena are invariably replicated under the same physical, chemical, and anatomical conditions. Bernard pointed out that in higher animals these conditions are largely determined by the existence of a *milieu intérieur*, a liquid internal environment that bathes the tissues, maintains for them a dynamic equilibrium of chemical and physical conditions, and mediates the influences of the external environment. The concept of the *milieu intérieur* enabled Bernard to safeguard the possibility of experimental determinism while recognizing the relative independence and spontaneity of higher organisms in relation to their external environments. In *Introduction* and in Bernard's other writings, the theme of power over nature characteristic of modern science and of the industrial societies of the nineteenth century found appropriate expression in biology and medicine.

Between 1865 and his death in 1878 Bernard's stature as spokesman for science was recognized and enhanced by numerous honors. President of the Société de biologie and commander of the Légion d'honneur in 1867, he was made senator of the Empire and member and president of the Académie française in 1869. In the wake of the Franco-Prussian War, Bernard, with his younger contemporary Louis Pasteur, made use of his fame to call for increased support for French science as a means to strengthen the nation. By according to him a national funeral in 1878, an honor hitherto reserved for political and military figures, Bernard's countrymen indicated that they valued not only the man but also the science that he represented.

G. Canguilhem, *Etudes d'histoire et de philosophie des sciences*, 3d ed. (Paris, 1975); M. D. Grmek, ''Bernard, Claude,'' *Dictionary of Scientific Biography* (New York, 1973), *Catalogue des manuscrits de Claude Bernard* (Paris, 1967), and *Raisonnement expérimental et recherches toxicologiques chez Claude Bernard* (Geneva and Paris, 1973); F. L. Holmes, *Claude Bernard and Animal Chemistry* (Cambridge, Mass., 1974); J. M. D. Olmsted and E. H. Olmsted, *Claude Bernard and the Experimental Method in Medicine* (New York, 1952); J. Schiller, *Claude Bernard et les problèmes scientifiques de son temps* (Paris, 1967); R. Virtanen, *Claude Bernard and His Place in the History of Ideas* (Lincoln, Neb., 1960).

J. E. Lesch

Related entries: LEGION OF HONOR; PASTEUR; POSITIVISM; SCIENCE AND TECHNOLOGY.

BERNHARDT, SARAH (1844–1923), actress. Born Henriette Rosine Bernard in Paris on 22–23 October 1844, the daughter of a Dutch courtesan (Judith Van Hard) and a law student (Edouard Bernard), the future Sarah Bernhardt was reared in a convent school. From 1858 to 1860, at the suggestion of the duc de Morny, one of her mother's lovers, she studied at the Paris conservatoire and made her debut at the Comédie française in Racine's *Iphigénie en Aulide* in 1862 to indifferent reviews. After a brief affair with Henri, prince de Ligne, which produced an illegitimate child (Maurice), and influential introductions, she transferred to the Odéon in 1866. Success there in *Kean* (Alexandre Dumas, *père*), *Le Passant* (François Coppée), and a revival of *Ruy Blas* (Victor Hugo) ensured her triumphal return to the Comédie française in 1872. Immense popular acclaim greeted her performances in Racine's *Phèdre* and Hugo's *Hernani*, and by 1879 she was sufficiently famous to ensure an independent career and so left the Comédie.

In 1880, with the American impresario Edward Jarrett, she undertook a spectacularly successful tour of the United States (the first of nine), starring in *La Dame aux camélias* (Alexandre Dumas, *fils*). On her return to Paris, she began a collaboration with Victorien Sardou in his *Fédora*, *La Tosca*, and *Cléopâtre*. Her sensational popularity permitted her to open a theater of her own in Paris, the Théâtre de la Renaissance, in 1893. Six years later in 1899, she established the Théâtre Sarah Bernhardt, which she owned and operated until her death. Her physical beauty, grace, and lyrical voice attracted immense audiences for Edmond de Rostand's *L'Aiglon*, *La Samaritaine*, and *Cyrano de Bergerac*. She also provoked a vogue for Shakespeare with her portrayal of *Hamlet*. In 1905, she suffered an injury to her right knee that never healed and necessitated the amputation of her leg in 1915. She nevertheless continued to act and produce her final sensation, in Louis Verneuil's *Daniel*, during the last year of her life.

Bernhardt was a talented amateur painter and sculptress. She also published her autobiography, *Ma double vie; mémoires de Sarah Bernhardt* (1907), and a novel, *Petite Idole* (1920), both of which present idealizations of her career. Her treatise on acting, *L'Art du théâtre* (1923), contains a revealing discussion of voice techniques. She was a fervent French patriot, opening a military hospital in the Odéon during the Franco-Prussian War and visiting the front lines during World War I. Bernhardt died in Paris on 26 March 1923.

A. Castelot, *Sarah Bernhardt* (Paris, 1961); J. Richardson, *Sarah Bernhardt* (London, 1959).

B. F. Martin and J. C. Overton

Related entries: COPPEE; DUMAS; THEATER.

BERR, HENRI (1863–1954), professor, philosopher of history, and editor. After preparation at the Lycée Charlemagne, Berr entered the Ecole normale supérieure in 1881 where he was a literature major. Except for the profound impression the historian Fustel de Coulanges had on him, Berr's normalian years were uneventful. In 1884 he passed the *agrégation* and served in provincial lycées as a professor in rhetoric. He was called to the Lycée Henri IV at Paris in 1896 where he remained until 1926. During this period he failed two times to be elected to a chair at the Collège de France. Early in the 1890s Berr published articles critical of the positivistic philosophy that dominated the academic circles of the early Third Republic. Under the influence of the neo-Kantian philosopher Emile Boutroux, Berr received the doctorate in 1899 from the University of Paris with two ambitious theses: "Gassendi est-il un sceptique?" and "L'Avenir de la philosophie: Esquisse d'une synthèse des connaissance fondée sur l'histoire."

The next year, in the wake of excitement created by the Paris Exposition of 1900, Berr founded the *Revue de synthèse historique*, which aimed to provide a forum for historians and social scientists increasingly separated by the boundaries of academic disciplines and specialization. Berr's call for a *synthèse historique* precipitated a fierce methodological debate that resounded deeply within the French university. But as Berr noted in his book, *La Synthèse en histoire* (1911), the majority of historians rejected or neglected to follow his lead in the creation of a truly integrated scientific history (*synthèse scientifique*).

After World War I, Berr began editing "L'Evolution de l'humanité," a project of a hundred volumes with long introductions keyed to his program for the coordination of social and historical research. Rising young talents like Lucien Febvre and Marc Bloch published their first works in the series. Berr retired from his teaching post in 1925 and became the director of a unique Centre international de synthèse: fondation pour la science at Paris in 1926. Housed after 1929 in the Hôtel de Nevers next to the Bibliothèque nationale, Berr and a small devoted staff persisted in disseminating the ideas of the *synthèse* program for a new history in the journal, which in 1931 became simply *Revue de synthèse*. Support came primarily from outside the university; a consortium of French banks provided yearly donations, and friendship with President Paul Doumer cleared the way for grants from the Ministry of Education. With the active partnership of influential professors like Lucien Febvre and Abel Rey, Henri Berr's Centre became a unique think tank for the exploration of the growing scientific culture in France and Europe in the 1930s.

In 1942 Berr published the autobiographical *L'Hymne à la vie*, a valuable study of the psychological impact of science and technology on humanistic and religious culture. By the time of his death in 1954, Henri Berr had completed almost three-quarters of the prefaces to his hundred-volume series, "L'Evolution de l'humanité." Though still relatively unknown among scholars, Berr's important contributions to the transformation of the social sciences and the success of the *Annales* school of social history in contemporary France have been clearly established.

S. Delorme, "Henri Berr," *Osiris* 10 (1951); M. Siegel, "Henri Berr's *Revue de synthèse historique*," *History and Theory* 9 (1970).

M. Siegel

Related entries: BLOCH; FEBVRE; HISTORIOGRAPHY: *ANNALES* SCHOOL.

BERT, PAUL (1833–1886), scientist, deputy, minister, educational reformer, colonial administrator. Three dominating passions—science, politics, and anticlericalism—shaped Bert's career. As deputy (1872–86), as member of Léon Gambetta's circle and minister of education and religion in his cabinet, and as leader of the Chamber of Deputies' educational committee, Bert played a central part in the campaign for free, secular education. The Republic depended on education, he argued, to make citizens and to resurrect France after the defeat in 1870. Under the motto "Through the schools, for the nation," he sought compulsory and free primary education with a secular curriculum that protected the family's primacy in matters of conscience and defended the Republic against the Catholic church. The Ferry Laws (1880–86) made these principles reality. To attract good teachers, Bert proposed departmental normal schools and legislation improving teachers' salaries and status. He also sought to strengthen secondary education for girls and to free higher education from church influence.

Bert's fervent attachment to laicism reflected the anticlericalism common to militant republicans and the rationalism typical of scientists. He had earned doctorates of medicine (1863) and natural science (1866) and in 1869 succeeded to his mentor Claude Bernard's chair in general physiology at the Sorbonne, a position he held throughout his political career. In his research, he explored the impact of the environment on organisms through specialized studies of animal transplantation, the comparative physiology of respiration, and anaesthesia. He published scientific treatises, including the important *La Pression barométrique* (1878), primary and secondary textbooks in the natural sciences, and articles on science in the press. In 1881 he became a member of the National Academy of Sciences.

In January 1886 he agreed to serve as first resident general of Annam and Tonkin. He worked to reestablish civilian authority, develop commerce, and implant French culture through the schools. Overwork weakened his resistance, and he died in Hanoi of dysentery at age fifty-three.

L. Dubreuil, *Paul Bert* (Paris, 1935); N. Mani, "Paul Bert," *Dictionary of Scientific Biography* (New York, 1970).

S. A. Ashley

Related entries: ANTICLERICALISM; BERNARD; EDUCATION: GOVERN-MENTAL POLICIES CONCERNING; FERRY; GAMBETTA; OPPORTUN-ISTS; OVERSEAS EMPIRE: COLONIAL ADMINISTRATION; OVERSEAS EMPIRE: SOUTHEAST ASIA; SCHOOLS, PRIMARY.

BERTHELOT, MARCELLIN (1827–1907), chemist, senator and governmental minister, positivist philosopher, and historian of science. Pierre-Eugène-Marcellin Berthelot (by error, Marcelin on the birth certificate) was born 25 October 1827 at place de Grève in Paris, the site of the future Hôtel de Ville. Here his father, a republican, practiced medicine. After studies at the Collège Henri IV, Berthelot took a *licence* in 1849 and a doctorate in 1854 at the Paris Faculty of Sciences. In 1858 he graduated from the Ecole de pharmacie, and in 1859 he was appointed to the school's newly created chair of organic chemistry. From 1865 he also held a new chair of organic chemistry at the Collège de France, relinquishing the pharmacy chair in 1876. In 1870–71 he was president of the Comité scientifique pour la défense de Paris, and from 1874 he served on the War Ministry's Commission on Explosives. As Inspecteur général de l'enseignement supérieure (1876–88), member of the permanent section of the Conseil supérieur de l'instruction publique (from its creation in 1880), member of the Senate (from 1871), and minister of education (1886–87), Berthelot exerted powerful influence in education and notable control over the appointments of science faculty members. He supported laicization of primary education and educational secularization in the years of the young Republic's struggle with the church. He served briefly as foreign minister in 1895 under Léon Bourgeois.

An ally of the European tradition of positivism and scientific materialism, a close friend of Claude Bernard and Ernest Renan, Berthelot advocated the application of scientific methods to the solution of social and ethical problems. He took the Comtian view of scientific method, stressing unity of scientific knowledge and the idea that scientific theories are series of relationships between observed phenomena. He resisted the use of the atomic hypothesis in chemistry and rejected structural hypotheses like Auguste Kekule's benzene ring. He opposed Louis Pasteur's argument that fermentation is the result of the action of living organisms and angered Pasteur after the death of Claude Bernard by publishing some of Bernard's notes supporting Berthelot's position that fermentation ultimately must be the result of purely chemical processes.

Berthelot's program of chemical synthesis decisively undercut the traditional vitalist view that organic compounds associated with vegetable and animal substances are the result of a set of natural laws completely different from the laws of inorganic nature. In 1854 he successfully prepared ethyl alcohol independently from the fermentation of a sugar solution. He synthesized in the laboratory methane, ethylene, propylene, butylene, amylene, ethane, propane, benzene, and naphthalene, converting them all into corresponding alcohols and demonstrating the open avenue for synthesis of an indefinite number of organic compounds. He was the first chemist to produce acetylene electrically and the first to synthesize formic acid (previously derived from ants). He demonstrated the feasibility of converting aliphatic hydrocarbons (like acetylene and ethylene) to aromatic ones (like benzene). Applying studies of heats of combustion to organic reactions, Berthelot's work included many researches in thermochemistry, and it was in the Physics Section that he was elected to the Academy of Sciences in 1873. Among his most important chemical texts were *Chimie organique fondée sur la synthèse* (1860) and *Essai de mécanique chimique fondée sur la thermochimie* (1879). In addition to researches in chemistry, Berthelot contributed to the history of alchemy and wrote the valuable historical study *La Révolution chimique. Lavoisier* (1890).

M. Crosland, "Marcellin Berthelot," *Dictionary of Scientific Biography*, vol. 2 (New York, 1970); C. Graebe, "Marcelin Berthelot," *Berichte der Deutschen Chemischen Gesellschaft* 41 (1908); E. Jungfleisch, "Notice sur la vie et les travaux de Marcellin Berthelot," *Bulletin de la Société chimique de France* 13 (1913); L. Velluz, *Vie de Berthelot* (Paris, 1964); R. Virtanen, *Marcelin Berthelot* (Lincoln, Nebr., 1965).

M. J. Nye

Related entries: ANTICLERICALISM; BERNARD; EDUCATION: ADMINISTRATION OF; PASTEUR; POSITIVISM; RENAN; SCIENCE AND TECHNOLOGY.

BESLAY, CHARLES (1795–1878), socialist friend of Joseph Proudhon and oldest member of the Paris Commune of 1871. Delivering the Commune's inaugural address, he interpreted its role as favoring decentralization and municipal liberties. A Breton engineer, son of a businessman and a deputy elected under three regimes, Beslay himself became a deputy in 1830 for having preserved Pontivy (Morbihan) from labor violence. Denied reelection because of his radicalism, he nevertheless served on Morbihan's departmental council and in 1848 became the department's general commissioner. Heading its list to the 1848 constitutional assembly, Beslay sided with the moderate republicans. Not reelected, he came increasingly under Proudhon's influence. Beslay lost a fortune applying socialist theories to his Parisian enterprises, the most notable failure being an attempt to found an exchange bank in accordance with Proudhon's ideas.

A Freemason and early adherent to the First Workingmen's International, Beslay opened his Paris home to the republican opposition under the Second Empire. In spite of his age, he sought enlistment during the Franco-Prussian War. A founder of the Vigilance Committee of the Sixth Arrondissement and its delegate to the Central Committee of the Twenty Arrondissements, he supported the uprising of 31 October 1870. But within the Commune Beslay exerted a moderating influence joining the minority faction. While the Commune rejected as too complex his proposal for a national exchange bank, it appointed him a delegate to the Bank of France. There he acted to preserve France's financial integrity by protecting the institution from his more extreme colleagues. Adolphe Thiers allowed Beslay free passage to Neuchâtel, Switzerland, where until his death he remained a respected and active member of the International.

R. Duthil, "Centenaire de la Commune de Paris: Comment un Dinannais, Charles Beslay, contribua au relèvement de la France," *Annales de la société d'histoire et d'archéologie de l'arrondissement de Saint-Malo, 1971* (Laval, 1972); J. Maitron, ed., *Dictionnaire biographique du mouvement ouvrier français*, vol. 1 (Paris, 1964); B. Noël, *Dictionnaire de la Commune* (Paris, 1971).

L. M. Greenberg

Related entries: COMMUNARDS; COMMUNE OF PARIS; INTERNATIONAL, FIRST WORKINGMEN'S; SOCIALISM (1870–1914).

BETOULLE, LEON (1871–1956), socialist leader, mayor of Limoges, deputy and senator of the Haute-Vienne. He participated in a succession of socialist groups in the 1890s. A moderate socialist in the tradition of Jean Jaurès, he supported Alexandre Millerand's participation in the 1899 René Waldeck-Rousseau administration. Betoulle joined the newly unified Socialist party (SFIO) in 1906 and repeatedly represented the Haute-Vienne at party congresses. Betoulle wrote regularly for several Radical and Socialist newspapers, including the influential *La Dépêche de Toulouse*. In 1905, he founded the regional socialist daily *Le Populaire du Centre*.

Elected to the Limoges city council in 1900, Betoulle became deputy mayor (*premier adjoint*) under Radical-turned-Socialist Mayor Emile Labussière. Betoulle was elected to the Chamber of Deputies in 1906, a position he held until becoming a senator in 1924. He was first elected to the department's *conseil général* in 1921, serving as its president from 1929 to 1940. Despite his long parliamentary career, he is most known for his accomplishments as Limoges' mayor (1912–40, 1947–56). His administration was dedicated to implementing municipal socialism: social welfare programs (child care and unemployment compensation, for example), construction and modernization of public facilities (parks, streets, and so on), support for working-class institutions (such as unions), and improvement of the local economy. Betoulle decisively contributed to the building of Socialist party political hegemony in Limoges and its region. As leader of the area's socialists for nearly half a century, Betoulle presided over the SFIO's most solid electoral stronghold.

P. Cousteix, "Le Mouvement ouvrier limousin de 1870 à 1939", *L'Actualité de l'histoire* 21 (1957); J. Lenoble et al., *Etudes sur la vie politique et les forces électorales en limousin (1871–1973)* (Limoges, 1978).

D. Wright

Related entries: JAURES; MILLERAND; SOCIALISM; SOCIALISM, MUNICIPAL; SOCIALIST PARTY; WALDECK-ROUSSEAU.

BIETRY, PIERRE (1872–1918), early national socialist and leader of the Fédération nationale des Jaunes de France. Although he began his career in the 1890s as a revolutionary socialist, within a few years Biétry had taken over leadership of an independent and antisocialist federation of trade unions, popularly known as the Jaunes. In its heyday, between about 1904 and 1907, the Jaunes seemed to possess at least the potential to challenge the Confédération générale du travail (CGT), France's largest labor organization. Although figures are notoriously unreliable, there is some scholarly consensus that the pre-1914 CGT never surpassed 350,000 members, whereas the Jaunes, at its height, could count about 100,000. Biétry's influence peaked in 1906 when, in the wake of his election to the Chamber of Deputies, he was touted by virtually all of the nationalist Right as the man who could save the working class for the nation. This salvation was deemed necessary to most on the Right because the leaders of the CGT were openly promoting class warfare and the general strike and called themselves revolutionary syndicalists.

Biétry's alternative to revolutionary syndicalism—in both its essentials and many of its particulars—foreshadowed much of later fascism. His program was a militant version of that of Edouard Drumont: nationalist and antiparliamentary, vehemently anti-Semitic, and vaguely anticapitalistic. Like later fascists, Biétry became convinced that Marxian socialism was a conspiracy against the nation and that France could be made strong only through some form of corporatism and the destruction of the liberal-democratic state. The problem with contemporary socialism, according to Biétry, was that it promoted class warfare by its hostility to the idea of private property. His solution was not the abolition of property but the transformation of workers into property owners.

Although a capable organizer and a talented orator, Biétry was not able to establish his Jaunes on a solid foundation. The problems were manifold: lack of general enthusiasm among both industrial and governmental elites, an increasing hostility among the rank-and-file Jaunes disconcerted by Biétry's involvement in politics, and, finally, the failure of his political strategy to build a great rightist coalition. This coalition, had it materialized, would have been based on opposition to socialism and anticlericalism, would have emphasized patriotism and anti-Semitism, and would have been orchestrated by Biétry himself. Like many other attempts to unite the Right, this effort ended in squabbling and recrimination among what would have been its component parts. Biétry, defeated and disgusted, not only bowed out of politics but left France in 1912.

G. Mosse, "The French Right and the Working Classes: Les Jaunes," *Journal of Contemporary History* 7 (1972); Z. Sternhell, *La Droite révolutionnaire, 1885–1914* (Paris, 1978).

P. Mazgaj

Related entries: CONFEDERATION GENERALE DU TRAVAIL; DRUMONT; SYNDICALISM; TRADE UNION MOVEMENT.

BINET, ALFRED (1857–1911), psychologist of learning. He was born in Nice but moved with his mother to Paris so that he might attend the Lycée Louis-le-Grand. He studied law and medicine at the Sorbonne but was most attracted by the work on hypnosis of Jean Charcot. In 1878 he abandoned law to read psychology by himself at the Bibliothèque nationale. He followed the English associationist school of psychology stemming from James and John Stuart Mill and Herbert Spencer, but by 1886 and in his work *La Psychologie du raisonnement*, he saw the limitations of the mechanist approach of the associationists. He also appreciated the importance of experiments in psychology but disliked the German experimental tradition, which emphasized the physiology of sensations. Binet was interested in the higher mental processes, in reasoning ability, and in the emotional and nonrational responses to sensations. He began to devise experiments designed to measure individual responses to pictures, inkblots, and different objects. In 1891 he joined the Laboratory of Physiological Psychology at the

Sorbonne and from 1895 to 1911 was director of the laboratory. He also founded a center in Paris for studying children and for experimental teaching.

Binet is best remembered for his scales to measure intelligence, developed between 1905 and 1911. He had been impressed by Sir Francis Galton's attempts to develop standardized tests, and he devised tests that provided data on both the intelligence and the educational progress of school children. His close observation of the development of his own two daughters resulted in his work *L'Etude experimentale de l'intelligence* (1903). He also tried to apply his tests to writers, artists, mathematicians, and chess players. His interest in normal as well as abnormal mental processes and his continued interest in suggestibility and hysteria set him apart from the mechanists and associationists in his time. He died in Paris, 18 October 1911.

A. Binet, *La Psychologie du raisonnement* (Paris, 1886), and *L'Etude expérimentale de l'intelligence* (Paris, 1903); R. H. Pollack, and M. W. Brenner, eds., *The Experimental Psychology of Alfred Binet: Selected Papers*, trans. F. K. Zetland and C. Ellis (New York, 1969); T. H. Wolf, *Alfred Binet* (Chicago, 1973).

H. J. Steffens

BING, S. (1838–1905), a major French exponent of Japanese art and the organizer of the salons of Art Nouveau. From a wealthy, entrepreneurial background, he trained as an industrial designer and established a thriving Oriental trading business, which led to the opening in Paris during the 1870s of an Oriental crafts shop. Bing had acquired much of the merchandise on his Japanese tours. He also founded a periodical, *Artistic Japan* (published simultaneously in English, French, and German between 1888 and 1891) and organized some tasteful, rare Japanese art exhibitions, featuring much that was fresh to European eyes.

By 1893, Bing, tired of his mercantile life-style, was sent by his government to the United States to draft a report, eventually published as *Artistic Culture in America*. This fired his interest in industrial art, giving rise to the December 1895 reopening of his shop at 22 rue de Provence as the first salon of Art Nouveau. This controversial first exhibition was critically acclaimed and consolidated the opinion that commissioned decorative designers could create room ensembles harmonious in style and motif. His support for the Nabis, Henry van de Velde, Louis Comfort Tiffany, and many others launched modernism under thoughtful auspices.

Bing's success among devotees of Art Nouveau climaxed with the opening of his own pavilion, Art Nouveau Bing, at the Paris World's Fair (1900). It incorporated rooms designed by three artists in his sole employ: Georges de Feure, Edouard Colonna, and Eugène Gaillard. Ceramics designed by Colonna and de Feure and produced by G.D.A. in Limoges were well received. Five years later, having sold his furniture manufactory to Majorelle of Nancy, Bing died. His place as an importer of Oriental art was assumed by his son Marcel.

R. Koch, "Art Nouveau Bing," *Gazette des beaux-arts* (March 1959); G. P. Weisberg, "Samuel Bing: International Dealer of Art Nouveau," *Connoisseur* (March, April, May,

July 1971), and "Gerard, Dufraissex and Abbot: The Manufactory of Art Nouveau Bing Porcelains in Limoges, France," *Connoisseur* (February 1978).

G. P. Weisberg

Related entries: ART NOUVEAU, *BELLE EPOQUE*; GUIMARD.

BLANQUI, AUGUSTE (1805–1881), renowned patriot, revolutionary militant, and elder statesman of the French Left. He played a major, ongoing role in the revolutionary movement in nineteenth-century France, from its early manifestations in the secret societies of the Restoration era, through the revolutionary days of 1830, 1848, and 1870–71, to the domestication of the revolutionary movement to the political processes of the Third Republic in the late 1870s. As the most notorious of France's nineteenth-century revolutionaries, he was destined to become a legend in his time.

A brilliant student with promising opportunities for a professional career, he abandoned the study of law in the mid-1820s to devote himself completely to the revolutionary cause. Henceforth he played an overt role as a republican journalist and a covert one as a revolutionary conspirator and organizer of secret revolutionary societies. He is best known for the courage with which he held fast to his commitments through forty-three years of imprisonment on a variety of charges by four different political regimes. By the early years of the Third Republic, he was as important for his reputation as the "imprisoned one," a martyr for the radical republican cause, as he was for his actual political activities. So great was his prestige for the Communards as a potential lawgiver for the Commune that his followers worked tirelessly to exchange hostages for him, all to no avail. Blanqui remained incarcerated through the 1870s, but he was not forgotten. Freedom for Blanqui became the watchword of the campaign for amnesty for the Communards in the late 1870s. While still imprisoned, he was elected to the Chamber of Deputies by the citizens of Bordeaux in 1879, and his candidacy in other cities assumed the proportions of a plebiscite for amnesty and was a contributing factor in its success in 1880. Blanqui was freed in 1879 and was hailed as a national hero on his nationwide speaking tour in 1880, shortly before his death. Pilgrimages to his gravesite on the anniversary of his death became an important rite for his followers during the 1880s.

Feared at mid-century by all but the extreme Left as a sinister revolutionary conspirator breeding discontent, he was honored during the Third Republic as the elder statesman of the Revolutionary tradition. Judgments about Blanqui have always had to come to terms with his ascetic manner. Public opinion was struck by his eccentricities and his stylized posture as a pariah. Regarded as severe and aloof by outsiders, nonetheless he was found to be genial and deeply humane by his close companions. In a larger historical perspective, Blanqui enjoys respect for the quality of his polemical journalism and for his contribution to the theory of revolutionary organization. He inspired Lenin and other twentieth-century revolutionaries who have emphasized the crucial role of the revolutionary party in the radical reconstruction of society. His contribution to social theory was less important than his disciples believed it to be. Depicted by sympathetic historians as a forerunner of Marxian socialism, he in fact drew his political and social ideas from the radical republican conceptions of the *sans-culottes* of the French Revolution. Blanqui's atheism in turn underpinned his political creed, and his struggle against the church was his deepest crusade.

The meaning of Blanqui's life is derived less from his ideas or his activities than it is from his idealism, the stoic courage with which he faced all his trials, and which inspired the generation of republican youth that came of age about the time of the Paris Commune of 1871.

S. Bernstein, *Auguste Blanqui* (Paris, 1970); M. Dommanget, *Auguste Blanqui au début de la IIIe République (1871–1880)* (Paris, 1971); P. H. Hutton, *The Cult of the Revolutionary Tradition* (Berkeley, 1981); A. Spitzer, *The Revolutionary Theories of Louis-Auguste Blanqui* (New York, 1951).

P. H. Hutton

Related entries: BLANQUISTS; COMMUNARDS; COMMUNARDS: AMNESTY MOVEMENT FOR; COMMUNE OF PARIS; DOMMANGET; JACOBINISM.

BLANQUISTS, a revolutionary faction devoted to the person and especially to the ideals of Auguste Blanqui. Their activities extended from the 1860s through the 1890s. The group was sustained throughout by personal bonds uniting a core of militants, although there was considerable movement in and out of its ranks. In the late 1860s and again in the mid-1880s, the Blanquists may have numbered as many as 2,000. Within the group there were different kinds of commitment. One contemporary observer, Arthur Ranc, drew a distinction between Blanquists of the first (disciples) and second (fellow travelers) degrees. Although the group displayed more of the characteristics of a sect than those of a political party, it exercised far-reaching influence on the revolutionary movement in the early years of the Third Republic because of the fervor with which it promoted revolutionary politics. Successively a radical student society during the Second Empire, a political faction in the Paris Commune of 1871, a band of exiles in England during the 1870s, and a political committee (the Central Revolutionary Committee) in Paris during the 1880s, the Blanquist party acquired a reputation for being the most zealous defender of the French Revolutionary tradition. The Blanquists preached an ideology that taught that community is forged through revolutionary struggle. A patriotism founded on comradeship was its essential element, although it favored popular democracy and egalitarian reforms as complementary ideals. The Blanquists conceived of themselves as a vanguard of the revolution, but they stressed that their mission was to catalyze rather than to direct the revolution. They praised the ideals of Jacques Hébert, Pierre Chaumette, and the Revolutionary Commune of 1793 as the source of their politics and correspondingly condemned the politics of Maximilien Robespierre and the Committee of Public Safety as an elitist betrayal of the revolutionary ideal. Their political ideology was derived from their radical atheism, which divided believers and unbelievers as the constituent elements underlying the political struggle. The former were condemned for their passiveness and resignation, which rendered them obedient to authority. The latter were praised for their willpower and independence of mind, which enabled them to fight against oppression. The participation of the Blanquists in the Free Thought movement (to propagate atheist ideas) provided a continuous thread to their activities apart from their political objectives.

The original circle of Blanquists, formed in 1864 to visit Blanqui in prison, was composed of medical and law students at the University of Paris. While the Blanquist party would subsequently include many workers, its leadership was drawn from the middle class. The only genuine theoretician among the Blanquists was Gustave Tridon, who systematized the Blanquist viewpoint in *Les Hébertistes* (1871), a political tract, and *Le Molochisme juif* (1884), a work on religious anthropology that established the foundation of the group's attack on Judeo-Christian values. Others played important roles as journalists (Albert Regnard, Henri Place, Alfred Breuillé) or as political organizers (Théophile Ferré, Ernest Granger, Emile Duval), and several held important posts during the Commune (especially Emile Eudes, Ferré, Raoul Rigault). Somewhat apart was Edouard Vaillant, a Communard who joined the Blanquists during their London exile. As one of the best educated and best known of the Blanquists, he was the first among them to be elected to political office (Municipal Council of Paris, 1884) during the Third Republic. Vaillant was destined to become one of the most important leaders of the Socialist party in the era before the First World War, and his political attitudes were subsequently interpreted as being representative of the Blanquist viewpoint. Yet he was regarded by the surviving founders of the Blanquist party as an outsider, and his sympathies for Marxism, together with his ambition to turn the Blanquist circle at Paris into a national party, promoted a quarrel that led to the division and eventually to the disintegration of the Blanquist cause. The decision of several Blanquist leaders to participate in the Boulangist campaign in 1888, and Vaillant's refusal to follow them, precipitated the schism. It effectively ended the party's existence. Vaillant's faction was absorbed into the socialist movement during the 1890s. The other faction, which included most of the party's old guard, gravitated toward the radical nationalist (protofascist) movement, which led the campaign against Alfred Dreyfus. The schism of the Blanquists crystallized the dilemma of many revolutionaries in an age when mass politics was superseding the politics of popular insurrection. The choice of the Blanquists between new (Marxist) and old (Jacobin) approaches to the radical reconstruction of society prefigures that of the revolutionary movement at large between revisionist socialism and radical nationalism on the eve of the twentieth century.

C. Da Costa, *Les Blanquistes* (Paris, 1912); G. Da Costa, *La Commune vécue* (Paris, 1903); M. Dommanget, *Blanqui et l'opposition à la fin du Second Empire* (Paris, 1960); P. H. Hutton, *The Cult of the Revolutionary Tradition* (Berkeley, 1981).

P. H. Hutton

Related entries: BLANQUI; COMMUNARDS; DOMMANGET; EUDES; FREE THOUGHT MOVEMENT; GRANGER; JACOBINISM; LEFT, THE; ROCHE, ERNEST; TRIDON; VAILLANT.

BLOC NATIONAL (1919–1924), the nationalist and conservative electoral coalition that won a majority in the Chamber of Deputies after World War I. A change in voting procedure, issuing from the prewar campaign for proportional representation, in 1919 provided for departmental-wide voting with additional seats awarded to parties best able to combine in electoral coalitions. Parties on the Right were able to do so; those on the Left could not. Traditionally anticlerical moderates and Catholics made mutual concessions, while Radicals feared possible Socialist support for Moscow and dared not join them. In addition to these structural reasons for the victory of the most conservative coalition since the National Assembly (1871), the Left was accused of inadequately preparing France for war in 1914 and of being sympathetic to communism in 1919. Bloc candidates and sympathizers won about 433 seats to the 180 won by the opposition. Because many of the new deputies were former army officers, the Chamber was nicknamed "sky blue," after the color of their uniforms.

Early Bloc governments, those of Alexandre Millerand (1920), Georges Leygues (1920–21), and Aristide Briand (1921–22), profited from the large legislative majority. It was the Radicals' mounting disillusionment with the majority and their return to the Left opposition that led to the disintegration of the Bloc national and the success of its replacement, the Cartel des gauches, in the subsequent (1924) election. Radicals particularly opposed the majority's determination to enforce vigorously the provisions of the Versailles Treaty, which led to the occupation of the Ruhr in 1923. It is also true that the Radicals' own determination to politicize all issues in the interest of partisanship (admittedly easier to do in a multiparty, as opposed to a two-party, system) destroyed the coalition's chances to reach agreement on the bipartisan program. Radicals refused to participate in the third Raymond Poincaré cabinet (1924). President Millerand's insistence on seeking reinforcement of the presidential powers and an unpopular increase in taxes (the *double décime*) needed to bolster the country's finances contributed significantly to the dislocation of the Bloc, while Poincaré's refusal to campaign for it in the 1924 election helped to bring the rival Cartel des gauches to power.

G. Bonnefous, *Histoire politique de la Troisième République*, vol. 3 (Paris, 1973); R. Simonsson, *Millerands Presidentur* (Uppsala, 1938); Frédéric Wurzburg, "The Politics of the Bloc National" (Ph.D. dissertation, Columbia University, 1961).

L. Derfler

Related entries: BRIAND; CARTEL DES GAUCHES; CLEMENCEAU; CONSERVATISM; MILLERAND; POINCARE, R.; PRESIDENT OF THE REPUBLIC, OFFICE OF; RADICAL AND RADICAL-SOCIALIST PARTY; RUHR OCCUPATION.

BLOCH, MARC (1886–1944), medievalist, social and economic historian, editor. Bloch's formal education at the Lycée Louis-le-Grand at Paris led to acceptance in 1904 at the Ecole normale supérieure, where his father was professor of Roman history. Passing his *agrégation* in 1908, Bloch spent a year in Germany perfecting his research techniques in seminars at Leipzig and Berlin. A three-year fellowship at the Fondation Thiers in 1909 kept him in Paris where he worked on his doctoral thesis while remaining in close contact with the advanced circles of historians and social scientists led by Henri Berr and the young Lucien Febvre. While teaching at lycées in Montpellier and Amiens from 1912 to 1914, Bloch published his first work in social history in the pages of Berr's *La Revue de synthèse historique*; it called for a new history of the regions of France based on close cooperation with geographers and sociologists.

Service in the war was followed by an appointment to teach medieval history at the University of Strasbourg together with an elite corps of French specialists in an attempt to strengthen the French cultural roots of that disputed frontier. His thesis, "Rois et serfs, un chapitre d'histoire capetienne", presented to the Sorbonne in 1920, was followed four years later by *Les Rois thaumaturges*, a brilliant investigation of the role of magic and ritual within the French monarchy. For the next seventeen years Bloch produced at Strasbourg an impressive series of provocative and reformist articles and books. Bloch and his friend Febvre, a colleague at Strasbourg, formed one of the most productive partnerships in the history of scholarship. Both of them had worked closely with Berr hoping to awaken French scholars to the challenge of a comparative and interdisciplinary history of humanity. In 1929 they struck out alone to found the *Annales d'histoire économique et sociale* through which they promoted their new critical history in an extraordinary stream of articles and book reviews that laid the foundation for the transformation of French historiography in the 1930s.

After reaching the pinnacle of professional success as a medievalist with the publication of *Les Caractères originaux de l'histoire rurale française* in 1931, Bloch became professor of economic history at the University of Paris in 1936. He was reunited (at Paris) with Febvre, who had been appointed professor at the Collège de France three years before. Their commitment to a new history made them and their students the bêtes noires of the French university.

Ironically, the *Annales'* "new history" was to achieve its greatest successes after Bloch's death in 1944. He was captured during the last weeks of World War II by the Germans as a member of the Resistance; tortured, he was shot near Lyons, the place of his birth. Two of his last works, *Strange Defeat* (1946) and *The Historian's Craft* (1949), were published after his death by students and friends. They are unique contributions to the study of French social history and the creative possibilities of the historical profession. Bloch has become one of the saints of contemporary French scholarship and remains one of the most widely read among the *Annales'* French historians, both in France and the rest of the world.

M. Aymard, "The Annales and French Historiography (1929–1972)," *Journal of European Economic History* 1 (1972); M. Bloch, *Memoirs of War, 1914–15*, trans. Carole Fink (Ithaca, 1980); C. E. Perrin, "L'Oeuvre historique de Marc Bloch," *Revue historique* 199 (1948).

M. Siegel

Related entries: BERR; FEBVRE; HISTORIOGRAPHY: *ANNALES* SCHOOL; WORLD WAR I, FRANCE'S ROLE IN.

BLUM, LEON (1872–1950), socialist leader, jurist, and man of letters. Educated at the lycées Charlemagne and Henri IV before entering the Ecole normale supérieure in 1890, Blum turned away from an academic career and received degrees in law and literature from the Sorbonne. Pursuing simultaneous careers in literary criticism and the judiciary, he won distinction in both before abandoning them for politics in the course of World War I.

Blum achieved his earliest eminence as literary critic of the *Revue blanche* (1894–1900) and made an equally strong mark as drama critic of *Comoedia* (1908–11). His venture into social criticism, *Du mariage* (1907), outraged conservatives, but his *Stendhal et le beylisme* (1914) was well received. The most enduring product of his literary years was *Nouvelles conversations de Goethe avec Eckerman* (1901), a remarkable pastiche of literary criticism and social philosophy.

Entering the Conseil d'état in 1896, Blum became *maître des requêtes* in 1907. Appointed a *commissaire du gouvernement* in 1910, he became known as a progressive jurist.

The Dreyfus affair was Blum's political initiation. His outspoken defense of Dreyfus then led him to follow Lucien Herr and Jean Jaurès into the socialist unity movement. Blum's contribution was largely confined to intellectual circles in activities such as the formation of a socialist publishing house and the Société nouvelle de librairie et d'édition (1899). Once unity was achieved in 1905, his militancy became dormant.

World War I decisively changed Blum's life. Chef de cabinet to Marcel Sembat, socialist minister of public works (1914–16), Blum plunged full time into politics and was elected to the Chamber of Deputies as a Socialist in 1919. The lucidity and courage with which he defended the *vieille maison* of French democratic socialism against the Communist challenge catapulted him into a position of leadership.

After the socialist-communist split at Tours (1920), Blum devoted himself to rebuilding the Socialist party, the Section française de l'internationale ouvrière (SFIO). Rapidly accepted as leader of the parliamentary delegation, he became the intellectual leader of the SFIO through his frequent editorials in the party daily, the *Populaire*. His doctrine of the exercise of power provided the socialists with a rationale for nonparticipation in bourgeois governments in the 1920s and later proved compatible with their role in the coalition government of the Popular Front. Blum's tactical doctrine and political leadership were major forces in the party's revival.

The SFIO unexpectedly emerged as the leading partner in the victorious Popular Front coalition, and Blum became France's first Jewish and first socialist premier (4 June 1936). Greeted by a massive wave of sitdown strikes, Blum brought labor and management together at the national level for the first time, negotiating the Matignon Accords. The Popular Front's reformist legislative program was quickly enacted. By adhering strictly to this clearly stated program, Blum hoped to calm middle-class fears of social revolution, but with little success.

The Spanish Civil War proved the undoing of the Popular Front coalition. Despite close ties with the Spanish republican government, Blum feared aid to it would lead to both civil war in France and war against Germany and Italy, with France isolated. His reluctant policy of nonintervention alienated the Communists, much as his initial efforts to aid the Spanish republicans had frightened most Radicals and the pacifist wing of the SFIO. Long an advocate of peace through disarmament, Blum came to realize that France needed to strengthen its defenses, and after 1937 he turned increasingly to promoting national unity.

France's defeat in 1940, as he had feared, splintered the SFIO. Blum courageously chose to remain in France, and he was soon arrested and brought to trial at Riom by the Vichy government. In prison he helped to inspire the organization of the Resistance, gave his support to de Gaulle, and composed the credo of his mature years, *A l'échelle humaine*. Taken hostage by the Gestapo (1943), he spent time in Buchenwald and Dachau.

Blum's last years were those of a widely respected elder statesman. He formed an all-socialist caretaker government in 1946–47, led a delegation to Washington that secured U.S. aid for postwar reconstruction, and continued to write for the *Populaire* until his death.

J. Colton, *Léon Blum* (New York, 1966); W. Logue, *Léon Blum* (DeKalb, Ill., 1973).

W. H. Logue

Related entries: CHAUTEMPS; COLLECTIVE BARGAINING; DALADIER; DEAT; DESROUSSEAUX; DREYFUS AFFAIR; GIDE, A.; HERR; HERRIOT; JAURES; MATIGNON AGREEMENTS; PEGUY; POPULAR FRONT; SOCIALIST PARTY; THOREZ.

BONAPARTISM, the set of political ideas associated with the movement to restore the regime of the Bonapartes in France. For reasons both of history and political sociology, it was arguably the only political doctrine capable of successfully challenging the durable establishment of the Third Republic. Its origins, long antedating 1870, associated it more closely with republican than with monarchist ideas. Napoleon insisted that his historical role had been to provide effective government for a society based on revolutionary principles; Republic and Empire alike were offspring of 1789. Napoleon III had based his regime even more explicitly on democracy, though it was a democracy that found its fullest expression in plebiscites rather than parliamentary elections.

Bonapartism was thus the doctrine of the regime that claimed to combine the defense of social and political equality for which the Republic stood with effective political authority. The Second Empire had thus had a tremendous appeal for the people who continued to make up the majority of France's population under the Third Republic. Peasants and small-town tradesmen and artisans generally wanted a government that would thwart challenges from either the reactionary Right or the revolutionary Left to the consensus that had emerged after 1848.

The Third Republic's strongest appeal was to the same constituency of striving and succeeding lower middle classes. Yet it is not surprising that many of them perennially deserted it (as in the Boulanger crisis or the growth of the leagues of the 1920s and 1930s) once the ideal of the Republic had become a reality, for the Republic's ideology and system, shaped precisely in reaction to Louis Napoleon's executive coup d'état of 1851, interdicted the incarnation of authority and equality in a charismatic leader in the Bonapartist manner. Some commentators have pointed to this fear of the appearance, even more than of the reality, of executive authority as the Republic's most damaging weakness.

Yet the pattern of the past was not repeated. The Third Republic was not replaced by a Third Empire as the First Republic had been replaced by the First Empire and the Second Republic by the Second Empire. The reason is partly that by 1870 Bonapartism was no longer, as it had been in 1848, a set of political ideas associated with an individual's name. Bonapartism in 1870 was embodied by the Bonapartists, the personnel of the fallen regime.

H. A. L. Fisher, *Bonapartism* (Oxford, 1905); J. Rothney, *Bonapartism after Sedan* (Ithaca, N.Y., 1969); T. Zeldin, *The Political System of Napoleon III* (New York, 1958).

J. Rothney

Related entries: BONAPARTISTS; BOULANGER AFFAIR; NAPOLEON-JEROME, PRINCE; PRINCE IMPERIAL.

BONAPARTISTS, the name given to those who favored the imperial regime of the Bonapartes in France. The term applies to anyone so inclined but here is limited to the politicians who comprised the Bonapartist party under the Third Republic.

Contrary to what might have been expected, the defeat of 1870 did not preclude all hope of an imperial restoration. Although few Bonapartists ran and fewer were elected in the general elections of February 1871, by-elections turned increasingly in their favor throughout the duration of the National Assembly (1871–75). The party of the *Appel au peuple*, so named for its demand for a plebiscite to determine France's political future, came to comprise some thirty deputies, led by the former "vice-emperor," Eugène Rouher. The votes of this group were decisive in overthrowing the presidency of Adolphe Thiers early in 1873. They also contributed to the downfall of the cabinet of Duc Albert de Broglie, who had followed Thiers, in 1874. Bonapartist votes thus helped to block the realization of the conservative Republic under his own leadership to which Thiers aspired and to thwart whatever possibility remained of a restoration of the Bourbon or Orleanist monarchy. Having helped to eliminate its rivals, the Bonapartists probably also helped inadvertently to create the Third Republic that did emerge in 1875. Its constitution—the fundamental laws reluctantly enacted by a National Assembiy dominated by nonrepublicans—probably won the necessary votes because of growing fears that a political groundswell for a Bonapartist restoration might be developing.

The Bonapartist cause needed such a groundswell because, barring a new return from Elba backed by military complicity (something that became much less likely after Napoleon III's death in January 1873), the only way to demonstrate

France's desire for a restored Empire would be to produce the effect of a successful plebiscite by winning a general election. The results of the election of 1876 showed this to be impossible. Bonapartists and sympathizers captured over one hundred seats in the new Chamber of Deputies. This was a remarkable achievement six years after the debacle of Sedan, but it was vitiated by the fact that the party had contested fewer than half of France's constituencies.

Such abstention was understandable in some regions of France, especially the east and south, where defeat would have been virtually inevitable; the Republic had already sunk deep roots among the electorate before or after 1870. But there were other parts of France where latent sympathy for the imperial cause was not mobilized, the consequence of the nature of the Bonapartist party. Its failure revealed it to be a diverse collection of aging provincial notables, ill-equipped even after a quarter-century of universal suffrage to fight a democratic election. Relatively few of them had developed the kind of village-by-village constituency-wide organization needed to mobilize and maintain the loyalty of the masses. Lacking such a machine, many made compromising alliances with their fellow conservatives (Legitimists or Orleanists) that not only failed to offer the electorate a clear Bonapartist alternative but also did not get them elected. Unable to amass a treasury that could control candidates' behavior by the threat of withholding funds, the party's central committee could no more prevent such alliances than it could fund a local paper in every department to guarantee effective electoral propaganda.

For all of these reasons, the elections of 1876 were an appeal to the people that failed. The Bonapartists in the Senate helped prepare the way to a second electoral fiasco for their party in 1877 by providing the necessary votes to enable President Maurice de MacMahon to dissolve the Chamber of Deputies after his coup of May 16. Although the Bonapartists won thirty additional seats in the ensuing elections, they could take no satisfaction from them, for the Republican victory had once again given the new regime the legitimation of universal suffrage.

After 1877 Bonapartism under the Third Republic gradually faded away. Discouraged by their party's impotence, embarrassed by the confrontation (after 1879) between two rival pretenders, Bonapartist deputies retired from politics or converted to Republicanism. Even rural southwestern France, the Bonapartists' perennial electoral stronghold, eventually converted to the radical brand of republicanism.

The story of the Bonapartists of the Third Republic was merely an epilogue to the history of the Second Empire. The Third and indeed the Fourth Republic would continue to be challenged by ideas that owed much to the presence in the French political heritage of the Bonapartist concept of plebiscitary, authoritarian democracy. A genuine Bonapartist of the 1870s—though not many of the party's conservative parliamentarians—would have found much in the constitution of the Fifth Republic to approve of. But by 1900 the appellation *Bonapartist* could be applied properly only to a few nostalgic candidates and voters in places like

Corsica and to a few bands of trouble-making students battling their many rivals in the streets and cafés of the Latin Quarter.

R. Hudemann, *Fraktionsbildung im Französischen Parlament* (Munich, 1979); J. Rothney, *Bonapartism after Sedan* (Ithaca, N.Y., 1969); T. Zeldin, *The Political System of Napoleon III* (New York, 1958).

J. Rothney

Related entries: BONAPARTISM; NAPOLEON-JEROME, PRINCE; NAPOLEON-VICTOR, PRINCE; NOTABLES, THE; ORLEANISM; PRINCE IMPERIAL; *SEIZE MAI* CRISIS.

BONNARD, PIERRE (1867–1947), painter, illustrator, printmaker, designer, and member of the Nabis. Bonnard was greatly influenced by the Japanese print and the exotic atmosphere of the fin de siècle, and his work later influenced the fauves. He studied for one year at the Ecole des beaux-arts and failed in his efforts for the Prix de Rome. Attending the Académie Julian in the late 1880s, Bonnard was absorbed into a new group calling themselves the Nabis, a closely-knit fraternity of aspiring artists.

In the 1890s, Bonnard became involved in the applied and deocrative arts that were an integral part of the Nabi aesthetic. Essentially a colorist, Bonnard was also an artistic innovator, his experiments with non-naturalistic use of space and color resulting in highly decorative works that showed affinities with Art Nouveau in their flat planes and sinuous lines. Painting numerous tiny interiors and street scenes commemorating everyday life (*The Barrel Organ Grinder*, 1895), Bonnard emphasized visual pleasure, and his basically clear palette derived from Paul Gauguin and the Japanese print, both compatible with his essentially cheerful outlook. He exhibited at the Salon des indépendants in 1891, at Durand-Ruel's in 1896, and in England and Belgium during the same decade. After 1905 he spent most of his time in the country; this influence is evident in his work. In 1915 he attempted to break away from his fascination with color only to succumb once more to its lures.

J. Rewald, *Pierre Bonnard* (New York, 1948); C. Wheeler, *Pierre Bonnard* (London, 1966).

J. K. Franklin

Related entries: ART: MAJOR STYLES AND MOVEMENTS; ART NOUVEAU; FAUVISM; GAUGUIN; NABIS, THE.

BONNET, GEORGES (1889–1973), Radical-Socialist politician, advocate of appeasement of Adolf Hitler. Born in Bassilac (Dordogne), Bonnet began his career in government as auditor to the Council of State in 1913. Decorated for his service in World War I, he subsequently participated in the Paris Peace Conference as a member of the French delegation. Elected as a Radical-Socialist deputy from the Dordogne in 1924 and again in 1929, he became a frequent participant in government posts during the interwar period. As under secretary of state in the second Paul Painlevé government (1925) he created the Economic

Council; as minister of finance (1933) he reestablished the national lottery; and as minister of commerce and industry he organized the International Exposition of 1937. In the diplomatic arena he presided over the Stresa Conference of 1932 and participated in the London Conference of 1933 as a member of the French delegation. Sent as ambassador to the United States by the Popular Front government (1936–37), Bonnet subsequently became foreign minister in the third Edouard Daladier government (April 1938–September 1940). With the outbreak of World War II he remained in the government as minister of justice until Daladier's resignation in March 1940. Upon the defeat of France, he sought refuge in Switzerland. During the postwar period he devoted much of his time to defending his record as foreign minister and returned briefly to the National Assembly as deputy from the Dordogne (1957–58).

In domestic politics Bonnet was regarded by observers as an opportunist consumed by ambition. Although supported by a faction in the Radical party, he was never entirely trusted or liked by his political colleagues. His orthodox conservative tendencies were reflected by his actions as finance minister in 1938 to dismantle the programs of the Popular Front. It was his role as foreign minister during the last year before the outbreak of World War II that made him a controversial figure. His defeatist mentality and his conviction that close cooperation with Britain was vital to French security led him to become one of the most ardent appeasers in France and a defender of the capitulation to Hitler's demands at the Munich Conference of September 1938.

A. Adamthwaite, *France and the Coming of the Second World War* (London, 1977); G. Bonnet, *Défense de la paix*, 2 vols. (Geneva, 1946–48); P. Larmour, *The French Radical Party in the 1930's* (Stanford, 1964); L. Namier, *Europe in Decay* (London, 1950); J. Néré, *The Foreign Policy of France from 1914–1945* (Boston, 1975); Ministère des affaires étrangères, *Documents diplomatiques français, 1932–1939*, 2e série, vols. 9, 12 (Paris, 1974–78); T. Taylor, *Munich* (New York, 1979).

J. E. Dreifort

Related entries: CZECHOSLOVAKIA, ALLIANCE WITH; DALADIER; GERMANY, RELATIONS WITH (1914–1940); GREAT BRITAIN, RELATIONS WITH; MUNICH CONFERENCE: FRENCH ROLE IN; POLISH AGREEMENT; RADICAL AND RADICAL-SOCIALIST PARTY.

BORDEAUX, a major seaport and commercial and industrial center that grew rapidly during the Third Republic in the midst of an otherwise remote, rural region of southwestern France. The city's commerical preeminence dated from the eighteenth century, when it was second only to London among European cities in the importance of its overseas trade. Although its position as a French port of international commerce was surpassed by Marseilles, Rouen, and Le Havre in the course of the Third Republic, Bordeaux was still the hub of a trading network wider, more intensive, and more diverse than ever before. Bordeaux merchants trafficked in such exports as timber, wine, and chemical products and imported coal, grain, phosphates, and exotic tropical foodstuffs.

Their shipping routes spanned the globe, although they profited especially from their commercial ties with West Africa and Latin America. Fifty-five overseas shipping companies were registered in Bordeaux in 1921.

The growth of Bordeaux's population paralleled its rising prosperity. The city's population tripled from 88,202 in 1821 to 267,409 in 1921. The full measure of population increase during the Third Republic can be appreciated only by including the eleven suburban communes into which the population sprawled as space within the city limits disappeared by the turn of the century. Greater Bordeaux expanded by 60 percent from 245,000 in 1872 to 391,000 in 1936. Bordeaux, moreover, was a city that grew through immigration. In 1911, 49 percent of its population were immigrants, the vast majority young adults from the surrounding rural departments who came in search of work.

The city's economy offered these newcomers diverse opportunities. If Bordeaux had long been a great entrepôt, it was in the Third Republic on its way to becoming an industrial center of some importance; 44 percent of the work force was employed in industry by 1911. Shipbuilding, an old and flagging industry in the early years of the regime, was given new life by governmental contracts for warships in the era of naval expansion before World War I. Pottery, glass, barrel and box making, textiles, and construction were small-scale industries with deep roots and enduring importance in the city's economy. But industrial growth was tied especially to the inauguration of heavy industries based on new technologies, notably processed foods, chemical products, and automobiles, which flourished in the early twentieth century.

Despite an interlude of economic recession in the 1880s and a difficult readjustment from wartime to peacetime industry in the immediate aftermath of World War I, Bordeaux's economic growth during the Third Republic was steady until the onset of the worldwide depression in the 1930s. Even then, the enduring buoyancy of the city's West African trade in some measure compensated for the slump in its domestic and northern European markets. Its overall prosperity notwithstanding, Bordeaux never exploited the full possibilities of industrial development during this era, in part because of a dearth of energy resources, raw materials, skilled manpower, and nearby markets, in part because the city's financiers trusted more in commercial than in industrial expansion.

The role of these economic directors set the style of politics in the early years of the Third Republic. The political majority in Bordeaux was republican from the regime's founding, but political power at least until World War I was held by moderate republicans loyal to the wealthiest financiers and merchants. Because of the large number of commercial employees and industrial workers in the city, however, a vibrant radical faction and a well-organized socialist party emerged early to challenge the moderate republican office-holders. Bordeaux politics in the prewar Third Republic was particularly animated because of the periodic alliance of socialists, radicals, and conservatives to outvote moderate republicans in local elections. This coalition made possible the election of Auguste Blanqui, the renowned revolutionary, to the Chamber of Deputies in 1879, of supporters of General Georges Boulanger to local and national offices in 1889, and of the entire opposition slate to the thirty-six-member municipal council in 1896. The steady growth of the parties of the Left in the early twentieth century reflected the transfer of political power from the magnates of commerce and industry to their employees and workers. By the mid-1920s, the Left was capable of winning elections without the aid of the Right. Radical-Socialist coalitions decisively won both the legislative elections of 1924 and the municipal elections of 1925.

If prewar politics in Bordeaux had been distinctive for its electoral coalitions, postwar politics was conspicuous for its commanding personalities, who were often capable of turning elections in Bordeaux against national patterns. Particularly important in this respect were Georges Mandel, who persuaded the Bordeaux electorate to endorse candidates loyal to Georges Clemenceau in the immediate postwar era; the abbé Daniel Bergey and Philippe Henriot, who together gave new life to conservatism in city politics in the late 1920s and early 1930s; and especially Adrien Marquet, Bordeaux's socialist mayor from 1925 to 1945. Like Raymond Lavigne, who first organized a socialist party in Bordeaux in the 1880s, Marquet favored strategic alliances with radical and even moderate republicans over doctrinaire political independence. Cashiered from the Socialist party (SFIO) in 1933 for this attitude and openly opposed by it for the rest of the decade, Marquet continued to be elected to both local and national offices, thanks to his immense popularity in the city.

In addition to its role as *chef-lieu* of the department of the Gironde, Bordeaux served as the seat of the national government in three brief but critical episodes that punctuated the Third Republic: in 1871 for the opening sessions of the National Assembly; in 1914 while the first wartime cabinet planned its strategy; and in June 1940 while the last government of the Third Republic agonized over the terms of a humiliating armistice with Nazi Germany. While never a rival of Paris, Bordeaux was a city whose distance from that metropolis enabled it to play a distinctive and occasionally independent role in the definition of the urban society which was emerging during the Third Republic.

L. Desgraves and G. Dupeux, ed., *Bordeaux au XIXe siècle* (Bordeaux, 1969); E. Ginestous, *Histoire politique de Bordeaux sous la IIIe République* (Bordeaux, 1946); J. and B. Guérin, *Des Hommes et des activités d'un demi-siècle* (Bordeaux, 1957); P. H. Hutton, "The Boulangist Movement in Bordeaux Politics" (Ph.D. dissertation, University of Wisconsin, 1969); J. Lajugie, ed., *Bordeaux au XXe siècle* (Bordeaux, 1972).

P. H. Hutton

Related entries: BLANQUI; HENRIOT; LAVIGNE; MANDEL; MARSEILLES; PARIS; ROCHE, ERNEST; URBANIZATION AND THE GROWTH OF CITIES.

BOUGLE, CELESTIN (1870–1940), sociologist and educator. He was born in St. Brieuc (Côtes-du-Nord). A gifted student, he enrolled in the Ecole normale supérieure in 1890, earned his *licence ès lettres* in 1891, and passed his *agrégation* in philosophy in 1893. After a sojourn in Germany for travel and study, he returned to St. Brieuc, where he taught philosophy at the lycée. Advancing quickly through a succession of academic positions, he taught at the University of Montpellier, then at the University of Toulouse, before being invited to teach at the Sorbonne in Paris in 1901. Along the way, he completed his *doctorat ès lettres*; his thesis was entitled "Les Doctrines égalitaires, études sociologiques." In 1920 he founded the Centre de documentation sociale at the Ecole normale supérieure; subsequently he was appointed assistant director (1927) and director (1935) of that school. In these posts, he inaugurated a number of curricular and pedagogical reforms and strove to enhance the school's reputation.

Deeply influenced by the social theories of Emile Durkheim, Bouglé worked actively to promote sociology as an academic discipline and as a practical philosophy for creating a more democratic society. His theoretical contributions to sociology were substantial. A founder of *L'Année sociologique*, a leading journal in this field, he also wrote a number of important books, notably *Les Idées égalitaires* (1899) and *Essais sur le régime des castes* (1908). His interest in the history of social theory prompted him to write *La Sociologie de Proudhon* (1912) and to edit Joseph Proudhon's writings (1930–35). In collaboration with Elie Halévy, he also edited the writings of Henri de Saint-Simon (1924).

In addition to his intellectual endeavor, Bouglé became openly involved in the political issues of his day. He worked actively to reverse the verdict against Alfred Dreyfus from the time of his conviction for espionage (1894). He was also a spokesman for the peace movement and an advocate of an international organization to promote that cause. Bouglé's progressive attitudes also enabled him to establish links between the theoretical interests of sociologists and the practical work of socialist politicians.

R. d'Amat, ed., *Dictionnaire de biographie française*, vol. 6 (Paris, 1954); T. Clark, *Prophets and Patrons* (Cambridge, Mass., 1973); P. M. Sturges, "Social Theory and Political Ideology: Celestin Bouglé and the Durkheim School" (Ph.D. diss., City University of New York, 1978); K. Wolff, ed., *Emile Durkheim* (Columbus, Ohio, 1960).

M. Chase and P. H. Hutton

Related entries: SCHOOLS, HIGHER EDUCATION: ECOLE NORMALE SUPERIEURE; DURKHEIM; HALBWACHS; HALEVY, E.; SAINT-SIMONISM; SOLIDARISM.

BOULANGER, GEORGES (1837–1891), professional soldier, minister of war, political personality of the early Third Republic. He was born in Rennes (Ille-et-Vilaine), the son of a lawyer. On graduation from Saint-Cyr in 1856, he pursued a career as a professional soldier. In a variety of campaigns abroad during the Second Empire, he was wounded, decorated, and promoted through the ranks. During the Franco-Prussian War, he helped defend Paris; during the ensuing civil war, he helped invade it. In 1874 he was promoted to colonel, in 1880 to general.

Thenceforth Boulanger's ambitions extended beyond his professional calling. Making known his republican opinions, he cultivated political friendships among the radicals and, as a protégé of Georges Clemenceau, was named minister of war in the cabinet of Charles de Freycinet in January 1886. During his eighteen-month tenure, he publicized his activities and did his best to ingratiate himself with a variety of constituencies: the enlisted soldiers by making the conditions of their service more tolerable, the workers by his sympathy for the striking miners in Decazeville, the republicans by dismissing eminent royalists from their military commands, the nationalists by his bellicose rhetoric during the Schnaebele affair, and nearly everyone with his lavish military parades. Boulanger's skill in enhancing his own popularity worried the Opportunist leaders of the government. When the cabinet in which he served fell from power in May 1887, he was relegated to an army command in Clermont-Ferrand. On his departure in July 1887, enormous crowds gathered to see him off and to cheer him along the way. Not only had he acquired a political following; he had become a popular hero.

Back on active duty, Boulanger spent as much time furthering his rising political fortunes as he did tending to his military responsibilities. He frequently traveled to Paris in disguise to confer with his political supporters. For these unauthorized absences, he was retired from his command in March 1888. From that time on, he campaigned openly for vacant seats in the Chamber of Deputies. With the support of a committee of radical politicians, he staged what was in effect a plebiscite, ostensibly for a more democratic constitution but tacitly to explore the dimensions of his personal popularity as a candidate for the presidency of the Republic. Standing for the Chamber of Deputies in a series of special elections, he was victorious in seven diverse departments, culminating in an overwhelming triumph in Paris in January 1889. Rallying support among the discontented from all quarters, Boulanger's personal campaign for the presidency became a major movement of political protest against the Opportunist leaders of the Third Republic.

In the face of the gathering momentum of Boulanger's campaign, the government took measures to stay its force. The League of Patriots, a mainstay of Boulanger's support, was dissolved for being a secret society, and Boulanger himself was threatened with arrest for a plot to overthrow the state. Intimidated, Boulanger fled to Belgium. Despite a lack of incriminating evidence, he was tried in absentia by the Senate sitting as a high court and was condemned to life imprisonment. Boulanger issued a brave defense from abroad, but his radical followers were dispirited by his decision to flee, and his popular support began to weaken. The government's success in winning passage of a bill forbidding multiple candidacies in the legislative elections nullified his bid to transform these into a national vote of confidence in himself. In the legislative elections of October 1889, his supporters won only 42 of 576 seats. Thereafter the Boulangist movement quickly fell apart. Boulanger's republicanism was called into question by revelations that he had received subsidies from the royalists. Despondent over the death of his lover, Marguerite de Bonnemains, he committed suicide on her grave in Ixelles, Belgium, on 30 September 1891.

Although he failed to realize his ambitions, Boulanger was important as a new kind of political personality. Without deep attachment to principle, he was highly sensitive to public opinion and knew how to manipulate it to his advantage. He epitomized the modern political hero who prefers to appeal to a mass electorate on the basis of his superficial charm rather than the substance of his ideas.

A. Dansette, *Le Boulangisme* (Paris, 1946); P. H. Hutton, "Popular Boulangism and the Advent of Mass Politics in France," *Journal of Contemporary History* 11 (1976); P. Levillain, *Boulanger, fossoyeur de la monarchie* (Paris, 1982); F. Seager, *The Boulanger Affair* (Ithaca, 1968).

P. H. Hutton

Related entries: ANTI-SEMITIC LEAGUE; BARRES; BOULANGER AFFAIR; DEROULEDE; LAGUERRE; LAISANT; LAUR; LEAGUE OF PATRIOTS; NAQUET; SCHNAEBELE AFFAIR; WILSON SCANDAL.

BOULANGER AFFAIR (1886–1889), a political crisis centering on the campaign of General Georges Boulanger, a career army officer, to become president of the Third Republic. Boulanger first received wide publicity for reforms he instituted while serving as minister of war in 1886, reforms that eased the life of enlisted soldiers. His popularity was soon manifested in the enthusiastic support lavished on him by crowds who cheered him at military reviews and parades and in the unsolicited electoral support he began to receive in special elections for the Chamber of Deputies in the spring and summer of 1887. Transferred to an obscure military command, he resigned his commission so that he might campaign more seriously for public office. His victories in a succession of special legislative elections in the spring and summer of 1888 transformed his personal popularity into a political plebiscite. Boulanger offered the appeal of the respectable civil servant, progressive and idealistic, who stood above the petty intrigues and scandals that had tarnished the reputations of so many moderate republican (Opportunist) governmental leaders. So great was his popularity that his enemies feared he might attempt a coup d'état following his triumph in a legislative election at Paris in January 1889. But his supporters, and Boulanger himself, were convinced that the tide of popular enthusiasm would sweep him into the presidency by legal means.

Popular adulation of Boulanger notwithstanding, his campaign was more important as a protest movement, drawing together a number of not-always-compatible elements. His campaign organizers were Radical politicians dissatisfied with the elitist (Orleanist) cast of the institutions of the Third Republic, who backed Boulanger as the standard-bearer of constitutional revision in order to create a more democratic republic. Boulanger also enjoyed the vigorous support of nationalists, still harboring ambitions of revenge on Germany for the loss of Alsace-Lorraine during the Franco-Prussian War. The League of Patriots, a gymnastic society organized along paramilitary lines, became a shock force for Boulangist demonstrations and an organizational apparatus on which to build an electoral campaign in outlying cities. Those who voted for Boulanger, however, were often the dispossessed—artisans and shopkeepers, as well as the new cadres of industrial workers—whose grievances were economic rather than political and who supported him as a means of protesting the government's unwillingness to deal directly with unemployment, low wages, and other problems resulting from the economic depression of the mid-1880s. Some revolutionary groups, notably the Blanquists, supported him in the hope that the crisis he had precipitated would prepare the way for a Parisian insurrection and hence provide an opportunity to restore the Commune. But the monarchists supported him too, with lavish, secret funding of his candidates' campaigns, in the hope that a Boulangist victory might eventually lead to a restoration of the monarchy. By virtue of his broad appeal to the politically disenchanted with the catchall slogan of national reconciliation, Boulanger forged a heterogeneous alliance of those who had some grievance against the existing regime.

The gathering momentum of Boulanger's electoral plebiscite was abruptly halted in March 1889 when Boulanger, intimidated by threats of prosecution, surprised his friends and enemies alike by fleeing to Belgium. His supporters continued the campaign by placing candidates in nearly all of the country's constituencies for the legislative elections of September 1889. But Boulanger's departure robbed the movement of its mystique of inexorable victory. The Boulangist candidates won elections in a scattering of cities, among them Nancy, Bordeaux, Lille, and Paris. But rural France voted solidly for the moderate republicans, and the Boulangists won only 42 of the 576 seats in the legislature. The Boulangist movement disintegrated quickly, its adherents finding their way into other protest causes, significantly in those identified with the new radical right wing that coalesced during the Dreyfus affair.

To some extent, the Boulangist crisis resolved issues of long standing. The defeat of the Boulangist movement confirmed popular support for the political institutions of the Third Republic. Constitutional revision did not again become a serious issue during its seventy-year history. The crisis marked as well the monarchists' last political stand, as it did the last attempt of social revolutionaries to turn Parisian protest toward political insurrection. Still, the most enduring significance of the Boulangist movement was its experimentation with new political methods. The Boulangist campaign was conspicuous for its use of public rallies, popular journalism, photos, songs, café concerts, and other forms of publicity designed to arouse popular emotions and to deepen ordinary people's concrete sense of participation in a political cause. As a nationwide campaign coordinated by unprecedented political organization, Boulangism was France's first mass political movement, offering techniques of propaganda that would be appropriated by both the radical Left and the radical Right with the approach of the twentieth century.

M. Burns, *Rural Society and French Politics* (Princeton, 1984); A. Dansette, *Le Boulangisme* (Paris, 1946); P. H. Hutton, "Popular Boulangism and the Advent of Mass Politics in France, 1886–90," *Journal of Contemporary History* 11 (1976); J. Néré, *Le*

Boulangisme et la presse (Paris, 1964); F. Seager, *The Boulanger Affair* (Ithaca, 1968); Z. Sternhell, *La Droite révolutionnaire, 1885–1914* (Paris, 1978).

P. H. Hutton

Related entries: BOULANGER; GERMANY, RELATIONS WITH (1871–1914); LAGUERRE; LAISANT; LAUR; LEAGUE OF PATRIOTS; NATIONALISM; POLITICS; ROCHEFORT; SCHNAEBELE AFFAIR.

BOURDELLE, ANTOINE (1861–1929), one of France's leading sculptors of the late nineteenth and early twentieth centuries. Bourdelle's reputation is on a level with that of his mentor, Auguste Rodin, although his work generally avoided the controversy aroused by the latter's. Bourdelle went beyond Rodin's romanticism by integrating elements of the romanesque and classical into a monumental style appropriate to his time.

He was born on 30 October 1861 in Montauban (Tarn), the son of a cabinetmaker and the nephew of a stonecutter. At the age of fifteen his precocious talent earned him a scholarship to the Ecole des beaux-arts in Toulouse, and at twenty-four he went to the Ecole des beaux-arts in Paris to study briefly under Alexandre Falguière. Shortly after, he began to work under the guidance of Rodin. After various exhibitions he was awarded a commission for a Franco-PrussianWar memorial at Montauban. His first masterpiece, it required eight years to complete.

In 1896 Bourdelle was invited to work in Rodin's studio, and in 1900 he started to teach in Rodin's academy. In 1901 he began work on a Beethoven monument, a subject that remained a constant preoccupation throughout much of his career. At the same time he developed *Heracles the Archer*, which remained one of his more widespread and popular achievements. In 1909 he was nominated instructor at the Grande-Chaumière, a post he held until the end of his career. Rodin was so impressed by Bourdelle's genius that he was convinced his style would be dominant in the future. For the type of monumental sculpture in which he specialized, this evaluation would largely hold true.

Bourdelle's natural inclination was toward the romantic tradition, a tendency influenced and guided by Rodin's temperament; however, his tastes were eclectic, and Bourdelle gradually developed the native romanesque tradition of his home region. Of particular importance was his adaptation of classical models and the integration of sculpture and architecture. Because of his growing reputation, more commissions were forthcoming. In 1911 he received a contract for the bas-reliefs on the facade of the Théâtre des Champs-Elysées, and from 1913 until 1923 he prepared a monument to General Carlos de Alvear in Argentina.

Other works for which he is chiefly remembered are the *Madonna of the Vosges* in Alsace and the *Birth of Aphrodite* in Marseilles. In 1917 he started to sculpt a monument to Adam Mickiewicz, the Polish poet, which was not exhibited until the year of his death, 1929. Bourdelle died on 1 October near Paris. Although his posthumous fame did not equal that of his lifetime, he is to be counted among the leading sculptors of this century.

   Antoine Bourdelle (New York, 1962); G. Varenne, *Bourdelle* (Paris, 1977).

                                                                        F. Busi

Related entries: RODIN; SUARES.

BOURGEOIS, LEON (1851–1925), radical politician, a founder of the Radical party, advocate of peace. He was born on 29 May 1851 at Paris. He did not pursue the trade of his father, a clockmaker, but preferred to study law, a profession that he never practiced as such. Rather, he used his legal training in a long career in public administration and politics. In the 1870s and 1880s he entered the legal branch of the Ministry of Public Works, then rose from the rank of prefectural general secretary to that of prefect. During this time he made a marked impression on the republicans of the department of Marne and in February 1888 won a seat in a by-election to the Chamber of Deputies. This was the beginning of a thirty-seven-year career in parliament. Until 1905 he represented the arrondissement of Châlon-sur-Marne, and in that year he won a seat as senator from the department that remained so faithful to him. Although he is generally classified as a Radical, he served in many cabinets, save those of conservatives. He was interior minister (1890), minister of education and fine arts (1890, 1892, 1898), minister of justice (1892–93), minister of foreign affairs (1901, 1914), minister of labor (1912, 1917), and minister of state (1915, 1917).

   He was already a highly experienced administrator when he became premier in November 1895. Succeeding three conservative prime ministers, he formed a predominantly Radical government and put forward three goals: a progressive income tax, worker retirement pensions, and a law on associations that he intended to be the first step toward the separation of church and state. He immediately ran into a solid block of opposition to his fiscal proposal. In the Chamber, his supporters formed a somewhat slim majority. His real opposition came from the Senate where he could not muster more than a third of the members. It was there that he was confronted with a grave constitutional issue: did it, as well as the Chamber, have the right to force a premier's resignation once he no longer commanded a majority of the votes?

   The extreme Left urged him to resist the senators, but, with a bare majority in the lower house, he finally resigned on 23 April 1896. He never again accepted the premiership. Nonetheless he was, after serving as president of the Chamber (1902–4), elected senator and became president of that body (1920–23).

   The spirit behind Bourgeois' action was mainly an ideal he called *solidarité*. All people are bound to one another by a quasi-contract to help and defend one another. He opposed the extreme individualism of laissez-faire economists, emphasizing instead that each person is in debt to society. All that people know, their essence, is the product of past generations; they must repay this wealth and knowledge back to others—hence, the need for a progressive income tax, for mutual aid societies, and for cooperatives of production, exchange, and credit.

Bourgeois was an active proponent of world peace. As one of France's delegates to the Hague peace conferences in 1898 and 1907, he helped set up an international court of arbitration. He also became an advocate of a league of nations, to the creation of which he contributed and in 1920 presided at its first meeting. In that same year he won the Nobel Peace Prize.

M. Hamburger, *Léon Bourgeois* (Paris, 1932).

L. A. Loubère

Related entries: RADICAL AND RADICAL-SOCIALIST PARTY; SOLIDARISM.

BOURGET, PAUL (1852–1935), novelist and essayist. Born 2 September 1852 in Amiens (Somme), he studied the humanities, medicine, poetry, and literary criticism in Paris. In his moralistic novels and essays, he reacted against the modern pessimism and scientific determinism that prevailed in French intellectual circles at the turn of the century. In his first collections of writings, *Essais de psychologie contemporaine* (1893) and *Nouveaux essais de psychologie contemporaine* (1895), he examined the philosophies of contemporary literary critics such as Hippolyte Taine and Ernest Renan and accused them of causing the moral degeneration of French society in the late nineteenth century. In his novels, *Cruelle Enigme* (1885), *Crime d'amour* (1886), *André Cornélis* (1887), and *Mensonges* (1888), Bourget further attacked the naturalistic school of scientific determinism by developing tragic themes through psychological portraits of his characters.

The turn in his writings came with his completion of *Le Disciple* (1889), in which traditional values triumph over the materialistic and deterministic philosophies of modern intellectuals. In this tragic novel, Bourget asserted his intellectual commitment to traditional morality. In 1893, he wrote *Cosmopolis*, in which he attacked the corruption of aristocratic living. Following his conversion to Roman Catholicism in 1901, Bourget spent the rest of his life writing novels that promoted conservative Catholic values and pointed out the social evils of his day. Such novels include: *Un Divorce* (1904), which revealed the domestic tragedy of a modern French family; *L'Etape* (1907), which explored the injustice of class distinctions and the failure of upward social mobility in French society; and *L'Emigré* (1907), which proclaimed the worthlessness of the French nobility. In *Le Démon du Midi* (1914) and *Le Sens de la mort* (1915), he examined the spiritual aspects of Catholicism. He published sixty volumes before his death in Paris in 1935.

E. M. Bowman, *The Early Novels of Paul Bourget* (New York, 1925); A. Feuillerat, *Paul Bourget: histoire d'un esprit sous la Troisième République* (Paris, 1937); R. Raffetto, *L'Evolution du roman de Paul Bourget* (Toulouse, 1938).

B. F. Martin and L. C. Chewning

Related entries: CATHOLIC LITERARY RENAISSANCE; TAINE.

BOURSE DU TRAVAIL, an important institution in the development of the labor movement in the Third Republic. It was originally a center for job placement but acquired other functions as its numbers grew and its influence spread. The first Bourse du travail was founded at Paris in February 1887. In 1892, fourteen Bourses throughout the country formed the Fédération des bourses du travail; in 1902, the ninety-six Bourses in the Fédération merged with the Confédération générale du travail (CGT), the most important coalition of trade unions.

The strategies and guiding ideals of the Bourse movement were designed by Fernand Pelloutier, secretary of the Fédération des bourses du travail from 1895 until his death in 1901. Pelloutier believed that the Bourses should be worker-run agencies to assist fellow workers in their search for employment and to provide them with accident and unemployment insurance. He also envisioned that the Bourses might provide educational and cultural services for workers (such as libraries, humanities and vocational courses) and that they might ultimately serve as models of local community in a new, socialist society. In keeping with syndicalist theory, Pelloutier stressed the importance of the workers' autonomy and scorned the efforts of the Guesdist (Marxist) socialists to absorb the labor movement into their political organization.

In the early years of its existence, the Fédération ironically found itself in competition for recruits with the CGT, which shared its syndicalist philosophy. But the two organizations worked out their respective spheres of influence, and in 1902 the Fédération became an autonomous section of the CGT. Leaders agreed that the trade unions would focus on relations with employers (including strikes), while the Bourses would devote their energies to workers' education.

While the Bourse movement played a crucial role in the early organization of French labor, its significance is to be found not only in its efforts to aid workers in immediate and practical ways but also in its vision of a future, socialist society. The movement hoped to inspire in workers that mix of pride in work and cooperation in common tasks through which the socialist ideal might become a reality.

J. Juillard, *Fernand Pelloutier et les origines du syndicalisme d'action directe* (Paris, 1971); F. Pelloutier, *Histoire des bourses du travail* (Paris, 1971).

N. Papayanis

Related entries: CONFEDERATION GENERALE DU TRAVAIL; LABOR MOVEMENT; PELLOUTIER; SYNDICALISM; TRADE UNION MOVEMENT.

BOUTMY, EMILE (1835–1906), political scientist, founder and director of the Ecole libre des sciences politiques. Influenced by English empiricism and by his friend Hippolyte Taine, Boutmy wrote works on Greece, England, and the United States that attributed national behavior to a deep-seated collective psychology. He was critical of French deductive reasoning that produced such abstractions as the "rights of man" and "sovereignty of the people." A single code of laws or rights, he thought, could never apply to all the diverse peoples of the globe. Yet he realized that it was impossible for even the most diligent social scientist to master all of the facts about even a single nation. Facts were indispensable, but as the basis for an intuitive leap rather than for an inescapable conclusion. From a broad spectrum of evidence such as geography, climate, demography, social structure, political institutions, and intellectual life, Boutmy found the elements that pointed to the psychological key to a nation's character and behavior. At the same time he refrained from using this method to draw general conclusions about humanity as a whole.

Like other French educators in 1870, Boutmy blamed the French defeat in large part on deficiencies in the education of the ruling class. Therefore, encouraged by François Guizot and supported by Taine and a number of wealthy bankers and aristocrats, he founded the Ecole libre des sciences politiques in 1871 to provide "those classes who should rule" with the practical knowledge they required to do so effectively. A liberal of the Orleanist tradition and an admirer of English culture and society, Boutmy placed his stamp on the institution, which he directed for thirty-five years. The Ecole libre became known for its classical economics and conservative social ideas but also for its empiricism and its openness to the expression and examination of diverse opinions. Boutmy's greatest legacy was this school, which soon practically monopolized the preparation for several of the *grands corps*.

E. Boutmy, *Le Développement de la constitution et de la société politique en Angleterre* (Paris, 1887) and *Eléments d'une psychologie politique du peuple américain* (Paris, 1902).

R. J. Smith

Related entries: SCHOOLS, HIGHER EDUCATION: ECOLE LIBRE DES SCIENCES POLITIQUES.

BOUTROUX, EMILE (1845–1921), philosopher and teacher. Born at Montrouge, near Paris, he passed his *agrégation* in philosophy at the Ecole normale supérieure under Jules Lachelier. Appointed by Victor Duruy to prepare a report for the government on the teaching of philosophy in German universities, Boutroux studied mainly at Heidelberg between 1869 and 1870 and then taught at Caen (1871), Montpellier (1874), and Nancy (1876), successfully defending his doctoral thesis in 1874. He returned to the Ecole normale supérieure in 1877 as *maître de conférences*, taught philosophy at the Sorbonne in 1885, and held the Sorbonne chair of history of modern philosophy from 1888 until 1907. He was elected in 1914 to the Académie française.

Boutroux's *On the Contingency of the Laws of Nature* (1874) and *Idea of Natural Law* (1895) were crucial in the revival in France of neo-Kantian, idealist philosophy, and his ideas exerted special influence on his brother-in-law Henri Poincaré and his students Henri Bergson, Maurice Blondel, and Emile Durkheim. Boutroux's 1874 thesis followed from an examination of the claims of post-Comtian positive science for extending mechanical reductionism and deterministic scientific laws to psychology. In France this movement was associated with the materialist psychology of Hippolyte Taine. What concerned Boutroux were the implications of scientific determinism for doctrines of moral freedom and responsibility. He rejected the Kantian distinction between a phenomenal world, which is the abode of absolute determinism, and a noumenal world, which gives rise to liberty. By using the notion of scientific creativity, Boutroux argued that there is harmony between the scientific order of things and the moral order of things through similar foundations in reason and liberty.

Specifically Boutroux argued that the necessity in mathematical and scientific laws is a logical necessity and not a necessity in phenomena themselves. While mechanical analogies and scientific laws are valid schemata for aiding the mind in understanding nature, we have freely chosen this means. Scientific laws change in time both because they are imperfect representations of relations in nature and because nature itself is evolving and developing. Drawing on Aristotle, as well as on nineteenth-century evolutionary biology, Boutroux argued that nature is like an organism, with its parts organized hierarchically and holistically. Drawing on Blaise Pascal, Boutroux argued that modern-day philosophy is not merely the synthesis of the positive sciences, as Auguste Comte would have it, but philosophy is an inquiry into goodness and purpose in the universe.

L. Brunschvicg, "La Philosophie d'Emile Boutroux," *Revue de métaphysique et de morale* 29 (1922); L. S. Crawford, *The Philosophy of Emile Boutroux* (Ithaca, 1924); M. J. Nye, "The Boutroux Circle and Poincaré's Conventionalism," *Journal of the History of Ideas* 40 (1979); M. Schyns, *La Philosophie d'Emile Boutroux* (Brussels, 1923); C. Smith, "Emile Boutroux," *Encyclopedia of Philosophy* 1 (1967).

                                                                                    M. J. Nye

Related entries: BERGSON; BOURGET; DURKHEIM; POINCARE, H.; POS-ITIVISM; TAINE.

BOYER, ANTIDE (1850–1918), socialist militant in Marseilles. Of working-class origins, the son of a potter, Boyer received a Catholic education, first in his native town of Aubagne and later in a Marseilles seminary. He was not interested in a religious vocation and left his studies for a job on the railroad. By the end of the Second Empire his sympathies were republican, and he participated in the communal rising in Marseilles in 1871. Thereafter he gradually evolved toward socialism and took an active role in the socialist congress at Marseilles in 1879. In 1884 he was elected to the Marseilles city council and in the following year to the Chamber of Deputies on the departmental list of the Radicals. He was returned in succeeding elections until 1906 and elected to the Senate in 1909.

Boyer remained a maverick throughout his career, an example of that Midi socialism which found organizational loyalty and doctrinal orthodoxy constricting. In 1907 he broke with the united Socialist party (SFIO) to join the Independent Socialists. When he was defeated in the senatorial election of 1912, he retired from active public life.

J. Maitron, ed., *Dictionnaire biographique du mouvement ouvrier francais*, vol. 11 (Paris, 1974).

T. Moodie

Related entries: MARSEILLES; SOCIALISM, 1870–1914.

BRANCUSI, CONSTANTIN (1876–1957), Rumanian-born sculptor. The son of well-to-do Rumanian peasants, he left home at the age of eleven, worked in factories and shops, and studied at the Craiova School of Arts and Crafts (1894–98), graduating with honors, and then at the Bucharest School of Fine Arts (1898–1902). He arrived in Paris, having walked much of the way, in 1904, and studied at the Ecole des beaux-arts (1905–7). He was briefly influenced by Auguste Rodin. He settled in Montparnasse, was befriended by Henri Rousseau, Henri Matisse, Fernand Léger, and Amedeo Modigliani (1907–9), came under the influence of African art, and began to create the elegant, ultrasimplified abstractions of birds, animals, and human heads for which he is best known. His sculptures—made in marble, bronze, often with African-inspired wood pedestals—are so simple and abstract that U.S. Customs in 1926 accused Brancusi of attempting to smuggle a piece of bronze (*Bird in Space*) into the United States by declaring it a work of art. Brancusi won the case only with the testimony of collectors and fellow modernist artists during a lengthy trial.

S. Geist, *Brancusi: The Sculpture and the Drawings* (New York, 1975), and *Constantin Brancusi, 1876–1957* (New York, 1969); C. Giedion-Welcker, *Constantin Brancusi* (New York, 1959).

T. Shapiro

Related entries: ART: MAJOR STYLES AND MOVEMENTS; LEGER; MATISSE; MODIGLIANI; RODIN; ROUSSEAU.

BRAQUE, GEORGES (1882–1963), renowned modernist painter. Born in Argenteuil-sur-Seine and raised largely in Le Havre, he was the son and grandson of house painters who were also Sunday painters. He was apprenticed in the same trade and studied easel painting on the side, and also music, in Le Havre and after 1900 in Paris. In 1906–7, influenced by Henri Matisse, André Derain, and Raoul Dufy, he exhibited brightly colored landscapes as a member of the fauve movement. In 1907 he was influenced by the work of Paul Cézanne. After being introduced to Pablo Picasso by the poet Guillaume Apollinaire, he sobered his palette and began the exploration of spatial relationships that was to lead him and Picasso to cubism by 1909 and to the invention of the collage in 1912–13.

After being wounded in the First World War and discharged from service in 1917, Braque developed a personal version of cubism, henceforth little affected by changing art styles and group activity. His work after 1920 features a somber but rich palette, a thick paint surface, and a special preoccupation with spatial relationships—explored both in small, intimate canvases and on a monumental scale—and with the textural beauty of fruit, flowers, birds, and other natural forms. His major subject was the still life, but he periodically re-introduced the human figure, as in a series of canephores (1922–27) inspired by the contemporary classical preoccupations of artists and in the silhouetted models of eight monumental *Studios* in the 1950s. In 1930 he built a studio in Varengeville, near Dieppe, and thereafter his works increasingly reflected the Norman landscape and seascape.

G. Apollinaire, *Chroniques d'art, 1902–1918* (Paris, 1960); *Catalogue de l'oeuvre de Georges Braque* ([Paris], 1973); D. Cooper, *Braque: The Great Years* (Chicago, 1972); S. Fumet, *Georges Braque* (Paris, 1965); D. Vallier, "Braque, la peinture et nous," *Cahiers d'art* 29 (1954).

T. Shapiro

Related entries: APOLLINAIRE; ART: MAJOR STYLES AND MOVE-MENTS; CEZANNE; CUBISM; DERAIN; DUFY; FAUVISM; MATISSE; PICASSO.

BRASILLACH, ROBERT (1909–1945), novelist, literary critic, and historian of film; journalist and exponent of French fascism. Born in 1909, Brasillach lost his father, a French army officer killed in Morocco, when he was five. Despite this loss, he retained visions of a happy childhood and youth spent in the company of his beloved sister Suzanne, who later married Brasillach's close friend and colleague, Maurice Bardèche. As a student at the Ecole normale supérieure, Brasillach indulged his passion for the nascent cinema and the theater, forming a close relationship with the theatrical couple Georges and Ludmilla Pitoeff. Throughout his life, he remained committed to the bohemian life of his student years, spent in the company of a tightly knit group of friends. This nostalgia for youth gave a characteristic tone to his fiction and had an influence on the development of his political ideas.

A lover of the classics, Brasillach published his first book, a study of Virgil, with the aid of the right-wing journalist Henri Massis. Through Massis' influence, Brasillach began publishing essays and reviews in various periodicals, all identified with the philosophy of the French Right. At the age of twenty-two, he became editor of the literary page in the well-known *Action française*. As a literary critic, Brasillach is known particularly for his alertness to the phenomena of his own time. In 1929, for example, he was among the first to note the emergence of the new politically committed literature that would come to dominate the 1930s. He early recognized the importance of the cinema, and his *Histoire du cinéma* (1935), written in collaboration with Bardèche, remains a classic in in the field.

Brasillach was known for his enthusiastic support of French fascism, an attitude that finds expression in his best-known novel, *Les Sept Couleurs* (1939), in his memoirs, *Notre Avant-guerre* (1941), and in much of his journalistic writing. His first personal contact with a foreign fascist movement took place in 1936, when he met and wrote about the energetic young leader of the Belgian fascists, Léon Degrelle. In 1937 he reported on the Nazi Party Congress in Nuremberg, appreciating the theatricality of the mass rituals and particularly the enthusiastic atmosphere of the Nazi youth camps. It was this spirit of youthful comradeship, rooted in national tradition, that most attracted Brasillach to the various fascist movements he wished to transplant to France. His particular brand of fascism, never embodied in any clear political philosophy, found its most appropriate expression in the literary forms he chose.

Brasillach's attraction to youthful camaraderie was also an important factor in his involvement with the young team that directed the increasingly anti-Semitic and pro-German newspaper, *Je suis partout*, of which Brasillach became editor in 1937. He continued to write for *Je suis partout* even under the German occupation, and some of these articles were cited by the prosecution in his postwar trial as a collaborator. Despite a petition for clemency signed by a number of important French intellectuals, Brasillach was executed in Fresnes prison in 1945, thereby attaining the status of a young martyr to fascism.

Brasillach published six novels, a play, and a collection of poems, as well as his memoirs and various literary and cinematic studies.

G. Bernard, *Brasillach* (Paris, 1968); G. de Jubécourt, *Robert Brasillach, critique littéraire* (Lausanne, 1972); J. Madiran, *Brasillach* (Paris, 1958); W. R. Tucker, *The Fascist Ego* (Berkeley, 1975); P. Vandromme, *Robert Brasillach, l'homme et l'oeuvre* (Paris, 1956).

M. J. Green
Related entries: ACTION FRANCAISE; CINEMA; FASCISM; MASSIS; NOVEL, POLITICS AND THE.

BRAZZA, PIERRE SAVORGNAN DE (1852–1905), explorer and creator of the French Congo. Born in Rome on 26 January 1852 into an aristocratic family, Brazza became a French citizen in August 1874 while serving as a career officer in the French navy in equatorial Africa. During three expeditions under official auspices between 1875 and 1883, he founded the French post at Franceville on the upper Ogooué River in June 1880, made a treaty with the *makoko* of the Téké (Tyo) at the Stanley Pool on 10 September 1880, and helped to secure a treaty with the ruler of Loango on 12 March 1883. Brazza's explorations showed that the Ogooué River was not part of the Congo River system and that there was no direct water route from Gabon into the Congo interior. At the same time Brazza discovered that the headwaters of the M'Passa River, an Ogooué tributary, rose only a few miles from the headwaters of the Alima River, a northwestern tributary of the Congo. Brazza's expeditions, in which he successfully avoided the use of force, laid the bases for French sovereignty in the middle and upper Ogooué River system, on the Loango coast and up the Kouilou-Niari River, and in the Congo River system north of the Pool. From 1886 to 1897 Brazza served as commissioner general of the French Congo, which included the colonies of Gabon and the Middle Congo. During this decade he spent much of his energies in extending French control and claims into the areas that would become Ubangi-Shari and Chad. In 1905 Brazza was summoned from retirement to head an inquiry into the abuses of the concessionary regime that the French government had installed in 1899 to promote economic development by private companies. He died at Dakar, Senegal, en route to France on 14 September 1905, heartsick over the injustices and brutalities of the system, to which his own exaggerations about the potential riches of equatorial Africa had inadvertently helped to give support. The previous year the capital of the French Congo had been transferred to Brazzaville, the city he founded at the Pool and whose name has survived the Africanization of place names in the era of decolonization.

H. Brunschwig, ed., *Brazza explorateur: L'Ogooué, 1875–1879*(Paris, 1966); C. Coquery-Vidrovitch, ed., *Le Congo au temps des grandes compagnies concessionnaires, 1898–1930* (Paris, 1972), and *Brazza et la prise de possession du Congo: La Mission de l'ouest africain, 1883–1885* (Paris, 1969); R. West, *Brazza of the Congo: European Exploration and Exploitation in French Equatorial Africa* (London, 1972).

D. E. Gardinier

Related entries: OVERSEAS EMPIRE: FRENCH IMPERIALISM; OVERSEAS EMPIRE: EQUATORIAL AFRICA AND CAMEROON.

BREMOND, HENRI (1865–1933), abbé, historian of religious thought, and literary critic. Born in Aix-en-Provence (Bouches–du–Rhône) in 1865, Bremond entered the Society of Jesus in 1882. He spent ten years in England and Wales and taught in Jesuit schools from 1892 to 1899. In 1899 he became part of the editorial staff of the review *Etudes*, to which he made numerous contributions. Bremond left the order in 1904 for the secular clergy. During this period he gradually turned his attention to the mystical and lyrical aspects of Catholic religious thought with which he felt a close affinity. His books *Newman* (1905) and *Fénélon* (1910) reveal his evolution away from the concerns of traditional dogma.

Bremond's importance is founded on his eleven-volume *Histoire littéraire du sentiment religieux en France, depuis la fin des guerres de religion jusqu'à nos jours* (1916–36). Never finished, the work redefined the nature of religion and religious experience in seventeenth-century France. Although Bremond based his work on an enormous amount of unpublished material, this was not an empirically oriented study. Bremond described his method as the drawing forth from the style, method, and spirit of the principal religious works of the period the essence of the religious genius of the seventeenth century. Bremond succeeds in conveying to readers the nature of religious mysticism in the so-called age of classicism.

Elected to the Académie française in 1923, Bremond published a number of more strictly literary works in the later years of his career: *Pour le romantisme* (1923), *La Poésie pure* (1926), *Prière et poésie* (1927), and *Racine et Valéry* (1930). Bremond occasioned an important literary debate in the 1920s over the nature of pure poetry. Showing again his affinities with mysticism and the spiritual side of romanticism, Bremond maintained that the pleasure evoked by poetry is due to a spiritual reality (pure poetry) mysteriously transmitted through the words of a poem but apart from the apparent meaning of those words.

A. Autin, *Henri Bremond, l'homme, l'oeuvre* (Paris, 1946); A. Blanchet, *Henri Bremond: 1865–1904* (Paris, 1975); C. Moisan, *Henri Bremond et la poésie pure* (Paris, 1967); M. Nédoncelle and J. Dagens, ed., *Entretiens sur Henri Bremond* (Paris, 1967).

P. A. Ward

Related entry: LITERARY CRITICS AND CRITICISM.

BRETON, ANDRE (1896–1966), writer, poet, theoretician, and charismatic leader of the surrealist movement. His early medical training led Breton to be assigned in 1915 to military neuropsychiatric wards. In that environment he came in contact with Freudian theories and psychiatric methods of examination, as well as with a wounded soldier, Jacques Vaché, whose special brand of nihilism prepared him for the dadaist experience. Once the war was over, Breton engaged in both Freudian-inspired experiments and dada activities. The former enabled him to draft the first piece of genuinely surrealist writing, a collection of "automatic texts" (writings which express spontaneous personal visions and fantasies) produced in collaboration with Philippe Soupault, published in part in 1919 in the avant-garde review *Littérature*. Out of the dada participation he developed an iconoclastic strain, which, together with his faith in the redeeming power of the subconscious, became a basic feature of his surrealism. Yet it was only in 1924 that the publication of his *First Surrealist Manifesto* officially established the surrealist movement. The *Manifesto* expressed revolt against the prevailing logical and utilitarian framework of thinking and asserted the necessity of expanding the perception of reality through attention to the subconscious and its manifestations.

By mid-1925 Breton was drawn to communism. He joined the party in 1927 but did not think that allegiance to Marxism entailed renunciation of surrealist ideas and undertakings. This explains the abundance of texts he published while affiliated with the Communist movement in which he tried to demonstrate that it was possible to be both a surrealist and a Marxist (*Légitime défense*, 1926; *Second manifeste du surréalisme*, 1930; *Qu'est-ce que le surréalisme?* 1934; *Position politique du surréalisme*, 1935). Yet his persistent refusal to give up surrealist activities led in 1933 to his expulsion from the Communist party and in 1935 to the definitive break between surrealism and communism. This prompted him to turn to Trotskyism with whose leader he collaborated in the foundation and the drafting of the *Manifesto* of the Fédération internationale de l'art révolutionnaire indépendant. During World War II he sought refuge in New York City. He returned to Paris in 1946 and continued as the undisputed leader of surrealism until his death in 1966.

In addition to theoretical texts, Breton wrote poems (*Clair de terre*, 1923; *Le Revolver à cheveux blancs*, 1932; *L'Air de l'eau*, 1934), all fine examples of surrealist imagery, and published autobiographical novels and essays that illustrate surrealist ideas. *Nadja* (1928) describes his strange attraction to a woman who hovers on the verge of insanity and for that reason possesses unusual psychic capacities. *Les Vases communicants* (1932) challenges the traditional conception of an antinomy between dream and wakeful life and argues that, like communicating vessels, these two aspects of reality are in permanent correspondence. *L'Amour fou* (1937) analyzes, among other coincidences, the anticipation in an "automatic" poem of a love encounter and suggests a close relationship between openness to the subconscious and receptivity to the fantastic (*merveilleux*). His *Anthologie de l'humour noir* (1940), one of the last works to be printed before he left France, contains a preface that describes black humor as a supreme gesture of defiance. Because it allows the individual to laugh at the tragic aspects of existence, the practice of black humor fosters the triumph of the principle of pleasure over that of reality.

An intense personality with forceful convictions, Breton often excommunicated from the surrealist movement those who did not abide by its precepts. For this reason he appeared to many as an authoritarian pope, while to others as an incorruptible and inspiring leader. Rarely did he leave a contemporary indifferent.

A. Balakian, *André Breton* (New York, 1970); M. Bonnet, *André Breton* (Paris, 1975), A. Breton, *Les Pas perdus* (Paris, 1969), and *Point du jour* (Paris, 1970); G. Legrand, *André Breton* (Paris, 1976); F. Rosemont, ed., *André Breton* (London, 1978).

M. D. Maayan

Related entries: ARAGON; COMMUNIST PARTY; DADAISM; SURREALISM.

BRIAND, ARISTIDE (1862–1932), quintessential Third Republic politician and statesman. After growing up near the sea in Nantes and Saint-Nazaire where his parents were proprietors of cafés and a wine shop, he became a lawyer and a political journalist. In 1889 he ran unsuccessfully for the Chamber of Deputies as a Radical and Boulangist. Influenced by Fernand Pelloutier and attracted to the syndicalist idea of the general strike, which he saw as a nonviolent means to overturn capitalism, Briand turned toward socialism. Prosecution for a passionate love affair with a married woman further distanced him from respectable society.

In 1893 Briand moved to Paris where he worked as a journalist and rose to prominence in the socialist movement. He favored Alexandre Millerand's participation in a bourgeois ministry; in general, he allied with Jean Jaurès against Jules Guesde and the more doctrinaire Marxist wing of French socialism. From 1901 to 1903 he successfully defended at the bar Gustave Hervé and the newspaper *Le Pioupiou de l'Yonne* against charges of encouraging defeatism in the army. Finally, after failures in 1889, 1893, and 1898, he became a deputy from Saint-Etienne in 1902. As Briand's political prestige increased, he slowly moved away from socialism. In 1906 he joined the cabinet of Ferdinand Sarrien as minister of public instruction and religion and resigned from the Socialist party.

Acute political and psychological instincts, flexibility, and talents as a conciliator raised Briand quickly to power. In the Sarrien and Clemenceau cabinets, he guided the separation of church and state with tact. Briand sensed the viability of a broad centrist coalition with a Center-Right axis. He himself became premier in July 1909, and appealed for an easing of clerical-anticlerical conflicts.

In the years immediately preceding World War I, Briand became increasingly conservative. He spoke of the need for authority and social progress but emphasized the former. In October 1910 Premier Briand broke a railroad strike by mobilizing the strikers into the army. He appealed to national security and asserted that if the government had not found legal remedies, it would have turned to extraordinary measures, possibly military force. During his year and a half in power, Briand followed a foreign policy of Franco-German rapprochement. He tried unsuccessfully to create a Franco-German economic consortium to exploit central Africa; the project became mired in the N'Goko Sangha affair, which involved contention over an indemnity to a French company of that name operating in the Congo.

From 1912 to 1914 Briand played major roles in the nationalist revival and in conservative politics in general. In 1912 he entered Raymond Poincaré's government as a minister of justice. In January 1913 he virtually managed Poincaré's successful campaign for the presidency of the Republic and succeeded him as premier. He introduced the controversial three-year military service law but fell from power in March 1913 over his attempt to alter voting procedures. In 1914 Briand led the conservative coalition against Joseph Caillaux's Radicals and Jaurès' Socialists.

Briand was premier (and foreign minister for the first time) from November 1915 until March 1917. During World War I he sought a more efficient army command structure and smoother cooperation within the Entente. He advocated introducing troops at Salonika (Greece); in general, allied relations with Greece generated great controversy. Briand mixed firmness with an openness to conciliation. Fearing the effects of retreat on morale, he strongly urged standing firm at Verdun. But in 1917, when a German diplomat approached him about peace, he unofficially explored this possibility, although by then he had left power.

By the time he was again named premier in January 1921, Briand had become a legend, the man who read little but understood everything. Neither a naive idealist nor a pure opportunist, he was an artist of compromise who sought a middle ground, phrased in a bland, often ambiguous rhetoric. He voiced aspirations for peace in humanistic terms while seeking to preserve French interests by negotiations and international agreements.

The relationship between France's position in the world after the war and the pressures of domestic politics provide the keys to Briand's foreign policy. The United States and Great Britain had guaranteed France's security during the Paris Peace Conference but had reneged on the promises afterward. Financial clout lay in Washington and to a lesser extent in London rather than in Paris. Bolshevized Russia ceased to be a possible ally for French conservatives. Above all, the specter of German recovery haunted French leaders.

Containing Germany became the focus of Briand's foreign policy. In 1921 when the conservative Bloc National dominated the Chamber of Deputies, Briand ordered the occupation of three German towns as sanctions against German failures to carry out provisions of the Versailles Treaty. In November 1921 he briefly led the French delegation at the Washington naval conference, hoping to strengthen Franco-American ties and perhaps even to recover the lost U.S. security guarantee. His acceptance in December of a formula that limited the tonnage of French battleships elicited sharp criticism from rivals and enemies, but Briand had conceded little. He next marked out the terrain for a trade-off of French concessions in Europe in return for a renewed British security guarantee. At Cannes in January 1922, however, when President Millerand and other conservatives thought that he was offering too much to Britain's David Lloyd George, he resigned before he had actually been defeated in parliament. When Briand faced a wall, he stopped and probed for a way around it.

The Locarno Treaty of October 1925 saw Briand's emergence as one of the foremost internationalists of his times. During the election campaign 1923–24, he had moved away from the Bloc National toward the Cartel des Gauches. He was appointed a delegate to the League of Nations and in April 1925 returned to the foreign office. The Locarno negotiations had already begun, and Briand (and his close aide Philippe Berthelot) carried them to fruition. The accord offered the British guarantee, even though it was limited to Germany's western frontier. U.S. loans, which Briand viewed as a means to stem the French inflation (thereby bolstering his political fortunes), depended on a Franco-German rapprochement. Locarno had wide support from the Left, Center, Center-Right, and segments of the French business community that wanted Franco-German economic collaboration. Briand hoped to sever German ties with the Soviet Union. Finally, Briand offered concessions as a means of limiting future German demands. He shared the 1926 Nobel Peace Prize.

While Briand was premier and foreign minister from November 1925 to June 1926 and foreign minister in Poincaré's National Union government from 1926 to 1929, the Locarno spirit bubbled on the surface, but hard bargaining went on in private. Germany entered the League of Nations in 1926. Shortly after at Thoiry, Briand and Gustav Stresemann considered inconclusively major French concessions in exchange for immediate German reparations payments that could help France overcome the worst moment of the inflation. In late 1927 Briand proposed, unsuccessfully, a restoration of the Polish corridor if Stresemann would make extensive concessions on other Eastern European issues. In 1929 Briand agreed to withdraw French troops from the Rhineland the following year; in return Germany accepted the Young plan on reparations.

Briand sought to bolster French security in other ways. In 1927 and 1928 he pursued a type of bilateral Franco-American nonaggression pact, but Frank Kellogg, the U.S. secretary of state, extended the Kellogg-Briand Pact to many countries, thereby weakening it. In 1929 Briand appealed dramatically for European union and a United States of Europe, which would deepen Franco-German cooperation and might also strengthen the competitive economic position of Europe in relation to the United States. Throughout the 1920s Briand developed French relations with the new states of Eastern Europe and the Balkans, often placing agreements with them under the umbrella of the League of Nations. He also attempted to maintain harmonious relations with Benito Mussolini's Italy under fascism, although not with the Soviet Union under communism. Increasing German strength and nationalism made Briand's last years somber.

Failing health forced Briand to resign from the Foreign Ministry in January 1932; he died in March. He had been premier for the eleventh and last time in 1929. A bas-relief showing Briand addressing rapt crowds and including excerpts from his speeches now adorns the outer wall of the Quai d'Orsay. Inside, his photograph bears this caption: "Aristide Briand, Minister of Foreign Affairs, 1915–1932, Sixteen Times."

Briand's political saga reveals a pliability typical of many professional politicians during the Third Republic. An astute politician who made no gratuitous enemies, he straddled the center of the political spectrum, adopting conservative domestic and flexible foreign policies. After World War I he sought reconciliation with Germany within the framework of the defense of French interests.

E. Keeton, "Briand's Locarno Policy: French Economics, Politics, and Diplomacy, 1925–1929" (Ph.D. dissertation, Yale University, 1975); S. Marks, *The Illusion of Peace: International Relations in Europe, 1918–1933* (New York, 1976); G. Suarez, *Briand*, 5 vols. (Paris, 1938–41).

J. Blatt

Related entries: BLOC NATIONAL; BRIAND-KELLOGG TREATY; CAILLAUX; CARTEL DES GAUCHES; CLEMENCEAU; CZECHOSLOVAKIA, ALLIANCE WITH; GERMANY, RELATIONS WITH (1914–1940); GREAT BRITAIN, RELATIONS WITH; HERRIOT; HERVE; ITALY, RELATIONS WITH; JAURES; LOCARNO ACCORDS; LOUCHEUR; MILLERAND; NATIONALISM; NAVY: GOVERNMENTAL POLICY ON NAVAL WELFARE; PELLOUTIER; POINCARE, R.; RADICAL AND RADICAL-SOCIALIST PARTY; REPARATIONS POLICY; RIBOT; SUAREZ; SYNDICALISM; TRIPLE ENTENTE; UNITED STATES, RELATIONS WITH; WORLD WAR I, FRANCE'S ROLE IN.

BRIAND-KELLOGG TREATY (1928), a pact between France and the United States, subsequently endorsed by sixty-three other nations, outlawing war as an instrument of national policy. The Locarno Agreements of 1925, which ensured the integrity of national boundaries in Europe, raised hopes for stability and peace. Attempting to capitalize on this promising development, French Foreign Minister Aristide Briand proposed a separate pact to the U.S. secretary of state, Frank B. Kellogg, in 1927. Briand's goal was to ensure U.S. neutrality in Europe. Pressure by pacifist and isolationalist elements in the United States led, however, to the pact's being completed in a different, and more ambitious, form. As approved in August 1928 the treaty was essentially a general denunciation of war as an instrument of national policy. Eventually sixty-three nations, including the Soviet Union and Japan, agreed to the Briand-Kellogg. Japan became the first nation to violate the treaty when it invaded Manchuria in 1931.

The pact may be considered the last of the post-1918 attempts, which included the Versailles Treaty, the Covenant of the League of Nations, the 1922 Naval Accords, and the Locarno Agreements, to restrain nations in the use of force and acts of war. In the minds of many observers, the Briand-Kellogg Treaty is considered to represent the naive idealism of the 1920s. The treaty failed France as a sought-for instrument of collective security and carried no provisions for its enforcement.

D. W. Brogan, *Development of Modern France* (New York, 1966); L. E. Ellis, *Frank B. Kellogg: American Foreign Policy, 1925–1929* (New Brunswick, N.J., 1961); D. H. Miller, *The Peace Pact of Paris: Study of the Briand-Kellogg Treaty* (New York, London, 1928); G. Suarez, *Briand*, 5 vols. (Paris, 1938–41).

P. Monaco

Related entries: BRIAND; DISARMAMENT CONFERENCE; LOCARNO ACCORDS; UNITED STATES, RELATIONS WITH.

BRISSON, HENRI (1835–1912), radical republican deputy and prime minister, influential Freemason and anticlerical, journalist. Deputy (1871–1912), twice prime minister, perennial president of the Chamber of Deputies (1881–85, 1894–98, 1904–5, 1906–12), frequent chairman of the budget commission, president of the parliamentary commission investigating the Panama scandal, unsuccessful radical candidate for president of the Republic (1894, 1895), Brisson stood at the center of political life for four decades. His Masonic ties and broad friendships proved to be an asset in divided chambers. He campaigned with radical republicans for anticlerical and reform legislation, yet he maintained the respect of Léon Gambetta and his friends. In 1885 he succeeded Jules Ferry (6 April) with a slightly more radical government under his direction. It continued Ferry's Indochina policy, establishing protectorates in Annam and Cambodia, and kept the government neutral in the 1885 legislative elections. The new Chamber of Deputies, dominated by royalists and radicals, endorsed the cabinet by a close margin. Brisson waited until after Jules Grévy had been reelected to a second term and then resigned (29 December).

In 1898 (28 June), he brought the radicals back to power with a moderate program. The discovery that evidence used to defend the verdict against Dreyfus had been forged prompted Brisson to order the courts to review the case. Three successive war ministers resigned to protest his decision. Over the cabinet's objections, the deputies instructed it to stop attacking the army, and Brisson resigned (26 October). The following June, during a bitter debate over René Waldeck-Rousseau's Dreyfusard cabinet, Brisson made a dramatic appeal to vote for the Republic, closing with a gesture initiates recognized as the Masonic distress signal. Most radicals responded by voting for the new cabinet.

Brisson remained politically active until his death, helping to establish in 1901 the Parti républicain-radical et radical-socialiste.

A. Robert and G. Cougny, eds., *Dictionnaire des parlementaires français*, vol. 1 (1889); J. Jolly, ed., *Dictionnaire des parlementaires français*, vol. 2 (Paris 1962); J. Kayser, *Les Grandes Batailles du radicalisme* (Paris, 1962).

S. A. Ashley

Related entries: ANTICLERICALISM; DREYFUS AFFAIR; FREEMASONS; RADICAL AND RADICAL-SOCIALIST PARTY.

BRITTANY. Relations between Brittany (divided since 1790 into the five departments of Finistère, Côtes-du-Nord, Morbihan, Ille-et-Vilaine, and Loire-Atlantique) and Paris have never been easy since the incorporation of the Armorican peninsula into the French state at the end of the fifteenth century. Efforts to extend the central authority of France throughout the province invariably provoked stubborn acts of Breton resistance: the revolt of the Bonnets Rouges in 1685; the Pont-Callec affair of 1718–19; the La Chalotais controversy of 1764–65; the protest movement of Houssaye, Bothorel, and La Rouërie in 1790–92; the Chouannerie of the early 1800s; and the Cadoudal conspiracy of 1804. Mutual hostility and suspicion were reinforced when Paris authorities interpreted these acts of Breton defiance as evidence of the persistence of reactionary particularism or even outright separatist sentiment that must be stamped out.

This reciprocal pattern of French suspicion and Breton resistance continued to characterize relations between Paris and Brittany throughout the Third Republic. The first incident came with the formation by the Breton general Emile de Kératry of a volunteer army of 100,000 men against the advance of the Prussians into western France. This force, however, was viewed with alarm by Léon Gambetta and his government, who saw in it a Breton army whose leadership harbored autonomist or even separatist motives. War minister Charles de Freycinet accordingly telegraphed to Kératry urging him to forget that he was a Breton and to remember only that he was a Frenchman. Then the government failed to provision or adequately arm Kératry's troops billeted in winter camp at Conlie. This contributed to their crushing defeat by the Prussians at the Battle of Le Mans on 10–12 January 1871. Although patriotic Breton historians have since viewed the entire affair as a cynical French maneuver against Brittany, it seems more likely that Gambetta and his colleagues feared the royalist bias of the commanders of this volunteer force far more than they did any particular Breton character that it may have possessed. It was well known, for example, that Kératry was a rich Breton landowner and loyal partisan of the Bourbon pretender. That monarchism was a powerful political force in Brittany and hence a legitimate cause for concern on the part of the republicans around Gambetta was, in any event, amply demonstrated when elections for the National Assembly in February saw Breton constituencies return five times as many royalist as republican deputies.

For the next half-century, Brittany's political representatives in the French parliament constituted a more or less permanent right-wing opposition to the Third Republic, a reflection of the local ascendancy on the peninsula of a long-entrenched clerico-aristocratic ruling elite. The anticlerical legislation sponsored by Jules Ferry in the 1880s thus found some of its most determined opponents in Brittany, while the Dreyfus affair in the next decade showed that there was scant support for the Republic in the five Breton departments. The subsequent separation of church and state in 1905, moreover, encountered fierce resistance in Brittany where numerous priests and their faithful barricaded themselves in local churches against implementation of this measure. No incident better showed that a moral gulf existed between Brittany on the one hand and the French state on the other—a situation exemplified by the virtual absence of Bretons from the ranks of the *grands notables* who governed the Third Republic. (Aristide Briand, a native of the nominally Breton city of Nantes, and the communist leader Marcel Cachin who hailed from Brittany are but partial exceptions to this rule.)

The moral separation between Brittany and France was also expressed in the decades before 1914 by the efforts of local patriotic societies—the Association bretonne, the Union régionaliste bretonne, the Gorsedd des bardes, Bleun-Brug—to defend Breton language, culture, and history against French centralization and to promote the cause of regional reform. In 1911 these efforts were joined by a more radical group when several young Breton nationalists headed by Camille Le Mercier d'Erm organized the Francophobe and separatist Parti nationaliste breton. Although this group never attracted more than a few hundred supporters and did not survive the 1914–18 war, its appearance nonetheless heralded the emergence of militant Breton political action that continues to this day.

The loss of nearly one-quarter million Breton dead in the battles of the First World War and the heady talk of national self-determination that accompanied the end of hostilities encouraged the resumption of Breton political action in 1919. Numerous publications appeared—*La Bretagne intégrale, An Oaled, Buhez breiz, Foi et Bretagne*—to plead the cause of Brittany in terms of regional reform, language maintenance, and Catholic defense. The most important by far of these was *Breiz Atao* founded by Fanch Debauvais and Olier Mordrel. Though at first the champion of a relatively moderate form of regionalism, *Breiz Atao* was by the late 1920s advocating a militant brand of autonomism that with the foundation of the Parti national breton in 1932 became scarcely disguised separatism. At the same time *Breiz Atao* was able to attract several thousand adherents and to shoulder aside all other competing forms of Breton action. By the end of the 1930s, *Breiz Atao* and the Breton movement had become synonymous terms.

Debauvais and Mordrel concurrently emerged as the most resolute and influential Breton nationalist leaders. Both were politically conservative and admirers of the formula of their Irish cousins in the Sinn Fein: the enemy of our enemy is our friend. This was a combination that inevitably inclined the two men toward support of and eventually tacit alliance with Nazi Germany. These positions they impressed on *Breiz Atao* and the Parti national breton so that by the end of the interwar period, both became the targets of repressive action by Paris officials already worried by the violent exploits of a clandestine terrorist group in Brittany called Gwenn-ha-Du. Debauvais was arrested for sedition in June 1938, brought to trial, and convicted, a sentence he evaded by flight. Having in the meantime surrendered to French authorities in order to exploit the propaganda opportunities to be offered by a new trial, Debauvais along with Mordrel was once more tried for and convicted of sedition in December. Although the sentence for Mordrel was suspended, Debauvais remained in prison until July 1939 when he was released after a hunger strike.

Breiz Atao applauded each new instance of Nazi aggression and encouraged the development of defeatist attitudes in Brittany. This sort of provocation could not for long go unpunished by Paris. When on 27 August 1939, a few days after the signature of the Nazi-Soviet pact, *Breiz Atao* called on Bretons not to die for Danzig, the government suppressed the separatist organ by administrative decree and forbade the holding of the upcoming congress of the Parti national breton at Pontivy. Mordrel and Debauvais fled to Belgium and then traveled to Berlin where they remained during the months of the so-called *drôle de guerre*. On 7 May 1940, both men were tried in absentia at Rennes for treason, found guilty, and placed under sentence of death. Thus, no one praised more loudly the German offensive against France that began three days later and the fall of France six weeks after that than did Debauvais and Mordrel. The fortunes of Breton nationalism were thereafter joined in collaboration with those of German national socialism. Hence was created a doleful legacy that for more than a generation hung heavy over the post-1945 Breton movement.

J. E. Reece, *The Bretons against France* (Chapel Hill, 1977).

J. E. Reece

Related entry: AUTONOMIST AND SEPARATIST MOVEMENTS.

BROCA, PAUL (1824–1880), medical doctor, founder of the Société d'anthropologie de Paris. Born into a Protestant family in Sainte-Foy-La-Grande (Gironde), Broca was attracted to Voltairian views of the world and attempted to develop his scientific work independently of philosophical or theological systems. At an early age he won attention by publishing his medical research. He had a brilliant career as a medical practitioner and teacher. His most important medical contribution was his location of the area in the human brain that is the central organ of speech; he also made contributions to the understanding of cancer cells and a definition of the processes that cause rickets. Broca, a member of the Biological Society, led a breakaway group in 1859 that founded the Paris Anthropological Society, a model for other societies in the world. Under Broca's leadership a separate discipline of scientific anthropology developed in France. The society's meetings were recorded in the *Bulletin* of the society; in 1878 Broca founded the Institut d'anthropologie, which joined the society, the laboratory, and the *Revue d'anthropologie* (founded in 1875) into one institution, later to develop into the Musée de l'homme.

Broca was one of the earliest to try to develop physical anthropology on a scientific basis, perfecting various instruments of measurement and insisting on statistical rigor in describing human groups. French anthropology was to be heavily influenced by the weight Broca gave to human physical aspects, and until the 1890s it tended to underwrite a racist emphasis by seeing physical variations among human groups as the cause of the observable differences among races.

For his outstanding contributions to science and his lifetime attachment to republican ideas, Broca, a Gambettist, was elected by the National Assembly as a life member of the Senate. He served as *rapporteur* for a bill on the establishment of *lycées* for women. He sat only five months in the Senate, dying in July 1880.

W. B. Cohen, *The French Encounter with Africans* (Bloomington, 1980); C. Sagan, *Broca's Brain* (New York, 1979); F. Schiller, *Paul Broca, Founder of French Anthropology, Explorer of the Brain* (Berkeley, 1979).

W. B. Cohen

Related entries: LEBON; MEDICINE: DEVELOPMENTS IN; POSITIVISM; SCIENCE AND TECHNOLOGY.

BROGLIE, ALBERT, DUC DE (1821–1901), Orleanist theorist and politician. Son of Victor de Broglie, Albert followed politically and literarily in the footsteps of his father and grandmother, Germaine de Staël. He became a leader of the Orleanist cause in the 1870s. Of great intellectual ability and a prolific author, he wrote on subjects ranging from the ideas of Gottfried Leibniz to the role of Christianity in the fourth-century Roman Empire. He was elected to the Académie française in 1862. By the 1860s he sided with Bishop Félix Dupanloup in advocating a policy of a free church in a free state. The return of the Orleanists to power in the early Third Republic gave him his political opportunity.

Elected to the National Assembly in 1871, he became the leader of the Center-Right faction, which favored the restoration of the monarchy. Because Adolphe Thiers leaned toward the establishment of a conservative republic, Broglie played a significant role in his overthrow. As prime minister under President Maurice de MacMahon during 1873–74, he supported the cause of the Orleanist pretender, Philippe d'Orléans, the comte de Paris. His downfall came in 1877 when, as prime minister again, he collaborated with MacMahon in the *seize mai* affair, the last serious effort to transform France from a republic to a monarchy.

Broglie was a careful man in all matters but far removed from most people. A colorless personality and a poor speaker, he labored in a studied way for the solution he desired. He was a traditionalist in many ways but also at times a man of expediency. He believed a traditional monarchy to be superior to a republic but was unable to accept totally traditional monarchist values. He personified the strengths and weaknesses of the Orleanists as well as anyone in that camp.

J. de La Varende, *Les Broglie* (Paris, 1950); C. Muret, *French Royalist Doctrines since the Revolution* (New York, 1933); S. Osgood, *French Royalism under the Third and Fourth Republics* (The Hague, 1960).

M. L. Brown, Jr.

Related entries: MACMAHON; ORLEANISM; PARIS, PHILIPPE D'ORLEANS; *SEIZE MAI* CRISIS; THIERS.

BROUSSE, PAUL (1844–1912), member of the First Workingmen's International, anarchist, and from 1882 leader of the Possibilist socialist party. Born in Montpellier (Hérault), the son of a university professor, and himself trained as a doctor, Brousse was involved in activities of the First International in the Midi in 1871–72. Involved in feuds between Marxists and anti-authoritarians and wanted by the police, he took refuge in Spain. Here he came into contact with disciples of Mikhail Bakunin. After leaving Spain for Switzerland he played a prominent part in the Jura Federation of the International, the center of federalist and anarchist ideas within the international socialist movement. For a while, he became an extreme exponent of the anarchist doctrine of propaganda by the deed, and he was finally expelled from Switzerland for having written articles sympathetic to political assassination.

After brief sojourns in London and Brussels, he returned to France in 1880. He joined the Parti ouvrier, broke with the anarchists, and in 1882 led the opposition to Jules Guesde and the Marxists by forming the Possibilist party (Fédération des travailleurs socialistes de France), which preached municipal socialism. In due course Brousse was elected to the Paris municipal council, of which he became its vice-president in 1887. His espousal of reformist municipal socialism and his willingness to make electoral alliances with radical politicians alienated segments of the party, and a dissident group, headed by Jean Allemane, broke away in 1890. Although his party subsequently steadily declined in influence, Brousse remained a municipal councillor; he was eventually elected on the Socialist (SFIO) platform to the Chamber of Deputies in 1906, losing the seat in 1910.

Brousse's significance lies primarily in his formulation of the reformist notion of possibilism, the argument that socialists should work for progress within the capitalist system although without necessarily abandoning a revolutionary perspective. In particular he believed that valuable progress could be made at the municipal, or communal, level, where socialists could gain control and create public services in the interests of the working class. He inherited much of this perspective from his anarchist past, and he gave it theoretical expression in his pamphlet *La Commune et le Parti ouvrier* published in 1882. The doctrine separated him sharply from Marxists such as Guesde and Paul Lafargue. This, combined with the legacy of personal rivalries dating from the First International and strong Proudhonist-federalist sentiments among the Parisian working class, led Brousse and his supporters to expel the Guesdist faction from the Parti ouvrier at its St. Etienne Congress in 1882.

During the Boulanger crisis Brousse took an active part, with Jean Allemane, in forming the Société des droits de l'homme to defend the Republic. But his increasing immersion in Parisian politics, his willingness to contemplate electoral arrangements with the radicals, and his bourgeois background caused suspicion within the party and led to accusations of opportunism. Allemane and his supporters consequently left the party in 1890. This destroyed the Possibilists as an effective political force, and they never regained the prominence they had enjoyed (at least in Paris) as the largest of the various factions of the socialist movement.

Brousse remained active on the municipal council, while at the national level he supported the Jean Jaurès wing in the slow struggle to achieve socialist unity, which culminated with the formation of the SFIO in 1905.

J. Maitron, ed., *Dictionnaire biographique du mouvement ouvrier*, vol. 4 (Paris, 1967) and vol. 11 (1973); S. Humbert, *Les Possibilistes* (Paris, 1912); D. Stafford, *From Anarchism to Reformism* (Toronto, 1971) and "Paul Brousse", *1871, Jalons pour une histoire de la commune de Paris*, ed. J. Rougerie (Paris, 1973).

D. A. T. Stafford
Related entries: ALLEMANE; ALLEMANISTS; GUESDE; POSSIBILISTS; SOCIALISM, 1870–1914; SOCIALISM, MUNICIPAL.

BRUNETIERE, FERDINAND (1849–1906), literary critic and historian, essayist on social and moral issues. Born in Toulon (Var), Brunetière was educated in Lorient, in Marseilles, and at the Lycée Louis-le-Grand in Paris. With only the *baccalauréat* he eventually was named to the faculty of the Ecole normale supérieure in 1886 and became the most famous of a group of literary critics known as *normaliens* (because of their connection with the Ecole normale). After the end of the Franco-Prussian War (for which Brunetière had volunteered), he began to write articles on nineteenth-century theories of evolution for the *Revue bleue* and on literature for the *Revue des deux mondes*. He became director of the latter journal in 1893, the same year he was elected to the Académie française. As a young man, Brunetière was an ethical pessimist, influenced by the philosophy of Schopenhauer and by Buddhism. After an audience with Pope Leo XIII in 1894, he moved toward conversion, making public statements in favor of a brand of Catholicism that would address the social issues of his day, at the same time trying to reconcile religion and science. In his 1895 tract, *La Science et la religion*, Brunetière spoke of the bankruptcy of science because of its failure to fulfill its promises of progress and of improvement in the lot of humanity.

Brunetière had over thirty books published, many of them collecting his critical and polemical essays or his lectures. Among the most noteworthy are *Le Roman naturaliste* (1883), *Les Epoques du théâtre français* (1892), *L'Evolution de la poésie lyrique en France* (1894), *Etudes critiques* (8 volumes, 1880–1907), *Manuel de l'histoire de la littérature française* (1898), *Balzac* (1906), and *Discours de combat* (3 volumes, 1900–1907).

A traditionalist and classicist by taste who admired seventeenth-century French literature and also encouraged the rise of the study of comparative literature, Brunetière condemned the naturalist movement, particularly as represented in the work of Emile Zola. He similarly condemned the movement of art for art's sake and the impressionistic criticism of his contemporaries, Jules Lemaître and Anatole France. Yet Brunetière was distinctly a thinker of his own age, for he was profoundly influenced by the evolutionary theories of Charles Darwin, Aldous Huxley, and Herbert Spencer, which he applied to literary history and to literary genres. Although Brunetière saw literary genres as developing and changing like the evolution of an organism, he made room for the individual genius in literary history, claiming that every new species has as its point of departure the appearance of a new detail in the work of a specific individual. Literary history reveals how works are linked to one another, how the past always weighs on the present. Above all, Brunetière saw the critic as making value judgments—as classifying, judging, and setting up hierarchies.

J. Clark, *La Pensée de Ferdinand Brunetière* (Paris, 1954); E. R. Curtius, *Ferdinand Brunetière. Beitrag zur Geschichte der Französischen Kritik* (Strassburg, 1914); E. Hocking, *Ferdinand Brunetière, The Evolution of a Critic* (Madison, Wis. 1936); J. Van der Lugt, *L'Action religieuse de Ferdinand Brunetière (1895–1906)* (Paris, 1936).

P. A. Ward

Related entries: LITERARY CRITICS AND CRITICISM; ROMAN CATHOLICISM: CHURCH-STATE RELATIONS.

BRUNHES, JEAN (1869–1930), geographer and professor. An early disciple of Paul Vidal de la Blache, he elaborated the view that man is free in his relationship with nature. Livelihood, including its cultural and ritualistic aspects, was his core concern in the man-nature interplay. More than his mentor, Brunhes was concerned with typologies, as outlined in his seminal work, *Géographie humaine: Essai de classification positive* (1910). Rather than organizing geographic facts by regions as had previously been the rule, Brunhes systematized six essential types of phenomena: houses, roads, cultivated fields, domesticated animals, exploitation of minerals, and devastation of biota. Two other works, both prepared with coauthors, stand as monuments to his thought: *Géographie humaine de la France* (1920) and *La Géographie de l'histoire* (1921). Brunhes' considerable oratorial and literary skills were put to use as professor of human geography at the Collège de France, a post he held from 1912 until his death. Henri Bergson, Frédéric Le Play, and John Ruskin influenced his conceptions of knowledge, thought, and action.

A. Buttimer, *Society and Milieu in the French Geographic Tradition* (Chicago, 1971).

D. W. Gade

Related entry: VIDAL DE LA BLACHE.

BRUNSCHWICG, CECILE (1877–1946), feminist activist. Against the wishes of her father, Arthur Kahn, an industrialist and chevalier de la Légion d'honneur, but with strong encouragement from her philosopher husband, Léon Brunschwicg, she made a career for herself as one of the Third Republic's foremost feminists. An equivalence theorist who called for women's rights in the name of women's different but complementary qualities, Brunschwicg, politically awakened by the Dreyfus affair, initially focused on such long-standing feminist issues as unequal pay, inadequate education, child labor, and the civil incapacity of married women. Within a decade, however, she shifted focus to women's political rights and, from its inception in 1909, served for years as the general secretary of the Union française pour le suffrage des femmes, the French national affiliate of the 1904 International Women's Suffrage Alliance. Simultaneously, as the delegate of both the Réchauds de Midi, which she set up in 1909 to provide working women with a warm place to eat, and the Union des femmes de France de tours, she participated in the suffrage section of the Conseil national des femmes françaises, founded in 1901 as the French affiliate of the 1888 International Council of Women. By 1914, drawing primarily from the ranks of liberal Protestants, Jews, and free-thinkers, the Union through which she worked had roughly 14,000 members, while through the Conseil national she could reach nearly 100,000.

From 1914 to 1918, Brunschwicg, like most other French feminists, accorded priority to mollifying the effects of the First World War. At the outset of hostilities, she created a housing and jobs program for refugees, which eventually served 25,000 people and earned her the Croix de la Légion d'honneur. In 1917 she founded at Paris the Ecole des surintendantes d'usines, a school designed to train women to deal with social problems arising out of large-scale public and private employment. In the immediate aftermath of the war, she helped to secure the right of women to take examinations for positions in governmental ministries and for the *agrégation*. The mother of three children, she also enlisted as a propagandist in the struggle against depopulation, alcoholism, and prostitution.

As before the First World War, however, Brunschwicg's principal concern during the interwar years was woman's suffrage. In the mid-1920s, chagrined at the senate's refusal to ratify the Chamber of Deputies' endorsement of women's right to vote, she assumed the presidency of the Union française pour le suffrage des femmes, took on the task of directing *La Française*, and tried by joining the Radical party to counter its longstanding opposition to women's suffrage. In 1929 she helped to organize the Etats généraux du féminisme and presided over its Section du travail. With Edmée de la Rochefoucauld and Louise Weiss, she thus emerged as one of the three dominant figures of French feminism between the wars. As one of another threesome, she also obtained in 1936 the highest public office held by women under the Third Republic, serving in Léon Blum's first Popular Front government as under secretary of state for national education, alongside under secretaries of state Irène Joliot-Curie for scientific research and Suzanne Lacore for public health. In 1937 she was promoted to Officier de la Légion d'honneur.

Acting in assisting refugees from German racism in the late 1930s, Brunschwicg fled south when Franch suffered defeat in 1940, while her daughter joined Charles de Gaulle in England. During the German occupation of Vichy France, she worked at a girls' school in Valence under the name of Mme. Léger. From 1944 until her death two years later, she served on various United Nations reconstruction committees, sat on the executive committee of the Fédération démocratique internationale des femmes, assumed the honorary presidency of the Conseil national des femmes radicales socialistes, and generally sought to prepare women to exercise responsibly their recently won right to vote.

M. Albistur and D. Armogathe, *Histoire du féminisme français* (Paris, 1977); C. Brunschwicg et al., *La Femme emancipée* (Paris, 1927); J. McMillan, *Housewife or*

Harlot (New York, 1981); J. Rabaut, *Histoire des féminismes française* (Paris, 1978); L. Weiss, *Combat pour les femmes* (Paris, 1970).

P. K. Bidelman

Related entries: MISME; WOMEN: MOVEMENT FOR CIVIL RIGHTS; WOMEN: MOVEMENT FOR POLITICAL RIGHTS; NATIONAL COUNCIL OF FRENCH WOMEN; ROCHEFOUCAULD.

BUCARD, MARCEL (1895–1946), an organizer of veterans' groups and France's purest fascist. Born in Saint-Claire-sur-Epte, where his father was a prosperous horse dealer, Bucard was destined for the priesthood, only to have his seminary studies interrupted by the war. At the front he displayed exceptional heroism, was promoted captain, and named chevalier of the Legion of Honor. After a short postwar service in Germany and an unsuccessful bid for election to the Chamber of Deputies on the Tardieu list in 1924, Bucard in 1925 joined the Faisceau of Georges Valois where he was a leading propagandist: his speciality, impassioned and pathetic speeches evoking the camaraderie and heroism of the front. In 1927, Bucard left the now-crumbling Faisceau, where he had earned a reputation for dubious sexual and financial morality, to join forces with François Coty. Bucard wrote for several of Coty's newspapers, acting as a bridge between the nationalist millionaire and veterans' groups.

In 1933, after Coty had lost most of his fortune, Bucard founded the Parti franciste (distinct from Henry Coston's party of the same name). This openly fascist group, which probably never attracted over 10,000 members, was dissolved in 1936 along with the other leagues, only to be replaced by the Amis du francisme and, in 1939, the Parti Unitaire français d'action socialiste et nationale. Supported financially by Benito Mussolini, Bucard represented France at the international fascist congress at Montreux in 1935 and was active in the short-lived movement for universal fascism. As the war approached, however, he came increasingly under the influence of nazism and became increasingly anti-Semitic.

After the defeat, Bucard became an enthusiastic collaborator for which he was executed in 1946. His career of isolation and frequent failure shows the difficulties involved in organizing a purely and overtly fascist movement in France.

A. Deniel, *Bucard et le Francisme* (Paris, 1979); A. Jacomet, "Les Chefs du francisme: Marcel Bucard et Paul Guiraud," *Revue d'histoire de la deuxième guerre mondiale* 97 (1975); J. Plumyène and R. Lasierra, *Les Fascismes français, 1923–1963* (Paris, 1963).

A. Douglas

Related entries: ANTI-SEMITISM; COTY, F.; FASCISM; TARDIEU; VALOIS.

BUISSON, FERDINAND (1841–1932), educator, politician, and social reformer. One of several Protestants who exercised significant influence on the development of public education in the Third Republic, Bussion returned to France from four years of voluntary exile in Switzerland after the Second Empire collapsed and in short order became the secretary of the Commission de statistique de l'enseignement primaire, inspector general of public instruction, and director of primary education. During his seventeen years at the last post, he worked closely with Jules Ferry and others in creating a free, obligatory, and law school system, the rationale for which he simultaneously set forth in his *Dictionnaire de pédagogie*. Five years after receiving a doctorat ès lettres in 1891, he resigned as director in order to assume the chair of pedagogy at the Sorbonne.

Buisson also served for seventeen years as a Radical-Socialist deputy, representing Paris' Thirteenth Arrondissement from 1902 to 1914 and again from 1919 to 1924. A supporter of Emile Combes, Buisson acted as *rapporteur* for the law that forbade religious orders to teach and held the post of president of the Chamber of Deputies' Commission de la séparation des églises et l'état. His other Chamber posts included vice-presidencies of both the Commission d'assurance et de prévoyance sociale and the Commission du suffrage universel. He sat on the Commission de l'enseignement, the Commission des associations et congrégations, and the Commission de l'hygiène publique. Defeated for reelection in 1924, he retired to the village of Thieuloy-Saint-Antoine, serving there as a municipal councillor and from there as honorary president of the Fédération radicale-socialiste de l'Oise.

Buisson began a lifelong involvement in social reform in 1867 by attending the first Congrès de la paix at Geneva and by writing articles such as "L'abolition de la guerre par l'instruction." On returning to France in 1870, he founded an asylum for war ophans and then became the director of the Orphelinat de Cempuis. An ardent Dreyfusard he helped to create the Ligue des droits de l'homme and in 1913 succeeded Francis de Pressensé as its president. An equally ardent advocate of women's rights, he championed women's suffrage in the Chamber of Deputies, wrote *Le Vote des femmes* (1911), served as president from the outset of the 1911 Ligue d'électeurs pour le suffrage des femmes, and sat on the Comité d'honneur of the 1929 Etats généraux du féminisme. After the First World War he became president of the Ligue de l'enseignement. Although excoriated by clericals as one of the principal ringleaders of a Masonic plot against god and country, Buisson received the plaque de Grand-Officier de la Légion d'honneur from Edouard Herriot's ministry in 1924 and the Nobel Peace Prize in 1926.

Dictionnaire de biographie française, vol. 7 (Paris, 1956); J. Jolly, ed., *Dictionnaire des parlementaires français*, vol. 2 (Paris, 1962); *Grand Larousse* Vol. 2 (Paris, 1960).

P. K. Bidelman

Related entries: ANTICLERICALISM; ASSOCIATIONS, LAW OF; COMBES; DREYFUS AFFAIR; EDUCATION: ADMINISTRATION OF; FEMINISM; FERRY; FREEMASONS; HERRIOT; PROTESTANTISM; RADICAL AND RADICAL-SOCIALIST PARTY; SCHOOLS, PRIMARY; SEPARATION OF CHURCH AND STATE, LAW OF.

BURGUNDY. The four departments of the Burgundy region—the Côte-d'Or, Saône-et-Loire, Nièvre, and Yonne—followed different paths of development during this period. The population of Burgundy as a whole declined from 1.7 million in 1872 to 1.4 million in 1936, but while the population of the Yonne dropped and that of the Nièvre rose only slightly, that of the Saône-et-Loire and the Côte-d'Or increased more substantially. The first two departments remained predominantly rural and agricultural, whereas greater urbanization and industrialization took place in the Saône-et-Loire and the Côte-d'Or. Falling birthrates and large-scale migrations to Paris, Lyons, and other factory cities account for the demographic decline; the expansion of Dijon, which had 100,000 residents by 1940, could not make up for the rural exodus.

The routing of a major railway through Burgundy in the 1850s spurred economic growth in those towns it served, such as Dijon, but sped up emigration and economic dislocation in areas it bypassed. Furthermore, the disappearance of rural industries (particularly the closing of artisanal forges), the phylloxera epidemic of the 1870s and 1880s and competition for winegrowers from the Midi, and the depression all brought distress to the rural economy. The area worst affected was the Morvan, the forest preserve at the junction of the four departments; a half-century of emigration left it almost bereft of inhabitants. Many Burgundian villages were depopulated; only those towns that served as centers of government or commerce for their hinterlands—Auxerre, Beaune, Nevers, Mâcon—were able to hold their own. Major industrial centers, such as Montceau-les-Mines, fared better.

Although the number of persons engaged in agriculture dropped, as did the number of farms, crop specialization and the growth of medium-sized holdings aided agricultural modernization. Sales from wine, Charolais beef, and grain ensured the continuing importance of agriculture. Industry was most developed in the Saône-et-Loire, where the Le Creusot-Chalon-Montceau-les-Mines triangle was one of the most important industrial concentrations in France. (The Creusot factory alone employed 15,000 workers in 1915.) The Schneider factories and the Commentry-Fourchambault firm manufactured steel, railroad machinery, and armaments. Light industry predominated in the Côte-d'Or: food industries, chemicals, wood products, ceramics. There was some industrialization in the Nièvre, along the Loire, but both the Nièvre and the Yonne remained areas of farming. The third sector, services, expanded rapidly throughout the region, particularly in Dijon.

Politically, Burgundians were republican and anticlerical; twenty of twenty-six deputies elected in 1876 were republicans. The Côte-d'Or and Yonne elected Opportunists, the Nièvre and Saône-et-Loire Radicals. Socialism rapidly gained strength, and by the 1920s, the Saône-et-Loire was the second strongest socialist department in France. After World War I, many Burgundian districts became more conservative, but in 1936 fifteen of twenty-three deputies supported the Popular Front. Labor unrest was confined largely to the Saône-et-Loire. There were major strikes at Le Creusot in 1899 and 1900; however, the Confédération générale du travail increased its membership from 15,800 in 1935 to 92,000 in 1937.

Among notable Burgundians were the sculptor François Pompon (1855–1933), the painter Félix Ziem (1821–1911), the photographer Jules Marey (1830–1903);

the authors Jules Renard (1864–1910), Colette (1873–1954), Edouard Estaunié (1862–1942), and Romain Rolland (1866–1944); and Gustave Eiffel (1832–1923). The region produced two presidents of the Third Republic, Maurice de MacMahon (1808–93) and Sadi Carnot (1837–94). Traditions of popular culture, such as the charivari and the *veillée*, disappeared, perhaps even more rapidly in Burgundy then elsewhere because of the lack of a regional language, a disinterest in religion, and the diversity of the Burgundian geography and population.

R. Aldrich, *Economy and Society in Burgundy since 1850* (New York, 1984); P. Dibie, *Traditions de la Bourgogne* (Verviers, 1978); J. Richard, ed., *Histoire de la Bourgogne* (Toulouse, 1978); H. Vincenot, *La Vie quotidienne des Bourguignons au temps de Lamartine* (Paris, 1976).

R. Aldrich

Related entries: CARNOT; COLETTE; DIJON; EIFFEL; MACMAHON; ROLLAND; VITICULTURE.

BURTY, PHILIPPE (1830–1890), a highly influential art critic who supported japonisme and impressionism. With articles in the newspaper *Le Rappel* (1869) and the journal *La Renaissance littéraire et artistique* (1871–72), Burty passionately espoused Japanese art. His home, which contained a vast collection of Japanese artworks, attracted many prominent artists, among them the writer Edmond de Goncourt, the etcher Félix Bracquemond, and the painter Edgar Degas. Burty's explanations and advocacy of japonisme influenced many impressionists, in whose compositions may be perceived the subtle assimilation of Japanese design.

Burty avidly championed the impressionist cause through such periodicals as *La République française* and the English *Academy* (1874). He staunchly defended, against the prevailing critical reserve, their spontaneous appreciation of nature, their light-filled canvases, and their sketch-like compositions. As a result, he is acknowledged to be one of the few critics of his era to have openly advocated innovation and independent creativity.

G. P. Weisberg, "Philippe Burty and a Critical Assessment of Early 'Japonisme,' " in *Japonisme in Art, An International Symposium* (Tokyo, 1980).

G. P. Weisberg

Related entries: DEGAS; IMPRESSIONISM; PISSARRO.

BUSINESS ORGANIZATION. The rise to dominance of the joint stock, or corporate, form of business organization took place during the Third Republic. The first half of the twentieth century was also the golden age of small businesses, mostly commercial establishments. The basic texts governing business organization during the Third Republic were the Code de commerce of 1807, the law of 24 July 1867, a codifying statute for joint stock companies, and the law of 7 March 1925, introducing the *société à responsabilité limitée*. The Code recognized two types of partnerships: the ordinary partnership (*société en nom collectif*), in which all the partners were subject to unlimited liability, and the limited partnership (*société en commandite simple*), in which the active partner(s) who managed the enterprise were subject to unlimited liability but in which the passive, or silent, partner(s) possessed limited liability (that is, they were not liable beyond the amount of their investment in the enterprise). The Code permitted two types of joint stock companies. One was the *société en commandite par actions* (CPA), which resembled the *commandite simple* except that the capital of the enterprise was divided into freely transferable shares; the managing director (*gérant*) of the CPA was subject to unlimited liability, but the ordinary shareholders enjoyed limited liability. They were, however, prohibited from exercising any control over the omnipotent *gérant*. The other type was the *société anonyme* (SA), a regular corporation in which the managers and stockholders were covered by limited liability and in which the managers were responsible, at least in theory, to the stockholders. Until 1867, an SA could be formed only by the express authorization of the government, which was difficult to obtain. Between 1807 and 1867, the formation of SAs averaged only eleven per year, but the law of 1867 freed the SA from the requirement of governmental authorization. Since they could be freely formed, SAs appeared in increasingly large numbers during the Third Republic and came to dominate the economy before 1914. With the freeing of the SA, the CPA, which had been used for large numbers of enterprises from the mid-1830s, was reduced to a minor role. The CPA was, in spite of its inconveniences, a corporate substitute, which owed its popularity before 1867 to the difficulty of obtaining governmental authorization as an SA. For the period 1852–67, the formation of CPAs averaged almost two hundred annually. From this peak the creation of CPAs fell to an average of eighty-eight annually for the period 1877–97 and to eighty-two for the period 1898–1913. Further, the large CPA (capitalized at 5 million francs or more) virtually disappeared. Many existing CPAs, especially large ones, hastened to transform themselves into SAs, though there were a few exceptions: the Schneiders' huge metallurgical enterprise, Le Creusot, remained a CPA throughout the Third Republic.

The formation of SAs jumped to an annual average of 380 for the period 1868–97 and to 953 for the period 1898–1913. The SA became almost de rigueur for any large enterprise and convenient for medium-sized enterprise (capitalized from 1 million to 5 million francs). With each passing generation there was an inexorable tendency for large and medium-sized family enterprises, which had been proprietorships, partnerships, or CPAs, to adopt the SA form, especially since it was not incompatible with family control and offered the advantage of separating the family's wealth from the vicissitudes of the enterprise.

The dominance of the corporation over financial and industrial enterprises and the strong foothold it had acquired in commerce gave rise to a debate, particularly acute from the 1880s to 1914, over the nature and role of the corporation. The collapse of the speculative boom of 1879–81 brought about an attempt to establish elaborate safeguards over the creation of SAs in order to crack down on speculation and fraudulent promotions. Some questioned the efficiency of large corporate enterprise; others feared the consequences of concentration of economic power.

Partisans of the corporation supported further liberalization of company law (following the example of Belgium or England), arguing that the SA was indispensable to economic growth and that rather than being a means of concentration of economic power, the SA would democratize the economy by diffusion of shareholding among all classes.

Although the restrictionists held the upper hand in the 1880s, the tide turned in the 1890s. The law of 1 August 1893, a modest reform, lowered the minimum par value of shares from 500 to 100 francs for larger companies and from 100 to 25 francs for small ones—to expand the benefits of shareholding to almost everyone—and eliminated the provisions of the 1867 law, which provided exorbitant penalties for failure to observe certain formalities at the time a company was founded. From the 1880s on, public policy tolerated the development of cartels, usually in the form of common sales agencies (*comptoirs*) that set production quotas, on the grounds that these introduced production and price stability in place of the anarchy of the market. While the government acquiesced in the creation of large financial and industrial corporations, and in the formation of cartels among them, the appearance of large commercial SAs (such as department stores) was a cause for great concern and resulted in tax and other legislation discriminating against them in favor of *les petits*.

The most important innovation in company law during the Third Republic was the introduction of the *Société à responsabilité limitée* (SARL), which permitted the extension of limited liability to even the smallest partnerships and family enterprises. Based on the German law of 1892, the SARL was introduced into France, via Alsace-Lorraine, in 1925. The SARL proved to be an instantaneous success, as small business rushed to take advantage of the shelter of limited liability. For the period 1926–38, over 84,000 SARLs were founded, an average of more than 6,400 per year.

Increasing concentration in the financial and industrial sectors and the proliferation of small commercial enterprises underlay many of the domestic tensions and conflicts of the later Third Republic.

F. Caron and J. Bouvier, in F. Braudel and E. Labrousse, eds., *Histoire économique et sociale de la France*, vol. 4 (Paris, 1979); J. Houssiaux, *Le Pouvoir de monopole* (Paris, 1955); G. Ripert, *Aspects juridiques du capitalisme moderne* (Paris, 1946).

C. E. Freedeman

Related entries: BANKS AND BANKING; COMMERCE: DEPARTMENT STORES; COMMERCE; RETAIL MERCHANTS.

BUSINESSMEN. The category *businessman* encompassed a wide variety of entrepreneurial activity during the Third Republic. The village grocer and the director of a Parisian department store, the local notary and the millionaire banker were all businessmen. Diversity arose from different types of economic activity such as commerce, manufacture, transportation, service, and finance. Within each of these activities, businessmen were further distinguished by form of enterprise, sector, scale of operation, geographic location, scope of market, level of technology, and managerial style. Even religion divided businessmen. The pious Catholic textile manufacturers of the Nord, for example, marked themselves off from the clannish Protestant industrialists and bankers known as the *haute société protestante*.

Of all these distinctions perhaps the most fundamental was the scale of enterprise. A few large-scale enterprises functioned among a multitude of small- and medium-sized firms. Such a dual structure is not uncommon in industrial economies, but in the Third Republic the proportions were one-sided and certainly more durable than elsewhere. As late as 1906 the census showed a swarm of tiny firms in the food, wood, and clothing trades. In representative manufacturing sectors like textiles and automobiles, business was widely dispersed among medium- and small-scale companies. There were, for example, 86 woolen manufacturers in Roubaix, the center of this industry, while nationwide some 150 companies assembled automobiles. Only in a few sectors like mining and metals did large-scale enterprise dominate at the turn of the century. France had 13 truly big firms (over 5,000 employees) in 1896 and only 44 as late as 1931. But even these giants were often dwarfs when compared to their British, German, or U.S. counterparts.

Despite this diversity businessmen shared a common belief in the virtues, if not the sanctity, of individual effort, the free market, and a hierarchy of responsibility culminating in the authority of the employer. This individualism, or liberal economic philosophy, was expressed in a passion for secrecy about business affairs and in a deep suspicion of competitors, trade unions, and the state. Self-discipline in the form of cartels, however, did not violate this libertarian code. Nor did protection from the state.

Within the overall structure of society, businessmen ranged from the lowest to the highest ranks of the bourgeoisie. At the level of the boutique distinctions with the working class were blurred. At the other extreme, the fortunes of some bankers, merchants, and industrialists eclipsed those of the landed aristocracy. And with vast wealth came power. Yet wealth itself was insufficient for the acquisition of status in this traditionally stratified society. High social standing also required education, family, manners, and a certain style of life. As an occupation, business was still associated with pecuniary self-interest. During the Republic the most eminent business families could not command the prestige of the titled aristocracy. It was characteristic of French society that though it was seemingly obsessed with the pursuit of wealth, it was also slow to grant deference to the *nouveaux riches*.

Until the last two decades of the Third Republic, the most representative type of enterprise was the family firm or partnership. Limited liability companies arrived slowly and concentrated in a few sectors like railways or utilities. This was the era of entrepreneurial or family capitalism. The family-owned and -operated textile mill was the archetype of this kind of entrreprise. Here the individual talents of the owner-manager determined success or failure, and family interests and status were closely identified with the fortunes of the enterprise.

Even many big companies in newer industries or trades began as family firms. Thus the Boucicauts blended innovative forms of mass retailing with old-fashioned paternalism in the Bon Marché department store.

Paternalism, which took the form of such practices as company housing, medical care, and pension programs, was typical of French employers in the early Third Republic. Even such a massive operation as the iron and steel works at Le Creusot, including the town government, was run as a private patrimony by the Schneider family. The ubiquitous family firm contributed to this style of industrial relations since it was assumed labor and management were members of the extended economic family guided by a patriarchal employer. There were, of course, other reasons besides the form of enterprise that explain this paternalistic strategy. The need, for example, of holding scarce skilled labor by developing identification with and dependence on the enterprise also contributed. Given the strength of paternalism, it should come as no surprise that French employers on the whole were determined opponents of trade unions. In more anonymous forms of organization, where family control never existed or had disappeared, a strong authoritarian and bureaucratic strain characterized French management. The Napoleonic model of centralized and hierarchical authority was representative of the newer corporations. In these managerial firms the *président-directeur général* concentrated authority much as the owner did in the family firm.

Over the seven decades of the Republic, the traditional *patronat* gradually lost ground. After 1900 the importance of family and inherited wealth declined as the social basis for the recruitment of business leaders. Even before 1900 in sectors like railroads and mining and later in the burgeoning newer industries like chemicals, electricity, and oil, the business elite became populated by experts, especially graduates of technical schools. Professional salaried managers replaced members of entrepreneurial families and the older elite of merchants and bankers in directing business. Top employers became more highly educated. Between 1890 and 1920 in particular, there was a substantial influx of engineers. This professionalization of the *patronat* did not mark, however, a true democratization since employers continued to be drawn narrowly from the upper social strata. Recruitment opened slowly, but privilege still determined access to the business elite.

Changing recruitment patterns were linked to a more profound shift in business. From 1890 on managerial capitalism tended to replace entrepreneurial or family capitalism. Although it occurred belatedly in France when compared with other advanced economies, the modern, integrated corporation run by a hierarchy of managers made its appearance in certain sectors. The increasing scale, pace, and complexity of business activity and the need to secure resources and markets in advance were some of the reasons for the rise of this new type of enterprise. Where such firms already dominated U.S. business by 1920, they had made their debut in France only by the interwar years and then often in the form of loosely articulated holding companies rather than vertically integrated corporations. While entrepreneurial capitalism continued to be the most typical form of French enterprise, managerial capitalism was on its way to gaining control of many strategic industrial sectors.

Under the Republic businessmen were loosely organized as a community of interests. Their diversity and individualism resulted in a poorly developed institutional structure. Weak associational life characterized business as it did labor. Trade associations developed relatively late, and when they did surge forward after 1890, they were, with few exceptions, facades without substance. Employers organized mainly in self-defense against the dangers posed by trade unions, foreign competition, or the state. While businessmen might mobilize for broad economic or social goals, they rarely collaborated successfully in sharing markets or setting prices. Cartels, for example, proliferated, but they were notoriously fragile and short-lived. A peak employers' association, the Confédération générale de la production française, was formed, but only in 1919 and then in response to the government's initiative. This body encompassed too many competing interests for it to speak with a loud voice. Real power remained with a few specialized trade associations like the Union des industries métallurgiques et minières, which often also functioned as cartels. A lack of solidarity, or what was called the *poussière patronale*, hounded the business class and hampered its effectiveness as an interest group.

Business was well treated by the Republic without ever commanding much respect. Several notorious scandals such as the Panama affair of 1892–93 involved the corruption of politicians by business lobbyists. The Left suspected the business elite of sinister plutocratic powers. In the interwar years, for example, the 200 Families (the largest shareholders of the Bank of France) allegedly checked the efforts of left-wing governments and subsidized fascist movements. Most of these allegations of business conspiracy were unfounded or exaggerated, as were the charges that business controlled national elections or political parties. Yet fear of the plutocracy's antidemocratic inclinations and its alleged interference was sufficiently credible to help mobilize voters against the Right and arouse small businessmen against the *mur d'argent* in the election of 1936.

For its part big business did not view the Republic as a sympathetic regime. The mildly leftist complexion of many governments between 1900 and 1914 worried business. Heavy industry, when it compared its situation with that of its rivals in imperial Germany, believed the Republic lacked a coherent industrial policy. Similarly in the 1920s French employers saw the United States as far more responsive to business interests than the French Republic. Perhaps this perception of an indifferent republic was part of the *patronat*'s inferiority complex, its abiding sense of being disadvantaged with respect to resources and markets. Whatever the reason, there is a paradox. In spite of perceptions of an apathetic republic, the interests of business were well guarded. There was relatively little legislation that could be construed as antibusiness. Social programs that might have burdened business rarely became law, and the rules against cartels were unenforced. Small business, in particular, enjoyed a privileged position. When lobbies sought protection, the regime tended to accommodate them with tax breaks, subsidies, and tariffs. On the election of the first Socialist premier in 1936–37, business panicked. Many employers believed government and labor were about to liquidate their authority. As it turned out, this Popular Front government, like its predecessors, did very little to weaken the position of capital.

A persistent controversy about business under the republic has been generated by the charge of Malthusianism. Critics accuse businessmen of a lack of true entrepreneurial spirit. According to this view businessmen lost their taste for venture, shirked investment, relied on the sheltered domestic market, and sought protection from the state whenever they were in distress. This deficiency of entrepreneurship, labeled *Malthusian* after the pessimistic doctrines of Thomas Malthus, is held responsible for the relative decline of the French economy. Whereas France may have been the world's second industrial power as late as 1870, it forfeited this high standing before the turn of the century. By the end of the Republic the economy suffered from a low level of concentration, a dearth of plant capacity, obsolescent equipment, and reduced international competitiveness. Responsibility for this relative backwardness rests, according to critics, with anemic entrepreneurship.

Recent historiography has challenged this contention and diminished, without entirely eliminating, its force as a causal explanation for economic decline. As a stereotype the Malthusian reputation of businessmen is inaccurate in several ways. First, on a per capita basis the French economy grew between 1870 and 1930 on a par with that of Great Britain and Germany. Moreover, within this period there were surges of expansion, such as the one between 1895 and 1913, that contradict a consistent Malthusian pattern. Second, it has been argued that, given economic circumstances, the *patronat* performed well. The multitude of small firms, for example, filled the need for specialized products and volatile consumer tastes in widely dispersed local markets. These firms, furthermore, employed a labor force known for its artisanal skills. Later, with the gathering momentum of economic concentration, small firms continued to multiply because they served as subcontractors for large concerns. Similarly, it can be argued, French exporters wisely avoided trying to break into world markets where they lacked comparative advantage; instead they continued to sell more traditional luxury items. In this view French entrepreneurs adapted to circumstances, seized available opportunities, and gradually introduced appropriate techniques and products. A third line of argument points out that the Malthusian model underestimates the entrepreneurial talent of a steadily growing minority of business leaders after 1890. If in periods of economic attraction like the 1880s or the 1930s Malthusians set the pace, then in cycles of expansion like the years prior to 1914 or the decade after 1919 a dynamic *patronat* was in charge. *Patronats* tended to work in newer industries like automobiles, chemicals, and electricity. They owed more to the technocratic inspiration of Henri de Saint-Simon than to the gloomy theories of Malthus. In the 1920s, for example, these managers expanded the scale of production, put together mergers, introduced mass production, adopted the latest technology, and redefined managerial authority.

The accomplishments of managers like André Citroën and Ernest Mercier contradict a Malthusian stereotype.

Responsibility for whatever backwardness existed in the economy on the eve of the Second World War must be shared. While the economy's overall performance was not impressive, businessmen alone were not at fault. They faced severe constraints, especially those set by a slowly developing and highly fragmented domestic market. Relatively high production costs and high barriers to entry in many export markets were also handicaps. And each period of expansion like that of 1895–1913 or the 1920s was cut short by external forces like war or global depression. For its part labor tended to resist changes such as Taylorism, which streamlined the production process. Nor did the state do much to promote industrial or commercial development. Thus Malthusian entrepreneurship will not suffice as the causal explanation for the economy's performance.

Business nevertheless cannot escape responsibility altogether. The lags and weaknesses that had accumulated by 1940 were real enough, and entrepreneurs are supposed to lead. The conservative temperament of most businessmen was exposed by a pattern of failure for those aggressive entrepreneurs who tried to change prevailing attitudes among employers. Businessmen, like most other Frenchmen under the Third Republic, were unwilling to plunge into the unknown of an industrial society. To most, economic progress meant growth with stability. It meant all kinds of enterprise, big and small, efficient and marginal, marching forward without displacing one another. Factory chimneys, a proletarianizedwork force, and global trading were not elements of the French vision of a healthy economy. When prosperity flagged in the 1930s, business became defensive. One dynamic and reflective manager of the time observed that businessmen thought of France as a *pays de bonheur* rather than as a *grand pays*. At heart they did not want to compete against industrial conquerors like the Germans or the Americans. They preferred, according to this observer, a happy mediocrity to the risk, upheaval, and self-discipline that global competitiveness entailed. If a Malthusian stereotype is false, the basic conservatism of most businessmen, which turned into pessimism and rigidity in the 1930s, is not.

By 1940 the business community was heading in a new direction. The momentum for overhaul had been gathering for decades, but it would require a military defeat, foreign occupation, and massive destruction before the need for change became compelling. Deficiencies had been noticed as early as the 1890s, but only from the First World War on was there a discernible movement among employers for renovation. In the 1920s progressive managers organized to move France toward a high-consumption, American-style, standard of living and championed such innovations as mass marketing and high wage policies. These neoliberals shed old-fashioned paternalism and endorsed a measure of enlightened state intervention. In the 1930s the failure of the self-adjusting mechanisms of the market convinced these managers of the need for national economic planning as a means of guiding and expanding economic activity. A growing minority of the business elite during the last years of the Republic widened their perspective, shed their conservatism, and moved toward a partnership with public authorities. The historian can see in the Third Republic, especially after 1920, a stage of preparation for the great transformation that was to come when the French businessman traded his Malthusian reputation for that of a technocrat.

J. Boudet, *Le Monde des affaires* (Paris, 1952); J. Bouvier et al., *Histoire économique et sociale de la France*, vols. 1–2 (Paris, 1979–80); F. Caron, *An Economic History of Modern France* (New York, 1979); E. Carter et al., eds., *Enterprise and Entrepreneurs in Nineteenth- and Twentiety-Century France* (Baltimore, 1976); H. W. Ehrmann, *Organized Business in France* (Princeton, 1957); A. François-Poncet, *La Vie et l'oeuvre de Robert Pinot* (Paris, 1927); P. Fridenson, *Histoire des usines Renault* (Paris, 1972), and "Le Patronat," in *La France et les français en 1938–1939* (Paris, 1978); J.-N. Jeanneney, *L'Argent caché* (Paris, 1981); R. F. Kuisel, "Business History in France," *Business and Economic History* (Urbana, Ill., 1978), *Capitalism and the State in Modern France* (Cambridge, England, 1981), and *Ernest Mercier* (Berkeley, 1967); D. S. Landes, "French Entrepreneurship and Industrial Growth in the Nineteenth Century," *Journal of Economic History* 9 (1949); G. Lefranc, *Les Organisations patronales en France* (Paris, 1976); M. Lévy-Leboyer, "The Large Corporation in Modern France," in *Managerial Hierarchies* (Cambridge, Mass., 1980), and "Le Patronat français, 1912–1973," in *Le Patronat de la seconde industrialisation* (Paris, 1979); M. Miller, *The Bon Marché* (Princeton, 1981).

R. F. Kuisel

Related entries: BUSINESS ORGANIZATION; CITROEN; COMMERCE: RETAIL MERCHANTS; INDUSTRY: FORMS OF PRODUCTION; MERCIER; SAINT-SIMONISM; SHOPKEEPERS; WORKERS, INDUSTRIAL.

C

CACHIN, MARCEL (1869–1958), journalist, politician, socialist, then communist, leader. He was born in 1869 in Paimpol (Côtes-du-Nord) to a poor, piously Catholic Breton family of peasant stock; his father was a gendarme. Outstanding as a pupil, Cachin was guided by his teachers into the lycée, given a classical education, and matriculated at the University of Bordeaux in 1890 where he studied classical languages and philosophy. He was very early attracted to socialist student groups and came under the spell of Jules Guesde, whose loyal disciple he remained through the First World War. A founding member of Guesde's Parti ouvrier in Bordeaux, Cachin abandoned a promising academic career in 1895 to devote himself to party organizing, first for the Parti ouvrier, and then for the unified Socialist party (SFIO) after 1904. Cachin quickly rose to the leadership in Paris, debating Jean Jaurès as a representative of the Guesdist faction in 1903, serving as a delegate at the International Congress of Amsterdam in 1904, and becoming known as a skilled propagandist and expert on peasant questions. He was first elected to parliament in 1910, but his seat was invalidated. He nevertheless served as secretary to the Socialist parliamentary group from 1911 and won election again in 1914, serving in parliament thereafter with only one peacetime interruption until his death in 1958.

Cachin's simple, modest, and courteous manner made him a favorite for delicate missions involving persuasion. A firm partisan of the *union sacrée* during World War I, Cachin was sent to Italy in April 1915 to convince or bribe a maverick Italian socialist named Benito Mussolini to support his country's entry into the war. In 1917 Cachin went to revolutionary Russia in an effort to persuade the Russian socialists not to abandon their war effort. Cachin's most critical mission came in May 1920 when, as director of the socialist newspaper *L'Humanité*, he accompanied Louis-Oscar Frossard to Moscow to report back to the French on the Bolshevik experience. Once in Moscow, Cachin abandoned Guesde for Lenin, becoming an unconditional partisan of the Third International and, at age fifty-one, a founding member of the French Communist party. The only ranking socialist leader to join the Communist party in 1920, Cachin became a venerated figure who, although occasionally suspect as an intellectual with a social-democratic past, nevertheless symbolized the party's claim to continuity with the French revolutionary tradition.

Cachin was a member of the Communist party's political bureau, a deputy, and director of the party organ *L'Humanité* through the interwar period and after. He was primarily a propagandist, however, and disdained factional conflict. He was never an organizer in the party's inner council or a candidate for the top leadership, like Maurice Thorez or Jacques Duclos. Cachin was twice imprisoned: for opposing the Ruhr campaign and supporting the Rif rebellion. He was shunted aside during the sectarian period when the party was led by Henri Barbé and Pierre Célor (1929–31) but became an avid party spokesman during the Popular Front (1936–38). He served in the executive of the Communist International from 1935 to 1939 and simultaneously won election to the Senate, the first Communist to enter that body. A loyal Communist until his death, Cachin was never known to have expressed any hesitation about following the numerous twists and turns in his party's line. He joined in the personality cults of Josef Stalin and Thorez, and naively sang the praises of the USSR while serving as the National Assembly's *doyen d'âge* after the war. Throngs attended his funeral in February 1958.

M. Hertzog-Cachin, *Regards sur la vie de Marcel Cachin* (Paris, 1980); M. Cachin, *Marcel Cachin vous parle* (Paris, 1959).

I. M. Wall

Related entries: COMMUNIST PARTY; GUESDISTS; LAVIGNE; SOCIAL-IST PARTY.

CAGOULE PLOT (November 1937). The Comité secret d'action révolutionnaire (CSAR), or Cagoules ("hooded ones"), as it was jokingly called by Maurice Pujo (a leader of the Action française), was an anticommunist, anti-Jewish, antiparliamentary, secret right-wing terrorist organization created by Eugène Deloncle. Dissatisfied with the Action française's insistence on legality, Deloncle patterned the CSAR after the general staff and subdivided it into cells, complete with codes, rituals, passwords, and disguises. Aided by high-ranking army officers, it was financed by leading French capitalists and industrialists. The CSAR drew up elaborate plans, utilizing the Parisian sewer system to overthrow the Republic and replace it with a Mussolini-type fascist state. The military arm of the CSAR conducted assassinations for the Italians, sabotaged operations for Franco's Spain, and acted as agents provocateurs by bombing the buildings of employers' associations in France. A related army organization, the Corvignolles, was formed by Marshal Philippe Pétain's aide, Commandant Georges Loustaunau-Lacau, to purge the army of suspected communists, but it refused to join the CSAR. Alerted to the existence of the CSAR by a mysterious "lady in black" following the execution of one of its traitors, the police made their first arrests in November 1937. In response, a coup was scheduled for the night of 15–16 November, but

Deloncle lost his nerve when he did not receive the active support of the army. A two-year investigation uncovered seven CSAR arms caches (one that blew up), but prosecution of the conspirators was delayed by the coming of war. After the fall of France (1940), some Cagoules fought on the Free French side, but most were active around Pétain in Vichy. Deloncle was killed by the Gestapo, but other Cagoulards (notably Joseph Darnand of the Milice) collaborated actively. A 1948 trial of Cagoule survivors resulted in few convictions.

P. Bourdrel, *La Cagoule* (Paris, 1970); H. Charbonneau, *Les Mémoires de Porthos* (Paris, 1967); G. Loustaunau-Lacau, *Mémoires d'un français rebelle* (Paris, 1948).

M. L. Mickelsen

Related entries: ACTION FRANCAISE; ANTI-SEMITISM; CAMELOTS DU ROI; CROIX DE FEU; FASCISM; LA ROCQUE; PETAIN; RIGHT, THE.

CAILLAUX, JOSEPH (1863–1944), fiscal reformer, minister of finance, premier, and senator. He was born in Le Mans on 30 March 1863 the son of Eugène Caillaux, an Orleanist deputy, who was minister of finance in the *Seize mai* 1877 cabinet of duc Albert de Broglie. After a ten-year career as inspector of finance, Joseph entered politics as a moderate republican and was elected to the Chamber of Deputies from his father's former district of Mamers in 1898. The following year, he was appointed minister of finance in the cabinet of René Waldeck-Rousseau. In this capacity he effected minor reforms in indirect taxation.

In 1903 Caillaux published his major work, *Les Impôts en France*, in which he argued that the fiscal burden on the productive elements of society had to be lightened and some of it transferred to those who lived on unearned income. The chief vehicle for such reform was to be the income tax, which Caillaux duly presented to parliament as finance minister in the Georges Clemenceau government in February 1907. Despite strong opposition from moderate and conservative deputies, the bill was passed by the Chamber in March 1909.

On becoming premier on 30 June 1911, Caillaux was initially diverted from domestic politics by the sudden appearance in Agadir of a German gunboat, the *Panther*. After negotiating a colonial settlement with Germany, he presented his domestic program in November 1911. It included subsidies to low-rent housing, aid to food cooperatives, and greater state control over railways. Opposition to this program from moderate elements within his own parliamentary majority led to Caillaux's resignation on 10 January 1912, ostensibly over the negotiations with Germany.

Conservative and moderate opposition to Caillaux's fiscal and economic reforms had the effect of driving him further to the left. In October 1913, as the newly elected president of the Radical-Socialists, he pushed through the party congress a program identical to that of the Socialist party (SFIO) in two important respects: opposition to the three-year law and a call for passage of the income tax by the Senate. An electoral alliance with the Socialists in the general elections of May 1914 enabled both parties to register significant gains. Caillaux was prevented from becoming premier, however, by his wife's fatal shooting, on 16 March

1914, of Gaston Calmette, editor-in-chief of *Le Figaro*, following the latter's vitriolic slander campaign against him. Mme. Caillaux was acquitted of murder on 28 July 1914, thereby releasing her husband for further political activity. But the war, and the government of *Union sacrée* that it fostered, prevented the formation of a leftist ministry in France at that time.

Caillaux's wartime contacts with German agents in order to seek a negotiated peace led to his imprisonment and trial for treason before the Senate in April 1920. Although acquitted of treason, he was found guilty of "harm to the external security of the state" and deprived of his civic rights for five years. He returned to politics as minister of finance under Paul Painlevé in 1925 but was unable to restore confidence in the franc or arrive at a settlement of the war debt issue. As a senator, Caillaux opposed the economic policy of the Popular Front government. During the Second World War, he wrote his memoirs, laying great stress on his role as peacemaker, while avoiding political contact with Vichy. He died at his home in Mamers on 22 November 1944.

J.-C. Allain, *Joseph Caillaux: Le Défi victorieux, 1863–1914* (Paris, 1978); R. Binion, *Defeated Leaders: The Political Fate of Caillaux, Jouvenel, and Tardieu* (New York, 1960); J. Caillaux, *Mes Mémoires*, 3 vols. (Paris, 1943); A. Fabre-Luce, *Caillaux* (Paris, 1933); F. Seager, "Joseph Caillaux as Premier, 1911–1912: The Dilemma of a Liberal Reformer," *French Historical Studies* 11 (1979).

F. H. Seager

Related entries: CLEMENCEAU; GERMANY, RELATIONS WITH (1914–1940); JAURES; RADICAL AND RADICAL-SOCIALIST PARTY; WORLD WAR I, FRANCE'S ROLE IN.

CAMBON, JULES (1845–1935), administrator, diplomat. Licensed in law (1866), he saw active service as a captain in the Garde mobile during the siege of Paris (1870–71). He rose rapidly thereafter to occupy with distinction a series of prominent posts: prefect of Constantine (1878–79); secretary-general at the prefecture of Police, Paris (1879–82); prefect of the Nord (1882–87) and the Rhône (1887–91); governor-general of Algeria (1891–97); ambassador to the United States (1897–1902), Spain (1902–7), and Germany (1907–14); first secretary-general at the Foreign Ministry (October 1915–December 1917); plenipotentiary (one of France's five) at the Paris Peace Conference (1919–20); and president of the Conference of Ambassadors (1920–31), which supervised application of the treaties. In Washington he served as Spain's designated intermediary in arranging the armistice ending the Spanish-American War (1898), in Madrid engaged in negotiations concerning the Franco-Spanish Agreement on Morocco (1904) and the Algeciras Conference (1906), and in Berlin earned high regard in negotiations surrounding the Casablanca Deserters affair (1908), the Bosnian crisis (1908–9), the Franco-German Morocco Treaty (1909), the Agadir crisis (1911)—which he considered his most signal service toward keeping the peace—and the crisis of July 1914. Although deeply patriotic, he sincerely desired good relations with Germany and worried about the influence of bellicose elements in both countries. His warnings about German military preparations (1912–13) greatly influenced his government's advocacy of the three years' service bill. At the Peace Conference he chaired the commissions on Polish, Czechoslovak, and Greek and Albanian affairs, but he exerted at most a modest influence on policy.

With his older brother Paul (at London) and Camille Barrère (Rome), he was one of the triumvirate that crowned France's exceptionally able diplomatic corps from the 1890s into the 1920s. He was a model professional of the old school: polished, tactful, patient, seasoned in judgment, adroit and dryly humorous, with a daunting fund of dignified self-esteem to match his talents and high offices.

J.-M. Cambon, *The Diplomatist* (London, 1931); F. Charles-Roux, *Trois ambassades française à la veille de la guerre* (Paris, 1928); G. R. Tabouis, *The Life of Jules Cambon* (London, 1938).

D. S. Newhall

Related entries: BARRERE; CAMBON, P.; GERMANY, RELATIONS WITH; MOROCCAN CRISES; OVERSEAS EMPIRE: COLONIAL ADMINISTRATION; PREFECTS; SPAIN, RELATIONS WITH; UNITED STATES, RELATIONS WITH.

CAMBON, PAUL (1843–1924), civil servant, Tunisian proconsul, and ambassador. Cambon was born 20 January 1843 at Paris. He and his younger brother Jules followed parallel careers as prefects, colonial administrators, and diplomats. Jules Ferry, mayor of Paris in September 1870, made Paul Cambon his secretary. Cambon's early career advanced with that of his mentor. In 1882 Cambon became resident-minister in Tunisia, where he regularized the 1881 protectorate. When he left Tunis in 1886, French rule there had become stable. Cambon served as ambassador to Spain (1886–91), Turkey (1891–98), and England (1898–1920). In the course of events and from the perspective of each of these posts, his views of the European power balance evolved. But his policy was constant: to build alliances for France that would protect it against humiliation (such as had followed diplomatic isolation in 1870). As ambassador Cambon tried to guide weak foreign ministers; he worked with strong ones as a collaborator.

He arrived at London during the Fashoda crisis, which Théophile Delcassé soon resolved. One must not exaggerate Cambon's initiative during the period from Fashoda to the conclusion of the 1904 Entente cordiale, for he visited Delcassé frequently. Nonetheless, these years saw Cambon shrewdly, patiently, and meticulously bring the two countries to an understanding; on that foundation he built an alliance. An exchange of visits by Edward VII and President Emile Loubet in 1903 symbolized the rapprochement between the former colonial rivals. The Entente resolved overseas differences between them, particularly regarding respective interests in Egypt and Morocco. Cambon helped preserve the Entente following the Dogger Bank incident (involving England with France's ally Russia) and during the 1905 Moroccan crisis (intended by Germany to wreck the Entente). Cambon encouraged Anglo-French military staff talks, as well as the conclusion of England's 1907 Persian-Afghanistan Agreement with Russia. Foreign Secretary Sir Edward Grey resisted French bids for a firmer military commitment, but in 1912 naval talks brought the issue into sharper focus and led to an exchange of letters engaging England's honor. During the crisis of July 1914, Cambon pressed the faltering Grey to stand by his country's commitment to the alliance that now existed. During the war Cambon continued at London. He observed peacemaking at Paris uncomfortably in 1919. He retired in December 1920 and died at Paris 28 May 1924.

P. Cambon, *Les Conditions du travail en Espagne* (Paris, 1890), and *Correspondance, 1870–1924*, 3 vols., ed. H. Cambon (Paris, 1940–46); H. Cambon, *Histoire de la Régence de Tunis* (Paris, 1948), and *Paul Cambon, ambassadeur de France* (Paris, 1937); K. Eubank, *Paul Cambon, Master Diplomatist* (Norman, Okla., 1960).

J. D. O'Donnell

Related entries: CAMBON, J.; DELCASSE; ENTENTE CORDIALE; FASHODA INCIDENT; FERRY; FRANCO-PRUSSIAN WAR; GREAT BRITAIN, RELATIONS WITH; LOUBET; MOROCCAN CRISES; OVERSEAS EMPIRE: TUNISIA; PARIS PEACE CONFERENCE; SPAIN, RELATIONS WITH.

CAMELINAT, ZEPHERIN (1840–1932), Parisian labor and socialist activist, communard, and later a member of the Socialist party (SFIO) and the Communist party (CP). Born in the Yonne department, the son of a wine grower and stonecutter, Camélinat went to Paris at age seventeen, where he became a bronze worker. He was an early member of the First International Workingmen's Association. He was tried and imprisoned for his activities in the International but resumed his political activity during the Paris Commune, for which he became director of the mint. With the fall of the Commune, he fled to England, where he remained until 1880. In the legislative elections of 1885, he won a seat for the Seine department and joined the small group of socialists who actively defended workers' causes in the Chamber. He was not reelected in 1889 and failed on other occasions to win public office. As a member of the SFIO and, after 1920, the CP, he became an elder statesman of working-class politics, revered for his early militancy. At his death in March 1932 he was given a hero's funeral.

J. Maitron, ed., *Dictionnaire biographique du mouvement ouvrier français*, vol. 11 (Paris, 1974).

T. Moodie

Related entries: COMMUNARDS; COMMUNE OF PARIS; COMMUNIST PARTY; SOCIALIST PARTY.

CAMELOTS DU ROI (1908–1936), a paramilitary group that acted as the tactical arm of the royalist Ligue d'action française. The title *Camelots du roi* (often sarcastically spelled, with intended archaism, *Camelots du roy*) translates as "street vendors of the king." The group was formed in 1908 by a union of Action française students and a group of vendors of royalist newspapers. Although the Camelots were presided over by Maxime Réal del Sarte and Marius Plateau (until his death in 1923), their real chief was Maurice Pujo. In 1910 an elite corps of Commissaires was created for more reliable or demanding service.

The functions of the Camelots included hawking the daily *Action française* (which could itself involve conflict with other vendors), protecting royalist meetings and disrupting those of opponents, as well as directing violence against politicians (and statues of politicians) hated by the Ligue. Although they occasionally fought alongside other right-wing leagues, as at the wrecking of an international disarmament congress in Paris in 1931 and the brutal quashing of an autonomist meeting in Colmar in 1926, the Camelots more often worked alone or with the Etudiants d'action française who helped them dominate the Latin Quarter between the wars.

The Camelots slapped some republican politicians (Aristide Briand in 1910), assaulted others (Marc Sangnier), and intimidated many more. They broke up pacifist meetings, blocked the showing of films and plays they considered unpatriotic, smashed the premises of hostile newspapers, and disrupted university lectures. Camelot weapons included the ubiquitous cane (often armed), clubs, smoke and stink bombs, castor oil (for purges), and their own jeering songs. Membership was mixed, ranging from well-born youths and students, to shop clerks, employees, and skilled workers. Although the Camelots probably never exceeded 1,500 for the Paris area, their organization and discipline and the imaginativeness of their tactics gave them a force beyond their numbers. The Camelots du roi were dissolved by government order, along with the rest of the Ligue, in 1936 following an attack on Léon Blum by Action française sympathizers.

Through their regular intimidation of foes both in and out of government, the Camelots were the most fascist element in the generally reactionary Ligue and can be seen as pioneers of fascist paramilitary tactics. As such, they contributed heavily to the creation of a climate of violence and interclass hatred in Third Republic France.

E. Nolte, *Three Faces of Fascism* (New York, 1969); M. Pujo, *Les Camelots du roi* (Paris, 1933); E. Weber, *Action Française, Royalism and Reaction in Twentieth-Century France* (Stanford, 1962).

A. Douglas

Related entries: ACTION FRANCAISE; FASCISM.

CANADA, RELATIONS WITH. Relations were principally cultural and economic, since Canada was a British colony until it gained dominion status by the Treaty of Westminster in 1932. From the Second Empire on, France maintained consulates at Quebec and Montreal. By 1914, seven others had been added at Halifax, Chatham and St. John (New Brunswick), Toronto, Winnipeg, Vancouver, and Victoria. By 1882, in turn, Canada established a nondiplomatic commissioner-general in Paris to foster French commerce, investment, and emigration. A Canadian-French tariff and commercial treaty, the first treaty negotiated by Canadians with a foreign power, was ratified in 1895. The treaty provided both countries with most favored nation status. In 1928, the commissioner-general became a full-fledged diplomatic representative, an action that had quickly followed the establishment of diplomatic relations with the United States.

The Canadian hopes for French investment never came to much. With 85 percent of foreign investment composed of British and American capital, French investment never constituted more than 5 percent of the total. By 1902, France had only 138 million francs invested in Canada, roughly the same amount invested in Denmark and Venezuela. That investment was focused on railroads and street railways, hydroelectrical power, and mining.

French immigration to Canada was even less successful than investment. French Canadians hoped to attract massive numbers of Francophones to offset the flood of immigrants into English Canada, but economic opportunity in the Francophone province of Quebec was slight from the Long Depression (1880s) to the Great Depression (1930s). No more than 2,000 or 3,000 Frenchmen dribbled into Canada each year, and the total number living in Canada at one time never exceeded 25,000. Frenchmen preferred to emigrate to the more lucrative fields of North Africa or South America. A few thousand Frenchmen did settle either as professionals in Quebec or as farmers on the Canadian prairies, particularly near Winnipeg, where they rapidly assimilated into English Canada. The Associations Law of 1901 brought 2,000 French clerics to Quebec, where they met a critical staffing shortage in schools and hospitals. Indeed, by 1914 one-seventh of the members of Quebec's religious orders were of French origin.

Unhelpful in attracting French immigrants was Frenchman Louis Hemon's novel on French Canada, *Maria Chapdelaine* (1916). Its depiction of struggle against the harsh nature of the late nineteenth-century Quebec pioneer region of Lac St. Jean made the novel one of France's best-sellers in the twentieth century. At the same time, it surely reinforced Voltaire's view that Canada was merely *quelques arpents de neige*. The most celebrated French work on Canada was André Siegfried's *Le Canada, les deux races* (1906), a scholarly analysis of French-English relations.

Probably the most important connection between France and Canada was cultural and ideological. This was made possible by the existence of 3 million Francophone Canadians constituting almost 30 percent of Canada's total population by the end of the Third Republic. Because of the language tie, French Canadian intellectual and political leaders frequently studied in or visited France, closely followed French intellectual and political life, and were influenced by it. Province of Quebec premiers regularly visited France after 1880, as did Wilfred Laurier (1841–1919), the first French-Canadian prime minister of Canada (1896–1911). By the 1880s the Quebec French-language press was served by telegraphic reports from Agence Havas. The poetry of Louis Frechette (1839–1908) was honored by the Académie française. *La Vérité* of journalist Jules Tardival (1851–1905) was so closely associated with the French ultramontane press and the efforts of Leo Taxil that it occasionally broke stories too sensitive for initial Parisian publication. The French ties of Henri Bourassa (1868–1952), a principal nationalist leader and founder-editor of the influential daily newspaper, *Le Devoir*, extended from the pre–World War I *Libre Parole* to the Fédération Républicaine of the 1930s. Yet Bourassa opposed Canada's entry into World War I and led opposition to conscription in 1917. Nationalist historian and journalist Lionel Groulx (1878–1967) founded a separatist Quebec Action française sympathetic to the French organization of the same name until its papal condemnation. Especially influential in French Canada during the Third Republic were such thinkers as Louis Veuillot, Joseph de Maistre, Paul Bourget, René Bazin, Jacques Maritain, and Emmanuel Mounier.

In this association, French Canadians regularly pointed out to France that they were loyal to French culture and British rule. While French Canadians could deplore the German victory at Sedan, they had no enthusiasm for the principles of 1789 in either their Opportunist or Radical incarnations or for defending either Britain or France in World War I, despite considerable French propaganda to the contrary.

Colloque: Les relations entre la France et le Canada au XIXe siècle (Paris, 1974); G. Laperrière, " 'Persécution et exil': La Venue au Québec des congrégations françaises, 1900–1914," *Revue d'histoire de l'Amérique française* 36 (December 1982); P. Savard, *Jules Tardival, la France et les Etats-Unis, 1851–1905* (Quebec, 1967), and *Le Consulat Général de France à Québec et à Montréal de 1859 à 1914* (Quebec, 1970); S. M. Trofimenkoff, *The Action Française* (Toronto, 1975).

C. S. Doty

Related entries: COMMERCE: FOREIGN; GREAT BRITAIN, RELATIONS WITH; OVERSEAS EMPIRE: AMERICAS; ROMAN CATHOLICISM: OVERSEAS MISSIONS; UNITED STATES, RELATIONS WITH.

CAPITAL PUNISHMENT, the supreme form of punishment in France during the Third Republic. By maintaining the guillotine as the instrument of punishment for capital crimes throughout the Third Republic and until this writing (1983), the French simultaneously illustrate two remarkably consistent aspects of their character and modern institutions: their abiding unwillingness to make major departures from the theory and practice of the Napoleonic Code and the willingness to maintain this punishment though it has been abandoned by virtually all other nations of the industrialized world.

French magistrates applied the penalty in a sparing manner during the Third Republic. Excluding the years of the First World War, 1871, and 1939, when special measures were in effect *la veuve* claimed only 519 victims, or an average of about 8 per year. These figures are roughly similar to the figures from Great Britain for the same period and are much lower than the French figures from the first half of the nineteenth century, when the average was about 45 each year. Between 1870 and 1939 13 crimes in common law required the death penalty. Most of these covered such special varieties of premeditated murder as parricide, poisoning, or infanticide or obsolete measures applying to railway deaths or explosive devices. The two most important categories were assassination, the French term for premeditated murder, and murder committed in the course of another crime whose intention was to facilitate flight or suppress witnesses.

The efforts to abolish capital punishment in modern France have been especially notable during two periods: the period from 1815 to 1870 and from 1960 to the present. The most serious efforts in the earlier period were sponsored by republican politicians and intellectuals to embarrass the tyranny of monarchs and emperors. Once in power themselves, however, the Radicals and Opportunists of the Third Republic preferred to retain the republican concept of social defense against political and civil enemies.

The efforts of the abolitionists—an alliance of Catholics, humanitarians, and leftist politicians—took two forms during the period 1870 to 1940. The lesser strategy endeavored to suppress public executions, still allowed under the law, though banned in Paris after 1898. This aim was finally achieved in 1939. Outright abolition was proposed in Georges Clemenceau's reform program of 1906. Chances for passage seemed excellent at first, but by 1908 when the measure was finally debated, the political atmosphere had so altered that the bill was decisively defeated by Radical centrists on whose loyalty Clemenceau did not insist. It was the last time an abolition measure was debated in a French assembly until 1979.

E. Garçon, *Le Droit pénal* (Paris, 1921); A. Lacassagne, *Peine de mort et criminalité* (Paris, 1908); P. Savey-Casard, *La Peine de mort* (Geneve, 1968).

R. A. Nye

Related entries: CRIME, PATTERNS OF; PRISONS.

CARNOT, SADI (1837–1894), president of France from 3 December 1887 to 24 June 1894. He is generally described as the republicans'—and particularly Georges Clemenceau's—choice for the presidency precisely because he was not expected to exert authority, being merely the possessor of a prestigious republican name. (His grandfather was Lazare Carnot, the Revolution's "organizer of victory," and his father was a revolutionary in 1830 and then a republican minister.) An engineer by training, Carnot was elected deputy from the Côte-d'Or. In this capacity he was modest and hard working. Possessing more technical skill than political vision, he produced clear and concise reports and speeches and in a time of rampant corruption showed total integrity in both political and private life.

Like his predecessor in the Elysée, Jules Grévy, he interested himself in matters of foreign policy and defense and played a part in the early negotiations for an agreement with Russia (corresponding with the czar and arranging for mutual visits with high-ranking military and naval officers). Regarding the political issues of the day, Carnot firmly opposed the political campaign of General Georges Boulanger. He persuaded the baron Armand de Mackau and his conservative friends to abandon Boulanger and worked closely with the Tirard government to intimidate him into fleeing France. He also showed understanding and even sympathy for the Ralliement. Breaking with Grévy's practice of remaining within the confines of the Elysée, he made numerous trips throughout the country. It was on one such trip in 1894 that he was assassinated by the Italian anarchist Santo Caserio.

A. Dansette, *Histoire des présidents de la République de Louis-Napoléon Bonaparte à Charles de Gaulle* (Paris, 1960); L. Derfler, *President and Parliament* (Boca Raton, 1983); P. Lesourd, *Les Présidents de la République dans l'histoire de la France* (Paris, 1960).

L. Derfler

Related entries: ANARCHISM; BOULANGER; CLEMENCEAU; GREVY; PRESIDENT OF THE REPUBLIC, OFFICE OF; RUSSIA, RELATIONS WITH.

CARTEL DES GAUCHES, a coalition of radical and moderate republican parties in the French parliament during the interwar years. This left-of-center political alliance was a major force in the politics of the era and formed ministries in 1924 and 1932. The Cartel was the chief rival of the Bloc national, the right-of-center coalition that formed most of the ministries during these years.

During the 1924 parliamentary elections, the Left was for the first time well organized and cohesive and as a result was voted into office with 328 of the 582 seats, with most of the support coming from the south of France. The Cartel then forced the resignation of President Alexandre Millerand and presented Paul Painlevé as a candidate for the presidency. The National Assembly refused Painlevé and elected Gaston Doumergue instead. Doumergue then called on the Radical Edouard Herriot, leader of the Cartel, to form a ministry.

The 1924 Herriot ministry, supported mainly by the Radicals, was faced with a series of major problems, the most serious of which were financial. In international affairs, however, they actively pursued peace initiatives, such as the Locarno Accords (1925) and the Dawes Plan (1924) dealing with German reparations. They were also involved in the February 1925 abolition of the French embassy at the Vatican (in keeping with their anticlerical views) and the official recognition of the Soviet Union (28 October 1924).

The Cartel, however, was faced with an overwhelming fiscal crisis. The state treasury was in a very serious situation, inflation was on the rise, and the franc was plummeting against both the British pound and the U.S. dollar. The monetary difficulties worried both the government and the public and came to dominate all other problems. In 1925 the pace of the franc's decline quickened, and political disorder began. On 10 April 1925 the Herriot ministry was overthrown by the Senate on the budget question. The four short-lived ministries that followed (P. Painlevé, 17 April–25 October 1925 and 29 October–22 November 1925; Aristide Briand, 28 November 1925–6 March 1926; Herriot, 20–21 July 1926) were unable to control the financial problems, and during the first two years of the Cartel government, the franc declined from 90 to 240 francs against the British pound. The Cartel could not persuade a majority to vote for its budget, and this was the main reason for its demise. On 22 July 1926, the Cartel was overthrown, and Raymond Poincaré, leader of the Bloc national, was elected premier.

The 1932 ministry, again formed under Herriot, fared no better, for the fiscal crisis this time was aggravated by worldwide depression. Four ministries (Joseph Paul-Boncour, 18 December 1932–28 January 1933; Edouard Daladier, 31 January–24 October 1933; Albert Sarraut, 26 October–23 November 1933; Camille Chautemps, 26 November 1933–27 January 1934), all sponsored by the Cartel, followed one another in rapid succession; none was able to balance the budget or devise measures to resuscitate the stagnant industry.

The politics of the Cartel makes manifest the drift of the Radicals from their left-wing reformist posture before World War I to centrist compromise and accommodation during the interwar years. The failure of the Cartel des gauches, and of the Radicals who were its sustaining force, to exhibit bold or imaginative leadership contributed to the disillusionment with parliamentary politics during this era and to the psychological defeatism in the face of economic crisis and Nazi aggression.

J-P. Azéma, *La Troisième Republique* (Paris, 1970); G. Bonnefous, *Histoire politique de la Troisième République*, Vol. 4 (Paris, 1960); J. Chastenet, *Cent ans de la République*, vols. 5–6 (Paris, 1970); F. Goguel, *La Politique des partis sous la Troisième République* (Paris, 1958); J. Néré, *La Troisième République* (Paris, 1970); J. Touchard, *La Gauche en France* (Paris, 1977); G. Wright, *France in Modern Times* (Chicago, 1981).

A. J. Staples

Related entries: BLOC NATIONAL; BRIAND; CHAUTEMPS; DALADIER; DOUMERGUE; HERRIOT; LEBRUN; LEFT, THE; PAINLEVE; PAUL-BON-COUR; POLITICS; RADICAL AND RADICAL-SOCIALIST PARTY; SARRAUT.

CASIMIR-PERIER, JEAN (1847–1907), deputy, prime minister, president of the Republic, wealthy industrialist. His family, the Périers, held controlling interests in the Anzin mines. His grandfather had served King Louis Philippe as prime minister, and his father Adolphe Thiers as minister of the interior. Casimir-Périer's social position, close ties with moderate republicans, and his reputation for energetic, authoritative action helped make him deputy (1876–94), under secretary of education, religion, and fine arts (1877–79) and of war (1883–85), and president of the Chamber of Deputies (1893, 1894).

When moderate republicans gained a parliamentary majority in 1893, he formed a government (3 December) without the radical republicans. The cabinet pushed through strong anti-anarchist legislation, signed the secret alliance treaty with Russia, and called for an *esprit nouveau* to foster closer ties between republicans and the Right. Alarmed by his conservatism, radicals and some moderates defeated his cabinet (23 May 1894). The next month, after President of the Republic Sadi Carnot's assassination, he reluctantly agreed to stand for the presidency.

His election (25 June 1894), with votes from the Right, outraged the radicals who launched a vicious press campaign against him. Six months later (15 January 1895), after the Chamber unexpectedly defeated the Charles Dupuy cabinet, Casimir-Périer resigned. His unprecedented action provoked widespread criticism.

In public, he invoked the president's powerlessness; to his friends, he explained that the radical attacks and the efforts of Dupuy and Gabriel Hanotaux, foreign minister, to exclude him from decisions prompted him to end his political career.

A. Dansette, *Histoire des présidents de la République* (Paris, 1960); L. Derfler, *President and Parliament* (Boca Raton, 1983); J. Reinach, *Histoire de l'Affaire Dreyfus*, vol. 1 (Paris, 1901).

S. A. Ashley

Related entries: DUPUY; OPPORTUNISTS; PRESIDENT OF THE REPUBLIC, OFFICE OF; PROGRESSISTS; RUSSIA, ENTENTE WITH.

CASSAGNAC, PAUL DE (1842–1904), Bonapartist, Catholic journalist, deputy, and unrelenting critic of the parliamentary Third Republic. He was the eldest son of Bernard-Adolphe de Granier de Cassagnac, a Gascon with family ties to Maréchal Soult, and Rosa de Beauvallon, the daughter of a West Indian planter. He was a cousin of Prosper-Olivier Lissagaray, chronicler of the Commune of Paris, on his father's side. Cassagnac's father had established a powerful political fiefdom in the department of Gers, to which Paul de Cassagnac fell heir. Although young Cassagnac had to fight to establish his own personal and political identity independent of his father, he nevertheless inherited the latter's combative temperament (he had been one of the most controversial political journalists of the July Monarchy) and assimilated his political ideology, which posited the necessity of a strong national leader, chosen by the people and sustained by a supportive sociopolitical elite. Both Cassagnacs were thus committed to a radical monarchical theory of authoritarian plebiscitary democracy, grounded in their interpretation of France's political history since 1789 as a descent into political and social anarchy. The regime of their choice was the authoritarian Second Empire of Napoleon III, which from 1867 on they defended vigorously against those who sought to liberalize it and, after 1870, sought no less vigorously to reinstall.

After studying law in Paris and a short stint as a civil servant in the Ministry of the Interior, Paul de Cassagnac made his debut in the Parisian press in 1866 as his father's second at *Le Pays*. He soon acquired public notoriety as a polemicist in the heroic romantic mode, a young eagle poised to pinion liberals, anticlericals, proto-Prussians, or enemies of Empress Eugénie. In 1869 he had been elected to the general council of Gers, on which he served throughout his political career. After the fall of the Empire and many months as a prisoner of war in Silesia, he returned to France, took over the editorship of *Le Pays*, and ran successfully for reelection to the general council. In 1876 he was elected to the Chamber of Deputies as a proponent of what he called imperialism, the conservative alliance of all monarchists (irrespective of dynastic allegiance) behind the seven-year presidency of Marshal Maurice de MacMahon.

A charismatic figure, a feared swordsman, and one of the most eligible bachelors in Paris (before his marriage to the Catholic heiress Julia Acard in 1878), Cassagnac threw his support as a deputy behind the defense of religious, educational, and political freedom for Catholics, as the republicans consolidated their anticlerical attacks after 1876. Two of his favorite targets were the republican leaders Léon Gambetta and Jules Ferry. After the death of Napoleon III's only son and heir in 1879, Cassagnac tried to rouse support for Prince Victor-Napoleon Bonaparte as pretender to the imperial title. In the meantime he became one of the chief promoters (along with Baron Armand de Mackau) of an alliance of monarchist deputies in the Chamber of Deputies, which made an impressive comeback in the elections of 1885 and hoped to win a majority in 1889. After 1885 Cassagnac espoused *n'importequisme*, which signified his support for any providential leader who could lead France out of the republican morass; in 1887 he established his own newspaper, *L'Autorité*, to promote this faceless authoritarianism. When General Georges Boulanger appeared as a possible "man on horseback," Cassagnac was one of the twelve members of the monarchist committee who convinced the comte de Paris to undertake a "parallel march" with the general in his plebiscitary campaign for revision of the Third Republic's constitution. Following the Boulanger fiasco in 1889, Cassagnac led the resistance to the Vatican-inspired movement to rally French monarchist Catholics to the republic. But with his own support in Gers seriously split, he lost his seat in the Chamber in the 1893 elections.

Although Cassagnac was reelected to the Chamber in 1898, ill health prevented him from again assuming a leading role in the vanguard of the conservative opposition. After his death in 1904, his two sons Paul-Julien and Guy carried on the family political tradition. Guy de Cassagnac was killed in the First World War, but Paul-Julien continued to uphold his father's fiercely independent brand of authoritarian democracy until his own death in 1966. Paul de Cassagnac is best remembered as a colorful political personality in his own right and as a transitional figure in the development of a secular French nationalist authoritarian democracy. He was one of the last truly popular spokesmen for the authoritarian and antiparliamentary democratic tradition in its monarchist-Catholic form.

P. de Cassagnac, *Oeuvres*, 8 vols. (Paris, 1905); K. M. Offen, "The Political Career of Paul de Cassagnac" (Ph.D. diss. Stanford University, 1970).

K. M. Offen

Related entries: BONAPARTISM; BONAPARTISTS; BOULANGER; MACKAU; LISSAGARAY; NAPOLEON-VICTOR, PRINCE.

CATHOLIC LITERARY RENAISSANCE. By the late 1880s it was evident that there was a generalized revolt against the positivist mentality of the French intellectual establishment in three areas: literature, philosophy, and the social sciences. Soon young writers like Charles Péguy and Ernest Psichari (grandson of Ernest Renan) would announce their break with the older generation, their "taking sides with their forefathers against their fathers." By the late nineteenth century, antireligious and anticlerical thought were not nearly as vigorous as they had been earlier. There were imaginative efforts to create a scientific morality, particularly on the part of Emile Durkheim, but his originality figures as an exception in the period. More spiritually oriented thinkers such as the American pragmatist William James, Henri Bergson, Maurice Blondel, and Edouard Le Roy began to have a direct influence on literature. After 1890 the exclusive reign of scientism or positivism was directly challenged by figures such as the prominent critic Ferdinand Brunetière whose article "After a Visit to the Vatican" (1 January 1895) caused a great uproar as this sardonic, yellow waist-coated intellectual, successor to Renan and Hippolyte Taine, declared that "a morality is nothing if not religious." Brunetière's denunciation of the pretentious failures of the natural sciences to account for human origins and ends, and of the moral sciences of the Third Republic to provide viable guidance to the new generations, dovetailed with other phenomena of the period: with the enthusiasm of Péguy, Jacques and Raïssa Maritain, and Georges Sorel for the "liberating" antipositivist lectures of Henri Bergson, and with the new generation of self-consciously nationalistic writers such as Charles Maurras, Maurice Barrès, and Edouard Drumont. Religion in general, and France's Roman Catholic traditions in particular, came to be valued just when the government of Emile Combes began its great effort to eradicate their influence.

The attraction of the Catholic church for literary figures at the end of the nineteenth century lay partially in the fact that the church represented values antithetical to those of a nineteenth-century bourgeoisie enamored with scientific and technological progress, if not antithetical to those of the century as a whole. There were more miracles and saints in nineteenth-century France than at any other time since the Middle Ages. Were the miraculous apparitions of the Virgin at La Salette and at Lourdes a response to Renan's *Vie de Jésus*? These events and the devotion to Jean Vianney, curé d'Ars, and to the Sacred Heart of Jesus, the veneration of Theresa of Lisieux, were popular, plebeian phenomena, but they harmonized with the serious antipositivist literature of the period and *la grande révolution bergsonienne* at the end of the century. The Catholic literary renaissance, however, was not, in the main, a movement of intellectuals. Rather it tended to be rooted in a traditional Christianity, relying on revelation and simple faith. Traditional Catholicism's chief priorities were litanies to deliver humanity from sudden death, the devil, storms, plague, hunger, war, and eternal death. The Roman church had demonstrated an astonishing force for stability that allowed it to digest, if not impose, change. In 1854 Pius IX had proclaimed the dogma of the Immaculate Conception: a symbol of a church and for a church confronting a world that was, in the words of Drumont, "subjected to the triple law of gold, of mud and of blood." After having been in a position of authority for such a long time, the church of the nineteenth century discovered the virtues of being of the opposition; it never felt more virtuous. *Pure et dure*, sure of the future that it saw revealed in signs from heaven, the church rediscovered the mysterious power of the rosary, to which Pope Leo XIII consecrated fifteen encyclicals.

In this context a deep involvement in religious matters became associated with works of genuine literary value for the first time in two centuries. The mystical and the miraculous were the elements that made up the literary and the religious originality of the Catholic literary renaissance. The men of the Catholic revival avoided the sentimentalism of Chateaubriand and the romantic Catholics, the rationalism of Louis de Bonald and Joseph de Maistre, the liberalism of Felicité de Lamennais and the modernism of their contemporaries. Their ideal was a return to what they considered to be the traditional values of the church, and their practical method was a renunciation of all compromise with any of the forces opposed to this aim. According to some historians the great revival of Catholic literature, and the immense spate of conversions among the literary elite from the 1880s to the First World War, constituted not only a literary but also a social revolution.

Louis Veuillot, Ernest Hello, and Antoine Blanc de Saint-Bonnet have been cited as the three writers of the Second Empire who most influenced (in very different ways) the revival of Catholic literature that began in the late 1870s and early 1880s. Veuillot's intransigent, violent polemic, Hello's rejection of the "Reign of Science" and interest in extreme forms of mysticism, Blanc de Saint-Bonnet's partisanship of legitimism, infallibility, and a hierarchical society based on work, the family, and a Christian acceptance of suffering were reflected to a greater or lesser extent in the Catholic authors who followed them.

Barbey d'Aurevilly's (1808–89) novel *Un Prêtre marié* (1865) revolved around a specifically religious subject, although it was treated with a certain dilettantism rather than religious conviction. Nevertheless, Barbey d'Aurevilly fired the imagination of widely different figures in the younger generation, such as Paul Bourget, "Sar" Péladan, J.-K. Huysmans, and Léon Bloy. In fact, Barbey, although he considered Catholicism merely "a magnificent balcony from which one could spit down on the masses," was a cause of the conversion of the young Léon Bloy in 1869. Bloy's great autobiographical novel *Le Désespéré* (1886) was "a milestone in the history of the French Catholic novel" (R. Griffiths) and the first in a series of autobiographical religious novels that would include those of Huysmans, as well as Bloy's own later *La Femme pauvre* (1897). The explosion of Catholic literature in the 1880s saw the poet Paul Verlaine (1844–96) produce a volume of Catholic poetry, which was followed by another eight years later and paved the way for the first-rate but less self-conscious Catholic poetry of Germain Nouveau (1852–1920) and Francis Jammes (1868–1938). In 1886 Vicomte Eugène-Melchior de Vogüé produced his influential study of the Russian novel, *Le Roman russe*, in which he pleaded for a novel free from the constraints of naturalism, a mystical novel that would deal with the things of the spirit as well as the flesh. The young novelist J.-K. Huysmans, immersed in occultism and satanism, echoed the sentiments of Vogüé in his novel *Là-bas* (1891) and then described his tempestuous route from the prostitutes of Pigalle to the contemplatives of La Trappe in the story of his conversion, *En route* (1895). Another great religious literary event was the publication of Paul Bourget's novel *Le Disciple* (1889). Bourget (1852–1934), successful novelist and disciple of Taine, in this and a succession of subsequent novels proclaimed the emptiness of positivist doctrines, the dangers of life unsupported by fixed moral values, and the way in which the solution to various problems could be found in the traditional values of the church. At the Christmas midnight Mass at Notre-Dame in 1886, Paul Claudel (1868–1955), a man who would revolutionize the French stage, experienced his conversion. His first play, *Tête d'or* (1889), reflected the spiritual struggle that led him to it. The very successful later plays—*Partagede Midi* (1905), *L'Annonce faite à Marie* (1910), and *Le Soulier de satin* (1924)— reflected a more confident certainty.

The new century, which in the wake of the Dreyfus case started with the violent anticlericalism of the Emile Combes administration, was also the scene of another large wave of conversions. Bloy played an important role in the conversion of Jacques and Raïssa Maritain, Huysmans in many others—the critic and novelist Adolphe Retté among them. While Huysmans, Bloy, Bourget, and Claudel continued their extensive output, new stars of great importance were rising—Charles Péguy (1873–1914), Francis Jammes (1868–1938), and Emile Baumann (1868–1941). Other novelists whose work stressed more conventional Catholic values and piety, such as René Bazin and Henri Bordeaux, became extremely popular. Péguy's main output, both in prose and verse, appeared in his review *Les Cahiers de la quinzaine*, which drew a host of young writers of talent around it, many of them influenced by the philosophy of Bergson: Ernest Psichari (1883–1914), who fused patriotic and religious fervor, and the witty and brilliant Henri Massis converted in 1913. A few of the participants in the Catholic literary renaissance before World War I, like the young novelist François Mauriac, were interested in social Catholicism and progressive Catholic movements like Le Sillon, but they were the exception rather than the rule. Most of the Catholic writers, particularly those affected by the "rude shock of conversion" (R. Maritain), held to Catholicism's radical rejection of the bourgeoisie and its transvaluation of the values of the modern age. After World War I, their ranks were joined by the "French Dostoevsky" Georges Bernanos, the theater of Gabriel Marcel, and the remarkable early novels of Mauriac. By that time sophisticated Catholic literature had become an important and accepted part of French culture and of a distinctive French approach to spiritual matters.

R. Bessède, *La Crise de la conscience catholique* (Paris, 1975); R. Griffiths, *The Reactionary Revolution* (London, 1966); E. Poulat, *Eglise contre bourgeoisie* (Paris, 1977).

J. W. Hellman

Related entries: BERGSON; BERNANOS; BOURGET; CLAUDEL; DRU-MONT; MARCEL; MARITAIN; MASSIS; MAURIAC; MOUNIER; PEGUY; POSITIVISM; THOUGHT AND INTELLECTUAL LIFE; VERLAINE; WEIL.

CELINE, LOUIS-FERDINAND (1894–1961), pseudonym of Louis-Ferdinand-Auguste Destouches. Céline was a novelist of exceptional creative power and originality whose pro-German comments and anti-Semitic writings, *Bagatelles pour un massacre* (1937), *L'Ecole des cadavres* (1938), and *Les Beaux Draps*

(1941), made him seek refuge near the end of World War II in Germany and later in Sweden where he was imprisoned for over a year. Tried in absentia and convicted of collaboration by the French courts, he was pardoned in 1951 and allowed to return to France that same year.

Born in Paris into a family of modest means, he served in World War I, was wounded, and was decorated for bravery. Céline's first major piece of writing, "La Vie et l'oeuvre de Philippe Ignace Semmelweis" (1924), was submitted as a thesis for the degree of doctor of medicine and contains important Célinian themes, such as man's inhumanity to man, especially regarding the man of genius, and a pervasive pessimism about human destiny.

Céline's first two books, *Voyage au bout de la nuit* (1933) and *Mort à crédit* (1936), are generally regarded by critics as his greatest achievements, probably because they contain recognizable plots that make them more readily accessible than such later works as *Guignol's Band I* (1944), *Guignol's Band II* (1963), *Féerie pour une autre fois* (1952), *D'un Château l'autre* (1957), *Nord* (1963), and *Rigodon* (1969). In these later novels, conventional plots disappear under the influence of unreliable narrators who cannot, or refuse to, distinguish fact from fancy or the past from the present.

Céline's novels offer a pessimistic portrayal of man as besieged from within and without. Human nature is corrupt and deceitful, and the individual, like Semmelweis, is crushed from the outside by the maliciousness and stupidity of others. Céline's view of a world in which there is no hope for humanity and where the only certainties are suffering and death forms a sharp and provocative contrast with the optimistic views of such contemporaries as Albert Camus, André Gide, André Malraux, and Jean-Paul Sartre who contend that man has, at least, the inner strength to make life bearable and occasionally happy despite the hostility or indifference of an incomprehensible universe.

A balanced evaluation of Céline's fictional works has been obscured until recently by critics who have insisted on the autobiographical content of his novels and rather neglected Céline the highly conscious literary craftsman whose concern for and control of style transmuted the events of his own life into the renderings of his fictional first-person narrators. Céline's innovations with the novel must be sought more in the style of his works than in their content. He had only contempt for those writers who composed novels of ideas. In his own works he attempts to create an emotive style through a written language modeled on a spoken and colloquial idiom that captures and conveys the raw and sometimes frenzied emotions of life.

M. Hindus, *The Crippled Giant* (New York, 1950); B. Knapp, *Céline* (University, Ala., 1974); J. H. Matthews, *The Inner Dream* (Syracuse, 1978); P. McCarthy, *Céline* (London, 1975).

                                                                                                                R. F. O'Reilly

Related entry: LITERATURE.

CEMETERY, CULT OF THE. During the first half of the Third Republic, the cemetery played a unifying role in the nation's public life. Throughout the nineteenth century a secular cult of the dead had evolved independently of the church. In part a popularization of an earlier romantic fascination with death, the cult found its most effusive expression in the large municipal cemeteries of Paris. On the wane in the twentieth century, it nevertheless took on political significance in the military cemeteries of the First World War.

In the century preceding the Third Republic, the cemetery had been attacked as a place of exceeding insalubrity. Eighteenth-century science had argued that cemeteries poisoned the air, and decrees of the late *Ancien régime* and Revolution began to force burial grounds outside city walls. Napoleon Bonaparte created large suburban cemeteries outside Paris, but the growth of the city brought the living and the dead in contact once again. During the Second Empire, when Baron Georges Haussmann proposed an even more distant necropolis in Méry-sur-Oise to be reached by train, Parisians protested. When variations on Haussmann's plan reappeared in the Third Republic, the Parisian population was no less adamant.

The Parisian municipal council studied the problem from 1872 to 1881 and in 1879 created a commission to study related questions of public health. Now scientific opinion found no danger in urban cemeteries. Moreover, scientists, moralists, clerics, and the general public agreed on the importance of the cemetery as a cultural institution.

Disagreements arose concerning the particular role of the cemetery. Catholics charged that the cemetery would be the last battleground in the war against secularism, anticlericalism, individualism, and solidarism; they mocked self-proclaimed materialists whose concern for the cemetery indicated an underlying belief in spiritual life. Indeed positivists were as protective of the cemetery as were Catholics; sometimes their reasoning was identical. Both sides defended the cemetery as a fundamental institution that recognized the continuity of generations by allowing the expression of family bonds that survived individual deaths. Even supporters of cremation proposed that urban cemeteries be used for the procedure and for the permanent repose of funerary urns. One plan delivered to the Parisian municipal council proposed that the grounds surrounding the crematorium be marked by monuments to the dead.

Noteworthy in the literature on the cemetery at the end of the nineteenth century is a concern for the survival of the family. That concern can also be seen in the care given previously neglected cemeteries all over France. Cemeteries became populated with family plots rather than individual graves. Bourgeois families etched their lineages in stone for whose maintenance they paid dearly. The vast national burial grounds of the First World War temporarily replaced family allegiance with national allegiance. After the war, cemetery plots reunited husbands and wives, but geographic mobility prevented the maintenance of ties of lineage.

Throughout the Third Republic, though, the cemetery played an important role in the lives of otherwise divergent groups. The cemetery became park, art gallery, pilgrimage site, and tourist attraction. The discovery of a Gallo-Roman cemetery in Paris in 1878 provoked public interest. The French national horticultural society published a booklet on flowers and tombs in 1902. Tourist guides devoted chapters to the cemeteries, and Hachette published a volume that treated *les tombes célèbres*.

While some urban cemeteries took on the landscaped look of the American park cemetery, French taste ran more often to the sculpture garden variety. These collections of stone became veritable cities of the dead. Tombs gained addresses, including street names and numbers. Maps were required to find one's way around. Administrators of the larger cemeteries held advanced degrees in engineering. Most popular of all Parisian cemeteries was Père Lachaise, whose variety made it an attraction for visitors of diverse interests. One could attend religious or secular burials, pay one's respects to any number of dead celebrities of the nineteenth century, visit the presumed remains of Abélard and Héloise, ponder the political significance of the Communard Wall, or meditate before the *Monument aux morts* of A. Bartholomé, a sculpture that mixed classical and Christian imagery.

If the cult of the cemetery represented a popularization of a romantic fascination with death, the fact that that fascination was limited to a prescribed arena perhaps foreshadowed the more recent taboo surrounding the subject of death.

P. Ariès, *L'Homme devant la mort* (Paris, 1977); R. Bertrand, "Cimetières marseillais aux XVIIIe et XIXe siècles," *Provence Historique* 23 (1973); R. Bertrand and M. Vovelle, *La Ville des morts: Essai sur l'imaginaire urbain contemporain d'après les cimetières provençaux* (Côte d'Azur, 1982); A. Cadet, *Des cimetières de Paris et de la crémation* (Paris, 1874); Msgr. Gaume, *Le Cimetière au XIXe siècle* (Paris, n.d.); G. Gibault, *Les Fleurs et les tombeaux* (Paris, 1902); L. Gosset, *Tout Paris par l'image* (Paris, 1937); L. Landau, *Un Coin de Paris. Le Cimetière Gallo-Romain de la rue Nicole* (Paris, 1878); M. Levaillant, *Les Tombes célèbres* (Paris, 1926); F. Zonabend, "Les Morts et les vivants. Le Cimetière de Minot en Châtillonnais," *Etudes rurales* 52 (1973).

D. G. Troyansky

Related entries: FALLEN SOLDIER, CULT OF THE; FUNERALS, STATE; POSITIVISM; WORLD WAR I, FRANCE'S ROLE IN.

CEZANNE, PAUL (1839–1906), leading painter of the impressionist and post-impressionist generations. Born in Aix-en-Provence (Bouches-du-Rhône), the son of a banker, he was a boyhood friend of Emile Zola. In 1861 he abandoned his law studies and went to Paris to join Zola and become a painter. In 1870, still engaged in the dark, often violent, and erotic manner that characterized his youthful painting, he returned to the south to avoid conscription for the Franco-Prussian War. During the 1870s he worked closely with Camille Pissarro, gradually altering his style and lightening his palette and participating in the first and third impressionist exhibitions in 1874 and 1877. Of the impressionists the most consistently rejected by the Salon juriés, Cézanne retired in the late 1870s to Aix, where he worked in relative isolation for the rest of his life. Concentrating on a variety of subjects—landscape, portrait, still life, and multi-figure bather scenes—he gradually elaborated a style of painting that combined the interests of the impressionists in light and color and atmosphere with his own ideas on structure and composition. He is generally considered to be an important forerunner of cubism, although his last paintings also display a strong expressionist quality in color and design. He may be said to have had a greater influence on twentieth century painting than any other artist of his time.

A. Chappuis, *The Drawings of Paul Cézanne*, 2 vols. (Greenwich, Conn., 1973); R. Fry, *Cézanne, a Study of His Development* (London, 1927); W. Rubin, ed., *Cézanne, the Late Work* (New York, 1977); M. Schapiro, *Cézanne* (New York, 1952); L. Venturi, *Cézanne, son art, son oeuvre*, 2 vols. (Paris, 1936).

J. Isaacson

Related entries: CUBISM; IMPRESSIONISM; POSTIMPRESSIONISM; ZOLA.

CHAGALL, MARC (1887–1985), lyrical, visionary Russian-Jewish painter. Born in Vitebsk, Russia, to a large, poor Jewish family, he studied painting in Vitebsk and in St. Petersburg (1907–10), where he was influenced by the lush orientalism of his teacher, Leon Bakst, painter and celebrated designer for theater and ballet. Having learned about impressionism and postimpressionism from Bakst, he went to Paris in 1910, settling in Montparnasse along with many other Eastern European artists of the time. Influenced by the fauves' use of color and the cubists' analysis of space, he subordinated these models to his whimsical, protosurrealistic vision in works dealing with his village childhood, Hasidic folklore and religious practices, human relationships, and modern Paris. His radiantly colored works depict a topsy-turvy dream world, humorously fusing symbol, memory, and desire and prominently featuring animals and flowers.

Having gone to Russia to marry in 1914, he was unable to return to Paris and became caught up in the artistic euphoria of the early USSR. He served as art commissar for Vitebsk province (1918–20) until ousted by the more radical constructivists and then designed sets and a curtain for the Jewish Kamerny Theater in Moscow. Disillusioned, he returned to Paris in 1922. From then until 1940, he continued to paint in his inimitable style, influenced the surrealists (though he never joined their movement), and completed several book illustration projects commissioned by the art dealer Ambroise Vollard: Gogol's *Dead Souls* (1924–25), the fables of La Fontaine (1926–31), and the Bible (1931–39, reworked 1952–56). He became a French citizen in 1937, spent 1941 through 1948 in exile in New York, and after 1950 lived in Vence on the Côte d'Azur.

S. Alexander, *Marc Chagall* (New York, 1978); M. Chagall, *Ma vie* (Paris, 1957); W. Haftmann, *Marc Chagall* (New York, 1972); F. Meyer, *Marc Chagall* (New York, n.d.).

T. Shapiro

Related entry: ART: MAJOR STYLES AND MOVEMENTS.

CHAMBER OF DEPUTIES (1876–1940), the lower house of parliament created by the Constitution of 1875; the center of French political life. The Chamber of Deputies was created by the constitutional laws of 1875 to replace the National Assembly and to provide direct representation of the nation through universal suffrage. It remained the center of French political life from the first election in 1876 until a joint session of parliament conveyed power to Marshal Philippe Pétain in July 1940.

The Chamber sat for a four-year term (*législature*) except in unusual circumstances (such as dissolution in 1877, prolongation by World War I). Annual sessions began in January for a minimum of five months (*session ordinaire*) and usually continued for several weeks in the autumn (*session extraordinaire*). Debates at these sittings were open to the public and published in the *Journal officiel*.

The membership of the Chamber changed with each census but averaged about 600. All seats were contested at each election (*renouvellement intégral*), but electoral practices varied greatly. Most elections were conducted with single-member constituencies (*scrutin d'arrondissement*), although multimember constituencies (*scrutin de liste*) were tried twice (1885–89, 1919–27), the last time with proportional representation. Candidacy in more than one constituency was permitted until 1889. Electoral law excluded several groups of citizens from eligibility for office or from voting, notably men on active military service and all women.

Formal political parties appeared in the Chamber of Deputies only after the chartering of the Radical and Radical-Socialist party in 1901. Throughout the Third Republic, deputies affiliated with less structured factions whose names and identity changed with almost every election; deputies sat with these factions on the semicircular floor of the Palais Bourbon (*hémicycle*) in approximate ideological array from left to right. Deputies also belonged to *groupes*, which cut across party lines to bring together supporters of some special interest (such as the colonial group).

The primary function of the Chamber of Deputies was legislative. The entire body was divided by lot into eleven *bureaux*, which elected members (usually two) to the standing committees (*commissions*). A bill (*projet de loi*) first went to the Commission of Initiative and then to the appropriate committee, which designated a *rapporteur* to present its conclusions to the Chamber for debate. Bills normally had to be read two times, but the second could be skipped if a declaration of urgency was voted. Those adopted went to the Senate.

The Chamber of Deputies also exercised control over the cabinet, which needed the support of a majority to be invested and to retain office. Cabinet policies were controlled a posteriori in three ways: (1) the *enquête*, a rare commission of inquiry; (2) questions on details of administration, answered on the floor until 1909 and thereafter in the *Journal officiel*; and (3) most effectively, through interpellations demanding the explanation of a policy, leading to debate and a vote of confidence. The Chamber's special functions included joint sessions with the Senate for constitutional revision (*Assemblée nationale*) or presidential elections (congrès).

While the Chamber of Deputies was the public arena of French politics, the focus on its debates obscures the location of great power elsewhere: in the constituency committees and regional federations of political parties, which kept deputies responsive to local interests; in the commissions that controlled the flow of legislation; in the ministerial under secretaries and civil service, which established more law than did the Chamber through the interpretation of vague legislation and powers of decree; in the extraparliamentary associations to which deputies belonged, such as Masonic lodges; and in the close link between deputies and special economic interests, through devices such as hiring a *député-avocat* as a corporation's attorney (for example, Raymond Poincaré and the Creusot arms works).

H. Bergasse, *Histoire de l'assemblée* (Paris, 1967); P. Campbell, *French Electoral Systems and Elections* (London, 1958); R. Gooch, *The French Parliamentary Committee System* (Charlottesville, Va., 1935); R. Poincaré, *How France Is Governed* (London, 1913).

S. C. Hause

Related entries: CONSTITUTIONAL LAWS OF 1875; DEPUTIES OF THE THIRD REPUBLIC; NATIONAL ASSEMBLY; SENATE; VOTING PROCEDURES.

CHAMBERS OF COMMERCE, official organizations representing local business interests and providing commercial services. In 1900, there were 143 chambers in France—at least 1 per department—plus 44 smaller, consultative chambers. The most active of these were in Paris, Lyons, Marseilles, Bordeaux, Rouen, Lille, Saint-Etienne, and the Vosges (Epinal). Each chamber had nine to twenty members, except Paris, which was allowed forty. In the 1870s, these members were chosen by a select group of business notables designated by the prefect. By 1908, however, all businessmen voted for members in their district. Legislation in 1898 allowed chambers to organize nationally, and the National Assembly of Chamber Presidents was created. In 1919, twenty regional groupings of chambers were formed to coordinate postwar reconstruction.

In the early Third Republic, chambers of commerce served as advocates for local interests on matters of national economic policy. In the debate on tariffs from 1871 to 1892, the chambers of Rouen, Lille, and the Vosges led the protectionist forces, while Paris, Lyons, and Bordeaux sought freer trade. All chambers were concerned with railroad rate determination, and a number of chambers (Lyons, Bordeaux, Marseilles) promoted colonial ventures. After 1900, business interest representation fell increasingly to new industrial associations such as the Union des industries métallurgiques et minières, and chambers of commerce concentrated on providing local business services. All chambers issued import licenses, certificates of origin for exported goods, and identity cards for salesmen. In addition, the Paris chamber ran a commercial library, underwriting laboratories for paper and firearms, bonded warehouses, and business schools. The Lyons chamber administered a silk rating and conditioning bureau, a silk underwriting laboratory, and a textile museum. In the sea and river ports, chambers formed semipublic corporations to build docks and warehouses and oversee port services. Many chambers issued paper money to replace scarce coinage during World War I and administered currency controls during the financial crisis of the mid-1920s. In the 1930s the chambers of Lyons, Bordeaux, and Marseilles served as concessionaires for the airports in their regions.

E. P. Herring, *"Chambres de commerce*: Their Legal Status and Political Signifi-cance," *American Political Science Review* 25 (1931); B. Ippolito, *Les Chambres de commerce dans l'économie française* (Bordeaux, 1945); J. Laffey, "Municipal Imperi-alism in Nineteenth Century France," *Historical Reflections* 1 (1974); A. J. Wolfe, *Commercial Organizations in France* (Washington, D.C., 1915).

M. S. Smith

Related entries: BUSINESS ORGANIZATION; BUSINESSMEN; COM-MERCE: RETAIL MERCHANTS; ECONOMIC POLICY.

CHAMBORD, HENRI (V), COMTE DE (1820–1883), duc de Bordeaux, posthumous son of the duc de Berry; Legitimist pretender. The comte de Chambord had offered a rallying point for the Legitimists from 1830 to 1870, but an opportunity for a restoration never presented itself, partly because of the success of Napoleon III in gaining clerical support during the Second Empire and partly because of the division among the monarchists. With the fall of the Second Empire in 1870 and the calling of a National Assembly in 1871, a monarchist restoration was again a possibility. The reaction of rural France against the Commune (1871), together with a conservative Catholic movement, greatly favored the chances of restoration. The hopes of restoration were complicated by the candidacy of two pretenders: the Orleanist comte de Paris and the legitimist Chambord. Some monarchists favored a fusion, that is, a compromise in which the childless, aging Chambord would be named king, to be succeeded on his death by the comte de Paris and his progeny.

Chambord, however, was ill disposed toward this compromise. He made an incognito visit from his Austrian exile to the Chateau de Chambord in early July 1871, where he dramatically wrote, "Henri V cannot abandon the flag of Henri IV." Chambord's objection to a fusion was thus symbolized by his refusal to accept the tricolor flag as his emblem, insisting instead on the traditional Bourbon fleur-de-lis.

The monarchist politicians, a majority in the National Assembly, nevertheless persisted. They could not believe that Chambord would continue to refuse a compromise on the issue of the flag. Despite concerted attempts by the Orleanists to persuade Chambord, he reiterated his stand of 1871. In the face of this intransigence, the National Assembly voted the law of the Septennat, which provided for a seven-year presidency. Thus with such a reluctant candidate for king, France became a republic in 1875, and Adolphe Thiers dubbed Chambord the "George Washington of France" for making the republic possible.

In the late 1870s, Chambord's health failed, and he abandoned all hope to become king. His death on 24 August 1883 in Goritzia, Austria (his residence in exile), effectively ended the Legitimist cause in France. The Spanish Carlists inherited his claims, but the bulk of the French Legitimists either retreated from political life or supported the comte de Paris. Monarchism thus continued in France well into the 1880s but only in the Orleanist tradition.

Chambord, steeped in a traditional conception of absolutist monarchy, waited and dreamed of the moment when he would return to the throne and France would accept a regime like that of 1815–30. His uncompromising, inflexible position ruined the possibility of France's once again becoming a monarchy in the 1870s.

M. L. Brown, *The Comte de Chambord* (Durham, N.C., 1967); R. de Castries, *Le Grand Refus du comte de Chambord* (Paris, 1970); C. Muret, *French Royalist Doctrines since the Revolution* (New York, 1933); S. Osgood, *French Royalism under the Third and Fourth Republics* (The Hague, 1960).

M. L. Brown, Jr.

Related entries: CLERICALISM; LEGITIMISM; ORLEANISM; PARIS, PHILIPPE D'ORLEANS.

CHARCOT, JEAN-BAPTISTE (1867–1936), oceanographer. As the son of Jean-Martin Charcot, the noted neurologist, Jean-Baptiste studied medicine at the Faculty of Medicine of Paris, where his father was a professor. He interned at the Hôpital de Paris and received the M.D. in 1895. Charcot succeeded his father in the department of neurology of the Faculty of Medicine. He also studied at the Pasteur Institute in Paris. He did research in neurology and published articles on such topics as epilepsy, aphasia, and various nervous disorders that result from physiological causes. He continued his father's pioneering emphasis on the connections between physiology and psychology.

In 1901 Charcot gave up his medical career to devote himself to exploration and the study of oceanography. He was responsible for the planning and building of the first polar exploration and oceanographic research vessels built in France, the *Français* and the *Pourquoi Pas?* The *Pourquoi Pas?* became the research vessel for the Ecole pratique des hautes études and for the Muséum national d'histoire naturelle, with Charcot as its director. Under Charcot's leadership, courage, and scientific ability, modern French oceanography flourished. Charcot commanded the first French Antarctic expeditions, in 1903–5 and 1908–10, involving the French in the international exploration of the Antarctic.

Charcot led numerous expeditions to the North Atlantic, to the Arctic, to the North Sea, and to Greenland between 1912 and 1936. He died in a shipwreck off Iceland in 1936. Charcot's expeditions captured the public's interest. The extensive researches carried out aboard the *Pourquoi Pas?* helped establish two new areas of oceanographic research, submarine geological mapping and geological oceanography. Charcot was also interested in the possible practical application of oceanographic knowledge, especially to the fishing industry. He published the first French fishing map of the North Sea in 1923 and helped to establish the Office scientifique et technique des pêches.

"Hommages au Commandant Charcot et aux victimes du naufrage du *Pourquoi Pas?*" *La Géographie* 66 (1936); "Hommage national à J. Charcot et à ses compagnons," *Bulletin du Muséum d'histoire naturelle*, 2d ser., 8 (1936); A. Tétry, "Charcot, Jean-Baptiste," *Dictionary of Scientific Biography*, vol. 3 (New York, 1971).

H. J. Steffens

Related entry: CHARCOT, J.-M.

CHARCOT, JEAN-MARTIN (1825–1893), one of the founders of modern neurology. His work demonstrated the connection between physiological disorders and psychological disturbance. Charcot's work on hysteria interested Sigmund Freud, and his neurological investigations influenced the development of Freud's psychology. Charcot's work also stimulated interest in brain function and intelligence. Alfred Binet studied with Charcot in Paris.

Charcot was a student at the Faculty of Medicine of Paris and became an intern in the hospitals of Paris in 1848. He presented a doctoral thesis on gout and rheumatism for the M.D. in 1853. In 1862 he began a department of neurology at the Salpêtrière clinic. He developed this department into an important center of neurological study when he accepted a chaired position there in 1882. Charcot served as professor of anatomical pathology on the Faculty of Medicine of Paris between 1872 and 1882. His work there demonstrated the close relationship between anatomical irregularities and neurological disorders. A neurologic disease of the joints is now known as Charcot's disease. Charcot also studied the neurological effects of disorders of the spinal cord, especially the results of infantile paralysis. His investigations of progressive neuropathic muscular disorders led to the identification of the disease known as Charcot-Marie amyotrophy. Charcot's studies of disorders of the spinal column and the brain convinced him that disorders in specific areas of the nervous system produce specific neurological effects. This important new orientation proved the key to the better understanding of neurological problems, such as aphasia and epilepsy, and for an understanding of the source of learning disabilities.

Charcot's studies of hysteria, initiated and continued after 1872, had an important influence outside the practice of medicine. He was interested in the identification of the physiological causes of hysteria and the possible treatment of hysteria by hypnosis. This work most interested Freud.

J. Charcot, *Oeuvres complètes*, 9 vols. (Paris, 1886–90); G. Guillain, *J.-M. Charcot, La vie, son oeuvre* (Paris, 1955); A. Tétry, "Charcot, Jean-Martin," *Dictionary of Scientific Biography*, vol. 3 (New York, 1971).

H. J. Steffens

Related entry: BINET.

CHAREAU, PIERRE (1883–1950), modernist designer and architect. He was born in Bordeaux (Gironde) in 1883 and educated at the Paris Ecole des beaux-arts, where he studied painting, music, and architecture (1900–1908). In private practice in Paris from 1918 to 1940 and subsequently in New York, Chareau earned his living mainly as a decorator, designing interiors for many modernist houses (particularly those of Robert Mallet-Stevens) and for the Exposition des arts décoratifs in 1925 and the 1937 Paris World's Fair.

As an architect he is known for just one house, built in 1930 in collaboration with the Dutch architect Bernard Bijovoet: the house of Dr. Dalsace on the rue Saint Guillaume in Paris, nicknamed the *maison de verre* for its structure of iron girders and glass bricks. This house, ingeniously built on a difficult site to provide maximum light while ensuring privacy for the house and clinic, is today considered one of the masterpieces of modern architecture, due to its frank use of industrial materials and its brilliant inventiveness.

M. Emanuel et al., eds., *Contemporary Architects* (New York, 1980); Y. Futagawa and F. Montes, "Maison Dalsace," *Global Architecture* 46 (1977).

T. Shapiro

Related entries: ARCHITECTURE AND URBAN PLANNING; LE CORBU-SIER; MALLET-STEVENS.

CHATEAUBRIANT, ALPHONSE DE (1877–1951), Breton novelist, mystical Catholic, and admirer of national socialism. Born in Rennes (Ille–et–Vilaine) to the Breton aristocracy, Chateaubriant established himself as a provincial novelist of talent by winning the Prix Goncourt with his first novel, *Monsieur des Lourdines* (Paris, 1911). Mobilized as an ambulance driver during World War I, he underwent a religious experience in 1915 that would henceforth dominate his thought. Although his close friendship with Romain Rolland led to his association with several communist-related enterprises, including the founding of the review *Europe*, his spiritual meditations found a more natural home in the Maurrassian *Revue universelle*. He vigorously pursued his studies of the mystical tradition in Christian thought, which set the background for his rapturous reaction to the more pagan mysticism of national socialism. A visit to the Black Forest in 1935 and a more extensive tour of Germany the following year formed the basis for his *La Gerbe des forces: Nouvelle Allemagne* (Paris, 1937), a veritable manifesto for a Catholic, mystical fascism. An interview with Adolf Hitler in 1937 sealed an infatuation that led Chateaubriant to assume a major collaborationist role during the Occupation as director of his own weekly, *La Gerbe*. His writings include *La Brière* (Paris, 1923), *La Réponse du Seigneur* (Paris, 1933), and *Cahiers, 1906–1951* (Paris, 1955).

B. M. Gordon, *Collaborationism in France during the Second World War* (Ithaca, 1980); L.-A. Maugendre, *Alphonse de Chateaubriant, 1877–1951* (Paris, 1977).

J. R. Braun

Related entries: FASCISM; ROLLAND.

CHAUTEMPS, CAMILLE (1885–1963), four-time Radical-Socialist premier and minister in eleven interwar cabinets. An opportunistic master of subtlety, he subordinated conviction to expediency, using his consummate skill at compromise to smooth over problems. His second cabinet (November 1930) fell in the wake of riots over the Serge Stavisky affair when he refused to appoint an investigatory commission because his relatives and ministers were implicated. Adept at covering his tracks, Chautemps resigned following charges by the Right that he had instigated the murder of Stavisky's prosecutor, who had "committed suicide" under mysterious circumstances. Later joining Léon Blum's government, Chautemps opposed aiding the Spanish Republic during the civil war (1936–39).

After breaking with the socialists, he succeeded Blum as premier in 1937 but avoided taking any position on major issues. Chautemps contrived to resign without seeking a vote of confidence in order to avoid confronting the *Anschluss* crisis of March 1938. He reemerged as vice-premier in Edouard Daladier's third cabinet where he quietly favored appeasement of Adolf Hitler and advocated a negotiated peace during the *drôle de guerre* of late 1939 and early 1940. As vice-premier in Paul Reynaud's cabinet, Chautemps secretly supported Marshal Philippe Pétain's program of ending the war. On 15 June 1940, he proposed the formula of asking the Germans for their conditions without asking for an armistice. This proposal brought Pétain to power as premier. Continuing as vice-premier for a month, he left for the United States, where he remained after finally breaking with the Vichy regime.

C. Chautemps, *Cahiers secrets de l'armistice, 1939–1940* (Paris, 1963).

M. L. Mickelsen

Related entries: ARMISTICE OF 1940; BLUM; DALADIER; FALL OF FRANCE, 1940; LEBRUN; PETAIN; POPULAR FRONT; REYNAUD; RADICAL AND RADICAL-SOCIALIST PARTY; STAVISKY AFFAIR.

CHEVALIER, MAURICE (1888–1972), France's leading entertainer of the twentieth century. Chevalier owed his remarkable fame to his ability to project a certain theatrical image of Gallic insouciance and sentimentality, which appealed to generations of French and foreigners. For more than seven decades he was admired for his image as France's unofficial ambassador of goodwill abroad.

Maurice Auguste Chevalier was born 12 September 1888 in the Paris district of Ménilmontant on the same day, he liked to recall, that the Eiffel Tower was first illuminated. His father was an alcoholic house painter who early abandoned the family. Maurice and his brother Paul decided to become circus acrobats but abandoned the idea. At the suggestion of his mother, Maurice tried his hand as a music hall singer. After a slow start he gradually improved his act and obtained better billings in Montmartre clubs and tours in the provinces.

In 1904 Chevalier received an engagement in a higher-class Parisian boulevard music hall. At this time he added elements of the American music hall tradition to his repertoire to create the novel blend that would be his international trademark.

At the age of nineteen he played the Alcazar in Marseilles, and when his act was cheered by Sarah Bernhardt, his name was solidly established. Later he had a brief affair with Colette and a longer liaison with Mistinguett.

After the First World War Chevalier entered the realm of stardom. It was then that he adopted the straw hat and tuxedo. He played the lead in *Dédé*, an operetta, which endeared him to American tourists in Paris. His reputation preceded him to the United States. There his stage appearances strengthened his new world reputation.

In 1927 Chevalier married his costar, Yvonne Vallée, and the following year he agreed to work for Irving Thalberg in sound films. The 1930s were the high point of his cinematic career. When war broke out in 1940, he was back in France, and he volunteered to entertain French prisoners in the detention camp where he had been interned two decades earlier. During these years he was attacked by Nazis and communists, and in the Marcel Ophuls's film, *Le Chagrin et la pitié*, it was unfairly suggested that he had collaborationist sympathies. His name was completely cleared.

During the McCarthy period, he was refused entry to the United States for having signed a peace petition. But Chevalier's public demanded his return to work on Broadway and in Hollywood. After a brief illness, he died on 1 January 1972. His voluminous memoirs constitute a valuable chronicle of French and American popular entertainment for most of the twentieth century.

D. Bodeen and G. Ringgold, *Chevalier* (Secaucus, New Jersey, 1973); M. Chevalier, *The Man in the Straw Hat* (New York, 1949), and *I Remember It Well* (New York, 1970).

F. Busi

Related entry: CINEMA.

CHILDREN: ATTITUDES TOWARD. The 1880s and 1890s witnessed a major change in attitudes toward children. The importance of children was reaffirmed, stress was placed on the importance of doctors and science in raising infants, and obedience to authority became the prime virtue that both authorities and parents wished to inculcate in children. The middle classes recognized adolescence as a stage of life. Education of children was seen as the key to social progress.

The importance of children was affirmed and reaffirmed from the 1870s to the 1890s. A recrudescence of children's literature both for and concerning children began in the 1870s and increased rapidly. Many novels and scientific books about children were published each year. The books stressed parental and state authority over children, obedience of children to that authority, scientifically based methods of child rearing, and the proper moral behavior of children. Children were to be supervised and controlled to ensure that they grew up obedient and well-mannered.

Attitudes toward children also reflected the growing public support for population growth. The awareness of France's slow population growth in contrast to that of a more rapid population increase in other nations, a military loss to Germany in 1871, and a relatively slow industrial growth contributed to this change. Authorities aimed to increase the population by encouraging rural, working-class, and bourgeois families to have more children and by protecting those already born from death in infancy and early childhood. Since governmental policy encouraged population growth and an increase in the numbers of children among the working classes, it also accepted the obligation to nourish and control these children by education and various social services. This led to intervention in the lives of children by a host of public and quasi-public officials: doctors, pediatricians, specialists in infant welfare, social workers, psychologists, and teachers. The idea of the state as protector of the children because they were weak and victims of society began to win acceptance in the early decades of the Third Republic.

Children from birth to age nineteen constituted about one-third of the entire population during the Third Republic, and authorities began to recognize them as a sizable social group. This percentage, however, was declining. Children under nineteen represented 37 percent of the population in 1852, 35 percent in 1891, and only 30 percent in 1948. While people in traditional rural areas (where children represented farm hands) continued to have many children until World War I, families in the cities frequently had only one child. The 1891 population of Paris under nineteen years of age was only 27 percent. This figure cannot be taken at face value since many of the newborns of Paris were sent to the countryside to be wet nursed. Nevertheless, the ideal family of the bourgeoisie had only one child. Governmental authorities saw this declining population as family limitation by the predominantly urban parents who preferred to nurture a few offspring carefully rather than to procreate great numbers.

As family size became smaller, parents offered their children more affection and nurturing. Still, in 1900, many children did not have a full family life. For every fifteen families with both father and mother alive, six families were incomplete, with either father or mother dead. At the turn of the century, as many as 45 percent of all French children lost at least one parent before their adulthood.

Specific attitudes toward children varied with the age of the child, according to the three perceived stages of childhood. From birth to age six, the period known as early childhood (*petite enfance*), the child was completely dependent on adults. In the next stage, from six to fourteen years of age, that of childhood (*enfance*), the youngster attended school, often worked, and enjoyed some independence. From fourteen to adulthood (usually perceived as attained at marriage), the stage of youth (*jeunesse*), the child was almost totally independent, either working or attending school, depending on the socioeconomic status of the family.

Early childhood was divided into two stages: birth to age two and two to six. For the under-two group, wet nursing of infants flourished until World War I. Artisan and working-class mothers frequently sent their nurslings to wet nurses who lived in rural France where the infants stayed, usually for one to two years.

In these cases mothers had little contact with their infants. Middle- and upper-class mothers often hired a wet nurse from the countryside to nurse an infant in the baby's home in the city. These wet nurses sent their own babies back home as soon as they got a position in a bourgeois home. Some authorities see the lack of maternal nursing of biological babies as evidence of maternal indifference toward children. Others see the institution of wet nursing in a different light. Artificial feeding was neither safe nor sanitary until the end of the century, and doctors felt that breast feeding an infant, even by a wet nurse, was preferable to bottle feeding a child cow's milk. In addition, working-class families experienced acute economic difficulties when their children were under five; mothers with such young children found it difficult to be wage earners outside the home, but working for wages was a necessity; sending offspring to wet nurse was often essential for the economic survival of the family. Wet nurses themselves nursed another's baby because they needed the income. Bourgeois women frequently employed a wet nurse in their home on the advice of their doctor, but in such circumstances, bourgeois women could supervise the wet nurse's feeding and habits. Despite the higher-than-average mortality rate for babies sent to wet nurses, wet nursing represented less an attitude of indifference toward children and more an economic necessity for working women.

Doctors, equipped with their new scientific knowledge of pasteurization, germ theory of disease, and pediatrics, felt it desirable to assume a greater role in the lives of infants. They saw the infants as having special needs and instructed mothers to carry out scientifically determined schedules and amounts of feeding, to weigh infants periodically on home infant scales, to have separate beds for infants, and to reduce or eliminate the practice of swaddling. Doctors also asked to be summoned for consultation whenever a child became ill.

Doctors and parents were preoccupied with the health of the children from age two to age six and with teaching morality and obedience. Doctors looked after the health of the bourgeois children by working directly with the mother—the doctors prescribed and the mothers acted. Doctors influenced the health of working-class children by their educative surveillance as consultants in the free infant health clinics (*instituts de puériculture*) and in the preschools (*écoles maternelles*), which had begun to proliferate toward the end of the century.

Working-class and bourgeois parents had different attitudes toward teaching obedience. Middle-class parents believed that constant surveillance of the children was essential. They did not believe in striking the children, holding that discipline and good behavior should be internalized. Working classes had few rules for their children but believed that corporal punishment was essential for raising a well-behaved child.

The stage from age six to fourteen was seen as the time when children joined groups of peers and went to school, where teachers and other professionals exerted quasi-parental authority over the children. The evolution of attitudes toward children of this age group was affected by the growth of cities and of factories and by an increasing concern about childhood as a separate stage with its own special needs. Within this larger framework, rural, urban working-class, and bourgeois society exhibited three different types of attitudes. In rural, traditional society, children worked and played in groups with their own hierarchy, rules, and rites. But by the end of the nineteenth century, this gradually gave way to school and to adult society's organization of after-school activities.

For urban working-class children, factories vied with the schools for the children's time, just as in rural areas farm work vied with school. Despite compulsory education, urban working-class children sometimes did not go to school until parents had extra income provided by the work of other children in the family. By the beginning of the twentieth century, however, attitudes changed, in part due to laws for compulsory education. Parents began sending their children to school regularly and for more years. After, or in lieu of, school or work, children organized themselves into peer groups and often wandered the streets as gamins. Authorities viewed these children as a potentially dangerous element of neglected or delinquent youths who needed to be controlled. By the late 1880s, there was concern about child abuse, neglect, and juvenile delinquency.

Bourgeois children in the six to fourteen age bracket engaged less in mutual education with peers than did children of other social groups and spent more time with their families, especially their mothers. They were to imitate and emulate adults more readily. Parents chose their children's acquaintances, and their mothers supervised their homework. The family and schools complemented each other in establishing rules of discipline for children.

It was generally accepted that doctors, psychologists, and teachers were to observe, guide, enrich, and mold children through family, school, and leisure (organized clubs, sports, and summer camps) activities. Pauline Kergomard, general inspector of preschools in the early years of the Third Republic, dreamed of influencing the family's behavior through the schools. To that end, primary and secondary schools stressed conformity and discipline.

Youth, or adolescence, which began when a person reached fourteen or the end of compulsory education and usually lasted until marriage (twenty-four to twenty-six for women, twenty-five to twenty-eight for men), was the third stage of childhood. Adolescence began to receive the special attention of the middle class in 1880s and 1890s when their own children stayed in school longer and often became more knowledgeable than the parents and yet remained dependent on them for support for a longer period. The middle classes were also chary of the adolescents of the urban working classes. The awakening of sexual desire was seen as one of the greatest dangers facing young people of all social groups, and parents and society expressed concern over the sexuality of adolescents. In general, attitudes toward adolescence were to encourage obedience to the adult world through long periods of work on farms, in factories, or in schools. Youths did not always accept this subordinate role and often rebelled and were frequently accused of disrespect to authority.

Attitudes differed toward rural, urban working-class, and bourgeois youths. Rural youths were expected to, and did, spend their time at home working on their family farm or in the trade of their fathers. Marriages were endogamous, and people usually married those in similar occupations. These youths were socially and culturally isolated and usually pursued no education beyond age fourteen. After 1918, more migrated to cities, where they sometimes continued their education. The rate of exogamous marriage increased. Urban working-class youths spent their adolescence in apprenticeships or, more frequently, in paid work. They too usually ended schooling at age fourteen, but after World War I many sought postsecondary education. Most of the bourgeois adolescents were students in postsecondary education.

The number of undergraduate postsecondary students, excluding those in professional schools or private colleges (*étudiants*), increased from 29,000 in 1900 to 73,600 in 1936. Such an increase is partially due to a new value placed on education by and for all youths. Furthermore, after 1918 more youths attended secondary school, and people saw an increased need for trained and qualified specialists. Starting in the 1880s education was seen as necessary for girls as well as boys. Camille Sée best exemplified the new attitudes by saying in the early 1880s that France was not a convent and women were not put in the world to be nuns. Education of children was viewed as a force for progress.

The most striking aspect of attitudes toward children during the Third Republic was the greater attention devoted to this stage of life. Authorities saw children of all ages as needing expert nurturing, protection, and education. Governmental policies concerning children are rooted in this attitudinal change of the 1880s.

A. Armengaud, "L'attitude de la société à l'égard de l'enfant au xixᵉ siécle," *Annales de démographie historique* (1973); L. Clark, *Schooling the Daughters of Marianne* (New York, 1984); M. Crubellier, *L'Enfance et la jeunesse* (Paris, 1979); J. Donzelot, *The Policing of Families* (New York, 1979); R. Fuchs, *Abandoned Children* (New York, 1983); H. Hatzfeld, *Du paupérisme à la sécurité sociale* (Paris, 1971); G. Sussman, *Selling Mothers' Milk* (Urbana, Ill., 1982); L. Tilly and J. Scott, *Women, Work and Family* (New York, 1978); E. Weber, *Peasants into Frenchmen* (Stanford, 1976); T. Zeldin, *France*, vol. 1 (Oxford, 1974).

R. G. Fuchs

Related entries: CHILDREN: GOVERNMENTAL POLICIES CONCERNING; CHILDREN: IN THE LABOR FORCE; EDUCATION: GOVERNMENTAL POLICIES CONCERNING; FAMILY: ATTITUDES TOWARD AND GOVERNMENTAL POLICIES CONCERNING; SOCIAL WELFARE: FAMILY AND CHILDREN.

CHILDREN: GOVERNMENTAL POLICIES CONCERNING. The Third Republic supervised and educated children by exerting the influence of the state on almost every facet of their lives through intermediaries—doctors, teachers, psychologists, social workers, legislators—who regulated education and the rights of parents such that the government and quasi-public social welfare agencies generally sapped paternal authority and usurped the father's prerogatives by protecting children at home, at work, at play, and in school.

Governmental authorities increasingly saw themselves as protectors of children and their rights and as defenders of them against the neglect or aggression of adult society. Because of growing industrialization and urbanization, a greater number of parents worked outside the home than ever before. Thus, many children in the cities were left to themselves. The first legislation to safeguard children was the Roussel Law of 1874 for the protection of nurslings; it regulated the wet nursing industry and sought to control abuses in order to reduce the high rate of infant mortality among children sent out to wet nurse.

The most important, radical, and far-reaching governmental policy toward children was the much-debated law of 24 July 1889 for the protection of neglected and abused children (*moralement abandonnés*). By this measure, the state was enabled to deprive parents of their authority in cases of perceived immorality— vice, drunkenness, crime. Authorities presumed that such depravity resulted in unwholesome upbringing, neglect, or abuse of children. The law defined the conditions under which fathers could be stripped of parental rights. It enabled police, social service, and medical authorities to determine which children should be taken away from their parents and made wards of the state with an official of the Bureau of Public Assistance (*L'Assistance publique*) as their guardian. This law was augmented by one in 1898 that gave power to a judge to confer the guardianship of children to an official of public assistance or to another third party and provided punishment for parents who abused, beat, starved, or otherwise ill treated their children. The government transferred authority from a family found morally lacking to a body of notable officials—public assistance personnel, judges, social workers, and philanthropists.

The year 1912 marked the official inauguration of a system of juvenile justice with separate courts and judges. Juvenile judges had power not only over the children but also over their families. Children could be brought before the judge by fathers, mothers, guardians, the police, or the Republic's prosecutor for everything from disobedience to homicide. The juvenile judge heard all suggestions and evidence about the situation of a given minor and all recommendations from professional personnel about the youth's future. The judge investigated the personality and actions of the minor and the family environment. The judge then had the responsibility to take any measures necessary for the protection of the child, the family, or society. Disciplinary incarceration for adolescent children was no longer seen as the best solution for those who were abused by or who had abused society. The juvenile court sought to replace punishment with prevention and prison with supervision.

The judge had many options in the disposition of minors. He could order that the child be placed in an institution for further medical or social observation or in one for the education or reeducation of the child. Such placements included a prison facility for juveniles, remedial classes, boarding schools, and annexes of elementary schools where children whom the judge ruled unstable, feebleminded, perverse, or aggressive could be placed. The judge could prescribe educative assistance for the child in a noninstitutional, homelike environment or placement in a home with foster parents. The child also became a ward of the state under the guardianship of an official of the Bureau of Public Assistance, who could also place the child in a specialized institution or with foster parents. If conditions warranted, the judge could order a child confined to a medical hospital or award custody to a relative. The courts determined if a child could return to the family, which had to provide evidence of moral probity for a favorable decision. Governmental authorities returned children to their parents infrequently. Child psychiatry, which became established in France with the 1914 publication of *Enfants anormaux et délinquents juveniles* by Georges Heuyer, promulgated the theory that the origin of children's troubles lay within the family.

Between the wars, authorities further criticized the family for the ills of children. During the 1930s a plethora of articles blamed separation, divorce, widowhood, and poor, large families for childhood disturbances. The interwar period also saw a decline in the use of penal institutions for children, with a corresponding increase in the number of private, philanthropic, protective societies for abused or abusive children, and in special prisons for juveniles.

The state limited paternal authority in a relatively minor way by a decree in 1896 and by the Lemire Law of 1907, which abridged the father's right to prevent his children's marriages and which protected illegitimate children. The 1907 law abrogated the requirement of paternal authorization for marriage after the child reached legal majority. By the end of the Third Republic, paternal authority had been effectively restrained in the presumed interest of the child.

Education was the means by which governmental policies directly affected most children; the crucial legislation was that of 1882. Secular education for boys had been in existence since the Guizot laws of 1833. The Ferry Law of 28 March 1882, however, established that public schools be free, nondenominational, and secular, and it made attendance compulsory for children of both sexes from ages six through thirteen. The law provided penalties for heads of families who failed to send their children to school.

Although the number of boys in primary schools hardly changed after 1882, compulsory education seems to have affected literacy rates; at least, the literacy rate for recruits increased from 82 percent in the 1870s to 95 percent in 1913. For girls, the law made a big difference, even in attendance. Their numbers in public primary schools doubled, although in 1900 girls still constituted only 12 percent of the children in secondary schools (*étudiants*). There were, however, significant variations in school attendance according to gender, region, and socioprofessional class background. The higher the socioeconomic echelons and the farther north or northeast, the greater the frequency of attendance and the higher the literacy rates.

Attendance at the lycées, generally frequented by the middle classes, grew by roughly 2 percent per year from 1881 to 1930 and then almost doubled from 1930 to 1939. Attendance in the upper primary school (*écoles primaires supérieures*, EPS) increased almost fourfold for boys alone and six times for boys and girls together between 1881 and 1938. From 1901 to 1930 the number of girls in lycées increased fourfold, and their numbers in the EPS increased almost three and a half times. Demand for professional education (law, science, letters, medicine, pharmacy) multiplied eight times from 1870 to 1930. Such increases in school attendance reflected positive attitudes on the part of parents and youth, and governmental policies responded by providing education for the increasing demand.

Governmental policies fostered vocational or technical education as well as the more traditional forms. In 1882 Jules Ferry advocated that three hours per week be allocated to manual work in the elementary schools (*écoles primaires élémentaires*). The bourgeoisie did not send their children to these schools but rather to lycées and were unaffected by the proposed labor. Ferry's proposal led to a debate on vocational training, which in turn led to the establishment of the professional schools of commerce and industry (*écoles professionnelles de commerce et industrie*) in 1892. Despite their high cost, they had an initial enrollment of 1,300 boys in 1893 and 11,800 by 1913. For girls during the same period, the enrollment increased from 400 to 2,900.

The practice of apprenticeship continued to decline throughout the Third Republic, and governmental authorities became concerned with the number of boys without a skill or the means of acquiring one. In 1919 the Astrier Law stipulated that all children under eighteen employed in commerce or industry, either as apprentices or under contract, be required to take a professional course organized in each commune by the Ministry of Commerce and Industry. They were to attend this course from four to eight hours a week for three years to get a certificate of professional ability (*certificat d'aptitude professionelle*). The law had only moderate success.

Governmental authorities viewed education as a means to mold and control children ages six to fourteen, predominantly those in urban areas. To be completely effective, social workers, psychologists, and teachers trained in psychology worked in the schools to supervise and train working-class children to become hard-working, productive, law-abiding citizens who would contribute to rather than drain the economy. The state aimed to supervise the children by direct surveillance in the schools. Such surveillance necessarily involved regularization of the school day and of leisure-time activities. To this end, the state supported the establishment of clubs and sporting activities, and during the 1880s gymnastic and sporting societies proliferated. By 1913, the Federation of Sport and Gymnastic clubs (*Fédération gymnastique et sportive des patronages*) of France had 130,000 members. Summer camps (*colonies de vacances*), founded by religious leaders and philanthropists, consisted of organized, educative, and sports programs during three to four weeks of summer school vacation. The activities or games at the camps were designed to teach obedience, discipline, loyalty, initiative, and endurance. In 1900, 25,000 children attended summer camps; by 1913, the figure was 100,000. Between the wars nearly 500,000 children attended.

Governmental policies concerning children were designed to supervise and train them to enter the adult world. By the end of the Third Republic—through the influence of doctors, judges, psychologists, and teachers—the government had entered into the area of raising the children and had appropriated much of the authority and many of the duties previously held by parents.

M. Crubellier, *L'Enfance et la jeunesse* (Paris, 1979); J. Donzelot, *The Policing of Families* (New York, 1979); H. Hatzfeld, *Du paupérisme à la sécurité sociale* (Paris, 1971); R. Fuchs, *Abandoned Children* (New York, 1984); G. Sussman, *Selling Mothers' Milk* (1982); T. Zeldin, *France*, vol.1 (Oxford, 1973).

R. G. Fuchs

Related entries: CHILDREN: ATTITUDES TOWARD; CHILDREN: IN THE LABOR FORCE; EDUCATION: GOVERNMENTAL POLICIES CONCERNING; FAMILY: ATTITUDES TOWARD AND GOVERNMENTAL POLICIES CONCERNING; SOCIAL WELFARE: FAMILY AND CHILDREN.

CHILDREN: IN THE LABOR FORCE. The participation of children in the French labor force, and especially their participation in industrial labor, came under increasing restriction during the Third Republic. At the start of the Third Republic, there were about 125,000 children under sixteen in France's industrial work force, representing about 14 percent of all French industrial workers. In addition, there were untold numbers of children working in agriculture, in commerce, or in a small-scale production, often under the supervision of their parents. Though there were virtually no legal restrictions on the labor of most young workers, those children working in shops that were mechanized or had twenty or more workers were subject to the minimal standards of the child labor law of 1841. The 1841 law set a minimum age for employment of eight years and prohibited children under twelve from working more than eight hours a day. The law allowed children twelve to sixteen a maximum workday of twelve hours, and it severely restricted the employment of youngsters at night and on Sundays and holidays. Enforcement of the child labor law, originally left to locally appointed voluntary inspectors, had been placed in the hands of France's mining engineers in 1868, but the law remained widely ignored nonetheless.

A major new French factory law was enacted on 19 May 1874. This law was the only significant piece of social legislation adopted under the provisional Republic, and its passage was motivated in large part by Catholic pro-family sentiment and by a belief that the Franco-Prussian War had demonstrated France's need to be more careful in the treatment of its children. The 1874 law was applicable to all industrial establishments, and although it allowed for the employment of ten year olds under exceptional circumstances, it raised the basic minimum age for employment to twelve. The maximum workday set by the 1874 law was six hours for children under twelve and twelve hours for older children. The law banned the employment of males under sixteen and of females under twenty-one in nighttime labor. Perhaps the most important feature of the 1874 law was its establishment of an extensive system of enforcement and its provision for the appointment of fifteen salaried factory inspectors. France's first legislation governing children in itinerant trades was also passed in 1874, but for the most part children outside purely industrial employment remained unprotected by the law until the twentieth century.

The 1874 factory law was the basic child labor law of France until 1892, when yet another major factory act was passed. The 1892 act, which remained the fundamental law governing the participation of children in the work force throughout the remainder of the Third Republic, raised the minimum age for employment in industrial establishments to thirteen generally and to twelve for those children who had completed their primary education by that age. The law set the maximum workday for children under sixteen at ten hours and for those sixteen to eighteen at eleven hours. Although the 1874 factory act had barred all women from employment in mines, the 1892 law was the first to include major restrictions governing the employment of adult women, and in subsequent years most of the special legislation applied to children in industrial employment contained provisions applicable to women as well. Because the 1892 law set maximum limits on the workdays of children and of women that differed from the standard twelve-hour workday of adult men, it created serious problems of implementation. For this reason, legislation introducing a uniform ten-hour day in all plants where women or children worked was passed in 1900.

In the early twentieth century, numerous measures were adopted to restrict further the employment of children and to protect those who did work. An administrative decree of 1909 limited the weights that could be carried by youngsters, for example, and decrees of 1914 and 1926 forbade or restricted the participation of children under eighteen in many types of dangerous work. In addition, as more and more laws were passed to protect workers generally, the lot of child laborers improved. Child laborers benefited from the various workmen's compensation measures adopted beginning in the 1890s and from the general eight-hour workday imposed in 1919. The effect of international conventions concerning child labor also began to be felt in the early twentieth century. For example, the French law of 1925 prohibiting virtually all workers under eighteen from working between 10 P.M. and 5 A.M. was enacted in response to decisions reached at the Washington International Labor Conference of 1919.

While the labor of young industrial workers was covered by a wide variety of restrictions by the 1920s, the labor of young workers in other sectors of the economy was still largely unregulated. It was not until 1928, for instance, that the minimum age requirements established for industry in 1892 were applied more widely. The law of 30 June 1928 extended the basic minimum age of thirteen to all commercial establishments and also to industrial establishments that had previously been exempt, such as those whose main function was educational or charitable. In 1929, children in agricultural labor came under the protection of a law that sought to guarantee them some technical training, but in general the protection of children employed in nonindustrial labor, and especially of those working under the supervision of their families, lagged far behind the protection of children employed in industry.

Throughout the Third Republic, the child labor issue was closely tied to that of primary education; one intention of France's child labor laws was to guarantee that employment would not deprive children of their opportunity for schooling. The Factory Act of 1874 stipulated that all children under twelve employed in factories attend school for part of the day, and it also limited the workday of children over twelve who had not completed their primary education. The compulsory education law of 1882 reenforced some of the education provisions of the 1874 law, though it complicated the interpretation of others, and one goal of the 1892 Factory Act was to bring child labor legislation into complete harmony with the government's education policy. Indeed, enforcement of the laws requiring school attendance became a major factor in keeping children out of paid employment in the late nineteenth and early twentieth centuries.

The problem of vocational training was also closely tied to the issue of children's participation in the work force. At the beginning of the Third Republic, those children employed as apprentices were under the theoretical protection of the apprenticeship law of 1851. The 1851 law spelled out the mutual obligations of apprentices and masters, and it stipulated that apprenticeship contracts had to be agreed on in writing. There was little compliance with the apprenticeship law, however, and already in the 1870s new methods of providing vocational training were being sought. More and more, that training was entrusted to schools and formal courses. Although private initiatives to advance professional education proliferated in the early decades of the Third Republic, increasingly it was the government that stepped in to fill the void created by the deterioration of traditional apprenticeship, and by the end of the Third Republic government involvement in vocational education was extensive. World War I had confirmed France's critical need for new ways to prepare skilled workers, and in 1919 the Astrier Law was enacted, organizing a complete system of technical education for children under eighteen. In 1928 a new apprenticeship law applicable to both commercial and industrial establishments was adopted to regulate what remained of traditional apprenticeship.

In the early decades of the Third Republic, it was sometimes difficult to enforce compliance with all the provisions of France's child labor laws and especially with those provisions that conflicted with prevailing industrial practices, so that some children continued to work under abominable conditions even in protected shops. The six-hour day for workers between ten and twelve was constantly ignored between 1874 and 1892, for example. On the other hand, there were always some paternalistic employers who went beyond the requirements of the law in attempting to protect young employees and provide for their welfare. Some employers in the early twentieth century went so far as to send their young workers on paid vacations arranged by their firms, and others hired female superintendents whose task was to look after the well-being of young workers. By the last decade of the Third Republic, the evils inherent in child labor and the benefits to be derived from an extended education were widely recognized, and with general public support the various laws covering child labor, education, and the protection of workers were having the desired effect of reducing the participation of children in the work force. In 1931 the roughly 327,000 working children under fifteen in France constituted only about 1.5 percent of all gainfully employed persons in the country, and these children were far better protected on the job than child laborers had been at the inception of the Third Republic.

S. Béziers, *La Protection de l'enfance ouvrière* (Montpellier, 1935); C. van Overbergh, *Les Inspecteurs du travail* (Paris, 1893).

L. S. Weissbach

Related entries: CHILDREN: ATTITUDES TOWARD; CHILDREN: GOVERNMENTAL POLICIES CONCERNING; EDUCATION: GOVERNMENTAL POLICIES CONCERNING.

CINEMA (1895–1945). There are four relatively distinct eras in the cinema of the Third Republic: the archaic period prior to 1918, the troubled era of the silent feature in the 1920s, the comparatively successful epoch of the sound feature in the thirties, and the lean years of the German Occupation, 1940–44.

The first public presentation of motion pictures in France took place in a Parisian café on 28 December 1895. The exhibitors, Auguste and Louis Lumière, however, saw no commercial promise in the cinematograph and soon lost interest in it. Their loss became the gain of Léon Gaumont, Charles Pathé, and Georges Méliès. Gaumont and Pathé, working independently and in competition with one another, came to control the business side of the fledgling industry. Méliès pioneered camera devices and techniques that established the fiction film as fantasy and spectacle.

In the first decade of the twentieth century, movie making in France was dominated by Méliès, a competitor named Ferdinand Zecca, and a production company founded in 1908, Film d'Art. The one-reelers produced by Film d'Art followed closely the conventions of filmed state drama. Méliès's work, too, reflected his experience in the theater before coming to movies. This linking of the motion picture and the theatrical in France in the archaic period established conventions that long persisted.

Gaumont and Pathé prospered, invested abroad, established branch firms, and became internationally preeminent as producers. By 1914 90 percent of the movie production in the world was French. In France, however, the burgeoning popularity and increasing respectability of the cinema evident on the eve of the First World War fell victim to the economic hardships brought on by the conflict. The majority of young film artists and technicians were conscripted, many to serve in the army's Photographic Section (SPCA). Nitrate, used for film stock but also for explosives, became prohibitively expensive or unavailable. The foreign markets for movies either shrank or were cut off from French distribution entirely. Domination of motion picture production internationally passed quickly to the United States after the war began.

With the end of the war, there was a staggering demand for motion pictures. French producers were in no position to respond. Pathé and Gaumont had retrenched and settled on conservative business practices for the coming years.

The competition of Hollywood movies seemed insurmountable, not only in the world market but even in France itself. In Europe, German movies quickly became the most successful, both artistically and commercially.

In the 1920s movie theaters in France were being built swiftly, attendance at movies was high, and substantial profits were being made by both distributors and exhibitors of motion pictures. Movie production, however, stagnated. The bulk of it was taken up with adventure films (which failed to match the visual excitement of Louis Feuillade's pre-World War I serials), sentimental dramas (often based on the orphan theme), adaptations from literature (which suffered badly in adaptation), and light comedies (which could hardly compete with the popular Charlie Chaplin of Hollywood or even with France's own Max Linder of the archaic period). Throughout the decade the government refused to limit the importation of foreign films or to support the native industry financially. Business and banking circles in France (significant investors in motion pictures in Germany and the United States) were unresponsive to movie producers. Foreign audiences were indifferent to French imports or even hostile to the slow pace of many French features.

The French cinema of the 1920s survived, and in the light of its liabilities remarkably well. Movies of genuine artistic merit were made by Louis Delluc, Germaine Dulac, Jean Epstein, and Marcel L'Herbier; spottier successes were achieved by Jacques de Baroncelli, Jacques Feyder, and Abel Gance; René Clair and Jean Renoir launched their directorial careers. Paris became the center for the viewing and appreciation of esoteric movies with the opening of a number of art movie theaters. Moreover, the making of avant-garde movies was centered in Paris, although the best were made by foreign-born directors: Luis Buñuel, Alberto Cavalcanti, and Man Ray.

The fortunes of the French cinema altered drastically after the coming of sound production in 1929. The number of features produced in France during the 1930s was about double annually what it had been for each year of the 1920s. Not only did the quantity soar, but the quality improved as well. In the early 1930s investment capital flowed into motion picture production, suggesting that the reluctant financiers of the twenties were not anti-cinema but rather were waiting for a product they felt to be worthwhile. The relatively late impact of the worldwide economic depression in France meant that the transition for the industry to the production of sound films was smooth.

The early 1930s saw the production of movies that were visually exciting and deftly edited and in which the sound track became an integral part of the whole. The comedies of René Clair were masterpieces. Even more significant, the French cinema managed to produce a number of movies of serious social commentary or satire, the best remembered of which were directed by Clair, Jean Renoir, and Jean Vigo.

In late 1934 and throughout 1935 the economic and political instability in France took its toll on the movie industry. At this juncture, however, the artistic ingenuity and energy of those involved in production (as well as the enthusiasm of at least one newcomer to the movies, Marcel Pagnol) meant that the cinema not only survived but flourished. The features of the last years of the 1930s, directed by Marcel Carné, Julien Duvivier, Pagnol, and Renoir, mark a cinema that was original, capable of projecting authentic social significance onto the screen, and remarkably successful commercially. In these movies the viewer discovers a cinematic naturalism, often dominated by scenes of the sea, pastoral landscapes, the earth covered by snow, or atmospheres of fog and mist. This naturalism of setting is integrated in these movies with the thematic material so as to create a lingering fatalism within the framework of a subtle and pervasive social commentary.

With the fall of France in 1940 and the coming of the occupation, the French cinema went into eclipse. Jean Benoit-Lévy, Feyder, Duvivier, and Renoir chose exile. The studios remained open, but the productions from them explored only timeworn themes and in a highly stylized manner. This marked a break with the late 1930s of such magnitude that regaining a continuity with them was nearly impossible. The triumphs of the late 1930s influenced far more the Italian cinema than they did French productions after 1945. The burst of creativity of the New Wave in France after 1959, moreover, was more indebted to the American *film noir* than to the French naturalism of the late 1930s.

H. Agel, "La France et le cinéma français," *Chronique sociale de France*, no. 4–5 (1954). M. Bardeche and R. Brasillach, *Histoire du cinéma*, 2 vols. (Paris, 1964). P. Cowie, ed., *A Concise History of the Cinema*, vol. 1 (London, 1971); R. Jeanne and C. Ford, *Le Cinéma et la presse* (Paris, 1961); P. Leglise, *Histoire de la politique du cinéma français* (Paris, 1970); P. Monaco, *Cinema and Society* (New York, 1976); G. Sadoul, *Histoire du cinéma français* (Paris, 1962); J. Sidier, "Dans le cinéma français l'aventure ne dépasse pas le coin de la rue," *L'Ecran*, (January 1958); E. Strebel, "French Social Cinema and the Popular Front," *Journal of Contemporary History* 12 (1977).

P. Monaco

Related entry: COMMUNICATIONS.

CITROËN, ANDRE (1878–1935), automobile manufacturer. He was the son of a Paris diamond merchant of Dutch-Jewish background who committed suicide after being deceived by swindlers. After graduating from the Ecole polytechnique and serving a brief term in the army, young Citroën established a machine shop making gears with teeth cut in a new chevron-style pattern. In 1907–8 he became president of the Mors automobile company but was unable to raise this firm above mediocrity before the First World War.

After several months of duty as an artillery officer in 1914, he persuaded the government to finance a large shell-making factory on the Quai Javel in Paris. Using mass production techniques that he had seen in the United States before the war, Citroën's firm soon produced thousands of shells a day with a largely unskilled labor force, including many women. When the war ended, he turned back to automaking, offering one low-priced model put together on a moving assembly line. Citroën soon became the largest auto producer in France, with just one or two models produced with up-to-date equipment and sold by imaginative and aggressive methods. In 1926 he established four assembly plants elsewhere in Europe, and in 1929, his best year, he made 62,000 cars.

When the French auto market declined in the Great Depression, Citroën's sales stopped expanding, and he found it more and more difficult to keep his creditors at bay. The introduction of a new front wheel drive model in 1934 proved to be a technical success, but it came too late. The company was placed in judicial liquidation in December 1934. The largest creditor, Michelin, took over, and Citroën had to leave. He died in July 1935.

J.-L. Loubet, "La Société André Citroën (1924–1968)" (dissertation, University of Paris-Nanterre, 1979); M. Norroy, *André Citroën le précurseur* (Paris, 1973); S. Reiner, *La Tragédie d'André Citroën* (Paris, 1954).

J. M. Laux

Related entries: INDUSTRY: AUTOMOBILE; RENAULT.

CLAUDEL, PAUL (1868–1955), dramatist, poet, diplomat. On Christmas Day 1886 Claudel had a mystical experience in Notre-Dame Cathedral; on Christmas Day 1890 he formally returned to communion, never to waver again. Earlier that year he had placed first in the entrance examination for diplomatic service. He held consular posts in New York and Boston from 1893 until 1895 when his first Chinese tour of duty occurred. Returning to China from France in 1900, he met the prototype for Ysé, his 1905 heroine of *Partage de midi*. The play's symbolist lyricism does not conceal Claudel-Mesa's unhappy love affair. Sin, separation, guilt, and expiation are Claudelian hallmarks.

Instead of rereading and correcting, Claudel wrote completely new versions of his plays. *Partage de midi* had a 1948 version and another in 1949. His most famous play, *L'Annonce faite à Marie* (1910–11), had two predecessors, both titled *La Jeune fille Violaine*, and was followed by another version in 1948. Claudel's masterpiece, *Le Soulier de satin* (1919–24), was written mostly during his Japanese ambassadorship (1921–27). A Washington ambassadorship followed from 1927 to 1933.

Claudel continued to write poetry. His finest, *Cinq Grandes Odes* (1908) and *La Cantate à trois voix*, are written in the *verset claudélien*, a long, free, irregular rhythm determined by respiration. Claudel's dramatic dialogue is also written in *versets claudéliens*. His purely theatrical innovation was not widely appreciated at first because of production difficulties. Eventually Jean-Louis Barrault dazzled Paris by his imaginative staging of Claudel plays. For example, the waves in *Le Soulier de satin* were effectively rendered by dancers. In this play the themes of separation, sacrifice, nobility, and salvation are intertwined in a panegyric to Catholicism. As in *Partage de midi*, the heroine is involved with three men, but in *Le Soulier de satin* there are numerous other characters, an epic scope, and an intentionally episodic structure. Lyrical scenes with a guardian angel and with the moon contrast with comic interludes involving stupid pedants. Other characters prevent the audience from empathizing. Such techniques later made the German dramatist Bertolt Brecht and his epic theater famous, but appreciation of Claudel's theatrical genius has been hampered by widespread dislike of his religiosity.

J. Chiari, *The Poetic Drama of Paul Claudel* (New York, 1969); H. A. Waters, *Paul Claudel* (New York, 1970); H. Watson, *Claudel's Immortal Heroes* (New Brunswick, N.J. 1971).

C. F. Gerrard
Related entries: CATHOLIC LITERARY RENAISSANCE; THEATER.

CLEMENCEAU, GEORGES (1841–1929), politician, journalist, called "the Tiger", twice premier (25 October 1906–20 July 1909; 17 November 1917–18 January 1920). Born at Mouilleron-en-Pareds (Vendée) to a line of physician-landowners, he earned a medical doctorate (Paris, 1865) while engaging in radical political activity inspired by his father and, for a time, Auguste Blanqui. Disappointed in love, he emigrated to New York (1865–69), where he wrote on political life for *Le Temps*, taught at a Stamford (Connecticut) girls' school and married a pupil, Mary E. Plummer (a son, two daughters; divorced, 1892). He returned to the Vendée to practice medicine but was drawn to Paris by the Franco-Prussian War. He participated in the Revolution of 4 September, was appointed and then elected mayor of Montmartre during the siege of Paris, elected to the National Assembly (February 1871), voted against the cession of Alsace-Lorraine, was nearly lynched while trying to rescue Generals Claude Lecomte and Clément Thomas at the outset of the Commune in Montmartre (18 March), and after resigning his posts tried to mediate between Adolphe Thiers and the Commune. In 1871–76 he practiced medicine and represented Montmartre on the Paris Municipal Council (president, 1875). He was elected deputy from Montmartre in 1876, 1877, and 1881 and from the Var in 1885 and Draguignan (Var) in 1889. Defeated in 1893, he was elected a senator from the Var in 1902 and 1909, retiring in 1920.

As a journalist, the role he most enjoyed, he was a columnist for numerous papers, notably *La Dépêche* (Toulouse, 1894–1906) and *L'Aurore* (1897–99), publisher-editor of *La Justice* (1880–97), *Le Bloc* (1901–2), *L'Aurore* (1903–6), *L'Homme libre* (1913–14), and *L'Homme enchaîné* (1914–17), its retitled continuation, and he lent his name to André Tardieu's *L'Echo national* (1922–24). He wrote a novel (*Les Plus Forts*, 1898) and a one-act play (*Le Voile du bonheur, 1901*) and published nineteen volumes of collected articles, seven on the Dreyfus case. In retirement he wrote *Demosthène* (1926), a philosophy entitled *Au soir de la pensée* (2 vols., 1927), *Claude Monet: Les Nymphéas* (1928), and *Grandeurs et misères d'une victoire* (1930), an unrevised set of essays on World War I and its aftermath. His writing, while sometimes prolix, was marked by ironic wit and acute observations on a host of subjects. A sparkling conversationalist, he was a formidable public speaker and devastating in debate.

In the Chamber of Deputies (1876–93), as leader of the left-wing radicals (Radical-Socialists), he earned repute as a ministry wrecker while advocating a more thorough democratization of political and social life through such measures as separation of church and state, recognition of trade unions, social insurance, nationalization of utilities, and an income tax. He opposed imperialist ventures overseas, especially Jules Ferry's, and urged an entente with Britain to oppose German power. To republicanize the army, he recommended General Georges Boulanger as minister of war (1886–87) but subsequently took alarm at his ambitions and worked to defeat his movement. A campaign engineered by Boulangists defeated him in turn (1893), using unproved corruption charges connected with the Panama Canal Company scandal and forgeries (the Norton Papers) naming him as a paid agent of England.

He then turned full time to journalism, playing a leading role in securing a retrial for Captain Alfred Dreyfus (1897–99). Persuaded to stand for the Senate (1902)—which he had sought to abolish when a deputy—he supported Emile Combes' anticlerical campaign there and in the press. His prominence brought him to the Interior Ministry under Ferdinand Sarrien (14 March–19 October 1906), whom he overshadowed. His ensuing premiership, unusually long and controversial, coincided with the apogee of anarchosyndicalist influence in the unions, a drive to organize minor civil servants (such as teachers and postal workers), and a wave of strikes. His peremptory ways, general combativeness, and stern responses to violence—strike-breaking, according to his critics— provoked the newly unified Socialists, disconcerted the Radicals, and spawned endless interpellations that impeded his highly ambitious legislative program. Its key items, an income tax and a workers' pensions bill, finally cleared the Chamber, but the Senate stalled them, and despite a successful foreign policy— closer ties with Britain, peaceful settlement of the Casablanca Deserters (1908) and Bosnian (1908–9) crises and conclusion of the Franco-German Morocco Treaty (1909)—his ministry was generally regarded as a disappointment.

His warnings of a growing German menace, which he underscored by provoking Joseph Caillaux's fall (1912), foreshadowed his role as an outspoken, frequently censored critic of the government's conduct of the war, criticism given added weight because of his presidency of the Senate's Army and Foreign Affairs commissions. But President Raymond Poincaré, a long-time foe whose election (1913) he had opposed, had resolved to summon him only as a last resort. A long-maturing crisis involving General Robert Nivelle's failed offensive, the ensuing army mutinies, a train of spy scandals, the Italian defeat at Caporetto, and the Bolshevik coup presaging Russia's withdrawal finally led Poincaré in November 1917 to send the call.

The Allies' victory in 1918 owed much to Clemenceau's ability to inspire confidence and drive his countrymen forward despite their terrible weariness, for a French collapse would have doomed the Allies' chances. His dramatic arrest of Caillaux on (somewhat flimsy) subversion charges (14 January), vigorous measures against malingerers, and close attention to the army's morale and leadership braced the nation to meet the great German offensives of the spring. He emphasized inter-Allied cooperation and was instrumental in putting the armies under Ferdinand Foch's direction. At the Armistice (11 November) his prestige at home and abroad was immense.

It paled during the Peace Conference (1919–20), over which he presided, because he neither adopted Woodrow Wilson's theses outright, which would have pleased his left-wing critics, nor broke with the Allies to please the Right when he could not obtain a permanent occupation of the Rhineland and reparations in amounts the public had thought possible. The complex problems attending demobilization and economic readjustment also eroded his standing. These factors plus his age (seventy-eight), anticlerical views, and hesitation about posing his candidacy helped bring about his startling defeat by Paul Deschanel for the presidency in January 1920. He retired, having previously decided to resign the premiership.

In retirement he said little publicly about the mutilations of the peace treaties, but on a visit to the United States (1922) he implored the United States not to desert its late allies. He died (24 November 1929) convinced that Germany would seek revenge and deeply troubled over the Allies' weakness and disunity. He was buried, at his request, in a nameless grave beside his father at Le Colombier, a farm near Mouchamps (Vendée).

Endowed with prodigious reserves of energy and will, intelligent, courageous, highly cultured yet earthy, witty and sensitive yet capable of brutally riding over anyone or anything in his way, he was the most striking political figure of the Third Republic. His unsurpassed ability as a critic, intense individualism, and willingness to make enemies overshadowed his gifts for constructive activity. Although a founder and the leading spokesman of Radicalism, he was a lone fighter, at bottom little interested in party organization. Firmly committed to democratic values (notwithstanding his methods and mannerisms), he was superbly equipped for the role that fell to him in old age: the leader of a great democracy in the crowning crises of a world war. He exercised a virtual dictatorship, yet by later standards he requested and employed remarkably few special powers. At the Peace Conference he was a hard but not an unreasonable negotiator, basically agreeing with Wilson on aims and values but disagreeing on the role of force in human affairs. He sought, with only passing success, to ensure postwar Allied cooperation to achieve international stability and to meet France's security requirements at a time when its industrial and military potential had plainly become inferior to Germany's.

G. Geffroy, *Georges Clemenceau*, rev. ed. (Paris, 1932); J. Martet, *Georges Clemenceau* (New York, 1930); G. Michon, *Clemenceau* (Paris, 1931); G. Monnerville, *Clemenceau* (Paris, 1968); J.-J.-H. Mordacq, *Le Ministère Clemenceau*, 4 vols. (Paris, 1930–31); D. R. Watson, *Georges Clemenceau: A Political Biography* (London, 1974); G.-M. Wormser, *La République de Clemenceau* (Paris, 1961).

D. S. Newhall

Related entries: ANTICLERICALISM; ARMISTICE OF 1918; BLANQUI; BOULANGER; CAILLAUX; COMMUNE OF PARIS; DREYFUS AFFAIR; FOCH; GERMANY, RELATIONS WITH; GREAT BRITAIN, RELATIONS

WITH; JACOBINISM; MANDEL; MOROCCAN CRISES; NEWSPAPERS, ROLE OF; OVERSEAS EMPIRE: FRENCH IMPERIALISM; PANAMA SCANDAL; PARIS PEACE CONFERENCE; POINCARE, R.; RADICAL AND RADICAL-SOCIALIST PARTY; ROMAN CATHOLICISM: CHURCH-STATE RELATIONS; RUSSIA, RELATIONS WITH; SEPARATION OF CHURCH AND STATE, LAW OF; SYNDICALISM; TARDIEU; *UNION SACREE*; UNITED STATES, RELATIONS WITH; WORLD WAR I, FRANCE'S ROLE IN.

CLERICALISM, ideology associated with the Catholic church that defended the rights of the clergy to influence French political and social institutions. Throughout the Old Regime the Catholic clergy had been a privileged order, the First Estate, which controlled the educational system of France, supervised the distribution of charity, monitored the religious and moral behavior of laymen, and officiated at rituals that sanctified critical moments in the lives of individuals, local communities, and the French state. Resentment of clerical power led to the abolition of this privileged status during the Revolution. Although the Concordat of 1801 reestablished official ties between church and state, many clergymen, recalling their former positions, sought a restoration of their influence in French society.

Education was the major area in which the clergy asserted their claims. Convinced that God judges people according to the state of their souls and not their minds, clergymen argued for the inclusion of the religious and moral doctrines of Catholicism in the instructional programs of French schools. The clergy were given a major role in inspecting primary schools in the Guizot law (1833) and were allowed to establish their own secondary schools outside the state system as a result of the Falloux law (1850). In the early years of the Third Republic, the National Assembly moved to expand the influence of the clergy in education. The composition of the Conseil supérieure de l'instruction publique was altered in 1873 to include four bishops. Two years later the Assembly granted the church the right to open universities despite the strong opposition of anticlericals. Proponents of Catholic higher education such as Monsignor Maurice d'Hulst, rector of the Catholic University in Paris, made it clear that they saw their task as one of combatting the dangers of materialistic science with faith informed but not dominated by reason.

Other legislation passed by the Assembly in the early 1870s added to the power and prestige of the Catholic clergy. With Monsignor Félix Dupanloup playing a major role, *curés* were placed on local welfare boards, soldiers were guaranteed the time and opportunity to attend Sunday Mass, and a reformed chaplain corps was established for the military services. Outside of the Assembly, the clergy, cooperating with Catholic laymen like Albert de Mun, organized associations of Catholic youths and workers. Clerical influence was also extended through the numerous devotions and shrines that flourished in the Third Republic.

The political, organizational, and devotional activity of the 1870s reflected the opinion prevalent in the Catholic clergy that they merited a position as the moral and religious tutors of the French state and its citizens. The failure to acknowledge the importance of the clergy was believed to have led to the political and social disorders of the nineteenth century, and the restoration of clerical authority was deemed the best guarantee of public tranquility. This utilitarian argument in favor of clericalism was accompanied by an insistence that the salvation of individual souls and of France as a nation was dependent on the favorable disposition of God's will, which could be won only by granting the clergy the respect and attention they deserved.

Anticlericals responded to the advance of clericalism in the 1870s by describing it as a threat to the liberty and independence of France. The clerical legislation of the 1870s was abolished in the 1880s, and clericalism was dealt a crushing blow when the church was separated from the state in 1905. Following World War I, Catholics continued to insist on their rights to a religious education, and the bishops issued a condemnation of state-run schools in 1925. But in general a new sense of toleration replaced the rancor of the prewar years as Catholics and the clergy gradually came to accept a secular state.

J. Brugerette, *Le Prêtre français et la société contemporaine*, 3 vols. (Paris, 1933–38); J. Gadille, *La Pensée et l'action politiques des évêques français au début de la IIIe république (1870–83)*, 2 vols. (Paris, 1967); R. Rémond, *L'Anticléricalisme en France de 1815 à nos jours* (Paris, 1976).

T. A. Kselman

Related entries: ANTICLERICALISM; DUPANLOUP; PIE; ROMAN CATHOLICISM: CLERGY; ROMAN CATHOLICISM: POPULAR DEVOTIONS; SCHOOLS, ROMAN CATHOLIC.

COCTEAU, JEAN (1889–1963), considered himself above all a poet and accordingly classified his works as poetry of the theater, cinema, and novel. Born in Maisons-Lafitte near Paris, Cocteau was associated with many different avant-garde artistic groups. The quantity and diversity of his creative production and his refusal to limit himself to any one artistic school make it difficult to determine the extent of his influence. Some critics see much of Cocteau's work as superficial, derivative, and unimportant. The fact remains that he was a talented and innovative artist who made enduring contributions to drama, film, poetry, and the novel.

Cocteau collaborated with such important artists of his day as Pablo Picasso and Erik Satie on the ballet *Parade* (1917) and with Darius Milhaud on *Le Boeuf sur le toit* (1920). With Francis Poulenc, Milhaud, and Sergei Diaghilev he worked on the ballet *Les Biches* (1924), and he wrote the text for the opera-oratoria *Oedipus-Rex* (1927) with music by Igor Stravinsky. Best known among his own dramatic works are *La Voix humaine* (1930), a tour de force one-act monologue for actress, and *La Machine infernale* (1934), based on the Oedipus theme. In the 1930s Cocteau turned his hand to the cinema, distinguishing himself as a filmmaker. He is well known for his motion pictures *Le Sang d'un poète* (1932) and *La Belle et la bête* (1945).

His poetry is composed in a traditional style but is personalized by the originality of his themes, images, and myths. The purity and cruelty of childhood, the angel-poet, Heurtebise, sleep, dreams, and death are among the topics in his early poetry that recur in his other works.

Cocteau's debut with the novel in *Le Grand Écart* (1923) reveals an interest shared with André Gide and Marcel Proust in the passage from adolescence to adulthood, which he explored in two subsequent novels. In *Thomas l'imposteur* (1923), the adolescent hero, dressed in a borrowed military uniform and pretending to be the nephew of a famous general, treats illusion and reality as one even at the moment of death. Cocteau's most successful novel, *Les Enfants terribles* (1929), is an interesting experiment in poetry of the novel. Caught up in the enchanted world of childhood, the children remain in touch with their primal urges, communicating through arcane symbols and obscure rituals. With fiercely protective animal instincts, they resist the intrusion of the adult world at the price of death by suicide. The poetic purity that Cocteau found in the theme of childhood is self-limiting and reaches its climax in the premature deaths of his young heroes whose spirits are thereby saved from the corruption of the adult world. In 1955 Cocteau's achievements were recognized by his election to the French Academy.

C. Borgal, *Cocteau, poète de l'au-delà* (Paris, 1977); B. Knapp, *Jean Cocteau* (New York, 1970); N. Oxenhandler, *Scandal and Parade* (New Brunswick, N.J., 1957); F. Steegmuller, *Cocteau* (London, 1970).

R. F. O'Reilly

Related entries: CINEMA; GIDE; PICASSO; PROUST; SATIE; THEATER.

COLETTE, SIDONIE (1873–1954), writer. Born in Saint-Sauveur-en-Puisaye (Haute–Saône), she spent her childhood in the Burgundian countryside, where she developed a love of rural ways. At the age of twenty, she was married to the literary critic Henri Gauthiers-Villars, known as "Willy," and moved to Paris. Notorious for his use of ghost writers, Willy ordered Colette—as she was called—to write a memoir of her schooldays. At first he dismissed the work as worthless, then changed his mind and published *Claudine à l'école* under his own name in 1900. The book was an immediate success and was followed by *Claudine à Paris* (1901), *Claudine en ménage* (1902), and *Claudine s'en va* (1903), all of which Collette wrote and for which Willy claimed credit.

Cruelty and infidelity drove Colette from her husband. (She married twice again, to the politician Henry de Jouvenel and to Maurice Goudeket.) She then started her own career as writer, critic, journalist, and, from financial necessity, music hall performer. It is for her personal independence, earned after her separation from Willy, as well as for her writing that Colette is honored; she has perennially been rediscovered, most recently as a feminist author. Her characters, such as the doomed lover of *Chéri* (1920) and *La Fin de Chéri*

(1926), the schoolgirl of the Claudine series, and the ingénue of *Gigi* (1944) quickly became literary standards and have also been translated to the screen.

Much of Colette's greatest work is autobiographical. In *La Maison de Claudine* (1922), she celebrates the Burgundian countryside, and *Sido* (1929) is an endearing portrait of her mother. Other books describe Brittany and the Midi, where she spent vacations. Books such as *Dialogues des bêtes* (1904) and *La Chatte* (1933) take animals for their subject, particularly Colette's beloved cats. Colette took great joy in anything sensual, from a flower to a lover. She wrote as eloquently of her mother's garden as she openly defended the love of a young man for an older woman in *Chéri* or homosexual love in *Le Pur et l'impur* (1932). She perfected the genre of the novella, and her novellas wed a lyrical evocation of French landscapes with deft characterizations of her friends and the honest recollections of a woman whose independence sometimes caused scandal.

Colette, *Oeuvres complètes* (Paris, 1973–75); M. Raaphorst-Rousseau, *Colette, sa vie, son oeuvre* (Paris, 1964); M. Sarde, *Colette, libre et entravée* (Paris, 1978).

R. Aldrich

Related entry: BURGUNDY.

COLLECTIVE BARGAINING. The process of collective bargaining—negotiations between workers' unions and employers—was not well established during the Third Republic. Systematic collective bargaining became common in France only after the Second World War and some observers argue only after 1968. The rarity of collective bargaining prior to 1940 reflects the particular characteristics, perhaps the weaknesses, of industry, employers, workers, and unions in the Third Republic.

Collective bargaining can succeed only when employers are willing to view their work force as a collective unit and recognize a union as a legitimate representative. Unions must pursue objectives limited to a particular factory or at most a national industry. Furthermore, union leaders must agree that their conflicts with employers can be resolved. Neither the pre–World War I Confédération générale du travail (CGT) nor the postwar Confédération générale du travail unitaire (CGTU) was willing to endorse these principles fully. In addition, the numerical weakness of all unions made it difficult to engage in collective bargaining until the last years of the Third Republic. Employers on the whole were even more resistant to collective bargaining than workers. Although unions had been declared legal associations in 1884, most employers continued to ignore their existence or view them as dangerous trespassers on their property. *Liberté de travail* and *maître chez soi* were the twin standards of French employers until after the Second World War. The weakness of collective bargaining efforts is documented by the evidence that only 2,500 contracts were concluded over the twenty-six-year period from 1919 to 1935.

Despite the infrequency of collective bargaining prior to 1945, certain employers, unions, and the state did make efforts to introduce this form of labor relations during the Third Republic. The first collective contract was signed in 1891 following a coal miners' strike in the north. Until 1900 this Convention d'Arras, which covered miners in the Nord and Pas-de-Calais, was regularly renegotiated without strikes. However, the mining industry with its large labor force participating in a well-established reformist union, its greater degree of capital investment, and its tradition of employer paternalism, was an anomaly in France. One year after the Convention d'Arras, the state tried to encourage collective bargaining by establishing voluntary arbitration boards. The failure of this approach influenced the reform socialist Alexandre Millerand to propose obligatory arbitration. Millerand designed an elaborate method of negotiations that would have imposed collective bargaining on workers and employers. The Millerand plan, proposed in 1901 and again in 1906, gained little support among workers or employers. It was never presented on the floor of the Chamber of Deputies.

Collective bargaining was promoted by very different conditions in the 1910s and the 1930s. Beginning about 1910, employers in certain industries sought out collective contracts. The disarray of the syndicalist movement and the industrial boom of the period gave employers a new confidence in their ability to control unions. But this trend among some large industrialists to accept collective bargaining did not grow after the First World War. In 1936 only 7.5 percent of the labor force had a collective contract. The year 1936 is the most important date in the development of collective bargaining. The election of the Popular Front government and the great sitdown strikes of the spring placed collective bargaining at the head of the workers' demands. The Matignon Agreements of 7 June 1936, concluded between the CGT and the large employers' organization, the Confédération générale des producteurs français, had as its first article the acceptance of collective bargaining. Immediately after Matignon the number of collective contracts increased to 5,000 in two years; however, economic, international, and political conditions made it impossible to maintain the workers' gains. In 1939 fewer than 500 contracts were negotiated.

Although collective bargaining does not dominate the history of labor relations during the Third Republic, the efforts to introduce it reveal much about labor conflict prior to 1940 and much about the bases for the eventual acceptance of collective bargaining after 1945.

P. Stearns, "Against the Strike Threat," *Journal of Modern History* 40 (1968); G. Lefranc, *Juin 36* (Paris, 1966); J. Colton, *CompulsoryLabor Arbitration in France, 1936–9* (New York, 1951).

J. F. Stone

Related entries: BASLY; BLUM; CONFEDERATION GENERALE DU TRAVAIL; CONFEDERATION GENERALE DU TRAVAIL UNITAIRE; DEPRESSION OF THE 1930s; INDUSTRY; MATIGNON AGREEMENTS; MILLERAND; POPULAR FRONT.

COLLECTIVISM, a term embracing the entire history of the French labor movement during the early Third Republic. Broadly it defines an alternative to capitalism in the social or collective ownership of land and capital. Originally delineating a federalist socialism based on associated trades and communes, it came to signify in the hands of the Guesdists, the first French Marxists, a centralized state socialism, the very opposite of its original meaning in the socialist lexicon.

Rather than an abstract doctrine elaborated by intellectuals, collectivism was an ideology that grew out of the discussions and experience of the International Workingmen's Association, founded by French, British, and German workers in 1864. The term originated with Baron Hippolyte de Colins, the Belgian socialist who advocated the collectivization of land through the gradual abolition of inheritance. It was introduced by the Belgian César de Paepe to the International's congress (Brussels, 1868), which approved his resolution for the collectivization of land along with industrial capital. The majority of French delegates, usually classified as Proudhonians, who voted this resolution reflected the emerging collectivist consensus in the French labor movement.

Although a majority of labor militants remained committed to the cooperative program of the Second Republic through the 1870s, a vocal minority, led by Eugène Varlin and Benoît Malon, began to advocate the necessity for a violent revolution to break the rule of the bourgeoisie and collectivize land and capital. These revolutionary collectivists saw the *syndicat*, or trade union, as the main instrument of revolution and unit of production in a federation of trades and communes. These revolutionaries became associated with the anarchist Mikhail Bakunin in 1869 and, after the suppression of the Paris Commune, joined the Swiss Jurassian Federation in its revolt against Marx's authoritarian leadership of the International.

After returning to France in 1877, the revolutionaries, led by Jules Guesde, were soon able to triumph over the cooperators in the trade unions and to establish the Parti des travailleurs socialistes de France, the first French socialist labor party, at the Congress of Marseilles in 1879. In 1880 the Parisian federation of the party approved a minimum electoral program, drafted anonymously by Guesde and Marx, declaring that "the collective appropriation [of capital] can only result from the revolutionary action of the producing class."

Disagreements soon erupted between Guesde, who came increasingly under the influence of Paul Lafargue, Marx's son-in-law, Malon, and Paul Brousse, the former leader with Prince Pyotr Kropotkin of the anarchist communist French Federation of the International. When Guesde lost his bid for stronger leadership of the party, he withdrew with his coterie to found the Parti ouvrier français in 1882. Guided by a rudimentary Marxism, the Guesdists repudiated the federalist heritage of the skilled trades and sought to create a centralist party oriented toward factory workers in industrial regions of France.

Despite the shift toward centralism, the Guesdists continued to call themselves collectivists in contradistinction to Brousse, who retained the communist appellation from his anarchist days. From a term designating the federalist trade socialism of skilled workers, collectivism thus came to signify a highly centralized state socialism that even latter-day Marxists would find objectionable.

J. Guillaume, *L'Internationale: documents et souvenirs (1867–1878)*, 4 vols. (Paris,

1905); J. Maitron, *Histoire du movement anarchiste en France, 1880–1914* (Paris, 1955); B. Moss, *The Origins of the French Labor Movement, 1830–1914: The Socialism of Skilled Workers* (Berkeley, 1976); *La Prèmiere Internationale: recueil de documents*, ed. by J. Freymond, 4 vols. (Geneva, 1962–71); D. Stafford, *From Anarchism to Reformism* (Toronto, 1971); C. Willard, *Les Guesdistes* (Paris, 1965).

B. H. Moss

Related entries: BROUSSE; GUESDE; GUESDISTS; INTERNATIONAL, FIRST WORKINGMEN'S; LAFARGUE, P.; MALON; MARXISM; VARLIN.

COLONIALISM. Throughout the Third Republic *colonization* was the word used to describe the process of establishing overseas settlements of Frenchmen or controlling foreign lands and peoples. In the aftermath of the acquisition of a new empire in Africa and Asia, critics of French colonial policies and practices came to employ the term *colonialism* to mean a defective or abusive colonization. *Anticolonialism* most often meant a criticism of the shortcomings of colonization rather than complete opposition to such involvement.

French colonial expansion between the 1870s and the First World War derived both from the general European setting that produced the so-called new imperialism of those decades and from the particular French situation in the aftermath of the Franco-Prussian War of 1870–71. Nationalist rivalries among the industrialized states, involving considerations of power, prestige, and wealth, precipitated the scramble to partition and to occupy Africa and Asia. Given its colonial involvement on four continents since the seventeenth century and its acquisition of additional territories in Africa, Asia, and the Pacific in the period from 1815 to 1870, France very likely would have become a major participant in any competition among the Western nations. But the revived and strengthened nationalism emanating from its defeat in 1871 ensured a much more vigorous and extensive participation. At this time a minority of nationalists, particularly leftists, urged concentration on building up French power on the Continent as the best means of regaining Alsace and Lorraine. But the majority of nationalists came to see colonial expansion as an even superior means through the acquisition of fields for investment, markets for French goods, and sources of raw materials, as well as military manpower from overseas areas. They saw French prestige, power, and wealth enhanced by extension of their rule over additional lands and peoples to whom they would bring the material and moral benefits of Western civilization and French culture. They insisted that the costs of expansion had to be reckoned in long-term gains and benefits and not merely in short-term financial expenses or immediate advantages.

In administering the vast new territories it acquired in Africa and Asia between 1871 and 1919, the Third Republic drew on earlier colonial experiences in several important respects. First, it retained the traditional economic policy that subordinated the interests of the colonies to those of the mother country or metropole. The colonies were supposed to send France noncompetitive exotic products while receiving French manufactures. Preferential arrangements gave

French interests the bulk of the colonial markets while limiting or excluding the activities of foreigners. Colonies were expected to be financially self-sufficient and to generate locally their own funds for development. Thus despite the oft-professed liberalism of the Republic, mercantilist concepts from earlier eras governed the economic aspects of the colonial relationship.

Second, the Republic maintained the tradition of political centralization of earlier regimes, whether monarchical or republican, by ruling the colonies from Paris and through local officials appointed by Paris. Representative bodies in the colonies had powers that were mainly advisory and limited in scope. The Third Republic also adopted the previous republican practice of granting the inhabitants of the so-called old colonies (Guadeloupe, Martinique, Guyana, the communes of maritime Senegal) both citizenship and parliamentary representation. But in Algeria it extended these privileges only to the European settlers, not to the Arabs and Berbers of Muslim religion who formed close to nine-tenths of the population. The Muslim Algerians, like the millions of Africans and Asians who came under French rule during the first half of the Republic, would be treated as French subjects under a paternalistic regime of mainly direct administration.

The policy applied to the European settlers, blacks in the old colonies, and a few thousand other Africans and Asians elsewhere whose educational level and life-style made them eligible for naturalization as French citizens was called *assimilation*. It derived from the eighteenth-century belief in the genetic equality of all human beings but the superiority of Western civilization, and thus not only the possibility but the desirability of turning the non-Western peoples of the empire into Frenchmen culturally and politically. The policy of *association*, which was applied to the masses of non-Western peoples from the 1890s, was influenced both by the French experience in Algeria and by late-nineteenth-century anthropological and psychological thinking. While continuing to believe in the superiority of Western civilization, associationists saw social and moral values in non-Western cultures that were worthy of preservation. Further, they recognized better than the eighteenth century the complex difficulties of assimilation, even if the resources had been available to undertake the task. Some advocates of association, influenced by the racism of social Darwinism, questioned the possibility of assimilating non-Westerners whom they saw as genetically inferior. Under the theory of association the masses of people would retain their own institutions, cultures, and languages but would participate in the administration of local affairs under French direction. An elite among them, generally drawn from the previous ruling classes, would receive a Western education sufficient to allow them to assist the French in administration and to serve as a link with the traditionally oriented masses.

Colonial questions in France were ordinarily the concern of only a minority of those involved in public affairs. From the 1890s within the two houses of parliament there was a colonial group, cutting across party lines but predominantly republican and centrist, which brought together those 75 to 150 representatives who supported expansion or had overseas interests. These politicians provided the bulk of the leadership for the partisans of colonization around the country who were collectively called the colonial party. Members of geographic societies, publicists, and politicians were the local elements within this grouping most active in trying to influence public opinion. Involved to a lesser extent were colonial administrators, military and naval officers, explorers, and missionaries. By World War I there were special interest groups concerned with particular geographic areas such as North Africa, Indochina, and the Pacific.

As a result of the war, France gained control of former German territories in Africa and former Turkish territories in the Middle East as mandates under the League of Nations. The war had the effect of accelerating a revaluation of colonial policies and practices that had been going on since 1900, as well as examining the role that the colonies could play in postwar recovery. During the interwar period socialist thinkers tended to emphasize the need for economic development (*mise en valeur*) that would benefit the colonies as well as France. Some of them, and most Catholic thinkers, emphasized that colonization must serve humanity and lead ultimately to emancipation involving a new relationship with France. Few interwar writers, whether critical on anticapitalist, antimercantilist, or humanitarian grounds, condemned colonization as an intrinsic evil in the manner of various liberal and Marxist-Leninist critics from other European and New World countries. The bulk of Frenchmen who were concerned with overseas matters continued to regard colonization as a positive good provided that it aided the development or advancement of the colonized and that it was a form of trusteeship leading progressively to emancipation. Few of them were prepared for the anticolonialism unleashed by the Second World War that sought during the superpower era to end all political ties between France and its overseas possessions.

H. Brunschwig, *French Colonialism, 1871–1914: Myths and Realities* (London, 1966); C.-R. Ageron, *France coloniale ou parti colonial?* (Paris, 1978), and *L'Anti-colonialisme en France de 1871 à 1914* (Paris, 1973); R. Girardet, *L'Idée coloniale en France de 1871 à 1962* (Paris, 1972); C. M. Andrew and A. S. Kanya-Forstner, *The Climax of French Imperial Expansion, 1914–1924* (Stanford, 1981).

D. E. Gardinier

Related entries: FERRY; OVERSEAS EMPIRE: COLONIAL ADMINISTRATION; OVERSEAS EMPIRE: FRENCH IMPERIALISM; SCHOOL, COLONIAL SERVICE: ECOLE COLONIALE.

COMBES, EMILE (1835–1921), radical republican politician, premier, anticleric. Born at Roquecourbe (Tarn), he attended the petit seminaire at Castres and was later sent to the Ecole Carmes in Paris. He also attended the grand seminaire at Albi, where, as a theological student, he wrote his thesis on the psychology of St. Thomas Aquinas (French thesis) and on the controversy between St. Bernard and Abelard (Latin thesis). Although he originally planned to become a priest, he abandoned this vocation by 1862 and ceased to practice Catholicism by 1879.

Combes studied medicine in Paris (1864–68) and set up his medical offices in Pons, the home town of his wife, but also turned to politics with vigor. He was elected mayor of Pons (1874), then senator of the Charente-Inférieure (1885–1921), vice-president of the Senate (1894–95), and minister of public instruction (1895–96). Reaching the apogee of his career at the age of sixty-seven, he was chosen to succeed René Waldeck-Rousseau as premier (7 June 1902).

Combes was known mainly for his anticlerical policies and the consequent deteriorating relations between France and the Vatican. Many felt that Combes was waging a fanatical campaign against the church he once dearly loved. The government nevertheless enjoyed broad support on the Left to carry out its policies.

In his pursuit of (some say obsession with) religious institutions, Combes sought a rigorous application of Waldeck-Rousseau's Association Law of 1901. Under its provisions, he closed over 1,500 unauthorized teaching establishments. It is estimated that by 1903, possibly 10,000 religious schools had been closed, though many were able to reopen under a laic facade.

Combes' policies caused civil disturbances and unrest all over France in the spring of 1903, as many people felt that he had taken Waldeck-Rousseau's law of regulation and transformed it into one of exclusion. On 7 July 1904, Combes won the abrogation of the Falloux Law of 1850 and forbade all religious bodies from teaching in France. On 30 July 1904, after a series of disputes and strained relations with Pope Pius X, France broke off all diplomatic ties with the Vatican, and a few days later Combes declared a separation inevitable.

Although the Combes regime did have its good points (a new demand for a revision of the Dreyfus trial, rapprochements with Italy and England), it was toppled by the fanaticism of Combes and the *Affaire des fiches* of October 1904. Following this scandal and the resignation of the implicated General Louis André, minister of war, the Combes cabinet resigned on 18 January 1905, before the separation of church and state was actually achieved.

R. D. Anderson, *France 1870–1914: Politics and Society* (London, 1977); J. Chastenet, *Histoire de la Troisième République* (Paris, 1955); E. Combes, *Mon ministère* (Paris, 1956); J. B. Duroselle, *La France et les français, 1900–1914* (Paris, 1972); M. Rebérioux, *La République Radicale?* (Paris, 1975).

                                                                              A. J. Staples

Related entries: AFFAIRE DES FICHES; ANTICLERICALISM; ASSOCIATIONS, LAW OF; ENTENTE CORDIALE; GREAT BRITAIN, RELATIONS WITH; ITALY, RELATIONS WITH; LEFT, THE; LOUBET; RADICAL AND RADICAL-SOCIALIST PARTY; ROMAN-CATHOLICISM: CHURCH-STATE RELATIONS; ROUVIER; SEPARATION OF CHURCH AND STATE, LAW OF; WALDECK-ROUSSEAU.

COMMERCE: DEPARTMENT STORES. In the 1840s and 1850s new merchandising techniques evolved that made possible the modern organization of retailing. The institutions responsible for the retailing revolution were the department stores. They were much larger than traditional retail establishments and united a wide variety of goods under one roof. Specialization was retained only in the *rayons* or departments into which the stores were divided. The department store evolved out of the dry goods business, but French stores were the first to institute the integration of dry goods with domestic paraphernalia and furniture. The Bon Marché in Paris, enlarged about 1852 by Aristide Boucicaut, was the world's first department store.

The innovations of the department store included fixed pricing, which eliminated bargaining in the sale process. Fixed pricing altered the buyer-seller relationship, reducing the buyer to a passive consumer whose only options were to buy or not buy what was offered. The tactics of large-scale retailing included publicity, display of goods, and low profit margins so that the merchandise virtually sold itself. In order to attract customers and facilitate the rapid turnover of merchandise, the stores needed to stimulate public demand by catalogs, newspaper advertising, and displays. Even the architecture of the department stores was an aspect of the presentation of the merchandise. The stores did not simply pose passively for the passers-by; display windows drew attention to the magnificence contained within. Special services to customers included tea rooms and restaurants, film showings and concerts.

By the end of the nineteenth century, the department stores were the largest enterprises in Paris; each employed between 2,500 and 4,500 salespeople. The stores recruited, trained, and treated their employees in ways that reflected their unique size and retailing practices. Clerks began as low-paid, unskilled assistants who carried items to the customers and took payments to the cashiers. Base salaries were low, but stores paid commissions on sales. Paid vacations, medical care, retirement benefits, maternity leaves, and other forms of compensation were provided in the hope of cultivating employee loyalty. Employees could be terminated with a few hours' notice, and work discipline was strictly enforced by roving inspectors. Single employees were generally housed by the stores, and all employees were entitled to take their midday meal on the premises. Women were recruited by the stores for their sales force after 1870 but did not come to predominate until after World War I.

The Parisian stores dominated the national market through an active mail order business; by 1911 mail order constituted one-third of the total sales of the Bon Marché. There were few provincial department stores until after 1927 and the creation of chains of *prix uniques* outlets.

T. M. McBride, "A Woman's World: Department Stores and the Evolution of Women's Employment, 1870–1920," *French Historical Studies* 10 (Fall 1978); B. Marrey, *Les Grands Magasins* (Paris, 1979); M. B. Miller, *The Bon Marché: Bourgeois Culture and the Department Store, 1869–1920* (Princeton, 1981); H. Pasdermadjian, *Le Grand Magasin. Son origine. Son avenir* (Paris, 1949).

T. M. McBride

Related entries: BUSINESSMEN; COMMERCE: RETAIL MERCHANTS.

COMMERCE: FOREIGN. During the Third Republic, foreign commerce was a factor in France's economic development, its foreign relations, and its colonial expansion. The following table indicates the dimensions of French foreign commerce in the early Third Republic.

Average Annual Foreign Trade, 1871–1914 (millions of francs)

	Imports	Exports	Total
1871–1875	$3,547	$3,599	$ 7,146
1876–1880	4,255	3,378	7,633
1881–1885	4,584	3,381	7,965
1886–1890	4,219	3,440	7,659
1891–1895	4,076	3,342	7,418
1896–1900	4,168	3,754	7,922
1901–1905	4,569	4,367	8,936
1906–1910	6,182	5,572	11,754
1911–1913	8,239	6,557	14,796

As the figures show, French commerce stagnated during the depression of 1876–95. Then, despite rising protectionism worldwide, the economic recovery of 1896–1913 brought a dramatic increase in both imports and exports. On the eve of World War I, French foreign commerce was at twice the level of 1871–75. Even so the period 1871–1914 saw France's share of world trade decline from 12.7 percent to 7.6 percent. In 1875 France's volume of trade was second only to Great Britain's. By the early 1900s, it had been surpassed by that of Germany and the United States as well.

Between 1876 and 1896, France's single biggest import was foodstuffs (35 percent of total value), especially grain and wine. With the return to agricultural protection in the 1890s, these imports declined to 24 to 25 percent of the total, and industrial raw materials (wool, cotton, silk, fuel) emerged as the dominant imports. By 1909 fuel (coal and heavy oil) constituted half of French imports by value. Among exports, one agricultural product—wine—was important, even though France fell from first to third place among wine exporting nations between 1876 and 1900 because of the phylloxera blight. The most important exports were manufactured goods, especially textiles (60 percent of total industrial exports), clothing, luxury goods (glass, perfume, leather), and transportation equipment (France was the leading exporter of bicycles and automobiles between 1899 and 1913).

World War I disrupted the existing pattern of trade in that exports decreased, the importation of foodstuffs and war materiel rose dramatically, and all trade fell under strict government control. Controls were lifted in 1919, and in the next decade France's volume of foreign commerce rose 49 percent above the prewar level (versus a world increase of only 27 percent above the prewar level). On the basis of constant francs, France exported 75 percent more textiles in 1930 than in 1913, 50 percent more clothing, and 100 percent more chemicals and machinery. Thus, the World War era notwithstanding, 1896 to 1930 stands out as a period of expanding foreign trade for France in contrast to the stagnation at the beginning and end of the Third Republic.

In the 1930s the depression and the French government's response to it (increased tariff protection, overvaluation of the franc) undercut France's foreign trade, particularly exports. Whereas in 1929 France furnished 11 percent of the manufactures exported by the industrialized nations (and 15 percent of the textiles), it furnished only 5.8 percent of manufactures (6 percent of textiles) exported in 1937. French foreign commerce also declined in relation to the domestic economy. Whereas annual imports had ranged from 15 to 20 percent of annual gross domestic product (GDP) in the 1870–1934 period, they totalled only 10 percent of GDP in 1935–38. Exports, which averaged 13 to 17 percent of GDP in the 1870–1934 period, fell to only 6.9 percent of GDP between 1935 and 1938.

In the 1920s and 1930s, French imports continued to be weighted toward industrial raw materials, especially fuel (60 percent of the total), and exports continued to be weighted toward manufactures. Within industrial exports, the importance of textiles declined, from 40 percent of the total in 1913 to 23 percent in 1938, while the importance of chemicals and metallurgical products increased. At the same time, the geographical pattern of French trade was changing. Between 1880 and 1913, France's six European neighbors and the United States received three-fourths of French exports and furnished over half of French imports. After World War I, the West Europeans remained important trade partners, but trade with the United States declined and France increasingly depended on its colonies. Indeed, by 1938, the colonies supplied 26 percent of French imports (versus 10 percent in 1921–22) and received 30 percent of French exports (versus 14.5 percent in 1921–22).

Annuaire statistique de la France 1–56 (1878–1940/45); R. Girault, "Place et rôle des échanges extérieurs," and "Marchandises et capitaux: les marchés et les placements extérieurs, 1919–1945," in *Histoire économique et sociale de la France*, vol. 4 (Paris, 1979–80); E. Levasseur, *Histoire du commerce de la France*, vol. 2 (Paris, 1912); M. Lévy-Leboyer, *La Position internationale de la France* (Paris, 1977); R. Poidevin, *Les Relations économiques et financières entre la France et l'Allemagne, 1898–1914* (Paris, 1969).

M. S. Smith

Related entries: ECONOMIC POLICY; INDUSTRY; OVERSEAS EMPIRE: FRENCH IMPERIALISM.

COMMERCE: RETAIL MERCHANTS (1870–1920). A new generation of French entrepreneurs emerged in the early years of the Third Republic who capitalized on French mercantile interests and modernized commercial institutions. In the 1850s the world's first department store had been founded by one of these entrepreneurs, Aristide Boucicaut. Boucicaut's rapid success was emulated by several other dry goods merchants in Paris: Ernest Cognacq and Louise Jay, who founded and directed the Samaritaine; Georges Dufayel, who began the first installment buying plans; Alfred Chauchard and August Heriot, who opened the Grands Magasins du Louvre; and Félix Potin, who in 1870 opened the first chain of grocery stores in Paris.

All of the department store entrepreneurs had worked their way up in the commercial hierarchy to head their own enterprises. Their successes were not unrelated: Ernest Cognacq worked with Dufayel at an earlier dry goods business; Cognacq married Louise Jay in 1872, who was then a department head at the Bon Marché; and Jules Jaluzot had headed the cashiers at the Bon Marché before founding his own store, Au Printemps.

This generation of department store entrepreneurs did not cease even in old age to direct their operations personally. They took great pride in the stores and in their personnel. The Boucicauts, Aristide and Marguerite, set up a provident fund, arranged for profit sharing by employees, and left their entire inheritance to various charities, including a hospital, day nurseries, and vacation cottages. In addition to their philanthropies, many of the department store owners took up art collecting; their own tastes and the marketing system of the stores encouraged the revival of interest in the decorative arts in the 1890s.

Despite the growth of the department stores, the number of small enterprises continued to increase during the early years of the Third Republic. In fact, the number of small shops nearly doubled between 1866 and 1906. The specialization of retail outlets and the rising level of consumption in the late nineteenth century reinforced the need for small commercial outlets in the cities. The largest growth of such outlets in Paris was in the suburbs where the working-class population was growing as this group moved out of the center city. During the Third Republic, shopkeepers formed professional organizations, which carried on the struggle to protect small commerce against the taxes they considered discriminatory and against the consumer cooperatives they believed hurt their business. Before 1900 small shopkeepers viewed the state as an enemy, aiding the expansion of larger enterprises. After 1900, however, fearing the increasing power of the labor movement, shopkeepers moved closer to their competitors, urging state intervention to ensure the continuing diversity of commercial distribution. Their political philosophy after 1900 was reflected in the growth of radicalism.

A. Boime, "Businessmen and the Arts in France in the Nineteenth Century," *Enterprise and Entrepreneurs in Nineteenth Century France*, ed. E. C. Carter et al. (Baltimore, 1976). J. Boudet, *Le Monde des affaires en France de 1830 à nos jours* (Paris, 1952);

H.-G. Haupt and P. Vigier, eds., "L'Atelier et la boutique," *Le Mouvement social*, no. 108 (1979).

T. M. McBride

Related entries: BUSINESSMEN; COMMERCE: DEPARTMENT STORES; SHOPKEEPERS.

COMMUNARDS. Unlike the more popular *communeux*, *communard* originated as the pejorative term for supporters of the Paris Commune of 1871, but unlike the label *communist*, it referred to those whose foremost aim was further autonomy for local government.

While it would seem appropriate to apply the term to the eighty-one who accepted election to the Paris Commune, the variety of principles and positions that they held indicates the difficulty in affixing any label implying structure and uniformity to this diverse and rapidly evolving movement. Only loose ties of identification with the revolutionary traditions of 1793 bound members of the largest of the Commune's several groups, the neo-Jacobins, while even those associated with the International, relatively united in principles and supportive of the ideal of local autonomy, split on the critical issue of the Commune's surrender of authority to the Committee of Public Safety. The difficulty becomes compounded when, as is often the case, historians include under the *communard* rubric those whom the troops from Versailles killed, estimated between 17,000 and 25,000, and the over 50,000 on whom the military courts passed sentence.

Jacques Rougerie's study based on the dossiers of the 36,306 whom the government arrested attempts a portrait of the typical communard. It describes him as a staunch patriot, the last revolutionary of the old school, opposed to all that was antirepublican: the military, the clerics, the rural aristocrats. If his social hatreds remained vague and unfocused, the typical communard, a salaried worker, already saw as the enemy his rich and complacent patrons, the bourgeoisie. Undoubtedly this remains the popularly accepted image of the communard, one that unsympathetic conservatives would only supplement with suitable amounts of dirt, violence, alcohol, and class hatred. A qualification of the portrait, however, calls attention to 20,000 of the dossiers that were of the acquitted and therefore cut by the archivists and unexplored by Rougerie. Many from the middle class, without a criminal record, thereby escaped justice, for the law weighed heaviest on the *classes dangereuses*. Thirty percent of the 10,000 actually condemned had a previous conviction. Moreover, to identify the Commune's supporters with the combatants of its final days is to refuse the movement a history, inasmuch as what gave the communalist uprising a unique character appeared less in evidence during the frenzied bloody week of its demise than earlier when it elicited wider sympathy.

The speedy collapse of the revolt of 31 October 1870 and the strong vote of confidence (321,373 to 53,584) given the Provisional Government of National Defense had revealed socialist weakness even in the great city's poorer quarters.

Predominantly petty bourgeois rather than working class, the Central Committee of the National Guard, the communalist insurrection's principal coordinator between 18 and 26 March 1871, acted in behalf of the Republic and the rights of Paris. Representative of 215 of the city's 250 battalions, its members differed somewhat in background and intent from the combatants of Bloody Week, but few would deny that their principles were communard. Scarred by the trauma of the recent siege and frustrated by the nation's surrender to Germany, fearful of a royalist assembly's designs, and provoked by the government's policies, Paris had risen in protest. A large part of its population was communard in principle on 26 March when elections to the Commune, endorsed by the city's mayors and deputies, as well as sanctioned by the moderate republican press, drew over 229,000 voters. The radical arrondissements, composed largely of workers, participated with enthusiasm, and although many from the middle class had purposely delayed their return to Paris, these figures compared favorably with the statistics of earlier balloting. Certainly they compared favorably with the scant 53,680 who took part in the by-elections of 16 April, for by then the new council, dominated by the authoritarian Jacobins and Blanquists and in reaction to the military defeat of 3 April, set on a course no longer in keeping with a city's legitimate rights. Yet on 26 March broader support had been there when Charles Beslay, in the Commune's inaugural address, had paid honor to the goals of a decentralized Republic and freedom for local government. Aware that such a program had considerable appeal not only for Paris but for the larger provincial municipalities, the Commune restated it in the Declaration to the French People of 19 April. But by then the end was near; the Paris council was in obviously desperate straits as it daily belied by its acts any commitment to the rights or liberties of others.

Without denying the Paris Commune's socialist tendencies or the indifference, even hostility, of its centralist majority toward the federalist dream of a free association of communes, what uniquely defined the term *communard*, and distinguished the uprising from its predecessors of 1830 and 1848, was the emphasis on communal rights and liberties. To focus solely on the immediate but insignificant repercussions in the departments to news of events in Paris on 18 March or on the isolated attempts to sabotage the transportation of support to Versailles during the actual conflict is to risk losing sight of a greater picture. That picture is the extent to which France's major cities, by the exercise of freedoms long sought and now acquired through the collapse of the Second Empire, were all part of a decentralist movement that openly challenged the structure of the French state.

Whether one elects to accept the more popular definition of communard as the description of those who for whatever reasons or circumstances fell victim to the struggle's last days, or as those who willingly supported the movement for the sake of local autonomy so long as that principle was respected, there do at least appear signs of a growing consensus among scholars that it is the history of France itself that ought to supply the term's definition rather than myths born of ideological motives and inattentive to historical reality.

G. Bourgin, *La Guerre de 1870–1871 et la Commune* (Paris, 1971); G. Del Bo, *La Commune di Parigi* (Milan, 1957); L. M. Greenberg, *Sisters of Liberty* (Cambridge, Mass., 1971); Jean-Léo, *Bibliographie de la Commune de 1871* (Bruxelles, 1970); B. Noël, *Dictionnaire de la Commune* (Paris, 1971); J. Rougerie, ed., *1871 Jalons pour une histoire de la Commune de Paris* (Paris, 1973), and *Procès des Communards* (Mesnil-sur-l'Estrée, 1964).

L. M. Greenberg

Related entries: ANARCHISM; BESLAY; BLANQUISTS; COMMUNARDS: AMNESTY MOVEMENT FOR; COMMUNE OF PARIS; DELESCLUZE; JACOBINISM; LEFT, THE; LISSAGARAY; MICHEL; SOCIALISM, 1870–1914.

COMMUNARDS: AMNESTY MOVEMENT FOR (1871–1880), various initiatives over a nine-year period for restoration of civil and political rights to persons convicted for acts during the Paris Commune. The later stages of the movement were identified with reviving the revolutionary collectivist movement. The republicans in the National Assembly proposed partial amnesty soon after the Commune's suppression. They gave a landslide victory in 1873 to Désiré Barodet, whose campaign featured amnesty. By the 1876 elections, the republican majority had dropped the amnesty cause as too dangerous in the face of the monarchist threat. Only the Radical republicans stood for general amnesty. The candidacy in the Sixth Arrondissement of Paris by Emile Acollas was significant for the amnesty platform of an old-line socialist activist. Leadership in demands for amnesty remained with the parliamentary Radical republicans until the resolution of the *seize mai* crisis in late 1877.

The growth of an extraparliamentary movement for amnesty (1878–80), was allied with the beginnings of organized socialism in France. Inspiration came mostly from the staff of Jules Guesde's newspaper, *L'Egalité*, with the tactic of running the imprisoned Auguste Blanqui in legislative by-elections (Marseilles, Roanne, Paris, Lyons) to embarrass the government. The enactment in March 1879 of partial amnesty (exclusion of those denied pardon for common law crimes) was the signal for escalation of agitation. The Central Socialist Committee for Aid to the Amnestied and Non-Amnestied coordinated fund raising; the newspapers *L'Egalité* and *Le Proletaire* helped finance the successful campaign in 1879 to elect Blanqui a deputy from Bordeaux; socialist candidates won on full amnesty platforms in municipal elections; mass demonstrations greeted the returning amnestied. The Congress of Marseilles (21–31 October 1879) was a turning point. The amnesty movement became an adjunct to the emerging socialist Workers party of France. Amnesty was now demanded as a vindication of the Commune. Socialists equated denial of amnesty to capitalist exploitation of the proletariat.

Pro-amnesty demonstrations proliferated during the spring of 1880 in Paris and the provinces. The high point of the amnesty movement came when the unamnestied Alexis Trinquet ran first of four candidates for municipal councillor in the Père Lachaise ward of Paris (13 June). For over a year the leftist press had linked Trinquet with the amnesty cause. His relative success at the polls was the catalyst of the government's full amnesty bill (19 June). The socialist leadership pressed its campaign for full amnesty while the bill was in parliament. It greeted the compromise (law of 11 July 1880), a measure short of full amnesty, with a reaffirmation of its faith in social revolution. But the amnesty movement was effectively over. The unity it had generated among the various collectivist lefts evaporated with the enactment of the 1880 law.

G. Jacquement, "Gambetta et ses électeurs bellevillois," *Revue d'histoire moderne et contemporaine* 18 (1971); J. T. Joughin, *The Paris Commune in French Politics, 1871– 1880* (Baltimore, 1955).

J. T. Joughin

Related entries: BLANQUI; BLANQUISTS; DEVILLE; GUESDE; GUESD- ISTS; HUGO; ROCHE, ERNEST; SOCIALISM, 1870–1914.

COMMUNE OF PARIS (18 March–28 May 1871), a revolutionary regime that reigned briefly in the unsettled early days of the Third Republic. Marx hailed it as a harbinger of the proletarian revolution. Most historians, however, have stressed its affinities with the popular insurrections at Paris earlier in the century (1830 and 1848) in terms of its leadership (Jacobin), its cadres (*sans-culottes*), and its objectives (the creation of a democratic republic with an enlightened social policy). In this sense, the Commune was the last of the Parisian insurrections modeled on the ideals and the experience of the French Revolution.

The Commune was created in the aftermath of the Franco-Prussian War (August 1870–January 1871) and was in many ways a response to the problems it raised concerning the nature of the postwar French government. In an immediate sense, the Parisian uprising of 18 March in which the Commune was proclaimed was inspired by a confrontation between the Provisional Government at Versailles (headed by Adolphe Thiers) and the people of Paris over housing policy (the termination of the wartime moratorium on mortgages and rents), the status of the National Guard at Paris (termination of pay for National Guard militiamen and the appointment of an unpopular general as National Guard commander), the arrest, conviction, and incarceration of popular left-wing leaders because of their opposition to governmental war policy (Auguste Blanqui, Gustave Flourens), press censorship, the decision to situate the government at Versailles rather than at Paris, and the government's attempt to seize from the bluffs of Montmartre the cannon forged by the Parisians for their self-defense during the war. This last measure triggered the uprising of March 18, in which officers leading the expedition were massacred by the Parisian crowd. But all of these grievances were more deeply rooted in the bitterness of the Parisians over the ineffectiveness of the Provisional Government's war policy, the humiliating peace terms dictated by the Germans that the Provisional Government was willing to accept, and ultimately the conservative cast of the regime that the Provisional Government seemed likely to inaugurate. In the deepest sense, the Parisian insurrection brought to a head an unresolved quarrel of long standing over the meaning of the republican ideal. The Commune of Paris represented an alternative vision of the Third Republic (politically democratic, socially egalitarian, and loosely confederated) to that instituted by the Provisional Government and the National Assembly (politically libertarian, socially conservative, and centrally organized).

Despite the fleeting existence of the Commune, its narrative history is customarily divided into four phases: an initial period (18–26 March), in which the lines of battle were drawn and efforts at negotiation by the mayors of the districts of Paris foundered; a period of definition (26 March–28 April) in which elections for a Communal Assembly were held, governmental officials appointed, and the institutions of the revolutionary government established; a period of crisis (28 April–20 May), in which the military command was revamped and existing agencies were superseded by emergency governmental committees; and a period of dissolution (21–28 May), remembered as Bloody Week, in which Versailles' forces invaded Paris and systematically reduced the Commune into submission.

Leadership among the communards was never definitively established. In the days following the spontaneous popular uprising of 18 March, political control was exercised by an ad hoc Central Committee of the National Guard, composed of officers of that militia, mostly obscure men who had exercised military authority during the siege of Paris and who now turned the network of defense once used to stave off the Germans to protect the Parisians from their own countrymen. With the election of a Communal Assembly on 26 March and the naming of its members to executive commissions, the leadership of the Commune divided into two recognizable factions, Jacobins and Proudhonists. The Jacobins favored an authoritarian government, modeled on the Committee of Public Safety of the French Revolution, to meet the emergencies of war and to inaugurate economic and civil reforms conducive to the making of an egalitarian society. Fiercely patriotic, the Jacobins identified the ideals of nationalism and fraternity with the community formed through revolutionary struggle. Within this faction, some historians distinguish the Jacobins from the Blanquists, who claimed to stand closer to the ideals of Jacques Hébert and the Revolutionary Commune of Paris of 1793 (popular democracy) than to those of Maximilien Robespierre and the Committee of Public Safety (authoritarian democracy). As disciples of the legendary professional revolutionary, Blanqui, imprisoned by the Provisional Government on the eve of the Commune, the Blanquists made sustained yet futile efforts to retrieve him as a potential statesman for the Commune. The Proudhonists, in addition to championing the rights of the workingman, resisted Jacobin policies of centralization and advocated instead the creation of a decentralized republican confederation, composed of autonomous, self-governing municipalities. It was in the name of this conception of the Republic that the Commune of Paris inspired the founding of similar revolutionary regimes at Lyons, Marseilles, Bordeaux, and St. Etienne.

The most pressing tasks facing the Commune were military. But the strategies devised to deal with civil war lacked imagination, and the enthusiasm of the revolutionary uprising of mid-March was not rekindled on the battlefields during the ensuing weeks. The only major offensive of the Commune, a strike through the western suburb of Courbevoie toward Versailles on 3 April, was quickly routed. Two of the commanders of the expeditionary force, Emile Duval and Gustave Flourens, were captured and summarily executed, while their forces straggled back to Paris in disarray. Despite repeated changes in military leadership (Gustave Cluseret, Louis Rossel, Jaroslaw Dombrowski, Alfred Billiorary), the Commune's war policy remained irresolute and defensive in character, relying on fortifications and barricades rather than sorties against the Versailles army. The military defeat of the Commune therefore was largely a function of the time it took the Provisional Government to mass the forces necessary to invade Paris.

The attempts to fashion a domestic policy for the new regime were similarly uninspired. Historians sympathetic to the Commune point out that there were some interesting projects. The Commission on Industry and Trade inventoried vacant ateliers with a view to transforming them into workers' cooperatives. The Delegate for Public Instruction, Edouard Vaillant, sketched plans for a more democratic and innovative educational system, one that would combine technical training with instruction in the humanities. The painter Gustave Courbet sought to revitalize public support for the arts. Yet it proved difficult to proceed very far with any of these ventures under wartime conditions. These projects were, moreover, vitiated by the ruthless campaign against the Commune's real and imagined enemies, led by the anticlerical fanatic, Raoul Rigault, first as prefect of police and later as prosecutor of the Commune. Under the provisions of the Law of Hostages (5 April), which set special rules for the arrest, trial, and detention of political suspects, more than 400 hostages, most of them policemen and priests, were incarcerated, among them the archbishop of Paris.

As the military situation of the Commune grew desperate by late April, the Communal Assembly succumbed to the demands of the more extreme Jacobins to create a Committee of Public Safety to coordinate governmental and military affairs. From that date the Communal Assembly lost much of its influence and ceased to meet regularly. But the committee lacked the resources to reverse the fortunes of the civil war. On 21 May, the armies of Versailles began a systematic assault on the city. Paris was rewon from its defenders street by street during Bloody Week, until the Commune's last defenders were struck down. In this last stand, the militiamen of the Commune, aided by the women of Paris, displayed a heroism that, in the commemoration of the regime, would blot out the timidity and ineptitude that had characterized the Commune's earlier efforts. In these last days of fighting, atrocities were committed on both sides. Some 100 hostages were executed by vengeful Blanquists and hostile mobs. Much was made of these acts by conservative historians afterward. But these figures pale before the estimated 25,000 Parisians summarily executed by the invading Versailles army and the 36,000 prisoners rounded up for trial and deportation.

Despite the thoroughness of these reprisals, most of the leaders of the Commune escaped into exile, grouping especially in London, Brussels, and Geneva, until amnestied in 1880. Returning to Paris in the 1880s, the veteran Communards enjoyed much respect among republicans, but their attempts to renew interest in the Commune were without marked success as political initiative on the Left passed to the new socialist movement.

One hundred years after the event, the memory of the Commune continues to inspire passion and partisan opinion. While never again seriously considered as a model for a revolutionary government, the Commune remained a souvenir of the Left's disappointment with the character of the Third Republic and an emblem of their ongoing struggle to create a more democratic social republic.

J. Bruhat et al., *La Commune de 1871* (Paris, 1970); S. Edwards, *The Paris Commune, 1871* (London, 1971); P. H. Hutton, *The Cult of the Revolutionary Tradition* (Berkeley, 1981); G. Laronze, *Histoire de la Commune de 1871* (Paris, 1928); P.-O. Lissagaray, *Histoire de la Commune de 1871* (1896); J. Rougerie, *Paris libre, 1871* (Paris, 1971); G. Soria, *Grande histoire de la Commune* (Paris, 1970); M. Vuillaume, *Mes cahiers rouges au temps de la Commune* (Paris, 1909); R. Williams, *The French Revolution of 1870–1871* (New York, 1969).

P. H. Hutton

Related entries: COMMUNARDS; COMMUNARDS: AMNESTY MOVEMENT FOR; COMMUNES IN PROVINCIAL CITIES; FRANCO-PRUSSIAN WAR; LEFT, THE.

COMMUNES IN PROVINCIAL CITIES, revolutionary movements, precipitated by the Paris Commune, in defense of the Republic and municipal liberties. When provincial France learned that Paris had revolted against the Versailles government and created the Commune, there was an immediate sympathetic response. Perhaps as many as fifty urban centers spawned a commune or a significant demonstration of support for Paris. Lyons, Marseilles, Toulouse, Bordeaux, Grenoble, Saint-Etienne, and Le Creusot, as well as numerous lesser provincial towns, were touched. Revolutionary support for Paris was confined almost exclusively to southern France, the rest of the country being either unsympathetic—as in the case of the traditionally clerical and conservative west—or prevented from doing anything because of the German occupation. All the communes had a fleeting existence of not more than three or four days in late March 1871, though the one in Marseilles did last from 23 March to 4 April. A few reverberations followed, the most serious one an uprising in Lyons' La Guillotière district on 30 April.

The provincial communes never acquired anywhere near the mass following that the Paris Commune achieved. Support usually came from local radicals, National Guardsmen and their officers, and, in a few instances, an elected municipal official. The typical commune consisted of a forcible occupation of the city hall, issuance of a number of proclamations in favor of the Republic, organization of a defense of the commune, then dissolution in the face of a display of force by the regular army. Several repressions ended in fighting, notably Lyons on 30 April (21 dead) and Marseilles (about 150 dead), incidents that would have received far greater attention at the time and subsequently had they not been overshadowed by the Paris Commune.

Only recently has scholarship highlighted the provincial communes. Their existence, however brief, demonstrates that the concerns of the Paris Commune were not limited just to the capital city; the Commune was not exclusively a Parisian event. What produced the surge of provincial communes in the wake of the Paris Commune was the fact that the capital and the major provincial cities had undergone a similar conditioning during the Second Empire. In all of these cities there existed large bodies of people favorable to a Republic and extensive municipal rights. The Versailles Assembly, by the monarchical sentiments of a majority of its deputies and by its actions and attitude toward Paris, seemed opposed to both. Spontaneously, then, when all that was known about the Paris Commune was that it stood for a Republic and municipal liberties, supportive insurrections broke out. Although these demands were almost exclusively political, the fact that they were sought by insurrection and used a title that recalled the Paris Commune of 1793 kept potential supporters away. Consequently the insurrections lacked weight and recognized and respected leadership (except for Marseilles with Gaston Cremieux, Le Creusot with Jean-Baptiste Dumay, and Narbonne with Emile Digeon). National and municipal elections of the late Second Empire and early Third Republic indicate that a majority in cities where communes were established supported the Republic and municipal autonomy, but the limited appeal of the provincial communes indicates how crucial was the catalyst of the Prussian siege in preparing the way for the Paris Commune.

J. Archer, "La Commune de Lyon," *Le Mouvement social* 77 (1971); J. Gaillard, *Commune de province, Commune de Paris* (Paris, 1971); J. Girault, *La Commune et Bordeaux* (Paris, 1971); L. Greenberg, *Sisters of Liberty* (Cambridge, Mass., 1971).

J.P.W. Archer

Related entries: COMMUNE OF PARIS; FRANCO-PRUSSIAN WAR.

COMMUNICATIONS. At the outset of this era, communication was largely restricted to the press. By the turn of the century, however, the advent of radio and, in the 1920s, the popularization of cinema, added new dimensions to the communications industry.

Newspapers. During the Second Empire (1852–70) journalism in France was strictly monitored and regulated. Bound by archaic techniques and the authoritarianism of the regime, newspapers had relatively low circulation and were almost all biased in the government's favor. This changed during the Third Republic. The principal reason was the law of 29 July 1881, which gave greater freedom to the press. This liberal law, which has remained virtually unchanged up to the present day, gave all citizens the right to establish a newspaper and also gave the right of response to all. Because of this law, the press began to burgeon, and in the period 1881–1900, the number of daily and weekly newspapers more than doubled.

Other elements also contributed to this rapid growth in the number and importance of newspapers: the cheapening of the cost of paper, the invention of the rotary press, the rapid spread of literacy during the early years of the Republic, and the completion of the railroad network, which sped Parisian dailies to the provinces. Toward the end of the nineteenth century, developments in telegraphic (1880s) and telephonic (1890s) systems made possible the reception of news direct from European capitals, and the reporter–international correspondent made his debut.

With the rapid reception of news and the regular distribution of journals to all parts of the country, the press moved into its golden age. During the period 1870 to 1910, the number of Parisian dailies jumped from thirty-three to over seventy. By the beginning of the twentieth century, every city of importance had at least three papers: one conservative, one republican, and one radical. In the early 1900s, Paris was the major center of journalistic activity. Many writers for the world press grouped there. The Parisian press was authoritative, enterprising, controversial, and very political. Many papers were identified with a specific political party. The provincial press, which had lagged far behind during the Empire, had come into its own during the Paris Siege and the Commune, when they could no longer depend on getting daily information from the capital. These newspapers, many of merit, included local and regional news and generally were not as controversial as the Parisian dailies.

Both the Parisian and provincial papers depended heavily on publicity and advertisements. The commercial organization Messageries Hachette handled the national distribution of the papers over the railroad network. Although each daily paper had its own highly competent correspondents, the French press as a whole had to rely on Agence Havas for the national and international news. This company, directed from 1897 to 1924 by Charles Lafitte, enjoyed great prestige and grew rapidly after the law of 1881; in 1913 it opened its first permanent bureau in the United States.

During this golden era of the press, the five leading Parisian information dailies were *Le Petit Journal* (founded in 1863), *Le Petit Parisien* (1876), *Le Matin* (1884), *L'Echo de Paris* (1884) and *Le Journal* (1892). The first two, the leaders in circulation, were fierce rivals. Both were directed to the popular classes and therefore kept their costs low. The techniques they used included reducing the length of the articles and editorials and multiplying news briefs and coverage of the scandals of the day. The newspapers reflected all of the social and political struggles and found rich material in the Panama scandal, Boulanger affair, and Dreyfus affair. The sensationalism of such papers greatly increased their sales at the newsstand. In addition, the introduction of the novel in serial form (the *feuilleton*) and later the *pages spéciales* dealing with theater, arts, and cinema attracted many readers.

The First World War brought the golden era of the press to a close. With the outbreak of war many protests arose about the government's censorship of newspapers. While all agreed to the military censure, critics charged that there was civilian censure as well and that the government was meddling in affairs that should not concern it. Many papers closed, and the level of production dropped drastically. During the interwar years many of the papers resumed publication, and by 1939 the number of papers published was back up, though it would never again reach the peak of the pre–World War I era. Though newspapers long remained the primary source for information, the increasing prominence of radio diffusion came to pose a threat and rival to the printed word.

Radio. First diffused at the turn of the century, radio gained an almost immediate success. The first wireless transmissions date from 1898. With this invention, news arrived directly from all over Europe. In 1903, experiments involving broadcasts were conducted from the Eiffel Tower under the direction of Captain Auguste Ferrié, one of the pioneers of radio techniques. French radio was born in November 1921 when the first regular radio program was broadcast from a military transmitter on the Eiffel Tower.

On 30 June 1923, finance laws were passed to make radio a recognized monopoly of the state, along with the postal and telegraphic services. This radio monopoly was nominal since the state sold permits to private companies, which were run by industrialists and newspaper owners. The following year, the private station Radio-Paris was established, and commercial radio was born.

Radio rapidly gained popularity during the interwar years. It obtained a vast public, growing from 500,000 receptors in 1930 to 5.5 million in 1939. Early programs were composed mainly of news information and music. The news was immediate, brief, and dealt mainly with headlines. It was simplified and easily understood. Although the rival newspapers charged that listeners could not choose what they wanted to know as newspaper readers could, radio came to be a serious threat to the written press.

During the early to mid-1930s, a regional network of stations was founded, and in 1935 the state gave up its monopoly to the private stations, receiving in return more governmental control. The government justified its increased surveillance by pointing to mounting international tensions. The government tightened control of financial, economic, and political programs in 1938.

In July 1939, radio was made a separate administrative department, under direct supervision of the prime minister. This new department, entitled the Central Administration of National Broadcasting, ran the state network (Radio-Paris, Paris PTT, Tour Eiffel and the colonial service, Paris-Mondial) and monitored the remaining twelve private stations.

As the country moved toward war, official news bulletins for all French radio stations were broadcast at specific times each day to keep the public informed of the situation, which by 1938 was grave. The private stations experienced growing financial trouble as their advertising revenues declined. Many stations could not afford to continue.

Radio played an important role in both the public and private sectors during the Third Republic. Its presence was everywhere and was once said to be the *décor sonore de la vie quotidienne*. Radio had the double advantage of being a source of information and entertainment, this being the major reason for its huge popularity.

Cinema. Radio's main rival in the entertainment field was cinema. A series of experiments and inventions led to cinematography as we know it today, including the inventions of the photographic revolver (Pierre Janssen, 1874), the praxinoscope (Emile Reynaud, 1877), the photographic gun (Etienne Marey, 1882), and the chronophotograph (Marey and Georges Demeny, 1887). This last device was used to photograph subjects saying such simple sentences as *je vous aime* and *vive la France*. From 1892 to 1900, Reynaud showed hand-drawn animated films at his Théâtre optique in Paris.

The real beginning of cinema, however, took place in 1895 when Louis and Auguste Lumière showed their first film, *La Sortie des usines lumières*. The Lumière brothers, already leading manufacturers of photographic equipment, made a fortune in the early film days. On 28 December 1895 they showed the first public film to thirty-five people in the basement of the Grand Café in Paris. The program consisted of *La Sortie* and *L'Arrivée d'un train en gare*, which terrified the audience as the train approached.

The Lumière brothers are also responsible for the first newsreel, a filming of the French Photographic Society's Congress, and the first documentary, a four-part series about the Lyons fire brigade, a film in which the process of editing was born. By 1896 they had gained such success that they took on two assistants and sent them filming around the world, searching for new shots and new material.

Two other important pioneers of French cinema were Charles Pathé (1863–1957) and Léon Gaumont (1861–1946). Pathé founded Frères Pathé in 1901 and was largely responsible for the industry's huge growth in the pre–World War I years. Pathé's films sold throughout the world, and by 1908 his company alone produced two times the total number of films made in the United States. He built his own cinemas and in 1907 initiated the practice of renting films instead of selling them. The company's newsreels, Pathé Gazette, gained a global reputation in the early years of the twentieth century. Pathé's main rival was Gaumont, founder of Gaumont Studios, who had a flourishing business selling cinema films and equipment.

Before World War I, France, not the United States, dominated the world film market. All of the other countries looked to France for new techniques and innovations in the industry. One such innovator was George Meliès (1861–1938). Meliès, known as the Father of Film Art, used his genius and imagination in advancing technical processes such as camera trickery and *mise en scène*. In his desire to advance the film industry as a whole, he was a script writer, director, and actor and produced hundreds of short films. Meliès was a huge financial success and therefore had the resources to build the world's first film studio

(1897). His films, which were mainly fairy tales and fantasies, reflected his vast knowledge of theater, where he had begun his career.

The 1920s witnessed much experimentation in the marketing of cinema. Technical film magazines appeared, and there was growing popular interest in film criticism. During this era, ciné-clubs, specialized cinemas, and film festivals (Cannes, Venice) were founded. With the introduction of talkies (1926–27), attendance once again made a huge leap. By 1929 France had 4,000 movie halls.

For all these innovations, though, French cinema had problems. The first setback came in 1897 when a fire broke out at a charity bazaar in Paris, reportedly starting in the film room there. Over 200 people died in the fire, and for the next few years, many people were afraid to go to the movies. In the 1920s, moreover, France was badly hurt by foreign competition. The main rival was Hollywood, and as early as 1920, there was a fall in French production in the face of American competition. In addition, sound track revolutionized the film industry, and France, having no patent for sound, had to pay vast sums for the expensive new equipment. By 1929 French film production, which for the previous fifteen years had been the largest in the world, dwindled to about fifty mediocre full-length films a year. The French film industry tried to revitalize itself with its "impressionist school" (mid to late 1920s) and its "renaissance period" (about 1935–40), but the attempts were not entirely successful. With the outbreak of World War II and the subsequent disruption of production and exile of many of the principal film makers, French cinema was forced to let go of its already weakened dominance in the film world.

In the course of the Third Republic, communications systems underwent profound changes. By the 1930s, information reached the public by a variety of new methods (radio, cinema newsreels, television), which provided intense competition for the once-dominant written press. Instead of an elite newspaper-reading audience, the new media were directed toward a virtually unknown mass public. The advantages of uniformity and passivity won the mass media huge audiences and thus shaped public opinion and cultural taste in a totally new way. The popular arts, especially in the motion picture field, acquired a higher esteem among the public.

These arts now touched almost everyone. This, together with the law of 1936 reducing the work week from forty-eight to forty hours and making mandatory the annual four-week vacation, revolutionized French society. Ordinary people had more leisure time for entertainment and relaxation. All classes went to the movies, relatively cheap entertainment, and the cinemas were packed at the end of the week. The radio was a source of both news and entertainment, and it grew by 5 million (radios) during the last decade of the Third Republic. The media were thus transformed and were in turn a major force in transforming French society. The new mass media contributed in a fundamental way to the democratization of culture. As a form of entertainment as well as one of art, the media reached a greater and broader audience than ever before.

C. Bellanger et al., *Histoire générale de la presse en France*, vol. 2 (Paris, 1972); P.

Cowie, *A Concise History of the Cinema* (New York, 1971); M. Crubellier, *Histoire culturelle de la France* (Paris, 1974); R. Desmond, *Windows on the World: The Information Process in a Changing Society* (Iowa City, 1980); L. Febvre, ed., *Encyclopédie française* (Paris, 1954); D. and M. Frémy, eds., *Encyclopédie QUID 1983* (Paris, 1982); H. S. Hughes, *Contemporary Europe* (Englewood Cliffs, N.J., 1961); *Larousse du XXeme siècle* (Paris, 1929); R. Manévy, *La Presse de la Troisième République* (Paris, 1955); G. Manvell, ed., *International Encyclopedia of Film* (New York, 1972); R. Recouly, *The Third Republic* (New York, 1967); G. Sadoul, *French Film* (London, 1953); P. Sorlin, *La Société française, 1840–1914* (Paris, 1969); R. Thomas, *Broadcasting and Democracy in France* (Philadelphia, 1977); G. Weill, *Le Journal* (Paris, 1955).

A. J. Staples

Related entries: CINEMA; NEWSPAPERS, ROLE OF.

COMMUNIST PARTY, a political party inspired by the Russian Revolution that advocated collectivization of the means of production and exchange. The French Communist Party (PCF) was founded in December 1920 as a result of a split at the Socialist Congress of Tours, when a majority of the delegates present voted to join the Third International. Studies of the beginnings of the party, especially those by Annie Kriegel, stress the conjunctural and accidental nature of the schism at Tours, which followed a defeat of the French reformist socialists in the elections of 1919 and of the syndicalists in the failed general strikes of 1919–20. The new party was not, however, an artificial Russian graft onto the French social organism. Rather it was an amalgam of French working-class traditions, which as late as 1924 included in its leadership a social democrat (Louis Sellier), an anarchosyndicalist (Alfred Rosmer), a Guesdist (Marcel Cachin), and a pacifist (Albert Treint).

The initial process of bolshevization was begun, under Russian impulse, in 1924. It had two key aspects. The first was the proletarianization of the party's leadership. This policy has been consistently adhered to since, and the PCF has therefore been perceived as the most effective agency in French society for promoting the interests of the working class. The second aspect was conversion of the party to cellular organization in the workplace, the "terrain of the class struggle," rather than in the neighborhood. Much more difficult to achieve in practice, the policy of factory organization failed to encompass more than 25 percent of the total cells in the party, although the PCF has managed to maintain over 50 percent working-class composition in its membership. Communists have preferred the convenience of engaging in party-related activities where they live rather than where they are employed.

By 1927 the French section of the Comintern, under the supple Bukharin-like leadership of Pierre Semard, had become habituated to the united front policy of entente with the socialists, and the party appeared to have achieved a rough balance between the Leninist imperatives of democracy and centralism. Party congresses were still forums for open debate and rival opinions. But as Josef Stalin prepared to embark on his ambitious program of collectivization and industrialization in Soviet Russia, he imposed the sectarian class-against-class policy on the Comintern in the so-called third period, 1928–34. The French leaders resisted the new policy, which prompted the Comintern to discipline its French section, inaugurating a real process of Stalinization. This involved the suppression of local initiative in decision making, the rigid application of strictures against factionalism in party organization, and the facade of monolithic unity in party congresses, meetings of the Central Committee, and the Political Bureau. In the 1930s and after, under the leadership of Maurice Thorez, the PCF indulged in personality cults, purge trials, self-criticism, and paranoia. These characteristics of the Stalinist mentality proved especially adaptable to the French revolutionary and bureaucratic tradition. This domestication of the French party was accomplished in two stages. In 1929 Comintern officials first allied themselves with a militant and sectarian group in the party's youth organization headed by Henri Barbé and Pierre Celor. Willing advocates of the new line, they were promoted to the Political Bureau and the Secretariat. Some of the most important of the party's leaders through the 1960s, including Thorez, Benoît Frachon, François Billoux, and Raymond Guyot, were brought forward under the tutelage of Barbé and Celor.

By 1931 party membership, estimated at 58,000 in 1928, fell to 30,000; some unofficial estimates place it as low as 18,000. The PCF was in danger of degenerating into an impotent sect. Alarmed at this situation, the Comintern engineered a new coup, which brought Thorez forward as party leader under the close supervision of a highly intelligent Comintern agent, Eugen Fried (alias Clement), and promoted with Thorez two staunchly pro-Russian loyalists, Jacques Duclos and André Marty. Barbé and Celor were eliminated in a Stalin-like maneuver, admonished to admit their sins, and ultimately branded as police agents. But the party line shifted only slightly in the 1932 elections during which the Socialists were still being castigated as social fascists. From 1,064,000 votes in 1928, the PCF fell to 796,630 in the 1932 elections, while failure to support the Socialists on the second ballot limited the party to a scant twelve seats in the Chamber of Deputies. Clearly something different was needed.

The PCF was converted into a mass party during the Popular Front, receiving over 1.5 million votes in the 1936 elections, 72 seats in the Chamber, and ultimately gaining a membership of 387,000. The turn to an alliance with the Socialists in the Popular Front, moreover, proved almost definitive; one could argue that except for 1939–41, and possibly 1947–53 and 1977–81, the PCF has pursued a policy of mutual support for the Socialists ever since. In terms of its adoption of Jacobin-nationalist rhetoric and its embracing of socially conservative attitudes on the issues of women, the family, sex, and birth control, moreover, the policy shift of 1936 has never been repudiated by the party at all. The standard interpretation, recently reinforced by Philippe Robrieux, insists on Soviet initiative for the shift; other historians like Louis Bodin (and the party itself) have insisted on the internal French origins of the change. Georgi Dimitrov and the Soviets would appear to have pushed Thorez into the unity-of-action pact with the Socialists in July 1934, fearing that the fascist riot of 6 February might lead to a repetition in France of events in Germany and Austria. On the other hand, the slogan of a Popular Front including the Radicals was very likely the invention of Thorez and Fried and launched at French initiative in October 1934. The Popular Front brought the party a new spurt of popularity, despite Thorez's cautious response to the unprecedented wave of strikes in June 1936. Electing not to participate in the Léon Blum government, the PCF was able to support it yet reap the benefits of criticizing its policies on Spain, the economy, and administrative personnel changes.

The benefits the party achieved during the Popular Front were almost squandered when the PCF rallied to the support of the USSR following the Nazi-Soviet pact (August 1939); the party, under Comintern urging, carried its policy shift so far as to denounce the war as the product of rival imperialisms, placing Adolph Hitler on a par with Winston Churchill. The Edouard Daladier government responded by persecuting and repressing the party, unwittingly collaborating in the party's feigned martyrdom and contributing to the confusion subsequently engendered by the party over its true role during this period. The PCF has not been able to deny, however, that elements of its leadership approached the Germans in June 1940, immediately after the Battle of France, in the hope that the occupation authorities would permit the legal appearance of L'Humanité, since the party organ had advocated a policy of peace with Germany after the signing of the Nazi-Soviet pact. The PCF was able to save its honor following the incident only by its heroic role in the Resistance; the defections caused by the Nazi-Soviet pact were more than compensated for by a new generation of enthusiasts who rekindled the party's ardor for a socialist model in Soviet colors. But the widespread disillusionment the Soviet Union has caused on the Left since 1956 has resulted in the party's almost continuous decline from the high point of 28 percent of the vote and 800,000 members it achieved in 1946. By comparison with the PCF's post–World War II strength, the election result of 1981 (15 percent) appears to be a setback of historic proportions.

L. Bodin, "De Tours à Villeurbanne: Pour une lecture renouvelée de l'histoire du PCF," *Annales: ESC* 30 (1975); D. Brower, *The New Jacobins: The French Communist Party and the Popular Front* (Ithaca, 1969); A. Kriegel, *Aux Origines du Communisme français*, 2 vols. (Paris, 1964); P. Robrieux, *Maurice Thorez, Vie secrète et vie publique* (Paris, 1975), and *Histoire intérieure du PC*, vol. 1 (Paris, 1980); R. Tiersky, *French Communism, 1920–72* (New York, 1974); R. Wohl, *French Communism in the Making* (Stanford, 1967); I. Wall, *French Communism in the Era of Stalin* (Westport, Conn., 1983).

I. M. Wall

Related entries: CACHIN; DUCLOS; LABOR MOVEMENT; LEFT, THE; MARTY; MARXISM; POPULAR FRONT; RUSSIA, RELATIONS WITH; SOCIALIST PARTY; THOREZ; TOURS, CONGRESS OF.

COMPERE-MOREL, ADEODAT (1872–1941), socialist politician and journalist, exponent of agrarian socialism. Born at Breteuil-sur-Noye (Oise), he left school at thirteen to work with his father, a nurseryman. He joined the Parti ouvrier in 1891 and began a long career as a socialist activist. He was elected to the village council of Breteuil in 1900 and became mayor two years later. Compère-Morel ran unsuccessfully several times as socialist candidate to the Chamber of Deputies in the Oise department before winning a by-election in the Gard in 1909. He was returned to the Chamber thereafter through the elections of 1932.

Compère-Morel became a major socialist spokesman on agrarian issues and regularly sat on the Chamber's Agriculture Committee. He believed that peasant small holdings should be protected and that socialists should work to develop a peasant constituency. Compère-Morel was a moderate socialist who supported the *union sacrée* government during the First World War and remained in the Socialist party after its split with the Communists following the Congress of Tours (1920). He wrote numerous articles for leading socialist newspapers, was on the staff of both *L'Humanité* and *Le Populaire*, and produced a number of books and pamphlets. In addition to titles dealing with agrarian questions, he authored a biography of Jules Guesde (1937) and the *Grand dictionnaire socialiste* (1924). Compère-Morel opposed the Popular Front policy of the socialists and left the party in 1932 to join the neosocialist movement. He did not seek reelection as a deputy in 1936.

J. Maitron, *Dictionnaire biographique du mouvement ouvrier français, 1871–1914*, vol. 11 (Paris, 1974).

T. Moodie

Related entries: GUESDISTS; SOCIALISM, 1870–1914; SOCIALIST PARTY.

CONFEDERATION GENERALE DU TRAVAIL (1895–1940). The French labor movement developed rapidly after 1884 when the formation of trade unions (*syndicats*) was legalized. Throughout the 1880s and 1890s, two organizational developments paved the way for the birth of the Confédération générale du travail (CGT) at the Congress of Limoges in 1895. The first was the vertical creation of national trade or industrial federations such as the typographers (1881). The second was the horizontal creation of local-based Bourses du travail, such as the Paris Bourse (1887). The fact that the nascent labor movement decided to concentrate on the creation of industrial federations at the national level (rather than more narrowly trade-based federations) was a reflection of the overtly ideological considerations that shaped its development. Every effort was made to structure the industrial federations in such a way that corporate self-seeking would be eliminated.

The predominance of ideology was also evident in the rise of the Bourses, which brought together workers from a broad range of professions around a common direct action approach to local labor militancy. While the industrial federations were inspired by the belief that professional action in defense of wages and in pursuit of better working conditions could effectively protect workers in a given industry from the ravages of unbridled liberalism, the Bourses were often influenced by the libertarian assertion of the rights of producers to the product of their labor and the anarchist rejection of all state-oriented politics.

Both of these objectives fell afoul of the emerging ideas of Marxism as expressed by the infant socialist movement. For a decade after 1884, the national labor movement (Fédération nationale des syndicats) fought a running battle against the hegemonic aspirations of the Guesdist Parti ouvrier français (POF), whose leaders believed that the activities of the union should be strictly subordinated to their party's frontal attack on the bourgeois state. It was through the vehement assertion of syndicalist autonomy (against both the state and the socialist POF that the CGT came into being and claimed victory over political socialism). At the same time, the creation of the autonomous CGT in 1895 contributed to the development of the ideology of revolutionary or anarchosyndicalism (a doctrine some scholars prefer to call direct action syndicalism).

At the outset, the CGT embraced only the industrial federations, but in 1902 the confederation was joined by the Bourses, and its real structure and history began. The doctrine of revolutionary syndicalism, which received its consecration at the 1906 Congress of Amiens, was predicated on the belief that direct action not only displayed working-class power but also educated the workers and prefigured the new society in which the *syndicat* was to be the basic element.

The assertion of the rights of minorities was a major determinant of the structure of the CGT in the years before World War I. The basic principle ("federalism based on the absolute autonomy of each and every *syndicat*") held that the smallest craft union should have the same voting rights at a congress as the largest industrial federation. Each *syndicat* had double representation in the confederation's proceedings: via the industrial federation and via the local Bourse. Syndicalist ideology posited that democracy was no more than the tyranny of unconscious majorities. The structure of the CGT was therefore a deliberate attempt to ensure that most decisions depended on the vote of the active minorities. Such a structure rapidly institutionalized what was to become a permanent feature of the French labor movement: a deemphasis on size, numbers, and funds in favor of activist dedication and revolutionary commitment. What the movement gained from this in terms of self-education, social and political critique, and self-image, it correspondingly lost in terms of strategies of negotiation and a spirit of compromise.

The CGT was deeply divided throughout World War I. Under the influence of general secretary Léon Jouhaux, the moderate wing embraced the *union sacrée* and sought the structures and procedures whereby labor could best negotiate wage settlements and other industrial agreements with the government and employers. This faction was comforted by the work of socialist armaments minister Albert Thomas, who was bent on showing that socialist direction of the economy was possible. At the same time, the radical wing, revolted by the mass bloodletting, came, through a sincere quest for peace, into contact with Leninism. The Russian Revolution bestowed on this instinctive revolt the aura of historical success. These seeds of division within the CGT bore fruit in 1921 when, after the failure of an ill-prepared and badly executed series of strikes (1919 and

1920), the CGT suffered its first major disruption. The revolutionaries broke away to form the Confédération générale du travail unitaire (CGTU).

Throughout the interwar years, the CGT, under the increasingly reformist leadership of Jouhaux, concentrated on what came to be known as *la politique de présence*: participation in every conceivable form of negotiation to further a limited number of basic CGT objectives, such as the nationalization of industries and the introduction of an embryonic social security system. This approach was denounced by the CGTU as class collaborationist. Although membership numbers gradually increased (370,000 in 1922 and 750,000 in 1930), especially as a result of growing public sector affiliation, the ability or even the desire of the CGT leaders to marshal, educate, and train these growing ranks of militants around some clearly defined social project became less evident. Jouhaux spent more of his time in Geneva where he put increasing faith in the infant International Labor Organization.

After fifteen years of internecine warfare, the labor movement was reunified in 1936 as a result of the euphoria attending the creation of the Popular Front. Both wings accepted the general title of CGT. Although the former *unitaires* (CGTU members) were a numerical minority at every level, the training in militant leadership they had received through their contacts with the international Communist movement stood them in good stead when the strike wave of 1936 broke out. Gradually the CGT, which had been born of virulent rejection of party politics, was brought under the wing of the French Communist party (PCF).

Despite a second split between 1939 and 1943 (when Communists were expelled from the CGT), the Jouhaux wing constantly lost ground. After the Liberation, Communist domination of the labor movement became inevitable. In 1947, a third split sent the supporters of Jouhaux into a self-imposed exile in a new confederation, the Force ouvrière. The CGT itself became inextricably integrated into the aims and policies of the PCF.

H. Dubief, *Le Syndicalisme révolutionnaire* (Paris, 1969); J. Julliard, *Fernand Pelloutier et les origines du syndicalisme d'action directe* (Paris, 1971); G. Lefranc, *Le Mouvement syndical sous la Troisième République* (Paris, 1967); V. R. Lorwin, *The French Labor Movement* (Cambridge, Mass. 1954); J.-D. Reynaud, *Les Syndicats en France* (Paris, 1975); G. Ross, *Workers and Communists in France* (Berkeley, 1981).

J. Howorth

Related entries: AMIENS, CHARTER OF; ANARCHISM; BOURSE DU TRAVAIL; CONFEDERATION GENERALE DU TRAVAIL UNITAIRE; GRIFFUELHES; JOUHAUX; LABOR MOVEMENT; STRIKE, GENERAL; SYNDICALISM; TRADE UNION MOVEMENT.

CONFEDERATION GENERALE DU TRAVAIL UNITAIRE (CGTU), a left-wing trade union organization that was formed by a schism in the Confédération générale du travail (CGT) at the end of 1921 and that survived until reunification in 1936, on the eve of the Popular Front. The new group professed, by its name, to represent a greater commitment to unity than that held by the reformists, on whom left wingers blamed the schism. But the CGTU itself was an uneasy alliance among disparate groups, and it experienced another schism when anarchosyndicalists left the organization after 1924 to remain in autonomy or to form a third body, the CGTSR (Syndicaliste révolutionnaire). By that time, the CGTU had come under the virtual domination of the Communist party and the Third International, whose trade union branch, the Profintern, claimed to honor French traditions of syndicalist autonomy but maintained a close liaison between party and union organizations. The resumption of unity in 1936 restored the old statutes of the CGT but soon worked to the advantage of the Communist faction, which retained control of the organization after yet another schism (which yielded the Force ouvrière) in 1947.

At the time of its founding congress at Saint-Etienne in 1922, the CGTU was still dominated by the syndicalist faction, and its statutes preserved the principles of federalism and direct action. But after the Communists won a majority at the Congress of Bourges in 1923, new statutes reorganized departmental unions into regional units more closely supervised by the central leadership and by representatives of the Communist party, whose concurrent reorganization aimed to maximize party union ties. From then on, most top officials, including Gaston Monmousseau and Benoît Frachon, sat on the party's central committee, and most decisions on strikes or other tactics aimed to serve the party's own interests. Only a small opposition remained, to fight from within rather than opt for autonomy or the CGTSR. Still, the party's victory was superficial, as the CGTU's membership (which peaked at some 430,000) trailed behind the CGT's and further declined (while the CGT's remained fairly steady) after the mid-1920s. Like its rival, the CGTU also recruited large numbers of public service employees (*fonctionnaires*) and failed to rally many unskilled industrial workers until after the reunification and the strikes of 1936.

A. Kriegel, *Aux origines du communisme français, 1914–1920*, 2 vols. (Paris and the Hague, 1964); G. Lefranc, *Le Mouvement syndical sous la Troisième République* (Paris, 1967); J.-L. Robert, *La Scission syndicale de 1921* (Paris, 1980); R. Wohl, *French Communism in the Making, 1914–1924* (Stanford, 1966).

K. E. Amdur

Related entries: COMMUNIST PARTY; CONFEDERATION GENERALE DU TRAVAIL; LABOR MOVEMENT; STRIKES; SYNDICALISM; TRADE UNION MOVEMENT.

CONSCRIPTION, MILITARY. Before 1789 conscription was used occasionally in emergencies. During the Revolutionary and Napoleonic wars (1792–1815), it was extensively employed but often resisted or evaded. Thereafter, until 1872, about 10 percent of males were conscripted by lot for a seven-year term, but inductees could pay for a substitute. Under the Third Republic substitution was abolished (1872), and a substantial majority of men had to serve. Evasion or outright resistance, nevertheless, was strikingly rare.

The 1872 law declared all males liable for service but compromised application of the principle because of financial considerations and conflicts between proponents (such as Adolphe Thiers) of a long service, basically professional force and those favoring a short service, mostly conscripted force. It divided the annual class by lot into two portions, one to serve five years and the other one year. Exemptions were numerous, including trainees for government service, teaching, and the clergy. University students, if they paid 1,500 francs toward uniforms and food, were allowed to volunteer for one year's service, after which they could become reserve officers by passing an examination. Liability for service was twenty years (ages twenty to forty), one to five years on active duty and the remainder in active reserve, territorial, and territorial reserve formations. Training of reserves, however, was often neglected under the Republic.

In practice no conscripts served actively as many as four years. In 1889 three years was made the upper limit. The one year volunteer scheme was abolished, but nearly a quarter of the annual class, chosen by lot, plus (at the Senate's insistence) university students, teachers, and seminarians, were required to serve only one year. University enrollments consequently rose dramatically in the 1890s.

The 1905 law marked a signal departure. In the name of equality, two years' service was made obligatory for all without exemption or reduction save for crippling physical defects, and liability was raised to twenty-five years. Students could get only a deferment. In 1913, responding to a worsening international climate, an increasingly unfavorable population disparity with Germany, and fear that a sudden attack could overwhelm covering forces before reserves could be mobilized, active service was raised to three years and liability to twenty-eight. The law, fiercely debated, dominated the 1914 elections. Rather than keep the 1910 class for a third year, two classes were called up in 1913. No more trained men were available at the outbreak of World War I than would have been under the 1905 law, but 50 percent more were on active duty, so complete covering forces were in position a day or two sooner. Whether this speed significantly affected ensuing operations remains unclear.

During World War I over 8 million men were mobilized and trained. After the war, active service was cut to two years (1919), to eighteen months (1923), and then to twelve (1928), but liability was raised to twenty-eight years. In 1935 two years' service was reinstated due to rising tensions and the onset of the lean years (1935–40), when classes would decrease by half owing to the demographic effects of World War I losses.

The navy relied mostly on volunteers but added conscripts, customarily from coastal departments, when needed. In the Empire conscription was applied by decree but with large variations among colonies and from regulations applying in France.

R. Challener, *The French Theory of the Nation in Arms, 1866–1939* (New York, 1955); G. Krumeich, *Aufrüstung und Innenpolitik in Frankreich vor dem Ersten Weltkrieg* (Wiesbaden, 1980); G. Michon, *La Préparation à la guerre: La Loi des trois ans* (Paris, 1935); G. Monteilhet, *Les Institutions militaires de la France*, 2d ed. (Paris, 1932); D. Ralston,

The Army of the Republic (Cambridge, Mass., 1967); J. Revol, *Histoire de l'armée française* (Paris, 1929).

D. S. Newhall

Related entries: ANTIMILITARISM; ARMY: ORGANIZATION; ARMY: PO-LITICAL ROLE; JACOBINISM; JUARES; MAGINOT LINE; MARNE, BAT-TLE OF THE; NAVY; OVERSEAS EMPIRE: COLONIAL ADMINISTRATION; SCHOOLS, MILITARY; THIERS; WORLD WAR I, FRANCE'S ROLE IN.

CONSERVATISM, a general term used to denote the theory and practice of political formations to the right of the radicals. Although there were many politicians and political parties in the Third Republic that are best described as conservative, the term itself was rarely part of the French political vocabulary. Only in the 1880s did the expression *conservateur* or *parti conservateur* have any currency. Then it was used (by those on the Right) to describe royalist and Bonapartist opponents of the Republic. The term allowed the Right to disguise electorally disadvantageous dynastic affiliations and permitted Bonapartists and royalists to unite under the label *union conservatrice.* Even then conservatives were as likely to describe themselves as liberals, an appellation meant to convey their opposition to administrative arbitrariness and anticlerical oppression. With the demise of the dynastic opposition after the Boulangist fiasco and the subsequent *ralliement*, the designation *conservateur* generally disappeared. Its occasional use in the twentieth century was limited to describing a moderate elder statesman of the Right (as in *conservateur chevronné*). After 1890 conservatives preferred to be called liberals (as with the conservative Catholic Action libérale populaire), *modérés, nationaux,* or even *républicains de gauche.* Everyone else designated them simply as the Right, a label that twentieth-century conservatives shunned.

Apart from a general desire to conserve the existing social order, there are few traits that characterize all French conservatives at all times. They were usually in opposition to the government (and before 1890 to the regime itself), but moderate conservatives like Jules Méline, Henri Poincaré, and André Tardieu were often mainstays of the Republic. Most conservatives were Catholic and staunch defenders of the church, their social doctrines heavily influenced by Christian corporatism. But the Center-Right Alliance démocratique made much of its laicism. Usually conservatives were thoroughly nationalistic, but the *conservateurs* of the 1880s and the *modérés* of the 1930s feared a neo-Jacobin nationalism as a prelude to or precipitant of social revolution.

One reason why French conservatism remains illusive is that during the Third Republic, conservatives never succeeded in forming an organized, disciplined, and highly articulate political party. Given their social and economic predominance and their natural allies in the church, army, and administration, conservatives initially saw no need for an effective political machine. These advantages, however, began to erode almost from the beginning, and from the 1890s on conservative commentators persistently decried the lack of political organization on the Right and insisted on the necessity of emulating the political zeal and organizational diligence of the Left. Yet despite unceasing laments about conservative apathy and appeals for an end to organizational anarchy, conservative parties remained invertebrate and lacking in cohesion both within and outside of the Chamber of Deputies.

All of the major conservative political parties of the Third Republic had pretensions of rectifying this situation. The Alliance démocratique (founded in 1901), Action libérale populaire (1901), Fédération républicaine (1903), and Parti démocrate populaire (1919) sought to create political organizations comparable to those on the Left. Only the very small Christian-Democratic Parti democrate populaire succeeded to any degree. The largest party, the Fédération républicaine, remained to the end a coterie of electorally secure deputies surrounded by a handful of departmental federations distinguished largely by their inactivity. The Alliance démocratique, despite periodic organizational efforts, never became much more than a convenient label for a loosely knit collection of Center-Right deputies. Significantly, the formations of conservative deputies within the Chamber rarely bore any direct relationship to the parties that existed outside.

There are a number of reasons for the organizational chaos on the Right. Political parties in France were generally less disciplined than elsewhere, and even the Radical party was hardly a model of cohesion. Deputies were extremely jealous of their independence and unenthusiastic about submitting to party discipline. The independence of conservative deputies reflected the fact that they rarely owed their election to the efforts of an organized party. The principal reason why conservative political organization remained rudimentary was because conservatives were elitist by temperament and conviction. Their idea of political organization was a meeting of a few self-appointed local notables to choose one of their number as a candidate and not the cultivation of a network of more or less popular and active committees.

In spite of their primitive political organization, conservatives retained important bastions of entrenched strength—notably in the Catholic west and, to a lesser extent, in the northeast and the southern fringes of the Massif central. Nonetheless their archaic political formations did leave them with a sense of impotence in an era of mass politics. Consequently, during periods of social and political crisis, real or perceived, their reflex was to search for allies who could provide a dynamism and a popular appeal that conservatives inherently lacked. At the end of the 1880s, royalists and Bonapartists, despairing of regaining power, financed and orchestrated the campaign of General Georges Boulanger and his coterie of political adventurers in an assault on the regime. At the end of the century, many conservatives, traditionally uneasy about the latent social radicalism in French anti-Semitism, began to support, covertly and overtly, the virulent anti-Semitic forces then emerging. In the 1930s, the *modérés* of the Fédération républicaine allied themselves with the mass antiparliamentary and protofascist formations like the Jeunesses patriotes, the Croix de feu, and the Parti social français. In all cases conservatives proved willing to ally with elements whose political style, social origins, and rhetorical emphasis were radically different from the image traditionally fostered by conservatives. If conservative discourse customarily stressed traditional religious and social values and hostility to social and political radicalism, their political reflexes often led them to associate with a so-called new Right whose values appeared to be fundamentally different. The fundamental conservative project, defense of the existing social order, was however, never forgotten, and what rendered cooperation with the new Right possible was the belief that the ideological gulf that separated it from traditional conservatives was often more apparent than real and the calculation that these allies could usually be controlled, manipulated, or corrupted.

Such alliances rarely yielded the anticipated returns and reflected the myopia of conservatives more than the objective reality of Third Republic France. Despite the fundamental political and cultural pessimism of conservatives and their sense of being beleaguered, France remained an essentially conservative society. Although the traditional elites were to some degree politically displaced by the *nouvelles couches sociales*, the latter rarely implemented significant social change. During periods of relative domestic tranquility, conservatives usually recognized this fact, and the result was a succession of *essais loyaux, ralliements*, or *unions nationales*. Only exceptionally, at the beginning and the end of the regime, did conservatives seek not to conserve but to destroy the existing political order.

M. Anderson, *Conservative Politics in France* (London, 1975); A. Bonnard, *Les Modérés* (Paris, 1936); W. D. Irvine, *French Conservatism in Crisis* (Baton Rouge, 1979); R. E. M. Irving, *Christian Democracy in France* (London, 1973); B. F. Martin, "The Creation of the Action Libérale Populaire: An Example of Party Formation in Third Republic France," *French Historical Studies* 9 (1976); R. Rémond, *Les Droites en France* (Paris, 1982); J.-P. Rioux, *Nationalisme et conservatisme* (Paris, 1977); R. Sanson, "L'Alliance démocratique," in R. Rémond and J. Bourdin, *La France et les Français en 1938–39* (Paris, 1973).

W. D. Irvine

Related entries: ACTION FRANCAISE; ACTION LIBERALE POPULAIRE; FASCISM; LIBERALISM; NOTABLES; ORLEANISM; PROGRESSISTS; RIGHT, THE.

CONSTITUTIONAL LAWS OF 1875, three laws voted by the National Assembly between 24 February and 30 November 1875, with the law of 30 December 1875 putting them into effect as the Constitutional Laws of the Third Republic. Although the final, very short document defines the executive and legislative branches of the government, it cannot properly be called a constitution; it contains no preamble and no declaration of the rights or sovereignty of the people, nor does it contain a preliminary statement naming the Republic as the accepted and official form of government. These shortcomings are best explained by the fact that the National Assembly, elected on 8 February 1871 and remaining in power until 1875, had as its primary task the ending of the Franco-Prussian War rather than the drafting of a constitution.

The Constitutional Laws of 1875 represent a series of compromises negotiated between the monarchists and the republicans once the basic principles had been agreed on: universal suffrage (limited to French males, twenty-one years or older), separation of powers, a bicameral parliament consisting of the Chambre des députés and the Sénat.

The law of 25 February 1875 (*relative à l'organisation des pouvoirs publics*) established the branches of government and determined the powers attributed to the executive branch (president elected for seven years) and the legislative branch.

The law of 24 February 1875 addressed the organization of the Sénat, naming this body also as the judicial branch (Cour de justice) empowered to judge the president, the ministers, and anyone else accused of jeopardizing the security of the state.

The law of 16 July 1875 (*sur les rapports des pouvoirs publics*) defined the relationship and the checks and balances of the branches of government.

The most serious shortcoming of these laws was the fact that executive authority was concentrated in the Conseil des ministres rather than in the president of the Republic. The ministers were at the mercy of the Chambre des députés, which by a vote of no confidence could topple the government. Inherent in the Constitutional Laws of 1875 was the possibility, therefore, of governmental instability under the leadership of a relatively weak president.

Les Constitutions de la France depuis 1789 (Paris, 1979); J. Ellul, *Histoire des institutions: Le XIXe siècle* (Paris, 1979); D. and M. Frémy, eds., *Encyclópédie QUID* (Paris, 1982).

J. D. Bragger

Related entries: NATIONAL ASSEMBLY; SEPTENNATE, LAW OF THE; WALLON AMENDMENT.

CONSUMER COOPERATIVES AND LEAGUES, the most important forms of consumer organization in France under the Third Republic. The concept of cooperation as a form for the social organization of modern industry was born in the era of utopian socialism in the early nineteenth century. Prior to 1870, however, consumer cooperatives were rare in France, and those that existed were for the most part dominated by political radicals. However, in the late 1870s and 1880s, leadership passed to an apolitical group near Nîmes, inspired by Fourierism and the more active English consumer groups. In 1885, under the leadership of the Nîmes group, a national federation of consumer cooperatives, the Union coopérative des sociétés françaises de consommation (later known simply as l'Ecole de Nîmes) was established.

Societies belonging to the Ecole de Nîmes in that era usually began as food cooperatives but later handled other staple items, such as furniture or clothing. The cooperatives sold at usual retail prices and then returned some of the surplus to individual members, reserving the rest to support programs of education or of production. The Ecole de Nîmes adhered strictly to a position of political neutrality, and its moderate program continued to attract new societies. The total number of consumer cooperatives grew to about 800 by 1889 and to twice that by 1900, but the societies adhering to the national union continued to be in a distinct minority.

The Union coopérative found it difficult to expand further without compromising its political neutrality. Overtures toward both the Right and the Left were unsuccessful. Simultaneously, however, the socialists, abandoning their hostility toward cooperatives, began to found such societies on their own. In 1895 they created the Bourse des coopératives socialistes. Unlike the Nîmois cooperatives, which were open to anyone, member societies of the Bourse usually admitted only workers.

For well over a decade, the Union coopérative and the Bourse exchanged long and bitter invectives, despite the fact that practical differences between their operations were few. A compromise was finally achieved by Jean Jaurès and other socialists who were influenced by utopian thought as well as by Marxism. In 1912 the two unions merged into the Fédération nationale des sociétés française de consommation. Although the manifesto on which the Fédération was based did not mention the class struggle or adhesion to the socialist party, the consumer cooperative movement eventually moved toward socialism without embracing it entirely.

During World War I consumer cooperatives multiplied rapidly and battled to keep prices and profits down when conditions of shortage encouraged inflation and profiteering. In 1922 there were close to 5,000 consumer cooperatives in France, but their growth stagnated thereafter as the state began assuming an ever larger role in the organization of consumer rights and responsibilities.

Early in the twentieth century another kind of consumer organization emerged. In 1903 Henriette Jean Brunhes, a Parisian housewife, established the Ligue sociale d'acheteurs in Paris. The basic principle of the Paris Ligue, and of others established throughout France, was that the shopper is ultimately responsible for working conditions. Its goal, which was to be achieved through methods of inquiry, intervention, and publicity, was to educate the shopper in her responsibilities so she could use her economic and social power wisely to encourage better working conditions. Although the Ligues started out emphasizing the responsibilities of consumers, they increasingly emphasized consumer rights. During the 1920s, in the face of massive postwar economic problems, however, the Ligues died out.

M. Deslandres, *L'Acheteur, son rôle économique et social; Les Ligues sociales d'acheteurs* (Paris, 1911); J. Gaumont, *Histoire générale de la coopération en France, les idées et les faits*, 2 vols. (Paris, 1924); B. Lavergne, *L'Ordre coopératif, étude générale de la coopération de consommation*, 2 vols. (Paris, 1926); Z. Strat, *Le Rôle du consommateur dans l'économie moderne* (Paris, 1922); R. H. Williams, *Dream Worlds* (Berkeley, 1982).

R. H. Williams

Related entries: GIDE, C.; SOCIALISM, 1870–1914.

COPPEE, FRANCOIS (1842–1908), popular writer; later in life, active Catholic, patriot, and anti-Semite. He was born in Paris to a family of moderate means. As a young man, he was first employed as a copying clerk at the Ministère de la guerre, next at the Senate Library in 1869, and then, from 1872 to 1883, he held a post as archivist at the Théâtre-français. His early verse, *Le Reliquaire* (1866) and *Intimités* (1868), was in the tradition of Leconte de Lisle and the Parnassians. But his later poetry—*La Grève des forgerons* (1869), *Les Humbles* (1872), *Le Cahier rouge* (1874), and *Les Récits et les élégies* (1878), for example— was more typical and earned him wide popularity and the soubriquet *le poète des humbles* for its simplicity, even naiveté, of expression, its sentimentality, and its evocations of the difficulties and joys of the common people of Paris and the *faubourgs*. Coppée's renown was enhanced by the success of his short romantic verse comedies, such as the very well-received *Le passant* (1869), played by Sarah Bernhardt, and *Le Luthier de Crémone* (1876). Following dramatic works included such plays as *Severo Torelli* (1883), *Les Jacobites* (1885), and *Pour la couronne* (1895). After his election to the Académie française in 1884, he continued to write plays, short stories, poetry, polemics, and novels, notably *La Bonne Souffrance* (1898), which reflected the new fervor of his Roman Catholicism after his conversion in 1898. The Dreyfus affair drew him into political involvement. He helped found and was *président d'honneur* of the anti-Semitic Ligue de la patrie française from 1899 until the elections of 1902, after which he resigned. Such nationalist and racialist activities caused a considerable diminution of his reputation in the twentieth century.

   R. N. Horry, "The Humanitarianism of François Coppée" (Ph.D. dissertation, New York University, 1949); L. Le Meur, *La Vie et l'oeuvre de François Coppée* (Paris, 1932).

G. Crichfield

Related entries: ANTI-SEMITISM; BERNHARDT; DREYFUS AFFAIR; LITERATURE; LITERATURE, PROLETARIAN.

COT, PIERRE (1895–1977), radical-socialist minister of aviation (1933–38), one of the organizers of the Popular Front, and an opponent of fascism. Attorney, professor of law and political science at Rennes, and mayor of Coise-Saint-Jean-Pied Gauthier, Cot was elected to the Chamber of Deputies from Savoy in 1928. More interested in foreign affairs than in domestic politics, he was named to the French delegation to the League of Nations (1929–32) and to the disarmament conference by Prime Minister Aristide Briand in 1929. In 1932 he was appointed under secretary of state for foreign affairs and championed reconciliation with Weimar Germany, disarmament, collective security, and close Franco-Soviet relations. In January 1933 Cot became minister of aviation in the first Edouard Daladier cabinet, a position he continued to hold under the Popular Front (1936–37). As a result of the Aéropostale scandal of 1933 (involving forgery and graft by the company's directors), Cot reformed French commercial aviation and created the government-owned Air France company, financed jointly by public and private sources. His outspoken denunciation of capitalistic monopolies for denying economic democracy and social equality led him to be singled out by the right-wing press during the 6 February 1934 riots. He succeeded in nationalizing the poorly run aircraft industry (1936–37) and secretly sent war materials to the Spanish Republic during its civil war (1936–39). Opposing the Maginot defensive strategy, he attempted to create an independent air army but was consistently blocked by the general staff and especially by Marshal Philippe Pétain.

Escaping to the United States in July 1940, Cot was tried in absentia by a Vichy court at Riom for weakening the French air force by his nationalization policies. In 1943 he was elected to the Consultative Assembly in Algiers and to the postwar Chamber of Deputies where his extreme leftist views led to his expulsion from the Radical party and to his creation of the small Progressive Union party.

P. Cot, *Triumph of Treason* (Chicago, 1944).

M. L. Mickelsen

Related entries: AIR FORCE: ORGANIZATION; BLUM; BRIAND; DALA-DIER; DEPRESSION OF THE 1930s; FASCISM; FEBRUARY RIOTS; GER-MANY, RELATIONS WITH (1914–1940); MAGINOT LINE; PETAIN; POPULAR FRONT; RADICAL AND RADICAL-SOCIALIST PARTY; RIGHT, THE; RUSSIA, RELATIONS WITH; SOCIALISM, 1914–1940; SPAIN, RE-LATIONS WITH.

COTY, FRANCOIS (1874–1934), a self-made billionaire who turned to journalism and the organization and subvention of radical rightist groups. Born François Spoturno in Corsica and orphaned at a young age, Coty by 1919 had built the well-known international perfume empire when he turned his ambitions to politics. Elected *conseiller général* in Corsica in 1920, he failed twice to enter the Senate. Defeated in 1921, his victory of 1923 was disqualified for electoral corruption, an event that helped to nourish his antiparliamentarism.

Meanwhile, Coty bought the *Figaro* in 1922, taking editorial and political control over the monarchist daily in 1927. Through subventions and promises, he sought to influence both the Action française and the Faisceau in 1925–27 and tried to seize control of the ailing Faisceau in 1927–28, helping only to scuttle the fascist organization.

Success in right-wing politics came after 1927. In that year he founded the veteran-oriented Croix de feu, later to become (in other hands) one of France's largest right-wing leagues. Coty added to his growing press empire in 1928 by creating *L'Ami du peuple*, a mass circulation daily that so far undersold its competitors that it was boycotted by the Havas and Hachette agancies, which monopolized the distribution of advertisements and newsstand copies.

Coty won his legal battle with the two agencies and, after his abandonment of the Croix de feu in 1930, continued to found a series of rightist leagues that became the Solidarité française in 1933, a group that survived his death. His program mixed anticommunism and a very vague corporatism with a program of constitutional reform bearing similarities to the Fifth Republic.

By 1933, Coty's political and journalistic ventures, a divorce, and some speculative setbacks were draining his fortune. When he died, both his money and most of his political influence had been spent.

A. Kupferman, "François Coty: Journaliste et homme politique" (troisième cycle thesis, Université de Paris, 1965); L. Latzarus, *Un Ami du peuple, Monsieur Coty* (Paris, 1929); R. Schor, "Xénophobie et l'extrême-droite: L'Exemple de 'L'Ami du peuple' (1928–1937)," *Revue d'histoire moderne et contemporaine* 23 (1976).

A. Douglas

Related entries: ACTION FRANCAISE; BUCARD; CROIX DE FEU; FASCISM; VALOIS.

COTY, RENE (1882–1962), the future president of the Fourth Republic (1954–58), who distinguished himself by the most forceful intervention into the political process undertaken by any other president since Maurice de MacMahon dissolved the Chamber of Deputies in 1877. Coty in 1958 threatened to resign if General Charles de Gaulle was not named by a hesitant parliament to head the government.

He was born in Le Havre (Seine Inférieure) into a family of school teachers and attended the University of Caen where he specialized in maritime law. In 1923 he entered national politics with his election to the Chamber of Deputies, a position he retained until 1936. As a deputy Coty showed interest in constitutional revision and proposed legislation calling for proportional representation. He favored a reinvigorated presidency and supported Raymond Poincaré's, and later André Tardieu's, efforts in this direction. In 1930 he served briefly as under secretary of state for the interior and in 1935 was elected to the Senate, where he remained until 1940.

M. D. Candée, ed. *Current Biography* (New York, 1954); J. J. Chevallier, "Le President René Coty," *Politique* 12 (1969); A. Dansette, *Histoire des présidents de la République* (Paris, 1960); L. Derfler, *President and Parliament* (Boca Raton, 1983); J. Jolly, ed., *Dictionnaire des parlementaires français*, vol. 3 (Paris, 1963).

L. Derfler

Related entries: POINCARE, R.; PRESIDENT OF THE REPUBLIC, OFFICE OF; TARDIEU.

COURBET, GUSTAVE (1819–1877), realist painter with socialist opinions. Courbet's ideas about art and politics suggest an extended childhood: the rebellious provincial boy with immense artistic talent at loggerheads with all established conventions and institutions, who remained the troublesome outsider for his entire life. His prosperous family endeavored to curb him through a religious education, which left him irreligious and anticlerical, and he would have none of the legal career they meant for him, taking lessons in painting in Besançon for three years at the expense of his legal studies. Whatever may have been his intelligence, it remained largely uncultivated. When he moved to Paris in 1840, he was indifferent to the literary and romantic subjects that then occupied more intellectual painters, probably accounting for his quick attraction to landscapes and portraits. Within a decade he had enlarged his topical scope to feature oversized canvases that focused on the daily exigencies of lower-class life, a realism concentrating on the sordid and the ugly. During the June Days of 1848, he instinctively sympathized with the mob against the established order, which gave focus thereafter to his adherence to radical causes. In 1850, he exhibited *The Stone Breakers*, portraying men he believed to be the personification of poverty. Proudhon later called it the first socialist painting and Courbet the first socialist painter.

Courbet made no such claim. What philosophizing he did about his art seems to have been done with the aid of literary friends. He wrote that realism is the negation of the ideal—an abandonment of art for art's sake. He believed that painting must tackle only concrete subjects—real and existing—and avoid anything abstract. For that reason, he considered realism the democratic art, consistent with the democratization of society in the nineteenth century and thus the art of the future. His critics answered that he recognized only the mundane aspects of life and external appearances. He ascribed such criticism to people having sold out to the imperial government. His canvases sold well and made him wealthy, partly because he produced masses of landscapes and portraits (and only an occasional depiction of the downtrodden), partly because he was unwittingly a more sophisticated painter than he claimed.

His hatred of authority in any form caused him to celebrate the fall of the Second Empire, and the minor posts he accepted from the subsequent provisional regime had been primarily created to dismantle fine arts institutions formerly financed by the state. He supported the Commune in 1871, evidently believing it represented the end of government. Brought to trial after the defeat of the Commune, he was fined and given a six-month term in prison. The ordeal undermined his health, but worse was to come. Shortly after Marshal Maurice de MacMahon took power in 1873, a royalist-Bonapartist coalition got a bill through the National Assembly making Courbet financially liable for the reconstruction of the Vendôme column, which had been pulled down during the Commune. There was no precedent for making an individual responsible for damage to public property during civil strife, but such retaliation was a measure of the bitterness in the aftermath of that conflict. Legal arrangements for paying off the obligation were not completed until mid-1877 (10,000 francs a year for thirty-two years), an impossible burden for a man of fifty-eight. He died on the last day of that year, having founded no school of painting or attracted disciples.

G. Boas, *Courbet and the Naturalistic Movement* (Baltimore, 1938); G. Mack, *Gustave Courbet* (New York, 1951).

R. L. Williams

COUTURE. The most well known of the French fashion houses were established during the Third Republic when designers such as Charles Frederick Worth, Paul Poiret, Gabrielle Chanel, Madeleine Vionnet, and Elsa Schiaparelli progressively moved from the restrictive, complicated, and tortured designs in women's clothing to the supple, simple, relaxed, and more comfortable lines. The early years of the Third Republic saw couturiers specializing in a particular article or accessory (dresses, hats, shoes), but with the 1920s and Chanel, diversification in production became increasingly important, and perfume emerged as a major sales item.

The history of French fashions between 1870 and 1940 may be divided into four periods, each identified with its particular trend-setting couturier: fin de siècle or the Gay Nineties (1870–99) with Worth; the *belle époque* (1900–14) with Poiret; the 1920s with Chanel and Vionnet; and the 1930s with Schiaparelli.

The Franco-Prussian War (August 1870–January 1871) temporarily put an end to the creation of fashions in France, but among the few who managed to keep their establishments open was Charles Frederick Worth (1825–97). The period from 1870 to 1899 was dominated by Worth, whose name came to symbolize haute couture and couture-création. After an apprenticeship in England, he settled in Paris, working first for Gagelin and Opigez. His unique designs and his fascination with materials quickly made him the favorite of the ladies of the Second Empire. His shop on the rue de la Paix was the first to use mannequins to display finished dresses. He became the court couturier for the Empress Eugénie and was sought after by the nobility and great ladies of the day. Among his most celebrated customers were the Princess Metternich, Queen Victoria, and, from the demi-monde, La Paiva. Worth originated the concept of the collection prepared for presentation to potential buyers. Although the name of Worth is also often associated with the crinoline, he was neither responsible for it nor used it in his fashions. He prided himself in imitating the full form in gowns without the aid of the crinoline.

Another couturier of note was Jacques Doucet (1853–1929) who established his shop on the rue de la Paix shortly after the Franco-Prussian War. A great admirer of French eighteenth-century painting, he was particularly inspired by Maurice Quentin de la Tour and Jean–Antoine Watteau, and his creations were dominated by the imaginative use of lace in an effort to make his clients look more seductive. His most famous client was the actress Réjane, and he counted among his friends Paul Valéry, Henri de Regnier, Pierre Louÿs, and Jean Cocteau.

In 1891, Madame Isidore Paquin (d. 1936) established her dressmaking firm on the rue de la Paix, and her elegant designs were soon sought after by the royalty of many European countries. In the faubourg Saint-Honoré, Madame Jeanne Lanvin (1867–1946) began designing and selling hats. She expanded her art to the *robes de style* for debutantes, elegant evening gowns with very full skirts requiring several petticoats. Her shop outlasted those of many of her competitors, and she became the most successful fashion creator during World War II.

The other famous houses established during this fin de siècle were Callot Soeurs, Beer, Martial et Armand, Doeillet, Jenny, Boué Soeurs, Drecoll, and Redfern. The newly wealthy industrialists ensured success for specialized shops: Reboux (hats), Mellerio, Cartier (jewelers), Révillon (furrier).

The *belle époque* (1900–14) was dominated by the extravagant personality of Paul Poiret (1879–1944). Apprenticed at the Maison Worth, he soon set out on his own with innovative styles that made him the most popular couturier in Paris. At the beginning of his career, he followed the trends of the late nineteenth century. His styles were elegant but comfortable and suited to women's increased desire for movement and freedom. Three-piece suits (jacket, skirt, blouse) were particularly popular, as were his more loosely fitting afternoon dresses. Poiret waged a relentless war against the corset but invented the *soutien-gorge* called, ironically, "Liberty." He began the rage for Oriental dress with the mandarin coat called Confucious, but, in spite of his desire for comfort in dress, he paradoxically promoted the tight skirt. He introduced the turban, became known in the art of theater decoration, and was the first to diversify his business to include perfume.

During this period, the House of Beer continued to be popular, the houses of Madeleine Vionnet and Amy Linker were just starting, and the men's tailor, O'Rossen, began manufacturing clothing for women. Shoes, more than any other part of a wardrobe, were indicative of the financial situation of the wearer. Hellstein, Gillet, Lobb were the principal outfitters in made-to-order shoes.

During World War I, sumptuous parties and ostentatious glamor were considered in bad taste, and many women were too busy with war work to worry about the latest styles. Only the darkest colors were acceptable in what was a dark period in French history. However, the necessities of wartime activities strongly influenced reform in women's clothing. For more comfort and ease of movement, skirts were made shorter, and walking shoes became the fashion.

Gabrielle "Coco" Chanel (1883–1971) made her debut in 1914. She had contributed to the war effort, and her inspiration came largely from the clothes (navy blue dresses, sweaters, shorter skirts) worn by women working as nurses and volunteers. After the war, she introduced the short pleated skirt with a straight jacket slightly longer than the waistline. Her lines were straight and simple, her colors dark with white accents. Her cloche hat contributed to the garçonne style imitated throughout the 1920s. This style influenced the wearing of short hair and gave increased importance to the Parisian coiffeurs.

Madeleine Vionnet (1876–1976) was Chanel's greatest rival. She was known for her bias-cut kimono sleeve, and her materials were more varied than those of Chanel. Vionnet's clientele came largely from the aristocratic circles of Paris.

With Chanel and Vionnet, a number of new big houses came into being. The most noteworthy of these were Jean Patou, Lucien Lelong, Robert Piguet, Louise Boulanger, Maggy Rouff, Marcelle Rochas, and Suzanne Talbot.

Piracy of models became particularly profitable during the 1920s. For many years, no laws existed to protect designers against copyists, and smaller houses were thus able to offer the less wealthy an array of clothes often indistinguishable from the original. Some of the medium houses in Paris succeeded in legitimizing this practice by entering into agreements with the large houses. They were able to reproduce and sell designs providing they did not release them before certain dates. Nina Ricci, Vera Borea, Madame Charpentier, Marcelle Dormoy, and Augusta Bernard were among the most well known of the Parisian medium houses during the post–World War I period.

The crash of 1929 and the subsequent depression brought profound changes to the fashion industry. American buyers dwindled, the tourist trade came to a standstill, credit was no longer available, fewer designs and more copies became the norm, only two instead of four collections (summer and winter) were presented each year. The boutique replaced the salon, and fashion houses had to concentrate on the foreign market to stay in business.

Foreign sales seemed to encourage eccentricity, and the first to see the advantage of this tendency was Elsa Schiaparelli (1890–1973). Black and white became her trademark, particularly in her sweaters with a large butterfly bow in front and in her suits and evening gowns. She appealed to foreign buyers with her original and unusual fashions and became the most popular couturière of the 1930s. Her designs were copied all over the world, and her boutique included many accessories previously scorned by designers: evening sweaters, blouses, jewelery, strange buttons, zippers (which she is said to have invented), raincoats, scarves, hats, aprons, kitchen dresses. With little regard for practicality, Schiaparelli set out to shock. Her collection introduced a new color, shocking pink, and her products set the trend in every area of fashion design.

Other major houses also made their debut during the 1930s. The most famous among these were Alix, Marcel Rochas, Jacques Heim, Drecoll, Jean Desses, Balenciaga, Madeleine Rauch, Carven, and Jacques Griffe.

The 1930s had a great impact on the French fashion world. Colors varied according to the season, knitted dresses and coats became popular, the cloche hat slowly disappeared in favor of hats that showed more hair, skirts became longer, the neckline dropped and the back was eliminated from evening gowns, sports clothes became more popular, and the simple, classical style was adopted to ensure longer wear.

As the 1930s drew to an end and war became once more inevitable, the great fashion houses were again forced to adapt to the economic crisis of the day. Many closed temporarily or permanently; some moved to the unoccupied zone; a few, such as Lanvin, managed to weather the storm in Paris.

K. Anspach, *The Why of Fashion* (Ames, Iowa, 1967); M. Beaulieu, *Le Costume moderne et contemporain* (Paris, 1951); C. Bertin, *Paris à la mode* (London, 1956); F. Boucher, *20,000 Years of Fashion* (New York, n.d.); E. Carter, *The Changing World of Fashion* (New York, 1977); E. Charles-Roux, *Chanel* (New York, 1975); M. Haedrich, *Coco Chanel* (Boston, 1972); A. Latour, *Les Magiciens de la mode* (Paris, 1961); M. Leloir, *Histoire du costume* (Paris, 1935–49); P. Morand, *L'Allure de Chanel* (Paris,

1976); H. Norris, *Costume and Fashion* (London, 1927–33); R. Riley, *The Fashion Makers* (New York, 1968); N. Waugh, *Corsets and Crinolines* (London, 1954).

J. D. Bragger

Related entries: BELLE EPOQUE; DECORATIVE ARTS; DEPRESSION OF THE 1930s; TOURISM.

CRIME, PATTERNS OF. Although there is some dispute among historians and sociologists, crime rates seem to have increased in most categories during the Third Republic. The problems confronting historians who wish to discover precise crime rates are many and profound. The French possessed the most thorough and uniformly recorded national crime statistics in the world during this period (Comte général de l'administration de la justice criminelle en France). But these figures include only those crimes reported to public prosecutors and exclude those known only by the police, those unreported to them, and whole categories of the so-called victimless crimes. Other problems include changes in reporting procedures, the creation and lapsing of whole categories of crime, and the formation in 1912 of a separate series of juvenile courts to try youths formerly tried in the regular courts. For these and other reasons, we may conclude that official statistics, although they may represent some trends fairly accurately, are useless for the real crime that never surfaced in legal processes.

It also seems more fruitful, as Michelle Perrot has pointed out, to regard extant judicial statistics not as facts but as judgments that reflect something of the character of those who make and administer the law. Thus, patterns of crime must include some account of what the French regarded as criminal behavior. Public drunkenness, never punished under the monarchy or the empire, became a crime only in 1873, reflecting the deep concern that many of the French felt for rising rates of alcoholism. We should also read infanticide statistics as judgments rather than real rates for this crime. During the first half of the nineteenth century, when we know from other evidence that infanticide was common practice, about 300 persons were brought to trial yearly on this charge. The rate fell to an average of 170 per year until 1913, when it climbed to 383 in the immediate prewar anxiety about France's low birthrates. The highest figures for this crime ever recorded followed the slaughter of the war years in 1920 (516) and 1921 (519). We are less likely to err, in short, when we consider the effects that the zeal of police, prosecutors, and judicial officials may have on legal statistics.

Some crime rates seem to be more directly tied to the modernization of French society than others. Fraud and embezzlement, modern crimes, averaged 6,600 cases tried per year in the 1870s and 13,400 in the 1930s, but arson, a distinctly rural and traditional crime, declined by 42 percent between the mid-nineteenth and early twentieth centuries. Rates of those tried for mendicity or vagabondage, often regarded as rural crimes, followed an expected downward trend during the Republic, from yearly averages of 20,000 to 35,000 per year in the period 1875 to 1895 to fewer than 15,000 a year after the war. But these figures are misleading since the highest rates of the nineteenth century were recorded between 1875 and 1895, suggesting that it was urban vagabondage that troubled contemporaries the most.

Crimes against property appear to reflect the growth of industrialization and the spread of personal wealth throughout France during the Third Republic. Some observers have concluded wrongly that theft rates declined during the period because the number of serious property crimes tried in assizes courts declined from figures over 2,000 per year in the 1880s to just over 1,000 in the 1920s. But in fact many of these crimes were being tried in the lesser, correctional courts where authorities believed convictions more certain and because in general the value of stolen goods in typical robberies had declined, reflecting a growth in common burglary as opposed to armed robbery. The number of individuals brought to trial in correctional courts averaged 40,000 per year in the 1870s and climbed gradually to 55,000 in the 1920s. Averaging serious and lesser property crimes reported to police (as opposed to those actually sent to trial) from the 1840s to 1910, Howard Zehr found an increase per capita of 230 percent. Making allowances for differing reporting and trial procedures elsewhere, similar patterns seem to have prevailed in England and Germany. When the effects of larger and more effective police forces are added to the equation, real property crime rates in the Third Republic may have changed little throughout the period.

Crimes of violence seem to have increased somewhat faster than population growth but in irregular patterns. Common assaults tried in court rose steadily from 25,000 per year in the 1870s and 1880s to 35,000 in the decade before the war and 39,000 in the 1920s. More serious assaults (with a deadly weapon) tried in the assizes courts changed little, remaining at just under 200 per year throughout the period. First- and second-degree murder fluctuated more radically. Zehr estimates a drop of 9 percent in the rates of persons tried for homicide between 1830 and 1910, but there appears to have been an upward bulge after 1905. The decade ending in 1905 averaged just 460 per year, but from 1905 to 1914 the average was 613 and was well over 500 per year in the 1920s. The generally downward trend in homicide typical of all other Western societies recommenced in the 1930s, however.

Rape and other serious sexual crimes seem to have declined significantly. Cases tried in this category exceeded 1,000 in some years during the 1870s but were averaging fewer than 400 in the years after the First World War. However, statistics in this area are most affected by prevailing social attitudes about all crimes and are probably less representative of real rates than any others. Juvenile crime rates are also difficult to describe because changes in the year of majority have occurred more than once since separate juvenile courts were established in 1912. Students of juvenile crime in nineteenth-century Europe have argued that the highest rates for juvenile crime were probably in mid-century during the peak years of urbanization and before primary schooling was made mandatory, but French proponents of separate courts after 1900 argued for this new jurisdiction because of the increases they observed in the number of young criminals.

Recidivism rates underwent a gradual decrease following a peak in the late

1880s and early 1890s when up to 45 percent of the suspects charged with crimes were found to have had prior convictions. The rate fell slowly to about 37 percent before the new juvenile administration took charge of youthful repeaters, after which the rate fell as low as 15 percent for certain years before 1939. The implementation of parole and conditional liberation in 1885 and 1892, respectively, probably had more effect in reducing recidivism than any other change in prisons or prior administrations.

Historians have debated the existence of predictors for crime trends in modern France, but few undisputed examples can be found. Most seem to agree that urbanity (as distinct from urbanization) is a mild predictor and that a similarly mild relation exists for areas in certain stages of industrialization. Even here distinctions must be made between theft and crimes of violence, the rates of which tended generally to be inversely related. Business or economic cycles are generally not good predictors. Perhaps the strongest positive correlations were those among food prices, real wages, and crime. During the Third Republic price indicators gradually shifted, as might be expected, from grain prices to a broader variety of staple foodstuffs.

A. Q. Lodhi and C. Tilly, "Urbanization, Crime, and Collective Violence in 19th Century France," *American Journal of Sociology* 79 (1977); R. A. Nye, "Crime in Modern Societies: Some Research Strategies for Historians," *Journal of Social History* 11 (1978): M. Perrot, "Délinquance et système penitentiaire en France au XIXᵉ Siècle," *Annales ESC* 30 (1975); D. Szabo, *Crimes et villes* (Paris, 1960); Yak-yon Chen, *Etudes statistiques sur la criminalité en France de 1855 à 1930* (Paris, 1937); Howard Zehr, *Crime and the Development of Modern Society: Patterns of Criminality in Nineteenth Century Germany and France* (Totowa, N.J., 1976).

R. A. Nye

Related entries: CAPITAL PUNISHMENT; JUDICIAL SYSTEM: COURTS; JUDICIAL SYSTEM: JUDGES; PRISONS.

CROIX DE FEU, a right-wing veterans' organization in interwar France. Founded in 1928 as a nonpolitical organization of World War I veterans, the Croix de feu became a significant force on the far Right after 1930 under the leadership of Colonel François de La Rocque. Initially restricted to decorated soldiers and combat veterans (the latter known as the Briscards), the league in 1934 created an auxiliary, the Volontaires nationaux, open to the postwar generation. The Croix de feu insisted that it was above politics and sought only to restore the discipline and spirit of national reconciliation that had existed in the trenches. It was hostile to the divisive spirit of political parties and contended that it stood for a social policy that transcended the sterile positions of Left and Right (hence its slogan, "ni à droite, ni à gauche"). In fact its stance on most issues of domestic or foreign policy was very like that of traditional conservatives, and, although the Croix de feu avoided any official association with conservative parties, a number of prominent right-wing deputies belonged to the league. What made the Croix de feu different was its dynamism and its talent for mass mobilization; its membership grew from a few thousand in 1930 to as many as 450,000 in 1936. What made the movement frightening was its cryptic references to a D day and an H hour, its penchant for convoys of automobiles and motorcycles, and its paramilitary parades. The opaque pronouncements of La Rocque could not disguise the overt contempt of many in the Croix de feu for parliamentary democracy.

The league was dissolved by the Popular Front government in June 1936 and reappeared as the Parti social français. In its new form the league founded a parliamentary group and actively sought to elect deputies. For about a year the Parti social français experienced dramatic growth, exceeding by 1937 the membership in the Croix de feu. By the end of the decade, however, internal rifts and the diminishing threat from the Left arrested both the growth and the dynamism of the new party. In 1941 the remnants of the movement were integrated into the Vichyite Légion français des combattants.

W. D. Irvine, *French Conservatism in Crisis* (Baton Rouge, 1979); P. Machefer, "Les Croix de feu, 1927–1936," *Information historique* (January–February 1972); P. Machefer, "Le Parti social français en 1936–37," *Information historique* (March–April 1972); A Prost, *Les Anciens Combattants et la société française* (Paris, 1977); P. Rudaux, *Les Croix de feu et le P.S.F.* (Paris, 1967).

                                                                              W. D. Irvine

Related entries: FASCISM; LA ROCQUE.

CUBISM, pivotal artistic movement of the first half of the twentieth century, which was ushered in by Pablo Picasso and Georges Braque in 1907 and continued as a coherent movement until about 1925. Conceptual in approach, cubism may be seen as the twentieth-century antithesis to (perceptual) impressionism and as the final consequence of the new direction taken by Paul Cézanne after the mid-1880s. In fact, the immediate impetus to the development of cubism was a retrospective exhibition of Cézanne's work at the Salon d'automne of 1907. The impact of this show, combined with the influences of ancient Iberian and African sculpture, led Picasso to paint his famous (unfinished) painting, *Demoiselles d'Avignon* (New York, Museum of Modern Art), generally considered the foundation stone of the cubist movement.

During the first (analytic) phase of cubism, Picasso, joined in 1907 by the former fauvist painter Braque, set out to revolutionize the representation of three-dimensional forms on the two-dimensional picture plane. Abandoning the traditional single fixed viewpoint for a number of different viewpoints, they fused multiple views of the subject into a single image. Simultaneously, conventional perspective was replaced by a new shallow space, extending both behind and in front of the picture plane, and forms were reduced to simple geometric shapes, following Cézanne's advice to "treat nature by the cylinder, the sphere, the cone."

As analytic Cubism moved from its early formative phase (c. 1907–09), during which it was still strongly influenced by Cézanne and African sculpture, to its mature hermetic phase (c. 1910–12), the paintings of Picasso and Braque became increasingly abstracted. The conceptual, intellectual approach toward their subject matter not only led to the abandonment of color (to the point where cubist paintings acquired a monochrome *grisaille* appearance) but also to an indifferent choice of subject matter, which was limited largely to half-length seated figures and still lifes. Nevertheless, Picasso and Braque were reluctant to sever the ties between observed reality and their art. By 1912, as their pictures became exceedingly difficult to decipher, they began to furnish them with recognizable elements such as a row of buttons, letters, words, musical notes, and the like— signs and symbols intended to provide clues to the interpretation of their paintings. By 1913, this pictorial device was taken one step further by the introduction of collage elements, such as strips of printed paper, textile, or chair caning, into the painting. The use of these extraneous materials clearly marked the beginning of a new phase in cubism—soon to be referred to as synthetic—which lasted from 1913 until 1925. During this phase the original cubists, Picasso and Braque, were joined by a third artist, the Spaniard Juan Gris, who not only carried the synthetic approach to its most logical conclusion but also became the spokesman and proselytizer of the movement.

During the synthetic phase of cubism, paintings or collages were made up of abstract shapes, which were put together in such a way as to suggest a particular subject. The nature of that subject was further defined by the use of clues (contours, words, details of anatomy or clothing) similar to the ones used earlier during the analytic phase. While during the beginning of the synthetic phase (1913–14), Picasso, Braque, and Gris preferred the collage technique, later they reverted toward pure painting, often applied in a textured way so as to suggest wood grain, marbling, and so on. At the same time color also made a comeback in their pictures.

It was synthetic rather than analytic cubism that had a following, both in France and abroad. In part this was due to the efforts of Gris, who more than Picasso and Braque was able to explain cubism to others. The influence of cubism was widespread but often superficial. The so-called Section d'or (Golden Section) group, which was founded in 1912 and included, among others, Jacques Villon, Marcel Duchamp, Francis Picabia, André Lothe, Auguste Herbin, Jean Metzinger, Louis Marcoussis, Albert Gleizes, Roger de La Fresnaye, and André Dunoyer de Segonzac, for the most part practiced a decorative, colorful cubism based on carefully calculated schemes of proportion and harmoniously balanced color schemes. For many of them cubism was merely a jumping board from which they ventured into new directions.

More important than decorative cubism was the work of Fernand Léger and Robert Delaunay. Léger came to cubism via the naive art of Henri Rousseau. From the start, he was interested in simple, primitive forms while his concern with modernity brought him close to futurism. Though before World War I he briefly ventured on the path of nonobjectivity, Léger's mature works show figures and objects transformed into streamlined, metallic forms with a precise machine-made look. Léger's preoccupation with precision of form relates him to the purist movement, another offshoot of cubism, founded by Amédée Ozenfant and Charles Edouard Jeanneret (Le Corbusier).

Robert Delaunay started out as an analytical cubist but unlike Picasso and Braque was interested in dynamic subjects evoking life in the modern city (hence, his preoccupation with the Eiffel Tower). By 1911, Delaunay became interested in color, which he approached in a pseudoscientific way, painting prismatic windows that break up the light into spectral colors, and entirely abstract series of color wheels, which he referred to as circular rhythms or simultaneous disks. It was the Orphist (Apollinaire) art of Delaunay rather than the orthodox cubism of Picasso and Braque that was most influential outside France. Particularly in Germany, where his paintings were shown as early as 1911, Delaunay's art had a major effect on several artists associated with the Blaue Reiter group, including Wassily Kandinsky, August Macke, Franz Marc, and Paul Klee.

Although the three founders of cubism never took the path toward nonobjectivity in art, cubism did give rise to several forms of abstraction. Besides the prewar abstractions of Léger and the Orphist color wheels of Delaunay, the art of the Dutch Stijl group (including Piet Mondrian, Theo van Doesburg, and Bart van der Leck) and the suprematist abstractions of the Russian artist Casimir Malevich were rooted in the cubist style. Cubist painting, moreover, gave rise to a cubist mode in sculpture, best represented in the works of Picasso, Alexander Archipenko, Julio Gonzalez, Henri Laurens, and Jacques Lipchitz.

D. Cooper, *The Cubist Epoch* (London, 1971); J. Golding, *Cubism: A History and an Analysis, 1907–1914* (London, 1968); C. Grey, *Cubist Aesthetic Theories* (Baltimore, 1953); R. Rosenblum, *Cubism and Twentieth-Century Art* (London, 1968).

P. t.-D. Chu

Related entries: APOLLINAIRE; ART: MAJOR STYLES AND MOVE-MENTS; BRAQUE; CEZANNE; DELAUNAY, R.; EXPRESSIONISM; LEGER; MONDRIAN; PICASSO; ROUSSEAU.

CURIE, MARIE (née MARIA SKLODOWSKA) (1867–1934), physicist. Maria Sklodowska was born and received her early education in Poland. She traveled to Paris, receiving her *licence* in physics in 1893, placing first with high honors, and her *licence* in mathematics in 1894. She took the women's *agrégation* in physics in 1896, placing first. Marie met Pierre Curie in 1894 and began working in the laboratory he directed at the Ecole municipale de physique et chemie. They were married in 1895. Wilhelm Röntgen of Munich had just discovered x-rays (1896), and Henri Becquerel of the Muséum d'histoire naturelle in Paris discovered that uranium compounds emitted these x-rays. Marie was fascinated by these discoveries and began a search for compounds of other substances that emitted these rays. She designed an electroscope apparatus to detect the presence of x-rays, using an electrometer and a piezoelectric quartz crystal to measure small currents, discovered by Pierre and Jacques Curie in 1881. She identified thorium as radioactive, a term she coined, and she realized that two kinds of uranium ore were more radioactive than uranium itself.

In 1898 Pierre set aside his own researches to help Marie with the chemical treatment of uranium ores. After hard work in poor conditions, they succeeded in identifying two new radioactive elements, polonium and radium. Marie set about attempting to isolate sufficient quantities of these new substances for study. By 1902 she had succeeded in isolating a tiny quantity of pure radium and in measuring its atomic weight as 225. Marie and Pierre shared the Nobel Prize for Physics with Becquerel in 1903.

Marie Curie continued her research on the atomic processes responsible for radioactivity. She was especially interested in Ernest Rutherford and Frederick Soddy's work on natural transmutation of thorium. She continued to study the processes of atomic disintegration and the natural transmutation of the radioactive elements. In 1911 she was awarded the Nobel Prize for Physics for the second time. She was also interested in the use of radium in medicine. She saw to the use of portable x-ray equipment during World War I, becoming head of the Radiological Service of the Union des femmes française. Marie and her daughter Irène (Joliot-Curie) began work at the newly founded Radium Institute in Paris in 1918. She continued her emphasis on the use of radioactive elements in medicine for the rest of her life, seeing the beginnings of the Curie Foundation in 1920 and the Radium Institute in Warsaw in 1932.

I. Joliot-Curie, *Oeuvres de Marie Sklodowska-Curie* (Warsaw, 1954); E. Curie, *Madame Curie* (Paris, 1939); A. R. Weill, "Curie, Marie," *Dictionary of Scientific Biography*, vol. 3 (New York, 1971).

H. J. Steffens

Related entries: BECQUEREL; CURIE, P.

CURIE, PIERRE (1859–1906), physicist. Pierre Curie was educated at home and developed an early interest in mathematics and experiments. He received his *licence* in physical science from the Faculty of Sciences in Paris in 1877. Pierre was appointed laboratory assistant at the physics laboratory of the Sorbonne from 1878 to 1882. He and his brother Jacques collaborated on the study of crystals, especially pyroelectricity, the production of electricity by certain crystals when heated. Together they discovered piezoelectricity, the property relating electricity and mechanical stress in crystals. The brothers designed and built experimental instruments based on piezoelectricity, especially the piezoelectric quartz balance used by Pierre and Marie Curie in their work on radioactivity.

In 1883 Pierre became director of laboratories at the newly founded Ecole municipale de physique et chemie. He remained there for twenty-two years, continuing work on crystallography and studying magnetism. His theoretical consideration of crystal structure led him to formulate general symmetry principles, known as Curie's symmetry laws, which applied to crystals, as well as to electric and magnetic fields. His investigation of the variation of magnetic properties with temperature resulted in his doctoral thesis in 1895. His experiments with strong magnetism (ferromagnetism), weak magnetism (paramagnetism), and weak magnetism with opposite polarity (diamagnetism) produced important discoveries. Curie's law states that paramagnetism varies inversely with absolute temperature. The Curie point of a magnetic substance is the absolute temperature where ferromagnetic properties change to paramagnetic ones. Curie's investigations, and the work by his student Paul Langevin, are central to a modern understanding of magnetism.

In 1895 Pierre married Maria Sklodowska, a student at the Ecole municipale. They collaborated on the study of radioactivity, in a laboratory at the Ecole, until 1905. Together they discovered polonium and radium. Their studies of uranium and radioactive substances established the discipline. They shared the Nobel Prize in Physics with Henri Becquerel in 1903. Pierre was killed by a truck in Paris in 1906.

P. Curie, *Oeuvres de Pierre Curie* (Paris, 1908); P. Langevin, "Notice sur les travaux de Monsieur P. Curie," *Revue du Mois*, 10 July 1906; J. Wyart, "Curie, Pierre," *Dictionary of Scientific Biography*, vol. 3 (New York, 1971).

H. J. Steffens

Related entries: BECQUEREL; CURIE, M.

CZECHOSLOVAKIA, ALLIANCE WITH (1924–1938), a major component of France's effort to maintain the post–World War I treaty structure. Although France was a victor in the First World War, the struggle had engendered concern for future security. Many in France felt that the Paris treaties did not provide adequate guarantees. Conventional wisdom has suggested that the failure of an Anglo-American treaty of guarantee against Germany led the French to seek security through a series of alliances with the newly created states in Eastern Europe. France's alliance with Czechoslovakia, which shared a common border with Germany and contained a substantial Sudeten German minority, is frequently cited as a case in point.

In fact, however, the Franco-Czech alliance, linking France to the Little Entente, was signed on 25 January 1924; military clauses obligating mutual support in case of aggression were added in 1925—after the period of extremely tense Franco-German relations in the Ruhr had run its course. In addition, close treaty relationships between France and the succession states enormously complicated France's relations with fascist Italy and Great Britain. The former resented French activities in the Danube area, regarded in Rome as an Italian sphere of influence, while the latter viewed commitments in Central and Eastern Europe with grave reservations. It seems clear, therefore, that Paris valued the connection to Prague and to the other Eastern capitals not because the alliance system represented a formidable military barrier to future German expansion but because the structure underscored the principle of opposition to any territorial revision. By supporting Czechoslovakia and its Little Entente partners in their drive to preserve the treaties of St. Germain and Trianon, France could act against the sort of revisionism that might lead Germany to call its own obligations into question.

Edward Beneš, president of Czechoslovakia, felt his country had little to fear from Germany. No part of it had ever been included in the Reich. Nevertheless, the Locarno Treaties of 1925, whereby Germany agreed to accept its western border as final but offered no such guarantees for its frontiers with Poland and Czechoslovakia, were viewed with serious misgivings by Beneš and other East European leaders. With the Franco-German frontier buttressed by an Anglo-Italian guarantee, how willing would France now be to stand by its military obligations should Germany commit an act of aggression against Czechoslovakia? The Czechs received their answer at Munich in 1938. Hitler's demands for the incorporation of the Sudetenland into the Third Reich raised the question of France's military pledge to Czechoslovakia. England's failure to support any such commitment in Eastern Europe led Premier Edouard Daladier to the Munich Conference where this strategically important part of Czechoslovakia was negotiated away without Czech participation. The failure of the Franco-Czech alliance (as well as those with the other succession states) weakened the Third Republic's strategic position in Europe in the months prior to World War II.

P. Wandycz, *France and Her Eastern Allies, 1919–1925* (Minneapolis, 1962); A. Werth, *France and Munich: Before and after the Surrender* (New York, 1939).

W. I. Shorrock

Related entries: FOREIGN POLICY; LITTLE ENTENTE; MUNICH CONFERENCE: FRENCH ROLE IN.

D

DADAISM (1916–1922), a nihilistic movement, predominantly in literature and art, whose repudiation of traditional forms and values prepared the ground for the modern revolution in sensibility and expression. Founded in Zurich, Switzerland, by a group of expatriates from various European countries as a protest against the First World War, the movement adopted as its label the word *dada*, whose dictionary definition was hobby horse but whose meaning the dadaists intended to be "nothing at all." Led by the Rumanian-born Tristan Tzara, the young nihilists tried to shock the citizens of Zurich through a series of stage performances that featured such eccentric numbers as brutist demonstrations (a cacophony of inarticulate sounds and mechanical noises) or simultaneous poetry (a concurrent reading by several voices of various texts in different languages). In 1917 Tzara issued a review, *Dada*, which brought the movement to the attention of the Parisian avant-garde. Three years later, he traveled to Paris where he found an enthusiastic following among the young poets Louis Aragon, André Breton, Philippe Soupault, and Paul Eluard who, also spurred by cultural revolt, had put together a nonconformist periodical ironically entitled *Littérature*. From then until its demise in 1922, dada made Paris its home and *Littérature* its main publication.

After a while, dada manifestations lost the capacity to arouse the public. This meant that the dadaists had either to change their tactics or to dissolve the movement. The dilemma produced a rift within their ranks, with Breton and the *Littérature* group opting for a more serious attitude toward cultural matters and Tzara determined to continue the playful nihilism of the Zurich period. The break became definitive in 1922 when Breton proposed a Congress of Paris to discuss "new directives for the modern mind." Since this positive program seemed incompatible with the whimsical spirit of dada, Tzara declined to attend. The majority followed Breton who in 1924 established a new movement under the banner of surrealism.

Although short-lived, dada functioned as a powerful catalyst in Western

European thought. It crystallized the crisis of moral and aesthetic values brought on by World War I and made room for new ideas and forms. It borrowed futurist and cubist techniques, which it used for iconoclastic purposes, and introduced the concept of the ready-made, that is, the notion that an ordinary object can become art if an artist decides to select it and to give it a title (for example, Marcel Duchamp's urinal exhibited as *Fountain* in 1917). In literature it adopted a form of collage that relied heavily on the workings of chance. Thus Tzara advised those who wished to compose poetry to cut words out of a newspaper, shake them in a hat, pick them out at random, and copy them in that order. All these techniques inspired the surrealists and other avant-garde writers and artists to develop new modes of expression.

Dada's radical assertion of artistic freedom and rejection of prevailing standards, while clearing the ground for new forms and values, served to express the frustration of a generation that had come of age in time of war and had experienced the bankruptcy of all the exalted principles their elders had taught them to respect.

M. L. Grossman, *Dada* (New York, 1971); G. Hugnet, *L'Aventure Dada* (Paris, 1957); M. Sanouillet, *Dada à Paris* (Paris, 1965); T. Tzara, *Oeuvres complètes* (Paris, 1975–79).

M. D. Maayan

Related entries: ARAGON; BRETON; CUBISM; SURREALISM.

DALADIER, EDOUARD (1884–1970), predominant republican political figure in the 1930s and prime minister who led France into war in 1939. He was born 18 June 1884 at Carpentras (Vaucluse). He became a history teacher and then entered politics as a Radical; in 1919 he was elected to the Chamber of Deputies. By the 1930s he had become one of the predominant political leaders of France, participating in the most consequential decisions of the time. Ultimately he was to bear a great share of the responsibility for the demise of the Third Republic. Daladier was popularly considered to be a strong man, an image reinforced by his powerful appearance, which led him to be nicknamed the "bull of Vaucluse."

A protégé of Edouard Herriot, Daladier served in his cabinet in 1924 as minister of colonies. Afterward he held portfolios in successive governments and in January 1933 became premier, holding this position until October. Daladier's career reflected the growing instability of the 1930s as political life in France polarized, aggravated by economic problems and heightened by increasing partisanship on the one hand for the Soviet Union and on the other for the fascist countries, Italy and Germany.

At the end of January 1934, Daladier resumed the premiership in the wake of the Stavisky scandal. The Action française and other right-wing groups seized on the Stavisky case as a pretext to revile the republican regime. Daladier, in his attempt to defuse the growing violence in the streets, dismissed the right-wing police commissioner of Paris, Jean Chiappe. This act led to an uprising whose violence had not been experienced in Paris since the Commune episode in 1871. On 6 February 1934, right-wing groups attempted to seize the Chamber of Deputies. This aborted coup was serious enough to cause Daladier to resign his premiership the next day. This threat to the Republic became a pivotal event, causing the left-wing parties to form the Popular Front. Daladier became an advocate of this coalition of the Radical, Socialist, and Communist parties.

Daladier returned to the premiership in April 1938, but thereafter international affairs became his paramount concern. Despite France's treaty obligations, Daladier, along with Neville Chamberlain, acquiesced to Adolf Hitler's demands for the Sudetenland from Czechoslovakia at the Munich Conference in September 1938. This policy of appeasement failed, for on 1 September 1939 Hitler attacked Poland. After the British declaration of war, Daladier also led France into the war against Germany. During the period of the phony war, France did little to engage the Germans. When the Soviet Union defeated Finland in March 1940, however, Daladier was criticized for not aiding Finland, and he was replaced by Paul Reynaud as premier. He remained in the cabinet as minister of war until June 1940, when France was defeated. With the establishment of the Vichy regime, he was arrested. Along with other leading republican figures, he was accused of having caused the defeat and was brought to trial at Riom. He defended himself well and so embarrassed his Vichy prosecutors that they suspended the political trials. In 1943 he was deported to Germany and remained there until he was liberated in 1945. After the war, he was reelected a deputy and served from 1946 until he retired in 1958. He died in Paris on 10 October 1970.

A. Adamthwaite, *France and the Coming of the Second World War* (London, 1977); R. Rémond and J. Bourdin, *Edouard Daladier, chef de gouvernement* (Paris, 1977); A. Werth, *France and Munich* (New York, 1969).

J. Szaluta

Related entries: CZECHOSLOVAKIA, ALLIANCE WITH; GAMELIN; GERMANY, RELATIONS WITH (1914–1940); MUNICH CONFERENCE: FRENCH ROLE IN ; REYNAUD; STAVISKY AFFAIR.

DALOU, JULES (1838–1902), decorative artist, communard, and sculptor contributing to a cult of the Republic and a cult of workers. Born in Paris of a glovemaker father, Dalou was discovered by Jean-Baptiste Carpeaux, studied at the Ecole des beaux-arts, and in the 1860s did decorative sculpture for sumptuous residences and competed for state prizes and medals. His early career in the Second Empire showed little hint of the democratic tradition of Parisian artisans from which he came.

In spring 1871 he joined the Paris Commune, in which the participating artists denounced "all government tutelage and all privileges." In the new order artists governed the arts; Dalou took the post of an assistant administrator of the Louvre. For that role he was sentenced in 1874 to forced labor for life, but he had escaped into exile in London in July 1871 and stayed there until he was amnestied in May 1879. He returned to Paris in April 1880.

Now began a career as dedicated artist for the Republic. In 1879 he had submitted to a jury for the Paris municipal council his sketch for a statue of the

Republic for the place de la République. Although his proposal did not meet the contest requirements and was not chosen, the councillors liked Dalou's idea so much that they commissioned it for the place du Trône, renamed the place de la Nation. The monumental *Triumph of the Republic* was his greatest contribution to the Third Republic. The largest bronze group in Paris, it took him twenty years to complete. It consisted of several allegorical figures: two lions guided by Liberty or Progress pull a cart carrying a standing female representation of the Republic. Accompanying the triumphant Republic are figures representing Work, Justice, and Peace.

The republican leaders wanted an imposing symbol of the Republic in the workers' east end of the capital, and they wanted it to be dedicated during the centennial of the Revolution in 1889. But Dalou was not finished and did not want to show partial work. In view of the Boulanger threat, however, he agreed to allow the plaster model with a bronze-colored coating to be dedicated in a ceremony on 20 September 1889. At that time President Sadi Carnot decorated the sculptor with the officer's cross of the Legion of Honor.

After several cost overruns and long delay, the completed monument was dedicated on 19 November 1899. President Emile Loubet gave Dalou the commander's cross of the Legion of Honor. Modest and retiring, the sculptor expressed embarrassment and put the decoration in his pocket. Republican leaders and workers turned the dedication into a festive counterdemonstration, protesting the reactionaries recently menacing the Republic. For five hours, an estimated 300,000 to 500,000 people, mostly unionists, marched past the monument.

While working on the *Triumph*, Dalou had turned out numerous sculptures celebrating revolutionary leaders and ideals and Third Republican figures; among them were bas-reliefs of Fraternity (1883) and of the comte de Mirabeau responding to the marquis de Dreux-Brézé (1884); statues of Pierre Vergniaud (c. 1892) and General Lazare Hoche (1902); statues of Auguste Scheurer-Kestner and Léon Gambetta (both unfinished); tombs of Auguste Blanqui (1885), Victor Noir (1890), and Charles Floquet (1899); and a bust of Victor Hugo now in the Comédie française.

Dalou disparaged allegory as outmoded bastard art, but he needed the income that came from satisfying the classic tastes of official committees ordering statues, and—he admitted—he was steeped in the Louis XIV style, despite his fervent republicanism. In the last decade of his career he moved toward modern, more realistic portrayals intended to promote a cult of workers and peasants to replace the old mythologies. He completed a model of a monument to workers in 1891, left a series of statuettes of workers (now in the Petit Palais), and completed a large bronze statue of a peasant (1899) now in the Louvre. He was not able to finish this important part of his *oeuvre* because of failing health and family cares.

H. Caillaux, *Aimé-Jules Dalou* (Paris, 1935); M. Dreyfous, *Dalou, sa vie et son oeuvre* (Paris, 1903); J. M. Hunisak, *The Sculptor Jules Dalou* (New York, 1977); *Le Triomphe de la République: Fête d'inauguration de ce monument place de la Nation*, compte rendu officiel (Paris, 1900).

C. W. Rearick

Related entries: COMMUNARDS; FESTIVALS: POLITICAL.

DARLAN, FRANCOIS (1881–1942), admiral; preeminent naval officer in the interwar years, commander in chief of the French Navy in 1939, and a leading opponent of the Third Republic in 1940. He was born 7 August 1881 in Nérac (Lot-et-Garonne). His father was a judge and served as a minister of justice in the Jules Méline cabinet from 1896 to 1898. Although he came from a republican family, Darlan decided to pursue a career in the navy, a service in France known for its royalist traditions. He graduated from the French Naval Academy in 1902.

During the interwar years, Darlan came to distinguish himself for his outstanding contribution in naval affairs, emerging as the preeminent officer of the French Navy. For nearly the entire period from 1926 to 1939, he served as head of the military cabinet of the minister of marine. In 1930 he acquired diplomatic experience by serving as a member of the French delegation to the London Naval Conference. In 1936 he became navy chief of staff, selected for this post by the Popular Front government. Darlan was a leading advocate of the modernization and growth of the navy, and under his direction it developed into one of the best in the world. In the 1930s, Darlan was noted to be politically right wing and an opportunist. These characteristics were intensified during the Vichy period as Darlan acted on these principles.

With the start of World War II in 1939, Darlan was promoted to commander in chief of the French Navy, with the rank of admiral of the fleet. Being able to escape German attacks, the navy was the only French service not to be defeated, and it emerged as the nation's strongest force. This course of events heightened Darlan's power and prestige, as the navy became the trump card of the newly established Vichy regime. When Philippe Pétain took power in 1940, Darlan immediately pledged his support to him.

Despite the destruction of the French fleet at Mers-el-Kebir by the British in 1940, Darlan became a dominant figure in the Vichy government, enjoying a unique and favored relationship with Pétain, and he was designated to be his eventual successor. In this preeminent capacity, he was the spokesman for Vichy at two important interviews with Adolf Hitler. He went as far as advocating military collaboration with Nazi Germany, which increased his notoriety. Coincidentally in Algiers when the allies invaded North Africa in November 1942, he repudiated Pétain's order to French Vichy troops to resist the Anglo-American invasion forces. Instead, Darlan negotiated a cease-fire with General Dwight Eisenhower, then committed the Vichy forces against the Axis, and finally took the side of the Allies. Nevertheless, these dealings with Darlan on the part of the Allies aroused protests. On 24 December 1942, Darlan was assassinated by a young anti-Vichy student, Bonnier de la Chapelle.

A. Darlan, *L'Amiral Darlan parle* (Paris, 1952); H. Michel, *Pétain, Laval, Darlan, trois politiques?* (Paris, 1972); R. O. Paxton, *Vichy France* (New York, 1972).

J. Szaluta

Related entries: LAVAL; NAVY; PETAIN.

DAUDET, ALPHONSE (1840–1897), popular but controversial novelist. Daudet was a fortunate writer in that his works made him wealthy. He was unfortunate twice over: each of his books made enemies, and the literary and political career of his son, Léon, tarnished the family name and served to diminish the father's reputation. The themes in Daudet's novels and stories were those of his own life and hint at unresolved dualities. He was a Provençal who lived his adult life in Paris and married a Parisian woman. One finds in his works a preoccupation with the differences and tensions between north and south and between urban and rural mores. He received a Catholic primary education but left the church in his youth. His books often revealed a Christian mentality or outlook but little sympathy for organized religion. He was nurtured and protected in the formative years of his literary career by the duc de Morny yet emerged from that period unallied to any political party or form and with a hostility to politics in general. During his later years in particular, he became the champion of strong family life and the enemy of divorce yet could not break his habit of sexual affairs that threatened the harmony of his own marriage until painful disease made such encounters impossible. Finally, although that pain made life nearly unendurable for most of his later years, he began to speak of himself as a merchant of happiness and meant to be—through his novels—the consoler of humanity. He believed that no one, no matter how destitute or base or sick, is beyond discovering joy and happiness in life.

His major works fall into three distinct periods. Between 1866 and 1869, he produced three autobiographical or subjective novels, the Parisian commenting on his native Provence: *Les Lettres de mon moulin, Le Petit Chose*, and *Tartarin de Tarascon*. Having exhausted that vein, Daudet turned to the alleged objectivity of realism for his subject matter. The novels of that period, 1874 through 1881, included *Jack, Le Nabab*, and *Numa Roumestan*. In the final period, beginning with *L'Evangéliste* in 1882, his books again became subjective: moralistic and polemical. But they were never political, and he took no open part during the Dreyfus affair despite Léon's anti-Dreyfus stance. In fact, Daudet's disapproval of Léon's private and public life in that period contributed to the tone and the subject matter in several of Daudet's later works—*L'Immortel*, for example.

Daudet contracted syphilis about 1861. Evidence of its tertiary stage appeared in 1878 and took the form of locomotor ataxia (tabes dorsalis), a crippling and extremely painful affliction. For some years he made notes on his reaction to pain and progressive paralysis under the heading *La Doulou*, extracts of which were published in 1931, a remarkable medical and moral document. Edmond de Goncourt was a confidant of Daudet for many years, and the notorious efforts of the Daudet family to suppress the publication of the unabridged Goncourt

Journal were simply an attempt to conceal suspected anecdotes about Daudet's illicit affairs. Literary historians now consider Daudet to have been a writer of the second rank, but his works to be important as a reliable mirror of life between 1860 and 1890.

A. Daudet, *Quarante ans de Paris, 1857–1897* (Geneva, 1945); M. Sachs, *The Career of Alphonse Daudet: A Critical Study* (Cambridge, 1965); R. L. Williams, *The Horror of Life* (Chicago, 1980).

R. L. Williams

Related entry: DAUDET, L.

DAUDET, LEON (1867–1942), nationalist anti-Semite and one of the leading figures in the Action française. Son of the noted writer, Alphonse Daudet, Léon began his career as a political journalist under the tutelage of Edouard Drumont. The latter's virulent and sentimental anti-Semitism, as well as his nationalism and indiscriminate conspiratorialism, became the center of Daudet's political vision; to these he added his own talents as satirist and polemicist. Alienated from his father's republicanism, he wandered in and out of the various nationalist leagues during the Dreyfus affair, until, shortly after the turn of the century, he was seduced by the royalism of Charles Maurras and found a home in the Action française. In 1908, using a substantial amount of his own capital, Daudet, together with Maurras, launched the neoroyalists' most successful project: the daily *Action française*. Daudet's regular columns in the *Action française* proved a perfect complement to those of Maurras. To the latter's dense, meticulously rigorous and sober prose, Daudet offered comic relief in what amounted to a political gossip column. He also brought to the royalist movement the ability to speak effectively to a large audience.

Daudet's career at the Action française had several phases. Until about 1912, he threw himself into the neoroyalist effort to win workers over to the social monarchy. Accompanied by a contingent of Camelots du roi, Daudet would sweep into working-class *quartiers* and stage well-publicized debates in which the bait of anti-Semitism was held out to workers. Although his success was limited among workers, the persistence of his efforts along these lines did much to separate the Action française from the stuffy traditionalism of the older generation of royalists.

Daudet's notoriety was at its height just before and during the First World War when his columns were filled with exposés of treason at the highest levels of French business and government. Although his proofs were flimsy, nonexistent, or even forged, his influence was such that, given the state of popular opinion overheated by wartime passions, he could force public officials, including cabinet ministers, out of political life. This influence reached its peak in 1919 when Daudet was elected to the Chamber of Deputies. Although isolated by his royalism, he became a force on the parliamentary Right because of his talent at violent invective and a feared figure among government ministers because of his easy recourse to character assassination.

By the 1930s his influence, along with that of the Action française, began to wane. His aging, portly figure, as well as his reputation as a gourmet and a bon vivant, made him seem an anachronism next to the fascists who placed a premium on youth and heroism.

L. Daudet, *Souvenirs des milieux littéraires, politiques, artistiques, et médicaux*, 2 vols. (Paris, 1920); E. R. Tannenbaum, *The Action Française* (New York, 1962); E. Weber, *Action Française* (Stanford, Calif., 1962).

P. Mazgaj

Related entries: ACTION FRANCAISE; ANTI-SEMITISM; CAMELOTS DU ROI; DAUDET, A.; DRUMONT; MAURRAS.

DAUTRY, RAOUL (1880–1951), one of the leading French administrators of the first half of the twentieth century. A graduate of the Ecole polytechnique, he worked for the railway company of the Nord for twenty-five years where, by virtue of his technological expertise and his advocacy of a progressive labor policy, he helped effect the merger of the six principal railroad lines in 1937 into the Société nationale des chemins de fer (SNCF). During the 1930s, he also reorganized both the French shipping company, the Compagnie générale transatlantique, and the French airline, the Compagnie aéropostale. He was in addition president of the Comité de coordination du rail et de la route, charged with coordinating the French transportation system. Dautry served as technical adviser to the Gaston Doumergue and Pierre Laval governments in 1934–35, helping to draw up the famous decree laws of those years and implementing the public works program to alleviate unemployment.

After retiring as head of the state network in 1937, Dautry went into private industry, until he was recalled to government service in September 1939 to head the newly created Ministry of Armaments in Edouard Daladier's wartime government. Vehemently opposed to the armistice in June 1940, he retired from public office under the Vichy regime. In November 1944 General Charles de Gaulle named him minister of reconstruction, responsible for raising France from wartime ruin. From 1946 until his death in 1951, Dautry served as administrator-general of the French Atomic Energy Commission.

Alongside his professional activities, Dautry had what amounted to a second career as a writer, public speaker, and member and founder of many private philanthropic and service organizations. In 1937 he published *Métier d'homme*, a collection of his speeches and articles, and in 1948 he was elected to the Académie des sciences morales et politiques.

Dautry had earned his appointment to the two most important administrative posts of his time as minister of armaments and then as minister of reconstruction by his work in reorganizing the State Railway network from 1928 to 1937. In less than ten years he transformed the rambling and ramshackle deficit-prone State Railway into the most technically modern and socially progressive network in France, laying the foundations of the SNCF's later reputation for technical proficiency and advanced social welfare policies.

J. M. Sherwood, "Rationalization and Railway Workers in France: Raoul Dautry and les chemins de fer de l'Etat, 1928–1937," *Journal of Contemporary History* 15 (1980).

J. M. Sherwood

Related entries: BUSINESSMEN; RAILROADS.

DEAT, MARCEL (1894–1955), a leading Socialist deputy and theoretician who, after his expulsion from the party, drifted toward wartime fascism and collaboration. He was born into a lower-middle-class family in Guérigny (La Nievre)and studied in provincial lycées before going to Paris in 1911 to prepare for the Ecole normale supérieure. In 1914 Déat, a brilliant student, joined the Socialist party (SFIO) and entered the Ecole, but he was mobilized immediately. Finding combat exciting and impressed by the camaraderie of the trenches, Déat was cited repeatedly for bravery, promoted to captain and named chevalier of the Legion of Honor. After the war, the veteran breezed through the Ecole normale earning his *licence* and *agrégations* in philosophy and sociology. After a short stint with Célestin Bouglé's Center for Social Documentation, Déat taught, from 1922 to 1925, at a lycée in Reims and married. Abandoning an academic career, however, and after an unsuccessful bid in 1924, he was elected deputy from Reims in a 1926 by-election. Déat's election was dependent on Radical support accepted in defiance of the SFIO, and in 1928 he was defeated at Epernay and then appointed administrative secretary of the SFIO parliamentary group.

By 1930 Déat, who favored participation in Radical governments, had established a position as the leading theoretician of the right wing of the SFIO. Blending Durkheim and Marx, he sought an anticapitalist coalition, including peasants and the middle classes, around a program that would socialize power first, then profit, and finally property, all to be carried out in a national framework.

In 1932 Déat was elected from Paris, but in parliament he and a group of deputies ran afoul of the SFIO executive over support for, and participation in, the Daladier government. At the national congress of July 1933, Déat was defeated after defending his neosocialism and in November was expelled with a group of followers for repeated indiscipline. With most of the SFIO's right wing (thirty-two deputies and seven senators), Déat founded the Parti socialiste de France-Union Jean Jaurès (PSDF). This new party included democratic reformist socialists like Pierre Renaudel as well as more authoritarian neos like Adrien Marquet, besides featuring a paramilitary defense group with fascist overtones. In the 1930s, Déat expanded his ideas into advocacy of Henri De Man's *Planisme*, corporatism, a social (or just) price and the abandonment of the socialization of the means of production.

In 1935 the PSDF joined with two other reformist socialist parties to create the Union socialiste et républicaine (USR), which participated in every government from 1936 to 1940. As air minister in 1936, Déat was among those who opposed unilateral resistance to Adolf Hitler's rearmament of the Rhineland.

Despite his desire for a Left-Center coalition, Déat and his party joined the

Popular Front, but he was defeated, after refusing to desist in favor of a Communist candidate, in Paris in 1936. Remaining general secretary of the USR, Déat returned to lycée teaching until April 1939 when he was elected, with right-wing support, in a by-election in Angoulême.

From the mid-1930s Déat was a leading anti-militarist who opposed sanctions against Italy and resistance to German expansion. His famous 1939 article "Die for Danzig?" was followed by active pacifism during the war. After the defeat Déat, who never called himself a fascist, urged a totalitarian government, a single party, and a policy of collaboration. Kept out of Vichy until all was lost, he was used by the Germans to pressure Philippe Pétain. After the liberation, Déat escaped to an Italian monastery, where he died in 1955. His doctrinal and political quarrels with the SFIO had led him to a quasi-fascism and collaboration.

E. H. Goodman, "The Socialism of Marcel Déat" (Ph.D. diss., Stanford University, 1973); S. Grossman, "L'Evolution de Marcel Déat," *Revue d'histoire de la deuxième guerre mondiale* 97 (1975); G. Lefranc, *Le Mouvement socialiste sous la IIIè République (1875–1940)* (Paris, 1963).

A. Douglas

Related entries: DALADIER; DURKHEIM; FASCISM; POPULAR FRONT; RADICAL AND RADICAL-SOCIALIST PARTY; SOCIALIST PARTY.

DEBUSSY, CLAUDE (1862–1918), most influential composer of the Third Republic. Debussy was born to humble parents at Saint-Germain-en-Laye (Seine-et-Oise) on 22 August 1862. His education outside of music was extremely limited. An early piano teacher, Antoinette Mauté de Fleurville, the mother-in-law of Paul Verlaine, recognized his talents and directed him to the Paris Conservatory, where he studied from 1872 to 1884. As a result of winning the first Prix de Rome for his cantata, *L'Enfant prodigue* (1884), he spent the next three years studying and composing in the Italian capital. There he was influenced by the music of Palestrina and the church modes. Earlier he had traveled throughout the Continent under the auspices of Nadezhda von Meck, Tschaikovsky's patron, and in Russia developed an interest in the whole-tone scale. At Bayreuth his confrontation with the music of Robert Wagner led ultimately to rejection of the great German romanticist's approach to orchestral music and contributed, in reaction, to his rediscovery of preromantic French musical traditions. From hearing Annamite and Javanese music at the World Exhibition in Paris in 1889, Debussy developed an interest in the pentatonic scale and the gamelan, a Javanese version of the xylophone. He came to know well the works of both the symbolist poets and the impressionist painters, which were to inspire his most important works for orchestra and for piano. He also composed songs on the texts of Stéphane Mallarmé, Charles Baudelaire, and Pierre Louÿs in the form of a supple recitative that is alive to the inflections of the French language. His contacts with the symbolists and impressionists contributed much to shaping his approach to form, harmony, and coloring.

Debussy's interest in Spanish music, particularly the distinctive elements derived from the Moors, and a milder one in the twelve-tone scale after the turn of the century, would round out the diverse influences that helped to shape his art. Although the performance of such orchestral works as *Prélude à l'après-midi d'un faune* (1894) and *La Mer* (1905) and of music for Maurice Maeterlinck's lyric drama, *Pelléas et Mélisande* (1902), brought Debussy fame amid controversy, he had to supplement his income as a composer by teaching piano privately, serving as a music critic, and giving concert tours as pianist and conductor. His liaison from 1903 and eventual second marriage to Mme. Emma Bardac, the mother of his only child and daughter, provided a stability in his personal life that he had not hitherto enjoyed. The rectal cancer that plagued the last decade of Debussy's life and ultimately killed him did not diminish his creative powers. He died on 25 March 1918 during a German bombardment of Paris.

Debussy's importance and his standing as the Third Republic composer of greatest influence on subsequent European and U.S. composers derive primarily from two related achievements. Through compositions for orchestra, piano, and voice, which were unusually independent of traditional norms in form, harmony, and coloring, he sought to evoke an atmosphere in the manner of the symbolists and impressionists. He therein succeeded in creating works that reached new levels of psychological penetration through understatement. By his use of the pentatonic scale and Gregorian modes and by his development of the whole tone scale, he enlarged the boundaries of European music to embrace medieval and Oriental traditions. At the same time the distinctions between dissonance and consonance that he challenged became the basis for many new harmonic developments, including the ones that resulted in atonalism. Both his search for freedom from tonality, which involved the liberation of harmony from traditional boundaries of keys and relationships of keys, and his pursuit of new rhythmic fluidity would influence practically every composer of distinction since his day. Thus, while expressing the quintessence of the sensibility of the pre–World War I generation, Debussy both revived preromantic French music and laid the foundations for the stylistic eclecticism of subsequent generations.

E. Lockspeiser, *Debussy: His Life and Mind*, 2 vols. (London, 1962); J. Barraqui, *Debussy* (Paris, 1972); S. Jarocinski, *Debussy: Impressionism & Symbolism* (London, 1976); A. B. Wenk, *Claude Debussy & the Poets* (Berkeley, 1976).

D. E. Gardinier and J. Z. Sevilla-Gardinier

Related entries: MALLARME; MUSIC; SATIE.

DECAZES, LOUIS-CHARLES, DUC (1819–1886), Duc de Glücksberg, diplomat, Orleanist politician, foreign minister, and industrialist. Decazes was born to a prominent Girondin family ennobled by Henry IV. His father, Elie Decazes, was an intimate associate and minister of Louis XVIII, who raised the family to a dukedom. Decazes joined the diplomatic corps in 1841 and served the July Monarchy at London, Madrid, and Lisbon. He entered the *conseil général* of the Gironde in 1846 but retired from public life in opposition to Napoleon III and devoted himself to the family business at Decazeville, which he inherited in 1860. After unsuccessful liberal candidacies for the Corps législatif in 1863 and 1869, Decazes participated in the revolution of 4 September 1870 as an officer of the National Guard.

Elected to the National Assembly in 1871, the Duc Decazes became a leader of the Orleanist Right-Center at Versailles. His greatest fame came after entering the second Albert de Broglie government of 1873 as foreign minister. Decazes remained at the Quai d'Orsay through seven consecutive cabinets (1873–77). He secured the diplomatic support of Britain and Russia to block the possibility of a German preventive war in the war scare of 1875, and he kept France out of major involvement in the eastern crisis of 1875–78. After being defeated for the Senate in 1878, Decazes retired from politics.

G. Hanotaux, *Contemporary France* (New York, 1905); W. Langer, *European Alliances and Alignments* (New York, 1962); A. Robert et al., ed., *Dictionnaire des parlementaires français* (Paris, 1891).

S. C. Hause

Related entries: BROGLIE; GERMANY, RELATIONS WITH (1871–1914); NATIONAL ASSEMBLY; ORLEANISM.

DECORATIVE ARTS (1870–1925). France experienced a renewed emphasis on the decorative arts in the late nineteenth century that emerged from two sources: the desire to promote French supremacy in craftsmanship and a revived focus on the interior. The retreat from the naturalistic world, which attracted the impressionist painters after 1880, was paralleled by the creation of intimate interiors by designers as a refuge from a chaotic world. The Art Nouveau movement organized the efforts of the decorative artists to revitalize the traditional crafts and to promote a greater sense of artisanal pride. The movement was inspired by a fear that the national aesthetic sense had been blunted by the mechanized mass production of domestic objects. Believing that both skilled craftsmanship and artistic discrimination would be the victims of industrialization, the decorative artists attempted to reassert the artistic character of their creations.

Among the leaders in this movement was Emile Galle, a native of Nancy and an amateur botanist, who pioneeered new processes in the production of colored glass, encouraging its widespread application in secular buildings and in domestic uses. The Ecole de Nancy became a center for the production of artistic glass, jewelry, and book illustration. Another leader in the movement, though not primarily an artist himself, Samuel Bing organized early exhibits of the new style and in 1895 opened a shop in Paris, La Maison de l'Art Nouveau.

In the 1880s, the Union centrale des arts décoratifs was organized to sponsor exhibits and competitions in the decorative arts. A school was founded to train the new generations of craftsmen, the Ecole Boulle, named for the renowned eighteenth-century cabinetmaker. The Union centrale also took up the campaign to lend the decorative arts a status similar to that of architecture and the visual arts, but the close relationship between the Union centrale and furniture dealers led to further attempts to produce artistic furnishings that could be duplicated for the mass market after 1900.

The craft most involved in the controversy over the new modern style was furniture making. A traditional craft in the faubourg Saint-Antoine of Paris, cabinetmaking suffered a profound economic crisis in the nineteenth century. Furniture styles were largely determined by the need for good investments and by the taste for traditional styles. Thus, cabinetmakers tended to duplicate popular eighteenth-century models or to produce for the active market in fake ''antique'' furniture.

The transformation of the furniture-making crafts occurred not with Art Nouveau, around 1900, but with the widespread application of mechanization in the early 1920s and the marketing of furniture by department stores and through installment buying. By the World's Fair of 1925, the modern style had become synonymous with simple, geometric designs that could be easily mass-produced by mechanized processes.

S. Bing, *Artistic America, Tiffany Glass, and Art Nouveau* (Cambridge, Mass., 1970); Paul Garenc, *L'Industrie du meuble en France* (Paris, 1958).

T. M. McBride

Related entries: ART: MAJOR STYLES AND MOVEMENTS; ART DECO; ART NOUVEAU.

DEGAS, EDGAR (1834–1917), painter. The son of a well-to-do family, Degas lived in comfortable financial circumstances throughout his life. Unlike many of his contemporaries in the arts, he displayed little hostility toward society and its conventions, avoided personal escape into decadence, and remained indifferent to the allure of traveling to exotic places.

After 1870 Degas became one of France's best-known and most influential painters. Often associated with impressionism, his work did not truly belong to the movement. His canvases display only a marginal concern with brushstroke and the arranging of dots and dabs of color to create a subtle and flowing pictorial composition. Most striking in his work are various compositional innovations, highlighted by his ability to depict a figure in a captured moment of swift and crucial movement.

Degas studied Japanese prints and was influenced by their elements of formal design. He also interested himself in photography, and many of his paintings are easily recognized as being composed like snapshots. Increasingly he took liberties in cutting off figures at the frame and in compositional arrangements, which capture a lively sense of unposed spontaneity. He also experimented with close-up paintings. His most mature work was distinguished by the subtle use of pastel colors.

His favorite subjects were found at the racetrack, in the theater, and, especially, at the ballet. In many of his paintings the viewer witnesses renditions of the late nineteenth-century demimonde, characterized by the accentuated facial expressions of figures in which Degas has captured a rare combination of fatigue and tension.

Much of his mature work documents the pace and the contradictions of a significant sphere of Parisian life during the first three decades of the Third Republic.

J. Bouret, *Degas*, trans. D. Woodward (New York, 1966); J. C. Canaday, *Mainstreams of Modern Art* (New York, 1959); D. C. Rich, *Edgar Degas* (New York, 1951); Alfred Werner, *Degas Pastels* (New York, 1968).

P. Monaco

Related entry: IMPRESSIONISM.

DELAUNAY, ROBERT (1885–1941), pioneering abstract painter. His parents were divorced during his childhood, and he was raised by his mother, a countess. He left school at seventeen and studied theatrical decoration for two years (1902–4). He was influenced by impressionism, Paul Cézanne, and neoimpressionism in turn and was early involved in the development of cubism (1909). In 1910 he married the Russian-born painter Sonia Terk; henceforth the two became leaders in the development of abstraction. Robert was the theoretician of the two. He quickly traversed several phases between 1909 and 1914, evolving from the cubists' geometric analysis of forms in space, through a cubic look at the play of light in the Paris streets (*Eiffel Tower* paintings), to totally abstract works in which contrasts of pure color entirely displaced drawing and spatial construction. Vestiges of reality persisted in Delaunay's art, and his most characteristic subject matter after 1909 was modernity: the products of industry (Eiffel Tower, airplanes) and aspects of mass culture (sport).

In the 1920s, the Delaunays were the center of an avant-grade circle that included the dadaists and surrealists. Although much of Delaunay's work was totally abstract, especially after 1930, he also painted many portraits, as well as illustrating books and designing theater sets and publicity. Toward the end of his life, he completed several monumental projects, above all the decoration of the aviation and railway pavilions of the 1937 Paris Exposition universelle. He died of cancer in 1941.

A. A. Cohen, ed., *The New Art of Color: The Writings of Robert and Sonia Delaunay* (New York, 1978); R. Delaunay, *Du cubisme à l'art abstrait* (Paris, 1957); B. Dorival, *Robert Delaunay, 1885–1941* (Paris, 1975); G. Vriesen and M. Imdahl, *Robert Delaunay* (New York, 1967).

T. Shapiro

Related entries: ART: MAJOR STYLES AND MOVEMENTS; CEZANNE; DELAUNAY, S.

DELAUNAY, SONIA (1885–1979), Russian-born abstract painter and designer. Born Sophie Stern to Jewish parents in modest circumstances in a small Ukrainian town, she was adopted at age five by an uncle, Henri Terk, a wealthy lawyer of St. Petersburg, and raised in luxury. She studied art in Karlsruhe (1903–5) and Paris, where she settled in 1905 and was soon influenced by Vincent Van Gogh and Paul Gauguin to paint violently colored portraits. While married to the German art critic Wilhelm Uhde, she met Robert Delaunay and promptly divorced Uhde and married Delaunay (1910). The marriage was to prove a lifelong collaboration in cubism, orphism, abstract art, and modern design in which each spouse continually influenced the other. Robert devoted himself almost exclusively to painting, whereas Sonia supported the family with her revolutionary designs for bookbindings, textiles, furs, fashion, automobiles, and furnishings after her Russian income was cut off in 1917. Basic to their art was the cubist breakdown of the naturalistic depiction of space and an interest in the refraction of light and the interaction of colors. By 1912–13 they were creating abstract works in which simultaneous contrasts of colored disks replaced drawing and perspective.

Sonia Delaunay's virtuosity is demonstrated by a list of some noted works: a pathbreaking edition of Blaise Cendrars' *La Prose du Transsibérien et de la petite Jeanne de France* (1913) in which the poem and abstract touches of color intermingle; a "simultaneous boutique" in collaboration with the couturier Jacques Heim at the 1925 Exposition des arts décoratifs; a prize-winning neon sign (1936); huge murals dealing with aviation for the 1937 Paris Exposition universelle. She outlived her husband by almost forty years, during which her art—largely pure painting in the spirit of their partnership—remained at a uniformly high level.

A. A. Cohen, *The New Art of Color: The Writings of Robert and Sonia Delaunay* (New York, 1978), and *Sonia Delaunay* (New York, 1975); J. Damase, *Sonia Delaunay* (London, 1972); *Sonia Delaunay* (Buffalo, 1980).

T. Shapiro

Related entries: ART: MAJOR STYLES AND MOVEMENTS; DELAUNAY, R.; GAUGUIN; VAN GOGH.

DELAVIGNETTE, ROBERT (1897–1976), colonial administrator and publicist. Entering the colonial administration of West Africa after World War I, Delavignette served in Niger and Upper Volta. In the latter he was especially well regarded for his ability to carry on an effective and humane administration. He published *Paysans noirs* (1931), a fictional account of an administrator's year in a district, very much modeled after the experiences he had had in the district of Banfora, Upper Volta. The novel won a prize in 1931 for the best novel with a colonial theme, was made into a movie, and had considerable influence in inspiring idealistic young Frenchmen to choose a colonial career.

In 1936 the Popular Front government appointed Delavignette director of the Ecole coloniale, the training school for administrators. He added to the curriculum of the school an emphasis on African languages and better training in ethnology and a year of on-the-job training in the colonies. A frequent contributor to *Esprit*, Delavignette shared the idealism of the personalists around Emmanuel Mounier. He tried to transfer liberal, social Catholic ideals to the colonial sphere. Publishing in the *Journal des débats* and *Temps*, in addition to more specialized journals, Delavignette stressed that the colonies were not arenas for exploitation but rather regions to which the French people owed long-term moral, financial, and political obligations.

After World War II Delavignette served as high commissioner to the Cameroon, 1946–47, and director of political affairs of the Ministry of Overseas France, 1947–50. After his retirement he continued to play an important role as a publicist in African affairs.

W. B. Cohen, *Rulers of Empire* (Stanford, 1971), and ed., *Robert Delavignette on French Empire* (Chicago, 1977); R. Delavignette, *Freedom and Authority in French West Africa* (London, 1950). R. Girardet, *L'Idée coloniale en France, 1871–1962* (Paris, 1972).

W. B. Cohen

Related entries: OVERSEAS EMPIRE: COLONIAL ADMINISTRATION; SCHOOL, COLONIAL SERVICE: ECOLE COLONIALE.

DELBOS, YVON (1885–1956), Radical-Socialist politician, statesman, journalist. One of the lesser though still influential figures of the interwar years, Delbos was born of middle-class parentage in Thonac in the Périgord region of southwest France. He earned the *agrégation* (letters) at the Ecole normale supérieure in 1911, and pursued the well-worn path from the university to journalism to politics. Upon graduation he worked for and became editor in chief of *Le Radical*, where he became acquainted with many leaders of the Radical party. His journalistic career interrupted by World War I, he returned after the war to join *La Dépêche de Toulouse*, one of the leading Radical papers in France. Although defeated in 1919, he was elected to the Chamber of Deputies in the leftist landslide of 1924 and held his seat from Sarlat for thirty years. Identified with the moderate Left among the Radical deputies, his election to the presidency of the Radical parliamentary group in 1934 was a good measure of his stature within the party. Although accepting the post of minister of public instruction in the third Paul Painlevé government (1925), he rejected subsequent cabinet posts, although he served as vice-president of the Chamber of Deputies from 1932 to 1936. With the advent of the Popular Front government led by his friend Léon Blum in 1936, Delbos became foreign minister, holding the post longer than any other interwar leader except Aristide Briand (June 1936–February 1938).

Although he saw more clearly than many others the international dangers confronting France, the diplomatic effects of Germany's remilitarization of the Rhineland and Delbos' determination to keep in step with Britain prevented him from pursuing an independent foreign policy regarding such crises as the Spanish Civil War and the Austrian *Anschluss*. Brought back into the government as minister of education with the outbreak of World War II, he opposed the surrender to Germany in 1940. Subsequently arrested by the Vichy regime, he was deported to Germany in 1943. After the war he regained his seat in the Chamber of Deputies. The apogee of his postwar career came with his unsuccessful bid for the presidency of the Fourth Republic in 1953.

A. Adamthwaite, *France and the Coming of the Second World War* (London, 1977); L. Blum, *Chef de gouvernement, 1936–1937* (Paris, 1967); J. Dreifort, *Yvon Delbos at the Quai d'Orsay* (Lawrence, Kans., 1973); N. Greene, *Crisis and Decline* (Ithaca, N.Y., 1969); P. Larmour, *The French Radical Party in the 1930's* (Stanford, 1964); Ministère des affaires étrangères, *Documents diplomatiques français, 1932–1939*, vols. 2–9 (Paris, 1964–74).

J. E. Dreifort

Related entries: BLUM; CHAUTEMPS; DALADIER; GERMANY, RELA-
TIONS WITH (1914–1940); GREAT BRITAIN, RELATIONS WITH; PAIN-
LEVE; POPULAR FRONT; RADICAL AND RADICAL-SOCIALIST PARTY.

DELCASSE, THEOPHILE (1852–1923), journalist, diplomat, and architect
of France's pre-1914 alliance system. Born in Paumiers (Ariège) in southwestern
France, Delcassé went to Paris as a schoolteacher but nursed ambitions to become
a playwright. Unsuccessful in his literary career, he turned to journalism and
politics, joining the many aspiring politicians attached to Léon Gambetta.
Throughout his career Delcassé displayed the mix of republicanism and patriotism
characteristic of the Gambettists.

In the 1880s Delcassé wrote for *La République française* where he specialized
in foreign affairs. His articles were read carefully at the Quai d'Orsay. In the
parliamentary elections of 1889 Delcassé won a seat that he was to retain for
the next thirty years. His maiden speech dealt with foreign policy, and he
supported France's alliance with Russia, despite republican fears of association
with reactionary czardom. In 1893 Delcassé became under secretary for colonies,
and the following year he headed the new colonial ministry where he pushed
for French expansion in Africa. As colonial secretary and later as foreign minister,
he insisted on the primacy of state interests in imperial expansion, and he kept
a tight rein on the ambitions of civilian and military colonists.

Delcassé became foreign minister in 1898 during the height of the Fashoda
crisis, in which Britain and France reached the brink of war over their African
rivalry. After negotiating the French withdrawal from Fashoda, Delcassé began
strengthening French ties with Russia. He also arranged understandings with
Italy and Spain over Morocco, now an object of French expansion. Briefly, he
sought accommodation with Germany, but the unwillingness of German officials
to bargain for the return of Alsace-Lorraine convinced him that Britain offered
better prospects for an alliance, despite years of colonial competition. The Anglo-
French Entente of 1904 (Entente cordiale) resolved outstanding differences
between the two countries on questions of empire and paved the way for
rapprochement in European affairs as well. Fearful of Delcassé's presumed anti-
German policies, the German government used the first Moroccan crisis (1905)
to force Delcassé's resignation from the Quai d'Orsay, but the understanding
with Great Britain was reinforced by Germany's action and remained a cornerstone
of French policy before and during the First World War.

Delcassé returned to government as naval minister between 1911 and 1913 in
the Joseph Caillaux and Raymond Poincaré ministries; he briefly served as
ambassador to Russia in 1913–14, and he returned to France in 1914 where he
again served as foreign minister in René Viviani's war cabinet. He worked to
bring Italy into the war on the Allied side but was unsuccessful in his attempt

to lure Greece from neutrality. He also failed to keep Bulgaria from siding with Germany and Austria-Hungary, and Bulgaria's entry into the war led to Delcassé's resignation from office on 13 October 1915.

C. M. Andrew, *Théophile Delcassé and the Making of the Entente Cordiale* (London, 1968); A. Neton, *Delcassé, 1852–1923* (Paris, 1967); C. W. Porter, *The Career of Théophile Delcassé* (Philadelphia, 1936).

J. K. Munholland

Related entries: CAMBON, J.; CAMBON, P.; ENTENTE CORDIALE; FASHODA INCIDENT; GAMBETTA; GERMANY, RELATIONS WITH (1871–1914); GREAT BRITAIN, RELATIONS WITH; MARCHAND EXPEDITION; MOROCCAN CRISES; RUSSIA, ENTENTE WITH; RUSSIA, RELATIONS WITH; TRIPLE ENTENTE.

DELESCLUZE, CHARLES (1809–1871), republican activist, journalist, communard. Born to a middle-class family in Dreux (Eure-et-Loir), he studied law at le Collège Bourbon in Paris. While still a student, he fought in the uprising of 1830 as a devoted republican. He was arrested in 1834 for his participation in republican secret societies. This was but the first in a long series of arrests, imprisonments, and exiles for his Jacobin activities.

Delescluze was present at the proclamation of the Second Republic at Valenciennes (25 February 1848). Three days later he was named a commissioner for the Nord and Pas-de-Calais departments by the provisional government.

Disenchanted with Napoleon III's Second Empire, he engaged once again in a republican conspiracy, for which he was imprisoned from 1853 to 1859. Although this long incarceration had a devastating effect on this health, the amnestied Delescluze returned to Paris to found his most significant newspaper, *Le Réveil* (1860).

With the founding of the Third Republic, Delescluze immediately assumed a leadership role. On 5 November 1870 he was elected mayor of the nineteenth ward of Paris. He resigned on 6 January because of the government's refusal to increase municipal power and to take measures of public safety. But he was soon to become a leader in the government of the Paris Commune (1871). He sat on the Foreign Relations Commission, the Executive Commission, the War Commission, and the Committee of Public Safety. His most ardent desire as a reformer was to unite society through a reconciliation of the bourgeois and working class. During the last days of the Commune, he died fighting on a barricade (25 May 1871). Viewed as a martyr for the revolution by surviving Communards, he was commemorated with a monument at the cemetery Père Lachaise during the 1880s.

R. D'Amat and R. Limouzin-Lamothe, eds., *Dictionnaire de biographie français*, vol. 10 (Paris, 1965); J. Bruhat et al., *La Commune de 1871* (Paris, 1970); M. Dessal, *Un Révolutionnaire jacobin: Charles Delescluze* (Paris, 1952); P. Larousse, ed., *Grand*

Dictionnaire universel du XIXe siecle, vol. 6 (Paris, 1865); J. Maitron, ed., *Dictionnaire biographique du mouvement ouvrier français*, vol. 5 (Paris, 1968).

L. LeClair

Related entries: COMMUNE OF PARIS; JACOBINISM.

DEMOLINS, EDMOND (1852–1907), conservative sociologist and educator. Son of a Marseilles physician and educated by Jesuits, he combined social analysis with conservative positions in the review *Science sociale*, cofounded with the abbé Henri de Tourville in 1886. Attracted by Frédéric LePlay's vision of using systematic studies of society as a basis for social regeneration, Demolins embraced LePlay's method of compiling detailed monographs on working-class and peasant families, but he rejected his mentor's obsession with restoring the extended patriarchal family. To make France economically competitive with rivals, Demolins advised individuals to free themselves from archaic restrictions imposed by families, social groups, and government. His best-selling *A quoi tient la supériorité des Anglo-Saxons* (1897) contrasted the merits of English individualism with the failings of French collectivism and recommended educational reform to alter French habits. In 1898 he opened L'Ecole des Roches, a high-priced experimental boarding school in Normandy that promised to prepare sons of bourgeois families for competitive careers by dispensing practical academic and physical training and avoiding the narrow intellectualism of traditional secondary schools.

T. Clark, *Prophets and Patrons* (Cambridge, Mass., 1973); "Edmond Demolins," *Science sociale* 22 (1907).

L. L. Clark

Related entry: LE PLAY.

DEPRESSION OF THE 1930s. The New York Stock Exchange crash of 1929 did not have immediate repercussions in France. Raymond Poincaré's economic policy had left the franc undervalued in 1928, so French products remained competitive on the market, and the export boom of the 1920s continued. When the British devalued the pound sterling in 1931, however, competition stiffened. But the French now resisted further devaluation and pursued deflationary policies until 1936.

Major economic indexes dropped by 1931, particularly in industrial production of the main export products: silk and other textiles, leather, and luxury goods. Total industrial production fell from the 1928 level, on an index of 100, to 94 in 1931 and 78 in 1932; after a rise to 88 in 1933, the index dropped again, to 82 in 1934, and bottomed out at 79 in 1935. There was an upturn to 85 in 1936 and 89 in 1937, a fallback to 83 in 1938, and a jump to 95 the following year. Production thus still fell short of the 1928 level at the outbreak of the war.

Consumer prices, at an index of 100 for 1930, fell to 97.2 in 1931, 89.9 in 1932, 85.2 in 1933, 82.1 in 1934 and 76.0 in 1935. Prices then rose to 79.8 in 1936, 99.7 in 1937, and 113.4 in 1938, surpassing the predepression level.

Salaries fell during the 1930s. In the Paris region, the average hourly wage for a male worker was 6.61 francs in 1931; for the next three years, it stagnated at 6.34 francs and then was reduced by government action to 6.23 francs in 1935. The average Paris wage rose to 7.06 francs in 1936, topped 10 francs in 1937 and 1938, and stood at 10.90 francs in 1939. In other French cities, the curve was similar, although salaries were only three-quarters as high as those in the capital. Purchasing power increased from a base of 100 in 1930 to 141.7 in 1939. If those holding jobs were able to get by in industry, farmers did less well, and the unemployed suffered.

The monthly average of unemployed Frenchmen receiving aid stood at only 54,600 in 1931. It rose to 273,800 in 1932, 276,300 in 1933, 341,600 in 1934, 425,800 in 1935, and 433,700 in 1936. It dropped to 351,300 in 1937, rose to 374,100 the next year, and ended at 356,400 in 1939. These rates of unemployment were low compared with those of other European nations, but there was a significant amount of disguised unemployment in France, and approximately half a million foreign workers had been sent out of the country.

The policies of the conservative governments in the early 1930s aimed above all at maintaining the value of the franc. They cut public expenditure and tried to balance the budget. Rising unemployment, growing budget deficits (8.9 million francs in 1934 and 10.4 million in 1935), and declining production showed the lack of effectiveness of these measures in ending the crisis. The government of Pierre Laval in 1935 made a more determined effort by cutting prices 10 percent and lowering salaries and rents, but that did little to stimulate production, and 1935 turned out to be one of the worst years of the depression.

Léon Blum's victory in 1936 brought the Popular Front into office. The Matignon agreements, signed in June 1936, raised workers' salaries 12 percent and gave workers a forty-hour week and paid vacations in an attempt to stimulate purchasing power. The government nationalized armaments production and extended its control over the Bank of France. Yet these policies proved unsuccessful, partly because of the necessity of increased government borrowing to finance the provisions of the Matignon accords. Finally, Blum was forced to devalue the franc by 30 percent in relation to the Poincaré franc, but he left office without having revived the economy. Not until 1938, with Paul Reynaud as minister of finance, did the outlook improve. His modifications of the forty-hour week law, changes in government restrictions, and a pro-investment policy stimulated the economy. Inflation eased, production rose, and the franc was stabilized. Even with these achievements, the economy had not entirely regained its strength by the end of the decade. Although the depression had come later to France than to other countries, it had lasted longer.

Neither the conservative policy of maintaining the value of the franc nor the socialist effort at intervention and social action had pulled France out of the depression. Various problems of the 1930s aggravated the difficulties. Frequent changes in ministries, periodic scandals, growing international uneasiness about Nazi Germany and war-torn Spain, and the effects on France of the depression elsewhere were all to blame for the lack of confidence in the franc, a root of the problem. In addition, specific actions, although innovative social measures, worsened the overall state of the economy. There were also structural problems—such as monopolization and restrictionism in industry—which hindered recovery.

The 1930s witnessed a stagnation of the French economy, which slid into a decline. France avoided some of the worst social effects of the depression felt in Germany and England, but the crisis was prolonged and recovery modest. The weakness of the economy at the end of the 1930s is thus cited as one reason for the failure of France to resist the German onslaught in 1940.

F. Caron, *An Economic History of Modern France* (New York, 1979); T. Kemp, *The French Economy, 1913–1939* (London, 1972); A. Sauvy, *Histoire économique de la France entre les deux guerres*, vols. 1–2 (Paris, 1965, 1967).

R. Aldrich

Related entries: BANKS AND BANKING; ECONOMIC POLICY; ECONOMY; INDUSTRY.

DEPUTIES OF THE THIRD REPUBLIC. A French deputy stood for election every four years, a term secured in practice after 1877 by the president of the Republic's extreme reluctance to dissolve the Chamber of Deputies. The number of deputies, all male French citizens, at least twenty-five years old, ranged from 768 (1870) to 533 (1876), 589 (1902), 602 (1914), and 612 (1936). Their indemnity of 9,000 francs increased to 15,000 in 1906, 60,000 in 1929, and 67,200 in 1937.

Deputies established their own rules and chose their own officers. Elections of the president and vice-presidents reflected the dominant currents of the majority and provided in newly elected chambers an initial measurement of political forces. The executive committees (*bureaux*), drawn by lot, validated elections and appointed commissions to review government bills. In 1902 the chamber replaced the large number of ad hoc commissions appointed to examine a particular bill with standing commissions, and in 1910 they decided to recruit commission members from political groups in proportion to their strength.

Good connections, eloquence, ambition, and a reputation for honesty helped win elections. Most deputies came from the middle class, and most ranked with the local notables. Men of law dominated the Chamber, particularly before the Dreyfus affair (1881, 41 percent; 1906, 37 percent); teachers gained prominence after it. In 1871, a third of the deputies probably were noble; after 1910 less than 10 percent had names distinguished by the *particule*. In 1881 only one peasant and one worker served; by the end of the Republic 110 deputies had proletarian origins, and 120 came from the lower middle class. Once elected, deputies frequently served several terms, usually for the same district. Of the 4,892 deputies serving between 1870 and 1940, over half (2,621) belonged to at least two legislatures, and four-fifths of these sat without interruption.

In theory, French deputies represented the whole nation rather than a particular region or political group. In practice, the usual electoral system—the single-member constituency, double-ballot system—encouraged deputies to cater to local interests. Deputies maintained close contact with their constituencies through correspondence and regular visits and intervened with the administration to secure favors or services for their voters.

French deputies earned a reputation for the jealous defense of their principal prerogatives. Sitting together with the senators, they elected the president of the Republic and amended the constitution; sitting separately, they made the laws and controlled cabinets. Deputies shared with the ministry the right to initiate legislation, and individuals exploited it with floods of private bills. They also controlled the budget and amended and voted the laws. The parliamentary commissions reviewed bills and conducted the general debate around their revised version of the proposal.

The Chamber subjected cabinets to close scrutiny. Deputies had plenty of opportunities to challenge ministries and, unrestrained by fear of dissolution, little reason not to use them. Any deputy could interpellate (challenge) the government any time (although, after 1909, only in writing). If a majority refused to accept the government's reply or its request to postpone the interpellation, the cabinet usually fell. If they anticipated trouble over a bill, an interpellation, or a point of procedure, prime ministers could call for a formal confidence vote, but a defeat compelled them to resign. In cases of criminal acts, the Chamber indicted the president or ministers, and the Senate judged the case.

Deputies collected in factions defined by principle and by personal affinities. Although these groups formed the currency of political calculation, they never commanded perfect loyalty from their adherents. Until factions gained official recognition in 1910, deputies sometimes belonged to no group or to several, and republicans at times temporarily renounced groups altogether in order to facilitate the formation of governments.

Differences over the nature of the regime and over reform created the deepest divisions. Moderate and progressive republicans faced socially conservative royalists and Bonapartists on the extreme Right and deputies committed to radical political and social reform on the extreme Left. The character of the extremes changed in the mid-1890s with the conversion of many monarchists to the Republic (the Ralliement) and with the election of socialists. The Dreyfus affair spawned a nationalist, anti-Semitic, authoritarian extreme Right influenced by the Action française and in the 1930s by fascist sympathizers. Socialists and, after 1920, communists dominated the extreme Left.

Several groups, defined roughly by their attitude toward change, occupied the center. Opportunist republicans, noted for their moderate policies, dominated politics until the Dreyfus affair. They pushed for free, secular education, limited colonization, and democratization of the Senate but regarded social and fiscal reform (the income tax) with suspicion. The Radicals and Radical-Socialists, anticlerical and democratic, though financially conservative, supplanted the Opportunists and controlled governments almost continuously until 1940.

The harsh divisions between antirepublicans and republicans and between those favoring and those resisting reform shaped parliamentary politics. The extremes usually opposed governments, although each one regularly joined factions from the Center on certain issues and occasionally even in governments. The extreme Right voted with moderate republicans to defeat radical reform initiatives, and the Radicals, and later the Socialists, rallied to defend the Republic when the extreme Right threatened. Thus two main constellations of deputies dominated legislatures: the Center against the extremes and conservatives against radicals. These broad coalitions, at least until 1902, coexisted in the Chamber. Cabinets officially depended on one of these recognizable coalitions, but on particular issues the other might emerge. Transitory combinations of deputies also formed on specific votes.

Their common calling also bound all deputies in a club-like atmosphere, cemented by private rites and unspoken rules. Even implacable political enemies mingled in the corridors and snack bar and addressed each other with the familiar *tu*. This camaraderie diffused ideological passions and, according to some critics, reduced politics to a game involving self-interest rather than principle.

Contemporaries and later observers commonly judge the deputies' performance severely on several counts. They blame delinquent deputies for endemic ministerial instability, for stalemated government, and for the growing challenge to parliamentary institutions. From 1870 to 1940, the French endured 108 cabinets, yet power returned repeatedly to the same factions and the same individuals. Not all cabinets fell to the blows of undisciplined and divided deputies. Some strong cabinets received loyal support, and many resigned without having been defeated in the Chamber. But the deputies cut enough cabinets short over trivial matters to appear at once tyrannical and irresponsible.

Critics generally attribute the weakness of majorities either to the deputies' refusal or to their inability to cooperate, to indiscipline, or to irreconcilable divisions. While divisions did promote ministerial instability, the existence of groups too hostile to the Republic to be entrusted with power also limited the extent of change by confining power to a few groups. Moreover, the threat of the disloyal opposition prompted republicans to overcome their rivalries and deliver disciplined support to some cabinets.

To their credit, republicans, until the military defeat in 1940 stirred a majority to vote special powers to Marshall Philippe Pétain, effectively defended the Republic against its adversaries. In spite of their disunity, they also managed to pass major reforms, although slowly, and to supervise the executive, although overzealously. Moreover, most deputies satisfied the basic expectations of voters by serving as honest and effective ambassadors to the remote and powerful centralized administration.

J. Bécarud, "Noblesse et représentation parlementaire," *Revue française de science politique* 23 (1973); M. Dogan, "Political Ascent in a Class Society," in D. Marvick, *Political Decision-makers* (Glencoe, Ill., 1961); F. Goguel, *La Politique des partis sous la IIIe République* (Paris, 1958); J. Jolly, ed., *Dictionnaire des parlementaires français* (Paris, 1960); A. Robert and G. Cougny, ed., *Dictionnaire des parlementaires français*

(Paris, 1889); P. Warwick, "Ideology, Culture, and Gamesmanship in French Politics," *Journal of Modern History* 50 (1978).

S. A. Ashley

Related entries: CHAMBER OF DEPUTIES; LEFT, THE; NATIONAL ASSEMBLY; POLITICS; RIGHT, THE; VOTING PROCEDURES.

DERAIN, ANDRE (1880–1954), fauve and cubist painter. Derain's parents, confectioners in Chatou, a village on the Seine near Paris, intended him for a career in engineering, and he enrolled in the Paris Ecole des mines but abandoned his studies in favor of painting after completing military service in 1904. Decisive for his artistic development was his encounter with Maurice Vlaminck in 1900; the two rented a studio in Chatou and here developed their emotional, highly colored approach to landscape influenced by Vincent Van Gogh that became one aspect of fauvism (1905–7). In 1907 Derain left Chatou for Montmartre, distanced himself from Vlaminck, and grew close to the artists and poets of the Bateau Lavoir. Along with Pablo Picasso and Georges Braque and under the influence of African art, he toned down his palette and began to concentrate on spatial rendition, though he stopped short of the cubists' nearly total disintegration of natural forms.

By 1912 and throughout the interwar period, various eclectic influences asserted themselves one by one in his art: fifteenth-century Italian and Flemish painting, Greek classicism, popular prints, nineteenth-century French art. His relative conservatism during the 1920s earned him critical acclaim but no lasting renown. He is more remembered for his theatrical work of the time, including sets and costumes for *La Boutique fantasque* (1919, Ballets Russes) and Erik Satie's *Jack-in-the-Box* (1926), and for his book illustrations (works by Apollinaire, Max Jacob, André Breton, Antonin Artaud, Ovid, and Oscar Wilde, among others).

André Derain (Paris, 1977); *Derain* (London, [1967]); *Les Réalismes, 1919–1939* (Paris, 1980); A. Derain, *Lettres à Vlaminck* (Paris, 1955).

T. Shapiro

Related entries: ART: MAJOR STYLES AND MOVEMENTS; BRAQUE; PICASSO; SATIE; VAN GOGH; VLAMINCK.

DERAISMES, MARIA (1828–1894), feminist militant. The recipient of an excellent education as well as a fortune made in commerce by her liberal republican father, she brought both talent and wealth to feminism, republicanism, and many other causes during the late Second Empire and early Third Republic. Acclaimed as a gifted orator after accepting an invitation in 1866 to participate in the philosophical conferences sponsored by Léon Richer and other Freemasons at the Grand Orient, Deraismes soon employed her fame and contacts to help lay the organizational and ideological bases of the liberal feminist movement in France. In 1869 she lent financial and literary support to Richer's *Le Droit des femmes* (1869–91), and in 1870 they cofounded the Société pour l'amélioration du sort de la femme, which merged in the 1880s with an older feminist group to which Deraismes also belonged, the 1866 Société pour la revendication des droits de la femme. In 1878, once beyond the turmoil of international and domestic strife, Deraismes and Richer cohosted the first French Congrès international du droit des femmes. A second Congrès français et international du droit des femmes resulted from a similar joint initiative in 1889. Like Richer and the majority of France's other early feminists, Deraismes subscribed to the *politique de la brèche*, a strategy that accorded priority to eliminating women's civil disabilities by breaching the wall of masculine discrimination at its weakest points. Yet unlike Richer, she also lent occasional support to the feminist minority that subscribed to Hubertine Auclert's suffragist *politique de l'assaut*. In addition to helping to secure a series of educational reforms beneficial to women in the 1880s and the reenactment of divorce in 1884, Deraismes played a pivotal role in obtaining the right of businesswomen (*commerçantes*) to vote for judges of Commerce tribunals, a right that passed the Chamber of Deputies in 1894 and became law with the Senate's approval in 1898. Rather than in the area of legislative reforms, however, Deraismes contributed most to the emancipation of French women by the example she set and the legacy she left. Not only did she inspire other privileged women to turn to feminism, but she also bequeathed to her successors an organization through which to act and a body of writings on which to draw. Especially important among the latter, which were compiled collectively by her feminist sister, Anna Féresse-Deraismes, were *Eve contre Dumas fils* (1872) and *Eve dans l'humanité* (1891).

Although convinced that only women's emancipation could guarantee republican stability, Deraismes saw the Third Republic as the essential precondition for all future progress. In pursuit of this precondition, she helped to popularize republican ideals through tracts such as *France et progrès* (1873) and rallied her home department of Seine-et-Oise to elect its first republican deputy during the *seize mai* crisis of 1877. In the 1880s she directed the *Républicain de Seine-et-Oise*, handpicked the local republican slate that swept to victory in 1885, and later turned her salon on the rue Cardinet into an anti-Boulanger headquarters. Meanwhile, persuaded that the Roman Catholic church threatened both feminism and republicanism, Deraismes published anticlerical works such as *Lettre au clergé français* (1879), presided as vice-president at the 1881 Congrès anticlerical, and served in 1885 as president of the Fédération des groupes de la libre pensée de Seine-et-Oise. Persuaded too that Freemasonry constituted a bulwark against clericalism, Deraismes sought to breach the tradition that forbade full Masonic membership to women. Such a breach momentarily occurred when a lodge at Pecq (Seine-et-Oise) formally initiated her in 1882, only to rescind her membership under pressure from its parent organization. With the help of Senator Georges Martin, however, Deraismes in 1893 achieved an alternative breakthrough by creating the Grande Loge symbolique écossais de France: Le Droit Humain, a lodge that admitted women and men as equals.

Closely connected to Deraismes' attempt to create a lay, republican France based on sexual equality were a variety of moral reform efforts. She helped to marshal support in France for Josephine Butler's campaign against governmental regulation of prostitution, repeatedly inveighed against novelists she considered decadent such as Emile Zola, and fought animal abuse through participating in the Société française contre la vivisection and the Ligue populaire contre l'abus de la vivisection. Connected as well to her vision was a strident anticommunism, although she granted that early utopian socialists had elaborated a "just and incisive critique of our current [social] organization."

Reactions to Deraismes' career proved as varied as the efforts into which, despite chronic illness, she poured her energies. Many objected to her laissez-faire opposition to protective legislation for women. Others blamed her for too personally imposing her will on French feminism and for confusing women's rights with anticlericalism and liberal republicanism. Some Freemasons saw her as a "kind of monster." Workers tended to suspect her class background, the bourgeoisie her call for women's emancipation. Still others faulted her for dissipating her energies and for hoarding her money. Yet what Léon Abensour said in 1921 about her efforts on behalf of women's rights might apply as well to the full range of her endeavors: "Many contemporary feminists have, without moreover always rendering unto Caesar that which belongs to him, borrowed ideas, facts, and arguments from the works of Maria Deraismes." During her lifetime, Deraismes earned admission to the Société des gens de lettres. Shortly after her death, the Paris Municipal Council renamed a street in her honor (rue Maria-Deraismes in Paris' Seventeenth Arrondissement), next to which in 1898 her friends further commemorated her memory by erecting a statue to her in the Square des Epinettes (only the pedestal remains today).

L. Abensour, *Histoire générale du féminisme* (Geneva, 1921); P. Bidelman, *Pariahs Stand Up!* (Westport, Conn., 1982); *Dictionnaire de biographie francaise*, vol. 10 (Paris, 1965); Jean-Bernard (Passerieu), "Notice," in *Oeuvres complètes de Maria Deraismes* (1895–1896); O. Krakovitch, *Maria Deraismes* (Paris, 1980); C. Moses, *French Feminism in the Nineteenth Century.* (Albany, 1984).

P. K. Bidelman
Related entries: AUCLERT; FEMINISM; RICHER; WOMEN: MOVEMENT FOR CIVIL RIGHTS.

DEROULEDE, PAUL (1846–1914), nationalist poet, veteran, founder of the League of Patriots, deputy from Angoulême 1889–93, 1898–1900. He divided his life between Paris, the city of his birth, and Langely, his provincial residence near Angoulême. This division reflected the passions of the man who was also known as the Don Quixote of France. Paris, the political arena, contrasted with the bucolic environment of traditional France, the source of inspiration for Déroulède's enormously successful verse.

Déroulède's early life was spend in pursuit of typically Parisian bourgeois conventions. His father, a lawyer, and his uncle, Emile Augier, a popular and successful Second Empire lyricist, provided the educational and financial resources requisite for a Parisian upper-middle-class youth. In 1868 at the age of twenty-two, Déroulède had his first play, *Juan Strenner*, produced at the Théâtre français.

By his own admission Déroulède's normal middle-class life pattern was irrevocably altered by the Franco-Prussian War (1870–71), the proclamation of the Republic (4 September 1870), and the experience of the Commune (1871). Déroulède was wounded and taken prisoner following the Battle of Sedan (2 September 1870). Engineering an escape from his Prussian captors, he joined Léon Gambetta's army of the Loire and proclaimed, for the first time, his allegiance to the Republic of 4 September. Loyal to the army, however, he participated in the repression of the Commune. Armed with a *légion d'honneur* for his exploits in the field and the epithet "butcher of the Commune," he spent the decade from 1872 to 1882 defining himself politically and poetically.

In Paris he associated with Gambetta's inner circle—Arthur Ranc, Juliette and Paul Adam, and Joseph Reinach—and supported the republicanism of his mentor. Similarly, he maintained a sentimental attachment to the army, whose prestige he identified with the nation itself. By 1881 he was firmly opposed to the politics of Jules Ferry and the Opportunist majority, especially to their foreign and domestic policies of conciliation with Germany and acceptance of the Constitutional Laws of 1875.

Déroulède expressed these positions most clearly through his poetry, the vehicle by which he became closely associated in the popular mind with *revanche* (revenge on Germany) and that rendered him wealthy at the same time. His first book of verse, *Chants du soldat* (1872), evoked the simple fellowship and bravery of war and promised national redemption only when the humiliation of 1870–71 was removed. Over a twenty-year period *Chants* passed through twenty editions and became required reading in French primary schools. Compared favorably to Victor Hugo, Déroulède never duplicated the success he achieved in this first book, despite an enormous production of poetry, plays, and essays during the remainder of his lifetime. For the moment, however, he had become the apostle of *revanche*.

In 1881–82 Déroulède joined Gambetta's short-lived government as a member of the Commission on Military Education, a post he resigned under pressure from Ferry. Subsequently he decided to continue Gambetta's policies outside government and helped to found, along with other Left republicans, the League of Patriots. The league called for a reversal of Opportunist policies, domestic and foreign, a more democratic parliamentary republic, and a strong position with regard to Germany. Déroulède assumed formal presidency of the league in 1885, a position he maintained until his exile in 1900.

In the late 1880s, Déroulède maneuvered the league into supporting Georges Boulanger and gained a seat in the Chamber representing Angoulême's second district in 1889. After Boulanger's prosecution and flight, Déroulède remained loyal to the Boulangist republican program, viewing it as an extension of Gambetta's earlier ideas. His famous temper and naiveté led him first into a duel with Georges Clemenceau (1893) and then into the embarrassment of the Norton affair, a scandal that forced him to resign his parliamentary seat.

Returning to his country residence at Langely, Déroulède spent the next five years as a gentleman poet and playwright. His intention was to renounce politics as theater and to develop a theater of politics. These plans were set aside, however, because of the impact of the Dreyfus affair on the political campaigns and legislative elections of 1898.

Following the Emile Zola trial (1898), public opinion divided on the question of the guilt or innocence of Captain Alfred Dreyfus. The response of many ex-Boulangists, including Déroulède, was that Dreyfus' innocence was a defamation of the army and hence the nation. They claimed that only a weak republic would reverse the guilty verdict. Entering the national political scene once again, now simply as a nationalist, Déroulède regained his old seat from Angoulême and in September 1898 revived the League of Patriots. Increasingly active and militant, Déroulède and the league provided the cutting edge of anti-Dreyfusard opinion from September 1898 to August 1899. Convinced that Dreyfus' revision was at hand and that such revision would bring calamity on France for a generation, Déroulède and his closest collaborators and friends, Marcel Habert and Maurice Barrès, hatched the ill-fated plot of 23 February 1899. The plot featured Déroulède's attempt to detain an army column and march on the Elysée on the day following the death of President Félix Faure. Probably entrapped by the prefect of police and some anonymous republican generals, Déroulède found himself instead under house arrest at a local armory. Acquitted in May 1899 of any wrongdoing, Déroulède quietly redefined the organization and doctrine of the league in July and August 1899.

Having already militarized the league in preparation for Dreyfus' retrial in August, Déroulède in a speech at Angoulême stole a page from the anti-Semitic book and called for a "France for the French." Urging the nation to cleanse itself racially, calling for support of imperialist policies, and proclaiming the Republic corrupt and decadent, Déroulède completed his transformation from a Gambettist-republican to an antiparliamentary, racist nationalist.

As a consequence, he and other dissident royalists and anti-Semites, including Marcel Habert and Jules Guérin, were tried and convicted before the Senate, convened as the Haute cour, for having plotted against the Republic. Exiled for ten years, Déroulède took up residence in Spain, wrote his memoirs, and returned to France under amnesty in 1906.

By that time he was largely forgotten, and neither his literary nor political talents found any public applause. He spent the last years of his life under the care of a devoted sister, Jeanne. Déroulède died in June 1914, barely six weeks before the outbreak of a war for which he had lived since 1871.

P. Déroulède, *Chants du soldat* (Paris, [1872]); R. Girardet, *Le Nationalisme français* (Paris, 1965), and "L'Idéologie nationaliste," *Revue française de science politique* 15 (June, 1965); P. Rutkoff, *Revanche and Revision* (Athens, Ohio, 1981); Z. Sternhell,

"Paul Déroulède: The Origins of Modern French Nationalism," *Journal of Contemporary History* 6 (1971).

P. M. Rutkoff

Related entries: BARRES; BOULANGER AFFAIR; DREYFUS AFFAIR; FERRY; GAMBETTA; LEAGUE OF PATRIOTS; NATIONALISM; RIGHT, THE.

DESCHANEL, PAUL (1856–1922), politician, writer, president of the Republic (18 January–23 September 1920). He was born in Brussels, Belgium, during the exile of his father, Emile (b. 1819), who was a noted literary academician, later deputy (1876–81) and life senator (1881–1904). A precocious student in letters and law, he became a secretary (1876–77) to Emile de Marcère and Jules Simon, served briefly in the prefectorial corps, and then represented Eure-et-Loir (1885–89) and Nogent-le-Rotrou (Eure-et-Loir, 1889–1920) in the Chamber of Deputies and Eure-et-Loir in the Senate (1921–22). He spoke and wrote abundantly on many subjects: tariffs, finance, social policy, and, especially, colonial and foreign affairs. His connections and a spate of books and articles brought him an early election to the Académie française (1899) and to the presidency of the Chamber (1898–1902, 1912–20). A lifelong Gambettist, a critic of socialism and syndicalism but a strong advocate of mutualism, he was among the moderates (Progressists) who opted, finally, for Alfred Dreyfus and a separation of church and state.

His election to the presidency of the Republic (1920) stunned the world, which expected Georges Clemenceau to be chosen. Aided principally by Clemenceau's liabilities—age, personality, the public's disappointment with the Versailles treaty, and especially his anticlericalism—Deschanel, who had obtained a quiet endorsement from Rome, carried the preliminary caucus (16 January) by 408 to 389 votes. Clemenceau withdrew so the official election (17 January) was a formality. Having attained his life's ambition, Deschanel, by a cruel irony, was obliged to resign eight months later due to bizarre manifestations of manic-depressive symptoms. These had become widely known when, en route to Montbrison (24–25 May), he fell through a window of his sleeping car, wandered the tracks in his pajamas, and finally identified himself to an incredulous crossing guard.

Like Jules Grévy, Deschanel won the presidency without ever serving, despite invitations, as a minister or premier. Handsome, urbane, somewhat dandyish, he was a polished speaker and an ideal presiding officer. His addresses as president of the Chamber are models of a genre of inspirational prose, admired at the time, which says little of substance but in a most elegant way. His writings were soon forgotten, but his biography of Léon Gambetta, although written with an eye to the presidential election, is still worth reading.

Centenaire de Paul Deschanel (Chartres, 1956); A. Dansette, *Histoire des présidents de la République* (Paris, 1981); L. Derfler, *President and Parliament* (Boca Raton, 1983); P. Deschanel, Deschanel Papers, Archives Nationales, *La France victorieuse, paroles de guerre* (Paris, 1919), *Gambetta* (Paris, 1919), and *La Question sociale* (Paris, 1898); R. Malliavin, *La Politique nationale de Deschanel* (Paris, 1925); X. Vallat, "Pourquoi le 'Tigre' ne logea pas à l'Élysée," *Ecrits de Paris* (October, 1970); D. Wormser, "Clemenceau et l'élection présidentielle de 1920," *Revue politique et parlementaire* 63 (1961).

D. S. Newhall

Related entries: BLOC NATIONAL; CLEMENCEAU; GAMBETTA; OPPOR-TUNISTS; PRESIDENT OF THE REPUBLIC, OFFICE OF; PROGRESSISTS.

DESROUSSEAUX, ALEXANDRE (pseudonym, BRACKE) (1861–1955), Hellenist savant and militant socialist politician. He was born in Lille (le Nord) on 29 September 1861, the son of a famous songwriter. He completed his secondary studies on a scholarship at the Lycée Louis-le-Grand, where he received his *bachelier ès lettres* in 1879. He entered the Ecole normale supérieure in 1881 and passed his *agrégation* in grammar there in 1884. Desrousseaux spent the next three years at the Ecole française in Rome studying archaeology before returning to teach Greek philology at the University of Lille (1887–91). In 1891 he took a teaching job at the Ecole pratique des hautes études in Paris, where he later became director of studies. During this period he was the author of many important philological works and translations of many Greek writers and philosophers.

Soon after his arrival in Paris in 1891, Desrousseaux met the socialist Jules Guesde and became committed to socialism after reading Karl Marx's *Capital*. Actively involved in socialist politics from 1898, he was a frequent participant in national and international congresses and from 1900 to 1905 served as secretary of the Parti ouvrier français and the Parti socialiste français.

Desrousseaux was elected deputy for the Seine in 1912 and was reelected in 1914 and 1919. During the First World War, he supported the Socialist party's politics of national defense. After failing to be reelected by the Seine in 1924, he was elected deputy of the Nord in 1928, a post he held until 1936.

Throughout this era he wrote and edited many newspaper articles, especially for *Le Socialiste* and *L'Humanité*, often under the pseudonym Bracke. He was a staunch advocate of proportional representation in parliament, socialist unity, and women's rights. All the while, he maintained his university post. Retiring from politics in 1936, he spent the last two decades of his life working on scholarly articles and translations of German and Greek works. He died in Paris on 25 December 1955.

R. d'Amat, *Dictionnaire de biographie française* (Paris, 1975); J. Jolly, ed., *Dictionnaire des parlementaires français, 1889–1940*, vol. 2 (Paris, 1962); *Larousse du XXe siècle* (Paris, 1928); D. Ligou, *Histoire du socialisme en France* (Paris, 1962); J. Maitron, ed., *Dictionnaire du Mouvement ouvrier*, vol. 11 (Paris, 1973); C. Willard, *Les Guesdistes* (Paris, 1965).

A. J. Staples

Related entries: GUESDE; GUESDISTS; SOCIALIST PARTY.

DEVILLE, GABRIEL (1854–1940), early Marxist; journalist, author, deputy, and diplomat. Born into a prominent republican family in Tarbes (Hautes-Pyrénées), Deville gravitated toward militant socialism in an era stunned by the excesses of the Paris Commune. At seventeen, he was a founder of a Marxist section of the First International in Toulouse and joined a clandestine circle of young radicals after moving to Paris in 1872. Deville's group gathered daily at the Latin Quarter Café Soufflet and became the nucleus of the first French Marxist party. Although Karl Marx's writings were largely unknown in France in the mid-1870s, Deville and his comrades initiated the campaign of a socialist candidate for parliament with a program (written primarily by Deville) containing the first electoral statement of collectivist principles. Upon returning from exile in 1876, a still anarchistic Jules Guesde was drawn to the revolutionary socialism of Deville and his group. Together, and with growing enthusiasm, they immersed themselves in Marx's philosophy under the tutelage of several foreign Marxists living in Paris. In November 1877, Deville and Guesde founded *L'Egalité*, France's first collectivist journal.

In a crusade for general amnesty for all political exiles, Deville wrote a series of articles in *L'Egalité* promoting the candidacy of Auguste Blanqui as a means of securing freedom for the old revolutionary. Continued in *La Révolution française* after the demise of the first series of *L'Egalité*, Deville's campaign resulted in Blanqui's election to the Chamber of Deputies in 1879. In the same year, the revolutionary propaganda of Guesde and Deville led to the formation of the first Marxist party in France, the Parti ouvrier français (Guesdists). Joined by Paul Lafargue, Deville and Guesde formed the leadership triumvirate of the POF for the next decade.

One year before his death, Marx commissioned Deville to undertake an abridgement of the first volume of *Capital*. First published in 1883, the abridgement was immediately popular, widely translated, and ensured Deville's reputation as a pioneer theorist of French Marxism. Although the abridgement remained his most noted achievement, Deville's literary talents produced numerous books and journal articles ranging from social and political commentary to the role of love in Balzac. *Thermidor et directoire* (1904), his contribution to Jean Jaurès' *L'Histoire socialiste* (1901–08), was hailed as a masterful economic interpretation of the French Revolution.

In 1889, Deville resigned from active membership in the POF. Disagreement with Guesdist tactics, especially the constant harping on cataclysmic and violent revolution, led him to disassociate himself from the party, although he remained close to Guesde and Lafargue and active as an independent. The evolution of his thought—or the maturation of his understanding of Marxism—was particularly notable in his *Principes socialistes* (1896). Elected as republican socialist, Deville served Paris' Fourth Arrondissement as deputy in 1896–98 and 1903–6.

When the *cas Millerand* split the socialists, Deville, an outspoken proponent of ministerialism, joined Jaurès' Parti socialiste français in 1902 and became an open opponent of his old Guesdist comrades. As intransigent a reformist as he had once been a revolutionist, Deville even broke with Jaurès' moderate faction over the questions of parliamentary collaboration and party discipline. Although he had long worked for unity, he refused to join the unified socialists in 1905 and retired from parliament after defeat in 1906.

A new career opened for Deville in 1907 with a diplomatic appointment to Ethiopia. He served as minister to Athens from 1909 until 1915, writing of his experiences in *La Grèce et la Bulgarie* (1919). Deville remained in the diplomatic service until 1929 when he retired to Viroflay. Deville's important contributions in introducing Marxism in France were largely forgotten by a new generation of socialists. Yet he maintained at the end of his life that he had never ceased to be republican, socialist, and Marxist.

J. Hall, "Gabriel Deville and the Development of French Socialism (1871–1905)" (Ph.D. diss., Auburn University, 1983); M. Dommanget, *L'Introduction du marxisme en France* (Lausanne, 1969).

J. H. Hall

Related entries: BLANQUI; COLLECTIVISM; GUESDISTS; MARXISM; SOCIALISM, 1870–1914.

DIJON, city in east-central France, the capital of the Côte-d'Or department and of the Burgundy region. The population of Dijon grew from 42,573 in 1872 to 96,257 in 1936, in large part due to the arrival of migrants from the surrounding countryside. The great stimulus to expansion was the train, as Dijon had become the chief stop on the line from Paris to Lyons and the Mediterranean in the 1850s. In addition, the Dijon depots handled much of the freight traffic between France and Central Europe. Consequently railway workers poured into the city, as did employees of train repair shops, hotels, and other auxiliary businesses. There were also refugees from Alsace and Lorraine after 1870. The western area of the city and neighboring suburbs began a steady expansion to house the new residents, culminating in the creation of an entirely new suburb in the 1930s.

The traditional industries of Dijon (mustard, spice bread, and black currant liqueur) remained productive, although most of the wine trade was now transacted in Beaune. New factories making train parts, bicycles, and pharmaceutical products were established in Dijon in the 1880s, but the city remained devoid of heavy industry. By 1936 only a third of the labor force worked in industry. More important was the tertiary sector. Dijon's position as departmental capital, seat of a university, an academy, and a court of appeals, and the financial and marketing center for much of Burgundy made it a service city par excellence. Lawyers, doctors, and businessmen, rather than industrialists, dominated the city.

Politically Dijon was traditionally on the Left, electing republican deputies and mayors after 1870 and socialist city governments in 1896 and 1904. After World War I, conservatives began to take over the political life of the city, and even leftists turned toward the Right. The mayor from 1919 to 1936, Gaston Gérard, was a Radical who became increasingly more conservative. However,

Dijonnais voters reverted to their old ways to support the Popular Front. Neither the Boulanger nor Dreyfus affairs caused a great stir in Dijon, and labor disputes were minor in this nonindustrial city. One local scandal of national consequence involved Albert Le Nordez, the bishop of Dijon. Accused of republicanism and Freemasonry, he was forced to resign in 1904; the summoning of Le Nordez to Rome was one cause of the breaking of relations between Paris and the Vatican.

Among notable Dijonnais cultural figures were the historian Gaston Roupnel (1871–1946), the philosophers Gaston Bachelard (1884–1962) and Maurice Blondel (1861–1949), and the novelist Edouard Estaunié (1862–1942). In *Les Choses voient* (1914) and *Tels qu'ils furent* (1927), Estaunié provided a mordant portrait of his bourgeois townsmen. A similar view is presented in *Le Solitaire*, the fictionalized autobiography of Marcel Martinet (1887–1944), a Dijonnais intellectual who became literary critic for *L'Humanité* and authored a study of proletarian culture. Gaston Gérard's *Dijon, ma bonne ville* is a complementary memoir of turn-of-the-century life in the Burgundian capital.

R. Aldrich, *Economy and Society in Burgundy since 1850* (New York, 1984); Centre régional de documentation pédagogique, *La IIIe République en Côte-d'Or, 1870–1914* (Dijon, 1969); P. Gras, ed., *Histoire de Dijon* (Toulouse, forthcoming).

R. Aldrich

Related entries: BACHELARD; BURGUNDY; URBANIZATION AND THE GROWTH OF CITIES.

DION, ALBERT DE, COMTE (1856–1946) (marquis from 1901), pioneer automobile manufacturer. An aristocratic playboy, de Dion liked mechanical contrivances and in the 1880s hired some Paris craftsmen to make several steam automobiles. After early failures, his steam buses were used in the late 1890s. More successful was an 1895 tricycle powered by a high-speed gasoline engine devised by de Dion's associate, Georges Bouton. As many as 15,000 of these gasoline tricycles were produced in the Paris suburb of Puteaux by De Dion-Bouton until 1901. Many other manufacturers imitated it or made it on license in these years. In 1899 De Dion-Bouton offered its first four-wheeled gasoline car. Light, inexpensive, and reliable, it was the largest-selling car in Europe for a few years, and many other early auto firms bought De Dion-Bouton engines for their cars. The company continued in the industry until 1927, eventually making large cars, including a V-8 from 1909, gasoline buses, and converting to aircraft engines during the First World War. De Dion was the most active leader of the industry until about 1910, helping to organize the Automobile Club of France in 1895, an automakers' trade association in 1898, *L'Auto* daily newspaper in 1900, and in 1907 a machine tool firm.

A Bonapartist in politics, he was twice arrested for violent opposition to the Republic. He became a deputy (Independent) from Nantes in 1902 and moved to the Senate in 1923 where he remained until 1940.

J. Laux, *In First Gear* (Montreal, 1976); *Dictionnaire de biographie française*, vol. 11 (Paris, 1967); J. Jolly, ed., *Dictionnaire des parlementaires français*, vol. 4 (Paris, 1966).

J. M. Laux

Related entries: BONAPARTISM; INDUSTRY: AUTO; RENAULT.

DISARMAMENT CONFERENCE (1932–1934), meeting to establish limitation and reduction of arms among sixty nations, including the United States and the Soviet Union. Preliminary talks had begun during the Versailles negotiations (1919) and continued with a special Preparatory Commission (1926). French suspicion of Germany's desire to remilitarize prevented any easy understanding. The failure of these deliberations marked the renewal of the arms race and growing tension between France and Germany. By 1931 France, already sensing the threat of German aggression (the rise of Adolf Hitler was only two years away), wanted to check German rearmament directly. The conference convened on 2 February 1932, with the French exerting leadership from the outset. Premier André Tardieu proposed the establishment of an international police force, under the control of the League of Nations, to which all states would submit weapons. Some governments (notably the United States and the Soviet Union) viewed this as a threat to their sovereignty, but U.S. President Herbert Hoover's alternate plan for the elimination of certain weapons and the reduction of standing armies was also rejected.

The third major proposal for disarmament was a French creation, the Herriot-Paul-Boncour Constructive Plan. Included in this was the maximum plan, which would allow each state to keep a militia rather than permanent national forces at its disposal (removing the possibility of large scale rearmament by Germany). These French statesmen also had a backup minimum plan, wherein permanent national forces would be maintained, but heavy bomber aircraft would be at the disposal of the League of Nations. This proposal too was modified to such an extent that it became meaningless, and the participants could agree only on a pact to consult one another.

Germany was finally promised military parity with France in the Ramsay MacDonald plan (16 March 1933), which also called for the reduction of European armies by almost half a million men. Germany continued to protest. Further attempts were made to reach a compromise when France, Great Britain, Italy, and the United States promised not to build up armaments for four years and agreed that after this period Germany would be allowed to possess the same capacity as the other powers. Germany refused, insisting on the right to possess defensive weapons immediately.

General frustration led to Germany's withdrawal from the conference and the League of Nations on 14 October 1933. The conference met briefly from 29 May to 11 June, but no further progress was made due to the unyielding French attitude. The final break was made when Germany formally denounced the disarmament clauses of the Versailles Treaty (16 March 1935). After this time both France and Germany began to rearm, paving the way for World War II.

R. Albrecht-Carrié, *France, Europe and the Two World Wars* (1961; rpt. Westport, Conn., 1975); J. Néré, *The Foreign Policy of France from 1914 to 1945* (Boston, 1975); F. Schuman, *War and Diplomacy in the French Republic* (New York, 1931).

L. LeClair

Related entries: FOREIGN POLICY; GERMANY, RELATIONS WITH (1914–40); HERRIOT; PARIS PEACE CONFERENCE; PAUL-BONCOUR; TARDIEU.

DIVORCE, instituted in France in 1792, modified and restricted by Napoleon (1799, 1804), and abolished in May 1816 by the restored monarchy. During the early years of the Third Republic, Senator Alfred Naquet pushed for the reinstatement of divorce. His law reestablishing divorce was passed on 27 July 1884. In one way this new law was more severe than its precursors because it excluded divorce by mutual consent or on the grounds of incompatibility (previously allowed in the law of 1792 and under Napoleon). It did, however, grant the courts greater latitude in interpreting the grounds of cruelty and serious injury, thereby making divorces much easier to obtain.

After its reinstitution, the number of divorces began a steady climb, peaking in 1921 and leveling off thereafter. Statistics show that in 1900 approximately 7,300 divorces were granted (about 6% of married couples) and approximately 15,000 in 1913. The year 1921 was the highest point for divorces during the Third Republic, with over 32,500 divorces granted. After this year, the figures remained rather stable at about 21,000 divorces per year until the end of the Third Republic in 1940. It is estimated that during the first fifty years following the reinstatement of divorce, approximately 500,000 French families were broken up by divorce.

D. and M. Frémy, *Encyclopédie QUID* (Paris, 1983); R. Naz, *Dictionnaire du droit canonique*, vol. 4 (Paris, 1949); T. Zeldin, *France 1848–1945*, vol. 1 (London, 1973).

A. J. Staples

Related entries: MARRIAGE; NAQUET.

DOMMANGET, MAURICE (1888–1976), schoolteacher, socialist, communist, revolutionary syndicalist, and historian. He was born 14 January 1888 in Paris. After becoming a primary schoolteacher in the Oise department, he joined both the Socialist party (SFIO) and the Fédération des instituteurs and in 1908 organized one of the first strikes of schoolteachers in France. An active journalist, he contributed articles on revolutionary syndicalist principles to a variety of left-wing papers, using various pseudonyms (Jean Prolo and Jean Social). At the same time, he published several historical works, which attracted the attention of Albert Mathiez, who unsuccessfully attempted to steer Dommanget toward a university career. Yet while remaining an *instituteur* for the sake of his revolutionary syndicalist principles, he was to become a leading historian of the French revolutionary tradition.

During the First World War, despite his mobilization, he rejected the *Union sacrée* and, in collaboration with Alphonse Merrheim, promoted Zimmerwaldien ideas among his entourage. He joined the Communist party (PCF) in December 1920 and in 1926 was elected general secretary of the Fédération unitaire de l'enseignement, a constituent element of the Confédération générale du travail unitaire (CGTU), striving in vain to unite the conflicting tendencies (revolutionary syndicalist and communist) within the union. After breaking with the PCF in 1930, he founded an opposition movement within the CGTU to promote the cause of revolutionary syndicalism. He was suspended from his teaching position by the Vichy regime but was reinstated in 1944. A leading theoretician of the Ecole émanicipée group, he remained a devoted syndicalist all his life.

Above all, Dommanget was the historian of the revolutionary tradition, the author of around fifty books on 1792, 1848, 1871, Gracchus Babeuf, Sylvain Maréchal, Eugène Varlin, Eugène Pottier, Edouard Vaillant, and, primarily, Auguste Blanqui for whom he remains the undisputed principal source. As Ernest Labrousse noted in his funeral oration, "He was the historian of men, of souls, of heroes, of flags, of great symbols." He died on 2 April 1976, leaving his books and papers, an unparalleled massive collection of primary historical material—the *Fonds Dommanget*—to the Institut français d'histoire sociale in Paris. A complete biography of Dommanget will be published in Volume 17 of Jean Maitron's *Dictionnaire biographique du mouvement ouvrier français*.

J. Howorth

Related entries: BLANQUI, COMMUNIST PARTY; CONFEDERATION GENERALE DU TRAVAIL UNITAIRE; MATHIEZ; MERRHEIM; SOCIALISM, 1914–1940.

DORIOT, JACQUES (1898–1945), a leading Communist who became one of France's most influential fascists. Born into a working-class family in Bresles (Oise), Doriot settled in 1915 in the Parisian suburb of Saint-Denis as a metal worker. After war service he became a leader of the recently formed Jeunesses communistes. Rising fast in the party, Doriot became secretary-general of the Jeunesses, engaged in antimilitarist agitation, and made trips to Moscow. Imprisoned for urging French soldiers in the Ruhr to fraternize with the Germans, Doriot was then elected deputy from Saint-Denis in 1924, which led to his amnesty. (In succeeding years he was frequently convicted but rarely imprisoned.) In the Chamber of Deputies, the young deputy, who had become an expert on colonial affairs, made a name for himself through his open support of the Moroccan insurgent Abd el-Krim.

By 1926, with his popularity in the party high, Doriot, already a member of the Politburo, intrigued unsuccessfully to be named secretary-general of the French Communist party (PCF). The following year, as a Comintern representative in China, he witnessed at first hand the debacle of Stalin's policy. On his return to France, Doriot vigorously opposed the International's new antisocialist tactic of class against class, only to be defeated within the party and obliged to make public self-criticism at the national congress in 1929.

Blocked on the national party level, Doriot built a local base at Saint-Denis, where he became mayor in 1931 and created a model communist municipality. By the fall of 1933, Doriot, concerned with the rise of fascism, sought again to change the party line but was rebuffed, in January 1934, by his long-time rival, Maurice Thorez. Following the riots of 6 February, Doriot broke discipline and sought to create a fait accompli by founding an action committee of local Communists and Socialists. After his refusal to take his fight with Thorez to Moscow, the deputy and mayor was read out of the PCF at the same congress (June 1934) that formally adopted the Communist-Socialist alliance he had so long sought. Doriot had been right too soon.

Though he left the PCF, Doriot brought the Communist organizations of Saint-Denis (the *neuvième rayon*) with him. Blocked by the Popular Front, Doriot found himself unable to act as the center for a leftist coalition and was obliged to look to the Right for allies in his vendetta against his former party. Accordingly, in June 1936 he founded the Parti populaire français (PPF) whose apparatus was dominated by ex-Communists but attracted leading rightist intellectuals like Drieu la Rochelle and Bertrand de Jouvenel. With anticommunism his major theme, Doriot may have attracted as many as 100,000 members, but, faced with the rivalry of François de La Rocque's Parti social français, he was as unsuccessful at coalition building on the Right as he had been on the Left. In 1938–39 the PPF disintegrated in fights between pro- and anti-Munichois. By this time, Doriot had lost both his post as mayor and his seat in parliament.

After the defeat, Doriot became one of the leading Paris collaborators and was eventually entrusted, in late 1944, with the creation of a French government in exile. He was shot by a plane in Germany in January 1945.

G. Allardyce, "Jacques Doriot et l'esprit fasciste en France," *Revue d'histoire de la deuxième guerre mondiale* 97 (1975), and "The Political Transition of Jacques Doriot," in W. Laqueur and G. L. Mosse, eds., *International Fascism, 1920–1945* (New York, 1966); J.-P. Brunet, "Réflexions sur la scission de Doriot (février–juin 1934)," *Le Mouvement social* 70 (1970); D. Wolf, *Doriot, du communisme à la collaboration* (Paris, 1969).

A. *Douglas*

Related entries: ANTIMILITARISM; COMMUNIST PARTY; FASCISM; FEBRUARY RIOTS; LA ROCQUE; POPULAR FRONT; RIF REBELLION; RUHR OCCUPATION; THOREZ.

DORMOY, JEAN (1851–1898), Parti ouvrier militant, Allier Department. A metallurgical worker, Dormoy became active in working-class politics during the closing years of the Second Empire. This activity continued in the 1870s, and he attended several early labor and socialist congresses. Dormoy was an early adherent to the Guesdists and served on the national council of the Parti ouvrier in the 1880s. His socialist views cost him his job in Montluçon. Blacklisted by other employers, he became a traveling salesman who dispensed cooking oil and his socialist ideas at the same time, a pattern not unusual for early socialist militants. In 1883 he was arrested with Jules Guesde and Paul Lafargue and charged with inciting to murder, pillage, and arson for the role he played in socialist meetings. Dormoy was convicted and sentenced to six months in prison. He continued to be active in both trade union and political circles throughout the 1880s and did much to develop the strength of the Parti ouvrier in the Allier. In 1888 he was elected to the municipal council of Montluçon and served as its mayor from 1892 until the time of his death. In 1898 he was elected to the departmental general council.

J. Maitron, ed., *Dictionnaire biographique du mouvement ouvrier français*, vol. 11 (Paris, 1974).

T. Moodie

Related entry: GUESDISTS.

DOUMER, PAUL (1857–1932), politician, colonial administrator, and president of the Republic. He was a man of modest origins, and his life demonstrates the possibility of advancement through politics in the Third Republic. Economic hardship compelled Doumer to earn his baccalaureat and teaching certificate at night through the Ecole des arts et métiers. Subsequently he taught mathematics and then entered politics through the influence of his father-in-law, who secured his appointment as editor of a republican newspaper.

When Doumer's views proved too radical for the paper's owners, he helped found the *Tribune de l'Aisne*, which became the voice of the radical party in that department. Doumer's energy and organizing ability gained him valuable allies among influential radical politicians. He entered the Chamber of Deputies in 1887 and became known for his expertise in financial matters. As finance minister under Léon Bourgeois (1895–96), Doumer pushed for an income tax, but conservative opposition defeated the measure and brought down Bourgeois' cabinet. The new government removed the inconvenient Doumer by appointing him governor-general of Indochina.

Doumer's tenure left a mark on the French colony. He promoted railway expansion, including a line into China's Yunnan province, imposed new taxes, secured loans to finance his projects, and centralized the administration. Although Doumer was proud of these accomplishments, the costs of his economic and administrative reforms fell heavily on the Vietnamese population and left a simmering resentment beneath the colony's outward calm and prosperity.

On his return to France, Doumer abandoned his earlier radicalism and was elected president of the Chamber of Deputies with conservative support. His first bid for the presidency of the Republic failed in 1906, however. During the First World War Doumer organized civil defense in Paris, and after the war he twice served as finance minister under Aristide Briand. He became president of the Senate in 1927, and in 1932 he defeated his former colleague, Briand, for the presidency of the Republic. Shortly after taking office, Doumer was assassinated by a disturbed Russian exile who thought that this act would call attention to the plight of the Ukraine under Soviet rule. A major thoroughfare in the fashionable Sixteenth Arrondissement of Paris was renamed in honor of the martyred president.

P. Doumer, *Situation de l'Indo-Chine, 1897–1901* (Hanoi, 1902), and *L'Indochine française*, 2 vols. (Paris, 1905).

J. K. Munholland

Related entries: BOURGEOIS; OVERSEAS EMPIRE: SOUTHEAST ASIA; PRESIDENT OF THE REPUBLIC, OFFICE OF.

DOUMERGUE, GASTON (1863–1937), deputy, minister, senator, prime minister, and president of the Republic. Like several of his predecessors in the Elysée, he came from a rural petit-bourgeois background. Doumergue practiced law in Nîmes, where he was elected a deputy in 1893. He was a minister of colonies, commerce, and education in pre–World War I governments and was elected senator in 1913. Holding few strong ideological commitments, Doumergue readily found a place in the Radical party.

Pleased with Doumergue's advocacy of close ties with Britain and Russia as well as with his promise to support the newly enacted three-year military service, Raymond Poincaré asked him to head the government in 1913. As minister of foreign affairs in the René Viviani cabinet (1914) and then minister for colonies (1914–17), Doumergue concerned himself with recruiting colonial troops. As president of the Senate (1923–24) he secured de facto eligibility for the presidency of the Republic and replaced Alexandre Millerand, who was forced to resign on 13 June 1924.

During his *septennate*, Doumergue had to resolve fifteen ministerial crises. He was aided by his knowledge of human nature, by friendships in all political parties, and by a well-developed sense of *bonhomie*, which won him the epithets "le bon Gaston" and "Papa Doumergue." He first called on cartel leaders to form governments, but neither Edouard Herriot nor Paul Painlevé could bring a halt to inflation. Doumergue estimated that the time was ripe for a Center-Right coalition government, and he asked Poincaré, whom he respected, to form one. During his presidency he favored Poincaré and Aristide Briand, calling on the former twice and the latter four times.

Doumergue intervened in the political process but judiciously and seldom publicly. He asked the speakers of the two chambers to speed desired legislation, and he participated actively in the formation of ministries. He repeatedly offered advice to Herriot and Briand, until he replaced the latter with Poincaré, despite a left-of-center majority in the Chamber. He expressed his views at ministerial meetings and tried to prevent Briand, foreign affairs minister from 1925 to 1932, from pursuing appeasement too fervently. But he always did this privately and respectfully. Once an anticlerical, he now worked to ensure religious peace.

In the wake of the riot of 6 February 1934, President Albert Lebrun asked him to come out of retirement and form "a government of respite, appeasement and justice." Doumergue requested and won the right to decree laws necessary to secure financial and moral renewal. His coalition government included both Herriot and Philippe Pétain. During his tenure he went on radio to keep his listeners informed (by means of "family chats") of events and proposed remedies. His undoing issued from his awareness of the need to strengthen the executive branch. Pressing foreign threats, such as the assassination of Engelbert Dollfuss and Adolf Hitler's rise to power, as well as the inability of parliament to deal with events, prompted Doumergue to ask for presidential powers to dissolve the lower house on the sole recommendation of the prime minister (eliminating Senate consent) by the second year of each legislature. His decision to push for reform by means of radio speeches aroused old fears of authoritarian rule. Herriot resigned from the cabinet, and the Radicals dropped their support, forcing Doumergue's resignation shortly thereafter. His failure proved to be the last effort made before World War II to reinforce presidential power.

J. Barthélemy, "La Constitution Doumergue," *Revue politique et parlementaire*, 10 November, 1934; A. Dansette, *Histoire des présidents de la République* (Paris, 1960); L. Derfler, *President and Parliament* (Boca Raton, 1983); M. Verne, *Le Président Doumergue* (Paris, 1925).

L. Derfler

Related entries: BRIAND; CARTEL DES GAUCHES; HERRIOT; LEBRUN; MILLERAND; POINCARE, R.; PRESIDENT OF THE REPUBLIC, OFFICE OF; RADICAL AND RADICAL-SOCIALIST PARTY.

DREYFUS, ALFRED (1859–1935), army officer whose wrongful conviction on espionage charges precipitated a major social and political crisis. Dreyfus was born at Mulhouse on 9 October 1859, the youngest of seven children in a highly acculturated Jewish family prospering in the Alsatian textile industry. When Mulhouse was lost to Germany in 1871, Alfred moved with his parents to Switzerland. The young Dreyfus was sent to school in Paris beginning in 1873, and, rejecting a position in the family business, he entered the Ecole polytechnique at the age of nineteen in order to prepare for a career in the military. Dreyfus held several military assignments between 1880 and 1890, and in 1890 he entered the Ecole supérieure de guerre. In that same year Dreyfus married Lucie Hadamard. Two children were born of this marriage: Pierre in 1891 and Jeanne in 1893. When he graduated from the Ecole de guerre in 1892, Dreyfus was assigned to the Army General Staff, and it was while serving there that he became the center of the celebrated affair that bears his name.

Dreyfus was physically and emotionally exhausted by the ordeal of his trials and by his four years of confinement on Devil's Island in French Guiana (1895–99). Although he was finally exonerated and reinstated in the army with the rank of major in 1906, he remained on active duty only a year, retiring in 1907. Dreyfus spent the years between 1907 and 1914 in retirement, reading history and sociology. At the outbreak of World War I, he rejoined the army, and by the end of the war he had risen to the rank of lieutenant colonel and had been made an officer of the Legion of Honor. Dreyfus became increasingly frail in his final years, and he died after a long illness on 11 July 1935.

A. Dreyfus, *Cinq années de ma vie* (Paris, 1901); P. Dreyfus, *Dreyfus: His Life and Letters*, trans. B. Morgan (London, 1937).

L. S. Weissbach

Related entry: DREYFUS AFFAIR.

DREYFUS AFFAIR (1894–1899), a political and social crisis surrounding the arrest and imprisonment of a French officer wrongly accused of transmitting military secrets to Germany. In November 1894, Edouard Drumont's anti-Semitic newspaper *La Libre parole* announced that a Jewish officer had been secretly arrested for espionage and placed under interrogation by the army. For the next five years the case of Captain Alfred Dreyfus became the battleground for issues of nationalism, militarism, church and state, anti-Semitism, and more. Léon Blum spoke for many when he said that "life was as if suspended" during *l'affaire Dreyfus*.

In September 1894, a memorandum (*bordereau*) of French military data had been discovered by an undercover agent in the German embassy in Paris. After comparing the handwriting of officers attached to the French General Staff, suspicion fell on Captain Dreyfus, an Alsatian Jew with few friends and fewer supporters among militant Catholics who dominated the officer corps. On October 15 Dreyfus was summoned to the War Ministry. Commandant Mercier du Paty de Clam ordered the unsuspecting captain to take dictation and recited passages from the *bordereau*. When Dreyfus' hand began to shake—he later said it was cold in the room—the commandant formally placed him under arrest for the crime of high treason.

The evidence was thin, the investigation hasty, but the army rushed to prepare a court-martial. Officials refused the prisoner's requests to see his wife and two children and ignored his pleas of innocence. On 22 December, in a secret session from which Dreyfus' lawyers were barred, the army sentenced the "traitor" to life imprisonment. At a public degradation ceremony at the Ecole militaire, crowds chanted "Down with the Jews! Long live the Army!" while Dreyfus, stripped of sword and epaulets, cried, "I am innocent! Long live France!" A month later, he was transported to Devil's Island, a former leper colony off the coast of French Guiana.

In 1894–95 virtually no one rallied to the captain's side. The popular anti-Semitic press had been insisting for over a decade that Jews were quintessential traitors; moreover, most Frenchmen trusted the army beyond doubt and feared Germany beyond reason. Still, crucial questions concerning motive and evidence had been left unanswered. Dreyfus, son of a prosperous textile manufacturer, had no reason to profit from espionage; and his professional career, at the Ecole polytechnique and later as an artillery officer, had been exemplary. Motive remained a puzzle. Documents that army officials insisted confirmed Dreyfus' treason remained guarded for reasons of "national security." Only a small coterie on the General Staff knew that most of those documents were irrelevant and that others had been forged.

In the months that followed, Dreyfus' wife, Lucie, and brother, Mathieu, petitioned authorities for a retrial, but interest in the case did not reemerge until 1896 when Georges Picquart, new chief of Army Intelligence, found a suspicious German telegram addressed to a French officer, Commandant Ferdinand Esterhazy. After comparing samples of Esterhazy's handwriting with the *bordereau*, Picquart knew that the wrong man had been sent to Devil's Island.

A labyrinth of political intrigue, forgeries, lies, and violent anti-Semitism marked the next phase of the affair. In a pamphlet entitled "A Judicial Error," Bernard Lazare (French Jew, anarchist, and early Dreyfusard) exposed inconsistencies in the case; and, in turn, Colonel Hubert Henry, an officer in the intelligence service, added new forgeries to the secret Dreyfus file, "evidence" that would further incriminate Dreyfus were the case reopened. In 1897, Picquart convinced the vice-president of the Senate, Auguste Scheurer-Kestner, of Dreyfus' innocence. In a desperate and transparent move, the army ordered Picquart to a post in North Africa. But interest in the case continued to build. Late in 1897, Esterhazy, in secret and bizarre contact with Henry and du Paty de Clam (they wore dark glasses, wigs, and false beards to their clandestine meetings), denounced Picquart. Armed, no doubt, with knowledge of Henry's forgeries, Esterhazy asked to be brought before a court-martial to prove his innocence. On 11 January 1898, crowds outside the courtroom celebrated news of Esterhazy's acquittal with shouts of "Long live the Army! Death to the Jews!"

Two days later, on the front page of Georges Clemenceau's newspaper *L'Aurore*, Emile Zola published "J'Accuse," a scathing indictment of the General Staff. The case had become an *affaire*, and Zola's article triggered a rash of anti-Semitic riots. Gangs attacked Jewish homes and shops in Paris, Marseilles, Grenoble, and dozens of other cities, and demonstrations continued through February in response to Zola's trial. Again, "Death to Dreyfus, Zola and the Jews!" became a harrowing leitmotif in cities and towns.

Reviewing the Dreyfus file a few months later, an officer in the War Ministry discovered Colonel Henry's forgeries. On 30 August 1898 Henry was arrested and the following day committed suicide in his prison cell.

In the summer of the next year, Dreyfus, emaciated and barely able to speak after more than four years of isolation and forced silence, returned to France to face a new trial at Rennes. For the first time, he heard the details of the byzantine drama that had unfolded during his captivity. However, in yet another secret session, judges again condemned Dreyfus, this time with "extenuating circumstances." Two judges supported Dreyfus' innocence, while others remained either convinced of his guilt or wary of the social and political turmoil an acquittal might unleash. In the wake of this confusing verdict and after a half-decade of upheaval, René Waldeck-Rousseau's government pardoned Dreyfus. In November 1899 a general amnesty ended the most tumultuous phase of the affair.

During the next six years Dreyfus fought to clear his name. Esterhazy had fled to London and had admitted writing the *bordereau* in a convoluted plot of counterespionage. The secret file was exposed as a mass of forgeries. Finally, in 1906, a new, more responsive republican government, many of its members former Dreyfusards, reversed the Rennes decision. At the Ecole militaire, where twelve years before he had been degraded, Dreyfus was reinstated in the army and awarded the Legion of Honor. He served in World War I, became a lieutenant colonel, and retired to live peacefully in Paris until his death in 1935. "I was only an artillery officer whom a tragic error prevented from pursuing his normal career," Dreyfus wrote a supporter after the affair; "the symbol is not me. It is you who created that Dreyfus."

Histories of the fin de siècle stress the bifurcation of France during the affair. The nation was torn asunder, the story goes, families divided, old friendships ruined. For the most part and for many reasons, country people, still the majority of the nation, remained indifferent to the affair. But in cities and towns, militant anti-Semites, xenophobic nationalists, and members of the League of Patriots and Action française battled republican anticlericals, socialists, and members of the League of the Rights of Man. This familiar scenario of confrontation contains some truth and much oversimplification. Many nationalists and Catholics, like Charles Péguy, supported Dreyfus, while a significant number of socialists held to the anti-Jewish, anticapitalist equation and considered the affair bourgeois folly. Not until the eleventh hour did they rally to Dreyfus, led, not surprisingly, by Jean Jaurès.

In the end, justice and reason prevailed, and the Third Republic survived the affair. But in the process, racism, political corruption and cowardice, social and religious conflict, and more had surfaced. Many of those who had come to the affair with a clear, often noble enthusiasm looked back on the struggle confused and disillusioned. "Everything begins as a *mystique*," wrote Péguy, "and ends as a *politique*."

The impact of the Dreyfus affair reached beyond the borders of France and into the final years of the Third Republic. In 1894, when Theodore Herzl came to France to cover the trial for an Austrian newspaper, Vienna, not Paris, was the center of political anti-Semitism. Herzl, expecting tolerance and justice in the first nation to extend civil liberties to Jews, witnessed instead a bloody campaign of anti-Semitic violence. Modern zionism did not emerge directly from the affair, but Herzl confirmed that events in France gave immediacy to his quest for a Jewish state.

During the 1930s, a play entitled *L'Affaire Dreyfus* attracted bomb-throwing hooligans of the Action française, a group that had been formed during the affair. Through that decade and into the Vichy years, the memories, myths, vocabulary, and methods of the Dreyfus affair reemerged to help define a new civil war, a new struggle over the role of the state, the army, and the individual in modern France.

J. D. Bredin, *L'Affaire* (Paris, 1983); A. Dreyfus, *Cinq années de ma vie* (Paris, 1901); D. Johnson, *France and the Dreyfus Affair* (New York, 1967); J. Reinach, *Histoire de l'Affaire Dreyfus*, 7 vols. (Paris, 1903–11); S. Wilson, *Ideology and Experience: Anti-semitism in France at the Time of the Dreyfus Affair* (Rutherford, N.J., 1982).

M. Burns

Related entries: ACTION FRANCAISE; ANTICLERICALISM; ANTIMILI-TARISM; ANTISEMITIC LEAGUE; ANTI-SEMITISM; BARRES, M.; CLE-MENCEAU; CLERICALISM; DREYFUS; GERMANY, RELATIONS WITH (1871–1914); JUDAISM; REINACH; SCHEURER-KESTNER; WALDECK-ROUSSEAU; ZOLA.

DRIEU LA ROCHELLE, PIERRE (1893–1945), novelist, essayist, poet, and exponent of French fascism. He was born in Paris, the first child of a bourgeois family with unstable finances, a milieu he describes in his novel *Rêveuse bourgeoisie* (1937). A good student, he attended the prestigious Ecole des sciences politiques but surprised and disappointed his professors and himself by failing the final examinations. This early failure prevented him from undertaking a career in diplomacy and led him to consider suicide, a possibility that was to tempt and fascinate him throughout his life.

Called into military service with his class, Drieu was already a corporal when the First World War broke out. His first experience of combat in the Battle of Charleroi filled him with ecstasy and introduced him to the possibility of being a charismatic leader (*un chef*), a concept that was to remain central to his political thought. Drieu spent much of the wartime period convalescing from wounds received at Charleroi and Verdun. During his hospitalization, he began writing poetry about his personal response to the war. These early poems, published as *Interrogation* (1917) and *Fond de Cantine* (1920), gained him his first literary recognition.

In 1917 he married Colette Jeramec, the sister of his best friend, who had been killed at Charleroi. Although the marriage, like all of Drieu's many relationships with women, was short-lived, this alliance with a rich Jewish family gave him the financial means to enter the fast-moving hedonistic society of the 1920s. During this time Drieu was involved with the surrealists through his brief friendship with Louis Aragon. Like many of his wartime generation, Drieu became increasingly disillusioned by the decadence of the immediate postwar world, and during this period he alternated essays on the future of Europe with fictional portrayals of the superficial society that surrounded him. The best known of these portraits, *Le Feu Follet* (1931), the story of the last days of a drug addict engaged in a futile search for meaning, was made into a film by Louis Malle in 1963.

By the end of the 1920s Drieu had become convinced of a need for political commitment. The protagonist of his 1930 novel, *Une Femme à sa fenêtre*, opts for communism, but in 1934 Drieu made his own position clear in a series of essays entitled *Socialisme fasciste*. Subsequently he became a leading spokesman for the fascist Parti populaire français founded by Jacques Doriot in 1936. Although he contributed regularly to the party's paper, *L'Emancipation nationale*, Drieu soon became disillusioned with this attempt to unite dream and action. Even before his resignation from Doriot's group in 1939, he had retreated to pour his energies into his major novel, *Gilles* (1939), a monumental autobiographical study of *l'entre-deux-guerres*.

Although he held little real optimism about the Nazis, Drieu accepted the editorship of the prestigious literary journal *Nouvelle revue française* under Nazi censorship. Depressed and in hiding at the end of the war, he finally, after several persistent attempts, committed suicide in 1945.

P. Andreu and G. Grover, *Drieu la Rochelle* (Paris, 1979); D. Desanti, *Drieu la Rochelle ou le séducteur mystifié* (Paris, 1978); F. Grover, *Drieu la Rochelle and the Fiction of Testimony* (Berkeley, 1958); R. B. Leal, *Drieu la Rochelle* (Boston, 1982); R. Soucy, *Fascist intellectual: Drieu la Rochelle* (Berkeley, 1979).

M. J. Green

Related entries: FASCISM; NOVEL, POLITICS AND THE.

DRUMONT, EDOUARD (1844–1917), anti-Semitic journalist. At age forty-two he gained notoriety for his book, *La France juive* (1886). The book, based on the anti-Semitic theory of Count Arthur de Gobineau (1816–82), argued that France was being ruled by Jewish interests, alien to its ethnic and cultural origins. Drumont called for a "France for the French" and proposed that French citizenship be restricted to those with at least four generations of French ancestors.

Drumont, in *La France juive*, was also trying to account for the fall of the Catholic bank L'Union Générale four years earlier. The publication of his book made him the most notorious anti-Semite of his generation. Although he had earlier adopted a reformist social philosophy as a writer for *La Liberté*—which had been published by Isaac Pereire, a Saint-Simonian and a Jew—Drumont from 1886 to 1902 became increasingly conservative, ultramontanist, and nationalistic as well as anti-Semitic.

In 1889 he launched the Ligue national antisémitique de France, dedicated to pursuing politically the ends envisioned in his book. He also founded *La Libre Parole* (1892) whose journalistic efforts were in large part responsible for the exposé known as the Panama affair. Two years later, with readership declining, *La Libre Parole* broke the story of the arrest and alleged treason of Captain Alfred Dreyfus.

Drumont stood by his story even as the forces of revision gathered strength. In 1898 he permitted the more violent and even less scrupulous Jules Guérin to eclipse him as France's premier Jew hater. In that year he took his anti-Semitic campaign to Algeria, whose citizens elected him to the Chamber of Deputies. Drumont served in the Chamber for four years, returned to literary-journalistic affairs in 1902, and was denied membership in the Académie française in 1909. He died in 1917.

G. Bernanos, *La Grande Peur des bien-pensants* (Paris, 1931); R. F. Byrnes, *Anti-Semitism in Modern France* (New Brunswick, N.J., 1950); L. Daudet, *Les Oeuvres dans les hommes* (Paris, 1922); L. Poliakov, *Histoire de l'antisémitisme* (Paris, 1968).

P. M. Rutkoff

Related entries: ANTISEMITIC LEAGUE; ANTI-SEMITISM; DREYFUS AFFAIR; GUERIN.

DUCHAMP, MARCEL (1887–1968), artist. Born in Blainville (Seine-Inférieure) in 1887, he came from an artistic family; his sister (Suzanne Duchamp) and two brothers (Jacques Villon and Raymond Duchamp-Villon) were also well-known artists. He attended the lycée Rouen and at a young age moved to Paris, where he taught himself to paint. Until 1910 he made his living by drawing caricatures.

His first major work was an original combination of cubism and futurism, *Nude Descending a Staircase*. First shown in New York City in 1913, the painting was the center of controversy and scandal. As the inventor of ready-mades (1915), common everyday objects on which he bestowed the name *art*, Duchamp anticipated dadaism. The two most famous of his ready-mades were a bicycle mounted on a stool, and a urinal entitled *Fountain*. These works, along with others such as his *L.H.O.O.Q.* (a painting of the Mona Lisa, with beard and mustache) won him considerable notoriety.

After 1915, he lived in New York. Cofounder of the Société anonyme (New York, 1920) and of the review *VVV* (1940–42), he was, with Francis Picabia, a leader of the New York dada movement and was closely related with the surrealists, though his independence kept him from aligning himself totally with any one group or movement. He was an artist capable of abstract, cubist, dadaist, futurist, and surrealist works.

From 1915 to 1923 he worked on his most important work, *The Bride Stripped Bare by Her Bachelors, Even,* a painting on glass he never completed. He gave up painting in 1923, turning to chess, and never worked seriously as an artist again, producing but a few ready-mades under the pseudonym Rrose Sélavy (a play on words for *arroser, c'est la vie*). He died outside Paris on 2 October 1968 and bequeathed almost all of his works to the Philadelphia Museum of Art.

M. Duchamp, *abecedaire* (Paris, 1977); J. Gough-Cooper, *Plan pour écrire une vie de Marcel Duchamp* (Paris, 1977); R. Lebel, *Marcel Duchamp* (New York, 1959); A. G. Marquis, *Marcel Duchamp: Eros. C'est la vie. A Biography* (Troy, N.Y., 1981); B. Meyers, *McGraw-Hill Dictionary of Art*, vol. 2 (New York, 1969); C. Tomkins, *The World of Marcel Duchamp* (New York, 1966).

A. J. Staples

Related entries: ART: MAJOR STYLES AND MOVEMENTS; CUBISM; DADAISM; PICABIA; SURREALISM.

DUCLOS, JACQUES (1896–1975), journalist, politician, and Communist leader. Like Maurice Thorez with whom his life was inextricably linked, he found in communism the means by which humble origins could be transcended and a career in journalism and politics achieved. Duclos was born 2 October 1896 in the town of Louey (Hautes-Pyrénées). His innkeeper family spoke dialect, Duclos learning his meridionally accented French in school. Apprenticed to a pastry cook, Duclos went to Paris to practice his trade, working in a bakery there and involving himself in socialist politics until 1914 when he was drafted into the army. The years in the trenches traumatized Duclos. Only lightly wounded himself, his brother returned from the war horribly disfigured. Captured in April

1917, Duclos heard of the Russian Revolution while laboring in Germany and immediately rallied to the Bolshevik cause. After his release at war's end, Duclos became a stalwart of the communist war veteran's association, serving as its president for most of his life. Duclos joined the Socialist party in 1919, followed the majority into the French Communist party (PCF) after the Congress of Tours in December 1920, and become party secretary of Paris' Tenth Arrondissement. He was first a candidate for the Chamber of Deputies in 1924 and was successfully elected in a by-election in 1926. In the interim he had completed a course of study in the first party school. Duclos quickly established a reputation in the Chamber as a gifted if bitingly sarcastic orator. He entered the PCF Central Committee in 1926 and was reelected a deputy in 1928, defeating Léon Blum. Duclos was a fugitive from justice for much of his second term, however, owing to his antiwar activities.

In 1931 Duclos entered both the Political Bureau and the Party Secretariat, where he supported Moscow's effort to regain control of the PCF after the sectarian Barbé-Celor interlude. He was defeated in the 1932 elections but was chosen for the executive bureau of the Communist International, where he assumed major responsibility for several of the West European Communist parties. Duclos, with Thorez, negotiated the unity-of-action pact with the Socialists in 1934, and he prepared the way for the Spanish Popular Front while on a mission to Spain in 1935. Elected to a safe parliamentary seat in 1936, Duclos became secretary of the Communist parliamentary group, the leading party spokesman in parliament, and vice-president of the Chamber of Deputies. After the Nazi-Soviet pact and Thorez's departure for Moscow, Duclos assumed leadership of the clandestine Communist party, guiding it through both its collaborationist (1939–41) and resistance (1941–44) activities. Unequalled in his mastery of French politics, Duclos remained the principal client of the Russians in France, and his name remains tied to the Stalinist phenomenon. Short, corpulent, jovial, and grandfatherly, he projected a benign public image, which led his party to present him as its presidential candidate in 1969. His importance in the PCF leadership, however, declined after Stalin's death in 1953.

J. Duclos, *Memoires*, 6 vols. (Paris, 1968–74), I. Wall, *French Communism in the Era of Stalin* (Westport, Conn., 1983).

I. M. Wall

Related entries: COMMUNIST PARTY; THOREZ.

DUFAURE, JULES (1798–1881), lawyer and moderate republican leader in the early years of the Third Republic. He was close ideologically and personally to Alexis de Tocqueville and was well known for his role in the 1848 republican government, as well as for his liberal opposition to the governments of the Second Empire.

A member of the Académie française from 1864, he was elected to the National Assembly in 1871 and played an important role in the formation of the Third Republic. Minister of Justice (1871–73) under Adolphe Thiers, he initiated reform of the judiciary, established laws for jury trials, reorganized the Conseil d'état, and led the prosecution of the Communards. At the same post in 1875, he influenced legislation regarding the establishment of electoral rules.

Dufaure supported the Wallon amendment (1875) and was elected senator for life in 1876. Between 1871 and 1879, he was three times chief of cabinet. In his third ministry (December 1877–February 1879), he pressed cautiously to take advantage of the republican victory in the *seize mai* crisis (1877). His effort to force the retirement of generals of doubtful republicanism led to the resignation of President Maurice de MacMahon (1879). His own cabinet fell shortly after. Somewhat too conservative to align himself with Léon Gambetta's Opportunist republicans, he ended his political career in 1879 and died in Reuil on 27 June 1881.

F. Brabant, *The Beginning of the Third Republic* (N. Y., 1972); J. Chastenet, *Cent ans de la République*, vol. 1 (Paris, 1970); R. D'Amat, ed., *Dictionnaire de biographie française*, vol. 11 (Paris, 1967); G. Picot, *Etudes d'histoire parlementaire: M. Dufaure, sa vie et ses discours* (Paris, 1883); R. Recouly, *The Third Republic* (New York, 1967).

A. J. Staples

Related entries: GAMBETTA; MACMAHON; NATIONAL ASSEMBLY; *SEIZE MAI* CRISIS; THIERS.

DUFY, RAOUL (1877–1953), fauve painter and designer. One of nine children of a poor but highly musical family of Le Havre, he left school at fourteen to earn a living, working for a coffee importer and studying painting at night at the Le Havre Municipal Art School. On a municipal scholarship, he went to Paris in 1900 for study at the Ecole des beaux-arts, settling in Montmartre. Despite the conservative training at the Ecole, he was soon influenced by the impressionists, especially Henri Toulouse-Lautrec, whose method of outlining his figures shaped Dufy's drawing style. Under the influence of Henri Matisse, Dufy became a fauve, though he was to retain a more structured drawing and composition than either the other fauves or the German expressionists, who were another influence, as was Paul Cézanne. He preferred subjects of leisure, amusement, gaiety: streets decorated for festivals, seaside scenes, the cityscape.

After 1912, Dufy's style lightened. His most characteristic works, painted between 1920 and 1940, feature strong drawing in sweeping, supple arabesques that function independently of planes of highly saturated color. He was a chronicler of the pastimes of the monied in the interwar period. He had a strong interest in decorative art, beginning in 1910. He illustrated many books (Apollinaire's *Le Bestiaire*, 1910; Alphonse Daudet's *Tartarin de Tarascon*, 1937); designed fabrics for the couturier Paul Poiret (1911–14) and for the Lyons silk firm Bianchini-Ferrier (1912–30); executed theatrical decors (Darius Milhaud's *Le Boeuf sur le toit*, 1920); and designed furniture, tapestries, and ceramics. For the Exposition des arts décoratifs in 1925 he designed fabrics for three barges displayed by Poiret. For the 1937 Paris Exposition universelle he produced an immense mural (60 by 10 meters) depicting the history of electricity.

P. Courthion, *Raoul Dufy* (Geneva, 1951); M. Laffaille, *Raoul Dufy. Catalogue raisonné de l'oeuvre peint* (Geneva, 1972–77); A. Werner, *Raoul Dufy* (New York, [1970]).

T. Shapiro

Related entries: ART: MAJOR STYLES AND MOVEMENTS; FAUVISM; MATISSE; TOULOUSE-LAUTREC.

DUHAMEL, GEORGES (1884–1966), biologist, doctor, surgeon, man of letters, lover of nature, patriot, and social critic. Trained both as a physician and a biologist, Duhamel worked in laboratory research before committing himself completely to a literary career. During World War I, however, he spent fifty-one months treating 4,000 casualties at the front and operating more than 3,000 times in a mobile surgical unit. Between the wars Duhamel tried to encourage harmony between France and Germany, but in 1939, his *Mémorial de la guerre blanche* denounced pacifism as an unacceptable response to Hitler and national socialism. Duhamel returned to surgery in the spring of 1940, treating the civilian victims of German aerial warfare. In the same year, the Nazis seized and burned three Duhamel books: *Positions françaises* (1940), *Lieu d'asile* (1940), and one of his masterpieces, *Civilisation 1914–1917*. The last (1918) constitutes, together with *Vie des martyrs, 1914–1916* (1917), Duhamel's eloquent tribute to the soldiers of World War I.

Even in peacetime, Duhamel was an unequivocal critic of twentieth-century technology, particularly mechanization, not in itself but as man's new idol. He was against the materialism of both the U.S.S.R. and the United States, but most scholars feel he was unfair to the United States when, in 1930, he published *Scènes de la vie future*, a scathing denunciation, which was awarded the Grand prix de l'Académie française. While Duhamel did revise his evaluation of the United States during another trip in 1945, his attack on the ubiquitous ugliness, noise, erosion, and pollution of modern life has been corroborated in the nearly fifty years since he wrote *Querelles de famille* (1932) and *L'Humaniste et l'automate* (1933). Duhamel was a scientist who, like Pascal, believed that reason and intellect have their limitations.

From an aesthetic standpoint, Duhamel's fame will rest on two fictional chronicles, *Vie et aventures de Salavin*, five volumes published between 1920 and 1932, and the *Chronique des Pasquiers*, ten volumes published between 1933 and 1944. The latter traces the rise of a lower-middle-class family from respectable poverty to material and professional success. The *Salavin* series is less traditional in theme and style. Particularly in *Confession de minuit* (1920) and *Journal de Salavin* (1927), the protagonist's seeming indifference but actual anguish, the meaning of existence, and the question of agnostic saintliness make Duhamel's hero a precursor of existentialist fiction.

Despite being a cooperative academician in learned societies, Duhamel stressed individualism, especially after the failure of the artistic, utopian community, l'Abbaye de Créteil (1905–1908).

Georges Duhamel (1884–1966) (Paris, 1967); L. C. Keating, *Critic of Civilization: Georges Duhamel and His Writings* (Lexington, Ky., 1965); B. Knapp, *Georges Duhamel* (New York, 1972).

                                                                                C. F. Gerrard

Related entry: NOVEL, POLITICS AND THE.

DUMAS, ALEXANDRE (DUMAS *fils*) (1824–1895), playwright whose dramas were among the most successful on the French stage throughout the second half of the nineteenth century. Born in Paris as the illegitimate son of Alexandre Dumas *père* and a seamstress, Alexandre Dumas *fils* turned to literature as a young man to earn a living and to express his ideas on social problems. He went on to become one of the most successful dramatists of the Second Empire and early Third Republic. After a volume of poetry, he published several novels; he soon adapted the most important one, *La Dame aux camélias* (1848), into a play of the same title (1852). This was one of the greatest theatrical hits of the nineteenth century in France and remains the best and most durable of all his dramatic works; further, it was the inspiration for Verdi's opera, *La Traviata* (1853).

Influenced by Saint-Simonism and positivism, Dumas *fils* became a strong proponent of utilitarian theater. Against art for art's sake, which he found meaningless, he thought drama should direct consciences, denounce social ills, and propound social virtues. His realistic "problem plays" or *pièces à thèse* attacked such vices and injustices as prejudice against illegitimate children (*Le Fils naturel* [1858], inspired by his own difficulties), the harm inflicted by unforgiving attitudes toward past transgressions (*Denise* [1885]), greedy financiers (*La Question d'argent* [1857]), marriage laws tying women to unfaithful husbands (*La Princesse Georges* [1871]), adulterous wives (*La Femme de Claude* [1873] in which the husband was justified in murdering such a spouse), and dissolute husbands (*Francillon* [1887]). In general, he promoted marital fidelity and the sacredness of the family and frequently denounced prostitution and the demimonde. His plays revealed a talent for dialogue, characterization, and logical and tightly knit construction, but they were flawed by heavy-handed didacticism, moralizing verbosity, and oversimplification of good and evil. Later in his career, he also collaborated on plays with George Sand, Emile de Girardin, and others. He wrote numerous polemical prefaces and brochures as well on such social, moral, and judicial questions as divorce, paternity, and the roles of husband and wife. He was elected to the Académie française in 1874.

Dumas *fils* had a very large audience; some contemporaries went so far as to consider him a major thinker of his era. However, his reputation has paled considerably over the course of the twentieth century. With the exception of *La Dame aux camélias*, his work is now viewed as being principally of historical interest.

P. Lamy, *Le Théâtre d'Alexandre Dumas fils* (Paris, 1928); H. Lyonnet, *"La Dame aux camélias" d'Alexandre Dumas, fils* (Paris, 1930); A. Maurois, *Les Trois Dumas*

(Paris, 1957); H. S. Schwartz, *Alexandre Dumas fils, Dramatist* (New York, 1927); F. A. Taylor, *The Theatre of Alexandre Dumas fils* (Oxford, 1937).

G. Crichfield

Related entries: GIRARDIN; LITERATURE; MARRIAGE; OPPORTUNISTS; POSITIVISM; PROSTITUTION; SAINT-SIMONISM; SAND; WOMEN: ATTITUDES TOWARD.

DUPANLOUP, FELIX (1802–1878), bishop, polemicist, senator. Born in Savoy the son of a peasant girl, he mixed in the fashionable circles of Paris as a young priest, becoming confessor and teacher of high nobles, director of St. Nicolas du Chardonnet (the seminary of Paris), and professor of sacred scripture at the Sorbonne in 1841, only to be suspended from the post for attacks on his *bête-noire*, Voltaire. In 1849, he gained the episcopacy of Orléans where his eloquence and talents made him a dominant figure within the French church, education, and politics for the next three decades. A liberal Gallican within the church but also a monarchist and a defender of the social order, Dupanloup searched for an accommodation with a secular order he disliked while retaining a nostalgic preference for Catholic France of the seventeenth century. Becoming a senator in 1871, he supported the restoration of the Bourbon monarchy but also urged the comte de Chambord to reign under the tricolor. As a member of the National Assembly, Dupanloup attempted to disassociate the French church from Vatican politics and to reassert its social and political role in France.

Mgr. Dupanloup was a preponderant figure in Catholic education: as a member of the Falloux Commission, as standard-bearer in the Catholic advocacy of liberty of higher education in 1875, and as a promoter of Catholic schools within his diocese. Throughout his life, he remained a defender of traditions of Catholic classical humanism—against Abbé Joseph Gaume's call (1852) for the exclusion of all "pagan learning" in schools; in 1876 against Jules Simon's efforts to substitute modern subjects. The themes enunciated in his three-volume *De l'éducation* (1849) continued to influence the policies governing Catholic secondary education at the time of his death.

Like most other French intellectuals of his time, Dupanloup believed that students had predestined occupational roles for which there was an appropriate education: primary for the "popular" classes, vocational for the "intermediate," literary for the "upper." Consequently, Dupanloup never questioned the structure of French schooling, only its moral direction. An elitist who acknowledged individual mobility, Dupanloup wrote mainly about secondary and higher education. Although he shared Catholics' emphasis on parental authority as prior and superior to the authority of the state, his concerns about increasing secularism in society and the malleability of children led him to recommend a greater emphasis on boarding schools.

In his own diocese, he established a modern administrative machinery, encouraged libraries, sodalities, and retreats, built schools and churches, and demanded good conduct from his priests. His self-stated goal was to rechristianize a diocese in which only one man in forty had been making the Easter Duty. During his episcopate, the physical and financial state of the diocese improved, as did priestly conduct; vocations rose while superstitious beliefs declined. After his death, the administrative machinery functioned less well. His success was ephemeral, barely lasting his lifetime. His larger hope for reconciliation of the church with the modern world must be deemed a failure.

Dupanloup was not a supporter of Vactican politics. He did not favor retention of the papal states and opposed in the National Assembly attempts to "recover Rome." His explanation of the infamous Syllabus of Errors as an ideal that was impracticable and impossible to implement rendered the encyclical innocuous and became a model adopted by liberal prelates throughout the world. At Vatican Council I he was a member of the *non expedit* group who accepted a doctrine of papal infallibility but opposed its proclamation. Although the French government promoted Dupanloup to succeed Darboy as archbishop of Paris, the opposition of the Vatican and French conservatives scuttled the idea.

A controversial man, Dupanloup made and lost friends and enemies within and outside of the church. A part of the intellectual establishment with membership in the Académie française, he was anathema to many within it. He has been harshly treated by conservative Catholics and anticlerical republicans alike because he searched for ways to reconcile mutually prejudiced, uncompromising, and irreconcilable groups. He became an obstructionist, a recalcitrant and obstreperous old man. His last battle was an unsuccessful attempt in 1878 to forestall public celebration of the centenary of Voltaire's death. Louis Veuillot's judgment that he failed in everything he did was too harsh; he was a greater success than was Veuillot. But his successes were short term. He could not reestablish the Catholic France of the seventeenth century, and in his dotage he forgot his professed goal of reconciling church and modern society.

C. Marcilhacy, *Le Diocèse d'Orléans sous l'épiscopat de Mgr. Dupanloup, 1849–1878* (Paris, 1962)

P. J. Harrigan

Related entries: ROMAN CATHOLICISM: CHURCH-STATE RELATIONS; SCHOOLS, ROMAN CATHOLIC; SCHOOLS, SECONDARY: *COLLEGES.*

DUPUY, CHARLES-ALEXANDRE (1851–1923), deputy, senator, prime minister, teacher, born in Le Puy (Haute–Loire). He passed the *agrégation* in philosophy (1879) but left teaching (1872–80) and educational administration (1880–85) for politics. He served as deputy (1885–1900), senator (1900–23), minister of education, fine arts, and religion (1892–93), and five times as prime minister between 1893 and 1899. Once elected, he rapidly gained influence in parliament, serving on commissions and as president of the Chamber of Deputies (1893–94). He presided the day the anarchist Auguste Vaillant hurled a bomb from the gallery, and stories of his orders to carry on enhanced his reputation for capable leadership. His integrity and his ability to persuade moderates and radicals to cooperate also explain his influence.

His cabinets spanned a period of diplomatic realignment and of domestic turmoil produced by social unrest and the Dreyfus affair. His first government (4 April–25 November 1893) repressed socialist demonstrations at home and courted Russia abroad. When the 1893 elections returned a moderate majority, his cabinet split, and Dupuy resigned. He returned the next spring (30 May) with a moderate cabinet and governed until President Sadi Carnot's assassination (27 June). The new president, Jean-Paul Casimir-Périer, invited Dupuy to remain (1 July), and his cabinet organized an expedition to Madagascar and passed stiff antianarchist laws. The Chamber overturned it unexpectedly (14 January 1895) over the issue of state contracts with the railroad companies.

At the height of the Dreyfus affair, he formed a cabinet (1 November 1898) committed to defending the army's prestige and to settling the Dreyfus case through the courts. The cabinet resigned when President Félix Faure died (18 February) and then returned under his successor, Emile Loubet. Dupuy presided over French withdrawal from Fashoda (November 1898) and reached agreement with England over African spheres of influence (March 1899). In a move condemned by the Dreyfusards, his government changed the judicial review procedures, but the United Appeals Court finally ordered revision (3 June 1899). The next day, right-wing gentlemen attacked President Loubet at the Auteuil horse races. When police intervened a week later against left-wing demonstrations hailing Loubet, Dupuy's majority collapsed (12 June).

Dupuy moved to the Senate in 1900, but his position during the Dreyfus affair, his campaign against the separation of church and state (1905), and his hostility to socialism isolated him from former allies and reduced his political influence.

A. Rivet, "La Jeunesse de Charles Dupuy," "La Carrière gouvernementale de Charles Dupuy," "Charles Dupuy dans son département," *Cahiers de la Haute Loire* (1974–76).

S. A. Ashley

Related entries: DREYFUS AFFAIR; FASHODA INCIDENT; OPPORTUN-ISTS; PROGRESSISTS.

DURAND, MARGUERITE (1864–1936), actress, journalist, feminist militant. The namesake and 1931 benefactor of the excellent feminist repository in the town hall of Paris' Fifth Arrondissement, she first achieved public recognition in the 1880s as an actress at the Comédie-française and then, abandoning the stage in order to marry deputy Georges Laguerre, as the "Madame Roland of Boulangism." Soon separated from Laguerre and later divorced, she turned full time to journalism, which brought her an assignment from *Le Figaro* in 1896 to cover the fourth French Congrès féministe international. Impressed by what she observed, Durand resolved to make the cause that she had come to cover her own.

A year later Durand's resolution assumed tangible form in *La Fronde* (1897–1905), the first daily newspaper entirely run by women. Intended to demonstrate the competence of women as well as to advance their cause, *La Fronde*, with an initial run of 200,000 copies, provided a forum through which women could reach a general audience. Stridently republican in tone, *La Fronde* eventually played a highly influential political role as a voice of Dreyfusardism. As a feminist tribune, *La Fronde* played an equally influential role in securing in 1900 the first governmental sponsorship of a feminist congress and a seat law requiring employers to provide chairs for sales personnel. Through *La Fronde*, Durand also helped to obtain such reforms as women's right to full status at the Ecole des beaux-arts, admission to the French bar, and equal consideration for the Légion d'honneur. Indeed, simply covering the news provoked a successful struggle by *La Fronde's* reporters for access to the male-only press facilities of the Chamber, Senate, Municipal Council, and Bourse.

Although Durand never abandoned journalism and even attempted in 1914 and again in 1926 to revive *La Fronde*, she also never limited her feminism to propaganda. Concerned with the plight of working women, she helped to found several women's unions, successfully sued the Bourse du travail to admit *La Fronde's* Syndicat des femmes typographes, and organized in 1907 the first Congrès du travail féminin. In 1910 she protested against women's disenfranchisement by posing a shadow candidacy for the Chamber in Paris' ninth arrondissement. During the First World War, despite expressing what critics castigated as pro-German pacifism in *Les Nouvelles* (which she directed with Jacques Stern from 1909 to 1914), Durand organized the Club féministe automobile to transport wounded soldiers.

In 1922 Durand hosted an Exposition des femmes célèbres du XIXe siècle, one purpose of which was to raise money for a rest home comparable to the male-only Maison des journalistes hommes. Success came when, after Séverine's death in 1928, Durand purchased her home at Pierrefonds, renamed it "Les Trois Marches," and opened it to her former colleagues. She also helped to organize the 1929 Etats généraux du féminisme. Always involved in party politics, Durand in 1930 served on the Commission administrative du parti républicaine-socialiste. Aside from the still-functioning Bibliothèque Marguerite Durand and from the general influence she exercised and the example she set, Durand launched another still functioning project: a pet cemetery that, reflecting the concern for moral regeneration of many nineteenth-century feminists, she founded at Asnières in 1899.

M. Colin, *Ce n'est pas d'aujourd'hui* (Paris, 1975); *Dictionnaire de biographie française*, vol. 12 (Paris, 1968); J. McMillan, *Housewife or Harlot* (New York, 1981); *Minerva*, 9 November 1930.

P. K. Bidelman

Related entry: FEMINISM.

DURKHEIM, EMILE (1858–1917), principal founder of modern sociology in France. The methodology of his work defined sociology as an empirical science, while the development of a closely knit team of collaborators and disciples, and his influential academic position furthered the new discipline's acceptance.

Born in Epinal (Vosges) of a poor but respected rabbinical family, Durkheim rejected his father's vocation, although his later concerns suggest that he pursued similar goals within a larger, secular context. A serious worker and somber personality, it was only with difficulty that Durkheim entered and graduated from the Ecole normale supérieure (class of 1879), a school whose intellectual atmosphere he labeled superficial. While majoring in philosophy, however, he came under the influence of Fustel de Coulanges and read deeply Herbert Spencer, Charles Renouvier, and Auguste Comte. Durkheim taught philosophy for several years at the secondary level, but his predilection for the social sciences received reinforcement from a leave of absence to study in Germany (1885–86). The three articles he wrote on the social sciences in that country secured him a post at the faculty of Bordeaux (1887) where he became a colleague of the sociologist Alfred Espinas.

During the next few years Durkheim published his major books. His thesis, "De la division du travail social" (1893), referred to a "collective conscience" and demonstrated how in advanced societies individual development related closely to social ties. *Règles de la méthode sociologique* (1894) reemphasized society's role and argued for sociology's independence from both philosophy and psychology, inasmuch as social facts were social things that the individual alone could not determine. *Le Suicide* (1897) attributed even the taking of one's life to social causes and provided a model for the type of fact-filled study that Durkheim favored. It appeared the same year that he founded *L'Année sociologique*, a collaborative journal about which his school of sociology formed and whose reviews and studies ranged from anthropology and the study of religions to critical philosophy.

The advancement of Durkheim's career coincided with efforts undertaken to modernize French education and to create a secular code of morality that could guide society in the new industrial era. Durkheim's sociology claimed to accomplish these ends by its scientific validity and its sensitivity to social crises accompanying society's evolution. Although Durkheim, a former classmate and friend of Jaurès, was socialist in his sympathies, he opposed class conflict, and his appreciation of society's collective constraints allied sociology to the more conservative movement in behalf of solidarity.

In 1902 Vice-Rector Louis Liard summoned Durkheim to the Sorbonne as a replacement for Ferdinand Buisson to teach the science of education, a chair to which he was permanently assigned in 1906 and which became the chair in education and sociology in 1913. Durkheim now devoted his attention primarily to teaching and to his journal. The only other major publication to appear in his lifetime—his lectures on education being published posthumously—was *Les Formes élémentaires de la vie religieuse* (1912). Religion increasingly had preoccupied him since 1896, the period of the Dreyfus affair and of his father's death. Durkheim exercised great influence within the Sorbonne in the decade preceding World War I and served on the university's council. The burden of additional wartime responsibilities, and the loss of his only son at the front, undoubtedly contributed to his own death in November 1917.

R. Bourdon, "Durkheim (Emile)," *Encyclopaedia Universalis*, Vol. 5 (Paris, 1975); A. Giddens, *Emile Durkheim* (New York, 1979); S. Lukes, *Emile Durkheim* (New York, 1972); Y. Nandan, *The Durkheimian School* (Westport, Conn., 1977); *Revue française de sociologie* 20 (1979).

L. M. Greenberg

Related entries: BUISSON; LIARD; POSITIVISM; SOLIDARISM.

E

ECONOMIC POLICY. The government of the Third Republic influenced economic activity in France through tariffs and trade policy, public works policies, banking and insurance regulations, and labor legislation; through the subsidization and regulation of some industries (shipbuilding, transport, mining, wine and sugar); and through the ownership and management of others (tobacco and matches, arms and munitions, the state rail system). Unlike later French regimes, the Third Republic never developed a comprehensive policy to encourage economic growth and modernization. Instead parliament made policy in each area on an ad hoc basis, often in response to political pressure and lobbying by the affected interests. The goal of most policies was conservative: to protect acquired positions, especially those of small and middle-sized producers; to preserve the traditional balance among agriculture, industry, and commerce; and in general to promote social as well as economic stability.

1871–1914. The tariff was the chief element in French economic policy before World War I. The Third Republic inherited the liberal tariff policy of the Second Empire in which a schedule of relatively low conventional duties, established in a series of bilateral trade treaties, had superseded the ultraprotectionist duties in the general tariff legislated earlier in the nineteenth century. Despite the efforts of President Adolphe Thiers to move France back toward high protection in 1871–73, the Third Republic sustained and extended the free trade policy of Napoleon III in the new general tariff of 1881 and the new trade treaties ratified in 1882. However, amid depression and the return to protection by other European countries in the 1880s, France moved away from free trade, starting with the legislation of higher import duties on livestock and foodstuffs and the tariff assimilation of its colonies (in effect, reserving them as markets for French goods). In 1892, passage of the Méline Tariff scrapped the system of trade treaties and substituted a legislated double tariff in which the minimum duties were granted only to countries offering France most-favored-nation status. Such reciprocal preferential treatment was eventually established with most other

European countries, although, in the case of Italy and Switzerland, only after a series of tariff wars. The Méline Tariff provided greater tariff protection for French farmers and some manufacturers, notably cotton spinners, but maintained low duties on raw materials and producer goods such as coal and steel. The Tariff of 1910 continued the minimum-maximum system while raising the level of both agricultural and industrial duties. Overall between 1871 and 1914, the Third Republic maintained relative free trade in industrial raw materials, moved toward greater protection of some producer goods (such as cotton yarn), and consistently provided high protection for finished manufactures. In agriculture, it moved from free trade to high protection as French farmers lost foreign markets and faced a growing threat to their domestic market from foreign products (U.S. wheat and livestock, Italian wine).

Next to tariffs, government policies dealing with transportation had the greatest impact on French economic development between 1870 and 1914. With the Freycinet Plan (1878–83), the Third Republic greatly expanded the national rail network and modernized the canal system so that most parts of the country were integrated into a truly national market by the 1890s. Meanwhile, the conventions with the railroad companies in 1883 gave the government increased influence over freight rates. By maintaining different rate schedules for the six major rail lines and by supporting the lowering of short-haul rates relative to long-haul rates, the government protected marginal producers operating in local markets from competitors in other parts of France while also protecting all domestic producers from foreign competitors. It similarly took a protectionistic approach to shipbuilding and the merchant marine. In 1881 parliament voted construction bounties to shipbuilders and navigation bounties to French shipowners. Since these bounties particularly favored the builders and operators of sailcraft, this policy contributed to France's failure to develop a modern steamer fleet and to its decline as a maritime power in the late nineteenth century.

A third important area of economic policy in the early Third Republic was labor regulation. While maintaining the long-standing pro-employer bias in French contract law and labor policy, the Third Republic assumed a larger role in the regulation of industrial employment. Notably an 1874 law created state inspectors to enforce earlier prohibitions on child labor in factories; an 1890 law abolished the *livret* (passport) system, which had previously restricted workers' freedom of movement and freedom of choice; laws in 1892, 1900, and 1905 reduced the maximum workday for children, women, and miners; and legislation in 1898 set up mandatory workmen's compensation insurance.

1914–1940. During the First World War, the focus of French economic policy shifted from the defense of private business interests to the marshaling of the nation's resources for total war, and by 1917 the tradition of laissez-faire had given way to unprecedented government control and management of the economy. In the name of national survival, various new authorities requisitioned and distributed food supplies and industrial raw materials, set wages and prices, managed foreign trade, monitored currency exchange, subsidized war industries, ran the railroads, and allocated the available work force to various employments. However, France quickly abandoned these wartime controls and dismantled the array of wartime agencies after the peace treaties were signed. By 1921, the prewar climate of economic freedom had been officially reestablished, and for much of French business, tariffs resumed their role as the chief element of economic policy. The 1920s saw a rapid rise in the level of import duties to offset the depreciation of the franc and the rise in prices. This was accomplished first by a set of multipliers applied to the tariff of 1910 and later by a comprehensive tariff convention with Germany in 1927. With the onset of the Great Depression and the widespread dumping of foreign goods in France, protective tariffs were augmented by a system of import quotas. First applied to agricultural products in 1931, these quotas were extended to most manufactures by the mid-1930s. Except for a brief experiment in trade liberalization by the Popular Front government in 1936, quotas remained the basis of French commercial policy to 1940.

As France moved toward more protectionistic, even autarkic, trade policies in the interwar years, it also embraced greater government control of the domestic economy in response to lingering problems caused by World War I and in spite of the reassertion of an official ideology of free enterprise. To finance postwar reconstruction, especially in the hard-hit northeast, the government created new state-run credit institutions (Crédit national, Crédit agricole), thereby permanently expanding the role of the public sector in banking and finance. Although renounced in 1919, state control of industry persisted, especially in transport. In the course of the 1920s and 1930s, the bankrupt railroads fell under increasing government tutelage and were finally nationalized in 1937. The Compagnie générale transatlantique (French Line) and Air France became state enterprises in 1932–33, and the government launched a national oil company, the Compagnie française des pétroles, to exploit the share of the Iraq oil fields acquired by France from Germany after the war (San Remo Agreement, 1922) and thereby to end France's dependence on outside suppliers of petroleum. The state also played an enlarged role in management of the chronically depressed wine, sugar, and alcohol industries after 1920. In 1923, the Service des alcools established a government monopoly in the distillation of industrial alcohol from beet sugar, and parliament mandated the use of this alcohol in motor fuel (*le carburant national*). In 1931 the government placed a ceiling on wine production and enforced mandatory distilling of surplus wine in order to keep prices up.

Stronger government policies to stabilize prices, promote production, and increase employment seemed unavoidable once the worldwide depression hit France in 1931. Yet for the next five years, the Radical-dominated parliament and cabinets did little to formulate such policies. Only with the advent of the Popular Front government of Léon Blum in 1936 did the state begin to assume responsibility for economic recovery. In 1936–37, Blum's government created the Ministry of the National Economy to coordinate government policy making; it nationalized the Banque de France and the munitions industry, as well as the railroads; it empowered the Wheat Office to buy up the annual harvest at fixed prices and to regulate grain imports and exports; and it sought to reflate the economy through public works spending, wage increases, and reduction of unemployment through enforcement of a forty-hour work week. These policies met strong opposition from much of French business, and many were renounced by the Camille Chautemps and Edouard Daladier governments in 1937–39. Still, the enlarged role of the state in economic management that emerged from World War I and the interwar years laid the foundation for the post–World War II system of state economic planning in France.

S. Clough, *France: History of National Economics* (New York, 1939); E. Golob, *The Méline Tariff* (New York, 1944); F. A. Haight, *A History of French Commercial Policies* (New York, 1941); *Histoire économique et sociale de la France*, vol. 4 (Paris, 1979–80); T. Kemp, *The French Economy, 1913–1939* (London, 1972); R. Kuisel, *Capitalism and the State in Modern France* (Cambridge, England, 1981); M. S. Smith, *Tariff Reform in France, 1860–1900* (Ithaca, 1980); C. K. Warner, *The Winegrowers of France and the Government since 1875* (New York, 1960).

M. S. Smith

Related entries: BANKS AND BANKING; BLUM; COMMERCE: FOREIGN; COMMERCE: RETAIL MERCHANTS; DEPRESSION OF THE 1930s; FREYCINET; INDUSTRY; LABOR MOVEMENT; MELINE; POPULAR FRONT; RAILROADS; SOCIAL REFORM: GOVERNMENT POLICIES AND ACTS; THIERS; VINICULTURE; WORLD WAR I: ECONOMIC ASPECTS.

ECONOMY. Growth, industrialization, and structural change are the main themes of the economic history of the Third Republic. These are recognized as such by all observers. Disagreement centers on the significance of these themes for fundamental, long-run transformation of the economy to a modern industrial form. This disagreement is reflected in at least two different periodizations of economic change. One sees the growth of national income, productivity, and structural transformation in spurts of short duration, bracketed by periods of economic stagnation or decline. Such periodization outlines the economic history of the Republic as a series of cyclical trends, commencing with the slowdown and stagnation of the 1880s and 1890s to 1896, followed by the first growth and industrialization spurt of 1896–1913 (the long crisis of 1901–5 excepted), interrupted by war and by the postwar adjustment and crisis to 1921, followed in turn by the second spurt of 1922–30, which was then sharply terminated by the depression of 1931–38, the latter consuming much of the fruit of previous growth. Such a view may be regarded as relatively pessimistic, for significant growth and structural change appear both exceptional and fragile and failed ultimately to remove the French economy from its nineteenth-century mold. Modern economic growth commenced, according to this view, only after 1950 and represented a sharp break with previous trends. Most defenders of the retardation–relative backwardness hypothesis about French industrialization and proponents of the malthusian interpretation of French growth, such as Alfred Sauvy, generally propose a variant of this periodization.

The second periodization emphasizes the continuity of these cycles of economic activity with preceding and subsequent growth and is therefore more optimistic. According to this view the economy of the Third Republic was situated at the transition from nineteenth-century development, characterized by secular falling prices, to twentieth-century growth, described as inflationary. The turning point was around 1896 or 1906. Until then industrialization proceeded amid rising productivity and increasing competition (both internal and external) in a context of stable monetary expansion, which translated into a slow decline of prices over the long run. Structural change during this period was limited, however; in particular, the share of the agrarian sector in product and employment remained quite large. After 1896–1906 the growth of productivity reflected a major change in economic structure. Growing demand put pressure on supply, and this fact, along with the monetary revolution and exchange depreciation after World War I, gave the period as a whole an inflationary hue. Only wartime controls and the depression of the 1930s produced a notable departure from this inflationary trend. This second period commenced the acceleration of the French growth rate culminating in the post-1950 harvest. Evidence for this second periodization has emerged from the continuous product series of the Institut de science économique appliqué (ISEA), under the direction of Jean Marczewski. Moreover, the studies of French growth in the twentieth century by J. J. Carré, P. Dubois, and E. Malinvaud generally conceive of French growth in this manner as well. The revisionist attack on the thesis of French retardation is also consistent with the same perspective, emphasizing the continuity between nineteenth- and twentieth-century growth.

Certain indicators of economic activity, subject as always to the errors or biases of overly broad aggregation and uncertain or missing data and to the possibility of several different readings, provide at least a general sense of the levels of activity and of the rates and components of change-defining periods in either case. Overall average annual per capita growth rates of national revenue (in constant francs) were of the following orders of magnitude: a high of 1.5–1.6 percent between 1830 and 1870—the peak period of nineteenth-century growth—followed by a decline after 1870 to 0.7 percent until the 1890s, followed in turn by a substantial rise to above 1.0 percent thereafter and culminating in a handsome 1.6 percent for the decade preceding World War I (Caron, based on ISEA and Sauvy). In terms of gross physical product, the mean annual growth rate declined gradually from a peak 2.4 percent between 1840 and 1860 to a rate above or near the 1815–24 to 1905–13 average of 1.5 percent through the 1870s. The rate subsequently fell below this average to 1896, after which recovery ensued at 1.8 percent (gross national product) to 1913 (Crouzet). During the 1920s average annual growth rates of gross domestic product were quite high, of the order of 7 percent in 1920–24 and 3 percent for 1924–29 (Carré et al.). After 1930 the rate fell sharply to negative values throughout most of the decade. Thus are defined cycles of slow growth and stagnation from 1860–70 to 1896, of recovery from 1896 to 1913, of intense growth during the 1920s, and of depression in the 1930s. Alternatively, average annual growth rates of 1.9 percent for 1896–1913 and of 1.7 percent for 1913–29 (Carré et al.) in gross domestic product suggest continuity over this period, while average annual rates of 1.5 percent for the period 1815–24 to 1905–13 in gross physical product (Crouzet), as compared with 1.7 percent for 1896–1929, 2.1 percent for 1929–63, and 4.6 percent for 1949–63 in total output (a concept close to GNP) (Carré et al.), underline the secular acceleration of growth since the nineteenth century.

Similar trends are evident in movements of industrial and agricultural product. For industry a decline of growth rates from 2 to 3 percent in the period 1815–65 to under 2 percent (1.6 percent according to Malinvaud) for 1870–96, recovering to 4 to 5 percent for 1906–13 and in the 1920s, followed by a negative rate of −1.1 percent for the 1930s, manifests the same general pattern. A rate of 2.4 percent per annum between 1896 and 1913 and of 2.6 percent between 1913 and 1929 (Carré et al.) reaffirms in French industrial history the continuity of the period after 1896. In agriculture the growth rate fell from around 1.1 percent between 1815–1819 and 1874–1878 to around 0.5 percent between 1874–78 and 1900–13, recovered to 1 percent during 1896–1913 and to 1.2 percent in 1924–29, and fell thereafter to 0.9 percent between 1929 and 1938. These figures reveal the sharp drop in the contribution of agriculture to growth throughout much of the Third Republic. This contrasted with its primary role in growth before this period and with its importance in French recovery after 1950. The great agrarian depression of the late nineteenth century was the main cause of this shift in agriculture's position. Transport, finally, grew more or less in tandem with industry but at slightly lower rates: around 1.8 percent before 1904, 2.7 percent between 1904 and 1913, around 3 percent between 1913 and 1929, and −1.7 percent between 1929 and 1938 (the last two periods include communications along with transport). Economic growth of the Third Republic was therefore concentrated largely in the industrial sector.

This focus on industry is reflected in a shift in the distribution of physical product between agriculture and industry, from around 60 percent agriculture, 40 percent industry in 1834–44 to 40 percent agriculture, 60 percent industry in 1905–13—in fact, a reversal of position. The relative shares remained around these levels during the interwar period, except for an increase in industry's share to 1929 and a probable decline during the 1930s. The distribution of the working population changed accordingly but not as dramatically before 1914, from 52 percent agriculture, 26 percent industry in 1840–45 to 43 percent agriculture, 28 percent industry in 1906. After the war the shift of working population to industry was more marked—to 33 percent as compared with 36 percent agriculture in 1931. In the transport and service sector, the share of working population was 22 percent in 1840–45, 28 percent in 1906, and 30 percent in 1931. Such movements suggest structural change as one of the sources of growth under the Third Republic.

Structural change was especially significant given the striking demographic stagnation of this period. While population had grown from 30 million to 36.5

million between 1816 and 1866, it increased to only 39.2 million by 1911 and to 41.9 million by 1931, despite the addition of nearly 1.7 million in three newly acquired departments at the end of the First World War. Mean annual rates of increase declined from about 0.50 percent between 1800 and 1850, to about 0.25 percent between 1846 and 1886, and to a mere 0.08 percent between 1886 and 1901. Beginning around 1900 the population growth rate recovered but not by much, to 0.20 percent through the late 1930s. As compared with rates of 1.10 percent, 0.80 percent, and 2.30 percent, respectively, for Britain, Germany, and the United States between 1850 and 1910, the French pace was barely a crawl.

The chief cause of stagnation was a secular decline in the birthrate, from 26 per thousand around 1850 to 14.8 per thousand by 1935–39; this decline was both earlier and steeper in France than in other industrial countries, where the rate was between 30 and 38 per thousand. The loss of 1.4 million to 1.5 million during the First World War, to which Sauvy adds another 1.4 million of wartime undernatality, constituted a further drain. Besides the direct effects of this loss on the size of population immediately after the war, the indirect impact on the birthrate of subsequent decades weakened the natural capacity of that population to grow then. Only a fall in mortality rates, notably during the 1890s and early 1900s, and immigration, especially during the 1920s, prevented population from falling absolutely. Indeed without the massive immigration of the 1920s, averaging 225,000 per year and making France second to the United States as a host country, population probably would have declined absolutely during this decade. Predictably these various demographic movements restricted the growth of the labor force rather severely. By one calculation, total working population increased from 16.2 million in 1952 to 17.4 million in 1882 and by 1896 reached 19.5 million. Between 1896 and 1931 it grew by no more than a million, accounted for largely by immigration. Between 1931 and 1936, partly due to slackening immigration—an effect of Malthusian labor policy by the government, among other causes—the labor force fell by more than a million. In short, population contributed very little to growth save as a stimulus for labor-saving investment. Moreover, as Sauvy emphasized, this population was progressively aging, and this characteristic may have explained a good part of the limited energy and vision with which French leaders and people responded to the crises of the interwar years, especially in the area of innovation.

In theory population contributes to growth in two ways: as a factor of production, enhancing output capacity, and as a market for final products, raising aggregate demand. Removing the demographic factor as a significant growth variable in either way raises the question of other sources of growth. On the side of production, growth is explained largely by a generally steady increase in efficiency-raising investment, in particular, that involving capitalization and mechanization of industry, and by a shift in working population to the more productive sectors of the economy. Both increased labor productivity to such an extent that significant growth was achieved despite the near stagnation of population. These factors operated especially strongly during the two major growth periods of the Third Republic: that of 1896 to 1913 and that of 1922 to 1929. Gross investment in fixed capital as a proportion of gross domestic production averaged annually 14.9 percent during the first period and 16.1 percent between 1922 and 1938; this proprotion reached a pre–World War II high of 18.3 percent and 20.8 percent, respectively, in 1929 and 1930. These were high investment levels not only for France but also in relation to other European countries and even to the United States. The character of this investment also had a strong positive impact on growth of productive capacity. The primary change before and after 1882 was a shift from basic investments in building and transport to a focus on industrial investments in plant, equipment, and power. The former laid the foundation of economy-wide productivity increases by lowering transport costs, increasing competition among industries and regions, and stimulating demand, mainly by widening markets. Such basic investments generated a type of industrial growth that might be described as nineteenth century: growth concentrated on consumer goods production with a large luxury or semiluxury component and catering to individualized tastes and local markets and on a limited expansion of heavy industries depending primarily on demand from the transport and urban public works sectors. The last burst of this type of investment was the biggest, the 4 billion franc Freycinet public works program of 1878–82.

Industrial investment, on the other hand, substituted capital for labor (hence capitalization) and expanded capacity and scale in producers' goods industries, especially metallurgy, chemicals, and mechanical and electrical industries; it fostered more extensive mechanization of certain consumers' goods industries, such as textiles; and it developed new sectors (electricity, petroleum) and new products (the automobile) with a relatively large capital component. This raised productivity in industries having the widest impact on the industrial sector as a whole and where, moreover, the probability of embodying the most advanced technique or leading product design was strongest. This investment pattern was reflected in the prominent place of capital equipment in the total investment package; this item more than doubled between 1905 and 1913 and nearly doubled again from 1913 to 1930, despite the war. As a result mechanization proceeded more rapidly in France than in England and the United States during this period, causing, more than any other factor, labor productivity to increase. Besides mechanization, the shift of workers into the more productive and capitalized sectors of the economy was a major cause of growing productivity, especially during the 1920s. Such a shift was the result of the rural exodus, of the deindustrialization of the countryside in most regions where industry had provided an important supplement to agrarian incomes, and of the decline of industrial crafts in favor of mechanized factory production. Together these factors induced an increase in the share of the labor force in industry, as compared with agriculture, in the new and highly capitalized industrial sectors, as compared with older, less efficient, and usually less concentrated sectors, and in the relatively capitalized and mechanized branches within a particular sector, as compared with their more labor-intensive counterparts. Both intensive investment in plant and machinery and structural change had their maximum impact during the 1920s, distinguishing this decade as the high-water mark of industrial capitalism under the Third Republic. The rate of growth of French industrial product then attained a level estimated by the Organization for Economic Cooperation and Development at a mean annual rate of 4.7 percent between 1924 and 1929, which was the highest in Europe. Within France itself the factory, the machine, and wage labor marked the industrial landscape with unprecedented clarity.

Significant pattern shifts also characterized movements of aggregate demand before and after 1880. Three sources of demand important in the earlier period—the expansion of agricultural product and incomes, the development of infrastructure (especially the building of railroads), and foreign trade—were secondary or negligible after 1880–84. The fall in agrarian incomes had the most negative impact on aggregate demand after 1880. Except during the 1920s and for a brief period in the decade before the First World War, the agricultural sector retreated from its earlier position as dynamic consumer of industrial products, even though it continued to harbor a large segment of France's population—between a half and a third. This retreat reflected the severity of the agrarian crises of the late nineteenth century and the resistance or inability of French peasants and farmers to make an adequate response. Ironically this was a period when the physical ties with urban markets and industry were closer than ever before as a result of the penetration of recently constructed rail and road networks deep into bourgs and villages. The agrarian crisis had three components: a sharp drop in prices, estimated at 33 percent for wheat, the main crop, between 1872–79 and 1892–96; a decline of output of the order of 0.80 percent annual average for foodstuffs between 1874–78 and 1889–93; and the destruction of the vine by the phylloxera epidemic (1875–1900), followed by overproduction and falling prices in the newly reconstituted wine industry (early 1900s). All three components produced a sharp depression in agrarian incomes, profits, and rents, which effectively diminished the capacity of the agrarian population to buy industrial products. The depression also discouraged investment in improvements in the sector, so that the technological level of French agriculture remained quite low even into the 1920s and 1930s. Indeed France was forced to rely on food imports to satisfy domestic needs. These provided 12 percent of domestic food consumption in 1913 and 25 percent in 1929–31. This was an especially striking development given the Méline tariff restrictions on food, which were maintained more or less continuously from 1892.

Foreign trade under the Third Republic departed from its earlier dynamism and leading position on the Continent. Before 1870 this sector had contributed significantly to French economic growth; the volume of foreign trade had accelerated progressively from around 13 percent of gross national product in 1830 to 30 to 40 percent in the 1860s. Export growth was especially strong, averaging an annual rate of 4.56 percent between 1815 and 1875; by 1860 French exports represented 60 percent of the total for Europe. This growth rested primarily on sales abroad of luxury, handcrafted items, notably textiles, rather than on exports of mass-produced manufactures. After 1875 exports grew by only 0.86 percent annual average to 1895 and recovered to only 2.74 percent average to 1913. By then the French share of European exports was a mere 12.6 percent. Luxury manufactures still prevailed in export sales, but apart from the motor car, where France gained a temporary supremacy, such manufactures no longer commanded the dominant position in world markets or even in French industry that had been their hallmark to 1870. French products also suffered from increasing competition, tariff barriers, and a shift toward colonial markets, where, outside of North Africa and Indochina, France's trading position was weak. Before World War I, then, exports no longer played the salient role in demand for French industrial products as they had before the Third Republic. They recovered during the 1920s, growing more rapidly than internal national product, as a result of productivity increases in export industries, low wage rates relative to those of France's major competitors, and the depreciation of the franc, which had its strongest stimulative impact on exports between 1924 and 1927. During this decade iron and steel products, machinery, and chemicals were added to the list of traditional exports, such as textiles, leather goods, and luxury manufactures, as major items of trade in foreign markets. Together with growing import volume, these restored France to a major position in world trade, where it ranked fourth overall. Thus trade and, especially, exports were significant components of aggregate demand spurring growth during the 1920s. In the subsequent decade, however, France lost this favorable position by adhering too long to the Raymond Poincaré franc while Britain and the United States devalued their currencies. After 1934 especially, France's trading position rapidly worsened as the export growth rate fell below that of internal product. Alongside this deterioration, sales to the French colonies intensified; these served as protected, privileged markets for French products, compensating somewhat for falling sales to the industrial world.

Imports generally held up better than exports throughout the Third Republic. Imports of agricultural products expanded up to the 1890s and grew, though less rapidly (because of protective tariffs), thereafter, except during the war. Industrialization, moreover, fostered increased imports through its needs for raw material, notably coal and textile fibers, and for capital equipment, which domestic resources or industry were unable to provide in sufficient quantities. Import growth was especially strong between 1905 and 1913, when it was correlated closely with industrial investment. In 1913 as much as 40 percent of French investment in mechanical and electrical products was supplied by imports, suggesting a certain dependence of French industrialization on the import sector. During the 1920s the same association between import expansion and industrial development was evident. Not surprisingly, a sizable trade deficit developed nearly every year before the war from intensive import demand coupled with a sluggish growth of exports. Only during the 1920s did exports perform well enough to reduce the trade deficit within range of balancing the trade account; in fact a trade surplus occasionally was realized during this period.

Normally, however, invisible earnings were required to save the overall balance of payments from deficit. Before the war these consisted largely of financial services of the Paris money market, second only to London as a world finance center, and of earnings on investments abroad. As is well known, the latter were quite extensive even before the Third Republic. Such investments quadrupled between 1880 and 1914, making France the world's second major capital exporter after Britain, and the total investment outlay earned more than enough income to fund each subsequent year's capital outflow. The geographical targets of this investment abroad were primarily Eastern and Central Europe, especially Russia after 1890, the Balkans, and the Americas, north and south. Among the primary destinations of previous investment, the Near East—especially the Ottoman Empire and Egypt—and southern Europe still harbored a significant share of the total outlay in 1914. Investments in these areas were primarily placements in fixed earnings securities, notably government bonds, and therefore were not necessarily motivated by the quest for higher returns per se. These were surely not funds seeking better industrial investment opportunities abroad than those offered by domestic industry. For this reason it is not only misleading but wrong to argue that French investors sacrificed the growth of domestic to foreign industry. Whether the French investment pattern reflected a diversion of capital, reducing supply for domestic purposes, or resulted from insufficient demand for outside capital by French firms—which did, by and large, finance investments from retained earnings—is still a matter of debate. Clearly capital movements and domestic investment were compartmentalized activities obeying different laws; financial institutions, notably banks, probably encouraged such separation of these two vital movements.

During the war most French assets abroad were consumed in the effort to finance the fighting; those lodged in Russia were immolated in the revolutionary conflagration of 1917, repudiated by the new Bolshevik regime along with all foreign debt. Emerging, moreover, from the war owing its allies a net sum of around 18 milliard francs, France was probably a debtor nation on balance, or at least very near to being such, whereas before the war it had been a leading creditor internationally. Renewed capital flows to Eastern Europe—only now to Poland, Rumania, Czechoslovakia, and Yugoslavia rather than to their eastern neighbor—and to the French colonies, especially Indochina and Morocco, restored some of the capital account abroad during the 1920s. The nature of these flows changed, moving more prominently into direct investment channels in industrial enterprise abroad than had prewar capital. Nonetheless, by 1931 the total sum of investment abroad amounted to no more than half that of 1913. This sum fell rapidly during the depression and with it the earnings that had previously helped to keep payments balanced. This factor, along with the steep drop in exports, left overall deficits on foreign account beginning in 1932; these remained a constant feature of the balance of payments throughout this depression decade, an unprecedented development. Payments deficits combined with speculative and politically motivated capital flights into short-term foreign securities during the Popular Front era forced the Léon Blum government to devalue the franc in September 1936 despite its earlier pledges not to do so. Only the Edouard Daladier government of 1938 could restore investors' confidence to check this flight of capital. Even so, neither this nor any other government could significantly reverse the trend toward deterioration of France's international position. France thus stood at the threshold of war not only weakened in its competitive trade position but also having less economic influence, through its investments abroad, than ever before within nearly a century.

Wellsprings of aggregate demand ran deep under the Third Republic, but their character was different from the agrarian, export, and transport investment demand of the preceding period. Urbanization, a product of the continuing rural exodus, and industrialization itself were two major sources after 1896. The first brought larger numbers of people into the market for consumers' goods and, especially between 1896 and 1913, stimulated urban infrastructure investment, including tramways and electrical generation for power and lighting. Such investment had a positive impact on demand for producers' goods as well as for consumables. Industrialization enhanced wage earners' incomes, notably those in cities where an increasing share of industry became located; these incomes induced more consumption, at least when inflation did not negate increased spending capacity of wage earners. Industrialization also created a specifically industrial demand for capital equipment, which stimulated domestic production and even exceeded the capacity of the latter, forcing some reliance on imports. This last fact was one indication of an important underlying structural feature of the Third Republican economy: the small size and rigidity of the productive base, limiting its capacity to respond sufficiently to demand once the sources of the latter were tapped. This characteristic, which might be conceived as a tautness of domestic production regarding aggregate demand, was especially signaled by the inflation accompanying industrialization under the Third Republic. Indeed inflation may have been the distinctive attribute of growth in this period.

Inflation was, however, not simply a consequence of growth. To some degree it may have been its cause, or at least a "grand permissive condition" (Bouvier et al., 2:641), especially during the 1920s. By then, inflation reflected, besides the pressure of excess demand on limited productive capacity, a transformation of the relationship of money to the economy, largely as a result of World War I and its aftermath. Before the war a fixed gold value of the franc (gold standard), long-run price stability, the pattern of international exchange, and the expansion and contraction of bank money in tandem with the rhythms of industrial growth generated monetary stability and a fixed exchange value of the franc without retarding economic progress. However, the war, reconstruction, indemnification of war victims, and the complexities of international trade and finance following the war, along with the illusions of German reparations to 1924, destabilized the relationship of money to the economy and injected into inflation a significant financial ingredient. The monetary revolution of the postwar era had several features, not all of which affected the economy in the same direction. Most prominent among these were the expansion of the monetary stock beyond the prewar gold cover, affecting the exchange value of the franc; the growth in volume and importance of bank notes (issued by the Bank of France), or fiduciary money, relative to bank money (commercial bank deposits and credits) in the total stock of money; the increasing part of government, especially government budget, in effecting monetary and currency (exchange) stability; and the inter-action of public opinion, perception, political ideology, and financial speculation as crucial determinants of major economic parameters, especially exchange rates. Implicitly these factors affected rates of economic growth by their impact on price levels, on import costs (and therefore, given the importance of imports to industry, on production costs), on export volume, and finally on the cost and supply of capital for investment. However, contemporaries generally perceived government finance and the security of rentier-type investments as the only affected parties; they were thus more preoccupied with means of funding the budget, with the distribution of the budgetary burden among the interested groups and social classes, and with the exchange value of the franc than with growth needs and transformation as such. The economy grew more or less independent of the currency, monetary, and fiscal crises of the 1920s—or so it seemed—along a more felicitous path of expansion and progress, especially industry. Clearly, however, the two arenas of economic activity were not unrelated. In-flation and exchange depreciation, the two main environmental features of the decade, had a significant impact, for instance—favorable by and large—on busi-ness confidence and on export promotion.

The sources of the several crises of the 1920s were war finance, postwar government expenditure and debt, and self-deceptive monetary, fiscal and ex-change policy. The government financed the war by borrowing from allies, from its own citizens, and from the Bank of France on an unprecedented scale. France's allies extended credit in the form of shipments of materials and advances via a common treasury to support the exchange value of the franc. France's citizens bought long-term government securities and short-term national defense bonds; the latter constituted the floating debt that covered budget deficits in the absence of increased taxation. The bank made extraordinary advances to the treasury, raising the share of the bank's investment portfolio held in government obli-gations from 6 percent to 62 percent between 1913 and 1918. These advances were in the form of extra note issue and therefore increased the fiduciary com-ponent of the money supply from 5.7 to 30.2 milliard francs in the same period. The stock of metallic reserves was not increased equivalently, however, as enjoined by the gold standard; in fact, it was reduced by some 3 milliards to meet wartime expenses. Therefore France abandoned the gold standard, while Allied credits artificially maintained the value of the franc. Various government regulations and interventions meanwhile controlled the inflation emerging from deficit finance and monetary expansion; these were employed only late in the war, however, and did not prevent some rise of prices. Once the war ended, the removal of these several restraints on market forces unleashed a flood of monetary and budgetary chaos. The termination of U.S. and British exchange support credits in 1919 suddenly revealed the weakness of the franc as an international currency. Its value fell to half that of the pound sterling and the dollar. The national debt assumed a dimension more than five times that of 1913 and burdened the budget with amortization and interest payments. To these charges were added the expenses of reconstruction, indemnification of war victims (including pensions), maintenance of a large defense sector, and social needs, doubling the ratio of government expenditure to national income over that of the immediate prewar period.

The response of policy makers to this postwar chaos was encumbered with illusion. First, they expected German reparations to fund a large share of government expenditures, and so taxes were not increased. Not until 1924, following the Ruhr crisis and the negotiation of the Dawes Plan, was this illusion broken. As a result of it, however, budget deficits continued to 1926 and reached very high levels, such as the 26 milliard franc deficit of 1919. As during the war, such deficits were financed by short-term borrowing, increasing public indebtedness and its service expense, and leading to a situation described by Sauvy as burdening the present and the future with charges of the past. A second illusion was the belief that inflation could be controlled by limiting the amount of currency in circulation to a ceiling and by the treasury's annual repayment of 2 milliard francs to the Bank of France for the latter's wartime advances, under the François-Marsal Convention of 1920. In fact such a policy of monetary deflation was inconsistent with the "fiscal inflation" reflected in the growing public debt (Schuker). A semblance of price stability during the early 1920s, which was helped considerably by the 1920–21 recession, only masked a substantial subterranean accumulation of inflationary pressure. The policies supporting this illusion made the treasury increasingly hostage to the speculative money market rather than rooting out the sources of rising prices. This illusion was broken in 1922 when wholesale prices began their steep ascent and when the François-Marsal Convention was circumvented by various expedients to keep the government solvent. A third illusion was the confidence placed in the ability of the franc to recover its prewar exchange value. Initially this illusion was shared by investors, who bet on an appreciation of the franc by investing in franc securities, as well as by policy makers, for whom pursuit of this goal became something of a fetish. The exchange crisis of 1924, provoked by speculators' shifting their bets against the franc, anticipating its imminent devaluation, failed, however, to break the sway of this illusion over policy makers. Not unlike their British counterparts, French leaders were blind to the international economic realities following the war, which had reduced permanently the true value of the domestic currency in foreign markets; also like their Anglo-Saxon fellows, they were committed to protecting the integrity of rentier investments in franc securities. Dogged adherence to the prewar franc and parliamentary indecision deriving from ideological division and economic ignorance caught French leaders in a whirlwind of exchange depreciation, inflation, and national debt that led, according to Schuker, to the diminution of French financial, political, and military autonomy internationally. International bankers and financiers increasingly shaped the conditions within which French diplomacy acted, as well as those of French economic activity abroad.

The whirlwind was checked finally by Raymond Poincaré's famous stabilization of the franc in 1926 and devaluation in 1928, which Sauvy heralded as an "isle of reason in an ocean of errors," referring to government economic policy during the interwar period. Poincaré's achievement, a story in itself, was as much a result of his ability to inspire investors' confidence as that of the currency and budgetary devices with which the actual stabilization was accomplished. Sauvy also credits Poincaré's pragmatic capacity to sidestep ideology and the vested interests he represented in order to tailor policy to immediate circumstance. Although the Poincaré franc was slightly undervalued and therefore, by inducing an accumulation of reserves, had perhaps a destabilizing effect on the international currency situation, it served, along with inflation, to relieve the French government of a large part of the excessive debt inherited from the war, liquidating the latter in effect (Sauvy). It also gave the French economy as a whole further stimulus to expansion by promoting exports during the few remaining, exceptionally vigorous years of recovery.

Much of the gain of the Poincaré franc was lost in the depression of the 1930s. The strength of the franc relative to the embattled pound sterling may have helped to maintain trade and investment in the early years of the depression decade. But soon the reduced differential between franc and pound values following the devaluation of the latter in 1931, and between the franc and the dollar after 1933, cut into the trading advantage that Poincaré's originally undervalued currency had secured. Exports fell by 60 percent between 1929 and 1935, while reserves that had been accumulated during the years of the undervalued franc rapidly diminished after 1932 as the franc became overvalued in relation to other, major currencies. The fall in export trade was matched by declining production and rising unemployment. Between 1929 and 1935 the number of unemployed, as measured by receipt of unemployment benefits—which surely understates the true figure—rose from zero to 426,000. The government's response to the crisis was initially deflationary. By cutting government expenditures and establishing price ceilings, it sought to encourage exports by forcing down domestic prices rather than devaluing the franc. These measures only worsened the decline in production, employment, and investment. At the same time the government pursued a contradictory policy of price maintenance through protective tariffs, subsidies, and encouragement to cartels in industry and to product quota agreements in agriculture. Under the Popular Front a different sort of contradiction blunted the effectiveness of government action: beefed-up expenditures on public works and social reforms, theoretically stimulative for the economy, and the forty-hour week, reducing the capacity of nonmodernized French industry to expand production in response to that stimulus. Budget deficits, larger than ever, again became the rule, making the functioning of government dependent on investors who voted their opinion of the regime in power through the flight of capital, a plague that lasted for nearly four years from 1934. Thus the depression in France came later than in other countries and was probably less severe, but it remained longer.

The economic history of the Third Republic has informed an important part of the discussion concerning the retardation, or relative backwardness, of the French economy as compared with other European countries during the nineteenth and twentieth centuries, especially for the period before 1914. The retardation hypothesis was originally framed in the 1940s and 1950s as a monocausal explanation of why French industrialization and growth were relatively slow. Inadequate coal deposits, entrepreneurial conservatism, resistance to innovation in agriculture, and misguided government policy were among the causes advanced, while the facts of slowness and tardiness remained unchallenged. As the causal explanation became more complex with focus on a combination of factors influencing the economy along a wide front, such as aggregate demand and the weight of institutional structures inherited from a long past, new evidence and theories began to challenge the very fact of retardation, or at least forced a revision of its chronology to the point of depriving the original hypothesis of substance. The continuous product series of Jean Marczewski's Institut de science économique appliquée and Rostow's stage theory were the most important of these novelties. Even though the evidence of the former was used by Marczewski to refute the take-off hypothesis of the latter in the case of France, both suggested that French growth performance during the nineteenth century compared much more favorably with that of France's contemporaries than proponents of the retardation hypothesis had claimed. Both Rostow and Marczewski relied heavily on measurable aggregate indexes of performance and in this sense set much of the standard for subsequent discussion.

Since the early 1960s, when this new work first bore fruit and began to command attention, the relative slowness assumption of the retardationists has been revised from two directions. One has been wedded to the concept of take-off in nineteenth-century France but has refined this concept to make it more suited to the French case. In this refined version the industrialization of the immediate prewar decades, especially 1905–13, was the second stage of the French equivalent of the take-off, focused on urban, industrial demand, following a first stage to 1870 based on rural demand. The other direction has emphasized continuity in French growth since 1815—or earlier—which was interrupted only temporarily by cyclical depression, notably that of the 1880s and 1890s, focused on agriculture, and that of the 1930s. From both perspectives the position of the early Third Republic economy (pre-1914) has been viewed in an essentially favorable light, despite the agrarian depression. French growth performance in this period has been described as respectable though not brilliant. In terms of growth of per capita income and labor productivity, France appears to have approached very closely, or even to have surpassed, its strongest competitors; by measures of aggregate product, capital intensity, and sectoral distribution of the labor force, it appears to have been further behind. There is, in short, an emerging consensus that earlier notions of retardation and relative backwardness need serious revision as a factual matter along lines more favorable to French economic performance before and during the period of the Third Republic.

More recently the revision of the factual record has led to even more radical interpretative onslaught against the retardation hypothesis. Acceptance not only of the British pace of industrialization but also of its very nature as the standard for assessing French (and other countries') industrialization processes has been the favored target of this more recent volley. One approach (Roehl) has reinterpreted French growth from that of follower to that of leader by assessing growth measures and processes according to Alexander Gerschenkron's criteria for relative backwardness. Regarded contrapositively, these criteria would seem to suggest that the French economy behaved as relatively advanced rather than relatively backward to 1914. This interpretation rests heavily on the recognition of protoindustry as a significant industrializing element and on a broader concept of industrialization than the technologically focused notion assumed in much earlier discussion. On both accounts the interpretation has been challenged. Another approach (O'Brien and Keyder) has employed a sophisticated reading of relative growth patterns of France and Britain between 1780 and 1914 in terms of welfare criteria and comparative advantage. From this reading British industrialization appears to have been a race to preserve per capita output against potential sinkage caused by social degradation and a rapidly expanding work force, while the French pattern reflected a choice by most French people (who were peasants, by and large) to retain existing means of earning income, as inefficient as these were, until the urban industrial economy gave reasonable assurance of providing equal or better opportunity from a welfare standpoint. The British advantage in per capita terms was reaped only as an unsought consequence of the means used to overcome what was essentially an economic and social crisis; the advantage was evident largely in relation to the initial stages of the French forward movement occurring simultaneously with the British harvest. In the end both Britain and France found their way into the modern twentieth-century economy by following different paths. From a social standpoint, at least, the path chosen by France may have been the more felicitous. At least some Englishmen—Morris Birkbeck, Samuel Cobbett, J. S. Mill, and William Thornton—probably would have thought so.

J. Bouvier et al., *Histoire économique et sociale de la France*, 4 vols. (Paris, 1979–80), vol. IV: *L'Ere industrielle et la société d'aujourd'hui (siècle 1880-1980)*; F. Caron, *An Economic History of Modern France*, trans. B. Bray (New York, 1979); J.-J. Carré, P. Dubois, and E. Malinvaud, *French Economic Growth*, trans. J. Hatfield (Stanford, Calif., 1975); F. Crouzet, "French Economic Growth in the Nineteenth Century Reconsidered," *History: The Journal of the Historical Association* 59 (1974); J. Marczewski, "The Take-Off Hypothesis and French Experience," in *The Economics of Take-Off into*

Sustained Growth, ed. W. W. Rostow (New York, 1963); P. O'Brien and C. Keyder, *Economic Growth in Britain and France, 1780–1914* (London, 1978); R. Roehl, "French Industrialization: A Reconsideration," *Explorations in Economic History* 13 (1976); A. Sauvy, *Histoire économique de la France entre les deux guerres*, 3 vols. (Paris, 1965– 72); S. Schuker, *The End of French Predominance in Europe* (Chapel Hill, N.C., 1976).

G. J. Sheridan

Related entry: ECONOMIC POLICY.

EDUCATION: ACADEMIC DEGREES. The Third Republic recognized three major post-*baccalauréat* degrees: the *licence*, the *agrégation*, and the *doctorat*. Between 1870 and 1940 diplomas conferred at the level of the *licence* and the *doctorat* numbered 53,973. Most academic degrees were awarded on the basis of results obtained in competitive nationwide examinations, thus emphasizing the ability to memorize and take tests rather than encouraging attendance and performance in the classroom.

Before 1880, academic degrees were actually professional diplomas intended to prepare students for a specific career, usually in law, medicine, or pharmacy. The pure mathematics or science student or the humanities student did not exist since these fields did not provide practical, career-oriented training. The 1880s represent a major turning point in French higher education. Academic degrees became more clearly defined, reorganized, and standardized, and students began to be prepared as researchers as well as practitioners. The *facultés* ceased to be solely professional schools; the competitive examinations for the various degrees became more serious and demanded demonstration of research and/or analytical ability.

The *baccalauréat* degree, culminating studies at the lycée (secondary education), was a prerequisite for university study. The *baccalauréat* examination, which consisted of an oral and written part as well as a translation (Latin), was generally taken at age eighteen. The examination was based essentially on memorized materials and required little or no original thought. In spite of this, the *baccalauréat* degree conferred a great deal of importance to an individual throughout the period of the Third Republic. According to the Falloux Law (18 March 1850), anyone twenty-five years or older with a *baccalauréat* and five years of teaching experience could open a secondary school. This same law specified that no teaching diploma was required to be a teacher in primary or secondary school. Consequently, until the 1930s, few teachers pursued a university degree before entering the teaching profession. Only those wishing to have the title of professor conferred on them continued their studies through the *licence* and the *agrégation*.

As of 1932, the primary and secondary school *instituteur* was required to have the *brevet élémentaire* and the *brevet supérieur*, and in 1940, the *baccalauréat* became mandatory. Both *brevets* comprised three years of study, with the third year devoted entirely to pedagogy (as of 1909).

In the humanities, the *licence ès lettres* consisted of one common examination (written and oral) and three options, each with its own examination according to the student's field of study: literature, philosophy, or history. In 1886, a fourth option, modern languages, was added to the *licence*. With the decree of 8 July 1907, these four options were divided into four distinct *licences*. From this point on, the *licence* was to remain a highly specialized degree. In 1920 a further reform reunited the four *licences* once again into one degree, and the system of *certificats* was instituted. Henceforth, four certificates were required to obtain the *licence*, with a fifth *certificat* in classical literature for those wishing to teach modern languages, history, or philosophy.

The *diplôme d'études supérieures* appeared in 1886. This degree was conferred without an examination and was based on the recommendation of a professor. Beginning in 1898 the *diplôme* became a prerequisite for the *agrégation* in many fields.

In 1885 the *agrégation* in the humanities was defined. The entire cycle took three years to complete: one year for the *licence*, one year for the *diplôme*, and one year for the *agrégation*. This degree included theoretical and practical (pedagogical) training, and the examination or *concours* was a nationwide competition.

In the sciences, the evolution of academic degrees was similar to that in the humanities. In 1896 the *licence ès sciences* was divided into three *certificats*: *sciences mathématiques*, *sciences physiques*, and *sciences naturelles*. The *agrégation* and the *doctorat* allowed the same type of specialization.

Medical studies required fewer reforms at the end of the century than the other fields. Medical training had been established long before, and the remaining change came about in 1878 when the sciences were more prominently included in the program. Physics, chemistry, and the natural sciences were included in an additional year in medical school, and in 1893, a *certificat* in these fields became a prerequisite for medical school. The *doctorat* in medicine required five years of study and a thesis in Latin. With this degree, an individual could practice medicine and surgery anywhere in France. A less rigorous program led to the *diplôme d'officier de santé*, which restricted its bearer to the practice of medicine in a specific department.

Pharmacy followed the same pattern. Three years of study led to a first-class diploma, valid nationwide; a shorter program led to a second-class diploma valid only in a specific department.

Law degrees developed along somewhat different lines. The *licence* resisted fragmentation into options. The *agrégation* was divided into four competitive examinations in 1896: *le droit privé*, *l'économie politique*, *l'histoire du droit*, and *les sciences administratives et politiques*. Finally, the *doctorat*, requiring four to five years of study and a thesis, completed the cycle in the field of law.

O. Gréard, *Education et instruction*, vol. 3, *Enseignement supérieur* (Paris, 1887); V. Isambert-Jamati, *Crises de la société, crises de l'enseignement* (Paris, 1970); E. Lavisse, *Etudes et étudiants* (Paris, 1890), and *Questions d'enseignement national* (Paris, 1885); L. Liard, *Universités et facultés* (Paris, 1890); G. Monod, *De la possibilité d'une réforme de l'enseignement supérieur* (Paris, 1876); A. Prost, *Histoire de l'enseignement en France*:

1800–1967 (Paris, 1968); A. Thibaudet, *La République des professeurs* (Paris, 1927);
T. Zeldin, *France 1848-1945*, vol. 2 (Oxford, 1977); T. Zeldin, "Higher Education in
France, 1848–1940," *Journal of Contemporary History* (November 1967).

J. D. Bragger

Related entry: EDUCATION: GOVERNMENTAL POLICIES CONCERN-
ING.

EDUCATION: ADMINISTRATION OF. The administration of the French
educational system is characterized by a high degree of centralization, with
authority concentrated in the office of the minister of education (minister of
public instruction during the Third Republic) who was assisted by a small number
of advisers. The greatest disadvantage of such an administrative system was that
education was subject to political fluctuations, making enlightened reforms more
difficult to enact. Each change of government was a potential threat to the stability
and continuity of the educational system, inadequate budgetary allocations
hampered progress, and political conflicts and conservatism maintained the status
quo. Until 1905 (separation of church and state), the rivalry between state-run
schools and church-run schools further complicated the questions of authority
and administrative jurisdiction.

In 1854, France had been divided into sixteen academic units (*académies*)
each headed by a *recteur* and each consisting of a variable number of *facultés*
(1855) or disciplines. The *recteur* was directly responsible to the minister, and
his political loyalties were therefore stronger than his concern for the *académie*.
As a representative of the minister, he was not only in charge of the *facultés* in
his city but also of all primary and secondary education in his region. In addition
to these regional representatives, the minister was seconded, in Paris, by the
Conseil supérieur de l'instruction publique made up of eight high-ranking university
professors forming the permanent council and nineteen representatives from
various public sectors, including advisers from the church. The council functioned
primarily in an advisory capacity to the minister. It addressed all questions
pertaining to national education and oversaw the various administrative units
(national, regional, municipal) of the country. It had the power to take disciplinary
action against administrators and all *instituteurs*, who had officially become civil
servants (*fonctionnaires*) in 1889. This same council determined the syllabi and
decided content and organizational questions at all educational levels.
Centralization of authority was deemed imperative to ensure equal standards and
learning experiences throughout the nation. Three directors were charged with
overseeing the council: *directeur de l'enseignement primaire*, *directeur de
l'enseignement secondaire*, and *directeur de l'enseignement supérieur*. This
administrative configuration ensured that all levels of education were controlled
directly from Paris and seriously limited the power of even the provincial
representatives.

The directors of primary, secondary, and higher education were by far the
most influential individuals in the administrative hierarchy. Many of the educational

reforms enacted during the Third Republic were due to the progressive ideas of some of these individuals or of the minister. Ferdinand Buisson (1841–1932) was director of primary education from 1879 to 1896. Under his leadership, primary education was updated, and pedagogical techniques were more closely scrutinized. His *Dictionnaire de pédagogie* (1882–93) was instrumental in creating a new attitude on the part of primary school teachers. For his work in education, Buisson was awarded the Nobel Peace Prize in 1926. Louis Liard, director of higher education between 1884 and 1902, was responsible for major reforms in higher education during the Third Republic. In 1885 he created a Conseil général des facultés in each *académie*, which was composed of representatives from each *faculté* in the same town. This was a modest attempt to establish coordination among the *facultés*, but its importance cannot be underrated. Liard eventually succeeded in officially uniting the *facultés* in 1896 when they assumed the designation of universities.

Each university continued to have a rector and vice-rector, both directly responsible to the ministry. The rector also continued to be the head of primary and secondary education in his own region.

On the local level, the administrative hierarchy manifested itself as progressively more complex, with fragmented jurisdictional authority. The Falloux Law (15 March 1850) had created departmental academic councils to supervise education in their own areas. This gave a great deal of power to the prefect who had the authority to appoint the *instituteurs* in his school district. In 1881 and 1882, the Ferry Law created municipal commissions in charge of primary education. As the laicization of primary schools was pursued by the state, more and more control was given to prefects, town mayors, and municipal commissions. In addition, each school had its principal and various other administrators (*proviseurs, censeurs*) who exercised a great deal of influence on administrative decisions.

To ensure uniformity and observance of rules, the state relied on a hierarchy of inspectors, whose chief responsibility was to visit schools and to send reports to the ministry. Local inspectors reported to the inspectors of the *académie*, who reported in turn to an *inspecteur-général*. More than any other administrative body, these inspectors kept the educational system conservative. The only changes they were authorized to make were mandated from above, and their jobs depended on strict observance of the rules.

Although the Third Republic did a great deal to further education in France and to stimulate more progressive attitudes, the highly centralized nature of the system seriously hindered innovations and academic freedom. The administrative hierarchy was not to be reformed until the revolution of May 1968.

O. Gréard, *Education et instruction*, vol. 3: *Enseignement supérieur* (Paris, 1887); V. Isambert-Jamati, *Crises de la société, crises de l'enseignement* (Paris, 1970); E. Lavisse, *Etudes et étudiants* (Paris, 1890), and *Questions d'enseignement national* (Paris, 1885); L. Liard, *Universités et facultés* (Paris, 1890); G. Monod, *De la possibilité d'une réforme de l'enseignement supérieur* (Paris, 1876); A. Prost, *Histoire de l'enseignement en France: 1800–1967* (Paris, 1968); A. Thibaudet, *La République des professeurs* (Paris, 1927);

T. Zeldin, *France 1848–1945*, vol. 2 (Oxford, 1977); T. Zeldin, "Higher Education in France, 1848–1940," *Journal of Contemporary History* (November 1967).

J. D. Bragger

Related entries: EDUCATION: ACADEMIC DEGREES; EDUCATION: GOVERNMENTAL POLICIES CONCERNING; FERRY; SCHOOLS, HIGHER EDUCATION: *GRANDES ECOLES*; SCHOOLS, MEDICAL; SCHOOLS, PRIMARY; SCHOOLS, SECONDARY: *COLLEGES*; SCHOOLS, SECONDARY: *LYCEES*; UNIVERSITIES.

EDUCATION: CURRICULUM AND TEXTBOOKS IN PRIMARY SCHOOLS. Compulsory primary schools provided children aged seven to thirteen with the rudiments of literacy and inculcated values prescribed by the state. Outlined by the law of 28 March 1882, the public primary school's curriculum was definitively shaped by the *arrêté* of 18 January 1887. During a thirty-hour week schools covered reading, writing, grammar and composition, history, geography, civic instruction, moral education, arithmetic, general science, drawing, singing, hygiene, physical education, and manual works. Two themes, France and work, united components of the encyclopedic curriculum. French received priority, the Ministry of Public Instruction allocating it eleven to fourteen hours a week, depending on grade level. Arithmetic rated an hour a day. The *morale* program was explicit about the traits of the good citizen. Teaching duties to self, family, country, and God, the school prized honesty, temperance, cooperativeness, respect for others, and uncomplaining acceptance of adversity. Aware that primary school pupils were mostly "children of the people" rather than bourgeois offspring sent to fee-paying elementary classes in secondary schools, the education ministry emphasized the virtues of hard work and thrift but advised against too much love of money. The curriculum provided the child with basic knowledge for many occupations, and the school's regimen promoted a work ethic. Patriotism in moral and civic instruction was reinforced by history and geography lessons, limited to France until the last grade when other parts of Europe and the world were covered.

Textbooks followed the official program's outlines and reproduced its didacticism. Typically they contained material likely to appear on examinations for the *certificat d'études primaires*, obtained by better students completing primary schooling. With their inspector present, public school teachers met annually at the cantonal level to select textbooks. Private schools could employ any book not banned by the education ministry. Public school pupils used a reader in the *cours élémentaire* (ages seven to nine); five books—a reader, an atlas, and grammar, arithmetic, and history books—in the *cours moyen* (ages nine to eleven); and the same five categories plus a *morale* book in the *cours supérieur* (ages eleven to thirteen). Among the classic textbooks selling several million or more copies were Ernest Lavisse's history offerings, Larive and Fleury's grammars, Pierre Leyssenne's arithmetics, and Pierre Foncin's geography books.

Bruno's *Tour de la France par deux enfants* (1877), the bestselling reader of the Third Republic (8 million copies), had heroes epitomizing the good worker, peasant, and patriot. Marie-Robert Halt's *Suzette* and Clarisse Juranville's *livres de lecture* were standard readers for girls.

Expected to attend separate schools in towns of 500 or more, boys and girls studied the same academic subjects but did not receive wholly identical educations. Assumptions about gender roles were prominent in the instructions of 1887 for *travaux manuels*: boys prepared for a future as workers and soldiers while girls mastered *ouvrages de femmes* and anticipated motherhood. Accordingly, girls learned sewing and rudimentary home economics, the latter often incorporated into science lessons. Boys learned to use common tools and received simple agricultural instruction. Textbooks, especially those for *morale* and reading, also depicted gender roles differently. Special girls' texts, more numerous before 1914 than after, delineated a feminine personality marked by sweetness, self-sacrifice, and—as the civil code required—obedience to the *chef de famille*. Textbooks endowed males with more forceful personalities and often with superior reasoning ability. The *foyer* was woman's domain; the *forum* of work and politics was for men.

Arrêtés of 23 February 1923 and 20 September 1938 retained the program of 1887 as the basis for primary education but made modifications. In 1923 the amount of weekly time for manual works was reduced by at least one hour, the ministry thereby meeting the complaints of many teachers who preferred academic subjects to practical ones. But heightened postwar concern about depopulation did lead to the addition of practical lessons in *puériculture* (the care of infants) to the girls' science program. The Popular Front raised the school-leaving age to fourteen in 1936 and for the added year created the *classe de fin d'études*, which placed more emphasis than did other grades on preparation for work. Boys would learn about the *métiers* common in their region, and girls would receive intensified training in home economics. While post-primary schools— vehicles for upward social mobility—enrolled record numbers of students aged twelve or thirteen by the 1930s, the six out of seven remaining in primary schools until age fourteen were recipients of practical and theoretical instruction about modest occupations.

A. Choppin, "L'Histoire des manuels scolaires," *Histoire de l'éducation*, no. 9 (1980); L. Clark, "The Primary Education of French Girls," *History of Education Quarterly* 21 (1981), and *Schooling the Daughters of Marianne* (Albany, 1984); A. Dupuy, "Les Livres de lecture de G. Bruno," *Revue d'histoire économique et sociale* 31 (1953); P. Gay and O. Mortreux, eds., *French Elementary Schools* (New York, 1926); D. Maingueneau, *Les Livres d'école de la république* (1979); J. and M. Ozouf, "Le Thème du patriotisme dans les manuels primaires," *Mouvement social* 49 (1964).

L. L. Clark

Related entries: CHILDREN: ATTITUDES TOWARD; CHILDREN: IN THE WORK FORCE; SCHOOLS, PRIMARY; WOMEN: ATTITUDES TOWARD.

EDUCATION: GOVERNMENTAL POLICIES CONCERNING. The fundamental laws and policies governing the French public education system were enacted during the period of the Third Republic. The Franco-Prussian War (August 1870–January 1871) convinced French authorities that they had been defeated by Germany's superior knowledge and more advanced scientific technology. This belief motivated the Ministry of Public Instruction to review its educational policies, to reorganize the school system, to develop true higher education, and to create more rigorous scholastic standards throughout the nation.

The most important reforms were enacted between 1872 and 1896, and they reflected the republican, democratic principles essential to the newly established government. According to these principles, education was to be free and compulsory, available to everyone, male and female, regardless of social status. Although the 1850 *Loi Falloux* had reaffirmed that education was the responsibility of the church, post-1871 laws progressively led to the laicization of the school system. Within this framework, the French government enacted a series of laws designed to realize these objectives.

27 September 1872   A memorandum, initiated by Jules Simon, reduced the importance of memorization and translation of Latin verse in the secondary schools. As a result, classical studies were now seen as a means of understanding antiquity and of forming the mind rather than as a simple mechanical exercise.

25 March 1873   A decree created the *comité consultatif*, which was to serve in a purely advisory capacity to the minister of public instruction. The Conseil supérieur was reestablished after having been discontinued in 1870.

9 April 1874   A decree divided the *baccalauréat ès lettres* into two parts, with one year between the parts and the last year of secondary education (*classe terminale*) concentrating on philosophy.

3 November 1877   The first scholarships for students pursuing a *licence* were awarded.

9 August 1897   A law that obliged each department to create and maintain an *école normale d'institutrices*.

27 February 1880   A law that limited membership on the Conseil supérieur to university professors.

18 March 1880   A law prohibiting nonstate institutions of higher education being called universities.

11 December 1880   A law created the *écoles manuelles d'apprentissage*.

21 December 1880   *Loi Camille Sée*. Established and organized secondary education for girls.

16 June 1881   *Loi Ferry*. Made public elementary education free and accessible to everyone.

28 March 1882   *Loi Ferry*. Elementary education became compulsory and was put under the control of municipal commissions.

28 December 1885   A decree creating the Conseil général des facultés, designed to coordinate the efforts of all the *facultés* within each academic jurisdiction.

28 July 1886   A decree created the *licence* in modern languages.

30 October 1886	*Loi Goblet*. Finalized the organization of elementary education.
18 January 1887	Various decrees put into effect the *Loi Goblet*, establishing schedules, a curriculum and administrative procedures.
19 July 1889	*Instituteurs* became civil servants paid by the state.
28 January–	
8 August 1890	Curriculum and budget of secondary schools were determined. The *baccalauréat* was reorganized.
10 July 1896	Law uniting the *facultés* of each city, thus establishing the provincial universities.
7 July 1904	Law prohibiting the opening of religious schools.
9 December 1905	Separation of church and state.
24 October 1911	Decree creating departmental committees in charge of trade schools.
25 July 1919	*Loi Astier*. Trade (technical) schools were organized.
15 July 1921	Organization of the *écoles maternelles*.
16 April 1930	Financial law making secondary education free and accessible to everyone.
9 August 1936	Education was made compulsory up to the age of fourteen.
21 September 1939	Decree creating centers of professional education.

R. Gal, *Histoire de l'éducation* (Paris, 1976); O. Gréard, *Education et instruction*, vol. 3: *Enseignement supérieur* (Paris, 1887); V. Isambert-Jamati, *Crises de la société, crises de l'enseignement* (Paris, 1970); E. Lavisse, *Etudes et étudiants* (Paris, 1890), and *Questions d'enseignement national* (Paris, 1885); L. Liard, *Universités et facultés* (Paris, 1890); G. Monod, *De la possibilité d'une réforme de l'enseignement supérieur* (Paris, 1876); A. Prost, *Histoire de l'enseignement en France: 1800–1967* (Paris, 1968); A. Thibaudet, *La République des professeurs* (Paris, 1927); T. Zeldin, *France, 1848–1945, vol. 2 (Oxford, 1977)*, and "*Higher Education in France, 1848-1940*," *Journal of Contemporary History* (November 1967).

J. D. Bragger

Related entries: FERRY; FRANCO-PRUSSIAN WAR; GOBLET; SCHOOLS, HIGHER EDUCATION: ECOLE NORMALE SUPERIEURE; SCHOOLS, HIGHER EDUCATION: *GRANDES ECOLES*; SCHOOLS, PRIMARY; SCHOOLS, SECONDARY: *LYCEES*; SCHOOLS, ROMAN CATHOLIC; SIMON; UNIVERSITIES.

EIFFEL, GUSTAVE (1832–1923), cultural hero of the early Third Republic, one of the most innovative and versatile engineers of the nineteenth century, and an important pioneer in the development of aerodynamics and meteorology. By 1869 he had established the methods and working procedures he would use in a series of spectacular structures erected during the Third Republic. The Maria Pia bridge in Portugal (1875), Garabit viaduct (1883), Tan an Bridge in Indochina (1880), Bon Marché department store (1879), dome of the Nice observatory (1885), armature for the Statue of Liberty (1883), and the Eiffel Tower (1889) were the products of Eiffel's knowledge of the structural properties of iron, careful attention to wind bracing, and novel methods of construction. His major contribution to engineering was the development of a firm theoretical basis for the design and construction of metal structures. His methods and his aesthetics strongly influenced the architects Auguste Perret and Le Corbusier (Charles-Eduoard Jeanneret).

Eiffel was the ideal self-made man of the industrial era. His ability to create sturdy structures using a minimum of materials was matched by the efficiency and economy with which he ran his firm and the restraint and order of his private life. Always meeting deadlines and remaining within his initial cost estimates, he became wealthy through activities he believed beneficial to society. Yet there is some indication that he was a highly sensitive individual who found in engineering a way to control his emotional energies. The Eiffel Tower, his most famous and least utilitarian project, symbolized for him man's ability to overcome the forces and difficulties that nature and life put in his way.

At the moment of his greatest success, Eiffel was implicated in the Panama Canal scandal and convicted of misuse of funds in 1893. The sentence was set aside, and he withdrew from active participation in his engineering firm, devoting his remaining thirty years to the study of air resistance and weather patterns. He received international recognition for this work, much of which he financed himself; for like the Curies, he had difficulty gaining governmental support for his experiments.

J. Harriss, *The Tallest Tower* (Boston, 1975).

M. R. Levin

Related entries: CURIE, M.; CURIE, P.; EIFFEL TOWER; PANAMA SCANDAL.

EIFFEL TOWER. Built for the Universal Exposition of 1889 celebrating the centennial of the French Revolution, the thousand-foot tower represented a significant contribution to engineering and the arts and symbolized the aspirations and values of the Republic. Drawing on procedures developed for the construction of iron bridges, the designer of the tower, Gustave Eiffel, was able to erect what remained the tallest structure in the world until the 1920s. An open latticework frame and pylons sunk deep into the banks of the Seine to absorb the downward thrust allowed him to overcome hitherto insurmountable problems of excessive weight and wind resistance. The tower strongly influenced the work of architects such as Auguste Perret and Le Corbusier, the Russian sculptor Vladimir Tatlin, and cubist painters interested in restructuring pictorial space.

The tower is rich in symbolic meaning. Generally thought of as an unabashed celebration of modern industrial society, it was originally intended as a form of integrative propaganda meant to narrow the gap industrialization had created between workers and the middle classes. Edouard Lockroy, the minister responsible for having Eiffel's design accepted, chose the project to demonstrate to the public that technology could strengthen the liberal democratic system. Special attention was paid to the organization of work crews so that they could provide a model of cooperation between workers and management using the latest building techniques. It was hoped that when completed the tower would provide a stage for an ongoing fête in which people of diverse socioeconomic backgrounds could participate. Climbing the tower was to be a modern form of the pilgrim's progress, with the platforms acting as way stations along the road to social unity. The form itself was symbolic of these aims. Its framework composed of small, interdependent parts is a metaphor for the liberal democratic system the tower was to secure, and the arches formed a triumphal gateway that opened onto an exposition filled with the products of science and industry.

During its first ten years, the tower drew millions of visitors. Despite a small group who opposed the tower, it was admired even by socialists who denounced the economic system it was to preserve. Since 1900 both the function and the symbolic meaning of the tower have changed. It has been used for aerodynamic and meteorological experiments and military and civilian radio, telegraph, and television communication. Illuminated advertisements, a giant clock, and a thermometer have adorned it, and it has served as a stage for pyrotechnic displays. Its association with the moral and social value of labor was soon lost. Now almost universally accepted as a symbol of Paris of *la belle époque*, the tower is losing visitors to the Centre Beaubourg, symbol of the consumer-oriented, technocratic Fifth Republic.

J. Harriss, *The Tallest Tower* (Boston, 1975); M. R. Levin, "Art and the Early Third Republic" (Ph.D. dissertation, University of Massachusetts, 1980).

M. R. Levin

Related entries: BELLE EPOQUE; CUBISM; EIFFEL; FESTIVALS: POLITICAL; INDUSTRY; LOCKROY; SEURAT; TOURISM.

ENTENTE CORDIALE, a diplomatic agreement signed on 8 April 1904 by representatives of France and Great Britain adjusting colonial disputes between the two signatories and paving the way for Anglo-French cooperation in preventing German expansion in Europe and in the colonial world. Ever since the British military occupation of Egypt and the termination of the Anglo-French condominium regulating the French-built Suez Canal in 1882, the French government had refused to recognize Great Britain's right to occupy militarily and control the finances of this strategic region linking the Mediterranean Sea and the Indian Ocean. In 1896 a French military expedition based in French Equatorial Africa was dispatched eastward toward the Upper Nile to lay claim to territory south of British-occupied Egypt. In the same year an Anglo-Egyptian military force began advancing up the Nile to assert a competing claim to the territory. In the autumn of 1898 the Anglo-Egyptian force under General Sir Herbert Kitchener and the French mission under Colonel Jean-Baptiste Marchand confronted each other at the town of Fashoda. In the aftermath of a severe crisis in Anglo-French relations, the French government backed down in humiliating fashion and ordered the evacuation of Fashoda on 3 November. Within two months Great Britain had established an Anglo-Egyptian condominium over the region of the Upper Nile that was to become known as the Anglo-Egyptian Sudan. The combined British occupation of Egypt, the Suez Canal, and the Sudan at France's expense produced an intense sentiment of Anglophobia in France that continued into the twentieth century.

In the meantime, France's efforts to gain a foothold in Morocco through economic penetration prompted opposition in London on the grounds that a French-controlled Morocco would threaten the security of the British naval base at Gibraltar. As was the case in the Egyptian-Suez region, British policy in the western Mediterranean was dictated by the necessity to protect the island-nation's lifeline to India and the Far East, a policy that conflicted with France's goal of extending the territory of its North African Empire. Moreover, the signing of the Anglo-Japanese alliance on 30 January 1902 threatened to draw France into a conflict with Great Britain in the event of a war in the Far East between France's ally Russia and England's ally Japan (both competing for hegemony over the Korean peninsula).

Fearful of such a confrontation with England and desirous of securing British support against Germany in Europe, French Foreign Minister Théophile Delcassé opened negotiations with London with the object of resolving the conflicts in North Africa that had poisoned relations between the two powers. The British government proved receptive to French overtures because of mounting anxiety over the German Empire's naval construction program begun at the turn of the century. Following an exchange of visits and expressions of mutual cordiality by Edward VII of England and President Emile Loubet of France, serious negotiations over Anglo-French differences were begun in July 1903. Hastened by the outbreak of the Russo-Japanese War in February 1904, an agreement was signed on 8 April of the same year. The provisions of the so-called *Entente Cordiale* ("friendly understanding") included French recognition of the British occupation of Egypt in return for British guarantees regarding the Egyptian debt and freedom of navigation in the Suez Canal; British recognition of a French sphere of interest in Morocco in return for a secret pledge by France to grant Spain an occupation zone across from Gibraltar in the event of the partition of the country; and several minor articles composing Anglo-French differences over Newfoundland, Siam, and West Africa.

Despite the military defeat of its ally Russia in the war with Japan, French security was considerably strengthened by the Entente Cordiale. Each time that France came into diplomatic conflict with Germany thereafter, it was supported by Great Britain. Moreover, the understanding between the two nations gradually developed into a general spirit of cooperation on a variety of issues. In January 1906 the British government authorized joint conversations between the British and French general staffs. In August 1907 Britain reached agreement with France's ally Russia on territorial issues in Central Asia. This diplomatic cooperation of France, England, and Russia was soon to become known as the Triple Entente. Although the British agreement with France contained neither military clauses nor the slightest hint of an obligation to defend France against aggression, it symbolized a community of interests between the two powers in opposition to the German Empire and its allies. It therefore served to prepare British public opinion for the eventual British intervention in the First World War on the side of France.

C. Andrew, *Théophile Delcassé and the Making of the Entente Cordiale* (New York, 1968); R. G. Brown, *Fashoda Reconsidered* (Baltimore, 1970); A. J. P. Taylor, *The Struggle for Mastery in Europe* (London, 1957.)

W. R. Keylor

Related entries: DELCASSE; GREAT BRITAIN, RELATIONS WITH; MOROCCAN CRISES; TRIPLE ENTENTE.

ERNST, MAX (1891–1976), painter, sculptor, and collagist; cofounder of the Cologne dada group and member of the surrealist school of Paris. He was born in Bruhl, Germany. In his early years, he was steeped in the fantastic images of Dürer, Bosch, and Brueghel of the late Gothic period and the more recent German romantic school. He had turned from the study of philosophy at Bonn to painting and in 1913 made his first trip to Paris where he met the poet Guillaume Apollinaire and the painter Robert Delauney. The following year he began a lifetime friendship with Jean Arp. After the war, he helped found in Cologne the Central Dada W/3 group, which expressed disenchantment with traditional moral and artistic values. With Arp and the painter and poet J. T. Baargeld, Ernst created a series of paintings and collages dubbed "Fatagagas" (*fabrications des tableaux garantis gazometriques*). Unlike Arp, Ernst often used clearly representational images. These realistic forms would be juxtaposed in bizarre ways to form a disquieting dreamlike effect similar to that evoked by the slightly earlier work of the Greek painter Giorgio de Chirico of the metaphysical school.

Through the organ of Ernst's *Schammade* magazine, the Cologne dadaist circle made contact with André Breton, the French poet and critic who would become the nucleus of the surrealist school. In 1920, Ernst was invited by Breton to exhibit at the first surrealist show. In 1922, Ernst took up residence in Paris and introduced use of nineteenth-century magazine engravings and images of microorganisms, which became mainstays of the surrealists' vocabulary.

In 1925, Ernst made his first *frottage*, a drawing made by placing paper over a textured object and rubbing over the paper with a pencil to create quasi-random outlines and unexpected spatial relationships. But in other works he often used refined sinuous outlines. He officially broke with the surrealists in 1938, and his work through the 1950s and 1960s was eclectic and reminiscent of late Gothic fantastic art, nineteenth-century romanticism and the avant-garde work of de Chirico, Francis Picabia, Yves Tanguy, and Salvador Dali. He turned to sculpture in the 1930s due to the influence of his friend Alberto Giacometti. These works in their elongation are reminiscent of Giacometti's own, and their primitive frontal qualities seem inspired by African tribal sculptures. His later works suggest a peaceful resolution and internal harmony in contrast to the horror and mockery evidenced in his creations of the surrealist period.

Although he had his first New York exhibit in 1931, Ernst did not achieve worldwide critical acclaim until the 1950s, having been blacklisted by the Nazis in 1933. He fled France in 1941 to live in the United States until 1955. He returned to France in 1955 and became a citizen in 1958. From 1956 to 1966, virtually every major museum of modern art staged a retrospective of his work, and numerous awards ensued. A comprehensive retrospective was held at New York's Guggenheim Museum the year before Ernst's death in 1976.

M. Ernst, *Beyond Painting and Other Writings by the Painter and His Friends* (New York, 1948); S. Hunter, ed., *Max Ernst: Sculpture and Recent Painting* (New York, 1968); P. Pritzker, *Ernst* (London, 1975); P. Schamoni, *Max Ernst: Maximilana* (Boston, 1974); U. Schneede, *Max Ernst* (New York, 1973); I. Turpin, *Max Ernst* (New York, 1979).

C. J. Hamm

Related entries: ARP; BRETON; PICABIA; SURREALISM.

EUDES, EMILE (1843–1888), Blanquist militant, Communard. He was born at Roncey (Manche). After attending secondary school in Saint-Lô, he moved to Paris to study pharmacy but became more involved in the activities of the republican opposition to the Second Empire. Noted especially for his bravado, he was one of the leading organizers of Blanquist secret societies in the late 1860s. A series of arrests and imprisonments for seditious activities culminated in a sentence of death in August 1870 for his participation in an abortive Blanquist raid on the fire station arsenal at La Villette, calculated to inspire a Parisian uprising against the Second Empire. Spared execution by the overthrow of the Empire on 4 September 1870, Eudes soon won high place in the National Guard of Paris during the Franco-Prussian War. By the eve of the Commune, he had been elected a legion commander and with the outbreak of civil war was named a war commissioner of the Commune by the Central Committee of the National Guard. On 3 April 1871 Eudes led a column in an unsuccessful military offensive against Versailles, for which he was relegated to lesser posts. He was named inspector general of forts on the left bank on April 20 and commander of a brigade of active reserves on May 5. A member of the Commune's Assembly, he was elected to its Committee of Public Safety on May 9. Eudes is reputed to have ordered the burning of a number of public buildings (among them, the Palace of the Legion of Honor, the Tuileries, and city hall) in the final days of fighting.

Escaping to England, Eudes was the acknowledged leader of the Blanquists in exile. Amnestied in 1880, he helped organize the Central Revolutionary Committee, a Blanquist society dedicated to commemorating the Commune and to rebuilding the revolutionary movement in its image. He died in August 1888 in the midst of a rally in support of striking workers in Paris. His funeral served as a display of revolutionary solidarity by veteran Blanquists, Communards, and other left-wing militants.

Remembered as the quintessential Blanquist activist, Eudes had a reflective side, revealed in his personal papers. These are housed in the Institut français d'histoire sociale, Paris.

M. Dommanget, *Hommes et choses de la Commune* (Marseilles, 1937); P. H. Hutton, *The Cult of the Revolutionary Tradition* (Berkeley, 1981); G. Laronze, *Histoire de la Commune de 1871* (Paris, 1928); J. Maitron, "A partir des papiers du Général Eudes," *L'Actualité de l'histoire* 5 (October 1953).

P. H. Hutton

Related entries: BLANQUISTS; COMMUNE OF PARIS.

EXISTENTIALISM, a philosophical current that takes human existence as the point of departure for reflection and action. Its focus on subjective experience exerted a particular attraction on French intellectuals between the 1930s and 1950s. Basically it represents a reaction against systems of thought that explain human beings according to abstract principles, or treat them as agents of larger natural or historical processes. Thus instead of asking questions about the essence or ultimate purpose of man, existentialist thinkers examine the individual in the concrete life experience. They see him as cast into a world whose existence cannot be understood rationally. They also view him as entirely free to decide what to make of his situation in the world. At the same time, they recognize that this freedom breeds anguish because the individual must bear the responsibility of his choices, whether these are explicit or implicit, as in the case in which he forgoes choosing anything at all.

This way of thinking has been traced to the Danish philosopher Søren Kierkegaard (1813–55) who, rejecting G.W.F. Hegel's rationalistic and idealistic system, submitted that religious belief was not a matter of metaphysical reflection but of subjective choice; it involved a leap of faith. This theistic orientation, which strips Christianity of metaphysical accretions and emphasizes subjective decision, characterizes the thinking of most religious existentialists, among them, Gabriel Marcel who, in addition, stresses the necessity of active communication with other selves as fundamental to authentic existence.

Unlike Marcel, the atheistic existentialist does not link his subjective world to that of an absolute deity. For him, the individual alone, through his projects and actions, gives significance to the life situations in which he is involved. If he declines responsibility for his decisions by alleging environmental, psychological, political, or other constraints, he acts in bad faith. According to Jean-Paul Sartre, for instance, not even a physical deficiency can be invoked as a limitation on one's freedom, for it is the individual's decision whether his physical condition should be an excuse for failure or an obstacle to overcome.

Although as a distinctive philosophical current existentialism emerged in France after World War II, the themes and mood associated with its outlook turn up in many prewar writings. Sartre's *La Nausée* (1938) relates the reactions of an individual who becomes aware of the absurdity of surrounding reality and of his freedom to decide what to make of his existence in it. Louis Ferdinand Céline's *Voyage au bout de la nuit* (1932) concentrates on an individual's experience as he goes through a series of situations that seem to have no meaning or purpose.

André Malraux's *La Condition humaine* (1933) portrays the efforts of various characters to transcend limitations imposed on them by nature or other people.

A clearer articulation of existentialist concepts emerges in Sartre's *L'Etre et le néant* (1943), which posits a duality between the *en-soi* and the *pour-soi* as a key to understanding the difference between individuals who live unconsciously, as things do, "in themselves," and those who, by consciously choosing the purpose of their existence, live "for themselves." A similar existentialist outlook informs Albert Camus' *Le Mythe de Sisyphe* (1942), which dwells on the absurdity of human life whose end in death renders the individual's projects futile but also suggests that, like Sisyphus, human beings enjoy their arduous and seemingly endless tasks.

Existentialism in France never grew into an organized philosophical system. It remained a philosophical attitude shared by a loose group of intellectuals whose writings reflect the moods of anguish and hope that marked the 1930s, the Occupation period and the decade following the Second World War.

H. J. Blackham, *Six Existentialist Thinkers* (New York, 1952); M. Charlesworth, *The Existentialism of Jean-Paul Sartre* (New York, 1976); L. Orr, *Existentialism and Phenomenology* (Troy, N.Y., 1978); R. Solomon, *From Rationalism to Existentialism* (New York, 1972).

M. D. Maayan

Related entries: BEAUVOIR; CELINE; MALRAUX; MARCEL; SARTRE.

EXPRESSIONISM, major early-twentieth-century artistic movement concerned with communication of subjective feeling and emotion by means of emphasis, exaggeration, and/or distortion for expressive purpose. Although primarily a movement in the visual arts, expressionism also manifested itself in other art forms, such as architecture, literature, music, drama, and film. A widespread European phenomenon, expressionism was nonetheless centered in Germany, Austria, and Switzerland. From there it fanned out to Scandinavia and Eastern Europe, while in France it took the form of fauvism. Though fauvism was not an outgrowth of expressionism or vice-versa, these parallel movements influenced and stimulated each other.

A movement rather than a grouping of artists, expressionism did not have a coherent program but took on many different shades depending, among other factors, on geographical location. Within the German-speaking world alone, at least four major centers of expressionism may be distinguished: Dresden, Munich, Berlin, and Vienna.

Although expressionism has many faces, several common characteristics may be noted. Expressionist painting developed out of the proto-expressionist art of the late nineteenth century, particularly the work of Vincent van Gogh, Ferdinand Hodler, and Edvard Munch, and to a lesser extent that of Henri de Toulouse-Lautrec and Paul Gauguin. The works of these artists became known in Germany in the early years of the twentieth century and had a strong impact on young artists. The expressionists, in addition, were influenced by late medieval and early Renaissance painting in Germany, and by various forms of primitive art, such as German folk art, children's drawings, and African and Oceanic sculpture.

One of the paramount characteristics of expressionism is a daring use of color. Early expressionist paintings by such artists as Ernst Kirchner, Wassily Kandinsky, and Alexej von Jawlensky generally show bright, gay colors on the warm side of the spectrum. Later expressionist paintings tend toward a cooler palette often with a predominance of blue (Oskar Kokoschka, Max Beckmann).

The expressionists tend to use bold contours often marked by a deliberate angularity. The predilection for angular lines can best be seen in the graphic work of the period, which consists almost exclusively of woodcuts, a medium well suited to the expressionist aesthetic. Linear angularity takes on many different aspects in expressionist painting, such as the jagged and frazzled contours of the mature work of Kirchner, the nervous febrile line of Egon Schiele and the early Kokoschka, the cubistic angularity of Franz Marc, and the awkward, primitive gauntness of Emil Nolde.

B. S. Myers, *The German Expressionists* (New York, 1957); P. Selz, *German Expressionist Painting* (Berkeley, 1957); J. Willett, *Expressionism* (New York 1970).

P. t.-D Chu

Related entries: ART: MAJOR STYLES AND MOVEMENTS; FAUVISM; KLEE; TOULOUSE-LAUTREC; VAN GOGH.

F

FABRE-LUCE, ALFRED (b. 1899), controversial and iconoclastic essayist. Born in Paris to the wealthy bourgeoisie, he was the grandson of Henri Germain, the founder of the Crédit lyonnais. After studies at the Sorbonne and the Ecole des sciences politiques, he served brief apprenticeships as an attaché with the French embassy in London, an assistant to a minister of the interior, and a collaborator of André François-Poncet's Société d'études et d'informations économiques. He then embarked on a precocious career as a writer, first attracting attention with his anti-Poincarist *La Victoire* in 1924. In addition to writing numerous books, he took up journalism, founding *Pamphlet* (1933–34), a collaborative effort with Pierre Dominique and Jean Prévost, serving as editor of *L'Europe nouvelle* (1934–35), and founding the violently anti–Popular Front *L'Assaut* (1936–37). Though long identified with the Left, he became fully committed to Jacques Doriot's Parti populaire français in 1937, contributing regularly to Doriot's *La Liberté* with which *L'Assaut* had merged. He broke with the party after Munich and began working closely with Georges Bonnet in support of appeasement. A highly original writer, brash and individualistic, Fabre-Luce suffered imprisonment both during and after the Second World War for his uncompromising views.

His writings include: *La Crise des alliances* (Paris, 1922); *Locarno sans rêves* (Paris, 1927); *Russie 1927* (Paris, 1928); *Après la législature des dupes. Le 22 avril* (Paris, 1928); *Pour une politique sexuelle* (Paris, 1929); *Caillaux* (Paris, 1933); *Révolution à Cuba* (Paris, 1934); *Le Secret de la République* (Paris, 1938); *Histoire secrète de la conciliation de Munich* (Paris, 1938); *Journal de la France* (Paris, 1940–47); *Anthologie de la nouvelle Europe* (Paris, 1942); *Vingt-cinq années de la liberté* (Paris, 1962–64); and *J'ai vécu plusieurs siècles* (Paris, 1974).

D. Wolf, *Die Doriot-Bewegung* (Stuttgart, 1967).

J. R. Braun

Related entries: BONNET; DORIOT; FRANCOIS-PONCET.

FAGUET, EMILE (1847–1916), political commentator, literary critic, savant. Born in La Roche-sur-Yon (Vendée) into an intellectual family, he entered the Ecole normale supérieure in 1867 and later passed his *agrégation*. He then attended the Sorbonne and received his *doctorat* in letters in 1883. During this same year, Faguet published his first work, his doctoral thesis, *La Tragédie française au XVIe siècle*.

Thus began Faguet's prolific literary career. A disciple of Hippolyte Taine, Charles Sainte-Beuve, Auguste Comte, and Ernest Renan, Faguet was to write over 200 volumes, some composed in weeks or months, dealing with an amazing variety of subjects. In his wish to understand and explain everything, Faguet dealt with literary, political, moral, and social questions. He was probably best known for his literary studies, including his four-volume series *Etudes littéraires*, one on each century from the sixteenth through the nineteenth.

Faguet was also a highly respected professor and was said to be clear and precise in his delivery of class material. He possessed an ability to analyze, synthesize, and systematize the character, general ideas, and tendencies of an author and his works.

One of the most eminent scholars of his time, Faguet was elected to the Académie française in 1901. Because of his incredible productivity, he is often accused of being too superficial and too impatient to finish one work before moving on to the next. The volume, diversity, and scope of his works, however, made of Faguet one of the last nineteenth-century savants, scholars who put breadth of vision before professional specialization. According to Gustave Lanson, when Faguet died in Paris in 1916, he had written more than both the famous Diderot and Voltaire had written in their lifetimes.

R. D'Amat, ed., *Dictionnaire de biographie française* (Paris, 1975); A. Belier, *La Critique française à la fin du XIXe siècle* (Paris, 1926); E. Faguet, *Drame ancien, drame moderne* (Paris, 1898); V. Giraud, *Les Maîtres de l'heure* (Paris, 1919); G. Lanson, *Histoire de la littérature française* (Paris, 1952); L. Petit de Julleville, *Histoire de la langue et de la littérature française*, vol. 8 (Paris, 1899).

                                                                        A. J. Staples
Related entry: LITERARY CRITICS AND CRITICISM.

FALL OF FRANCE (1940), an expression used to characterize the sudden and unexpected collapse of French resistance to Germany's invasion of Western Europe on 10 May 1940. The consequences of this collapse include the death of the Third Republic, the spread of the Nazi regime over the continent of Europe, and the expansion of the Second World War into the world's most devastating conflict.

The collapse was an indirect consequence of the price France paid for victory in the First World War. The revulsion at the horror and seeming futility of mechanized violence spanned the French political spectrum. The Treaty of Versailles restricted German armaments and thus offered security against German *revanche*, but the United States and Britain failed to ratify treaties guaranteeing

French security, while Soviet Russia seemed hostile. So France sought alliances among the new states of Eastern Europe and with Belgium; in 1923 the French government ordered the Ruhr occupied to enforce the settlement on a recalcitrant Germany. But the occupation disrupted the French economy and destroyed what remained of the coalition of 1918.

In 1925 France changed its tack by signing the Locarno Accords, by which Germany accepted its western frontiers and the permanent demilitarizing of the Rhineland. Amid the prosperity of the late 1920s, disarmament talks began under the auspices of the League of Nations. But in the early 1930s, the Great Depression helped bring Adolf Hitler to power in Germany; in 1935 Hitler began to rearm openly, with apparent British approval.

One direct cause of the fall was France's inability to face up to the need to act against Hitler while Germany was still too weak to fight. In March 1936, just after Belgium denounced its military accord with France, Hitler remilitarized the Rhineland. Having fortified the Rhineland, Hitler was free to rearm a population one-and-one-half times that of France and to draw on an industry two to three times stronger. He could then turn on France's eastern allies. The French public, divided by the effects of the depression and an election campaign that would bring the Popular Front to power, was in no mood to risk the horrors of another war to stop Hitler from occupying German soil. Nonetheless France began a major rearmament program.

By spring 1938, Hitler was strong enough to act. At Munich in September, Edouard Daladier joined Neville Chamberlain in abandoning Czechoslovakia rather than risk a total war in which the German Luftwaffe, which had engaged in terror bombing during the Spanish Civil War, threatened their population centers. But Hitler's seizure of the rump Czech state in March 1939 convinced almost all the appeasers that only force would stop Hitler: in June 1939, 76 percent of Frenchmen questioned in a Gallup poll favored the use of force to prevent further aggression.

In August 1939, the German-Soviet nonaggression pact freed Hitler to attack Poland; Britain and France declared war on 3 September. The mood in France was one of grim resignation to the new war. The slow mobilization of the huge French Army and French weakness in the air combined with Belgian neutrality to make an effective offensive against Germany impossible. By mid-October the front settled into the *drôle de guerre*: patrol actions along the Maginot Line and in the air with feverish activity in the rear as the Allies worked to match German armaments. Morale dropped during the period of inaction; in March 1940 Paul Reynaud came to power on a tide of public demand for some kind of action. Operations in Norway were, in part, a result.

A second direct cause of the fall limited the effectiveness of the Allied effort. Belgium and the Netherlands remained stubbornly neutral until actually invaded, and Britain withheld the bulk of its Royal Air Force (RAF) from the Continent while contributing only a small land force. The Allied coordinator, General Maurice Gamelin, planned to send most of the modern elements of the French

Army into the southern Netherlands and Belgium to meet the expected German invasion, to secure French territory, to preserve the substantial armies of the small powers, and to seize bases that would attract the RAF onto the Continent. These bases would also provide a springboard for an offensive into Germany. British reluctance and Belgian and Dutch neutrality made planning difficult, and Gamelin and Reynaud disagreed on strategy. Reynaud's government split over the issue of Gamelin's dismissal and fell from power before Germany struck on 10 May.

Reynaud resumed office, but his differences with Gamelin deepened as the expedition to the southern Netherlands failed and as the German Army unexpectedly broke the weak center of the French front on the Meuse River to the south and west of the Ardennes forests. The breakthrough threatened both Paris and the communications of the Allied armies in Belgium. On 14 May General Alphonse Georges, the Allied operational commander, collapsed under the pressure; salvation depended on Gamelin. Finally on 19 May Gamelin ordered an Allied counteroffensive. But Reynaud replaced him that same day with General Maxime Weygand. Weygand picked up Gamelin's plan, but precious time was lost. The Allied coalition unraveled; the Belgian Army capitulated, and the British and some French troops abandoned the Continent at Dunkerque, leaving most of the modern units of the French Army to be destroyed or captured in the north.

Outnumbered two to one, the remaining French forces were unable to halt the second German offensive, which began 5 June. On 10 June Italy joined the war against the Allies; on 14 June Paris fell. As French forces dissolved and millions of refugees fled south, the Reynaud cabinet split over the issue of continuing the fight from the French overseas empire. On 16 June Reynaud resigned and recommended Marshal Philippe Pétain, an aging defeatist reactionary, as his successor. On 17 June Pétain called for an armistice with Germany, which was signed on 22 June and put into effect on 25 June. By its provisions northern, eastern, and western France fell into German hands. Millions of refugees wandered in the countryside; the government was in chaos. With 120,000 soldiers dead and 250,000 wounded, losses greater than for a comparable period at Verdun, and 1.5 million captured, France was prostrate. Nor were many Frenchmen in a mood to respond to the appeal of 18 June from Charles de Gaulle for resistance. No regime could survive such a defeat. On 10 July, 569 of the 666 members present in the National Assembly voted to vest control of France in Pétain and his *Etat français*. The Third Republic was dead.

Successive political, economic, and military leaders of the Third Republic committed their share of hesitations and blunders in easing Hitler's way to victory in June 1940. It is clear in retrospect that France missed a great opportunity to stop Hitler in 1935 and 1936 when he threw off the restraints of Versailles and the Locarno Accords. The political leaders of the time, and particularly General Gamelin, bear a heavy responsibility for the failure to make clear to the public just how much France risked by allowing Hitler to exploit superior German resources to create his war machine without hindrance. Would the French public, preoccupied with the economic effects of the depression and justly horrified by the memories of the First World War, have responded? Probably not; and Hitler took care to cover his weakness by exploiting French and Western European pacifism to the fullest extent possible. By the time Hitler's aggressive intentions were clear, March 1939, it was too late for France to stop Hitler without outside help. But the record of the Third Republic in resisting Hitler was better than that of any other Western state; the failure of the Allies to form an effective coalition around France proved decisive in the spring of 1940. As for the Third Republic, it died in battle.

J.-B. Duroselle, *La Décadence* (Paris, 1979); J.A. Gunsburg, *Divided and Conquered* (Westport, Conn., 1979); H. Michel, *La Défaite de la France* (Paris, 1980); R. J. Young, *In Command of France* (Cambridge, Mass., 1978).

J. A. Gunsburg

Related entries: CZECHOSLOVAKIA, ALLIANCE WITH; DALADIER; GAMELIN; GEORGES; GERMANY, RELATIONS WITH (1914–1940); MAGINOT LINE; MUNICH CONFERENCE; PETAIN; REYNAUD; WEYGAND.

FALLEN SOLDIER, CULT OF THE. Following the loss of a generation of Frenchmen during the First World War, remembrance of fallen soldiers became the object of a secular, national cult. Honoring France's war dead gave individual deaths a national and political significance. The Third Republic was particularly disposed to raising monuments to itself. Monuments to its defenders provided the setting for the celebration of Armistice Day, 11 November, which quickly became as important a national holiday as 14 July. Whether in the spirit of revenge or simple commemoration, a national memory was created. The guarding of that memory was entrusted to veterans' organizations, but it encompassed everyone.

Equal treatment of the dead of all ranks expressed the growing democratization of French society. War memorials had previously honored generals and their victories. Such was the case of the Parisian Arc de Triomphe, identifying 386 generals and their battles. The monument's meaning changed in the wake of the First World War when the body of an unknown soldier was brought there on 11 November 1920 to be buried beneath an eternal flame.

War dead from the violent founding of the Third Republic had been honored in ways that presaged the new cult. The loss to the Prussians meant that memorials would honor all the dead, not only the victorious. In fact the French monument at Sedan resembles contemporary Prussian monuments marking the victory of 1871. Various groups in French society contributed to the emerging national cult. The church became involved, as the basilica of Sacré-Coeur in Paris was begun in 1876 as an act of national expiation. The Left honored the fallen Communard fighters of 1871 on the site of their death in the cemetery of Père Lachaise.

But it was the First World War that provided the greatest opportunity to honor the common soldier. Monuments appeared in every French village in the years immediately following the armistice. Typically placed opposite the town hall, identifying soldiers of the village by name, they became focal points of public life. As the war had been won, Marianne, the female symbol of the French Republic, sometimes became identified with Nike, Greek goddess of victory; more frequently, however, the monuments consisted of only a simple column. In some churches, depictions of soldiers replaced those of souls in purgatory.

The cult of the fallen soldier was not limited to the village. Battlegrounds became cemeteries, pilgrimage sites for the French nation. It was hoped that the burial ground would be perfectly democratic: one man, one stone. But the slaughter was too great, and many bodies remained unidentified. Consequently large single monuments marked some of the vaster battlegrounds.

The First World War is often seen as the event that unified the French nation. Military service united people who had previously been divided by class and geography. The cult that surrounded those who died in service to France reinforced national identification in the postwar period.

M. Agulhon, *Marianne au combat* (Paris, 1979), and "La 'Statuomanie' et l'histoire," *Ethnologie française* 8 (1978); P. Ariès, *L'Homme devant la mort* (Paris, 1977); B. Cousin and C. Richier, "Les Monuments aux morts de la guerre 1914–1918 dans les Bouches-du-Rhône," in *Iconographie et histoire des mentalités* (Paris, 1979); R. Koselleck, "Les Monuments aux morts depuis la Révolution française," in *Iconographie et histoire des mentalités* (Paris, 1979); P. Sorlin, *La Société française*, vol. 2 (Paris, 1971); G. and M. Vovelle, *Vision de la mort et de l'au-delà en Provence* (Paris, 1970).

D. G. Troyansky

Related entries: BLANQUISTS; CEMETERY, CULT OF THE; COMMUNARDS; FRANCO-PRUSSIAN WAR; FUNERALS, STATE; NATIONALISM; WORLD WAR I.

FALLIERES, ARMAND (1841–1931), provincial lawyer, mayor, deputy, six-time cabinet minister, prime minister, senator, and president of the Republic (1906–13). He thus followed the typical route to the Elysée established by the turn of the century. He was reputed to be impartial. Although slightly to the left of his predecessor, Emile Loubet, Fallières was elected a deputy from the Lot-et-Garonne in 1876 and represented the department until 1885. He then sat in the Senate from 1890 to 1906.

Fallières cut a corpulent figure with white beard, a southern accent, a taste for good food and wine, and strong paternal feelings. These traits made him as popular with his fellow politicians as with the public. He defeated the more conservative Paul Doumer, who had helped bring down Emile Combes and who was supported by the Right, for the presidency.

Aside from the Moroccan crisis of 1912 (in which he kept himself informed but played no part in the negotiations) his *septennat* was relatively free of international agitation. At home, social and fiscal issues replaced religious ones, and his administration was plagued by strikes and debate about taxes. On his many trips throughout the country, Fallières preached respect for the law. In

1912 he boasted of having kept peace with honor. The four prominent men whom he called to head the government, Georges Clemenceau, Aristide Briand, Joseph Caillaux, and Raymond Poincaré, were strong personalities, and whatever influence Fallières exercised was done privately.

Like his predecessors he showed most initiative in foreign affairs. He reassured foreign delegates to the Algeciras Conference (1906) of the continuity of French foreign policy. When the Moroccan settlement was ready for signature, the Rouvier government fell. Like Jules Grévy, who had signed peace overtures with China after the Jules Ferry government was ousted, Fallières accepted responsibility. At the time of the Agadir crisis (1912), he told members of the Caillaux government that in the event of war he would call for a coalition cabinet including Clemenceau and Paul Déroulède to govern the country.

J. Chastenet, *La France de M. Fallières* (Paris, 1949); A. Dansette, *Histoire des présidents de la République* (Paris, 1960); L. Derfler, *President and Parliament* (Boca Raton, Fla., 1983).

L. Derfler

Related entries: DOUMER; LOUBET; MOROCCAN CRISES; PRESIDENT OF THE REPUBLIC, OFFICE OF.

FAMILY: ATTITUDES TOWARD AND GOVERNMENTAL POLICIES CONCERNING. The family structure and function were similar for all social groups, but bourgeois and working-class families held different attitudes about the meaning of the family for themselves and for others. During the Third Republic the state became more involved in the private lives of families, either directly, in the case of working-class families, or indirectly, in the case of the bourgeoisie, to strengthen the units regarded as essential to maintaining the social order.

A hierarchical structure, based on the authority of the father, was the basis of traditional French family life. According to law, the husband was the head of the family and determined the family's place of residence, and the father exercised parental authority as head of the household and legal guardian of the children. In the absence of the father, guardianship usually fell upon the mother; also by law, a family council, composed of six relatives by blood or marriage (half from the paternal and half from the maternal side), confirmed the assignment of guardianship either to the mother or to another relative. Thus the family council assumed great importance in the rearing of a minor child in all circumstances in which the father was unable to fulfill his obligations.

Since one of the primary functions of the family, and of women within it, was reproduction, attitudes toward the family were intertwined with attitudes toward population growth. Anti-Malthusian and neo-Malthusian arguments represented two prominent positions on the subject of population growth. The neo-Malthusians saw birth control as the means to combat poverty and its consequences. They espoused the view that the excessive fecundity of lower-class families was a chief cause of their misery. Since many working-class husbands, moreover, could not fully support their families, any necessary state supplementary aid placed a strain on public finances. The increasing numbers of the urban working classes, the neo-Malthusians further maintained, led to unequal population growth: an overly large working class was perceived as a present political threat, and the children of working-class families were seen as a future political danger. The desire to control the population, especially to reduce the proportion of working-class births, was the predominant attitude of government officials until the 1880s.

The anti-Malthusian, familiast, or pronatalist movement gained ground in the 1880s when three events led to a revision of official opinion: (1) the crushing of the Commune in 1871 eliminated the problem of the internal threat posed by the working classes in the cities; (2) colonies overseas were being acquired, and these were seen as places to export the surplus working-class population; and (3) the loss of population vis-à-vis Germany promoted fears that the French population would be increasingly unable to provide necessary troop strength. Conjointly, in the 1880s and 1890s, with the advent of child labor laws and compulsory education for children through age thirteen, working-class families no longer saw increased numbers of children as an economic asset, and they began to limit family size. Thus, official policy shifted to encouraging the growth of population, particularly among the urban working classes.

Within this tradition, the bourgeoisie and working classes differed both in how their families functioned and in attitudes toward family life. To governmental policy makers, the social and economic usefulness of the bourgeois family constituted the ideal because it was built on the affective ties of its members, provided a place of privacy, and gave educational support to the children. In short, the bourgeois family allowed all of its members to thrive. The quality of relationships was important, and hence marriages were late (twenty-seven to twenty-nine years of age for men and twenty-three to twenty-four for women), not only to ensure a means of support for the family but also to limit family size, which in itself helped maintain a family's financial resources. One or two children were the norm. Family respectability meant upper bourgeois wives did not work for wages outside the home. Their main role was to manage the household and supervise the education of their children. Governmental authorities sentimentalized the functions of motherhood and saw the education of children as a means to inculcate certain personality traits useful to society.

The working-class family was a unit for economic survival. Unlike the women in the bourgeois household, working-class wives frequently held wage-earning positions outside the home, as well as having responsibility for household management. The authorities perceived deterioriation of traditional values in working-class family life. In the 1880s more men than women populated the cities, and consequently a greater number of men were eligible for marriage. Authorities feared further decline of the traditional legal family among the working classes because of the propensity for illicit unions, resulting in the increasingly younger age of marriage for women. Both were seen as threats to social stability since they would lead not only to an increase in the children of unwed mothers but also to a disproportionate increase in working-class children vis-à-vis their bourgeois counterparts. Women's need to work for wages also threatened traditional family life in that children were sent out to wet nurses until World War I, with the concomitant high infant mortality associated with wet nursing.

The prevailing policy in the 1880s and 1890s aimed to protect families financially and to encourage families of three or more children. To this end, the statistician Dr. Jacques Bertillon and the philanthropist Emile Cheysson created the National Alliance for the Increase of the French Population. In 1913, to encourage families to have children, the state began its program of financial assistance to *familles nombreuses* (those with three or more children) and in 1932 added a bonus to parents if the first birth occurred within two years of marriage. By the 1920s the pro-family movement had such a strong hold that a law in 1920 even prohibited any propaganda relating to contraception. Furthermore, the opposing neo-Malthusian movement had become discredited in governing circles because one of its leaders, Paul Robin, was associated with anarchism.

To support the pronatalist attitudes, governmental policies fostered marriage and the strengthening of family ties. But marriage did not seem to quicken the birthrate. Between 1860 and 1931, the proportion of women who married increased by 12 percent, and there was a decline in the percentage of unmarrieds in the twenty to forty age bracket. Nonetheless, fecundity decreased by 43 percent. Families had fewer children. Authorities attributed this to the increase in ambitions of individual families. Couples aimed to satisfy their social and economic aspirations and to ensure the success of their offspring. The marriage rate itself reflected outside economic events. It decreased slightly in the 1880s among agriculture workers during the economic crisis, which made furnishing a dowry difficult and hence was a deterrent to marriage. Urban workers did not experience this decline in marriage in the 1880s since their wages generally were not hurt by the economic crisis and since dowry portions were less essential to wedding vows. From 1896, when a period of prosperity began, the number of marriages increased until 1914. During World War I the marriage rate declined, although it increased dramatically immediately afterward. Throughout the Third Republic, however, the average age of marriage for women remained relatively stable at 23.8 years and declined from 28 to 27 years for men (except from 1914 to 1919, when the average age increased to 29 for men and 25 for women).

The reestablishment of divorce in 1884 might seem a direct contradiction of government policies aimed at strengthening the family and increasing children with the family. Divorce, however, was so difficult and so expensive to obtain that it was limited to the middle class. The divorce rate rose until 1920, when it stabilized at 5 percent of all marriages. Furthermore, divorce allowed remarriage and the creation of a new family unit, whereas separation did not, and separation without divorce served to weaken a family. The only grounds for divorce were adultery of either spouse, the sentencing of a spouse to degrading punishment, or violence or abuses when repeated, serious, and unbearable. In case of divorce, as in all other custody proceedings, guardianship of the child and his or her property belonged to whichever parent had the custody.

Although new values were attached to the privacy and intimacy of increasingly smaller families, the state increasingly invaded that privacy through its tutelary apparatus—doctors, welfare bureaucracies, psychiatric workers, counselors, teachers, and judges. For the bourgeois family, that intrusion came primarily with the medical personnel, who influenced family life by directing and advising mothers. Their advice began with regular prenatal care and increasingly and successfully encouraging mothers to give birth in hospitals. Doctors then prescribed pediatric care, which ranged from advising a mother to regulate the hours of sleep and the frequency of feeding she should allow her baby to examining and selecting the wet nurse who fed the baby in the mother's home. Doctors gave this advice and mothers accepted it in the name of the new medical science. The doctors made the wives and mothers the agents of their medical influence in the family.

For working-class families, the paternal power of the state was more pervasive. In many instances the state did not operate through the family, as in the case of doctors and middle-class mothers, but in lieu of the family. Such efforts were initially inspired by the ruling authorities' fear of class conflict and the government's attempt to educate and control the poor. Such governmental influence began with the social workers and doctors in special maternity hospitals (the Maisons maternelles) and in the free infant health and feeding clinics (Instituts de puériculture). As the child got older, governmental influence pervaded the preschools, (Ecoles maternelles), primary and secondary schools, and state-sponsored and regulated leisure activities for the children. In 1904 the state assumed authority for all parentless children and those with behavioral problems. With the establishment of a separate juvenile court system in 1912, there was no longer an adversary relationship between the children and the court, but the court acted in loco parentis as the protector of the child.

The rights of the family depended on cooperation with the social workers, law enforcers, judge, and court. The substitution of state for parental authority began in 1889 with the law that provided that in cases where the family was judged immoral, neglectful, or abusive of the child, the state could deprive the father of parental authority and assume it for itself. Offenses of adolescents were treated as symptoms of an unhealthy domestic environment. The state made inquiries into the family morality, demanded that families comply with principles of hygiene and child care, and removed the children from the family, if necessary, to protect the child from immoral or abusive parents and also to protect the other children in the family from the pernicious influence of that child.

For working-class families, then, outside intervention did not necessarily strengthen the family; instead it often transferred parental authority to a team of social service and medical professionals. Thus, despite the governmental laws and policies to strengthen the family and increase the number of children per family, another set of governmental policies served to extend the power and

influence of outside forces (doctors, teachers, social service personnel) within
the family and in the raising of the children.

J. Donzelot, *The Policing of Families* (New York, 1979); G. Duplessis-le Guélinel,
Les mariages en France (Paris, 1954); M. L. McDougall, "Protecting Infants: The
Campaign for Maternity Leaves, 1890s–1930," *French Historical Studies*, 13 (Spring
1983); M. Perrot, *La Mode de vie des familles bourgeoises* (Paris, 1961); J. Russotto
and F. Samuel, *French Family Law* (Cambridge, Mass., 1965); M. Segalen, *Mari et
femme dans la société paysanne* (Paris, 1980); L. Tilly and J. Scott, *Women, Work and
Family* (New York, 1978); E. Weber, *Peasants into Frenchmen* (Stanford, 1976); T.
Zeldin, *France* (Oxford, 1974).

R. G. Fuchs

Related entries: CHILDREN: ATTITUDES TOWARD; CHILDREN: GOV-
ERNMENT POLICIES CONCERNING; DIVORCE; SOCIAL WELFARE:
FAMILY AND CHILDREN; WOMEN: ATTITUDES TOWARD.

FASCISM. Though always a minority, this congeries of movements and
ideologues played a highly visible and occasionally influential role in interwar
France. Notoriously difficult to define or delimit, French fascism should be
distinguished from the prewar right-wing movements that did not combine
systematic economic and political antiliberalism with a revolutionary project
based on mass mobilization. Nevertheless, such movements, from Boulangism
to the Cercle Proudhon, were important precursors. Similarly, the development
of French fascism between the wars was paralleled by the rise of a series of
closely related more-or-less conservative authoritarian rightist groups like the
ideologically fuzzy Jeunesses patriotes (JPs) and Croix de feu (CdF).

The most important parallel movement, both before and between the wars,
was the royalist Ligue d'action française (AF). Backed by its newspaper, a daily
from 1908 through the Second World War, this authoritarian, traditionalist,and
violence-prone organization had an influence far outside its membership of over
60,000. The AF both helped and hindered the growth of French fascism. On
the one hand, many future fascists earned their stripes in the royalist league. On
the other hand, its uncommon vigor and longevity helped to block the formation
of a single, powerful fascist party.

Although most of the ideological components of French fascism had been
present for much of the history of the Third Republic, it was the two periods of
crisis, the monetary and political collapse of 1924–26 and the great depression
of the 1930s, which saw the birth and rapid growth of most French fascist
movements. These crises brought together the reality or threat of leftist governments
and economic distress that could generate both the popular base and the business
support necessary to organize any successful radical rightist movement.

The crisis occasioned by the victory of the Cartel des gauches in 1924 led not
only to the development of a new conservative paramilitary group, the JPs, and
the expansion of existing leagues but also to the birth of France's first openly
fascist party, the Faisceau of Georges Valois. A long-time AF militant, Valois

took from the parent organization both some of the leaders of his movement and the royalists' extreme antiparliamentarism. His original contribution was not only the domestication of the fascist name, adopted from Italy, but also the focusing on what would remain the preferred clientele of French fascist and right-wing movements: the veterans.

Ideologically, the Faisceau owed less to royalism. Valois called for a "national revolution," which would be led by a *chef* supported by the organized veterans but would leave the eventual political form of the French state open to future decision. His economic and social program was more specific. It called for integral syndicalism, involving the mutual constraint of workers and employers that would create increased productivity, lower prices, higher wages, and social peace. The Faisceau also eschewed the anti-Semitism that had been a mainstay of the prewar Right. After gathering over 60,000 members, the Faisceau declined following Raymond Poincaré's parliamentary and monetary stabilization. When it finally died in 1928, it had been scuttled as much by Valois' forced march leftward as by the end of the crisis. Its closest competitors, the JPs and the AF, survived though with reduced followings.

During the last years of prosperity, many former Faisceau members gravitated to the veteran-dominated organizations of the right-wing millionaire François Coty who had also been one of the Faisceau's major, though unfaithful, backers. Among these was the former Faisceau propaganda chief, and richly decorated war veteran, Marcel Bucard. In 1933 he founded France's second overtly fascist party, the Francistes. Its ideology was based on the Faisceau, corrected in a more authoritarian direction and with a vaguer corporative program. In addition, Bucard, who accepted Italian money, joined Benito Mussolini's fascist international as French representative and eventually, as the 1930s advanced, added an increasingly virulent anti-Semitism to his other negations.

The 10,000 members of the Parti franciste were overshadowed by two other, more conservative groups that emerged from Coty's wings. The largest, the CdF, was initially founded as an exclusively veterans' organization, but after being taken over by Colonel François de La Rocque in 1930, it was opened to nonveterans and grew to over 500,000. More faithful to Coty's ideas was the Solidarité française, which combined a program of strengthening the executive with anticommunism, antimasonism, and anti-Semitism.

Fascism in interwar France also drew from two cultural movements, both conceived in opposition to the fundamental conservatism of Third Republic society. The first movement, rooted in antiparliamentarism and seeking to transcend the traditional distinction between Right and Left while also eliminating liberal capitalism, called for economic expansion and technical progress largely through the implementation of a plan or plans. The *planiste* movement had followers on both the Left and Right and attracted many of the nonconformists of the 1930s. Closely related to this current were the neosocialists, the product of a schism in the Socialist party (SFIO). Although these heretics, led by Marcel Déat and Adrien Marquet, left the party in 1933 over the issue of support for, and participation in, bourgeois governments, their socialism rapidly evolved to the right from a tactical alliance with the middle classes to corporatism, a social or just price, and the creation of paramilitary groups.

The second major cultural movement was a revolt against a bourgeoisie overstuffed with wine, food, tobacco, and speeches and characterized by greed, physical cowardice, and an unhealthy sexuality. For some young intellectuals, like the brilliant writer Robert Brasillach and his fellow journalists at the right-wing *Je suis partout*, fascism promised to replace such decadence with a youthful cult of health, sport, virility, and communion in the great outdoors.

The second major wave of French fascism took place during the Great Depression, but its development was shaped by the events of February 1934 and their aftershocks. On 6 February, a large crowd of demonstrators that included members of the right-wing leagues and communists, as well as more respectable middle-class groups like the Taxpayers League, angry over the Stavisky scandal, demonstrated in front of the Chamber of Deputies and fought with the police. The result was a few dead, many more wounded, a Right-Center government of national union, and, for the Left, the myth of an attempted fascist takeover. This fascist threat then served as the basis for an alliance of socialists, communists, and radicals. The resulting Popular Front victory of 1936, greeted by a wave of strikes, badly frightened sectors of the French bourgeoisie. In addition, the accession of a Jewish socialist prime minister opened more opportunities for anti-Semitic agitation. In this sense, French fascism was also an anti-antifascism.

The political earthquakes of 1934–35 led in other ways to fascism as well. The popular Communist mayor of Saint-Denis, Jacques Doriot, who had attempted to provoke a communist-socialist alliance before 6 February 1934, in defiance of his party's line, was expelled for indiscipline at the same time the Communist party (PCF) was officially accepting the need for such a tactic. Vigorously denounced by his former comrades and blocked from any dealings with the Socialists by the Popular Front, Doriot had to abandon his original plans to serve as the unifier of the French Left. Starting with a program of a sort of national communism, he speedily evolved to the right and in 1936 founded the largely fascist Parti populaire français (PPF). This new group, which peaked at approximately 100,000 members, consisted of former Communists, many workers from Saint-Denis, former Radicals like Bertrand de Jouvenel, intellectuals like Pierre Drieu la Rochelle, and members of the middle classes. For several years, it also attracted important business support. PPF ideology was revolutionary and nationalist, but its socialism gradually gave way to corporatism and the defense of the middle classes. Anticommunism, almost an obsession with Doriot, was combined with antimasonism and anti-Semitism. Doriot's fascism, like Déat's, was that of a politician squeezed out by the workings of Third Republic politics.

The polarization of French politics during the mid-1930s, aided by vicious rightist newspaper campaigns like the one that provoked the suicide of a Socialist minister of the interior, led to increased political violence. A common pattern was that of right-wing meetings (of the PPF, the CdF, or JPs) that were met with leftist counterdemonstrations and led to violence.

French governments moved to halt the rising tide of violence by outlawing the paramilitary leagues. During the agitation preceding the 1936 election, a group of former AF members attacked Léon Blum, and as a result the royalist league was banned. Later the Popular Front government effectively outlawed all paramilitary groups. The principal rightist movements reorganized themselves as political parties. The CdF, which became the Parti social français (PSF), was the only one to exercise any serious influence.

One of the effects of this change was to put French fascists into more direct competition with the established conservative parties. Despite their fanatical opposition to the Popular Front and all its works, the French radical Right could not unite. A Front de la liberté to oppose communism was formed in 1937, but the largest movement, the PSF, refused to join.

By 1938 and 1939, with the parliamentary collapse of the Popular Front, the approach of war, and an improving economic situation, French fascism was clearly on the decline. It was only the defeat and German occupation that gave it a new lease on life but now as a tool of the Nazis, to be used as necessary to threaten the more conservative Vichy government.

P. Machefer, *Ligues et fascismes en France* (Paris, 1974); J. Plumyène and R. Lasierra, *Les Fascismes français, 1923–1963* (Paris, 1963); R. Rémond, *The Right Wing in France* (Philadelphia, 1969); Z. Sternhell, *Ni droite ni gauche, L'Idéologie fasciste en France* (Paris, 1983); "Visages de fascistes français," special issue, *Revue d'histoire de la deuxième guerre mondiale* (1975).

A. Douglas

Related entries: ACTION FRANCAISE; ANTISEMITIC LEAGUE; ANTI-SEMITISM; BRASILLACH; BUCARD; COTY; CROIX DE FEU; DEAT; DEPRESSION OF THE 1930s; DORIOT; FEBRUARY RIOTS; JOUVENEL; LA ROCQUE; NATIONALISM; POPULAR FRONT; RIGHT, THE; STAVISKY AFFAIR; VALOIS.

FASHODA INCIDENT (1898), the high-water mark of Anglo-French competition in Africa. The Fashoda incident was precipitated by the French occupation in 1898 of a fort on the Upper Nile abandoned by Anglo-Egyptian forces in 1885 as a result of the Mahdist revolt in the Sudan. Since the Sudan had been abandoned, France considered the area *res nilius*. By occupying some part of it, the French hoped to force the British to renegotiate their own control of Egypt. A widely held opinion in the 1890s was that whoever controlled the headwaters of the Nile controlled the future of Egypt. With this in mind, the French organized the Congo-Nile expedition under the command of Captain Jean-Baptiste Marchand in 1895. Marchand reached the Nile in 1898 where his men rebuilt the Fashoda fort. His group was to have been joined by a second expedition proceeding from Djibouti through Ethiopia, but this Clochette-Bonvalot mission failed to achieve the desired juncture at Fashoda.

The British, meanwhile, had organized an expedition of some 30,000 Egyptian troops to the Sudan regions the Marchand mission claimed for France. Marchand had only several hundred men under his command. The outcome was predictable: Marchand had to evacuate, and a diplomatic agreement eventually drew the border between the French and the Anglo-Egyptian spheres of influence in central Africa at the divide between the Nile and Congo basins.

In France, Foreign Minister Gabriel Hanotaux, who had presided over the challenge to British positions in Africa that climaxed in the Fashoda incident, was forced to resign. He was replaced at the Quai d'Orsay by Théophile Delcassé who, as colonial minister in 1894, had been the prime mover of the policy whose results were the Marchand Congo-Nile mission. Solving the French disagreement with the British over African issues, Delcassé was able to begin work on the Anglo-French entente of 1904.

C. M. Andrew, *Théophile Delcassé and the Making of the Entente Cordiale* (London, 1968); C. M. Andrew and A. S. Kanya-Forstner, "Gabriel Hanotaux, the Colonial Party and the Fashoda Strategy," in E. F. Penrose, ed., *European Imperialism and the Partition of Africa* (London, 1975); R. G. Brown, *Fashoda Reconsidered* (Baltimore, 1970); G. N. Sanderson, *England, Europe and the Upper Nile* (Edinburgh, 1965).

A. A. Heggoy

Related entries: DELCASSE; ENTENTE CORDIALE; GREAT BRITAIN, RELATIONS WITH; HANOTAUX; MARCHAND EXPEDITION.

FAURE, FELIX (1841–1899), sixth president of the Third Republic (1895–99), noted for effecting the Franco-Russian alliance, for his opposition to reopening the Dreyfus case, and for the romantic scandal attending his death. Faure was born in Paris, where he received a commercial education. He developed a major leather business in Le Havre, where he showed interest in local politics and became a lieutenant of Jules Siegfried, a leading republican figure in the area. Elected deputy in 1881, Faure sat with the Gambettists in the Union républicaine. He specialized in economic and colonial matters, taking a strong imperialist stand, and held occasional ministerial posts, including that of the navy in 1894, which he used to develop the port of Le Havre.

With the support of conservatives, he won the presidential election of 1895 (called after Casimir-Périer's resignation). Faure's detractors said that he owed his victory to his easy-going charm, his impeccable dress, and his likeable ordinariness. In fact, his fine presence and expansive manners enhanced his popularity and accounted for some influence exerted on his ministers, as well as his fellow (royal) chiefs of state. It was foreign affairs that most interested Faure. He saw the president as a guarantor of continuity, and he repeatedly reassured the czar and his advisers of France's long-term commitment to the alliance. Accordingly, he received Nicholas II in October 1896 and went to Russia the following year. He retained Gabriel Hanotaux as foreign minister through successive governments and gave him wide latitude in conducting foreign policy.

After the fall of the moderate Charles Dupuy and Alexandre Ribot governments, Faure called on the Radicals. His motives were not clear. He may have wanted to demonstrate his faith in the parliamentary system. Faure had spent time in England, presumably observing the British political system at work, and this may explain why, like Queen Victoria, he could designate two homogeneous governments representing opposed viewpoints, that of the Radical Léon Bourgeois and that of the moderate Jules Méline. Or the president may simply have wanted to show that an all-Radical government could not succeed. According to the historian of the Méline ministry (Georges Lachapelle), Faure's role was decisive both in choosing the prime minister and in getting Méline to resign after the 1898 legislative election produced no increase in the latter's majority. Faure's death in office came as a blow to anti-Dreyfusards, for he had worked to keep the case from being reopened, and his funeral provided the occasion for an aborted—and farcical—nationalist coup.

C. Braibant, *Félix Faure à l'Elysée* (Paris, 1963); A. Dansette, *L'Histoire des présidents de la République de Louis-Napoléon Bonaparte à Charles de Gaulle* (Paris, 1960); L. Derfler, *President and Parliament* (Boca Raton, 1983); F. Faure, "Mon élection à la présidence," *Revue hommes et mondes* 23 (January 1954).

L. Derfler

Related entries: BOURGEOIS; DREYFUS AFFAIR; HANOTAUX; MELINE; PRESIDENT OF THE REPUBLIC, OFFICE OF; PROGRESSISTS; RADICAL AND RADICAL-SOCIALIST PARTY; RUSSIA, ENTENTE WITH; RUSSIA, RELATIONS WITH; SIEGFRIED.

FAURE, GABRIEL (1845–1924), composer, musician, and administrator. Fauré was born at Pamiers (Ariège) in southwestern France on 12 May 1845. His mother came from the minor nobility, and his father directed a normal school. At the Niedermeyer School in Paris (1854–65), he prepared to become a Catholic church musician and studied composition with Camille Saint-Saëns. From 1877 Fauré served as an organist and choirmaster at the Church of the Madeleine in Paris. In February 1871 with Vincent d'Indy, Henri Duparc, and Immanuel Chabrier he organized the Société nationale de musique to promote the performance of contemporary compositions. At one of its programs, Marcel Proust heard the work by Fauré on which he based the description of Vinteuil's music in *A la recherche du temps perdu*. Despite his large output, Fauré was able to compose regularly only during his summer holidays. In 1896 Fauré became teacher of composition at the Paris Conservatory where his pupils would include Maurice Ravel, Georges Enesco, Jean Roger-Ducasse, and Nadia Boulanger. As director from 1905 to 1920, he revitalized the institution through curricular reforms and staff changes that made the Conservatory a center for innovation. Fauré died in Paris on 4 November 1924.

Fauré's stylistic development links the end of romanticism with the second quarter of the twentieth century. It covers a period in which the evolution of musical language was particularly rapid. The most advanced composer of his generation, he developed an identifiable style and created a personal musical language, primarily by widening the limits of harmony and tonality without destroying their senses. At the same time he proved a genius of melodic invention. His style had considerable influence on many early twentieth-century composers, and his harmonic and melodic innovations affected the teaching of harmony for later generations.

Fauré is most popularly known for his choral *Requiem*, which was composed from 1877 to 1890 and orchestrated in 1900. He is considered to be the greatest master of the French song, of which he wrote over sixty to the words of such romantic and symbolist poets as Victor Hugo, Charles Baudelaire, and Paul Verlaine. He is important for a wide range of chamber and piano compositions, as well as the music for two lyric operas, *Promethée* (1900) and *Penelope* (1913).

M. Long, *At the Piano with Fauré* (London, 1980); R. Orledge, *Gabriel Fauré* (London, 1979); N. Suckling, *Fauré* (London, 1946); J. Vuaillat, *Gabriel Fauré: musicien français* (Lyon, 1973).

D. E. Gardinier
and J. Z. Sevilla-Gardinier

Related entries: HUGO; IMPRESSIONISM; MUSIC; RAVEL.

FAURE, PAUL (1878–1960), journalist, deputy, and Socialist politician. Born in Perigueux (Dordogne) on 3 February 1878, the son of an ardent republican lawyer, he was attracted to socialism at a young age and became a member of the Parti ouvrier français in 1901. In 1904, at the age of twenty-six, he was elected mayor of Grignols (Gironde), becoming the youngest mayor in France. After serving as delegate to many socialist congresses, he became secretary of the Socialist party (SFIO) in 1905. During this period, he continued his career as journalist and wrote for many reviews, including the *Populaire du centre*, of which he became the editor-in-chief in 1912. An eloquent speaker, he served as deputy of the department of Saône-et-Loire from 1924 to 1932 and 1938 to 1942 and was also elected mayor of Le Creusot in 1924.

At the schism of the Socialist movement at Tours in 1920, Faure, with Léon Blum, assumed leadership of the reorganized SFIO. It was said that whereas Blum was the head of the party, Faure was its heart and soul. Ideologically, Faure was a disciple of Jules Guesde and held very traditional views regarding the role and formation of the Socialist party (including a growing hostility against the Communist party and a deep commitment to peace). Although Blum and Faure were closely allied, they often disagreed on domestic issues. Faure wanted the SFIO to remain autonomous and aloof; Blum wanted to broaden the alliance and build closer ties between Socialists and Communists. They disagreed, too, on foreign policy, with Faure supporting a more conciliatory stance toward Germany. Their differences reached the highest point of tension in 1938 over German aggression against Czechoslovakia (the Munich crisis). During Munich, Faure pushed for a policy of negotiation with Germany, which Blum opposed.

After that date, a reconciliation between the two Socialist leaders was no longer possible.

Faure's oratorial and journalist skills could always raise popular enthusiasm, and he traveled extensively to speak to socialist groups throughout the country. His deep pacifist convictions, fervent advocacy of nonintervention and of disarmament, and his staunch anticommunism made of Faure one of the two most important Socialist leaders in the interwar years, but his peace at any price policy finally alienated him permanently from Blum during the closing years of the Third Republic. He died in Paris on 16 November 1960.

N. Greene, *Crisis and Decline—The French Socialist Party in the Popular Front Era* (Ithaca, N.Y., 1969); J. Jolly, ed., *Dictionnaire des parlementaires français*, vol. 5 (Paris, 1968); G. Lefranc, *Le Mouvement socialiste sous la Troisième République (1875– 1940)* (Paris, 1963); D. Ligou, *Histoire du socialisme en France (1871–1961)* (Paris, 1962).

A. J. Staples

Related entries: BLUM; GUESDE; GUESDISTS; SOCIALISM, 1914–1940; SOCIALIST PARTY.

FAURE, SEBASTIEN (1858–1942), anarchist militant and publicist. Born in St. Etienne (Loire) into a comfortable and prominent bourgeois family, Faure was given a Catholic education. Although devout, he interrupted a novitiate in 1875 to assist in the family business and only gradually abandoned his religious convictions. In 1885 he moved to Bordeaux where he was attracted to the socialist doctrines of Jules Guesde and ran in the legislative elections of that year as a Guesdist. In 1888 he moved again, this time to Paris, where he evolved toward anarchism. Along with Louise Michel he founded the weekly, *Le Libertaire*, in 1895. Faure became a leading anarchist orator and pamphleteer, an ardent anticlerical and antimilitarist, who during the Dreyfus affair supported the Dreyfusards with attacks on both the church and the military hierarchy. In 1904 he opened an experimental school for orphans, run according to his principles of communal living. It survived until wartime stringency forced its closing in 1917. During the war Faure was an outspoken pacifist, whose weekly newspaper was finally suppressed in 1918. After the war Faure resumed his anarchist propaganda and undertook a number of publishing projects, of which his four-volume *Encyclopédie anarchiste* was the most ambitious. He remained an active champion of anarchist causes until the time of his death in 1942.

J. Humbert, *Sébastien Faure* (Paris, 1949); J. Maitron, *Histoire du mouvement anarchiste en France (1880–1914)* (Paris, 1955).

T. Moodie

Related entry: ANARCHISM.

FAUVISM, short-lived artistic movement that originated in France in 1905; marked by the use (often arbitrarily) of bright colors and simplified or distorted forms. In 1905 a group of young artists, which included Charles Camoin, André Derain, Othon Friesz, Kees van Dongen, Henri Manguin, Albert Marquet, Henri

Matisse, Jean Puy, Georges Rouault, Louis Valtat, and Maurice de Vlaminck, shared a room at the Salon d'automne, an annual juried exhibition in Paris, recently founded by the architect Frantz Jourdain. The works of these artists generally met with little critical success, and one critic referred to them as *fauves*, or wild beasts, an offhand remark that became the name of a movement. Among the most striking works at the 1905 exhibition were Matisse's *Green Streak* and *Woman with Hat*, the "nastiest smear of paint . . . ever seen," even to Gertrude Stein's brother Leo, who bought it. In spite of adverse criticism, the fauvists, joined by Georges Braque and Raoul Dufy, exhibited again at the Salon d'automne of 1906, a year that marks the zenith of the movement. The paintings shown in 1906 included vividly colored landscapes by Braque, Derain, and Vlaminck, as well as Matisse's famous *Joy of Living* (Meryon, Penn., Barnes Foundation).

It was perhaps in the nature of fauvism that the movement could not last long. By 1907 the first artists began to defect, and a year later the movement as such ceased to exist. Yet the fauvist principle was carried on in somewhat revised form by Matisse and Dufy, who developed a less violent and more decorative fauvist style. Fauvism, moreover, had some impact on the German expressionist movement and influenced such artists as Alexej von Jawlensky, Wassily Kandinsky, Ernst Kirchner, and Max Pechstein.

Inspired in part by postimpressionist artists like Paul Gauguin, Vincent van Gogh, and Georges Seurat, the fauvist felt that the main purpose of art is not to reproduce reality faithfully but instead to express by means of color, line, and brushwork the artist's sensations regarding subject matter. Fauvism, then, is subjective rather than objective and reflects the artist's temperament, whether it be gracious (Derain), lyrical (Matisse), or aggressive (Vlaminck). Like many other early twentieth-century artisitc movements, fauvism was strongly influenced by various forms of primitive art, including Japanese prints, Persian miniatures (Matisse), and African and Oceanic art. The fauvists admired the apparent spontaneity of these art forms and were encouraged by their example to depart from the imitation of nature and to give free rein to their natural impulses.

G. Duthuit, *The Fauvist Painters* (New York, 1950); J.-E. Muller, *Fauvism* (New York and Washington, 1967); J. Elderfield, *The Wild Beasts: Fauvism and Its Affinities* (New York, 1976)

P. t-D. Chu

Related entries: ART: MAJOR STYLES AND MOVEMENTS; BRAQUE; EXPRESSIONISM; GAUGUIN; MATISSE; VAN GOGH; VLAMINCK.

FAVRE, JULES (1809–1880), lawyer, politician, minister of foreign affairs (4 September 1870–22 July 1871). The son of a Lyons merchant, he was a leading lawyer from the mid-1830s and a member of the National Assembly (1848–51) and the Legislative Body (1858–70), where he led the Republican "Five" (Ernest Picard, Emile Ollivier, Jacques-Louis Hénon, Alfred Darimon, 1857–63) as a critic of the Second Empire, notably of the Mexican expedition (1861–67). He voted against the war with Prussia and played an important role in the revolution of 4 September 1870, when he was named vice-president and minister of foreign affairs in the Government of National Defense. Elected to the National Assembly (1871–75), he remained as foreign minister under Adolphe Thiers but resigned in July on a pretext because of fatigue and to combat slanders about his personal life. (He had falsely declared he was married to the mother of his children). He continued to support Thiers (1871–73) and in 1875 spoke frequently in debates on the constitution. As a senator (1876–80) he opposed Maurice de MacMahon during the *seize mai* crisis (1877).

By 1869 Favre's stock was falling in Paris, where more radical republicans (including Léon Gambetta, whose career he had fostered) were in the ascendant. His long service in the republican cause nevertheless ensured his inclusion in the new government. He was unpopular among the masses in besieged Paris, and his diatribe (21 March 1871) against the communard insurgents ("cannibals") earned him the undying hatred of the extreme Left. His actions as foreign minister—especially the circular (6 September 1870) vowing "We will not yield an inch of our territory nor a stone of our fortresses," his meeting with Otto von Bismarck at Ferrières (18–19 September 1870), and his negotiation of the armistice (23 December 1870–8 January 1871)—have all remained controversial. The circular, which affirmed the new Republic's innocence and firmness, was intended to win the sympathy of the neutrals and impress both German and, above all, domestic opinion. But it left him little trading room and later haunted his (and the government's) reputation when the armistice and peace treaty were signed. In the Ferrières interview, which he secretly arranged on his own initiative, he tried to persuade Bismarck to grant an armistice so elections could be held for a national assembly that could make peace. He hoped to get France off with only an indemnity and was profoundly shocked when Bismarck revealed that Alsace and Lorraine were at stake. Unwilling to bargain, Favre broke off, the interview was publicized, and the war now became a "war of peoples." Taking into account circumstances on both sides, however, it is doubtful that Ferrières was truly a great lost opportunity to end the war early. As for the armistice, he failed, incredibly, to inform the Bordeaux branch-government (Gambetta) that it would not apply in the three departments in the east where General Charles Bourkabi's army was still hanging on. The Germans consequently turned that army's incipient defeat into a tragic rout into Switzerland. Although Favre played a role in other parleys during the war, Thiers was more prominent and was the negotiator of the Treaty of Frankfurt (ratified 21 May 1871).

Notwithstanding his prominence as a critic of the Second Empire's foreign policy, Favre was miscast by temperament as foreign minister. He was accounted one of the great courtroom and parliamentary orators of his day. In ideas he was a moderate democratic liberal of no striking originality. Despite his sober-sided appearance and penchant for fiery phrase making, he was kind and sweet-tempered, a nobly patriotic man of sensitive nerves whom Bismarck himself came to like and respect (while exploiting, nonetheless, his deficiencies as a practitioner of high diplomacy).

J. Favre, *Discours parlementaires*, 4 vols. (Paris, 1881), and *Gouvernement de la défense nationale*, 3 vols. (Paris, 1871–75); R. Giesberg, *The Treaty of Frankfurt* (Philadelphia, 1966); M. Howard, *The Franco-Prussian War* (London, 1961); A. Mitchell, *Bismarck and the French Nation, 1848–1890* (New York, 1971); M. Reclus, *Jules Favre* (Paris, 1912).

D. S. Newhall

Related entries: CONSTITUTIONAL LAWS OF 1875; FRANCO-PRUSSIAN WAR; GAMBETTA; GERMANY, RELATIONS WITH 1871–1914; LIBERALISM; NATIONAL ASSEMBLY; *SEIZE MAI* CRISIS; SEPTEMBER 4, 1870; THIERS.

FEBRUARY RIOTS (1934), a highly publicized protest identified with the radical Right. Although not as well known as the anti-Dreyfus demonstrations, these riots constituted a serious challenge to the government of the Third Republic. As in the Dreyfus affair, a Jew stood at the center of events that radically polarized political life. By 1934 the worldwide depression had begun to make itself felt in France. The promise of postwar peace had faded, and the rise of fascism and communism threatened the foundations of the French state.

The immediate cause of the riots was the major scandal precipitated by Serge Alexandre Stavisky, a high society gangster and swindler of Jewish origins. He had bribed important government and police officials in an attempt to defraud investors in his municipal bond swindle scheme. In January 1934 Stavisky was found dead in Chamonix under suspicious circumstances. Rumors alleged that he had been killed by the police to protect implicated government officials.

Demands for dismissal of the government were fruitless. Because Stavisky was of Jewish origin, the most bitter criticism of those in power stemmed from the radical Right. The government exacerbated the matter by firing Jean Chiappe, the chief of the Paris police who was highly esteemed by the Right. To protest Chiappe's dismissal, several thousand demonstrators from various right-wing factions assembled in the place de la Concorde on 6 February 1934, intending to cross the Seine and invade the Chamber of Deputies in the Palais Bourbon. Contingents of police thwarted the rioters' plans, and violent clashes resulted in the deaths of fifteen demonstrators and the wounding of one thousand more.

It was never determined with certainty whether the demonstrators really intended to overthrow the government. This was the interpretation of the Left, which organized a general strike on 12 February. The fear of a right-wing coup d'état enabled the Left to consolidate its strength and later form the Popular Front. The initial Stavisky affair in itself was not unlike other scandals that had plagued the Third Republic. By 1934, however, France was sufficiently weakened to

permit this incident to be blown out of proportion. It revealed the instability of
the Republic and prefigured the polarized political positions in France during
the Second World War.

M. Chavardès, *Le 6 février 1934* (Paris, 1966).

F. *Busi*

Related entries: DREYFUS AFFAIR; FASCISM; POPULAR FRONT; STAV-
ISKY AFFAIR.

FEBVRE, LUCIEN (1878–1956), historian, geographer, professor, and editor.
Febvre's highly successful studies at the lycée at Nancy (where his father, a
graduate of the Ecole normale supérieure, taught grammar) were supplemented
by long vacations in the old province of the Franche-Comté at the home of his
uncle. It was here that he was introduced to Comtois local history and geography,
an interest that led him to choose history as a vocation. Febvre followed his
father into the Ecole normale after two years of preparation at the Lycée Louis-
le-Grand in 1899. He studied in the history section of the Normale; Daniel
Mornet, Henri Wallon, and Albert Thomas were classmates and friends. His
first formal essay for the *diplôme d'études supérieures*, "La Contre-Réforme en
Franche-Comté," was writtten in 1901. It was so highly regarded by his professors
that it was published in Paris two years later. By 1903 he became professor of
history at the lycée in Bar-le-Duc after passing his *agrégation* with distinction.
Here, on the eastern frontier of France filled with memories of war and rebellion,
Febvre published his *La Franche Comté* in 1905. He also found time to discuss
his Dreyfusard opinions in the local *Socialiste Comtois* from 1907 to 1909.

It was on the shelves of the library of the Ecole normale on the rue d'Ulm in
Paris that Febvre discovered the first issues of Henri Berr's *La Revue de synthèse
historique* in 1900. Febvre immediately responded to Berr's call for a new history
in France and in 1904 joined Berr's staff as a specialist on the regions of France.
However, unlike Berr, his intimate association with the "young Turks" of the
French university did not deprive Febvre of the rewards available to young
scholars of the period. For three years he was given the support of the Fondation
Thiers in Paris enabling him to complete the prescribed two theses for the *doctorat
ès lettres* in December 1911. Again, it was his beloved province that provided
the themes for this scholarly success; published as *Philippe II et la Franche-
Comté; Etude d'histoire politique et sociale* and *Notes et documents sur la
Réforme et l'Inquisition en Franche-Comté* in 1911, these books led to a teaching
post in the Faculty of Letters at Dijon where he taught the *histoire de la Bourgogne
et de l'art bourguignon*.

In August 1914 he was mobilized into the army as a sergeant; five years later,
after active service as an officer in a machine gun company, Febvre was appointed
professor at the Faculty of Letters at Strasbourg. His friend, the medievalist
Marc Bloch, arrived the next year as part of a plan to make this Alsatian university
a showcase of French culture and scholarship. Their partnership had begun before
the war at the side of Henri Berr; now they shared an interest in the reconstruction

of war-torn France and Europe with a liberal optimism that rejected the facile interpretations of the rise and fall of civilizations.

During the 1920s Febvre wrote two highly innovative books: *La Terre et évolution humaine* (1922) and the sociopsychological biography *Un Destin: Martin Luther* (1928). Like Marc Bloch's *Les Rois thaumaturges* (1921) these were models of a new kind of history, highly interdisciplinary and original, in which facts were subordinated to a search for a "wider, more human" structure. In 1929 Febvre and Bloch founded a journal to promote this new problem-oriented history, the *Annales d'histoire économique et sociale*, later *Annales: Economies, sociétés, civilizations*. In each volume, Febvre, a gifted polemicist, declared war against the "spirit of specialization" and the compartmentalization of the past. His trenchant book reviews and essays castigated the narrative, event-oriented history of his colleagues and offered instead the *Annales* paradigm of a new total history based on an active partnership with the social sciences (*sciences humaines*).

In spite of considerable opposition in the profession, Febvre was elected in 1933 to a new chair at the Collège de France at Paris for the study of the history of modern civilization. The 1930s also found him actively involved in Henri Berr's Centre international de synthèse while directing the multivolume *Encyclopédie française*, which appeared between 1935 and 1940.

During the war years Febvre divided his time between the Collège de France and Souget, his home in the Jura; there were also clandestine meetings with Bloch and other members of the underground. He passed the time in intense study of the religious ideas of a turbulent sixteenth-century France and published his last sustained scholarly works on which his reputation as a historian rests: *Le Problème de l'incroyance au 16e siècle* (1942), *Origène et Des Periers (1942)*, and *Autour de l'Heptaméron* (1944).

The end of the war and the last decade of Febvre's life marked a triumph for his combat for a new history in France. Elected to the Académie des sciences morales at politiques in 1950, Febvre played a key role in the reorganization of the Ecole des hautes études. Here, as president of its *sixièm⁻ section*, he led a new generation of historians, which included Charles Morazé, Fernand Braudel, and Pierre Chaunu in the creation of the *Annales* school of social research that continues to have significant impact on historical writings throughout the world.

H.-D. Mann, *Lucien Febvre: La Pensée vivante d'un historien* (Paris, 1971); P. Burke, ed., *A New Kind of History: From the Writings of Lucien Febvre* (New York, 1973); T. Stoianovich, *French Historical Method: The Annales Paradigm* (Ithaca, 1976).

M. Siegel

Related entries: BERR; BLOCH; HISTORIOGRAPHY: *ANNALES* SCHOOL.

FEMINISM. The organized feminist movement under the Third Republic displayed three distinct and frequently antagonistic tendencies: liberal, socialist, and Catholic. All three tendencies evinced a concern for improving women's status and for morally regenerating French society, but whereas the liberal tendency sought equal rights for women within the framework of a capitalist lay republic, the socialist tendency rejected capitalism, and the Roman Catholic tendency rejected both equality and laicism.

The liberal tendency, which most resembled contemporary Anglo-American feminism, received literary expression midway through the Second Empire in works such as Juliette Lamber's *Idées antiproudhoniennes* (1859) and Jenny d'Héricourt's *La Femme affranchie* (1860). A few years later it received organized expression through groups such as the 1866 Société pour la revendication des droits de la femme of André Léo and the 1870 Société pour l'amélioration du sort de la femme of Maria Deraismes and Léon Richer, with Richer's *Le Droit des femmes* (1869–91) supplying its voice. After the Franco-Prussian War (1870–71) and the Paris Commune (1871), Deraismes and Richer devised the *politique de la brèche*, a strategy that focused on obtaining women's civil rights by breaching the wall of masculine constraints at its weakest points while according political priority to defending the new Third Republic. Indeed, not until after republicanism triumphed in the *seize mai* crisis (1877) were Deraismes and Richer able to cohost the first French Congrès international du droit des femmes of 1878. Four years later Richer founded the Ligue français pour le droit des femmes, which still exists, and in 1889 he and Deraismes cohosted the second French Congrès international du droit des femmes.

Selectively assailing the Napoleonic Code, the two congresses demanded legal and moral reforms such as better education for women, reenactment of divorce, equal pay for equal work, equal access to all professions, abolition of state-regulated prostitution, as well as the right of wives to control their own income, of unwed mothers to file a paternity suit, of businesswomen to sit on *tribunaux de commerce*, of working women to sit on *conseils de prud'hommes*, and of all women to bear legal witness to public and private legal acts. Excluded was women's suffrage, an issue that most liberal feminists feared would alienate potential supporters and, if enacted, would reinforce clericalism with the votes of "priest-ridden" Catholic women. Opponents of the exclusion rallied to Hubertine Auclert, who, as founder of both the 1876 Société du suffrage des femmes and *La Citoyenne* (1881–91), formulated the *politiquede l'assaut*, an alternative strategy that focused on securing women's right to vote through public confrontation.

With Richer's retirement from feminism in 1891 and Deraismes' death in 1894, liberal feminism passed through a decade of crisis. After several years in Algeria, Auclert returned to suffragism but lost *La Citoyenne* to Maria Martin, who retitled it *Le Journal des femmes* (1891–1911) and aligned it with Eugénie Potonié-Pierre's 1891 Groupe de la solidarité des femmes. The Left-liberal Potonié-Pierre then organized the 1892 Fédération française des sociétés féministes, a short-lived coalition of sixteen-odd groups that cohosted with Marya Chéliga's 1899 Union universelle des femmes the third French Congrès féministe of 1892. A year later, repulsed by liberal feminism's radicalism, Jeanne Schmahl enlisted the Catholic Boulangist Duchesse Marie-Clémentine d'Uzès and the *révanchard* Madame Adam (the former Juliette Lamber) in the Right-liberal Avant Courrière, which demanded only witness and income rights. These and other newly formed groups collided in 1896 at the fourth French Congrès féministe, in reaction to which Marguerite Durand tried to bring order to the movement by founding the daily newspaper *La Fronde* (1897–1905) and arranging the fifth French Congrès international de la condition et des droits des femmes of 1900.

The disorder of the 1890s gave way within a year of the 1900 congress. In 1901 the leading liberal feminists helped to found the Conseil national des femmes françaises, whose member groups represented 100,000 individuals in 1914 and 250,000 in 1929. Although most National Council members came from the ranks of Jewish, Protestant, and freethinking women who saw women's rights as much in moral and social as in feminist terms, liberal feminists nonetheless gained a larger and better organized base, an official affiliation with the 1888 International Council of Women, and a springboard for regional feminist coalitions, such as the 1911 Fédération des groupes féministes du sud-est. The issue of women's suffrage came to the forefront as well when the Conseil national established a special section for it in 1907. The 1908 Congrès national des droits civils et du suffrage des femmes accorded it titular prominence, and the 1909 Union française pour le suffrage des femmes brought to it the support of a national coalition affiliated with the 1904 International Woman Suffrage Alliance.

The pre-1914 consolidation of liberal republican feminism constituted in part a reaction to the development of socialist and Roman Catholic feminism. Auclert induced the 1879 Marseilles socialist congress to endorse women's rights, and from 1880 to 1884 Léonie Rouzade's Union des femmes sought to unite feminism and socialism. Fifteen years later, Elisabeth Renaud and Louise Saumoneau founded the 1899 Groupe féministe socialiste, which, after heated debates at the liberal feminist congress of 1900, forbade class collaboration with bourgeois feminists. With socialist unification in 1905, however, the Groupe féministe socialiste disappeared, and, despite the militancy of socialist feminists like Madeleine Pelletier, a new one did not emerge until the Groupe des femmes socialistes of 1913, which under Saumoneau not only cut itself off from liberal feminism by maintaining the earlier ban on class collaboration but also had no separate status within the Socialist party (SFIO) itself. Hence, although it alarmed liberal feminists, this new group could neither attract broad support from outside the party nor prod the party into taking women's issues seriously.

In political reaction to the Dreyfus affair, Roman Catholic women organized by the tens of thousands in groups such as the 1900 Action sociale de la femme, the 1901 Ligue des femmes françaises, and the 1902 Ligue patriotique des françaises. To these women appealed Marie Maugeret, the founder of Catholic feminism who in 1896 established a group and a review called *Le Féminisme chrétien*. Desirous of improving women's status without jeopardizing the family hierarchy, Maugeret helped to organize the Congrès Jean d'Arc in 1904 (and annually thereafter) and a Fédération of the same name in 1905. Papal opposition to women's suffrage and a general identification of feminism with republican godlessness lessened Maugeret's effectiveness at first, but gradually other voices joined hers in a program that combined women's rights with anti-Masonic and anti-Semitic chauvinism.

During the First World War, aside from a few left-wing pacifists such as Saumoneau and Hélène Brion, the vast majority of feminists from all three tendencies subordinated women's rights and international sisterhood to national victory. This subordination supplied a patriotic rationale for women's suffrage, which the Chamber passed 334 to 97 in May 1919 but the Senate defeated 156 to 134 in November 1922. Coupled with successes in other areas, the war era thus had the effect of making suffragism virtually synonymous with feminism. Yet despite the emergence of a common objective, the three tendencies persisted.

Liberal feminism continued almost unchanged after the war, except for new leadership. Eager as in the prewar years to demonstrate women's competence, the old groups held Etats généraux du féminisme in 1929, 1931, and 1937, while Cécile Brunschwicg, an active member of the antisuffrage Radical party who had replaced Misme as director of La Française and had assumed the presidency of the Union française pour le suffrage des femmes, served as under secretary for state for national education in Léon Blum's first Popular Front government. Only the intervention of Louise Weiss' movement, La Femme nouvelle, in the mid-1930s pushed liberal feminism into public confrontation, one result of which was the unseating of the misogynist deputy Raymond Duplantier. Otherwise, despite several important legal reforms, a 1938 provision permitting women to serve as auxiliary municipal councillors constituted liberal feminism's sole political achievement before the regime collapsed in 1940.

Although split between advocates and opponents of the communist Third International, socialist feminism also changed little in the interwar years. On the socialist side, the Groupe des femmes socialistes reassembled in 1922, and in 1931 the party established a Comité national des femmes socialistes. But under Saumoneau's continuing influence, neither organization had any freedom of movement within the party, while both limited membership to regular party women and forbade class collaboration. Socialist-feminist Suzanne Lacore served as under secretary of state for public health alongside Brunschwicg, but neither she nor the party pressed Léon Blum on the issue of women's suffrage. By the late 1930s women constituted barely 3 percent of party members. On the communist side, women constituted slightly more than 4 percent, but no woman held a top post in the party's hierarchy. The party established a women's section at its 1921 Marseilles congress and fashioned links with Madeleine Vernet's 1921 Ligue des femmes contre la guerre, Gabrielle Duchêne's French section of the 1915 Ligue internationale des femmes pour la paix et la liberté, and Jeanne Buland and Antoinette Gilles' Union fraternelle des femmes contre la guerre imperialiste, which altered its name in 1932 to "contre la misère et la guerre." Yet not only did class solidarity take precedence over women's concerns, but the party also abandoned its initial support for sexual freedom in favor of a traditional emphasis on women's familial duties.

Due in part to a war-inspired reconciliation between the Republic and right-wing nationalism, as well as to a shift in papal attitude, only Catholic feminism, through a leap in popularity, significantly changed after 1918. In 1920 Catholic women led by Mme. Le Vert-Chotard founded the Union nationale pour le vote des femmes, whose presidency fell to the Duchesse Edmée de la Rochefoucauld from 1931 to 1939 and whose Center-Right political orientation bred close ties with the parties of order. The Union nationale also cooperated closely with André Butillard's 1925 Union féminine civique et sociale. Much less feminist but very active politically was the Ligue féminine d'action catholique, a million-strong fusion of the prewar Ligue des femmes françaises and the Ligue patriotique des françaises. Although provoking criticism from both liberal and socialist feminists for accenting women's traditional duties, Catholic feminists probably contributed more then either of the other two tendencies to paving the way for women's suffrage, which was granted at the end of the Second World War by Charles de Gaulle.

L. Abensour, *Histoire générale du féminisme* (Paris, 1921); M. Albistur and D. Armogathe, *Histoire de féminisme français* (Paris, 1977); P. Bidelman, *Pariahs Stand Up!* (Westport, Conn., 1982) and ''The Politics of French Feminism,'' *Historical Reflections* (Summer, 1976); H. Bouchardeau, *Pas d'histoire* (Paris, 1977); F. d'Eaubonne, *Histoire et actualité du féminisme* (Paris, 1971); R. Evans, *The Feminists* (New York, 1977); G. Gennari, *Le Dossier de la femme* (Paris, 1965); J. McMillan, *Housewife or Harlot* (New York, 1981); C. Moses, *French Feminism in the Nineteenth Century* (Albany, 1984); K. Offen, ''The Woman Question as a Social Issue in Nineteenth-century France,'' *Third Republic/Troisième République* no. 3–4 (1977); J. Rabaut, *Histoire des féminismes français* (Paris, 1978); C. Sowerwine, *Les Femmes et le socialisme* (Paris, 1978), and *Sisters or Citizens?* (New York, 1982); L. Weiss, *Ce que femme veut* (Paris, 1946), and *Combat pour les femmes* (Paris, 1970); M-H. Zylbergerg-Hocquard, *Féminisme et syndicalisme en France* (Paris, 1978).

P. K. Bidelman

Related entries: ADAM; AUCLERT; BRUNSCHWICG; BUISSON; DE-RAISMES; DURAND; MISME; PELLETIER; RICHER; ROCHEFOUCAULD; ROYER; SCHMAHL; WOMEN: MOVEMENT FOR CIVIL RIGHTS; WOMEN: MOVEMENT FOR POLITICAL RIGHTS.

FERROUL, ERNEST (1853–1921), socialist politician, doctor, militant leftist reformer. Born in Mas-Cabardès (Aude) on 13 December, he was the son of a middle-class merchant. The relative financial security that his father's income provided allowed the young man to attend the Faculté de médecine of Montpelier. Ferroul received his degree in 1880 and established a practice in Narbonne. A conscientious young man, he openly embraced socialist ideas and joined the Freemasons. Loosely affiliated with the Workers' party of Jules Guesde, Ferroul participated in various socialist and syndicalist congresses. During the 1880s he was a socialist member of the city council and mayor of Narbonne. In 1881 he was elected as a radical-socialist to the Chamber of Deputies.

In the 1890s and early 1900s Ferroul was particularly interested in the plight of rural workers, especially the Midi vinegrowers. His attempts to unionize the vinegrowers led to a conflict with the government of Georges Clemenceau. Ferroul sat with the extreme Left in the Chamber, always among the ranks of the socialists. The social concerns that he addressed there were the reduction of working hours, the rights of strikers, and social security for workers. In 1890, Ferroul (with Edouard Vaillant) was instrumental in establishing 1 May as an annual festival day for the recognition of the international solidarity of workers.

Because of his talents as an orator, Ferroul enjoyed a successful political career. But his socialist rhetoric eventually became timeworn, and his popularity declined. He died in Narbonne on 29 December 1921 at the age of sixty-eight.

J. Jolly, ed., *Dictionnaire des parlementaires français*, vol. 5 (Paris, 1968); J. Maitron, ed., *Dictionnaire biographique du mouvement ouvrier français*, vol. 12 (Paris, 1974); C. Willard, *Les Guesdistes* (Paris, 1965).

L. LeClair

Related entries: GUESDISTS; SOCIALISM, 1870–1914.

FERRY, JULES (1832–1893), Opportunist politician, promoter of imperialism and educational reform, twice premier (23 September 1880–14 November 1881, 22 February 1883–6 April 1885). Son of a prosperous, semi-retired lawyer in St.-Dié (Vosges), scion of an ancient clan of Lorrainers, he won national notoriety when, as a lawyer-journalist in Paris, he published a collection of articles for *Le Temps* entitled "Les Comptes fantastiques d'Haussmann"(1868), an exposé of the administration of the famous rebuilder of Paris. Elected to the Legislative Body (1869–70) from Paris as a radical Republican, he played a leading role in the revolution of 4 September 1870 and was made secretary to the Government of National Defense, its delegate to (prefect of) the department of the Seine (4 November 1870–6 June 1871), and mayor of Paris (16 November 1870–18 March 1871). His experiences during the siege, when he was in charge of supplies and police, and during the Commune, as the last high official to leave the city (in a daring night escape, 18–19 March), turned him toward a moderate republicanism expressive of his lifelong detestation of demagoguery and disorder. Deputy from the Vosges in the National Assembly (1871–75), he was one of "the four Jules" (Favre, Grévy, Simon), leaders of the moderates, and served Adolphe Thiers concurrently as ambassador to Greece (May 1872–May 1873). In the Chamber of Deputies (1876–89) he sat for Vosges and St.-Dié and headed the Republican Left—the right wing of the Opportunists (the left wing being Léon Gambetta's Republican Union). As minister of public instruction (4 February 1879–14 November 1881, 30 January–7 August 1882, 21 February–20 November 1883) and of foreign affairs (20 November 1883–6 April 1885) in his own cabinets and those of William Waddington and Charles de Freycinet (first and second), he was the prime mover of educational reforms (the Ferry Laws) and was much involved in extending the French empire: the conquest of Tunisia (1881); the development and expansion of the colonies of Senegal, Sudan, Guinea, Ivory Coast, Dahomey, Gabon, Somaliland, and French Oceania (Tahiti and the Leeward and Gambier isles); the founding of French Equatorial Africa through his promotion of Pierre de Brazza's expeditions and his role in the decisions of the Conference of Berlin (1884–85); the beginning of the conquest of Madagascar (1883–96); and the consolidation in Indochina of a protectorate in Annam and its dependency, Tonkin (1883–85).

A momentary military reverse at Lang-son (near Hanoi) furnished his opponents the opportunity to drive him from office in a tumultuous session on 30 March 1885. (Ironically he had China's confirmation of a settlement in his pocket but chose not to risk a last-minute rupture of the secret negotiations by revealing it.) But the more pertinent cause of his fall was the impending elections; many erstwhile supporters were worried over the effects of a lingering economic slump and unhappiness with his domestic policies. Ferry's unpopularity, concentrated largely in Paris, thereafter prevented his return to office. He remained, however, as he had since Gambetta's death (31 December 1882), the Opportunists' chief and as such fought the Boulangist menace from start to finish (1885–89). When Grévy had to resign the presidency (2 December 1887), he was the leading candidate (he had strong Senate support) but the National Assembly, cowed by violent street protests led by Paul Déroulède and Henri Rochefort, gave Sadi Carnot a plurality; he then withdrew to ensure Carnot's election. Defeated in 1889, he was elected by the Vosges to the Senate (1891–93), which, in tardy reparation, made him its president (24 February 1893). He died on 18 March, having never fully recovered from wounds sustained in an assassination attempt (10 December 1887) by a madman. He was given a national funeral and was interred at St.-Dié.

Ferry was born a Catholic (his sister, Adèle, remained very devout), but like many other advanced men in his milieu, he was influenced by positivism, Emile Littré, John Stuart Mill, and the Freemasons (joined, 1875). A man of ideals but no ideologue, he incorporated his beliefs in science, progress, and democracy into his reforms. He sponsored laws making public primary education free (16 July 1881), compulsory (either public or private) and moral and civic (28 March 1882) and requiring state certification (with some temporary exceptions) of all public school teachers (16 June 1881). He reformed the administration of higher education, created a nationwide system of normal schools, opened lycées (nationally funded secondary schools) for females, and promoted physical education, kindergartens, and training in technology and modern languages. He mined away at the Catholic church's influence in public life and in education removed clergy from inspection boards and promoted a law (30 October 1886) forbidding hiring of clerics by public schools. A clumsy attempt (1879–80), via a provision (article 7) inserted in a bill on higher education, to prevent all teaching, public or private, by members of unauthorized religious orders caused a storm. The Senate rejected the article, but decrees (29, 30 March 1880) banning the Jesuits—the real target—and requiring others to apply for authorization put some pressure on the religious orders. Ferry, however, backed off from strict enforcement. Other important legislation during his tenures included bills regulating freedom of association and the press (30 June, 29 July 1881), purging the judiciary of notorious nonrepublicans (30 August 1883), reorganizing municipal government (5 April 1884), and legalizing trade unions (6 April 1884).

In all instances save that of Equatorial Africa, the moves to expand the empire had begun under ministries preceding Ferry's. He showed no interest in the colonies before he took office, developed nothing resembling a doctrine of imperialism until well into his second ministry (speech of 24 March 1884), and made his most comprehensive statement (28 July 1885) only after he had departed. But he expended extraordinary energy in exploiting the opportunities presented him. His principal motive was to restore and ensure to France the standing it had enjoyed before 1870 as a great power. Economic factors, which figured importantly in the 29 July address, were much less significant in driving him forward than political motives and the entreaties of soldiers and colonial administrators. German Chancellor Otto von Bismarck's concurrent lack of interest in imperialism and his desire to turn France's attention away from Alsace-Lorraine unquestionably aided Ferry's enterprises. For his part, Ferry nourished some pale hopes that France one day might exchange some possessions for the lost provinces. The détente in Franco-German relations earned him wholly unmerited charges of treason, especially from Georges Clemenceau's Radicals. Nor was there any truth in accusations that he and his brother, Charles (1834–1909), a prominent businessman, deputy, and senator, profited from the ventures, though many others certainly did. Not infrequently Ferry acted without accurately reckoning the cost of future complications; in Tunisia, Madagascar, and above all Tonkin, where an undeclared war with China resulted (1883–85), he repeatedly presented parliament with faits accomplis together with overdue bills and demands for blank-check authority to continue operations. These sharp practices aroused fury and sowed distrust, even among his supporters.

From the siege of Paris, as "Ferry-Famine," through the anticlerical campaign, as "Nero" and "Anti-Christ," to the end, as "Ferry-Tonkin," he sounded the depths of unpopularity as have few other men in public life. He met criticism with a stoic calm or an infuriating disdain. Sensitive at heart ("my roses grow inward") and a talented amateur painter, he possessed an astonishing range of knowledge, a tenacious will, and courage both moral and physical. Idealistic in spirit, pragmatic in action, a fighter, tolerant in religion if anticlerical in politics, at his worst rigid, opinionated, and coldly sarcastic, "the kind of general that takes no prisoners" (Freycinet), no grand-style orator but one of the premier debaters of his time, Jules Ferry described himself as "a man of government," and was, with Gambetta, the most important founder of the Third Republic, above all of its educational system and its reincarnation of the French Empire.

P. Chevalier, *La Séparation de l'Eglise et de l'école: Jules Ferry et Léon XIII* (Paris, 1981); J. Ferry, private papers possessed by Mme. Fresnette Pisani-Ferry and the Bibliothèque Municipale, St.-Dié, *Discours et opinions de Jules Ferry*, ed. P. Robiquet, 7 vols. (Paris, 1893–98) and *Lettres de Jules Ferry, 1846–1893* (Paris, 1914); P. Guilhaume, *Jules Ferry* (Paris, 1980); L. Legrand, *L'Influence du positivisme dans l'oeuvre scolaire de Jules Ferry* (Paris, 1961); F. Pisani-Ferry, *Jules Ferry et le partage du monde* (Paris,

1962); anon., *Les Politiques d'expansion imperialiste* (Paris, 1949); M. Pottecher, *Jules Ferry* (Paris, 1930); T. Power, *Jules Ferry and the Renaissance of French Imperialism* (New York, 1944); A. Rambaud, *Jules Ferry* (Paris, 1903); M. Reclus, *Jules Ferry, 1832–1893* (Paris, 1947).

D. S. Newhall

Related entries: ANTICLERICALISM; BERT; BOULANGER AFFAIR; BUIS-SON; CLEMENCEAU; COMBES; DEROULEDE; EDUCATION: GOVERN-MENTAL POLICIES CONCERNING; FAVRE; FRANCO-PRUSSIAN WAR; FREYCINET; GAMBETTA; GERMANY, RELATIONS WITH (1871–1914); GOBLET; GREVY; LIBERALISM; LITTRE; MELINE; NATIONAL ASSEM-BLY; NATIONALISM; OPPORTUNISTS; OVERSEAS EMPIRE: FRENCH IMPERIALISM; POSITIVISM; RIBOT; ROCHEFORT; ROMAN CATHOLI-CISM: CHURCH-STATE RELATIONS; ROUVIER; SIMON; SPULLER; THIERS; WALDECK-ROUSSEAU.

FESTIVALS: POLITICAL, special days of political ritual, popular rejoicing, and demonstration by competing political movements. During its first seven difficult years, the Third Republic offered no occasion for public celebration. Not until France had recovered from the disasters of 1870–71 and republicans began taking over from monarchists did the state sponsor 30 June 1878 as a one-time civic holiday, a day free of divisive political memories. It was a day to celebrate the *exposition universelle*'s themes of work and peace. For monarchist and early republican leaders alike, work and order were the highest values. Public festivals were suspect, being too closely associated with profligacy, fighting, and troublesome political demonstrations. Most controversial of all were celebrations commemorating revolutionary anniversaries. In the first decade of the Republic, authorities not only refused to establish an annual national fete but also banned all public political celebrations. Paris police in 1878 even removed garlands from some popular quarters on 14 July.

Among Opportunists and Radicals, no date was so glorious as the day the Bastille was stormed. In private banquets republicans celebrated 14 July for years and campaigned to have the day given public recognition. Finally, republican victories in 1878 and 1879 cleared the way, and in May 1880 deputy Benjamin Raspail introduced a bill creating an annual 14 July holiday. The law was promulgated just about a week before the fete day itself. Like the law amnestying communards passed only five days later (July 11), the establishment of the national fete was in part an attempt to unite republicans and to appease Radicals and Socialists. Further, it was part of a program to create a popular cult of the revolution and Republic that would win people over from Catholicism and its deeply rooted feast days.

The day had many meanings. To the Right, 14 July was a bloody episode of insurrection; to the Left it was a popular conquest of liberty; moderates emphasized the commemoration of the 1790 fraternal fete of the federations. Republican liturgy for 14 July usually centered on the dedication of busts and statues of the

Republic, patriotic speeches and toasts, and a military review, which was the official event drawing the largest crowds in the nineteenth century. To the less politicized, the day was no doubt above all simply a holiday—a leisure time for drinking and dancing, attending free theater performances, and watching a parade and fireworks.

The first several Bastille Days in the 1880s appear to have evoked much spontaneous popular enthusiasm. With minimal official encouragement, citizens with republican sympathies decorated their houses and shops with the national colors, sang the "Marseillaise," and cheered the Republic and especially its troops. Workers' quarters in Paris and the provinces were more decorated and animated than those of the better-off classes. But within a decade after the first celebration, observers began noting a decline in the merrymaking. The repetition of stilted ceremonies was part of the problem. Feeling for the Republic was probably also cooling; in any event, the regime was established and flawed enough that there was less reason to rejoice in its triumph or its tenuous tie to a 1789 antecedent. Further, holiday excursions and alternative political festivals attracted increasing numbers toward the end of the nineteenth century, especially in Paris.

Following the model of the First Republic and even older royal precedents, republican leaders went on to offer many civic festivals besides 14 July. The larger state funerals took on some characteristics of festival. Centenaries of the 1789 meeting of the Estates General and the declaration of the First Republic were also national fete days in the Third Republic. One of the most joyous festivities of the period was the celebration of the Franco-Russian alliance during the czar's visit to France in 1896.

The First World War brought a suspension of merrymaking on Bastille Days. Finally, on 14 July 1919 Parisians gave themselves over to joyous release in a memorable victory celebration. In the wake of the war parliament created the new national holidays of 11 November (1921) and Jeanne d'Arc Day in May (1920), but neither became so basic a republican institution nor so popular a festival as Bastille Day. In the mid-1930s, after years of 14 July observances that were routine at best, the antifascist Left put new life into the day, stressing its importance in the revolutionary tradition of the people. Masses of street demonstrators in 1935 and 1936 brandished tricolors and red flags and then danced long into the night. With the demise of the Popular Front, the festival languished once more. The year 1939 was a time to celebrate the one hundred fiftieth anniversary of the storming of the Bastille; President Albert Lebrun called for a "fete of national unity," but the disunity of Right and Left was too great, official ceremonial was turgid, and the times signaled little cause for rejoicing.

For dissidents, the Republic's fetes were occasions for counterdemonstrations. Socialists, anarchists, and syndicalists cried that many bastilles remained to be taken; the bourgeois state could not obscure that fact by annually offering the poor some cheap amusements. So the police assiduously chased after white flags, red flags, black flags, and posters. Conspicuous abstention on 14 July was another form of protest, evident in the faubourg Saint Germain and the sixteenth arrondissement in Paris, for example, and in much of the conservative west of France.

The opposition also created rival political festivities with their own commemorative ritual. Partisans of the Commune solemnized 18 March each year. Monarchists used the day after Bastille Day, the feast day of Saint Henry, to celebrate their ideals. The clerical and monarchist Right also took over Jeanne d'Arc as a symbol in the 1890s, and on several days each May feted this heroine as emissary of God, patriotic savior, and devoted royal servant.

French socialists and syndicalists adopted 1 May as their special day following a resolution of the International Socialist Congress in Paris on 21 July 1889. In the early 1890s and occasionally thereafter (1906, 1919, 1920, 1936, and 1937 notably), workers engaged in strikes and large street demonstrations on this "revolutionary Easter," especially important in Paris and Saint-Etienne. Red flags and red banners, many inscribed with a demand for the eight-hour workday, festooned streets and work places. But it appears that in no year did a majority of workers take part in the demonstrations, and such rallies had less impact in France than in Germany.

The Left was divided on the question of whether May Day should be considered a fete. The 1889 Congress did not use such a term. 1 May 1891, which ended in the massacre of Fourmies, left reason to associate subsequent anniversaries with embittered mourning. Most early leftist appeals for May Day action in France did not call for a fete but rather for demonstrations and pressure on public powers; some socialist and syndicalist leaders explicitly rejected the idea of fete, deemed inappropriate until workers had some real triumph to celebrate. But other leaders such as Emmanuel Danflous and Jules Guesde called the day a *fête du travail*, as it was conceived in several other countries. After the First World War, the Confédération générale du travail, missing its extreme Left members, pushed for making 1 May a national holiday. Efforts in parliament to establish the new fete failed, but in 1937 Léon Blum on his own authority made the day a legal holiday—for the only time during the Third Republic.

M. Dommanget, *Histoire du premier mai* (Paris, 1953); C. Rearick, "Festivals in Modern France: The Experience of the Third Republic," *Journal of Contemporary History* 12 (1977); R. Sanson, *Les 14 juillet, fête et conscience nationale, 1789–1975* (Paris, 1976).

C. W. Rearick

Related entries: FESTIVALS: RELIGIOUS; FUNERALS, STATE; LABOR MOVEMENT; NATIONALISM; PARIS: UNIVERSAL EXPOSITIONS; SOCIALISM, 1870–1914.

FESTIVALS: RELIGIOUS. These were special holy days marked by Catholic ritual, popular merrymaking, pre-Christian customs, and sometimes political activity. French Catholics under the Third Republic celebrated religious fetes that were as richly varied and diverse as local secular traditions. In the church's festive calendar, local observances had little about them that was universal. Through the eighteenth century in Nevers, for example, Easter traditions included a procession to the Loire, which the clergy blessed to prevent floods. In the Berry, on what was called white Friday, nine days before Easter, shepherdesses had specially carved sticks blessed at a Mass to protect the sheep from harm and then broke fast with copious food and drink. Piety, magical utility, and popular reveling fit together easily in many popular traditions. In whatever ways local tradition dictated, the faithful at a minimum generally participated in the *grandes fêtes* of Christmas, Palm Sunday, Easter, Assumption (15 August), and All Saints' Day (1 November). But for much of the countryside the *fête patronale*, honoring the patron saint of the parish or a local occupational group, was the grand celebration of the year. Prayers, a Mass, and a procession through the village were usually followed by feasting, dancing, and games; often the celebration extended over several days.

In the period of the Third Republic, many religious festivities underwent what was from the religious point of view a decline, a continuation of an outward or public dechristianization already evident in the Old Regime. Violent interruptions of local routine and of relative isolation dealt sometimes fatal blows to communal observances; folklorists note that in some localities traditions such as bonfires were not renewed after the Franco-Prussian war and in other localities after the First World War. The Third Republic's anticlerical policies also worked against traditional fetes. As republicans triumphed over monarchists in the late 1870s, they took actions to suppress much of the external pomp of feast days. First state or local officials tried to prohibit religious processions in the streets of many towns; technically to maintain public order, mayors could take such action by law after 1884. Conflicts between church leaders and civil authorities ensued for many years, particularly over the *Fête Dieu* processions in larger towns. In addition, by a decree of 1883, marching troops, a great popular attraction in this period, were no longer permitted to take part in religious processions.

Except in devout strongholds like Brittany, Alsace, Lorraine, and the Basque country, the number of religious festivities generally declined. Twelfth Day (*jour des rois*) (6 January) and Candlemas (2 February) lost importance. By the late nineteenth century Rogation days (the three days before Ascension) saw fewer penitent processions through village fields. Assumption (15 August) went without notice in the Haute-Loire and the Creuse. From 1880 on, laic national education encouraged the dropping of local observances, now treated as signs of backwardness, just as the local patois was considered inferior to French. The clergy itself worked to restrain or even to suppress many traditional forms of celebration on holy days. Together with civil authorities, churchmen sought to promote morality and order by waging campaigns against animal blood sports, fights, the firing of arms, and pranks by disguised celebrants. To combat old superstitions, some clergymen also refused to participate in the lighting of ceremonial bonfires on Saint John's Eve (23 June) or Saint Peter's (29 June).

Religious feast days that continued to be observed were often overshadowed by the accompanying profane celebration. Priests who had long denounced games and dances during *fêtes patronales* met with new defeats. Commercial activities on fete days increased in scope. The state played a role by legalizing work on Sundays (law of 12 July 1880) and by making Mondays after Easter and Pentecost *jours fériés* (law of 8 March 1886); holy days were simply holidays or workdays for many. As the religious procession and sometimes even the Mass disappeared, people flocked to the itinerant merchants' stands, the spectacles of performers and animals, the exchanges at the fair, games of chance, and the ball. But these periodic village attractions had to compete with new civil celebrations like 14 July and with the more permanent spectacles offered in larger towns, made more accessible by trains, bicycles, and occasionally automobiles. Thus even secular amusements declined in many villages.

Some festive customs waned or disappeared as the agricultural traditions of which they were a part changed during the Third Republic. *Feux de joie* on the first Sunday in Lent (*Brandons*) and Saint John's Eve became rare in much of France. Disbelief in the fertilizing and purifying effects of such rites spread as teachers and priests taught that the old practices, which the church had taken over from pre-Christian magical beliefs, were not essential to good crops and healthy animals. Instead of giving lambs to the church on Saint John's Day (24 June), shepherds in the Dordogne around 1900 took them to market; instead of lighting a bonfire and risking its spreading, peasants saved their wood for household use and used fertilizer to improve the crops. As new agricultural techniques and mobility weakened the bond of the old communities, simple family observances, often with little religious content, became the new foci of fetes.

There was not, however, a simple movement toward the death of traditions and religious festivities in particular. In many rural areas and towns (such as Le Puy, Rodez, Mende, Angers) religious practice was more widespread at the end of the nineteenth century than earlier, when the weakened church was recovering from the French Revolution. Across France railways facilitated some new pilgrimages, like those to Lourdes, and a major new celebration took root in the late nineteenth century: Jeanne d'Arc days in May.

In the first two decades of the Third Republic, the Left was as ready as the Right to fete the patriotic heroine. The statue of Jeanne in Paris (erected February 1874) and the villages of Domrémy and Vaucouleurs became popular pilgrimage places; republicans moved in 1884 to create a national Jeanne d'Arc fete but backed away from the proposal when the clerical Right took up the cause as a substitute for *la fête des assassins*, the new 14 July holiday. In 1894 the church declared Jeanne venerable; Catholic and royalist youth organized well-attended festivals honoring her. The programs included religious solemnities but also popular entertainments such as races and even dances. Alarmed anticlericals stymied the legislative effort until 1920 when in a new spirit of *union sacrée* parliament passed the law creating the new May holiday.

Some partisans of the church and of folklore worked to revive ancient religious feasts also. Around 1900 in the west and center, for example, efforts were made to enliven waning patron saints' celebrations. And in the 1930s members of the *Jeunesse agricole chrétienne* worked to reintegrate seasonal labors with sacred rites for farm families; such practices as the blessing of seeds and harvest Masses took on some new life. Efforts of this sort notwithstanding, Catholic traditionalists, some of them to be early stalwarts of Vichy, were left with much to lament.

G. Duby and A. Wallon, eds., *Histoire de la France rurale*, vol. 4 (Paris, 1976); A. Varagnac, *Civilisation traditionnelle et genre de vie* (Paris, 1948); E. Weber, *Peasants into Frenchmen: The Modernization of Rural France, 1870–1914* (Stanford, 1976).

C. W. Rearick

Related entries: FESTIVALS: POLITICAL; ROMAN CATHOLICISM: POPULAR DEVOTIONS; RURAL SOCIETY, LIFE IN.

FEYDEAU, GEORGES (1862–1921), popular comic dramatist of the late nineteenth and early twentieth centuries. Born in Paris, Feydeau showed an early interest in the theater and was encouraged in this vein by his father, the writer Ernest Feydeau. Feydeau's first major success came with the production of *Tailleur pour dames* in December 1886. A madcap adventure of would-be adulterers and mistaken identities, the play scored a major triumph both with the theater-going public and with critics. Succeeding plays were much less well received, and in 1890 Feydeau temporarily withdrew from the world of the theater to study the art of comic playwriting in the works of Eugène Labiche, Ludovic Halévy, and Alfred Hennequin. Feydeau's return to the stage in 1892 revealed a *vaudevilliste* whose well-constructed, rapidly moving plays mocked the foibles of modern life with good-humored skill. *Monsieur chasse!*, *Champignol malgré lui*, and *Le Système Ribadier* premiered in 1892. These were followed by *Un Fil à la patte* and *L'Hôtel du Libre-Echange* (both 1894), *Le Dindon* (1896), and *La Dame de chez Maxim* (1897), which count among the most durable works in Feydeau's repertory of zany marital and extramarital misadventures. The appeal of these plays, like that of all other works written in the vaudeville genre, results from the close observation of contemporary mores and current events, from the stereotypical nature of the bourgeois characters, and from the comic exploitation of the situations and words.

After another fallow period, Feydeau returned to the stage in 1904 with *La Main passe*, a more subtle work than any he had written before, marked by special attention to personalities and human interaction. Feydeau reverted to his earlier vaudeville mode for the still popular *La Puce à l'oreille* (1907) and *Occupe-toi d'Amélie* (1908) but came more and more to write restrained one-act comedies in which complicated plots gave way to conflict of character. Among the major works in this genre, which Feydeau was to exploit until the years just prior to his death in a Paris sanitarium, are: *Feu la mère de Madame* (1908), *On purge Bébé* (1910), *Mais n'te promène donc pas toute nue!* and *Léonie est en avance* (both 1911), as well as *Hortense a dit: "Je m'en fous!"* (1916). As was true of his best vaudevilles, these works enjoyed enormous popular and critical acclaim not only in Paris and the provinces, but around the world.

Y. A. Favre, "Le Comique de Georges Feydeau," *Revue des sciences humaines* 150 (1973); H. Gidel, *Le Théâtre de Georges Feydeau* (New York, 1975); N. R. Shapiro, trans., *Four Farces by Georges Feydeau* (Chicago, 1970); A. Shenkan, *Georges Feydeau* (Paris, 1972).

B. T. Cooper

Related entry: HALEVY, L.

FLAMMARION, CAMILLE (1842–1925), astronomer. Born in Montigny-le-Roi (Haute-Marne), he exhibited an interest in astronomy at an early age. Two years after moving with his family to Paris (1856), he was hired as an apprentice at the Paris Observatory. He published his first book at the age of nineteen, *La Pluralité des mondes habités*, which marked the beginning of his career.

Flammarion was the author of many books, articles, and lectures dealing with the earth's atmosphere and with Mars. He also contributed an important study in 1870 on the rotation of celestial bodies, in which he formulated the simple but previously undiscovered relationship between the density of planets and the relative speed of their rotation.

In 1880, his famous *Astronomie Populaire* was published. The book was an instant best-seller and made of Flammarion one of the most important popularizers of science during his time. Three years later, he founded the Juvisy Observatory, which he directed until his death. In 1887 he founded the *Société astronomique de France*, which promoted the diffusion and popularization of science to the general public. Extremely intelligent and hard working, Flammarion wrote numerous works that were well received and often translated into other languages. He died in his observatory on 3 June 1925. Flammarion typifies the self-taught scientist of the late nineteenth century in his extraordinary intellectual curiosity and prolific scientific writings.

R. D'Amat, ed., *Dictionnaire de biographie française*, vol. 13 (Paris, 1975); P. Grimal, *Dictionnaire des biographies*, vol. 1 (Paris, 1958); T. Zeldin, *France 1848–1945*, vol. 2 (Oxford, 1977); *Dictionary of Scientific Biography*, vol. 5 (New York, 1972); *Grand Larousse encyclopédie*, vol. 5 (Paris, 1962) *Grand Larousse universel*, vol. 8 (Paris, 1865–90); *Larousse Encyclopedia of Astronomy* (New York, 1959).

A. J. Staples

Related entry: SCIENCE AND TECHNOLOGY.

FLANDIN, PIERRE-ETIENNE (1889–1958), centrist politician, statesman, and attorney. The son of a lawyer and politician who served as resident-general of Tunisia, Flandin was born in Paris, where he attended the Ecole libre des sciences politiques and the Faculté de droit of the Université de Paris. A pilot during World War I, he subsequently participated in the Paris Peace Conference as a French aviation expert. Flandin entered politics in 1914, when he was elected to the Chamber of Deputies, and served as the deputy from the Yonne until 1940. After the war he emerged as president of the centrist political party, L'Alliance démocratique, and participated in nine ministries during the interwar period. Flandin reached the pinnacle of his career when he became premier (November 1934–May 1935) following the collapse of Gaston Doumergue's government of union and reconciliation that had been organized after the riots of February 1934. He subsequently served as foreign minister in the second Albert-Pierre Sarraut government (January–June 1936). After the defeat of France in 1940, he remained in France and briefly acted as foreign minister in Philippe Pétain's Vichy regime (December 1940–February 1941). Tried for collaboration with the enemy by the High Court of Justice in 1946, he was sentenced to five years of "national indignity" but was granted a reprieve.

In domestic politics Flandin pursued conservative policies, typified by his unsuccessful deflationary attempts as premier to solve France's economic depression. In foreign affairs, although inclined as foreign minister to take strong action to oppose Adolf Hitler's remilitarization of the Rhineland in March 1936, he subsequently became an ardent advocate of the policy of appeasement. During the Czechoslovakian crisis of 1938, he publicly opposed resisting German demands, expressing the fear that only the communists would benefit from a war that might otherwise develop.

J.-B. Duroselle, "France and the Crisis of March 1936," in *French Society and Culture since the Old Regime* (New York, 1966); J. T. Emmerson, *The Rhineland Crisis* (Ames, Iowa, 1977); P.-E. Flandin, *Politique française, 1919–1940* (Paris, 1947); Ministère des affaires étrangères, *Documents diplomatiques français, 1932–1939*, 2 série, vol. 1 (Paris, 1963); L. B. Namier, *Europe in Decay* (London, 1950); J. Néré, *The Foreign Policy of France from 1914 to 1945* (Boston, 1975).

J. E. Dreifort

Related entries: DEPRESSION OF THE 1930s; DOUMERGUE; FEBRUARY RIOTS; GERMANY, RELATIONS WITH (1914–1940); MUNICH CONFERENCE: FRENCH ROLE IN.

FLOQUET, CHARLES (1828–1896), Radical republican politician, premier (3 April 1888–22 February 1889) during the height of the Boulangist agitation. As a young lawyer involved in left-wing causes, he was reputed to have greeted Czar Alexander II at the Palace of Justice (1867) with the words "Long live Poland, sir." As premier he lodged himself in memory for having leveled General Georges Boulanger in debate (4 June 1888) with a non sequitur—"At your age, General Boulanger, Napoleon was dead"—and for nearly killing him in an épée duel (13 July).

Floquet helped carry out the Revolution of September Fourth (1870), signed the protest against the cession of Alsace-Lorraine, and, after resigning his National Assembly seat, founded the League of Republican Union for the Rights of Paris, which tried to mediate between the Assembly and the Commune. As a left-leaning Radical, he represented Paris (1876–85, 1889–93) and Pyrénées-Orientales (1885–89) in the Chamber of Deputies. He was elected to the Senate from the Seine in 1894 after losing his Chamber seat as a result of unsubstantiated corruption charges arising from the Panama Canal Company scandal. He admitted, however, that while premier he had used money from the company to fight Boulangism.

As premier, Floquet sought to undercut the Boulangists' appeal by proposing reforms and constitutional revision. A bad wheat harvest damaged the economy and prospects for reform, and after Boulanger's Paris victory (27 January 1889), his ministry fell when the Opportunists took alarm at his continued advocacy of revision. Nicknamed "the Bombaster" because of his florid oratory and grand air, he was a man whose ambition (for example, for the presidency, 1887) exceeded his ability. He nevertheless won praise for his fairness and courtesy as president of the Chamber, to which office he was elected eight times (1885–88, 1889–January 1893).

G. Chapman, *The Third Republic of France: The First Phase, 1871–1894* (London, 1962); Floquet Papers, Archives Nationales; C.-T. Floquet, *Discours et opinions*, 2 vols. (Paris, 1885); H. K. Floquet, ed., *Choix de discours de Charles Floquet*, 2 vols. (Paris, 1904); M. Proth, *Ch. Floquet* (Paris, 1883).

D. S. Newhall

Related entries: BOULANGER AFFAIR; PANAMA SCANDAL; RADICAL AND RADICAL-SOCIALIST PARTY; SEPTEMBER 4, 1870.

FLOURENS, GUSTAVE (1838–1871), scholar, barnstorming revolutionary, and general of the Commune of Paris. Born in Paris, he came from an intellectual family and was a brilliant student and professor of physiology. Like his father, he taught at the Collège de France and also in London and Belgium. Deeply committed to the republican cause, he became involved in popular insurrections abroad, notably those in Poland and in Crete. Flourens was arrested and imprisoned many times for his political opposition to the Second Empire. As a National Guard commander in Paris besieged during the Franco-Prussian War, he clashed with leaders of the provisional government for his participation in the antigovernment demonstration of 31 October 1870, for which he was sentenced to death. Flourens fled to England and Holland and then returned to serve as a general of the Commune. He lost his life while leading the ill-fated offensive against Versailles of 3 April 1871.

J. Balteau, ed., *Dictionnaire de biographie française* (Paris, 1933–); J. Bruhat et al., *La Commune de 1871* (Paris, 1970); J. Chastenet, *Histoire de la Troisième République, 1870–1879* (Paris, 1952); S. Edwards, *The Paris Commune, 1871* (New York, 1971); G. Flourens, *Paris livré* (Paris, 1971); F. Jellenek, *The Paris Commune of 1871* (London, 1937); J. Maitron, ed., *Dictionnaire du mouvement ouvrier*, vol. 6 (Paris, 1969); E. S. Mason, *The Paris Commune* (New York, 1967); C. Prolès, *Les Hommes de la révolution de 1871: Gustave Flourens* (Paris, 1898).

A. J. Staples

Related entries: BLANQUISTS; COMMUNARDS; COMMUNE OF PARIS; JACOBINISM.

FOCH, FERDINAND (1851–1929), marshal, in 1918–19 commander in chief of the Allied Armies. Born in Tarbes (Hautes-Pyrénées) to a minor civil servant whose wife's family had a military tradition and educated mainly in Catholic schools, he enlisted during the Franco-Prussian War but saw no action. Commissioned (1874) in the artillery after attending the Ecole polytechnique (1871–73), he won wide notice as a professor of strategy and tactics at the Ecole supérieure de guerre (1895–1901) and returned there as commandant (1908–11) after his career had appeared threatened during the post-Dreyfus reforms because of his Catholic piety. His lectures, published as *Des principes de la guerre* (1903) and *De la conduite de la guerre* (1904), were much influenced by Karl von Clausewitz and stressed offensive tactics—"the will to conquer," as he expressed it—ideas that in exaggerated form became dogma among the General Staff's planners.

He owed his appointment in 1918 to the highest Allied command to his good relations with Georges Clemenceau and the other Allied leaders and to the reputation he had won during the war: at the Marne (6–9 September 1914), where his energy (and German confusion) had foiled a dangerous move on the French center; at the defense of Ypres (October–December 1914), where he coordinated Allied operations and thereby reinforced a favorable impression he had made among the British while serving in liaison and planning capacities before the war; as commander of the Northern Army Group, where he was a principal planner and executor of the great offensives in Artois (9 May, 25 September 1915) and on the Somme (1 July 1916), which, however, like the opening offensive in 1914, again demonstrated the limits imposed by machine-guns and artillery on "the will to conquer"; and as the successor to Philippe Pétain as chief of the general staff (15 May 1917), the army's top planning and administrative post, a position to which he was called after being shelved in the shake-up following General Joseph Joffre's removal (December 1916).

Foch was the consensus choice of a conference at Doullens (26 March) to coordinate the Allied defense when the German onslaught, beginning on 21 March, threatened to split the British armies from the French. His activity ensured that French reserves would continue to be used to maintain contact with the hard-pressed British. After being charged with the strategic direction of operations (3 April), he was formally titled (14 April) commander in chief of the Allied armies in France (extended to Italy, 2 May, and over the Belgians, 9 September). A great German success at the Chemin des Dames (27 May) caught him off balance and aroused criticism against him, but after the failure of the German offensive around Reims (15–17 July), he obtained the strategic initiative. Until the armistice, he directed an unrelenting series of alternating offensives that pinched off the Germans' salients and levered their tiring army toward the frontier. He was principally responsible for drawing up the terms of the armistice, which was signed (11 November) in his train at Rethondes.

During the Peace Conference (1919–20) he outspokenly advocated setting Germany's frontier at the Rhine, with the Rhineland detached and the Allies in permanent military control of the river. His criticisms of Clemenceau's compromises on this question embittered their relations. From 1920 Foch chaired the Allied Military Committee at Versailles, which enforced the military clauses of the treaties. He died on 20 March 1929 and was entombed at the Invalides near Napoleon.

Served by a tiny staff and a remarkable alter ego in General Maxime Weygand, Foch was a planner, arbitrator, and coordinator, not a true commander of combined forces such as was developed in World War II. Although his chief activity, the maneuvering of Allied reserves, played a capital role, his contribution to the victory owed more to his character than to his particular decisions or expertise. He was well grounded in the military science of his day and willing to learn, but he was not the Napoleon-like genius of war his admirers often proclaimed him to be. He found his true moment when at the darkest hour, in the maelstrom of the German offensives of 1918, as at Ypres in 1914, his fiery, unbending will and extraordinary ability to inspire confidence served to hold the Allied armies together and spur them to a victory that came sooner than even his quasi-mystical spirit had foreseen.

F. Foch, *Mémoires pour servir à l'histoire de la guerre de 1914–1918*, 2 vols. (Paris, 1931); T. M. Hunter, *Marshal Foch: A Study in Leadership* (Ottawa, 1961); J. C. King, *Foch versus Clemenceau* (Cambridge, Mass., 1960); A. Laffargue, *Foch et la bataille de 1918* (Paris, 1967); B. H. Liddell Hart, *Foch, the Man of Orleans* (London, 1931); R. Recouly, *Le Mémorial de Foch* (Paris, 1929); M. Weygand, *Foch* (Paris, 1947).

D. S. Newhall

Related entries: ARMISTICE OF 1918; ARMY: ORGANIZATION; CLEMENCEAU; DREYFUS AFFAIR; JOFFRE; MARNE, BATTLE OF THE; PARIS PEACE CONFERENCE; PETAIN; SCHOOLS, MILITARY; SOMME, BATTLE OF THE; WORLD WAR I.

FOREIGN LEGION, famous military organization enrolling foreigners for service outside France. Formed in 1831 after prior mercenary units had been abolished (1830), the Légion étrangère came to be stationed permanently in Algeria (from 1831), Indochina (1883), Morocco (1903), and Syria (1925). Most colonial campaigns employed legion units, and temporary *régiments de marche*, minus Germans, served in France during the Franco-Prussian War and both world wars.

French governments, sensitive to foreign criticism, were always closed-mouthed about the legion; it did not appear on the published Army List until 1931. As a rule it contained from two to six infantry regiments of varying size and (from 1922) a cavalry regiment, total establishments being about 6,000 in the 1870s, about 10,000 after 1900, perhaps 25,000 in the mid-1920s, and about 15,000 in the mid-1930s, with heavy influxes in World War I (approximately 43,000 served, with 35,000 casualties recorded) and 1939 (approximately 26,000). Wars and revolutions, political persecution, economic upheavals, and personal misfortunes were the legion's steadiest recruiters. Soldiers-of-fortune and cast-off lovers were common only in novelists' imaginations. At bottom, the legion served as a refuge for homeless, aimless men. Hence the consuming interest it always showed in fostering an intense loyalty to the corps, summed up in its doctrine, *Legion Patria Nostra* ("The Legion Is Our Country"), and its motto, *Honneur et fidélité*.

Enlistments were for five years. Exemplary service for one tour could earn French citizenship and three tours a pension. Most men enlisted under false names. No questions were asked, but serious criminals were regarded as unreliable and weeded out if discovered. After World War I enlistees had to be fingerprinted and cleared by the police. To avoid complications over citizenship, legionnaires took no oath to France, only to the legion. (In September 1908 a sharp diplomatic crisis between France and Germany arose over assistance to legion deserters by the German consulate at Casablanca.) Germans, notably Alsatians, usually were the most numerous nationality and always a majority among noncommissioned officers, who held extraordinarily broad authority. Swiss, Belgians, and Italians were common and in the 1920s and 1930s Russians and Spaniards owing to civil wars. English, Americans, and blacks were very rare, Orientals perhaps less so. French citizens were forbidden entry, but some always passed as Belgians, Alsatians, or Swiss. Most officers were French regulars—a prized assignment and after 1870 usually a permanent one—but former foreign officers could be commissioned, although they seldom were promoted beyond the rank of major. Commissioning from the ranks was exceedingly rare.

Legionnaires seldom fought in units larger than a company or two. In field armies for a campaign, an ad hoc *bataillon* or *régiment de marche*, composed of men selected from standing legion regiments, often was used as an elite striking force. Legionnaires also were employed in construction work of every description. Desertion, alcoholism, and bouts of a peculiar type of depression (*le cafard*) were perennial problems, abetted by hard duty in harsh climes. Moreover, French governments habitually treated the legion like an unwanted child, stinting its pay and equipment. Discipline was severe, not infrequently harsh, but inhuman brutality was not the rule despite reports to the contrary. The legion's feats of surpassing courage and endurance are well attested. It runs against reason to suppose that a rabble of damned and besotted renegades, so often depicted by sensation-seeking writers, could have earned the reputation the legion has long enjoyed among professional soldiers as a disciplined fighting force second to none.

G. Bocca, *La Légion!* (New York, 1964); L. Gauthier and C. Jacquot, *Honneur et fidélité*, 2 vols. (Paris, 1963); W. Kanitz, *The White Kepi* (New York, 1956); *Képi Blanc, journal mensuel de la Légion Etrangère* (Aubagne 13); "La Légion étrangère, 1831–1980," *Revue historique des Armées*, no. 1 (1981); E. O'Ballance, *The Story of the French Foreign Legion* (London, 1961).

D. S. Newhall

Related entries: ARMY: ORGANIZATION; GERMANY, RELATIONS WITH; LYAUTEY; MOROCCAN CRISES; OVERSEAS EMPIRE: FRENCH IMPERIALISM; RIF REBELLION.

FOREIGN POLICY. From 1871 to 1914, French foreign policy was dominated by a single imperative: to regain great power status in a German-dominated Europe. In practice, this meant working within the framework of the Treaty of Frankfurt, which imposed on France the cession of Alsace and two-fifths of Lorraine, as well as an indemnity of 5 billion gold francs. The indemnity was paid off in 1873, six months ahead of schedule, as a result of a public loan bearing tax-exempt interest at 5 percent. That the loan was fully subscribed can be explained in part by its relatively high coupon rate: French state bonds normally paid interest at 3 1/2 percent. Its success in French financial circles also reflected confidence in the conservative policies of the Adolphe Thiers government, whose repression of the Paris Commune in the spring of 1871 had effectively put to rest any notion that the new Republic might countenance revolution.

French diplomacy in this period reflected the regime's conservative nature. Like that of other European powers, it was the exclusive preserve of professional diplomatists, over whom public opinion exercised virtually no influence. In this context, it is easy to understand why the question of Alsace-Lorraine played no role in the formulation of French foreign policy. Although the loss of this territory stirred emotions in some intellectual and literary circles, French diplomatists tacitly recognized that any hint of irredentism on their part would be counterproductive. The only compelling claim the Third Republic had to Alsace-Lorraine was the desire of its inhabitants to remain French. But to raise the question of national self-determination would simply antagonize monarchical Europe. Nearly every European kingdom at the time had a national minorities problem, and none was eager to see a wholesale revival of this principle, which had been born of the French Revolution. Moreover, the French foreign ministry fully realized that an irredentist France could scarcely hope to win friends, let alone allies, among the great powers. No European country would risk being drawn into war over Alsace-Lorraine. Hence, the entire issue was effectively ignored.

The success of this policy can be seen as early as March 1875, when Otto von Bismarck provoked a war scare following the passage of a new army bill in the French parliament. Although the French government was initially tempted to yield to German pressure and withdraw the legislation, it decided instead to appeal to Great Britain and Russia for mediation. Both countries called on Germany to restore calm, which it did. Thus, France gained a small but decisive diplomatic victory, its first since the founding of the Third Republic.

Franco-German relations improved as a direct result of the republicans' political gains in 1877. Bismarck had made no secret of his preference for the French republicans, since he believed that they were less likely to find allies in the courts of Europe than their royalist adversaries. From 1878 to 1885, the moderate republicans under Jules Ferry pursued a tacit policy of entente with Germany, while committing France to colonial expansion in Tunisia and Indochina. Ferry intended to bolster the Republic's popularity and prestige through the acquisition of colonies.

Further drawing France and Germany together was the discovery in 1878 by two British scientists, Sidney Gilchrist Thomas and Percy Gilchrist, of a process whereby the iron ore of Lorraine could be purified of its phosphorus content. The richest deposits, which were just four kilometers on the French side of the 1871 boundary, provided Germany with an ideal complement to its western coal mines. Since steelmaking then required approximately five times as much coal by weight as iron ore, most of the French raw material was shipped to Germany for transformation into the finished product. French iron mining companies thus had a vested interest in the industrial expansion of Germany.

The Franco-Russian alliance, concluded in 1894 after nearly three years of negotiations, contributed to the stability of European affairs by making it clear that France was neither revolutionary nor irredentist. The failure of the Boulangist movement in 1889 removed any doubt as to the conservative nature of the Republic. As for Alsace-Lorraine, the czar made a pointed comment to the French ambassador: "You can wait with dignity." The alliance was severely criticized by the French socialists for tying France to a reactionary power. After Russia's defeat by Japan in 1904, critics emerged on the far Right, claiming that the commitment to Russia could drag France into war. Inasmuch as French diplomacy was well insulated from public opinion, however, such opposition had no practical effect on foreign policy. The alliance had support in French financial circles, since it facilitated the sale of Russian bonds in France.

France's search for closer relations with other European powers was rewarded in 1902 when Italy agreed in a secret treaty to remain neutral if France were attacked by Germany. The Entente Cordiale of 1904 with Great Britain initially was little more than a settlement of conflicting colonial claims, but it contained the seeds of a full-blown alliance. Perhaps the most remarkable of France's diplomatic achievements in the pre-1914 period was the treaty with Germany, negotiated in November 1911 and ratified early in 1912. Unlike the Algeciras Convention of 1907, this agreement was strictly bilateral. France, ostensibly the weaker of the two parties, got the better of the bargain, giving up a worthless strip of territory in the Congo in exchange for German recognition of French interests in Morocco. Thus was confirmed André Tardieu's boast of 1908: "Instead of seeking for her revenge on the field of battle, France has taken it in the Chancelleries."

On the eve of the First World War, France's diplomatic position was considerably stronger than in 1871 as a result of a policy of patient negotiations within the framework originally laid down by Germany. The Allied military victory in that conflict nullified France's earlier diplomatic gains. Germany in 1918 was potentially stronger, in relation to the rest of Europe, than in 1914. It was no longer saddled with the aging Hapsburg monarchy and the decrepit Ottoman Empire as allies. Its industries were intact, albeit somewhat worn out, and its combat losses were proportionately less than those of France. The French, on the other hand, had lost Russia as an ally, and Great Britain and the United States quickly reverted to their former isolationist positions. Moreover, the quiet diplomacy at which the French were so skilled was no longer possible. Since the citizenry of all belligerent nations had been drawn into the war effort, foreign affairs were now played out in the light of public opinion. The Treaty of Versailles received such bad publicity in the English-speaking world that France was almost alone in seeking to enforce its provisions.

Notwithstanding France's intrinsic weakness, the temporary power vacuum on the Continent made it the greatest European power throughout much of the interwar period. Until the mid-1930s, France was the only first-rank nation in Europe to possess a credible land army. Realizing the temporary nature of their predominance, the French tried to check a possible revival of German expansionism through a series of alliances with the successor states in East-Central Europe. The construction of the Maginot Line, which began in 1929, indicated that France did not consider its alliances to be sufficient security against a resurgent Germany. At the same time, the defensive posture adopted by the French army made it unlikely that France would be able to intervene effectively on behalf of its eastern allies.

In its relations with Germany, France sought to reconcile its need for security with fundamental economic realities. On the one hand, the French government had to enforce reparations payments in order to amortize its war debts to Great Britain and the United States. On the other, French industry—in particular the iron and steel sector—was mindful of Germany's importance as an economic partner. French business interests supported Raymond Poincaré's decision to occupy the Ruhr in 1923 until it became evident that the occupation, and the German government's reaction to it, were ruining the German economy. And although official French policy was to keep Germany disarmed as long as possible, Hitler's rearmament program did benefit France economically. Iron ore exports from Lorraine to Germany increased markedly from 1936 to 1939.

While trying to preserve the status quo on the Continent, French diplomacy sought above all to maintain good relations with Britain. The British military contribution, on both land and sea, had been decisive in the First World War, and French statesmen could not afford to lose Britain as a possible ally. This is apparent in France's readiness to sign the Locarno Accords of 1925. Earlier France had lost the possibility of establishing beachheads on the Rhine or of receiving an Anglo-American guarantee of military support in the event of German aggression. The Locarno treaties, while adding nothing to the provisions of Versailles, did seem to draw Britain closer to an eventual continental commitment.

Indeed from 1925 on, French foreign policy decisions were increasingly dependent on British approval. France's failure to enforce the Locarno Accords regarding the Rhineland, which the Nazi government remilitarized in March 1936, was due in part to fear of antagonizing Britain. This fear was largely responsible for France's nonintervention in the Spanish Civil War. The most important French diplomatic initiative in the 1930s was the pact with the Soviet Union in 1935, but this was negated by the Munich Accords three years later.

At Locarno, France ceased to be the arbiter of European affairs; at Munich it nearly ceased to be a great power. With Hitler in possession of the Sudetenland, Mussolini noisily revived old Italian claims to Tunisia, Nice, and Savoy late in 1938. This stiffened French resolve somewhat. France, after all, was still more important than Czechoslovakia, whereas Italy had nowhere near the strength of Germany. When the Nazis occupied Prague on 15 March 1939, French parliamentarians denounced Germany's violation of the Munich treaties as a humiliation for France. In an attempt to salvage what remained of its prestige, the Edouard Daladier government endorsed the hastily conceived guarantee offered by Britain to Poland two weeks later. The Polish guarantee was the first step in a diplomatic offensive known as the peace front in which Britain and France offered similar protection to other smaller countries, such as Greece and Rumania, in the spring of 1939.

The purpose of this diplomatic posturing, as initiated by British prime minister Neville Chamberlain, was to impress Hitler with the seriousness of the democracies' commitment to maintain the European balance and thereby to avert a general war. But only an alliance between the democratic powers and the Soviet Union would have deterred the Nazi dictator, and the Polish guarantee made such an alliance virtually unattainable. The French government gave high priority to negotiations with Moscow in the summer of 1939, but Chamberlain did not take them seriously. The Nazi-Soviet pact of 23 August 1939 revealed the fundamental error of peace front diplomacy: Hitler was not impressed. Britain and France would have to go to war over the Polish question after all.

France's entry into the Second World War was an avowal of its failure to maintain the peace of 1919. In order to avoid losing the next peace, French diplomacy during the "phony war" period was directed primarily toward Britain over the question of war aims. The French government sought what it called material guarantees against German aggression anytime in the future. In practice this meant the political division of the Reich and the stationing of Allied troops in its western regions. The British, fearful that the publication of such war aims would unite all Germans behind Hitler, refused to discuss them. Since 1945, however, France's war aims of 1939–40 have been effectively attained. A divided Germany dotted with foreign garrisons, its industrial heartland firmly linked to the French economy, has given belated vindication to the foreign policy of the Third Republic.

F. Goguel, *La Politique des partis sous la IIIe République* (Paris, 1958); P. Renouvin, *Histoire des relations internationales*, vols. 7, 8 (Paris, 1955); J. Néré, *The Foreign Policy of France from 1914 to 1945* (London, 1975).

F. H. Seager

Related entries: GERMANY, RELATIONS WITH; GREAT BRITAIN, RELATIONS WITH; RUSSIA, RELATIONS WITH.

FOUILLEE, ALFRED (1838–1912), well-known philosopher, creator of the philosophy of *idées-forces*. Forced to help support his family after the death of his father, Fouillée began his career as a secondary school teacher at the age of nineteen. While teaching philosophy at the lycée of Carcassonne, he entered the competition for the *agrégation* in philosophy and was received first in the nation (1864). This brought him for the first time in contact with the leading philosophers of the day and led to more prestigious positions at the lycées of Douai, Montpellier, and Bordeaux. His first book, *Philosophie de Platon*, won the Prix Bordin of the Académie française (1867). In 1872 Fouillée was named *maître de conférences* at the Ecole normale supérieure (ENS) and successfully defended his doctoral thesis, "La Liberté et le déterminisme," which challenged the views of the reigning eclectics and generated political controversy. Fouillée was able to teach at the ENS for only three years before his health failed; he spent most of the rest of his life in retirement at Menton.

Despite chronic ill health, Fouillée was a prodigious worker, turning out nearly a book a year plus numerous articles in the highly influential *Revue des deux mondes* until his death at Lyons in 1912. In these works, he developed and applied to a wide variety of subjects his philosophy of *idées-forces*, one of the most original conceptions of the nineteenth century. Fouillée attempted to synthesize materialism and idealism in philosophy; indeed he aspired to reconcile science and philosophy—one of the central problems of modern thought—by means of an approach that not only would resolve traditional problems, like the free will question addressed in his thesis, but would be effective in treating the unknown problems of the future as well. Something of a solitary figure because his philosophy challenged all the contemporary schools, Fouillée was nonetheless highly respected by contemporary philosophers as well as by the cultivated public. Through his writings on social and political issues, he exercised considerable influence on the new liberalism, especially on the solidarism of Léon Bourgeois. Mme. Fouillée was an influential author of laic, republican literature for children under the name G. Bruno. In France and abroad, Fouillée was one of the best-known French philosophers of his day.

A. Guyau, *La Philosophie et la sociologie d'Alfred Fouillée* (Paris, 1913).

W. H. Logue

Related entry: LIBERALISM.

FRANCE, ANATOLE (1844–1924), pseudonym of Jacques Anatole François Thibault, novelist, literary critic, renowned skeptic. The son of a Parisian bookseller, he was a master of satire and a prolific author of novels, essays, short stories, and literary criticism. Dissuaded from religiosity and philosophical spiritualism by his reading of Hippolyte Taine, Herbert Spencer, and Charles Darwin, he subsequently concluded that truths were as numerous as men. The skeptical France gained fame for merciless exposés of human stupidity and hypocrisy but later blended irony and pity. Contemporaries viewed him as a latter-day Voltaire. Initially focused on individuals' foibles, his fiction eventually included a social message, especially after he became a Dreyfusard. The four novels of *L'Histoire contemporaine* (1897–1901) depicted French society before and during the Dreyfus affair; M. Bergeret, their main character, was the author in disguise. *L'Ile des pingouins* (1908) also satirized the divisions engendered by the affair and attributed it to rivalries between social groups and institutions in need of change. *L'Affaire Crainquebille* (1901) and *Sur la pierre blanche* (1903) revealed socialist leanings that culminated in his eventual support for Russian communism. *Les Dieux ont soif* (1912) exposed the Reign of Terror's assaults on liberty in the name of liberty. He consistently favored individual freedom but often doubted man's ability to use it properly. A complex personality, France attempted to reconcile a skepticism fed by his understanding of history and natural science with a hope that humans could behave reasonably and change society for the better. Election to the Académie française (1896) and receipt of the Nobel prize for literature (1921) testify to his contemporary (but now faded) reputation as one of France's greatest writers.

M. Gaffiot, *Les Théories d'Anatole France sur l'organisation sociale de son temps* (Paris, 1928); C. Jefferson, *Anatole France* (New Brunswick, N.J., 1965); J. Levaillant, *Essai sur l'évolution intellectuelle d'Anatole France* (Paris, 1965).

L. L. Clark

Related entries: DREYFUS AFFAIR; LITERARY CRITICS AND CRITICISM; NOVEL, POLITICS AND THE.

FRANCOIS-PONCET, ANDRE (1887–1978), professor, politician, diplomat, and historian. Born at Provins (Seine-et-Marne) on 13 June 1887, he studied at the Ecole normale supérieure. He was professor of German at the Lycée Montpellier in 1911, and *chargé de conferences* at the Ecole polytechnique from 1911 to 1914. An infantry officer in the First World War commanding Company 304, he was sent to Switzerland in 1917 as an attaché to the French embassy. He was next a member of the International Economic Committee to the United States (1919) and in 1922 founded and directed for four years the Society for Economic Studies and Information, in Paris.

In 1924 he was elected to the Chamber of Deputies from the Seine and in 1928 from the Seventh Arrondissement in Paris. He served as an under secretary in the cabinets of Raymond Poincaré, Aristide Briand, André Tardieu, and Pierre Laval between 1928 and 1931. He represented France at the League of Nations in 1930 and at the grain conference in Rome in 1931.

In 1930 he opted for a diplomatic career, and Laval appointed him ambassador to Berlin in 1931. His warnings to the Quai d'Orsay about German armament and policy went unheeded. After Munich in 1938 he felt the only chance for peace was dependent upon the influence Benito Mussolini might have on Adolf Hitler. He asked for and was granted transfer to Rome.

He returned to France in 1940 after Italy's entry into the war and worked for the Vichy administration. Arrested by the Germans in 1943, he was imprisoned in the Tyrol.

In 1948 he was appointed adviser to the military governor of French-occupied Germany and in 1949 French high commissioner in the former Reich. After German independence he became ambassador to Bonn in 1955. He retired that same year and spent his time writing his memoirs and commentary on German literature.

He received the Croix de Guerre (1914–18) and the Grand Cross of the Legion of Honor, was elected to the Académie française (1952), and received an honorary degree from the University of Munich. He died in Paris, 7 January 1978.

A. François-Poncet, *De Versailles à Potsdam* (Paris, 1948), and *Souvenirs d'une ambassade à Berlin* (Paris, 1946); J. Jolly, ed, *Dictionnaire des parliamentaires français*, vol. 5 (Paris, 1968).

J. M. Rife, Jr.

Related entries: GERMANY, RELATIONS WITH (1914–1940); ITALY, RELATIONS WITH.

FRANCO-PRUSSIAN WAR (19 July 1870–28 January 1871), or Franco-German War, the war that brought the birth of the Third Republic and the loss by France of Alsace-Lorraine (1871–1918). On 12 July 1870 Prince Leopold of Hohenzollern-Sigmaringen, scion of the Catholic branch of the dynasty headed by William I of Prussia, withdrew his candidacy for the vacant throne of Spain after protests (4, 6 July) from France. On 13 July at Bad Ems, Ambassador Count Vincent Benedetti, on instructions, requested William to promise to decline any further Spanish offer. William politely but firmly refused and later sent word he would not grant a further audience Benedetti had requested to pursue this subject. Otto von Bismarck, Prussian minister president, received in Berlin a telegram relating the incident. He released an edited version (the Ems dispatch), which aroused both German and French opinion by making it appear that William had refused all further dealings with an impertinent ambassador. The Ems dispatch, reports that Prussia was arming, and a wave of war fever persuaded Napoleon III, with the Legislative Body's concurrence, to declare war (15 July). Prussia received official notice on 19 July.

Patriotic sentiment brought Bavaria, Saxony, Baden, and Württemberg to the side of Prussia and the North German Bund, an alliance that later led to the proclamation of the German Empire (1871–1918) at Versailles (18 January). France found no allies. Napoleon expected Austria to join him after he won some early victories; Italy occupied Rome (20 August) after the French garrison, which protected the pope's sovereignty there, was called home; Russia leaned toward Prussia because of the Polish question, and used the war as an excuse to abrogate (29 October, ratified 13 March 1871 at the London Conference) the clauses of the Treaty of Paris (1856) neutralizing the Black Sea. Great Britain, currently gallophobic, worried only about respect for Belgium's neutrality.

A swift mobilization might have enabled the French to disrupt Prussia's intricately planned mobilization and deployment, but it was abysmally mishandled. General Helmuth von Moltke's forces struck Marshal Maurice de MacMahon at Wissembourg (4 August) and Froeschwiller-Woerth (6 August), separating him from the other field force under Marshal Achille Bazaine. He retired through the Vosges, finally retreating to Châlons-sur-Marne to join an army being formed there. Bazaine fell back through Metz after actions at Spicheren-Forbach (6 August) and Borny (14 August) but abandoned the Verdun road after bloody, closely contested battles at Vionville-Mars-le-Tour (16 August) and Gravelotte-St.-Privat (18 August) and withdrew into Metz, which was put to siege (23 August). MacMahon left Châlons (21 August) with Napoleon in a forlorn attempt to join Bazaine. Moving swiftly, the Germans diverted him northward at Noart (29 August) and Beaumont (30 August). He retreated to Sedan, seven miles from Belgium. The Germans pressed in (Bazailles, 31 August). MacMahon, wounded at Bazailles, was replaced by General Emmanuel de Wimpffen, who refused advice to retreat while there was still time. The trap closed. Murderous fire annihilated desperate French charges, and Wimpffen then capitulated (83,000 men, 419 guns); Napoleon gave himself up separately the same day (2 September).

The German forces not besieging Metz and other fortresses now encircled Paris (19–20 September). The balance of the war amounted to a siege of Paris while new French armies, improvised from the debris of the old plus largely untrained reserves, volunteers, and conscripts, tried to compel the Germans to abandon it by attacks from bases in the Loire and Somme valleys or, at least, to gain time for the neutrals to bring Bismarck to soften peace terms. Bismarck meanwhile pondered the problem of finding a French government to negotiate with and whose orders would be obeyed.

On 4 September a Paris uprising had toppled the Empire, proclaimed a republic, and set up the Government of National Defense. A branch, the Delegation, was formed at Tours (to Bordeaux, 10 December), which Léon Gambetta, the interior minister, joined (11 October) after escaping Paris by balloon. Assisted by Charles de Freycinet, he took charge of the feverish attempts to raise new armies. Their prospects were gravely damaged by the release of a quarter million more Germans for field operations after the surrenders of Strasbourg (28 September) and Metz (29 October), where some 173,000 famished, disease-ridden regulars gave up after vegetating under Bazaine's inept command. They won short-lived successes, nevertheless, under General Louis d'Aurelle de Paladines at Coulmiers (19 November), capturing Orleans, and General Louis Faidherbe at the Hallue River (23 December) and Bapaume (2–3 January) in the north, but reinforced German armies retook Orleans (2–4 December) and drubbed Faidherbe at St.-Quentin (19 January). General Alfred Chanzy struggled gallantly on the Loire but finally had to retreat to Le Mans (mid-December). General Charles Bourbaki undertook a complex operation eastward to threaten supply lines to Paris but was defeated outside Belfort (15–17 January); under General Justin Clichant some 80,000 freezing survivors escaped to refuge in Switzerland. In the occupied regions, meanwhile, guerrillas (*francs-tireurs*) harassed the Germans, who, enraged by this violation of the rules of war, replied with burnings and summary executions.

At Paris, Moltke, with a quarter-million men stretched on a fifty-mile perimeter, had no intention of assaulting a city guarded by a moated, bastioned, thirty-three-foot wall and fifteen detached forts and garrisoned by about 95,000 regulars, 3,000 marines, 8,000 sailors (serving guns), 115,000 Gardes Mobiles (untrained reserves), and 200,000 or so volatile National Guards (volunteers and older reserves). Only at the insistence of Bismarck, who had grown anxious that the neutrals might intervene, did he begin (5 January) a long-range bombardment of the inner city. It achieved nothing militarily and was decried around the world as barbaric. General Louis Trochu, the French commander, tried three breakout attempts in force, at Champigny-Brie (29–30 November), which caused some alarm, Le Bourget (21 December), and Buzenval (19 January). They never penetrated the main German lines. He judged that untrained troops, although useful for defense and as a deterrent, were incapable of conducting complex movements needed to break a siege. In reply, frustrated National Guards twice revolted (31 October, 22 January), on the first occasion managing to hold the members of the government captive for some hours. Trochu finally gave some of the Guard a chance at Buzenval, to no avail—as he expected and perhaps as the government hoped. By then famine and cold (the winter was one of the century's severest), a climbing death rate, especially among children and the aged, the failures of the provincial armies, and fears of political agitation had sapped the government's will to continue. Believing starvation was hours away (actually about ten days' rations remained), they quietly sent Foreign Minister Jules Favre to Versailles, where he negotiated (23–28 January) an armistice until 19 February (later extended to 5 March) to permit election of a National Assembly (8 February) to decide whether to end the war.

Neither Gambetta nor a majority of Parisians wanted to believe or accept the armistice; bitterness over what they deemed a sellout contributed to the outbreak later (18 March) of the Commune. But the country gave peace-and-order candidates a crushing majority. At Bordeaux the Assembly commissioned Adolphe Thiers and Favre to negotiate at Versailles (22–26 February), and on 1 March it ratified (546 to 107) the preliminary terms. With retouches and detailed military, financial, and commercial clauses added, these terms were later embodied in the Treaty of Frankfurt (20 May). They entailed the cession of Alsace and about a third of Lorraine (including Metz), a 5 billion franc indemnity, and occupation of the northeastern departments, evacuation to follow in stages as the indemnity was paid. (Later revisions led to a final payment and evacuation in September 1873.) By conceding at Versailles a German march into Paris (1–3 March), however, Thiers had kept Belfort, an Alsatian border fortress at a gap in the Vosges that Colonel Pierre Denfert-Rochereau was still holding. Had Thiers suspected how keen Bismarck was to end a war whose continuance was becoming a drain on German resources and causing political and diplomatic rumblings, he might have extracted more concessions.

The war cost the lives of 140,000 French and 47,500 German soldiers. It ended a two-century reign by France as *la grande nation* in Europe, a fact that French leaders down to 1914 could neither forget nor quite forgive. The war's real issue was not the Hohenzollern candidacy, a pretext, but whether France would allow Bismarck to continue building Prussian power without a fight. Bismarck probably did not intend originally to provoke a war by the candidacy, but he was ready to accept one if the French insisted. Napoleon's victory in the 8 May 1870 plebiscite led Bismarck to worry that it would encourage him to stoke the south German states' growing resistance to inclusion in a Prussian-dominated Bund. The ghastly blunder at Ems, after the candidacy had failed, handed him a chance to recoup by inflicting on Napoleon a diplomatic or—if he took the bait—a military defeat.

Bismarck, and the German public, wanted Alsace-Lorraine, although he had included French-speaking Metz only at the insistence of Moltke and William. He expected France would not forgive a defeat whatever its cost and wanted a strong position for the future. He probably underestimated the resentment the annexation would bring and in later years had to resort to increasingly complex moves to keep France from finding allies to reverse the verdict.

The conflict, like the U.S. Civil War, revealed the effects on warfare of the current scientific and industrial revolutions. And after Sedan it became a modern-styled, nationalized "war of peoples." German successes and French failures waxed in legend. Most of the battles before Sedan were decided by narrow margins. The Germans' breech-loaded, precisely directed artillery was devastatingly effective, but the chassepot rifle in turn was murderous against exposed German infantry. French regular units man for man were usually superior to German units, which contained large numbers of reserves. The Germans won basically because of vastly superior planning and organization, rapid movement, strategical grasp, and a heavy preponderance of trained reserves. French élan could not overcome these advantages. France had ample supplies and got more by the seas, which it controlled, but logistics were left to *système D*—muddling through—which had sufficed in Algeria, the Crimea (1854–56), and, barely, in Italy (1859). The "Prussian schoolmasters" did not win the war, but the French undertook a needed educational reform thinking they had. More to the point, they began eventually to train large reserves, while the officers set themselves seriously to relearn their craft; the mobilization of 1914 bore little resemblance to the shambles of 1870.

For the rest, the French ran out of time. The politicians in Paris, weaned on laissez-faire liberalism, were disinclined to impose the kind of draconian controls a siege demands and feared political repercussions if they should try. Trochu was competent but lacked fire and imagination. Gambetta had both but lacked military expertise. Repeated defeats, cold, and hunger dissolved hope among his forces. The requirements of modern warfare resisted his attempt to repeat the miracle of 1792, but he saved his country's—and the Republic's—self-respect. So did Colonel Denfert-Rochereau. He surrendered (15 February) only on an order of the National Assembly. The Germans let him march out of Belfort armed and with uncased colors—undefeated.

R. Giesberg, *The Treaty of Frankfurt* (Philadelphia, 1966); H. Guillemin, *Les Origines de la Commune*, 3 vols. (Paris, 1954–60); M. Howard, *The Franco-Prussian War* (London, 1961); M. Kranzberg, *The Siege of Paris* (Ithaca, N.Y., 1950); P. Lehautcourt [Gen. B.-E. Palat], *La Defense nationale*, 8 vols. (Paris, 1893–98), and *Histoire de la guerre de 1870–71*, 7 vols. (Paris, 1901–8); L. Steefel, *Bismarck, the Hohenzollern Candidacy and the Origins of the Franco-German War of 1870* (Cambridge, Mass., 1962).

D. S. Newhall

Related entries: ALSACE; ARAGO; ARMY: ORGANIZATION; COMMUNE OF PARIS; FAVRE; FERRY; FLOURENS; GALLIFFET; GAMBETTA; GERMANY, RELATIONS WITH (1871–1914); ITALY, RELATIONS WITH; MACMAHON; NATIONAL ASSEMBLY; SEPTEMBER 4, 1870; THIERS.

FREE THOUGHT MOVEMENT (*La Libre Pensée*) (1870–1914), a social and intellectual movement of the early Third Republic, hostile to monotheistic religion and dedicated to proselytizing alternative secular faiths, among them ethical humanism, agnosticism, and atheism. Free Thought conceptions emerged out of the materialist and atheist doctrines of the Enlightenment of the late eighteenth century and the positivistic philosophy of the mid-nineteenth century. The movement took shape during the Second Empire because of antipathy in some intellectual circles toward the resurgent role of the Catholic church in public affairs and especially in education.

Two currents of Free Thought were in evidence at the outset of the Third Republic. The first was a viewpoint expressed by an older generation of intellectuals who championed secular humanism as the foundation of public morality. While opposed to a literal belief in Christianity as a divine revelation, they remained sympathetic to a symbolic interpretation of its teachings and pointed out the correspondences between humanist and Christian ethical precepts. Jules Michelet, Edgar Quinet, Victor Hugo, and especially Ernest Renan lent their intellectual stature to this position by teaching that Christ's life was morally edifying even if it was not invested with supernatural meaning.

The second current of Free Thought, and the one that inspired the founding of Free Thought societies, was identified with a youth movement that emerged in the student milieu of Paris in the mid-1860s. This younger generation of Free Thinkers (*Libres Penseurs*) was committed to an explicit atheistic materialism, derived from the writings of the German philosophers Ludwig Feuerbach and Ludwig Büchner. Conceived as agencies of intellectual liberation, these societies founded newspapers, sponsored conferences, devised secular rites of passage, especially for funerals, and laid plans to establish lay schools. Parisian leaders included Louis Asseline, Auguste Coudereau, and André Lefèvre; there were corresponding societies in Lyons, Marseilles, and Montpellier.

During the Commune of Paris (1871), the most militant elements of the Free Thought movement merged with the Blanquists, a secret society of political revolutionaries, whose faith in revolution was rooted in atheistic convictions. The Blanquists' vendetta against Catholic priests during the Commune was inspired by their belief that the clergy was an intellectually and politically subversive force.

The principal theorist of this radical atheism was Gustave Tridon, who identified atheistic and monotheistic thought with opposing mentalities that had rivaled one another since antiquity. Atheism for Tridon taught the affirmation of life, Christianity (and its antecedent, Judaism) its denial in favor of resignation to a priestly cult whose deity was a metaphysical fiction. Although Tridon died shortly after the fall of the Commune, Albert Regnard, a physician, scholar, and fellow Communard, popularized his ideas (and published some of his writings posthumously) during the 1870s and 1880s.

While few republican politicians were as doctrinaire as Tridon and Regnard, many (notably Jules Ferry, Paul Bert, and Ferdinand Buisson) shared their commitment to the creation of an intellectually enlightened secular society and worked actively to promote reforms designed to accomplish this end once they gained control of the government in 1879. Free Thought societies multiplied and flourished during the following decades, although they were increasingly domesticated as their agenda of educational reform (Ferry laws, 1882), civil divorce (1884), the vindication of Alfred Dreyfus (1899), and the separation of church and state (1905) were accomplished. Free Thought societies recruited and sought to further the interests of workers, but their emphasis was always on intellectual liberation rather than social reform.

The nature of this struggle for intellectual liberation was insightfully conveyed by Roger Martin du Gard in his novel *Jean Barois* (1913), whose hero is alternately drawn to Christianity and Free Thought without being able to choose between them. The poignancy of this dilemma, sensed by so many young people in the late nineteenth century, diminished in the twentieth as the emphasis on the spiritualist-materialist dichotomy was discarded in both scientific theorizing (as in relativity and quantum physics) and religious speculation, which turned from dogmatic theology to depth psychology (for example, the Catholic literary renaissance).

A. Bayet, *Histoire de la Libre-Pensée* (Paris, 1959); P. H. Hutton, *The Cult of the Revolutionary Tradition* (Berkeley, 1981); A. Lefèvre, *La Renaissance du matérialisme* (Paris, 1881); P. Lévêque, "Libre pensée et socialisme," *Le Mouvement social*, no. 57 (October–December 1966); G. Weill, *Histoire de l'idée laïque en France au XIXe siècle* (Paris, 1925).

P. H. Hutton

Related entries: ANTICLERICALISM; BERT; BLANQUISTS; BUISSON; CATHOLIC LITERARY RENAISSANCE; COMMUNE OF PARIS; DREYFUS AFFAIR; EDUCATION: GOVERNMENTAL POLICIES CONCERNING; FERRY; MARTIN DU GARD; POSITIVISM; PROTESTANTISM; QUINET; RENAN; SEPARATION OF CHURCH AND STATE, LAW OF; THOUGHT AND INTELLECTUAL LIFE; TRIDON.

FREEMASONS, a fraternal society that propagated progressive social and political ideas during the Third Republic. The first society of Freemasons was founded in England in the early eighteenth century to discuss and promote the doctrines of the Enlightenment. Masonic societies were formed throughout Europe in the late eighteenth century and were particularly active in France. Although the Freemasons did not engage in political conspiracy, as some conservatives believed, their social and intellectual activities did contribute to the broader intellectual movement that challenged and undermined the traditional values on which the Old Regime was erected and so indirectly made the French Revolution possible.

In the eighteenth century, Masonic societies attracted the elite from across French society: prominent middle-class lawyers and businessmen, as well as Catholics, clerics, and nobles. Its leaders were often eminent men of letters. In the Third Republic, in contrast, the vast majority of Freemasons hailed from the petty bourgeoisie. Rather than intellectuals, its leaders were middle-class professionals: doctors, lawyers, journalists, and academicians. Highly ritualistic, its fraternal role to some degree outweighed the intellectual role with which the Freemasonry of the eighteenth century had been identified. By the end of the nineteenth century, the society was more open toward minorities. Jews were admitted in considerable numbers, as were workers, particularly after World War I. A lodge that admitted women opened in 1893 but remained apart from the main network of Masonic societies. The size of the society grew steadily throughout France during the Third Republic. In 1862 its membership was 10,000; in 1908, 32,000; in 1926, 40,000; in 1936, 60,000. Freemasonry in the Third Republic was organized around two main groups: that identified with the Grand Lodge and the other with the Grand Orient.

As the composition of Freemasonry changed during the nineteenth century, so did its philosophy. Influenced by the growth of religious skepticism in the nineteenth century, some Freemasons favored discarding the society's commitment to deism for the positivist philosophy of Auguste Comte. Comte, a mid-nineteenth-century social thinker, taught that Western civilization, after passing through two stages of preparatory development, was at last entering a positive age, in which humanity would understand itself and formulate its values in terms of an empirical science of society rather than the metaphysical abstractions of medieval Christendom or the mythologies of antiquity. The acceptance and propagation of positivism in Masonic lodges in the early Third Republic was in effect an updating of the Freemasons' enduring commitment to advance rational values and socially progressive ideals.

The commitments of the Freemasons in the Third Republic are revealed in the causes they chose to support. The League of Instruction, designed to promote lay education, was one of the most important of these. They championed a number of political reforms, notably a progressive income tax, child labor laws, and social welfare legislation (particularly measures to aid the orphaned, the infirm, and the elderly), although they were not organized politically and advanced no official political creed. In practice, Freemasons tended to join the Radical party and, after the turn of the twentieth century, the Socialist party.

In comparison with its revolutionary origins in the Enlightenment, the Freemasonry of the Third Republic was thoroughly domesticated, but so too was the republican ideal itself. For this reason, the Freemasons' commitment to building an economically prosperous, socially advanced, politically democratic nation reinforced the basic commitments of the political leaders of the Third Republic. Without being an official arm of the Republic, the Freemasons contributed powerfully to its self-conception.

P. Chevallier, *Histoire de la franc-maçonnerie française* (Paris, 1975); M. J. Headings, *French Freemasonry under the Third Republic* (Baltimore, 1949); D. Ligou, *Frédéric Desmons et la franc-maçonnerie sous la 3ᵉ République* (Paris, 1966).

M. L. McIsaac

Related entries: AFFAIRE DES FICHES; ANTICLERICALISM; FREE THOUGHT MOVEMENT; POSITIVISM; RADICAL AND RADICAL-SO-CIALIST PARTY.

FREYCINET, CHARLES DE (1828–1923), engineer, organizer of defense in 1870–71, military reformer, and prime minister. Educated as an engineer at the Ecole polytechnique, he first came to prominence in 1870–71 as a member of the Government of National Defense where at Léon Gambetta's urging he assumed responsibility for organizing resistance to the German Army following the French defeat at Sedan. After the war Freycinet pursued a dual career in engineering and politics. Elected senator in the 1876 balloting, Freycinet participated in several cabinets during the 1880s and 1890s and headed four of them. In 1886 he selected General Georges Boulanger to be war minister. As minister of public works, Freycinet developed a program for completion of the French railway network and modernized the canal transportation system. He also improved port facilities and encouraged the expansion of heavy industry. Several appointments to the War Ministry allowed him to strengthen the French Army by creating a supreme war council, instituting a three-year draft, and reorganizing the eastern defenses.

In foreign policy Freycinet's record was mixed. He favored imperial expansion in Africa and Indochina but fell from office in 1882 when the Chamber of Deputies refused to follow his lead in Egypt, thereby alllowing Great Britain to gain dominance there. In the early 1890s he promoted French ties with Russia, ending French diplomatic isolation.

Freycinet returned to the War Ministry at the time of the Dreyfus affair, but he resigned after six months, claiming that the strain of office had become unduly burdensome. By this time he was seventy years old. Although no longer considered ministerial, Freycinet continued to serve on several important Senate committees. Between his seventieth and seventy-fifth birthdays, he published three books on mathematical theory. At the age of eighty-seven, he again returned to government as a member of Aristide Briand's wartime cabinet. He retired from politics in 1920 and died three years later at the age of ninety-five.

C. de Freycinet, *Souvenirs, 1848–92*, 2 vols. (Paris, 1912–13); E. L. Katzenbach, "Charles-Louis de Saulces de Freycinet and the Army of Metropolitan France 1870–

1918" (Ph.D. dissertation, Princeton University, 1953); W. B. Thorson, "Charles de Freycinet as Foreign Minister of France," *Historian* (Spring 1945).

J. K. Munholland

Related entries: BOULANGER; DREYFUS AFFAIR; FAVRE; FERRY; FOREIGN POLICY; FRANCO-PRUSSIAN WAR; GAMBETTA; OPPORTUNISTS; OVERSEAS EMPIRE: FRENCH IMPERIALISM; RAILROADS; SEPTEMBER 4, 1870.

FREYSSINET, EUGENE (1879–1962), engineer, inventor of prestressed concrete. Born in Objat (Corrèze) in 1879, he attended both of the French *grandes écoles* in engineering: the Ponts et chaussées and the Polytechnique. Between 1905 and 1918 he built bridges in central France and served as an army engineer. From 1929 until his death in 1962, he had a private practice in Paris.

He is especially known for his pioneering work in reinforced concrete and his development of prestressed concrete between 1928 and 1940, which paved the way for large-scale prefabrication of building elements. He built many public and industrial works, including bridges, factories, roads, and port facilities, in which he created vast, unencumbered spaces securely contained by concrete. His most famous constructions, built early in his career (1916–19), were two immense airplane hangars at Orly, 300 meters long and as high as the towers of Notre Dame de Paris. These, and many of his bridges, were destroyed during World War II. Although Freyssinet did little work in collaboration with architects, his construction methods have come into general use in postwar architecture.

J. A. Fernandez-Ordoñez, *Eugène Freyssinet* (Barcelona, 1978).

T. Shapiro

Related entries: ARCHITECTURE AND URBAN PLANNING; PERRET.

FROSSARD, LUDOVIC-OSCAR (1889–1946), journalist and politician of an unorthodox socialist tendency. Son of a Belfort saddler, he became a school teacher and entered socialist politics in the decade before World War I. Greatly influenced by Jean Jaurès, Frossard began writing for socialist newspapers, including *L'Humanité*. During the First World War Frossard's pacifism led him to join the minority faction within the Socialist party (SFIO) where he urged that socialists reconsider their unconditional support for the war effort and called for a negotiated peace settlement. By 1918 he had been elected secretary of the SFIO at the age of twenty-eight.

The Bolshevik triumph in November 1917 fascinated Frossard, who traveled to the Soviet Union after the armistice as a representative from the French socialists. On his return to France he urged socialist allegiance to the Third International. He helped found the French Communist party after the split within the SFIO at the Tours Congress of 1920, and he served as party secretary until 1922. In 1923 he left the Communist party, objecting to Moscow's increasing dominance of party affairs, and returned to the SFIO. In 1928 he was elected deputy from Martinique on the socialist ticket.

In parliament Frossard became known for his ability to interpellate governments with wit and irony. His sympathies for the Left were more emotional and pragmatic than doctrinaire, and he chafed at the socialists' refusal to participate in government. In 1935 he broke with the SFIO again when he accepted ministerial portfolios under Fernand Bouisson, Pierre Laval, and Albert Sarraut. Although a member of a splinter political party after his second break with the socialists, he served in the 1938 cabinets of Camille Chautemps, Léon Blum, and Edouard Daladier. In August 1938 he resigned as labor minister in protest over Daladier's modification of the forty-hour work week that had been part of the Popular Front reforms. He returned as a member of Paul Reynaud's cabinet in 1940, and he was Philippe Pétain's minister for public works in the last government of the Third Republic.

A. Kriegel, *Aux origines du communisme français, 1914–1920* (Paris, 1964); A. Rosmer, *Le Mouvement ouvrière pendant la guerre* (Paris, 1936); G. Suarez, *Nos seigneurs et maîtres* (Paris, 1937).

J. K. Munholland

Related entries: BLUM; CACHIN; COMMUNIST PARTY; DALADIER; JAURES; POPULAR FRONT; RUSSIA, RELATIONS WITH; SOCIALIST PARTY.

FUNERALS, STATE, final rites sponsored by the government to celebrate selected leaders and outstanding citizens and to promote the Republic. The Third Republic paid for and designed state funerals to honor prominent persons who were important to republican leaders, such as presidents of the Republic, generals (especially marshals of France), and cultural heroes (especially celebrated scientists and writers). These *fêtes funèbres* celebrated outstanding service to the Republic and the country with a pomp rivaling that of analogous church, royal, and revolutionary ceremonial.

The Third Republic offered two kinds of celebrations of its most admired dead: funerals designated simply "at state expense" and, more important, "national funerals," although sometimes the distinction was not clear even to functionaries. For national funerals the state spent more money on decorations and staging, and a law opening special credits had to be voted by parliament, whereas some funerals simply at state expense were so authorized by presidential decree with the necessary funds often found in existing budgets. In the early Third Republic the state commonly spent 5,000 to 10,000 francs on a funeral, like the one for Colonel Pierre Philippe Denfert-Rochereau in 1878 or Henri Martin in 1883. Spectacular national funerals like those for Victor Hugo and President Félix Faure cost over 100,000 francs. For any deputy's funeral, the state contributed 1,200 francs if the family so requested.

Funerals at state expense were held for such personages as Claude Bernard (1878), Louis Blanc (1882), General Alfred Chanzy (1883), chemist Eugène Chevreul (1889), Jules Ferry (1893), General Joseph Gallieni (1895), Théophile Delcassé (1923), Anatole France and Maurice Barrès (1924), Clement Ader and Jules Méline (1925), and Aristide Briand (1932). The Republic organized national funerals for such notables as Léon Gambetta and Martin (1883), Hugo (1885), Marshal Maurice de MacMahon (1893), President Sadi Carnot (1894), Louis Pasteur (1895), President Faure (1899), and Marcellin Berthelot (1907). After a hiatus occasioned by the carnage of the First World War, the tradition of grand national obsequies flourished anew with the rites for Marshal Ferdinand Foch (1929), Marshal Joseph Joffre (1931), André Maginot (1932), President Paul Doumer (1932), Paul Painlevé, Dr. Emile Roux of the Institut Pasteur and Georges Leygues (1933), former President Raymond Poincaré, Louis Barthou, and Marshal Hubert Lyautey (1934), the victims of the shipwrecked *Pourquoi Pas?* (1936), and former President Gaston Doumergue (1937).

Corteges through the streets, tributes and eulogies published in newspapers, lowered flags and functionaries in obligatory mourning signaled the importance of national funerals to the public at large. Religious services were commonly part of the program, but Gambetta, Hugo, and Jules Grévy had purely civil burials. In 1885 the Republic added a final highest tribute to its funereal ceremonial: transfer of the deceased's remains to the Pantheon. Hugo was the first to be so honored. In 1889 as part of the centennial of the French Revolution, the honor was extended to the revolutionaries Lazare Carnot, François Marceau, Théophile Corret de La Tour d'Auvergne, and the 1851 rebel Alphonse Baudin. Others given the Pantheon apotheosis were President Carnot, Emile Zola, Berthelot, Gambetta's heart (1920), Jean Jaurès (though not until 1924), Painlevé, and Doumer.

The early standard setter for an impressive funeral cortege was Adolphe Thiers' in 1877, although the family, not the state, paid for and made the arrangements. Gambetta's funeral was even grander; it became an important model in the planning of Hugo's. State funerals that seem to have evoked the greatest popular response were Gambetta's, Hugo's, Carnot's, and Foch's. Leaders who were assassinated or otherwise died in office received particularly lavish ceremonial homages and emotion-filled tributes. Since most of the major funerals were held in Paris, they involved predominantly Parisians as crowds participating in corteges, although the provinces commonly sent delegations and observed mourning forms locally.

A notable abstainer from the Republic's funeral customs was Georges Clemenceau, whose materialist free-thinking and democratic convictions militated against any solemnity, civil or religious. As he prepared for his death in 1929, he insisted, "pas de funérailles nationales! Rien." Accordingly, without ceremony or cortege, his body was taken to an unmarked grave in his native Vendée.

Politically, funerals served as occasions for republicans to demonstrate their strength and unity, particularly in times of crisis. Thiers' funeral had that function during the electoral campaign after *seize mai*, and so did Faure's funeral during the Dreyfus affair. Some death rites had the effect of distracting attention from critical problems; the passing of Foch, Joffre, and Lyautey for a time turned reflections toward past victories instead of intractable current economic and political troubles. State funerals could also become occasions for opponents of the Republic to express their hostility; the most famous example was Paul Déroulède's attempt to turn troops and the crowd against the regime during rites for President Faure. But generally police maintained tight control over dissidents and crowds to prevent the kind of disorders commonly associated with nonstate funerals of controversial political figures.

C. W. Rearick

Related entries: CEMETERY, CULT OF; FESTIVALS: POLITICAL.

FUSTEL DE COULANGES, NUMA-DENIS (1830–1889), classicist and social historian. He was born in Paris and became an orphan at an early age. Studies on scholarships at the Institution Massin and the Lycée Charlemagne were crowned by acceptance into the Ecole normale supérieure in 1850. He was a compulsive reader of history, triggered it seems by the reading of François Guizot's *La Civilisation en France*. Fustel's early liberalism was redirected by the rigid cartesianism and conservative eclecticism that pervaded the Normale at that time. Recognition of his skill as a classicist came in 1853 on graduation with his appointment to the Ecole française in Athens, Greece.

On his return to France in 1855 Fustel began to prepare for a university career while teaching at the lycées in Amiens and in Limoges. He passed his *agrégation* in letters in 1856 and two years later successfully defended his theses for the doctorate. These first scholarly works revealed his distinctive qualities as a historian: precise knowledge of Greek and Roman institutions, a low estimate of the work of contemporary scholars, and an obsessive belief in the need to return to the original texts for the unbiased truth.

Appointed to the chair in history at the Faculty of Letters of the University of Strasbourg in 1860, Fustel drew a large circle of students to his brilliant lectures. In 1864 he published at his own expense his pioneering study of religion in Roman and Hellenic societies, *La Cité antique*. This work, still widely read, rapidly became accepted as one of the masterpieces of the French language in the nineteenth century. Fustel's decade of success at Strasbourg brought him the support of Victor Duruy, Napoleon III's reform-minded minister of public instruction, who appointed him professor of history at the Ecole normale supérieure in 1870. For a few months before the German victory, he tutored the Empress Eugénie in history. The Franco-Prussian war had a profound effect on Fustel, and, like so many of his contemporaries, he plunged into the study of the roots of what seemed to be a decline of French civilization. He turned his scholarly energies to an often vengeful study of German scholarship and employed his pen in openly patriotic exchanges with leading German scholars. His talents as a historian, however, remained focused on the study of the origins of French political institutions in the Middle Ages, which led to his second and last great work, *Histoire des institutions politiques de l'ancienne France* (1875–89). In 1875 Fustel was given the chair in ancient history at the Sorbonne and in the same year was elected to the Académie des sciences morales where he had presented many of his most important papers.

Except for a brief period as director of the Ecole normale from 1880 to 1883 (where his presence inspired contemporary normalians like Henri Berr and Emile Durkheim), Fustel remained an august figure at the Sorbonne, towering over a historical profession that inspired the reformers of the early Third Republic.

Fustel's work was the focus of much controversy during his lifetime, and his impact on Third Republic historical thinking was not limited to academic circles. Members of the Action française attempted to draw political conclusions in support of their cause from Fustel's prestigious studies. But as the medievalist Marc Bloch noted, such political conclusions are negligible when one weighs the work of a historian who hated subjectivism, who rejected racial interpretations of the past, and who became the conscience of generations of French scholars dedicated to the ideal of a more scientific history.

H. Berr, "Une Léçon d'ouverture et quelques fragments inédits de Fustel de Cou-langes," *Revue de synthèse historique* 2 (June 1901); P. Giraud, *Fustel de Coulanges* (Paris, 1896); J. Herrick, *The Historical Thought of Fustel de Coulanges* (Washington, D.C., 1957); J. M. Tourneur-Aumont, *Fustel de Coulanges* (Paris, 1931).

M. Siegel

Related entries: ACTION FRANCAISE; BERR; BLOCH; DURKHEIM.

G

GALLIENI, JOSEPH (1849–1916), colonial soldier, administrator, and defender of Paris in 1914. Son of a naturalized Italian émigré, he rose to prominence as a builder of the Third Republic's empire. Upon the declaration of war against Germany in 1870, Gallieni, then a student at St.-Cyr, received his commission and was sent immediately to the front. He participated in the Battle of Bazeilles where he was captured after his unit had exhausted its ammunition supply. Following the war, he served in the colonial army. In Senegal and Tonkin, Gallieni developed a method of colonial warfare known as the "oil stain" technique that combined military force with negotiation to secure a gradual, systematic occupation and pacification of native territory. Success in Tonkin earned him an appointment as military governor of Madagascar in 1896, where he applied his precepts of colonial rule over the next nine years. He deposed the reigning Queen Ranavalo and initiated a series of administrative reforms and public works projects.

Hailed as a colonial hero, Gallieni returned to France in 1905 where he served as inspector-general for colonial troops, became a member of the supreme war council, and helped nominate a former subordinate from Madagascar, General Joseph Joffre, as supreme commander of the French Army. Gallieni retired from active duty in 1913 but returned the following year to organize the defense of Paris. His suggestion that Joffre counterattack against the exposed German flank enabled French forces to halt the German advance at the first Battle of the Marne. Troops from the Paris garrison were rushed to the front in taxis and buses. Gallieni became war minister under Aristide Briand until failing health forced his retirement in March 1916, just two months before his death. He received a marshal's baton posthumously in 1921.

R. Delavignette et Ch.-A. Julien, *Les Constructeurs de la France d'outre-mer* (Paris, 1946); J. d'Esme, *Gallieni* (Paris, 1965); V. L. Mathew, "Joseph Simon Gallieni (1849–1916)" (Ph.D. dissertation, University of California, Los Angeles, 1967).

J. K. Munholland

Related entries: ARMY: ORGANIZATION; JOFFRE; MARNE, BATTLE OF; OVERSEAS EMPIRE: MADAGASCAR; WORLD WAR I, FRANCE'S ROLE IN.

GALLIFFET, GASTON, MARQUIS DE (1830–1909), the general who distinguished himself at the Battle of Sedan in 1870, in the repression of communards the following year, and as minister of war in a republican defense coalition government (1899–1902). Galliffet rallied to the Republic and, as a friend of Léon Gambetta, was named military governor of Paris in 1880. René Waldeck-Rousseau, designated prime minister in June 1899, persuaded him to come out of retirement and serve as minister of war in a ministry that also included the leader of the parliamentary socialists, Alexandre Millerand. Galliffet's role was to reassure army leaders and to impose discipline on the army. (Two generals, Emile Zurlinden and Charles Chanoine, had previously accepted the controversial post and then, hostile to reopening the Dreyfus case, resigned.) Galliffet's appearance in the Chamber of Deputies on June 26 evoked a demonstration by left-wing deputies who denounced the "butcher of the Commune." On September 21, after Alfred Dreyfus accepted a pardon, Galliffet was reported as saying, "The incident is closed." As minister he reasserted governmental authority by forcing the three most outspoken antirepublican generals to resign. During his tenure, promotions were distributed on a more equitable basis. Defensive about his prerogatives, Galliffet himself suddenly resigned in 1900, when Waldeck-Rousseau insinuated that several army officers backed a new plot to overthrow the Republic. He was replaced by General Louis André.

L. Thomas, *Le Général de Galliffet* (Paris, 1910); H. de Rolland, *Galliffet* (Paris, 1945).

L. Derfler

Related entries: ARMY: POLITICAL ROLE; COMMUNE OF PARIS; DREYFUS AFFAIR; FRANCO-PRUSSIAN WAR; WALDECK-ROUSSEAU.

GAMBETTA, LEON (1838–1882), one of the founders of the Third Republic. Gambetta was born at Cahors (Lot), the son of an Italian grocer. After studying law in Paris, he became involved in politics during the Second Empire as a republican and as such was an outspoken opponent of the regime. Elected to the legislative assembly in 1869 as one of ninety republicans, Gambetta opposed the bellicose policy of the government toward Prussia in the summer of 1870. When the Third Republic was proclaimed on 4 September 1870, Gambetta was named minister of the interior in the provisional government whose primary responsibility was to carry out the disastrous war against Prussia. When the Prussians laid siege to Paris, Gambetta escaped the city in a balloon in order to mobilize the provinces and turn the tide of war in favor of France. Despite his heroic efforts in the cause of national defense, the government headed by Adolphe Thiers decided to sue for peace, and Gambetta was forced to accept France's humiliating defeat. In the elections of February 1871, he was chosen by nine constituencies and soon emerged as a leader of the republican forces in the National Assembly. His fiery oratory, personal popularity, and uncompromising republicanism made Gambetta a formidable political force in his own right. He vehemently resisted the efforts of royalists and Bonapartists to revive the monarchy in the period 1871–77, and he often opposed Thiers on the grounds that the chief of the executive power of the provisional regime was not republican enough. As head of the government between 1870 and 1873, Thiers had come to the conclusion that republicans would have to abandon their revolutionary heritage in order to attract the support of moderate political elements throughout the country and preserve the regime. By 1875 Gambetta had come to the same conclusion. He abandoned the radical republican insistence on a unicameral legislature, separation of church and state, and social legislation favorable to the working classes. Although he accepted the constitutional laws of 1875 that provided for a president and a bicameral legislature, he retained his anticlericalism. The survival of the regime, to his way of thinking, required the drastic curtailment of the political and cultural influence of the Catholic church in France. Gambetta's willingness to compromise republican principles for the sake of securing the Republic caused its more radical supporters to regard him as an Opportunist, a term that came to be applied to his followers who dominated the republican majority in the legislature during the 1880s and 1890s. By the mid-1870s Gambetta was clearly the leading republican politician in the country. Nevertheless, his heroic reputation earned during the Franco-Prussian War, his popularity, and his obvious qualities as a leader were looked upon with some suspicion by other republicans afraid that the tribune might eventually become another Bonaparte. When Jules Grévy was elected president of the Republic, he refused to invite Gambetta to become premier until the overwhelming republican victory in the elections of 1881 left him with no alternative. Gambetta's ministry, which he hoped would become a government of national union, lasted barely three months. At the end of his life, Gambetta had come to appear as a threat to the regime he had helped to found. Only after his death in 1882 were republicans willing to honor him as their leader by voting to have his heart buried in the Pantheon.

Gambetta's mature political opinions reflect the transition of republicanism from an essentially revolutionary to a conservative ideology. The people he represented—small proprietors and industrialists as well as shopkeepers—were on the whole excluded from the body politic in France until the advent of the Third Republic and therefore susceptible to revolutionary Jacobinism, which to them meant the establishment of a democratic republic respectful of property rights. These social elements—the *nouvelles couches sociales*, Gambetta called them—had acquired a far greater share of political power by the elections of 1881, when Gambetta's influence was at its height. Thiers' and Gambetta's espousal of a conservative Republic had great appeal to these small and medium property owners whose political ideals seemed more or less realized when the Republic took root in the 1870s. The emancipation of the individual by means of a free, compulsory, and secular education without the oppressive influence of the Catholic church, of equal participation in the political process, and with the material support of private property was Gambetta's ideal, which he believed was close to being realized at the time of his death. By that time the French revolutionary heritage had become a part of socialist ideology to which Gambetta and his followers were staunchly opposed.

J. P. T. Bury, *Gambetta and the National Defense* (London, 1936); J. Chastenet, *Gambetta* (Paris, 1969); J. Reinach, *La Vie politique de Gambetta* (Paris, 1919); H. Stannard, *Gambetta and the Foundation of the Third Republic* (New York, 1921).

A. Sedgwick

Related entries: FRANCO-PRUSSIAN WAR; *NOUVELLES COUCHES SO-CIALES*; OPPORTUNISTS; *SEIZE MAI* CRISIS.

GAMELIN, MAURICE (1872–1958), career army officer, finally general. As senior French military officer and Allied coordinator in Western Europe, Gamelin was responsible for the preparation and waging of the battle against German invasion in May 1940. Born in Paris into an old military family, Gamelin chose the military despite strong interests in art, philosophy, and history. His intelligence and capacity for work earned him promotion; in 1914 he was a principal aide to General Joseph Joffre and played a role in the Battle of the Marne. Subsequently he commanded the Ninth Infantry Division with distinction. After the war he commanded the French forces that pacified Syria. In 1930 he was named to the General Staff as a republican counterbalance to the appointment of General Maxime Weygand as chief of staff; from 1931 to 1935 Gamelin himself was chief of staff. The two generals added a mechanized and motorized maneuver force to the French Army, principally for use in Belgium, while filling out the Maginot Line along France's border with Germany. In 1935 Gamelin added the post of commander-in-chief-designate to his titles; his personal style of quiet reflection and tact aroused no fears of a military coup. Short and heavyset, seemingly modest and quiet, Gamelin was actually a calculating manipulator who used his intellectual dominance to influence policy.

During the Rhineland crisis of March 1936, Gamelin gave his government no encouragement to use force, but by the time of Munich he had changed his mind. As France rearmed, he supported Edouard Daladier in the foreign policy that brought France into the Second World War in September 1939, in spite of German numerical superiority, French weakness in the air, and limited support from Britain. Gamelin planned on a long war during which a German invasion through Belgium and the Netherlands would be halted by the French maneuver force and in part outflanked by a force rushed into the southern Netherlands. An Allied front there would attract British forces, particularly air forces, and keep the badly needed Dutch and Belgian armies in the fray. But Gamelin's subordinate, General Alphonse Georges, the Allied operational commander, considered this maneuver too risky, and Gamelin's superior after March 1940, Premier Paul Reynaud, also doubted the wisdom of this plan.

When Germany struck on 10 May 1940, the government had fallen over the issue of Gamelin's dismissal. Reynaud resumed office, but Gamelin's authority suffered—the more so when his maneuver failed before the unexpected German attack through the Ardennes forests and over the Meuse River. Georges collapsed under the strain on 14 May. For the next five days, the Allied High Command took no effective action as enemy spearheads raced to cut off the Allied armies in Belgium. On 19 May Gamelin intervened with a plan for a counteroffensive, but he was dismissed the same day in favor of Weygand.

There is much to admire in the way Gamelin built a smaller and industrially weaker France into a powerful military machine to oppose Germany. But Gamelin's strategic miscalculations created an opening for the blitzkrieg in 1940, and he intervened too late to save the situation.

M. Gamelin, *Servir* (Paris, 1946–1947); J. A. Gunsburg, "Coupable ou non? Le Rôle du général Gamelin dans la défaite de 1940," *Revue historique des armées* 4 (1979); P. Le Goyet, *Le Mystère Gamelin* (Paris, 1976).

J. A. Gunsburg

Related entries: ARMY: POLITICAL ROLE; DALADIER; FALL OF FRANCE; GEORGES; JOFFRE; MAGINOT LINE; REYNAUD; WEYGAND.

GARNIER, TONY (1869–1948), Lyons architect and urban planner. He was born in 1869 in the working-class Croix Rousse district of Lyons. His father was a designer in the silk industry. Garnier attended the Ecole nationale des beaux-arts in Lyons (1886–89), winning several architecture prizes, and then the Paris Ecole des beaux-arts (1889–99), where he won the Prix de Rome in architecture on his sixth try. While in Rome he produced the mandatory project, a reconstruction of the ancient city of Tusculum, but also began designing an industrial city, an unconventional pursuit for a graduate of the traditionalistic Beaux-arts, which caused a scandal when his sketches were exhibited in Paris in 1901. With the geography, industry, and hydroelectric possibilities of the Lyons area in mind, Garnier continued to elaborate this project until he published *Une Cité industrielle* in 1917. His ideas were revolutionary in that he accepted the high-density modern city but tried to make it livable through strict demarcation of residential, public, and industrial areas and by the provision of maximal sunlight and modern hygiene for all residents. Garnier was influenced by his childhood contact with a socialist, working-class milieu and also by the regionalism then current in France to plan a socialist city where land and the necessities of life would be communal property and where small cities would join in regional federations for trade, cultural exchanges, and mutually beneficial public works. Garnier greatly influenced Le Corbusier.

Although most of Garnier's projects for the industrial city remained unrealized, he received considerable support from the perennial mayor of Lyons, Edouard Herriot. He built various public buildings in Lyons between 1908 and 1940: a municipal cattle market and slaughterhouse at La Mouche (1908–24); the Edouard Herriot hospital at La Grange Blanche (1915–30); a stadium (1913–16); the War Monument in the Parc de la tête d'or (1918); the Central Telephone Exchange

(1922); the residential Quartier des Etats-Unis (1920–35); and the Textile School in La Croix Rousse. From 1912 Garnier taught at the Ecole régionale d'architecture in Lyons. His major building outside Lyons is the city hall of the Paris suburb Boulogne-Billancourt (1931–34).

T. Garnier, *Les Grands Travaux de la ville de Lyon* (Paris, 1920); C. Pawlowski, *Tony Garnier et les débuts de l'urbanisme fonctionnel en France* (Paris, 1967); anon., *Tony Garnier* (Lyons, 1970); D. Wiebenson, *Tony Garnier: The Cité Industrielle* (New York, 1969).

T. Shapiro

Related entries: ARCHITECTURE AND URBAN PLANNING; HERRIOT; LE CORBUSIER; LYONS.

GAUGUIN, PAUL (1848–1903), leading symbolist painter. He was born in Paris but spent the years 1849 through 1855 in Peru, where his mother's family lived. After several years in the merchant marine, he got a job as a stockbroker in 1871. In 1873 he began to paint and sculpt on a part-time basis, appearing at the Salon with a painting in 1876. In the late 1870s he befriended the impressionists and participated in the last five impressionist exhibitions from 1879 to 1886. In 1882 he lost his job due to an economic downturn, and in 1885 he left his Danish wife and five children in order to devote himself fully to his painting. Working mainly in Brittany in the second half of the 1880s, he became the leader of the so-called Pont-Aven group and along with Emile Bernard developed an art that combined imaginative and symbolic themes with a simplified, flattened treatment of figures and space, an amalgam generally known as synthetism. In 1891 he decided to put European civilization behind him in a search for more intuitive, primitive sources. He departed for Tahiti, where he lived until 1901. He died at Atuana in the Marquesas Islands.

W. Andersen, *Gauguin's Paradise Lost* (New York, 1971); M. Bodelsen, *Gauguin's Ceramics* (London, 1964); C. Gray, *Sculpture and Ceramics of Paul Gauguin* (Baltimore, 1963); M. Malingue, ed., *Lettres de Gauguin à sa femme et à ses amis*, 2d rev. ed. (Paris, 1949); G. Wildenstein, *Gauguin* (Paris, 1964).

J. Isaacson

Related entries: IMPRESSIONISM; POSTIMPRESSIONISM; SYMBOLISM.

GAULLE, CHARLES DE (1890–1970), general and strategist. The future leader of the free French and president of the Republic was born in Lille (Nord). His father, who had studied engineering and administration, taught in a Jesuit school and was profoundly affected by the French defeat in 1871. The household was strongly Catholic and nationalist, and Charles was taught to defend religion, army, and country. As a student he read the works of Maurice Barrès and Charles Maurras, men who demanded strong leadership to uphold the national honor and who expressed contempt for parliamentary democracy.

De Gaulle graduated from St.-Cyr (France's West Point) near the top of his class and then joined an infantry regiment commanded by Philippe Pétain, on whose staff he was to serve. During World War I, de Gaulle was wounded and taken prisoner by the Germans. In three books published in the 1930s (*Le Fil de l'épée*, 1932; *Vers l'armée de métier*, 1934; and *La France et son armée*, 1938) he called for the modernization and renovation of the French Army, specifically demanding greater mobility and professionalism. These ideas seem to have generated more interest in Germany than in France, although they won the support of Paul Reynaud. As head of the government, Reynaud invited de Gaulle, who had distinguished himself as general of an armored division after the German attack in May 1940, to serve as under secretary of state for war. De Gaulle rejected Pétain's armistice, having already left for England to ask for continued fighting and resistance.

E. Ashcroft, *De Gaulle* (London, 1962); A. Crawley, *De Gaulle* (New York, 1969); J. Lacouture, *De Gaulle* (Paris, 1969); P.-M. de la Gorce, *De Gaulle entre deux mondes—une vie et une époque* (Paris, 1964); J.-R. Tournoux, *Pétain et de Gaulle* (Paris, 1964).

L. Derfler

Related entries: ARMY: ORGANIZATION; ARMY: POLITICAL ROLE; PETAIN; REYNAUD.

GEORGES, ALPHONSE (1875–1951), career army officer, general. Deputy to General Maurice Gamelin during the late 1930s, Georges was the operational commander of the Allied armies facing the German invasion in May 1940. His personal collapse on 14 May was a critical factor in the scope and rapidity of the Allied defeat.

Of modest family origins, Georges distinguished himself at St.-Cyr and in combat in North Africa and was severely wounded in 1914. Then he served in Germany and overseas and was an assistant to War Minister André Maginot. In 1934 Georges was badly wounded in the assassination of King Alexander of Yugoslavia in Marseilles; he never completely recovered. A protégé of General Maxime Weygand, Georges was passed over when Gamelin became commander-in-chief-designate. But Georges became Gamelin's deputy, working on the development of doctrine and war plans. Relations between the two were cool, in part because of their differing personalities; Georges was an outspoken and politically conservative officer.

When the Second World War began, Georges received titular command of the forces facing Germany on the northeastern front, but the important decisions were made by Gamelin. Georges chafed at the restrictions and disagreed with Gamelin on strategy, fearing a German thrust toward the center of his front while Gamelin concentrated on Belgium. On 10 May 1940 Germany attacked; Georges' view proved more prescient than Gamelin's, but Georges never recovered from the shock of the initial German breakthrough at Sedan. Remaining closeted in his headquarters, unable to conceive the counteroffensive necessary to save the Allied cause, Georges pursued futile efforts to patch together a front until Gamelin and then his successor Weygand intervened to take effective control.

A. Georges, Preface to G. Roton, *Années cruciales* (Paris, 1947); J. A. Gunsburg, *Divided and Conquered* (Westport, Conn., 1979).

J. A. Gunsburg

Related entries: ARMY: POLITICAL ROLE; FALL OF FRANCE; GAMELIN; WEYGAND.

GERMANY, RELATIONS WITH (1871–1914). Defeated in the war of 1870, France was dominated in the following decades by the newly united German empire. The Treaty of Frankfurt in May 1871 ratified the forfeit of Alsace-Lorraine and imposed a reparations payment of 5 billion francs. To enforce this treaty, eastern portions of France were held hostage by German forces of occupation until early 1873. Thereafter German influence continued to weigh in favor of a compliant and moderate French Republic that would be militarily weak, diplomatically isolated, and psychologically vulnerable. These symptoms were apparent in the so-called war scare of 1875, such a flagrant example of German oppression that France received overt sympathy if not firm assistance from other European governments. When French conservatives then challenged republicanism during the *seize mai* crisis of 1877, Germany once more attempted to intervene with undisguised support for the Gambettists and with dire threats of armed conflict should the adherents of Marshal Maurice de MacMahon prevail. After the reactionaries were defeated and the Republic appeared secure, direct German interference in French internal affairs became more infrequent.

Meanwhile, France was obliged to construct a new system of defense and to rebuild its entire military structure. In these efforts, Germany served as both a model of efficacy and the major potential enemy. All efforts of rearmament necessarily had to be measured against France's most powerful neighbor, a discouraging comparison that still suggested a persistent French inferiority by 1890. This weakness was compounded by a growing demographic deficit. Whereas the French population virtually stagnated below 40 million inhabitants, Germany was burgeoning beyond 65 million. Hence France was motivated to conclude a military pact with Russia, which in turn stoked German fears of encirclement and thereby contributed to solidification of mutually hostile European alliances.

Economically France also fell far behind Germany. Slower to adopt protectionist tariffs, the French suffered a seriously unfavorable commercial balance with Germany in the 1880s and were less prepared to compete in European markets thereafter. France became more dependent on trade with colonial areas and decreasingly competitive in exporting finished goods to industrialized nations.

The trauma of defeat was consequently perpetuated by the rigors of competition. Several generations of French intellectuals were preoccupied by the phenomenon of Germany's material success and dazzled by the prestige of German philosophy, history, music, literature, and above all science. The model of German universities and laboratories could therefore be emulated or opposed, but not ignored, by the educational reformers of the French Republic.

Evidence does not support the view that after 1870 France was a nation incorrigibly and incessantly driven by a desire for revenge. Irredentist societies in fact declined notably during the period of rapprochement with Germany between 1878 and 1885. The Boulanger affair brought chauvinist passions back to the surface, but public rancor after 1894, despite xenophobia that accompanied the arrest of Alfred Dreyfus as a German spy, was centered primarily on internal issues and altercations. The loss of Alsace and Lorraine remained lamentable but seemingly unalterable. A significant revival of nationalism was not manifest until provoked by German intrusion into the French sphere of influence during the Moroccan crises of 1905 and 1911. France thereupon became a rabid participant in the European alliance system and arms race. Pacifist efforts by French and German socialists were insufficient to assuage the rising tide of militarism on both sides of the Rhine. In August 1914 the two nations, with their respective allies, thus faced each other in the decisive confrontation of World War I.

C. Digeon, *La Crise allemande de la pensée française (1870–1914)* (Paris, 1959); W. Langer, *European Alliances and Alignments, 1871–1890*, 2d ed. (New York, 1964); A. Mitchell, *The German Influence in France after 1870* (Chapel Hill, N.C., 1979); E. Weber, *The Nationalist Revival in France, 1905–1914* (Berkeley, 1959).

A. Mitchell

Related entries: BOULANGER AFFAIR; FRANCO-PRUSSIAN WAR; GERMANY, RELATIONS WITH (1914–1940); SCHNAEBELE AFFAIR.

GERMANY, RELATIONS WITH (1914–1940). Relations with Germany remained the central concern of French foreign policy after World War I. In the Treaty of Versailles, France succeeded in obtaining a substantial part of its war aims. Alsace and Lorraine were regained from Germany, the material damage wrought on French soil was to be repaired at German expense, and the great antagonist was greatly weakened militarily, politically, and economically. On the surface, France after 1919 was again the strongest European power. Its leaders, however, were painfully aware of the tenuousness and artificiality of this hegemony.

Only an alliance with three world powers had enabled France to prevail over the more populous, more advanced, and economically productive German empire. Only the continuation of that alliance, it was felt, could force Germany to abide by the terms of the peace. But Russia had dissolved in revolution and civil war, and no one could as yet discern its future shape. Britain and the United States quickly returned to their traditional positions of relative isolation from continental affairs. A treaty by which these powers were to guarantee France's eastern border, for the promise of which Georges Clemenceau had relinquished French demands for the separation of the Rhineland from Germany, was repudiated by the U.S. Senate and then by Britain. France, weakened by the enormous cost, human and material, of the war, would be left alone to contain an embittered Germany, whose resurgence most Frenchmen saw as only a matter of time.

Prior to 1924, France's rightist-nationalist governments sought to accomplish this by rigid enforcement of the treaty, especially the disarmament and reparations provisions. Various ultimata and acts of military force were climaxed by Raymond Poincaré's January 1923 invasion of the Ruhr, Germany's industrial heartland. By this action, France expected to extract reparations by force and perhaps after all to split the Rhineland from a chaotic, helpless Germany. The Ruhr adventure proved expensive for France, in economic terms as well as international isolation. It was the Third Republic's last attempt to use unilateral force in its dealings with Germany. After the withdrawal, brought about through British mediation, France reverted to diplomatic efforts to obtain British support for the maintenance of the peace settlement.

The long tenure of Aristide Briand as foreign minister (1925–32) was characterized by his attempt to reconcile the new democratic Germany, which seemed to gain some political and economic stability during the later 1920s, to a secondary position in Europe. The reparations issue was muted by the Dawes and Young Plan agreements. Under the 1925 Locarno Agreements, Germany accepted freely what Versailles had imposed: the new Franco-German boundary and the demilitarization of the Rhineland. An Italo-British guarantee partially met the French craving for security—but also imposed restrictions on France; unilateral military steps, as in 1923, were henceforth out of the question. With French support, Germany entered the League of Nations in 1926, thus achieving formal international equality with the victor powers. In 1930, France withdrew its occupation forces from the Rhineland, in advance of the date stipulated in the Treaty of Versailles.

Such a policy of conciliation, however, had rather narrow limits. Its aim was to reconcile Germany to the 1919 settlement, even while Briand's German counterpart, Gustav Stresemann, ultimately aimed at a gradual, peaceful undermining of that settlement. Trust was in scarce supply. In 1929, the year in which Briand made his celebrated proposal for a European union before the League of Nations, France also began the construction of the Maginot Line.

In the crucial years of the early 1930s, while the German Republic was being undermined by economic problems and Nazi extremism, France reverted to a policy of inflexibility, vetoing a proposal for an Austro-German customs union in 1931, refusing a German request for financial assistance, delaying the final settlement of the reparations issue, and displaying intransigence at the Geneva disarmament conference. Some historians argue that French policy thus contributed to weakening the last governments of the German Republic and easing Hitler's ascent to power.

In the face of Hitler's strident challenges, the hollowness of France's claim to power rapidly became manifest. While French military superiority remained overwhelming until at least 1937, the country's political and military leaders, blinded by an almost pathological pessimism and vastly exaggerating Nazi might, never considered taking forceful action without the support of allies. Hectic diplomatic activity designed to create paper obstacles to rising German power— including negotiations with Italy, the USSR, Britain, Poland, and the countries of Eastern and Central Europe—failed to impress Hitler. France accepted with no more than verbal protests the announcement of German rearmament and, in March 1936, Germany's military reoccupation of the Rhineland, which violated the Locarno Pact, as well as the Treaty of Versailles. Thereafter with its military and diplomatic position steadily deteriorating, France wholly subordinated its policy to Great Britain's so as to avoid any risk of having to face Germany alone. While French leaders, from Pierre Laval to Edouard Daladier and Léon Blum, were less sanguine about Hitler's ultimate intentions than their British counterparts, France nevertheless seconded the policy of appeasement, making no objection to the annexation of Austria in March 1938, and participating in the sellout of Czechoslovakia, France's most important Central European ally, in October.

When Britain stiffened its position following Hitler's occupation of Prague in March 1939, France followed suit, renewing commitments to Poland and other East European states and attempting, vainly, to reach a military agreement with the Soviets. Finally, two days after Hitler's invasion of Poland, on 3 September 1939, France followed Britain into what was to become World War II. Divided internally, paralyzed by wholly exaggerated visions of German military power and by its own generals' theories of the superiority of the defensive, France passively awaited the German offensive of May 1940. Within six weeks, it was to destroy the Third Republic.

R. Albrecht-Carrié, *France, Europe, and Two World Wars* (Geneva, 1960); J. B. Duroselle, *Histoire diplomatique de 1919 à nos jours* (Paris, 1962); J. Néré, *The Foreign Policy of France from 1919 to 1945* (Boston, 1975); P. Renouvin, *Histoire des relations internationales*, vol. 8 (Paris, 1957–58).

W. W. Schmokel

Related entries: BRIAND; CLEMENCEAU; CZECHOSLOVAKIA, ALLIANCE WITH; DISARMAMENT CONFERENCE; FALL OF FRANCE; FOREIGN POLICY; GERMANY, RELATIONS WITH (1871–1914); LOCARNO ACCORDS; MAGINOT LINE; PARIS PEACE CONFERENCE; POINCARE, R.; POLAND, RELATIONS WITH; POLISH AGREEMENT; REPARATIONS POLICY; RUHR OCCUPATION; WORLD WAR I.

GIDE, ANDRE (1869–1951), novelist. Honored with the Nobel Prize for Literature in 1947, Gide influenced a generation of readers and writers with his daring and provocative topics and his innovative literary techniques. His earliest work, the autobiographical *Cahiers d'André Walter* (1891), elucidates a conflict between the moral and sensual urges of the young Gide, a theme Gide transposed in a number of his works. Born in Paris into a strict Protestant family, Gide lost his father in 1880 and was raised by an austere mother whose severe piety left an enduring impression on his life.

Gide had the money, leisure, and dedication to devote himself earnestly to writing, and from a young age he wanted to become a novelist. His earliest works, *Le Traité du Narcisse* (1891), *Les Poésies d'André Walter* (1892), *La*

Tentative amoureuse (1893), and *Le Voyage d'Urien* (1893), reveal the influence of Stephane Mallarmé and the symbolists but did not attract much attention.

During a trip to North Africa in 1893, Gide realized his homosexual tendencies and experienced a moral and creative liberation that is reflected in his next two works. *Paludes* (1895), which he called a *sotie* (a simple satire on human frailty) together with *Le Prométhée mal enchaîné* (1899) and *Les Caves du Vatican* (1914), is a genial treatment of the stifling Parisian literary salon atmosphere with which Gide had been familiar prior to the voyage to North Africa. *Les Nourritures terrestres* (1897), the second important work of this period, is a lyrical exaltation of the sensual side of human nature. This theme of the liberation of the self is pursued in Gide's plays, *Philoctète* (1899), *Le Roi Candaule* (1901), and *Saül* (1903), as well as in his novels.

The *Immoraliste* (1902) is generally considered Gide's first masterpiece. Termed a *récit* (a more complex account of the interplay between character and circumstance), the *Immoraliste* demonstrates the tendency of his subsequent works to expose in an ironic and detached fashion those subjective motives that remain hidden from Gide's first-person narrators. The hero of the *Immoraliste* unwisely neglects the social and moral side of his life by placing too much emphasis on the sensual. The opposite occurs in *La Porte étroite* (1909), where characters suppress their sensual natures in favor of a strained piety that keeps them apart. In *La Symphonie pastorale* (1919), the charity of a minister for a poor blind girl evolves into a misguided love that separates him from his family and ends in the death of the girl he has tried to save. In a trilogy of *récits*, *L'Ecole des femmes* (1929), *Robert* (1930), and *Geneviève* (1936), Gide continued his experiments with narrative techniques while describing one situation from three different points of view.

Gide's interest in detective and adventure stories emerges in the *récit Isabelle* (1911) and in *Les Caves du Vatican*. Ever since the earlier *soties* Gide had been fascinated by the role of chance in human affairs. In *Les Caves* he develops the motif of the *acte-gratuit* or unmotivated act with his romantic hero, Lafcadio. The several stories that make up *Les Caves* unfold in an apparently haphazard and disjointed fashion with mock epic overtones until the end of the work when all the elements of the book coalesce around Lafcadio's gratuitous act of hurling one of the characters, whose identity is unknown to him, from a speeding train.

Les Faux-Monnayeurs (1926), the only work designated a novel by Gide, combines many of the elements that make up both the *soties* and *récits*. The frame story of this complex novel describes the passage from adolescence to adulthood. The theme of counterfeiting, disclosed in the title, is symbolic of the larger question of false versus real values with which all the characters must contend. The novel details characters who arrive at a sense of inner values through self-awareness as the means of surviving in a world that seems to operate in an inexplicable way.

Gide wrote some literary criticism, including a book on Dostoevsky (1923). He composed two works critical of French colonial practices in North Africa,

Voyage au Congo (1927) and *Le Retour du Tchad* (1928). His *Journal, 1885–1939* (1939), continued with a second volume covering the period *1939–42* (1944) and completed by a third for the years *1942–49* (1950), gives an interesting picture of intellectual life in Europe during the first half of the twentieth century.

G. Brée, *André Gide* (Paris, 1970); J. Delay, *La Jeunesse d'André Gide* (Paris, 1956–57); W. Holdheim, *Theory and Practice of the Novel* (Geneva, 1968); J. O'Brien, *Portrait of André Gide* (New York, 1953); V. Rossi, *André Gide* (New Brunswick, N.J., 1967).

R. F. O'Reilly

Related entries: LITERATURE; THOUGHT AND INTELLECTUAL LIFE.

GIDE, CHARLES (1847–1932), prophetic and creative economist of solidarism. Although Gide was educated in Paris in orthodox economic theory, he harbored reservations about the prevailing liberal doctrines from his student days on. His first significant deviation from orthodoxy came in 1884 with the publication of his *Principes d'économie politique*. Although this text was enormously successful, it scandalized liberal economists by according attention and even sympathy to socialism. On the other hand, Gide could never accept socialist doctrines of egalitarianism and violent expropriation. In 1885, while still trying to formulate his own alternative theories, Gide was attracted to a group trying to put its theory of social cooperation into practice. Within a few years he became a spokesman for the consumer cooperative movement in France.

Gide's involvement with cooperation enabled him to define a new type of economic thought independent of both liberal and socialist dogmas. Drawing on a wide variety of sources—Frédéric Bastiat, contemporary Swiss and Austrian economists, John Stuart Mill, and above all, Charles Fourier—Gide related them all to the concept of solidarism, which permeated the intellectual climate of his time. In 1889 he announced the formation of a new economic school of solidarism. According to Gide, cooperatives are the concrete expression of solidarism in the economic sphere.

Gide invented neither the concept of solidarism nor the advocacy of cooperatives. What is original with him is the application of solidarist principles to economic thought and practice and, even more, the insistence that consumer associations be the preeminent form of cooperativism.

A. Lavondes, *Charles Gide: un précurseur de l'Europe unie et de l'ONU* (Uzès, Gard, 1953); R. H. Williams, *Dream Worlds* (Berkeley, 1982).

R. H. Williams

Related entries: CONSUMER COOPERATIVES AND LEAGUES; SOLIDARISM.

GILLY, NUMA (1834–1895), radical politician, journalist. He was born 6 August in Sommières (Gard). Of humble origins, he worked as a barrel maker and eventually established a successful barrel factory (1859). As a laborer he developed a sympathy for the working class, which he maintained together with a fervent republican patriotism. In 1869 he founded with Yves Guyot *L'Indépendant* *du Midi*, a progressive newspaper. At the fall of the Second Empire (1870), he became vice-president of the patriotic association, La Ligue du Midi. In 1881 he was elected municipal councilor, then mayor, of Nîmes by the conservative Right and extreme Left groups that made up the anti-Opportunist coalition. In 1885 Gilly ran for the Chamber of Deputies on the Radical ticket in the legislative elections for the Gard. He was elected and sat with the extreme Left. While in the Chamber he helped found the Workers Group, a coalition of Radical deputies who advocated revision of the constitution and who inaugurated the electoral campaign of General Georges Boulanger as a figurehead for that cause. In the course of the campaign, Gilly gained notoriety by accusing Boulanger's Opportunist opponents of political corruption. Speaking at a public meeting in Alès (1888), he accused several members of the Chamber of Deputies of economic conflicts of interest and compared them to those deputies earlier compromised in the Wilson scandal (1887). He elaborated on these charges in his scathing exposé, *Mes dossiers* (1888). Those accused in the book filed suit against him. He denied authorship, which brought an additional case against him by his editor. Gilly lost both cases and was sentenced to a few months in prison. He was dismissed as mayor, but his critique of governmental corruption had given voice to the populist sentiments on which Boulanger built his campaign. With the support of the workers of Nîmes, he was reelected mayor against the Opportunist candidate on 20 January 1889. He ran in the legislative elections of 1889 and 1893 but lost. Still suffering from the controversies he incited, he died in Nîmes at the age of sixty-one.

A. Chirac, *L'Agiotage sous la Troisième République*, 2 vols. (Paris, 1888); P. Larousse, ed., *Grand Dictionnaire Universel*, vol. 17 (Paris, 1865–90); J. Maitron, ed., *Dictionnaire biographique du mouvement ouvrier français*, vol. 12 (Paris, 1974); A. Robert and G. Cougny, ed., *Dictionnaire des parlementaires français*, vol. 3 (Paris, 1891).

L. LeClair

Related entries: BOULANGER; BOULANGER AFFAIR; WILSON SCANDAL.

GIRARDIN, EMILE DE (1806–1881), probably the most important French newspaper innovator and magnate of the nineteenth century. He was among the first to bring down newspaper prices through printing advertising. He used polemic and sensationalism to increase reader interest and was a leader in making technical innovations in printing. His most creative period predates the Third Republic, but between 1870 and 1881 he owned (wholly or in part) a number of papers, including *La France* and *Le Petit Journal*, the latter the best-selling paper of the era.

Girardin had a trenchant journalistic style and in his periodicals emphasized such appealing interests as individualism, health, wealth, and happiness. In spite of his journalistic success, he believed that the influence of the press was ephemeral. From 1834 onward he often held a parliamentary seat, but the ministerial position he desired always eluded him. He sometimes advocated politically inopportune causes, such as women's rights and (in 1874) reconciliation with Germany. His political allegiances were often mercurial. He supported Emile Ollivier's liberal Empire, advocated war with Germany in 1870, and was one of the first to call for Napoleon III's abdication. He opposed Léon Gambetta's dictatorial government during the Franco-Prussian War and, after a brief flirtation with the early stages of the Paris Commune, rallied to the Versailles government and Adolphe Thiers. The political crisis of 1877 brought about a tactical reconciliation between Girardin and Léon Gambetta. Girardin's *La France* headed the coalition of powerful republican papers that opposed the authoritarian presidency of Marshal Maurice de MacMahon. Fittingly, in 1878, Girardin was the first chairman of the parliamentary committee that drew up the press law of 1881.

M. Reclus, *Emile de Girardin* (Paris, 1934).

J. I. Mather

Related entries: NEWSPAPERS, ROLE OF; PRESS, LEGISLATION CONCERNING.

GLEIZES, ALBERT (1881–1953), painter, theoretician of cubism, utopian socialist. The son of an industrial designer, he received his art training through apprenticeship. He was early influenced by impressionism and by socialism. He was a cofounder of the Association Ernest Renan, which promoted worker education (1905), and of the Abbaye de Créteil (1906–7), an intellectual phalanstery outside Paris, which failed for lack of means of self-support. Influenced by Fernand Léger and Pablo Picasso, he developed a personal approach to cubism and, with Jean Metzinger, became an influential theoretician of the new art *(Du "Cubisme,"* 1912). His cubism imposed an angular and dynamic treatment on scenes of daily life and communal activity. He was a member of the Section d'or movement (1912). Influenced by Robert Delaunay's orphism, he evolved a more abstract style and painted a series of geometric evocations of New York sights while in the United States during World War I. He underwent a religious conversion in 1918, and his work, strongly colored and alternately symbolic and abstract, henceforth was influenced by medieval and Celtic art. Combining religiosity with utopian socialism, he wrote a number of treatises on art, religion, and society and participated in humanitarian causes. In 1927 he founded Moly-Sabata, an artisanal and agricultural colony at Sablons (Isère), which survived, self-supporting, until 1940.

Albert Gleizes, 1881–1953 (Paris, 1964); *Albert Gleizes, 1881–1953: Retrospective* (Basel, 1969); *Albert Gleizes et le cubisme* (Stuttgart, 1962); A. Gleizes and J. Metzinger, *Du "Cubisme"* (Paris, 1912).

T. Shapiro

Related entries: ART: MAJOR STYLES AND MOVEMENTS; CUBISM; DE-LAUNAY, R.; LEGER, F.; METZINGER; PICASSO.

GOBLET, RENE (1828–1905), premier (11 December 1886–19 May 1887), founder of the Radical-Socialist party (1901). A lawyer and journalist from Amiens, he was a member of the National Assembly (July 1871–76), a deputy from Amiens (1877–85), the Somme (1885–89), and Paris (1893–98), and a senator from the Seine (1891–93). He entered politics as a Gambettist but moved leftward after 1881; while premier he was considered to be a radical, and after 1890 he was a leading exponent of radical socialism, taking particular interest in labor questions, education, civil liberties, and anticlericalism.

Goblet's sternly upright character, quick, clear mind, and precise, vigorous speech earned him a succession of ministerial posts in the 1880s, notably at Interior under Charles de Freycinet (1882), Public Instruction and Religion under Ferdinand Brisson and Freycinet (1885–86)—where he ably defended public elementary education and strengthened the provincial universities—and at Foreign Affairs under Charles Floquet (1888–89). His own government, a reshuffle of Freycinet's, became a holding operation while the parties decided what to do about General Georges Boulanger, the minister of war, who had rocketed to a controversial public prominence in that post under Freycinet. A frontier incident, the Schnaebele affair, found Goblet supporting Boulanger in that he saw the crisis to be a provocation engineered by Otto von Bismarck. Once it was settled, Jules Ferry and the Opportunists exploited the Radicals' growing doubts about Boulanger to bring about the fall of the ministry. Later in 1887 Goblet helped force President Jules Grévy to resign over the Wilson Scandal.

Goblet was an able, combative man of outspoken, independent views. Dedicating a moument to him at Amiens (6 October 1907), Georges Clemenceau eulogized his commitment to liberal ideals, which he had staunchly upheld even when opposed by colleagues in his own political entourage.

G. Chapman, *The Third French Republic: The First Phase, 1871–1894* (London, 1962); R.-M. Goblet, "Souvenirs de ma vie politique," *Revue politique et parlementaire* 136–137, 139–41, 145–149 (1928–31); B. Lavergne, *Les Deux Présidences de Jules Grévy* (Paris, 1966).

D. S. Newhall

Related entries: ANTICLERICALISM; BOULANGER; BRISSON; EDUCATION: GOVERNMENTAL POLICIES CONCERNING; FLOQUET; FREYCINET; RADICAL AND RADICAL-SOCIALIST PARTY; SCHNAEBELE AFFAIR; WILSON SCANDAL.

GOVERNMENT: CONSEIL D'ETAT, administrative court and advisory body to the government. A lineal descendant of the *conseil du roi* of the *ancien régime*, the Conseil was revived under the Consulate (1799) and has continued to exist in all subsequent regimes. The law of 24 May 1872 was the basic statute of the Conseil d'état during the Third Republic.

Composed of personnel divided into ranks of *conseillers d'état, maîtres des requêtes*, and *auditeurs*, those in the lowest rank, *auditeurs*, were selected by competitive examination and advanced within the Conseil, though some *maîtres des requêtes* and *conseillers d'état* were appointed from the outside to bring in individuals possessing a special knowledge in some field. During the Third Republic, members of the Conseil were recruited overwhelmingly from among the upper bourgeoisie, and, after 1900, most had attended the prestigious Ecole libre des sciences politiques. The Conseil served as a reservoir of trained personnel who could be detached for long periods to serve in the administration or as *chefs du cabinet* for ministers. Within the Conseil, members were assigned to different sections, and the advisory and judicial functions were separated. The regular membership of the Conseil grew from 76 in 1872 to 129 in 1937. There were also special members (*en service extraordinaire*), normally high administrators, who assisted in the Conseil's work. Many members left the Conseil to pursue lucrative careers in business or law, and a few made their mark in politics, among them, Léon Blum, André Maginot, and Michel Debré.

As adviser to the government, the Conseil assisted, when called on, in the drafting of government bills. It drafted regulations (*règlements d'administration publiques*) to complete and carry out laws and rules to guide the administration. It maintained close relations with governmental departments and was routinely consulted on legal and technical problems, such as the interpretation of laws. In some areas, the Conseil played an important role, such as church-state relations, particularly after the law of separation of 1905.

Since ordinary courts were prohibited from interfering with the administration, the Conseil d'état adjudicated in last-resort conflicts between individuals and the state. During the Third Republic, the Conseil significantly extended the protection afforded citizens from arbitrary administrative action and recognized the pecuniary liability of the state for damages caused by civil servants. This bold jurisprudence established the reputation of the Conseil as a defender of civil liberties.

C. Freedeman, *The Conseil d'Etat in Modern France* (New York, 1961); M. Letourneur and J. Méric, *Conseil d'état et juridictions administratives* (Paris, 1955); M. Rendel, *The Administrative Functions of the Conseil d'Etat* (London, 1970).

C. E. Freedeman

Related entries: GOVERNMENT: PUBLIC ADMINISTRATION; JUDICIAL SYSTEM: COURTS.

GOVERNMENT: MUNICIPAL ADMINISTRATION. While local officials gained increased autonomy and power after the early years of the Third Republic, municipal government continued to be supervised by the state. Local administration was exercised in over 30,000 territorial units called *communes*. With the exception of Paris, each commune, regardless of its size or population, was governed by an identical administrative structure. Communal government was composed of a municipal council (*conseil municipal*), mayor (*maire*), and one or more assistant mayors (*adjoints*).

The council was usually elected every four years by universal manhood suffrage. All candidates who won an absolute majority on the first ballot were elected. Those receiving the most votes on the second ballot obtained the remaining seats. The Orleanist-dominated Republic of Moral Order (1870–76) allowed only communes that were not administrative centers and that had populations of fewer than 20,000 to elect mayors. In these communes, municipal councillors elected one of their own members as mayor. In 1882 this prerogative was extended to all communes except Paris.

Limited decentralization of power was codified in the *loi municipale* of 5 April 1884. This law confirmed the right of municipal councils to elect the mayor and his assistants and specified what matters the council could consider. The legal limits of communal authority were ultimately determined by decisions of the Conseil d'état. While the commune could propose governmental action in a variety of areas, actual disposition often depended on central government approval, usually by its agent, the prefect. Municipalities had virtually no authority in the areas of public education, police service, or poor relief. The municipal budget was prepared by the mayor and debated by the council. But after the council passed a budget, it was still subject to approval by the prefect or, for large cities, the minister of the interior. A budget was composed of mandatory and voluntary expenditures. Since a variety of services (such as police protection and highway maintenance) were obligatory, their funding in a municipal budget was required. If they were not included by the council, the prefect had the power to do so. Voluntary expenses, such as park improvements, were still subject to prefectoral approval. Only actions without substantial monetary impact did not require the prefect's approval.

The municipal council met in four regular sessions annually. Regular sessions and any special meetings were always to be held in the city hall (*hôtel de ville*). The council's officers, the mayor, and the assistant mayors were elected in the session immediately after the elections. The mayor presided over all council meetings except when he presented his annual report. Like the parliament, council meetings were held on consecutive days. Except for the annual budgetary meeting, most regular sessions lasted no more than two weeks. Subjects for council consideration were severely limited. For instance, national and international matters were not to be considered. Article 43 of the *loi municipale* allowed the central government to suspend some or all of the councillors and to appoint an interim municipal commission if a council exceeded the scope of its powers or refused to undertake required duties. This procedure was used especially against socialist municipal regimes that attempted municipalization of enterprises or balked at budgeting funds for the police. Legally abuse of prefectoral power vis-à-vis municipal councils could be deterred only by appeal to the Conseil d'état. In practice the prefect usually was not anxious to arouse local ire by antagonizing duly elected officials. Furthermore, the commune's representative in the Chamber of Deputies, often also the mayor, was able to exercise considerable political power on behalf of the municipality.

The mayor was both the chief executive of the commune and agent of the state, responsible to the Ministry of the Interior. Since all mayors were chosen by municipal councils after 1882 and the bulk of mayoral duties involved local issues, mayors generally were not identified as agents of the central state. Instead they were perceived as the spokesmen for local prerogatives against a powerful interventionist state, personified by the prefect. Although the mayor received an allowance for expenses but not a salary, the power and prestige of his post made it highly desirable. It was a good base for securing positions in the Chamber of Deputies, the Senate, or even a ministry. The mayor's powers were extensive. He had responsibility for local appointments, administrative personnel, public property, municipal construction projects, communal expenditures, collection of revenues, the securing of loans, and promulgation of regulations. For larger communes many of the mayor's duties were discharged by his assistants. Usually each assistant mayor was responsible for overseeing a specific set of services; however, administrative decisions were largely determined by the permanent professional staff.

The national government had a preponderant influence in some areas of municipal administration. For all but a few cities, responsibility for public order was legally vested with the mayor. But actual direction of the police was done by superintendents (*commissaires de police*) who were appointed by the national government. Other police officials, and in small towns the communal clerk (*secrétaire*), were appointed by the mayor but only with prefectoral assent. In larger communes, the Ministry of the Interior appointed the *secrétaire de mairie*, who was responsible for numerous important administrative functions. A commune's financial officers (*receveur* and *percepteur*) were also appointed by national authorities or their agent, the prefect. After 1919, many other communal administrative posts were chosen according to civil service procedures instead of by mayoral appointment.

The mayor was symbolically the president of his *petite république*, the commune, but the national government intervened continually, usually through the prefect or sub-prefect. Central state control was limited by the desire of each national regime to secure the cooperation, if not allegiance, of local officials. Through shrewd use of patronage, astute handling of issues, effective administration, and exploitation of parliamentary connections, mayors could gain substantial political power. Hostile clergymen, schoolmasters, or prefects often undermined the power of less competent mayors, exposing their commune's affairs to intrusion by the central state. Local circumstances, not legal texts, ultimately determined the degree to which national government dominated local administration.

H. Detton and J. Hourticq, *L'Administration régionale et locale de la France* (Paris, 1972); M. Duverger, *The French Political System* (Chicago, 1958); P. Legende, *L'Administration du XVIIIe siècle à nos jours* (Paris, 1969); B. Singer, *Village Notables in Nineteenth-Century France: Priests, Mayors, Schoolmasters* (Albany, N.Y., 1983).

D. Wright

Related entries: GOVERNMENT: CONSEIL D'ETAT; GOVERNMENT: UNITS OF REGIONAL AND LOCAL ADMINISTRATION; PARIS: POLITICS AND ADMINISTRATION; PREFECTS; SOCIALISM, MUNICIPAL.

GOVERNMENT: PUBLIC ADMINISTRATION, the counterpart to parliamentary politics in the governance of France during the Third Republic. The parliamentary side of government was identified with the nineteenth-century Revolutionary tradition, for which representative government had been an essential cause. But the administrative side was derived from a much older tradition, identified with the absolutist kings in the seventeenth century and especially with Napoleon I in the early nineteenth, favoring the centralization of the state's power. Theoretically executive power emanated from the parliament, which elected the president of the Republic. Ordinarily a parliamentary politician himself, he in turn appointed a council of ministers, who also typically held seats in either the Chamber of Deputies or the Senate. But the president of this ministerial council (called prime minister after 1934) counted on the practical advice of the Conseil d'état, an ancient and prestigious administrative body, in drafting legislation and decrees. The ministries, too, were composed of administrative units staffed by distinct corps of high administrative officials (*fonctionnaires*), each with its own traditions and attachments.

The governance of France during the Third Republic was marked by a rivalry between these politicians and administrators, who represented the antipodes of French public life. The politicians were the more visible. Elected from diverse geographical, social, and professional backgrounds, they spoke for a spectrum of political viewpoints from radical to reactionary and were accustomed to the confrontations and compromises of the parliamentary arena. The high administrators were less obtrusive. Hailing from Paris in inordinate numbers, educated in select professional schools, they espoused the cautious and more nearly uniform viewpoints of the corps to which they belonged. The politicians were generalists and thrived on controversy as the stuff of democracy; the administrators were specialists and sought an arrival at consensus as the foundation of efficient government. Out of such a disagreement over method and purpose, the relations between parliament and administration in the Third Republic were frequently riled by the administrator's reluctance to endorse the politician's desire for changes in policy, especially if these tended in a leftward direction.

In the course of the Third Republic, the size of the administration and the scope of its activities expanded dramatically. There were 200,000 civil servants (*fonctionnaires* and *employés*) in 1871, 469,000 in 1914, 547,000 in 1927, and 1,095,000 in 1950. The average number of ministries doubled from nine in the 1870s to eighteen by the 1930s. There were nine original ministries: Justice, Foreign Affairs, Interior, Finance, War, Navy and Colonies, Education and Fine Arts, Public Works, and Agriculture and Commerce. In time, some of these ministries fissioned—for example, Commerce and Agriculture in 1881, Colonies and Navy in 1893. New ministries were created as governmental responsibility for public services was extended—among others, Post Office and Telegraph in 1879, Labor and Social Welfare in 1906, Pensions in 1920, and Public Health in 1930. Each ministry was organized in a vertical hierarchy of administrative units that carried out its mandated tasks (commonly, *directions, services*, and *bureaux*, in descending order of importance). This structure was complemented by a horizontal series of agencies that monitored the work of the ministry and offered the minister advice (*cabinets, inspectorats*, and *conseils*, in sequence of proximity to the minister). The ministries of the Third Republic, moreover, were conspicuous for the extent of their control over regional and local affairs. Offices dealing with these "external services" were an integral, and not necessarily inferior, part of the administrative network.

In theory, this organization was designed to serve the minister, who was responsible for the formulation and execution of public policy. But ministers were politicians sent to lead administrators, and their ministries were superstructures imposed on more cohesive administrative units. These units guarded their autonomy because their identity was so closely bound up with the corps of high administrative personnel that staffed them. There were several such *grands corps*, each identified with a major administrative institution, the most prestigious being the Inspection des finances, the Conseil d'état, the Cour des comptes, the Diplomatic Corps, and the Prefectoral Corps. Each had its traditions and exercised control over the recruitment and promotion of its own personnel. Nearly all members of these *grands corps* were graduates of either the Ecole polytechnique or the Ecole libre des sciences politiques. Hence leadership of the administration remained stable and unusually elitist, despite the burgeoning ranks of lower-level governmental employees.

In the face of such a network of common professional formation and deep corporate loyalties, there was little that ministers could do to impose significant procedural or organizational changes. In only a few instances did ministers institute general secretariats to coordinate the activities of their principal administrative units. Only the minister's *cabinet* was composed of advisers personally loyal to him, and even this body was infiltrated by professional civil servants in the later years of the Republic. Moreover, a minister, rarely serving in his post for more than two years, had neither the time nor the opportunity to accomplish structural changes even if he had been motivated to do so. The inertial power of long-standing traditions and procedures therefore thwarted political policies that departed radically from the wishes of the administration.

In the political and economic crises of the 1930s, moreover, many high administrators were impatient with what they regarded as the indecision and ineptitude of the politicians. Some, openly contemptuous of the parliamentary process, were not unhappy to see the collapse of the Republic in 1940. The Vichy regime (1940–44), however, proved to be a pyrrhic victory for the administrative model, and leaders of the Fourth Republic (1944–58), while reasserting the primacy of parliamentary government, were obliged to return to the task with which leaders of the Third Republic had earlier wrestled: how to expand the governmental bureaucracy while keeping it responsive to the democratic ideal.

F. Ridley and J. Blondel, *Public Administration in France* (London, 1969); W. R. Sharp, *The French Civil Service* (New York, 1931); E. N. Suleiman, *Politics, Power and Bureaucracy in France* (Princeton, 1974); David Thomson, *Democracy in France since 1870* (London, 1946).

P. H. Hutton

Related entries: GOVERNMENT: CONSEIL D'ETAT; GOVERNMENT: UNITS OF REGIONAL AND LOCAL ADMINISTRATION; GOVERNMEN-TAL EMPLOYEES; POLITICS; PREFECTS; PRESIDENT OF THE REPUB-LIC, OFFICE OF; SCHOOLS, HIGHER EDUCATION: ECOLE LIBRE DES SCIENCES POLITIQUES.

GOVERNMENT: UNITS OF REGIONAL AND LOCAL ADMINISTRA-TION (1870–1940). Local governments underwent a process of decentralization but generally remained subject to the authority of the central state. During the Third Republic, all local and regional government took place within the departments, districts (*arrondissements*), and communes—political subdivisions whose boundaries had changed hardly at all since the First Empire. Each department was divided into two or three districts, and each of these was composed of hundreds of communes. Each department was headed by a prefect (*préfet*) headquartered in its *chef-lieu*; districts were administered by sub-prefects (*sous-préfets*); and the communes were led by mayors (*maires*). The minister of the interior appointed the prefects and sub-prefects who were chosen both because of their ability and because of their loyalty to the regime in power. As the Third Republic matured, these administrators tended to be chosen more for their professional skills and less for their political loyalty. The sub-prefects were subordinate to the prefects, with no independent administrative authority, and both they and the prefects were regularly rotated to prevent them from developing strong political or personal ties to particular regions.

Republican principles were reflected in departmental government by the general council (*conseil général*), a representative body composed of one delegate from each canton of the department. (During the Third Republic the cantons were not administrative subdivisions but served as judicial circumscriptions and as electoral districts for general councillors [*conseilleurs généraux*].) Between 1871 and 1926 the general council was mainly of symbolic importance. Members usually met only once per year when they approved the prefect's budget for the coming year and heard him describe his administration of the department. The general council influenced the day-by-day functioning of the department only through the departmental commission, a committee that advised the prefect on local affairs. A decree of 5 November 1926, however, gave the general councils real power over internal departmental matters and permitted prefectorial intervention only when a council had acted illegally or when significant changes in departmental financing were being proposed.

The most important arena for the exercise of political power on the local level was the commune. France was divided into thousands of communes, each of which elected its own municipal council. Mayors were selected in varying ways during the Third Republic. Departing from practices generally followed since Napoleon I, which required all mayors to be named by the central government, the National Assembly's statute of 14 April 1871 permitted municipal councils to choose their mayors from among their own numbers in communes of under 20,000 that were not the *chef-lieu* of the department or a district. In these large and/or politically important communes mayors were still selected by the central government. In 1876 the law was liberalized to permit all communes not containing *chef-lieux* to choose their own mayors; this last restriction was lifted by the law of 28 March 1882, which gave the municipal councils (*conseils municipaux*) of all communes the right to select their mayors. (None of these provisions applied to Paris, which was administered according to an entirely different code of law.) The main political obstacle to the election of all mayors before 1882 was their traditional control over the police, a power many feared would permit them to obstruct national policies. This problem was resolved by vesting most police powers in the hands of superintendents (*commissaires de police*) named by the central government and responsible to the prefect.

Although local political battles were often spirited, France was a highly centralized state, and the real exercise of power generally took place along a chain of command that ran from the Paris ministries to the communes. As the central government's chief representatives on the local level, prefects supervised the work of all officials belonging to agencies of the central government who controlled revenue collection, public works, communication, public welfare, and education. Prefects also carefully supervised the internal operations of the communes. By law mayors were viewed as agents of the central state and were required to obey the orders of their superiors in the administrative hierarchy. If, in the opinion of the central government, a mayor did not adequately carry out laws, regulations, or measures of public safety, the prefect could intervene, demand action, and if necessary, remove him from office. This control was essential, argued Emile de Marcère, the *rapporteur* of the 1884 parliamentary committee charged with redefining the legal status of the commune, because "since the communes are dependent upon the general laws, it is necessary that the central government have guaranties against them [and] the means to force them to return to the rule when they depart from it."

In practice a prefect's power over his commune came from the right to oversee the preparation of communal budgets and the right to veto most decisions made by the municipal councils. Municipal budgets were divided into obligatory and voluntary expenditures. The *dépenses obligatoires* were those required by law such as the maintenance of roads, while the *dépenses facultatives* were those appropriated by the municipal councils for purely local purposes. The prefects had no control over the voluntary expenditures unless they required sizable tax increases or loans but had total control over obligatory expenditures. If a municipal council refused to fund its obligatory services properly, the prefect had the right to inscribe the necessary monies on the budget.

The prefect's control over the municipal decision-making process was just as great. Decisions of municipal councils were made according to the usual French rules of procedure. Questions were referred to the appropriate committee whose *rapporteur* presented recommendations to the council as a whole for discussion. All positive actions were then expressed as a *délibération*, a formal statement of the decision taken. Until the passage of the *loi sur l'organisation municipale* of 5 April 1884, which remained the basic statute of municipal government during the Third Republic, all *délibérations* required the prefect's approval. After 1884 only certain specified *délibérations* required prior approval. This list, however, was still very long and included most things a municipal council might want to do that had any long-term significance, such as the acquisition, construction, or repair of public buildings and the initiation of municipal improvement projects. Decentralization was a powerful code word during the Third Republic, and although decentralizers hailed both the 1884 law and the decree of 5 November 1926, which further extended local autonomy, communes were still subject to the administrative supervision of the central government, which, acting through the prefect, could still inscribe sums on budgets, annul *délibérations*, and remove mayors from office.

H. Detton and J. Hourticq, *L'Administration régionale et locale de la France* (Paris, 1972); J. Lafon, "L'Histoire de l'administration," in *L'Administration*, ed. J. Sallois (Paris, 1974); P. Legende, *L'Administration du XVIIIe siècle à nos jours* (Paris, 1969).

C. J. Haug

Related entries: GOVERNMENT: MUNICIPAL ADMINISTRATION; GOVERNMENT: PUBLIC ADMINISTRATION; PARIS: POLITICS AND ADMINISTRATION; PREFECTS.

GOVERNMENTAL EMPLOYEES, employees of the *fonction publique* or civil service. At the top administrative and technical posts were the high civil servants, the *hauts fonctionnaires*. Although all government positions were formally open to all citizens on the basis of merit, in actuality only training at the *grandes écoles* (the Ecole polytechnique, the Ecole des ponts et chaussées [for civil engineers] and the newly founded private Ecole libre des sciences politiques guaranteed passage of the examinations (*concours*) given by each ministry and entrance into the top levels of governmental service. This ensured that the *hauts fonctionnaires* would continue to be recruited from the wealthy and professional elites who were drawn to public service by its prestige and security.

Most significant in the political and economic life of the Third Republic was the growth in the number and importance of lower-level governmental workers, the *petits fonctionnaires*. The Third Republic, committed to serving the growing needs of an urbanizing and industrializing nation and heir to a highly centralized state, expanded governmental monopolies and public service, adding education to its services, making the state's fiscal control all encompassing, beginning state control of transportation, utilities, and new industries such as radio. Government employment increased rapidly. By the first decade of the twentieth century, the Republic had quadrupled the number of *fonctionnaires* to nearly 800,000, making it the most important employer in France. By 1940, approximately one of every twelve Frenchmen and Frenchwomen employed in nonagricultural activities was an employee of the national government. The largest employers were the Ministries of Education and Post, Telegraph and Telephone (PTT), with approximately 200,000 employees each, Finance with approximately 90,000, Public Works with over 20,000, and Interior and Justice with approximately 13,000 each.

The Third Republic *petits fonctionnaires* were not only more numerous than their counterparts in the nineteenth century; their class origins changed as well.

The expansion of the public schools brought into the state system not only a host of dedicated, republican teachers; it opened as well careers of public service to the children of peasants and village artisans. To become a *fonctionnaire* was one step, albeit a small one, up the ladder from poverty, tightening rural conditions, and job insecurity. The expansion of public education and public service had its greatest effect on women. Previously restricted to domestic or factory work, young women, armed with certificates and diplomas, rapidly feminized numerous sectors of governmental employment. Initially employed as telephone operators or as primary school teachers for girls, women gradually moved into all levels of the postal and educational systems, and finally, as clerical workers, into the offices that administered the finances and social services of the nation. This feminization of governmental service was accelerated by the labor shortages of World War I and ultimately by the wage policy of the government itself, which, attempting to run the state bureaucracy as cheaply as possible, paid wages guaranteed to drive out male workers and attract the normally lower-paid women who had few employment opportunities. By 1940, although women constituted one-third of the governmental work force, very few had advanced to supervisory positions; most remained low-paid, low-level employees. Except for teachers, the concept of equal pay for equal work would not be recognized by the Third Republic.

The rapid and penetrating growth of public service and employment affected the consciousness of the average citizen as the public became increasingly aware of the extent of the state's involvement in their daily lives. Critical of the inefficiencies of governmental services, the public was disturbed as well by the explosion in the number of *fonctionnaires*. Peasants in particular were incensed by the size of the state bureaucracy, paid for by their hard-earned and grudgingly paid taxes. The growth of bureaucracy beyond efficiency and control was derisively attacked as *fonctionnarisme*, and frustrations often found innocent victims; individual *fonctionnaires*, powerless themselves, were attacked for the faults inherent in the system. While some complaints about a bloated and lazy bureaucracy continued, particularly during the depression of the 1930s when the government began to reduce state employment, by the end of the Third Republic most citizens, many of whom had friends or family on the state payroll or were *fonctionnaires* themselves, accepted and even asked for expansion of governmental service and employment.

The state's involvement in public service and employment also opened for public debate the issue of whether *fonctionnaires*—citizens and employees of the state at the same time—would be permitted to organize to challenge collectively the authority of the state. The answer of the Third Republic to the question of *fonctionnaire* organization was a resounding no. Legally the *fonctionnaires* were denied the *droit syndical*, the right to unionize granted to blue-collar workers in 1884. Although *syndicats* (unions) were tolerated after 1925, *fonctionnaire* unionism remained technically illegal until 1946. *Fonctionnaires* enjoyed job security and were the first workers to receive pensions and paid vacations, but as services were expanded and governments reluctant to spend more money, *fonctionnaires* found their working conditions deteriorating and their salary advantages eroding. Promotion was determined mainly by examination and seniority, but *fonctionnaires* complained about favoritism and arbitrary administrators. By the turn of the century, the *fonctionnaires* began to organize. French *fonctionnaires* were the first civil service workers in the world to organize, to unionize, and to strike. A few teachers and postal workers formed illegal *syndicats*, and in 1909 there was a major postal strike, but the majority of *fonctionnaires* utilized the 1901 Law of Associations to form their organizations legally. By 1914, in contrast to the small number of unionized blue-collar workers, most *fonctionnaires* were organized; the umbrella organization, the Fédération des fonctionnaires, had almost 400,000 members. In the aftermath of the war, the *fonctionnaires* illegally transformed their associations into *syndicats* and in 1920 joined the major blue-collar labor federation, the Confédération générale du travail (CGT). Briefly independent in the early 1920s, the *fonctionnaires* reentered the CGT in 1927 where because of their numerical strength and their political experience they played a major role in the labor movement and in national politics.

Fonctionnaires, whose salaries and working conditions were determined by politicians, saw electoral politics as a necessary part of their activities. Throughout the life of the Third Republic, *fonctionnaires* had been active in political campaigns, running for office themselves, or campaigning for candidates, such as the cartel des gauches (1924), who supported their demands. In the 1930s, threatened by the economic depression and a resultant series of executive decrees cutting governmental employment and salaries and fearful of the rising tide of fascism, the *fonctionnaires* participated in strikes, demonstrations against fascism, and the campaign for the Popular Front government of 1936. By 1940, *fonctionnaires* were firmly placed in the mainstream of French economic and political life.

R. Bidouze, *Les Fonctionnaires, sujets ou citoyens?* Vol. 1 (Paris, 1979); G. Cahen, *Les Fonctionnaires* (Paris, 1911); R. Catherine, *Le Fonctionnaire* (Paris, 1961); G. Duveau, *Les Instituteurs* (Paris, 1966); P. Harmignie, *L'Etat et ses agents* (Louvain, 1911); Musée social, *Le Droit d'association des fonctionnaires* (Paris, 1912); J. Ozouf, *Nous les maîtres d'écoles* (Paris, 1967); F. Ridley and J. Blondel, *Public Administration in France* (New York, 1968); G. Thuillier, *La Vie quotidienne dans les ministères au XIXe siècle* (Paris, 1976).

J. Wishnia

Related entries: GOVERNMENT: PUBLIC ADMINISTRATION; LABOR MOVEMENT; SCHOOLS, HIGHER EDUCATION: *GRANDES ECOLES*; WOMEN: IN THE LABOR FORCE.

GRANGER, ERNEST (1844–1914), Blanquist militant, journalist, politician. The son of a wealthy lawyer, he was born in Mortagne (Orne). As a law student in Paris during the 1860s, he became affiliated with the young disciples of Auguste Blanqui and played a leading role in the formation of a secret society designed to overthrow the Second Empire. Granger helped organize a number of popular demonstrations against the imperial government in the late 1860s, culminating in an unsuccessful Blanquist raid on an arsenal in the La Villette quarter of Paris in August 1870. Granger was also a conspicuous participant in the uprising of 4 September 1870, in which the Third Republic was proclaimed.

During the Franco-Prussian War, Granger commanded the 159th battalion of the National Guard in Paris. He held no official post during the Commune of 1871 but was entrusted by his Blanquist companions with a mission to the Lot to ransom the imprisoned Blanqui, a venture that failed. As an exile during the 1870s, Granger traveled between London, Brussels, and Geneva to sustain solidarity among the Communards. Amnestied in 1880, he returned to Paris where he looked after the aging Blanqui during his last year. As executor of Blanqui's papers, he published an anthology of Blanqui's writings on social and economic issues (*Critique sociale*) in 1885 and bequeathed all of Blanqui's manuscripts and correspondence to the Bibliothèque nationale in 1899.

During the 1880s, Granger endeavored to revitalize the role of the Blanquists in left-wing politics, but most of these efforts were given to ceremonial commemoration of past revolutionary glories. His suspicion of Marxist socialism led him into an uneasy rivalry with Edouard Vaillant for control of the Blanquist organization. His decision to support General Georges Boulanger and to run himself as a revisionist candidate for the Chamber of Deupties split the Blanquists into opposing factions. Although Granger won election and retained the allegiance of most of the Blanquist veterans of the Commune, his faction did not fare well in the long run. Ostracized by Vaillant and the various socialist groups in the 1890s, Granger attempted to rebuild his party through an alliance with the emerging nationalist groups of the radical Right, but to no avail. Granger himself retired to his family's farm in 1893 following his term in the Chamber.

With his faith in insurrection as the way to revolution and his sympathy for the Jacobinism of the Revolutionary tradition, Granger epitomized a style of revolutionary militancy that made sense in the authoritarian world of the Second Empire but grew increasingly unrealistic in the democratic politics of the Third Republic.

M. Dommanget, *Blanqui et l'opposition révolutionnaire à la fin du Second Empire* (Paris, 1960); P. H. Hutton, *The Cult of the Revolutionary Tradition* (Berkeley, 1981); J. Maitron, ed., *Dictionnaire biographique du mouvement ouvrier français*, vol. 6 (*Paris, 1969*); W. Martel, *Mes entretiens avec Granger* (Paris, 1939).

P. H. Hutton

Related entries: BLANQUI; BLANQUISTS; BOULANGER AFFAIR; COMMUNE OF PARIS; JACOBINISM; VAILLANT.

GREAT BRITAIN, RELATIONS WITH. The relations between France and Great Britain from 1871 to 1940 were decisively influenced by the divergent geopolitical and economic situations of the two powers. Highly dependent on foreign trade for its economic prosperity and geographically protected from military invasion by the English Channel and the North Sea, Great Britain maintained as its principal foreign policy objective the preservation of naval superiority in the Channel–North Sea zone, as well as along the sea-lanes linking the mother country to its imperial outposts. France, less dependent on foreign trade and much more vulnerable to military invasion, was principally concerned with providing adequate security against German aggression on the Continent. These divergent conceptions of the national interest made cooperation between these two powers difficult, and Anglo-French conflicts over colonial matters seemed to make it impossible. The only circumstance that could (and did) produce a diplomatic entente between London and Paris was the prospect of a German challenge to British naval supremacy. Once that threat was temporarily removed by the destruction of the German fleet after the First World War, the two powers reverted to the acrimonious relationship of the earlier period. Only in the late 1930s did Britain and France belatedly embark on a cooperative venture to resist German efforts to revise the peace treaty of 1919.

In the last quarter of the nineteenth century, France and Great Britain acquired two of the largest colonial empires that the world has ever seen, dividing up most of the continent of Africa between them and establishing control over large sections of Southeast Asia and Pacific Oceania. This simultaneous colonial expansion inevitably produced tensions as territorial claims began to overlap. The major focal point of Anglo-French colonial competition was the Mediterranean Sea. The British objective of maintaining control of the strategic waterways at the two points of entry to the Mediterranean (Gibraltar and Suez) clashed with French efforts to expand the French North African Empire (Algeria and Tunisia). The compromise of 1904 that finally resolved this dispute (by granting England sole control of Egypt and France a sphere of interest in Morocco) was made possible by the two governments' shared concern about the growing naval and military power of Germany. Between 1904 and 1914 France and England developed a cordial relationship that matured into a cooperative military effort after the outbreak of the First World War.

Following the German invasion of Belgium in August 1914, a British expeditionary force was dispatched to northeastern France and fought side by side with French forces in a successful effort to halt the German advance in the west. Moreover, the British naval blockade of the Central Powers played a major role in straining the economic resources of Germany. In the realm of economic cooperation, Great Britain loaned France considerable sums for war-related expenditures. As the war dragged on, the two powers devised various plans for the postwar reconstruction of Europe, the partitioning of the Ottoman Empire, and the redistribution of German colonial possessions in Africa.

At the Paris Peace Conference (1919), the British government reverted to its traditional policy of isolation from continental affairs, refusing to cooperate in French schemes to divide Germany militarily and shackle it economically. Some historians have traced this new policy to a British concern for reviving the German economy in the interests of foreign trade. Others have cited the traditional British policy of supporting a continental balance of power between France and Germany. London repeatedly clashed with Paris in the years after the First World War, the former pressing for political and economic concessions to Germany and the latter insisting on strict enforcement of the Versailles Treaty.

This Anglo-French acrimony dissipated considerably during the second half of the 1920s. The Dawes Plan (1924) and the Locarno Accords (1925) promoted the type of economic and political stability on the Continent that Britain had been seeking since the end of the war. The two countries also cooperated in economic matters, supporting each other's currencies on world money markets and working closely to facilitate the transfer of German reparation payments to the allied countries and allied war debt payments to the United States.

With the onset of the world depression and the rise of German nazism, Britain and France were confronted with the challenge of devising methods for restoring European economic stability and deterring German aggression. The first objective was undermined by the rise of economic nationalism in the major countries of the world. England was compelled to abandon the gold standard and establish a system of colonial preference insulating the British Empire from foreign economic competition. France erected protectionist barriers around its economy, contributing to a dramatic decrease in world trade.

This turn toward economic warfare was accompanied by growing Anglo-French differences over the proper strategy for dealing with Hitlerian Germany. Time after time French officials attempted, in vain, to secure British support for a policy of resistance to German treaty violations. Adolf Hitler's abrogation of the disarmament clauses of the Versailles Treaty on 16 March 1935 elicited a joint protest from Britain, France, and Italy (the Stresa Conference, 11 April). But on June 18 Britain negotiated a separate bilateral naval agreement with Germany without informing France, thereby destroying the common front established at Stresa. In March 1936 France's request for British assistance in expelling the German military forces that had been illegally introduced into the demilitarized Rhineland zone was rejected, thereby helping to weaken French resolve to resist. In September 1938 British Prime Minister Neville Chamberlain masterminded a diplomatic solution to the German-Czechoslovak crisis that effectively destroyed the defensive capability of France's eastern ally. Some historians have held the French governments of the 1930s equally responsible for this policy of appeasement, contending that British pressure merely supplied French officials with a pretext for avoiding risks in foreign and defense policy that they were themselves unwilling to take.

After the German annexation of the rump Czech state in March 1939, the governments of Britain and France reversed the earlier policy, stepping up rearmament and issuing guarantees to Poland, the next likely victim of German aggression. The German attack on Poland on 1 September 1939 prompted an Anglo-French declaration of war on Germany two days later. When the German offensive against France began on 10 May 1940, British and French divisions had established positions in Flanders to the north of the French defensive fortification network, the Maginot Line. When that German tank and dive bomber offensive drove deep into northern France in late May, the British expeditionary force, together with detachments of the left wing of the French army, was cut off from the remainder of the French forces. These troops were evacuated to England from the channel port of Dunkirk (28 May–4 June), thereby terminating the British army's participation in the defense of France. As French forces reeled before the German blitzkrieg, British Prime Minister Winston Churchill refused to commit the royal air force to the battle of France in order to conserve it for the defense of the British Isles in the event (by then almost a foregone conclusion) of a French surrender.

H. Jordan, *Great Britain, France, and the German Problem, 1913–1939* (London, 1943); N. Waites, ed., *Troubled Neighbors: Franco-British Relations in the Twentieth Century* (London, 1971); S. R. Williamson, *The Politics of Grand Strategy: Britain and France Prepare for War* (Cambridge, 1969).

W. R. Keylor

Related entries: ENTENTE CORDIALE; TRIPLE ENTENTE; WORLD WAR I.

GREVY, JULES (1807-1891), politician, lawyer, president of the Republic (30 January 1879–2 December 1887). Jules Grévy, "the Fox of the Jura," son of a retired Revolutionary soldier and small landowner, practiced law in Paris and was a prominent republican in the National Assembly (1848–51) where, suspicious of Louis Napoléon Bonaparte's ambitions, he moved (6 October 1848) that there be no popularly elected president but instead only a president of the Council of Ministers elected by the Assembly. Briefly imprisoned after Bonaparte's 1851 coup, he resumed his law career, not reentering politics until 1869, when the Jura sent him to the Legislative Body as a firm opponent of the Empire. He remained aloof from the revolution of 4 September 1870 because of its illegalities. The Jura returned him to the National Assembly (1871-75); he was its first president (16 February 1871–2 April 1873) but resigned due to the waxing hostility of the Right and his growing discontent with Adolphe Thiers. Elected to the Chamber of Deputies (1876-79), he became on Thiers' death (3 September 1877) the nominal leader of the republicans (Léon Gambetta was the real chief) during the *seize mai* crisis. He was elected president when Maurice de MacMahon resigned and was reelected 28 December 1885. The Wilson scandal led to his resignation. He retired to his estate at his birthplace, Mont-sous-Vaudrey, and left a fortune acquired by saving a large part of his presidential stipends.

Grévy's presidency set the major precedents for that office until the Fifth Republic (1958–). He deprived it of all open implications of independent power, such as not using the rights to send messages to parliament or to dissolve it. But more perhaps than any of his successors, he exercised considerable backstage influence on cabinet formation, notably in his avoidance of forceful personalities as premiers (the supple Charles de Freycinet was his favorite) and on foreign policy, where he discounted revanchism and the seeking of alliances. He is usually held responsible for Gambetta's exclusion and for weakening his prospects when he finally called him (10 November 1881), but it is questionable whether Gambetta would have lasted long in any case in view of his lack of Senate support. In foreign affairs Grévy helped prevent a possible war with Germany over the Schnaebelé affair (April 1887) by advising against sending any ultimatum.

He was personally uninvolved in the schemes of Daniel Wilson, his son-in-law, who peddled influence from an apartment in the Elysée. But his mulish refusal—from the effects of age and family pride—to condemn Wilson's abuses or recognize their political implications, together with the public's mockery of his narrow, penurious ways, opened a major crisis, which was resolved by his resignation after an obstinate resistance to a "strike" by all potential premiers.

In his prime, Grévy was a coldly impressive speaker, devoid of the romanticism of other "48ists," and had a gift for lapidary summation. He commanded respect, was a fine conversationalist, and in counsel was wise and penetrating. But he grew prudent to the verge of immobility, resisting all change, and his parsimony, although exaggerated by repute, was well known. His brother Albert (1823–99) was a controversial administrator in Algeria (1879–81) and, as a senator, was implicated, though not tried, in the Panama scandal (1892-93). Another brother, Paul (1820–1914), was a general and senator.

D. Brogan, *The Development of Modern France*, (London, 1967); G. Chapman, *The Third Republic: The First Phase* (London, 1962); A. Dansette, *L'Affaire Wilson et la chute du président Grévy*, 2nd ed. (Paris, 1936), and *Histoire des présidents de la République* (Paris, 1981); J. Grévy, *Discours politiques et judiciaires, rapports et messages de Jules Grévy*, 2 vols. (Paris, 1888); B. Lavergne, *Les Deux Présidences de Jules Grévy* (Paris, 1966); E. Zevort, *La Présidence de Jules Grévy* (Paris, 1898).

D. S. Newhall

Related entries: BOULANGER; CONSTITUTIONAL LAWS OF 1875; FERRY; FREYCINET; GAMBETTA; GOBLET; NATIONAL ASSEMBLY; OPPOR-TUNISTS; PRESIDENT OF THE REPUBLIC, OFFICE OF; SCHNAEBELE AFFAIR; *SEIZE MAI* CRISIS; SEPTEMBER 4, 1870; THIERS; WILSON SCANDAL.

GRIFFUELHES, VICTOR (1874–1922), trade union militant and revolutionary syndicalist. He is one of the least known militants of the Confédération générale du travail (CGT). He was not a theorist and manifested a hard-bitten contempt for intellectuals of the Left, from Georges Sorel to Jean Jaurès. It was in the less conspicuous work of administration and organization that he left his mark. As secretary-general of the CGT (1901–9), Griffuelhes presided over the movement's emergence as the most powerful labor organization in France.

Griffuelhes was the son of a cobbler and himself worked in a shoe factory as a young man. He had belonged to a *compagnonnage* and flirted with Blanquism before turning in the 1890s to militant trade unionism. He served as an official of the Federation of Leather and Hides before acceding to the leadership of the CGT, the first worker to reach the upper echelons of the fledgling organization (the CGT was founded in 1895).

Griffuelhes brought with him a zeal for organization, deep-seated laborite convictions, and a thorough distrust of politicians. In 1902, the Bourse du travail united with the CGT, a merger negotiated by Griffuelhes that worked distinctly to the CGT's advantage. He planned the CGT's campaign against privately run placement bureaux, culminating in the general strike of May Day 1906. Griffuelhes shared the syndicalist vision of a future regime, planned and administered by the workers themselves through their trade unions. The administrative skills necessary to the task were to be learned in the day-to-day struggle to expand union membership, to organize strikes, and to win concessions. Griffuelhes rejected the politics of parliamentary reform as debilitating and distracting. Alexandre Millerand's presence in the René Waldeck-Rousseau cabinet (1899–1902) excited his disgust. Politicians, he felt, looked more to their own interests than to those of the working class. To maintain the labor movement's revolutionary élan, CGT militants ought to shun politics. To this end, Griffuelhes coauthored the Charter of Amiens (1906) which declared the organization's independence from political parties, including the Socialist (SFIO).

Griffuelhes resigned as secretary-general in 1909 but continued to exert an influence on the organization's policies through his protégé and eventual successor Léon Jouhaux. He was an ardent supporter of the *Union sacrée* but, like so many other syndicalist militants, welcomed unreservedly the Bolshevik Revolution of 1917. Combative and intelligent, a tough defender of working-class interests, Griffuelhes led the syndicalist movement through its heroic early years and established the CGT as the legitimate voice of organized labor in France.

E. Dolléans, *Victor Griffuelhes*, Conférences de l'institut supérieur ouvrier, série d'histoire syndicale, VIII (Paris, 1938); V. Méric, "Victor Griffuelhes," *Les Hommes du jour*, 13 February 1909.

P. G. Nord

Related entries: AMIENS, CHARTER OF; BOURSE DU TRAVAIL; CONFEDERATION GENERALE DU TRAVAIL; JOUHAUX, LABOR MOVEMENT; MILLERAND; STRIKE, GENERAL; SYNDICALISM; TRADE UNION MOVEMENT.

GRIS, JUAN (1887–1927), Spanish-born cubist painter. Born José Victoriano González-Pérez in Madrid, he was one of fourteen children of a paper and leather merchant. Gris attended the Escuela de Artes y Manufacturas in Madrid (1902–4) and then studied under an academic painter (1904–5). In 1906 he arrived in Paris, settled in Montmartre, and soon met Pablo Picasso and Guillaume Apollinaire and became part of the group that developed cubism. He supported himself with illustrations for Spanish and French literary and humoristic reviews (including *L'Assiette au beurre*, *Le Cri de Paris*, and *Le Charivari*). Beginning to paint seriously only in 1910, Gris by 1912 had a unique approach to cubism, featuring a highly structured, extremely rigorous organization of space. He was a founding member of the Section d'or group (1912).

During the 1920s, Gris designed sets and costumes for several Ballets russes productions and illustrated the works of many of his writer friends. He lived often in poverty and died of a lung illness caused in part by his privations.

D. Cooper, *The Cubist Epoch* (London, 1970); J. A. Gaya-Nuño, *Juan Gris* (Boston, 1975); J. Golding, *Cubism* (Boston, 1968); D. H. Kahnweiler, *Juan Gris* (New York, [1968]).

T. Shapiro

Related entries: APOLLINAIRE; ART: MAJOR STYLES AND MOVEMENTS; CUBISM; PICASSO.

GUERIN, JULES (1860–1910), leader of Parisian anti-Semitic organization, 1897–99; exiled in 1900 for plotting against the state; builder of Fort Chabrol. He was born in 1860. His father having died before his birth, Guérin was raised by his mother and a family friend, Mr. Mallet. His mother resided in Paris where Guérin attended school. He then joined Mallet's firm and by the age of sixteen achieved the post of managing assistant director, which paid him 6,000 francs annually. In the next ten years Guérin defrauded four companies, including his own, set fire to one of his factories in order to collect the insurance, and with his brother bilked the post office of 4,200 francs, which he claimed to have lost in the mail. A police report on his business activity rather underestimates his reputation: "Most of the businessmen with whom he had contact consider Guérin to be a man of bad faith, lacking scruples and propriety."

For most of his adult life, Guérin lived in the Nineteenth Arrondissement of Paris, quartier La Villette. There, in 1892, he tried to influence the local radical deputy to support a special business favor. When he refused, the deputy was severely beaten, and Guérin was sent to prison for a week. Politically Guérin associated successively with Radicals, Boulangists, Socialists, and finally anti-Semites. A man whose physical strength and will were feared, he dressed the part of a dandy: mustached, finely clothed, always sporting a felt hat.

In his *quartier*, he and his brother gained a reputation for their ability to organize street demonstrations during which Guérin was always surrounded by an entourage of La Villette's wholesale butchers. In 1893 Guérin became the friend of the marquis de Morès, himself a swaggering and unsavory con man who for a time had been a rancher in the United States. As Morès' lieutenant, Guérin also became associated with Edouard Drumont and *La Libre Parole*, for which he wrote a series of articles denouncing the company of Mallet. On Morès' death, Guérin obtained steady employment from Drumont, who in 1897 encouraged him to take over a small political organization, the Ligue anti-sémitique de France. Guérin was permitted by Drumont to use *La Libre Parole* to announce meetings and obtain initial financing.

In November 1897, Guérin led the Ligue anti-sémitique in the first organized protest against the possible revision of the Dreyfus affair. Guérin's reputation as a street demonstrator and leader was borne out in February 1898 when he daily led mobs of as many as 6,000 in protests during the trial of Emile Zola.

Several months later he and several of his elite Liguers accompanied Drumont to Algeria, where Drumont decided to stand for the Chamber of Deputies. Another violent riot in Algiers resulted in his imprisonment for a week. By late summer 1898 Guérin not only had become a celebrity in anti-Dreyfusard circles but had also launched his own paper, *L'Anti-juif*, and declared his independence from Drumont, who considered him a thug. In desperate need of money, Guérin turned to the Orleanists, who furnished him with almost unlimited funds for the next year.

Financially secure, working the street with great success, Guérin finally announced his program in August 1898. He declared that his goal was to defend the interests of *petit commerce, des employés et des ouvriers*. Further, *L'Anti-juif* embarked on a campaign designed to identify the Jews of Paris. Lists of Jews by profession were printed. The newspaper recommended that Jewish dwellings be marked and Jewish merchants boycotted.

Guérin's appeal to the working class was unsuccessful, however, as he and his henchmen were systematically turned away from striking building-trades workers' meetings in the fall of 1898. On the other hand, along with the Ligue des patriotes, Guérin's Ligue anti-sémitique was significant in turning Parisian lower-middle-class social and cultural resentment into anti-Dreyfusard protest.

Although not involved in the coup of 23 February 1899, Guérin was aware of its plan and, aided by royalist money, intended to subvert it should it succeed. Paul Déroulède's failure bound Guérin more closely to his financial backers, the royalists, who in March 1899 provided him with sufficient resources to construct the famous Fort Chabrol, an armored residence on a street of that name. There Guérin prepared for siege. Changing the Ligue's name to Grand Occident de France, Guérin waited for the retrial of Alfred Dreyfus at Rennes in August. On 10 August 1899, Guérin received word of his impending arrest for plotting against the state along with royalist and nationalist leaders. With several key associates, he locked himself in Fort Chabrol. Armed with revolvers, supplied with food delivered at night, Guérin and his men withstood for more than a month the siege at Fort Chabrol. In late September he gave himself up, was tried and convicted before the high court, and sentenced to ten years in exile. There is no official record of his subsequent existence. Organized political anti-Semitism would find its repose in other sanctuaries.

L. Poliakov, *L'Histoire de L'Anti-Sémitisme*, 3 vols. (Paris, 1968).

P. M. Rutkoff

Related entries: ANTISEMITIC LEAGUE; ANTI-SEMITISM; DREYFUS AFFAIR; DRUMONT.

GUESDE, JULES (1845–1922), socialist leader, founder of the Parti ourvrier, advocate of Marxian socialism. Born in Paris 11 November 1845, as Jules Bazile, the son of a private school teacher, François Bazile, and Eleanor Guesde, he took his mother's maiden name when he entered the world of opposition politics and journalism during the closing years of the Second Empire. Because of his articles defending the Paris Commune, Guesde was forced to flee France. During his exile in Switzerland and Italy he began to develop anarchist and later socialist ideas.

On his return to France in 1876, he resumed journalism and political activity, acquiring in the process a more thorough understanding of the ideas of Marx. He soon became one of the leading proponents of the creation of a working-class party along essentially Marxian lines. When the amnesty of the communards in 1879–80 brought a renewal of radical political activity, Guesde helped to establish France's first modern socialist party. Its stormy beginnings led to a schism in 1882 over issues of party organization and program between factions headed by Guesde and Paul Lafargue on the one hand and by Paul Brousse and Benoît Malon on the other. The Guesdistes, as they were soon called, took the name Parti ourvrier, adopted a Marxist program, and began the task of organizing working-class support.

Guesde devoted the next decade to building a working-class party. He made countless speeches and produced an array of articles and pamphlets outlining in simple Marxist terms the position and aims of the party. Success at the polls was meager during the 1880s, but Guesde and other leaders developed solid rank-and-file support. By the early 1890s the fortunes of the Parti ouvrier began to change. Guesde was elected to the Chamber of Deputies in 1893 from a textile district in the Nord department, which he was to represent again from 1906 until his death in 1922.

In the years leading up to the creation of a united socialist party, the Section français de l'internationale ouvrière (SFIO) in 1905, and within the party thereafter, Guesde remained a strong advocate of orthodox socialism against the reformist tendencies of such figures as Jean Jaurès and Alexandre Millerand and was largely successful in getting his position accepted as the official one of the party.

With the coming of the war in 1914 Guesde participated in the *union sacrée* government until the end of 1916. This apparent reversal of his earlier stance is perhaps best explained by an underlying patriotism and his devotion to the invaded regions of the North, which he represented in the Chamber. But Guesde's acceptance of a portfolio was largely symbolic. By 1914 his health, which had never been robust, began to fail, and he steadily withdrew from the center stage of socialist politics. He took no major part in the postwar debates over the future of French socialism and reacted to the schism between socialists and communists at the Congress of Tours (1920) with more disappointment than partisan feeling, although he did side with the socialist minority. He died 28 July 1922.

A. Compère-Morel, *Jules Guesde* (Paris, 1937); C. Willard, *Les Guesdistes* (Paris, 1965).

T. Moodie

Related entries: GUESDISTS; LAFARGUE; MARXISM; SOCIALISM, 1870–1914; SOCIALIST PARTY; *UNION SACREE.*

444 GUESDISTS

GUESDISTS, revolutionary faction of the socialist movement, founded and dominated by Jules Guesde. The group originated with the revival of socialist activity in the late 1870s and early 1880s. In 1877 Guesde and a small group of radical journalists founded a weekly newspaper, *Egalité*, and began to advocate the establishment of a socialist party. Trade union congresses in 1876 and 1878 revealed little inclination of workers to engage in socialist politics, but a congress held in Marseilles in 1879, at which political groups as well as trade unions were represented, called for the establishment of a socialist party. Given the diversity of the French radical tradition, however, ideas about what the party should stand for and how it should operate varied considerably. Some, including Benoît Malon and Paul Brousse, wanted a loosely structured organization and an eclectic program; some were anarchists. Others, among them Guesde and his supporters, favored a centralized organization and adherence of all members to a well-defined revolutionary socialist program.

Since the Marseilles congress specified nothing about the new party's program or organization, the party was thrown into an extended debate over these issues. Guesde took the initiative in developing a program and in early 1880 went to London to consult with Karl Marx, Friedrich Engels, and his future collaborator, Paul Lafargue, on a draft program. This London Program, whose preamble was drafted by Marx, outlined a revolutionary socialism based on class struggle and advocated collective ownership of the means of production. This statement of principle was followed by a set of immediate demands, both political and economic, that were to be the basis of the party's electoral politics. Guesde managed to get the program adopted at the socialist congress of 1880 despite resistance from other leaders, some of whom harbored a hostility to Marx dating back to the conflicts of the First International. Disputes continued during 1881 and 1882 and resulted in a schism at the St. Etienne Congress of 1882. Guesde and his supporters found themselves a distinct minority at the congress—perhaps, as they charged, owing to the manipulations of their opponents. Rather than accept defeat on major issues of doctrine and party structure, the Guesdists walked out of the congress and held a rival meeting at which they adopted the Marxist program and took the name Parti ouvrier for their diminutive band.

The party thus established under the leadership of Guesde and Lafargue became the vehicle for the introduction of Marxism into French socialist politics. The key to success, as Guesde often repeated, lay in strong organization—discipline, organization and concentration always, as he once said. The decade of the 1880s was devoted to building that solid organization. Guesde and Lafargue criss-crossed the country making speeches and recruiting local leaders. They sought to maintain a party press on a shoestring. At first progress was difficult. Groups were small and often geographically isolated. In the absence of dedicated local activists, they often melted away. Newspapers came and went with remarkable frequency as well—casualties of their financial weakness and the harassment of officials. Yet by the end of the decade the party's strength had measurably improved. Three centers of strength had developed: one in the industrial North;

one in the East, chiefly in the departments of Rhône, Loire, and Allier; and a third in the Paris region. The party created its own printing establishment in Lille, began to consolidate regional organizations, and initiated a system of national membership registration and dues collection. Two occupational groups figured prominently among the party's followers, textile and metal workers, occupations indicative of the proletarian character of the party's following.

With these foundations laid, the Guesdists' membership and electoral strength increased rapidly in the early 1890s. Several Guesdists were elected in the legislative elections of 1889, sometimes with the support of Boulangists. Lafargue was elected as a protest candidate in 1891 after a serious May Day incident and his subsequent jailing. Guesde himself, as well as several other party members, won in the legislative elections of 1893. At the same time, party membership rose rapidly—from 2,000 in 1889 to some 10,000 in 1893. After many years in which no national congresses were held, annual meetings were resumed in 1890.

The improved fortunes of the Guesdists contrasted with the declining influence of some of their rivals, notably the Possibilists. Thus, the Guesdists emerged in the 1890s as the dominant socialist organization, yet they had limited success in translating this strength into electoral victory or wide popular support. A relatively new and loosely organized group of independent socialists, headed by such figures as Jean Jaurès and Alexandre Millerand, eclipsed the Guesdists in this respect. The movement was increasingly polarized into the Guesdists, with their organizational strength, and the independent socialists, able to win elections but lacking a well-defined program or organization.

As some of the factional quarrels of the 1880s subsided and prospects for the future brightened, the impetus to create a united socialist party increased. Now that their own identity was clearly established, Guesdists became more willing to cooperate with other groups and to take electoral politics more seriously. In 1896 Millerand developed a minimum program of reforms he hoped all socialists could support in forthcoming municipal elections, and the Guesdists accepted this. Moves toward greater cooperation, if not unity, were interrupted by the Dreyfus affair and the subsequent participation of Millerand in the René Waldeck-Rousseau government. When a united socialist party (SFIO) was finally created in 1905, the Guesdists, with support from the German social democrats, were largely successful in getting their brand of socialist politics accepted as the official position of the party, despite the strenuous and eloquent objections of Jaurès.

Although the Guesdists ceased to exist as a separate organization after 1905, they retained important areas of strength (especially in the north) and continued to exercise a strong influence in party deliberations in the years preceding the First World War. The term *Guesdist* remained identified with party discipline and a politics based on class struggle.

S. Bernstein, *The Beginnings of Marxian Socialism in France* (New York, 1933); A. Compère-Morel, *Jules Guesde* (Paris, 1937); G. Lefranc, *Le Mouvement socialiste* (Paris, 1963); B. Moss, *The Origins of the French Labor Movement* (Berkeley, 1976); A. Noland,

The Founding of the French Socialist Party (Cambridge, Mass., 1956); C. Willard, *Les Guesdistes* (Paris, 1965); A. Zévaès, *Les Guesdistes* (Paris, 1911).

T. Moodie

Related entries: BROUSSE; DEVILLE; GUESDE; JAURES; LAFARGUE; LAVIGNE; MALON; MILLERAND; POSSIBILISTS; SOCIALISM, 1870–1914.

GUILLAUMIN, EMILE (1873–1951), rustic novelist. Ignored by many historians and literary critics, he made his living through farming and wrote on Sundays, holidays, and during the winter. His greatest work, *La Vie d'un simple* (1904), ranks as one of the great rustic novels of French literature. His many works reflected a lifelong concern with the conditions of the French peasantry. These include: *Notes paysannes et villageoises* (1925), *A tous vents sur la glèbe* (1931), *Panorama de l'évolution paysanne de 1875 à 1935* (1935), *François Peron, enfant du peuple* (1937), *Charles-Louis Philippe, mon ami* (1942), *Sur l'appui du manche* (1949), and (posthumously) *Paysans par eux-mêmes* (1953).

R. Mathe, *Emile Guillaumin, l'homme de la terre, l'homme de lettres* (Paris, 1966); P. Vernois, F. Masson, and S. Souchon-Guillaumin, eds., *Le Centenaire d'Emile Guillaumin. Actes du colloque de Moulins, 20 oct. 1973* (Paris, 1975).

R. E. Sandstrom

Related entry: RURAL SOCIETY, LIFE IN.

GUIMARD, HECTOR (1867–1942), Art Nouveau architect, designer of the first Paris Métro entrances. Guimard was the major exponent of Art Nouveau in France. He was born in Lyons in 1867 and educated at the Paris Ecole des arts décoratifs (1882–85) and the Ecole des beaux-arts (1885–89),leaving the latter before finishing his diploma. He built the Electricity Pavilion at the Exposition universelle of 1889. He was influenced by Eugène Viollet-le-Duc's neomedievalism and romantic rationalism, by the English arts and crafts movement, and by the Art Nouveau architecture of Victor Horta in Belgium. Through a series of suburban villas and apartment houses in and around Paris, Guimard developed his characteristic brand of Art Nouveau, featuring the juxtaposition of various building materials (rough and smooth stone, brick, iron, glass), the curving of brick and stone surfaces and of decorative elements to accord with natural forms (flower and plant motifs), asymmetrical composition, and the exposure of the iron support structure on the finished building. In 1895 Guimard developed his mature style in an apartment house in Auteuil, the Castel Béranger, for which he received a prize from the city of Paris. There followed many commissions, notably for a private concert hall (Humbert de Romans, built 1897–1901, demolished 1905), for a shop and dwelling in Lille (Maison Coilliot, 1898–1900), and for some ninety entrances to the new Paris Métro (1899–1905), of which about sixty are now extant. In 1909 he married an American painter, Adeline Oppenheim.

During the interwar period, Guimard continued to build apartment houses and to participate in the Salons and international exhibitions, but his simple, unremarkable postwar style had little impact. He received the Legion of Honor in 1929. He emigrated to New York in 1938 and died there in 1942.

F. Borsi and E. Godoli, *Paris 1900* (New York, 1977); *Hector Guimard* (New York, 1978).

T. Shapiro

Related entries: ARCHITECTURE AND URBAN PLANNING; ART NOU-VEAU; JOURDAIN; SAUVAGE.

GUYAU, JEAN-MARIE (1854–1888), social theorist. Guyau's dominant passion was to restore broken intellectual connections—between aesthetics and sociology, religious faith and scientific fact, individuality and solidarity. His ultimate goal was the synthesis of a new social morality appropriate to a secular and scientific age.

Chronic illness lent poignancy to Guyau's emphasis on the principle of life—both in its intensity and its expansiveness—as the basis of his moral and aesthetic philosophy. What Guyau accomplished during his brief period of productivity is astonishing in both volume and versatility. In his popular and influential *Esquisse d'une morale sans obligation ni sanction* (1884), he tried to demonstrate that the development of an instinct of moral obligation is part of the normal development of organic life; morality is thereby detached from metaphysical and religious doctrines and reestablished on the more solid foundation of scientific fact. In his aesthetic writings, Guyau suggested that aesthetic feelings may be transmitted to other people through vibrations similar to those of molecules of matter. Thus art can become a basis for social harmony through its capacity for communicating sympathy and sociability.

Guyau opened up more paths of thought than he had time to explore himself. More than any other French thinker of his day, he helped to reunite the concepts of beauty and utility, which had been divorced by neo-Kantians and advocates of art for art's sake. By doing so, Guyau made possible an appreciation of forms of beauty mediated through modern technology, and his theories on the communication of aesthetic experience opened up many possible relationships between aesthetic thought and theories of psychology and sociology.

G. Aslan, *La Morale selon Guyau* (Paris, 1906); A. Fouillée, *La Morale, l'art et la religion d'après Guyau*, 4th ed. (Paris, 1901); F. J. W. Harding, *Jean-Marie Guyau (1854-1888), Aesthetician and Sociologist* (Geneva, 1973).

R. H. Williams

H

HALEVY, DANIEL (1872–1962), historian, literary critic. He was born in Paris, the son of Ludovic Halévy, a playwright, and the younger brother of Elie Halévy, an eminent scholar. He was educated at the lycée Condorcet and the Ecole des langues orientales. He wrote for literary magazines from an early age and prepared studies and translations of the works of Friedrich Nietzsche and Hendrik Ibsen. He had a wide circle of friends among the artistic and intellectual elite of his day.

His active support for the vindication of Alfred Dreyfus led him into contact with left-wing intellectuals, notably Charles Péguy and Georges Sorel. Attracted to the democratic socialism of Jean Jaurès, he embarked on a study of its sources, which culminated in his *Essais sur le mouvement ouvrier en France* (1901). He contributed to Péguy's *Cahiers de Quinzaine* and obtained financial backing for the socialist newspaper, *L'Humanité*. But Halévy became progressively disillusioned with socialist ideology. While highly sympathetic to the cause of the working class, he believed that socialism contained authoritarian tendencies that would ultimately undermine its idealism.

His work during the interwar years reflects the libertarian viewpoint of his maturity. His brilliant studies of the early years of the Third Republic—*La Fin des notables* (1930) and *La République des ducs* (1937)—are sympathetic to government by elites. But even his faith in old-fashioned liberalism eroded as the end of the Third Republic drew near. He expressed interest in corporatist ideas during the 1930s and defended Philippe Pétain on the fall of Vichy in 1944.

A. Silvera, *Daniel Halévy and His Times* (Ithaca, N.Y., 1966).

M. Chase

Related entries: HALEVY, E.; HALEVY, L.; JAURES; PEGUY.

HALEVY, ELIE (1870–1937), historian and philosopher. He was born at Etretat (Seine-Inférieure) on 6 September 1870, the son of the playwright Ludovic Halévy. He was educated at the lycée Condorcet and the Ecole normale supérieure. He passed his *agrégation* in philosophy and earned his *doctorat ès lettres* in 1900. He became a professor at the Ecole libre des sciences politiques in 1898, where he taught British civilization and the history of labor and of socialism.

Halévy is best known for his monumental *History of the English People in the Nineteenth Century*, which he published in six volumes between 1913 and 1932. It is regarded as one of the most comprehensive studies in this field. His *Growth of Philosophical Radicalism* (3 vols., 1901–4), which analyzes the thought and influence of Jeremy Bentham and his followers, is also viewed as a classic. Halévy believed England to be the best example of a progressive, liberal society, a model against which revolutionary and reactionary alternatives compared unfavorably. Highly respected by English scholars, he was a close friend of Ernest Barker, Graham Wallas, Beatrice and Sidney Webb, Barbara and John Hammond, Bertrand Russell, and H. A. L. Fisher.

Halévy was actively involved in the intellectual life of his own country. With Xavier Léon, he founded and edited two scholarly journals, *Revue de metaphysique et de morale* (1893) and *Société française de philosophie* (1901), both important forums for current methodological discussions of the social sciences as well as for analyses of practical social problems. Halévy and his collaborators (among them Léon, Alain, René Berthelot, Célestin Bouglé, and Léon Brunschvicg) hoped that their scholarly investigations would lead their generation to a more scientific understanding of contemporary philosophical and political issues. Halévy and his circle had close ties with the sociologists of the Durkheim school. Politically, Halévy was a republican; he had been a supporter of the cause of Alfred Dreyfus.

Halévy served in a military hospital during World War I. After the war, he was a member of a commission headed by Paul Renouvin to investigate its origins. During the interwar years, he supported the League of Nations and advocated the continuation of close diplomatic ties with Great Britain. One of his last works was *The Era of Tyrannies*, which warned of the similarities between bolshevism and fascism.

Halévy died at Sucy-en-Brie (Seine-et-Oise) on 21 August 1937. His projected continuation of his *History of the English People* was left undone, but some of his lectures on socialism were published posthumously as *Histoire du socialisme européen* (1948).

M. Chase, *Elie Halévy: An Intellectual Biography* (New York, 1980).

M. Chase

Related entries: ALAIN; BOUGLE; HALEVY, D.; HALEVY, L.; LEON.

HALEVY, LUDOVIC (1834–1903), playwright, novelist, librettist. He was the son of Léon Halévy, a writer, and the nephew of Jacques Halévy, a composer and well-known music teacher. Educated at the Lycée Louis-le-Grand, he spent a number of years rising to the post of *secrétaire-redacteur* of the Corps législatif and serving as aide to his friend, the duc de Morny, president of that assembly. At thirty-one he left government to earn his living writing musicals, something he had already done under pseudonyms with Jacques Offenbach and Hector Cremieux. For more than twenty years, he and Henri Meilhac wrote operettas, farces, and comedies, sometimes two or three a year, which were the toast of the Second Empire. They were broad and clever satires of society, very popular and very profitable. The most artistically successful of more than forty shows were *La Belle Hélène* (1864), *Barbe Bleue* (1866), and *Frou-Frou* (1869). With Georges Bizet in 1875, Halévy adopted Merimée's novel *Carmen*, his major contribution as a librettist.

Halévy's politics were liberal, close to those of Lucien-Anatole Prévost-Paradol, one of the leading thinkers of the Second Empire and Halévy's illegitimate brother. Among his friends were the leading figures of the Empire and the Third Republic, including Edgar Degas, Hippolyte Taine, and Marcellin and Philippe Berthelot. During the Franco-Prussian War, Ludovic wrote articles on the war later published as *L'Invasion*, which reveal the thoughtful, observant, and liberal side of a man famous for his wit and frivolity. His *Cahiers* of that same period are a major source for historians. The success of his novel *L'Abbé Constantin* (1882) brought his election to the Académie française in 1884. His sons, Daniel and Elie, became eminent scholars.

A. Silvera, *Daniel Halévy and His Times* (Ithaca, N.Y., 1966).

M. Chase

Related entries: HALEVY, D.; HALEVY, E.

HANOTAUX, GABRIEL (1853–1944), historian, civil servant, foreign minister, polemicist, and member of the Académie française. He was born 19 November 1853 in Beaurevoire in northeastern France. After his father died (1870) and Prussians occupied his home town (1871), he moved to Paris. There he entered the Ecole des hautes études and discovered a passion for history. Historian Henri Martin, a distant relative on his mother's side, helped him transfer to the Ecole des chartes, where Hanotaux earned a degree as archivist in paleography (1880), and to secure a position in the archives of the Quai d'Orsay. Thus Hanotaux began his career as historian and civil servant. In 1893, he won the Grand Prix Gobert for the first volume of his biography of Cardinal Richelieu. Volume 2, published in 1896, earned the author membership in the Académie française (1897).

In 1894, Hanotaux became the youngest man ever appointed foreign minister; he was to hold the position longer than any of his predecessors: from 30 May 1894 until 1 November 1895 and from 2 April 1896 to 28 June 1898. Although he had served briefly as deputy from the Aisne in the Chamber elected in 1886, he was the only cabinet member who held no seat in the Chamber of Deputies. This weakened his position within the cabinet, as did the fact that, during his first month in office, he opposed the government's decision to prosecute Captain Alfred Dreyfus. His position was nevertheless strong because he was a thorough professional. He was not asked to stay on in the Radical cabinet organized by Léon Bourgeois in November 1895, although there is little doubt that the presence of a moderate like Hanotaux would have strengthened that government.

As foreign minister, Hanotaux presided over the most crucial period in the partition of Africa. With respect to Madagascar, Tunis, and West Africa, he was spectacularly successful. But on the issue he considered the most important, the Egyptian question, he failed. A French challenge to British domination of Egypt and of the Upper Nile, the Marchand expedition, led to the Fashoda crisis and to the end of Hanotaux's public career. From 1898 until he died in 1944, Hanotaux published numerous studies on contemporary history and tracts on the virtues of colonial expansion.

C. M. Andrew and A. S. Kanya-Forstner, "Gabriel Hanotaux, the Colonial Party and the Fashoda Strategy," in E. F. Penrose, ed. *European Imperialism and the Partition of Africa* (London, 1975); Peter Grupp, *Theorie der Kolonial-expansion und Methoden der imperialistischen Aussenpolitik bei Gabriel Hanotaux* (Frankfurt, 1972); A. A. Heggoy, *The African Policies of Gabriel Hanotaux* (Athens, Ga., 1972); T. M. Iiams, Jr., *Dreyfus, Diplomatists and the Dual Alliance* (Geneva and Paris, 1962).

A. A. Heggoy

Related entries: CARNOT; CASIMIR-PERIER; DELCASSE; DREYFUS AFFAIR; DUPUY; FASHODA INCIDENT; FAURE, F.; MARCHAND EXPEDITION; MELINE; RIBOT.

HENRIOT, PHILIPPE (1889–1944), right-wing politician. An English teacher from a Catholic college in Bordeaux, Henriot entered political life in 1925 in association with the conservative deputy from the Gironde, Daniel Bergey. He became vice-president of the conservative Fédération républicaine in 1932, when he was elected deputy from the Gironde. A member of the Jeunesses patriotes and contributor to the right-wing weekly *Gringoire*, Henriot soon became one of the acknowledged leaders of the extreme Right. Although his political ideas were nebulous, he was a forceful and effective public speaker and a favorite orator at right-wing rallies. Henriot came to national prominence by his savage attacks on the government's handling of the Stavisky riots and his impassioned defense of the extra-parliamentary leagues. After his reelection in 1936, he was outspoken in his opposition to the Popular Front and its foreign policy. An arch-appeaser, he denounced Czechoslovakia as a worthless ally and welcomed the 1938 Munich Accords. With the collapse of the Popular Front, his views changed and in September 1939 he advocated a firm stance against Adolf Hitler. After France's defeat, he rallied wholeheartedly to the Vichy regime, joined the Milice, and became famous for his pro-government radio broadcasts. He was executed by the Resistance in 1944.

J. Debû-Bridel, *L'Agonie de la Troisième République* (Paris, 1948); P. Henriot *Le 6 février* (Paris, 1934); W. D. Irvine, *French Conservatism in Crisis* (Baton Rouge, 1979);

F. Korber, "Philippe Henriot, 1940–1944," Memoire de maîtrise, Université de Paris (Paris, 1973); J.-P. Maxence, *Histoire de dix ans* (Paris, 1939).

W. D. Irvine

Related entries: BORDEAUX; CONSERVATISM; FASCISM; FEBRUARY RIOTS; STAVISKY AFFAIR.

HERR, LUCIEN (1864–1926), Dreyfusard, socialist, influential librarian of the Ecole normale supérieure. The son of an Alsatian primary school teacher who sided with France in 1870, Lucien Herr entered the Ecole normale supérieure in 1883 and three years later passed the philosophy *agrégation*. Yet he kept his distance from the idealist philosophy prevailing in the university and became instead something of a positivist. He was a complex man who loved music and admired Maurice Barrès before the Dreyfus affair but scorned rhetorical and literary studies. After a year of study and travel in Germany and Russia, in 1888 he took the post of librarian at the Ecole normale, where he remained until his death in 1926. Here he played a strategic role as a librarian in the narrow sense, as an academic and political mentor to generations of *normaliens*, and as a colleague of numerous professors, administrators, writers, and politicians. He made the library's collection reflect his own preference for scientific erudition, and his immense learning and scientific attitude had their effect on students who sought his advice. Thus he shared responsibility with men like Ernest Lavisse, Gustave Lanson, and Louis Liard for the scientific spirit of the *nouvelle* Sorbonne.

During the Dreyfus affair, Herr was largely responsible for coordinating the collection of signatures of professors and writers in favor of a new trial for Alfred Dreyfus, and in the library of the Ecole normale he often presided over discussions of the case with students and visitors such as Charles Péguy and Jean Jaurès. The *normaliens* rallied almost unanimously to the cause. Herr also recruited a significant minority of the *normaliens* to the Socialist party. Although he usually kept well out of the limelight, he was a friend and adviser of Jaurès, Léon Blum, and other socialist politicians. He expressed his anticlericalism, antimilitarism, and anti-imperialism in hundreds of short articles that appeared (often under a pseudonym) in left-wing journals. During the First World War, Herr, like most other French socialists, joined the *Union sacrée*; he cooperated with the *normalien* minister of armaments, Albert Thomas, by giving advice concerning which scientists should be recruited for sensitive projects for the war effort. Although he never wrote his projected study of Hegel, his prestige as a savant was immense.

C. Andler, *Vie de Lucien Herr* (Paris, 1932); L. Herr, *Choix d'écrits* (Paris, 1932); D. Lindenberg and P. A. Meyer, *Lucien Herr, le socialisme, et son destin* (Paris, 1977).

R. J. Smith

Related entries: DREYFUS AFFAIR; SCHOOLS, HIGHER EDUCATION: ECOLE NORMALE SUPERIEURE; SOCIALISM, 1870-1914.

HERRIOT, EDOUARD (1872–1957), Radical-Socialist politician, educator, writer, statesman. Born in Troyes (Aube), Herriot completed his studies at the famed Ecole normale supérieure, where he earned the high degree of *agrégé* of letters (1893). After he had embarked on a teaching career at the Lycée Ampère at Lyons, his political curiosity was piqued by the events surrounding the Dreyfus affair. He became a member of the Radical-Socialist party on its founding in 1901, and, plunging into local politics, he was elected mayor of Lyons in 1905. He was subsequently elected senator in 1912 and served in the second Briand war cabinet (1916–17). Elected in 1919 as deputy from the Rhone, he soon became president of the Radical party, holding the post until resigning in 1935. Leading the opposition against the postwar Bloc national, he became the head of the Cartel des gauches and led it to electoral victory in 1924. As premier and foreign minister for nine months (June 1924–April 1925), Herriot found his government beset by complex financial and diplomatic problems concerning reparations, the Ruhr invasion, and the Dawes Plan that he was ill prepared to solve. Moreover, he failed to secure the confidence of French and international financial circles necessary to implement his domestic program. Defeated in the Senate, he ultimately served in Raymond Poincaré's cabinet for two years as minister of public instruction (July 1926–November 1928). He returned to power in 1932 following another Cartel victory, but his predominantly Radical ministry proved unable to deal with the economic depression beginning to affect France, and, again, he was distracted by international issues generated by the disarmament conference in Geneva, the reparations conference in Lausanne, and war debts payments to the United States. Defeated over the last issue in December 1932, Herriot ultimately returned after the riots of February 1934 to serve in the government of union and reconciliation organized by Gaston Doumergue. In 1936 Herriot was elected president of the Chamber of Deputies, serving with distinction until July 1940, when he presided over its last session under the Third Republic.

Herriot typified the men of goodwill of the Third Republic. His extensive literary ability, considerable forensic skills, legendary gourmandism, omnipresent pipe, and political moderation made him a popular figure in France during the interwar years.

F. de Tarr, *The French Radical Party from Herriot to Mendès-France* (London, 1961); E. Herriot, *Jadis*, 2 vols. (Paris, 1948–52); S. Jessner, *Edouard Herriot* (New York, 1974); P. Larmour, *The French Radical Party in the 1930's* (Stanford, Calif., 1964); S. Schuker, *The End of French Predominance in Europe* (Chapel Hill, N.C., 1976); J. Touchard, *La Gauche en France depuis 1900* (Paris, 1977).

J. E. Dreifort

Related entries: CARTEL DES GAUCHES; DALADIER; DOUMERGUE; GERMANY, RELATIONS WITH (1914–1940); LYONS; RADICAL AND RADICAL-SOCIALIST PARTY; RUHR OCCUPATION; RUSSIA, RELATIONS WITH; UNITED STATES, RELATIONS WITH.

HERVE, GUSTAVE (1871–1944), journalist, historian, and political activist. He enjoyed a long public career that took him from revolutionary internationalism to conservative nationalism. Born into a modest Breton family, he was the second child of a quartermaster sergeant in the French Navy. Educated during his early years at a communal Catholic school, he showed unusual academic promise. When the local church schools were closed in 1882, Hervé continued his education at the secular lycée of Brest with the help of scholarships. After a year's study at the Lycée Henri IV in Paris, he was compelled by financial need to begin his teaching career as a tutor in various provincial and Parisian schools (1890–97). Becoming an *agrégé d'histoire* in 1897, Hervé was promoted to teaching positions at the lycées of Rodez, Alençon, and finally Sens in 1899. A socialist by 1898, he joined the Yonne Federation of Socialist Workers and undertook an active campaign of antimilitarism and contributed regularly to the *Travailleur socialiste* and *Pioupiou de l'Yonne* under the pseudonym "Sans Patrie" (1900–1901). His forceful articles attacking patriotism and military service soon attracted attention from all sides. His most celebrated writing, "The Anniversary of Wagram" (first published in July 1901), spoke of planting the flag in a dung heap, a phrase that made him notorious. By February 1901, he was prosecuted for antimilitarism but was acquitted thanks to the eloquence of his lawyer, Aristide Briand. Two similar efforts by the state to convict him failed in 1902 and 1903. Hervé was nonetheless suspended from teaching at Sens in June 1901 and after further hearings was dismissed in December. His efforts to spread his message throughout the Yonne earned him the title "traveling salesman of socialism." Attacks on him by conservatives and patriots in the local and Parisian press, as well as denunciations in the Chamber of Deputies, won him both national notoriety and a wide audience. In 1902 and 1903 he served as a delegate to the national congresses of the Socialist party of France (PSF), where he advanced his radical antimilitarism and denounced Alexandre Millerand's participation in a "bourgeois" government. Differences with the national organization caused him to found an independent socialist federation in the Yonne. By 1905 Hervé had established himself as a major figure in French socialism such that he was made a member of the five-man national unification commission of the newly founded Socialist party (SFIO). By now the eloquent spokesman for Hervéism, a mixture of antimilitarism, antiparliamentarism, insurrectionism, and antipatriotism, Hervé expressed his views in *Leur patrie* (1905), *Instruction civique* (1910), and his weekly newspaper *La Guerre sociale*, founded in 1906. Active in the Association internationale antimilitariste formed in 1904, he was prosecuted in December 1905 for signing an inflammatory red poster calling recruits to resist military service. Thus began a series of prison terms that totaled twelve years by 1912. Hervé recounted his trials in *Mes crimes* (1912), which reprinted the articles and speeches made against the army.

Weary from his long detention and influenced by the growing world crisis, Hervé abandoned his strategy of working-class insurrection to prevent war and shifted to the defense of France as the home of revolution. This is evident from a speech given in 1912 and published as *Notre patrie*. That he sought peaceful resolution of conflicts with Germany is evident from his *Alsace-Lorraine* (1913), but with the world war, Hervé became an ardent patriot, even volunteering for military service despite his age and poor vision. In 1916 he changed the name of his newspaper to *La Victoire*. Calling for the military defeat of Germany, he also attacked governmental incompetence and left-wing defeatism at home. After the war he proposed the formation of a nationalist socialist party that would strengthen France, an effort he revived in 1927 when his Parti national socialiste was formed, but he met with little success. In 1935 he published *C'est Pétain qu'il nous faut*, which sought the creation of an authoritarian and corporate state headed by the old marshal. Returning to his original Catholic faith, Hervé hailed the church for its traditionalism and in such works as *La France qui meurt* (1924) deplored the low birthrate caused by unbelief. At first enthusiastic about Adolf Hitler, whom he considered an embodiment of his own ideas, Hervé sought to win the Nazi leader over to a peaceful policy toward France in his *France-Allemagne: Réconciliation ou la guerre* (1931), which called for revision of the Versailles Treaty. Gradually disillusioned with the führer, Hervé came to consider him a threat to peace and French security.

   With World War II Hervé once more became an ardent patriot and supported the national war effort. Remaining in Paris during the German blitzkrieg of 1940, he sought to continue publishing *La Victoire* after the Occupation but was prevented after three unauthorized issues appeared in June. Left without a public voice, he sought to reach his audience through clandestine letters that were also soon banned by the German occupier. With the liberation, Hervé wrote to General Charles de Gaulle requesting permission to resume newspaper publication, claiming that he had begun the Resistance, but once again he was rebuffed. Hervé died forgotten or held in contempt by all but a few loyal followers, who published his *Epîtres de Gustave Hervé aux croyants* (1949) in his memory.

   V. Méric, *A Travers la jungle politique et littéraire* (1930); M. R. Scher, "The Antipatriot as Patriot: A Study of the Young Gustave Hervé, 1871–1905" (Ph.D. dissertation, University of California, Los Angeles, 1972).

                                                                                     J. Friguglietti
Related entries: ANTIMILITARISM; BRIAND; MILLERAND; PETAIN.

HISTORIOGRAPHY: *ANNALES* SCHOOL. The *Annales* school refers to the historians and social scientists whose work has been identified with the methods, approaches, and interests represented by the journal *Annales d'histoire économique et sociale*, founded by Lucien Febvre and Marc Bloch in 1929. Actually one cannot speak of an *Annales* school in the Third Republic. The journal was largely the creation of Febvre and Bloch who at the time were colleagues at the University of Strasbourg and only in the 1930s were able to transfer the journal to Paris after Febvre received a chair at the Collège de France and Bloch one at the Sorbonne. The challenge that the journal represented to the traditional narrative history of political events became a significant force in French scientific life only after World War II with the formation of the interdisciplinary Sixth Section of the Ecole pratique des hautes études in 1946 (since 1975 the Ecole des hautes études en sciences sociales), which became the home of the journal, now conceived as its new name, *Annales: Economies,* *sociétés, civilisations* suggested, as an organ for the study of all aspects of culture—except perhaps politics.

The discussions that led to the founding of the journal go back to the turn of the century. A number of sociologists (Emile Durkheim and François Simiand), geographers (Paul Vidal de la Blache), philosophers of history (Paul Lacombe), and historians (Henri Pirenne) began to question the methodology and conceptual framework of the scientific school of historiography, represented in France by Gabriel Monod, Ernest Lavisse, Charles Seignobos, and Charles Langlois, with its exclusive reliance on documents, its focus on politics, and its chronological recounting of events. History as a science, the critics held, must transcend pure narration of events and formulate questions that establish the relationship between these events. History, like all other sciences, must proceed with theoretical assumptions that are very different from the assumptions of natural science in taking into account the elements of uniqueness and nonrecurrence in all historical situations. Henri Berr in 1900 established the journal *Revue de synthèse historique*, an important forerunner of the *Annales*, dedicated to the discussion of the theoretical aspects of history and to the integration of history and the various social and humanistic sciences. Lucien Febvre became a collaborator of the journal in 1907, Marc Bloch in 1912. Febvre's doctoral thesis, "Philippe II et la Franche Comté" published in 1912, reflected the new concern to move from an event-oriented narrative history to an analysis of social structures in their historical context. Febvre here attempted the history of a region that explored the political struggles between nobility and bourgeoisie in the context of the Reformation but linked this conflict with a broad examination of economic, demographic, and cultural factors. The theoretical presuppositions of Febvre's approach were spelled out in his *La Terre et l'évolution humaine* in 1922 (prefaced by Henri Berr), in which he observed that historians conventionally had been interested only in the development of "the political, legal, and constitutional framework of the peoples of the past or the military and diplomatic events." The task now was to be "interested in the whole life of these peoples, in the material and moral culture, the total development of their sciences, arts, beliefs, industries, trade, social divisions and groupings."

It is important to keep in mind that the *Annales* historians have been concerned not only with material life (*vie matérielle*) but also with "mentalities" (*mentalités*). Febvre's great works,—his *Martin Luther: Un destin* (1928) and especially his *Le Problème de l'incroyance au XVIᵉ siècle: La Religion de Rabelais* (1942)— are works of intellectual history but do not attempt a history of ideas in the manner of Friedrich Meinecke or Benedetto Croce but seek to analyze an intellectual climate, a mentality, and to work out particularly the structure of thought of an age as reflected in what Febvre called its "mental tools" of concepts and language. Bloch's first major work, *Les Rois thaumaturges* (1924), is similarly an attempt to deal with collective mentality, the place of the popular belief in the miraculous healing power of the kings in the medieval conception of kingship. In his *Les Caractères originaux de l'histoire rurale* (1931), Bloch, in contrast to conventional agrarian histories, proceeded not from legal and institutional relationships but from agriculture as it had been practiced and took into consideration data on field patterns, cropping systems, and farming techniques in order to reconstruct a social history of agriculture since the Middle Ages. In his great synthesis, *La Société féodale* (1939–40), Bloch went beyond the conventional attempts to examine feudalism as a system of military, legal, and possibly economic relationships of dependence to a reconstruction of what he called a "total social ambiance," recreating the social climate and the mental structure of the time in which modes of work and thought and relations of domination and dependence were closely interwoven.

Febvre and Bloch began their fruitful collaboration when they became colleagues at the newly liberated University of Strasbourg. The journal was the outcome of careful planning, involving also the Belgian social historian Henri Pirenne. From the beginning the journal was intended as an alternative to the staid scholarship that focused narrowly on political, military, and diplomatic history. Bloch and Febvre were committed to writing about history from a more comprehensive perspective by studying the relationship between politics, society, culture, and psychology. The *Annales* are not characterized by any one approach. What makes the journal interesting is its many sides. It pursued Bloch's interests in agrarian structures and devoted space to the history of science and technology but remained interested at all times in the close relationship between economic and social history and the history of mentalities. The *Annales* followed with particular interest the beginnings of quantitative economic history, but its pages also reflected such anthropological interests as the significance of magic in European history.

The basic concerns of the later *Annales* were very much present in the 1930s. So was the interest in international scholarship and the attempt to make the *Annales* into a forum for international discussions in modern social history. Yet the *Annales* represented a minority orientation at the French universities in the late days of the Third Republic. The war—in which Marc Bloch lost his life as a member of the Resistance—may have contributed to the reorientation of historiographical thinking. With the establishment of the Sixth Section of the Ecole pratique des hautes études in 1946, the *Annales*, now directed by Febvre and renamed *Annales: Economies, sociétés, civilisations*, a title that more correctly reflected its interests, had a firm institutional basis. The Sixth Section made possible a collaboration among historians, economists like Ernest Labrousse, anthropologists including Claude Lévi-Strauss and Paul Bourdieu, and sociologists like Georges Friedmann.

The borderline between history and the various human sciences was blurred as history in France increasingly became a social science but a social science that maintained a pronounced humanistic core. *Annales* historiography has been marked by a pluralism of methods since World War II. The 1950s and 1960s were marked by a strong interest in the effect of quantifiable economic and demographic movements (*conjonctures*) on society and a relative neglect of political history. Fernand Braudel, Febvre's successor as director of the Sixth Section and author of the multidimensional synthesis, *La Mediterranée et le monde mediterranéen à l'époque de Philippe II* (1949), laid the basis in the *Annales* for an extensive study of material life, which combined quantification with qualitative description. Others, such as Emmanuel Le Roy Ladurie in his *Paysans du Languedoc* (1966) and *Montaillou; Village occitan* (1975), linked economic and social history with the analysis of popular consciousness. It is difficult to define the limits of *Annales* historiography. *Annales* historians have sought to apply the methods of social history to a large variety of facets of human existence, including basic existential concerns such as sexuality and death, which had previously been considered to lie outside the domain of historical scholarship.

L. Allegra and A. Torre, *La Nascita della storia sociale in Francia dalla Commune alle "Annales"* (Torino, 1977); H. S. Hughes, *The Obstructed Path: French Social Thought in the Years of Desperation 1930–1960* (New York, 1966); G. G. Iggers, *New Directions in European Historiography* (Middletown, Conn., 1975); T. Stoianovich, *French Historical Method: The Annales Paradigm* (Ithaca, N.Y., 1976).

G. G. Iggers

Related entries: BERR; BLOCH; DURKHEIM; FEBVRE.

HO CHI MINH (1890–1969), most prominent of Vietnam's nationalist leaders and communist revolutionary. Several times changing his name, and calling himself Ho Chi Minh only in 1945, Ho was born as Nguyen Tat Thanh in central Vietnam, the son of a mandarin. His father was part of the nationalist resistance to the French, common among the traditional educated elite in Vietnam at the turn of the century, and was dismissed from his post by the colonial authorities. Exposed to Western education, Ho received no diploma but was qualified to become a village teacher. Shunning such a career, he left Vietnam, working on board a French ship as a mess boy. In 1917 he arrived in France.

Ho came into contact with socialists such as Jean Longuet and adhered to the Socialist party. He made a living as a photographer's apprentice and as a decorator of imitation Chinese antiques. Fired with enthusiasm by the Bolshevik revolution, he seems—if one is to believe his testimony forty years later—to have been won over to Leninism by reading the Russian leader's *Theses on the National and Colonial Questions*, which *L'Humanité* reprinted. In 1920 Ho was struck by Lenin's notion that the struggle of the proletariat against capitalism and of the colonies for national independence was the same single struggle, each aiding the other. At the Congress of Tours, he sided with the majority in transforming the Socialist party into the French Communist party.

While strongly wedded to the idea of independence, Ho Chi Minh originally seems to have favored a program of political reform. In 1919 when the Peace Conference met at Versailles, he drafted a petition of eight points seeking Vietnamese representation in the French parliament, freedom of press and assembly, and other political freedoms. His appeal went unheeded. In Paris, he wrote for *L'Humanité*, *La Vie ouvrière*, and the anticolonial protest paper, *Le Paria*. By late 1923 he was in Moscow and as a Comintern agent traveled to China and Thailand. In Canton he organized the forerunner of the Indochina Communist party, the Association of Vietnamese Revolutionary Youth. The growth of several separate Communist factions in Vietnam led the Comintern to ask Ho Chi Minh to coordinate and unite them into a single political party, the Indochina Communist party, in 1930.

The popular uprising in 1929–30 by the Vietnamese Nationalist party (VNQDD), a group patterned after the Chinese Kuomintang, led to severe French repression. As a result the strongest non-Communist nationalist group was eliminated and— it has been averred—the only viable nationalist movement remaining was the better organized and more clandestine Indochina Communist party.

The outbreak of World War II and the Japanese occupation of Indochina in 1940 opened new opportunities for Ho Chi Minh, who returned to Vietnam in December 1940 after an absence of twenty-eight years and started a struggle that was to lead to Vietnam's independence.

L. Figuères, *Ho Chi Minh—notre Comarade* (Paris, 1970); J. Lacouture, *Ho Chi Minh— A Political Biography* (New York, 1968); B. B. Fall, ed., *Ho Chi Minh in Revolution, Selected Writings, 1920–1966* (New York, 1967)

W. B. Cohen

Related entries: COMMUNIST PARTY; OVERSEAS EMPIRE: SOUTHEAST ASIA; SOCIALIST PARTY.

HOARE-LAVAL PLAN (December 1935), a proposal by the British and French foreign ministers to recognize Italian territorial conquest in Ethiopia. On 3 October 1935 Benito Mussolini's Italy attacked Ethiopia in violation of the Covenant of the League of Nations. Mussolini's action placed the ministry of Pierre Laval in an awkward situation. Laval attached great importance to maintaining a Franco-Anglo-Italian front against Nazi Germany. Yet France had little choice but to join England in voting economic sanctions against the aggressor nation, the application of which risked alienating Italy from the West. The Hoare-Laval plan represented an effort to appease the Italians and thus maintain the anti-German coalition. Laval and Sir Samuel Hoare met in Paris in December 1935 and devised a scheme that would have given Italy some two-thirds of Abyssinia and a virtual protectorate over the rest. Evidence suggests that Mussolini might have welcomed such a solution. The popular indignation in both France and England that followed premature revelation of this proposal, however, forced its withdrawal and Hoare's immediate resignation. The Laval ministry shakily survived for another month. Historians have variously assessed Laval's role regarding fascist Italy, yet the failure of the Hoare-Laval proposal accelerated Mussolini's alienation from the other Western powers and assured the Third Republic's deepening diplomatic dependence on England.

G. Baer, *Test Case: Italy, Ethiopia and the League of Nations* (Stanford, Calif., 1976); H. de Lagardelle, *Mission à Rome: Mussolini* (Paris, 1955).

W. I. Shorrock

Related entries: ITALY, RELATIONS WITH; LAVAL.

HONEGGER, ARTHUR (1892–1955), major twentieth-century composer, conductor, and critic. He was born in Le Havre (Seine-Inférieure) on 10 March 1892, the son of Swiss parents. Interested in music at an early age, he spent two years steeped in German romanticism at the Zurich Conservatory before entering the Paris Conservatory in 1911. There and in private study with Charles Marie Widor and Vincent d'Indy, he was introduced to French impressionism.

Because of his friendship with his classmate Darius Milhaud, Honegger temporarily became part of the group of young followers of Erik Satie, Les Six. During the early 1920s, however, he gradually drifted away from their austere modernism and developed his own musical aesthetic. Convinced that a composer must both appeal to the tastes of a mass audience and make use of new musical discoveries, Honegger tried to be progressive but not unintelligible. He hoped to rejuvenate older familiar forms by infusing them with contemporary harmonic and rhythmic techniques. More a craftsman than an innovator, he admired Richard Wagner and Claude Debussy; his works had strong emotional undertones.

Honegger wrote for all musical genres but was especially interested in large-scale choral works and orchestral pieces. His most popular oratorio was *King David* (1921), which blended strong echoes of Handel and Bach with the stirring polytonalities of his day. Among his orchestral works, the short *Pacific 231* (1923) was hailed by audiences for its striking image of a speeding locomotive and by later scholars for its rendering in musical terms of the futurists' fascination with motion and machinery. Though most of his compositions were for the concert hall, he also wrote over thirty film scores. He died in Paris after a long illness, on 27 November 1955.

R. Myers, *Modern French Music* (New York, 1971); R. Shead, *Music in the 1920s* (New York, 1976).

P. V. Meyers

Related entries: DEBUSSY; IMPRESSIONISM; SATIE; SIX, LES; STRAVINSKY.

HUGO, VICTOR (1802-1885), poet, novelist, playwright, statesman, humanitarian; member of the French Academy. On 5 September 1870, one day after the proclamation of the Third Republic and after nineteen years of exile, Victor Hugo triumphantly returned to Paris where he was greeted by Georges Clemenceau, then mayor of the Eighteenth Arrondissement. One month later, the first French edition of *Les Châtiments*, a collection of poems critical of Napoleon III, sold out its first printing of 5,000 copies in two days. By the end of October 1870, 13,000 copies had been printed and sold. On 8 February 1871 Hugo was elected to the National Assembly as a delegate from Paris and left immediately for Bordeaux where he sat with the republican minority. By 8 March he had resigned from the Assembly because of the unseating of Garibaldi, which Hugo took as a personal offense in view of his longstanding support of the Italian statesman-soldier.

After a brief voluntary exile in Belgium and Luxembourg, Hugo returned to Paris and again stood for election to the Assembly in January 1872. In part because of his sympathy for the communards, he was defeated. On 28 April Hugo published *L'Année terrible*, a collection of poems evoking the French defeat in the Franco-Prussian War, the siege of Paris, and the Commune. In 1874, Hugo's last novel, *Quatrevingt-treize* [*sic*], a fictional treatment of the Vendéen insurrection during the Revolution, was published in Paris. On 30 January 1876 Hugo was elected to the Senate, where he would plead for amnesty for the communards and speak out against the death penalty. In 1877 Hugo published the second series of *La Légende des siècles*, which, along with the first series published in 1859 and the third series that appeared in 1883, illustrates the progress of the human conscience in a series of epic poems. Also published in 1877 were *L'Art d'être grand-père*, a collection of lyric poems celebrating the purity and innocence of children and childhood, based to a large extent on Hugo's observation of his grandchildren, and the first part of *L'Histoire d'un crime*, a polemical work describing the coup d'état of 2 December 1851. Together with the second part, published in March, *L'Histoire* proved immensely successful.

On 4 April 1879 Hugo moved to 130 avenue d'Eylau (today avenue Victor-Hugo) where he lived until the time of his death. On 27 December 1880, the city of Besançon unveiled a plaque marking the birthplace of Victor Hugo, and on 27 February 1881, public officials and private citizens paraded in front of Hugo's home on the avenue d'Eylau to mark the poet's eightieth birthday. In May 1883, Juliette Drouet, the woman whom Hugo had called his "true wife" and who had been his mistress and companion for over fifty years, died, leaving the poet grief-stricken and anxious for his own death. Hugo himself died on 22 May 1885. His body lay in state under the Arc de Triomphe where it attracted enormous crowds. After a secular state funeral, Hugo's body was buried in the Panthéon.

An important number of Hugo's works were published posthumously, including *La Fin de Satan* and *Le Théâtre en liberté* (both 1886), *Choses vues* (1887 and 1899), *Toute la lyre* (1888 and 1893), and *Dieu* (1891). Despite Hugo's unquestioned popularity, his literary status was often questioned by younger writers whose aesthetic practices were markedly different from his own. As a result, Hugo's works knew a period of relative eclipse even as they became a standard part of the school curriculum.

J. Gaudon, ed., *La Légende des siècles*, by V. Hugo (Paris, 1975); C. Gély, *Hugo et sa fortune littéraire* (Bordeaux, 1970); J. P. Houston, *Victor Hugo* (New York, 1974); P. de Lacretelle, *La Vie politique de Victor Hugo* (Paris, 1928); H. Meschonnic, *Ecrire Hugo* (Paris, 1977); M. Naudin, "Hugo et Camus face à la peine capitale," *Revue d'histoire littéraire de la France* 72 (1972); J. Richardson, *Victor Hugo* (New York, 1976); C. Roy, *Victor Hugo: Témoin de son siècle* (Paris, 1962).

B. T. Cooper

Related entries: COMMUNARDS: AMNESTY MOVEMENT FOR; FUNER-ALS, STATE; NOVEL, POLITICS AND THE.

HUGUES, CLOVIS (1851-1907), poet, journalist, and socialist politician. Born in Ménerbes (Vaucluse), he began his career in journalism and politics at an early age. Based in Marseilles, Hugues was actively involved in the republican fight against the Second Empire and also had a hand in the proclamation of the Republic on 4 September and in the 23 March proclamation of the Commune at Marseilles. In 1871, he was arrested and put in jail for the publication of a libelous article, "La Lettre de Marianne," in which he denounced wavering republicans as deserters. Much of Hugues' poetry was written during his stay in prison, with Victor Hugo as the model for his works. Released from prison in 1875, he returned to journalism in Marseilles and was married to Jeanne Royannez two years later. On 3 December 1877, he killed a Bonapartist adversary, Joseph Daime, in a duel over an apparent insult directed toward Mme. Hugues. He was acquitted of the crime on 22 February 1878.

In 1881, he was elected a deputy from the Bouches du Rhône for the second electoral district of Marseilles. As a deputy, Hugues was known for his forensic talents and his fiery and often sarcastic remarks. His eloquence and commitment to the cause made of Hugues an important figure in socialist meetings and congresses and among the Freemasons. Hugues was reelected in 1885 as a socialist but lost his seat in 1889 because of his loose affiliation with the Boulangist movement. Hugues then moved to Paris where in 1893 he was elected as deputy for the Nineteenth Arrondissement, a position he held until 1906. Hugues also ran in the 1904 senatorial elections in the Vaucluse but was not elected. In 1906, he chose not to renew his deputy's mandate. He died in Paris the following year. His poetic works include *Les Intransigéants, Poèmes de prison, Le Sommeil de Danton* and *Poésies socialistes.*

Grand Larousse encyclopédie (Paris, 1964); J. Jolly, ed., *Dictionnaire des parlementaires français, 1889–1940*, Vol. 6 (Paris, 1970); J. Maitron, ed. *Dictionnaire du mouvement ouvrier*, Vol. 13 (Paris, 1975); T. Zeldin, *France, 1848–1945* (London, 1973).

A. J. Staples

Related entries: BOULANGER AFFAIR; HUGO; SOCIALISM, 1870-1914.

I

IMMIGRATION. European immigrants filled the labor shortages due to declining population growth and the First World War. From 1870 to 1914, the foreign population increased slowly, from 655,036 or 1.7 percent of France in 1866 to 1,159,835 or 2.8 percent in 1911. From 82 percent to 90 percent of these immigrants originated in nations bordering France. Until the 1880s, Belgians (mostly of Flemish origin) and Germans predominated, but thereafter Italians and Spanish immigrants grew more important. Most immigrants settled in departments near the frontier or in Paris. By 1911, foreigners comprised 30 percent of the southeastern department of Alpes Maritimes and 11 percent of the Nord, which faced Belgium. Smaller numbers migrated to the regions of the Pyrenees and Moselle. Seven percent of Paris (1911) was non-French. While many were skilled artisans (especially in Paris), immigrants found jobs mostly in heavy industry, comprising 18 percent of the metallurgical, 10 percent of the chemical, and 9 percent of the construction work forces (1906). Belgian commuters (*frontaliers*) were important in the textile industry of the Lille region, as were Italian and Spanish seasonal farm workers in the south. None of the repeated efforts of both conservatives and leftists to restrict immigration was successful due to the political dominance of advocates of laissez-faire. Labor organizations were ambiguous toward immigrants. Formally, unions expressed solidarity with immigrants but frequently opposed the influx of foreign labor into local job markets because they feared a deterioration of wages and working conditions. Riots against foreigners occurred from the 1880s, especially in the Nord and southeast.

From 1914 to 1918, in order to replace French workers mobilized for war, the government recruited foreign labor for war industries and agriculture. Because of the invasion of Belgium and Italy's entry into the war, France had to seek new sources of European immigration. France imported Greek refugees as well as southern Europeans; 216,512 European immigrants worked in France during the war. The government recruited 222,758 colonial subjects from North Africa,

Indochina, and Madagascar, as well as Chinese workers. Because of the war emergency, the government abandoned its laissez-faire policy and strictly regulated immigration, for example, by requiring special identity cards and channeling foreign workers into low paying jobs. These controls remained after the war. Local opposition to non-European immigrants prompted the government to repatriate them in 1919 and to restrict non-European immigration in the interwar period to a small number of North Africans.

The period 1918 to 1931 witnessed a massive immigration owing to the labor shortage due to war losses and the expansion of the French economy. The immigrant population reached 2,714,697 by 1931 (6.7 percent of France), an increase of 77 percent in ten years. Immigration from Belgium and Germany declined absolutely while Spanish and Italian immigration rose, the latter leading other nationalities with 808,038 residents in France by 1931. Much of the growth was due to a commercial labor recruiter, the General Immigration Society, which imported miners, farm workers, and other manual laborers from Poland and other Eastern European nations. Polish immigrants became the second largest nationality in France with 507,811 in 1931. Immigrants contributed to French economic growth, especially in the burgeoning industrial regions of the north, Lorraine, and suburban Paris. By 1931, immigrants constituted large proportions of the heavy industries avoided by the French, including mining (40 percent), metallurgy (35 percent), quarries (26 percent), construction (25 percent), and shipping (20 percent). The General Immigration Society recruited Poles heavily for the coal mines of the Nord-Pas-de-Calais. Farmers in the northeast hired Poles as day laborers; Italians and Spaniards replaced French as sharecroppers in the southwest (Garonne). Government regulated foreign entry and access to jobs in order to prevent domestic opposition. It restricted immigration during the recessions of 1921 and 1927 and required immigrants to obtain work authorizations from government labor exchanges; this channeled foreigners into jobs many French avoided. The dominant reformist labor movement, the Confédération générale du travail, accepted immigration but lobbied to regulate it in order to ensure French priority in employment. The communist-dominated labor movement, the Confédération générale du travail unitaire, supported equality of opportunity for immigrants, but foreigners who joined the communists were subject to deportation. Although parliament reduced the requirements for naturalization in order to encourage assimilation in 1927, only 11 percent of the foreign population was naturalized by 1931.

From 1931 to 1940, immigration declined sharply due to the depression; foreigners suffered a disproportionate loss of jobs. Because of repatriations, the foreign population dropped to 2,198,236 by 1936. With the rise of French unemployment, anti-immigrant sentiment increased, producing legislation that imposed quotas on employing immigrants in selected industries (August 1932). The reluctance of French workers to take the more onerous and low-paying jobs that immigrants held prevented a more draconic purge of immigrants from the work force.

H. Bunle, "Mouvements migratoires entre la France et l'étranger," in *Statistique générale, Etudes et documents*, no. 4 (Paris, 1943); L. Chevalier, ed., *Documents sur l'immigration* (Paris, 1947); G. Cross, "Toward Social Peace and Prosperity: The Politics of Immigration in France during the Era of World War I," *French Historical Studies* 2 (1980); G. Mauco, *Les Etrangers en France* (Paris, 1932), A. Prost, "L'Immigration en France depuis cent ans," *Esprit*, no. 348 (1966).

G. S. Cross

Related entries: LABOR MOVEMENT; OVERSEAS EMPIRE: FRENCH IM-PERIALISM; POPULATION TRENDS; WORKERS, INDUSTRIAL.

IMPRESSIONISM, a style of painting in the final third of the nineteenth century characterized by vibrant colors, rapid brushstrokes, and a new treatment of light to achieve realistic depictions of optical responses. Paintings alive with primary colors and fleeting impressions; artists working in the open air, concerned more with atmosphere than text; observations of the world *sur le vif*—these traditional views capture the formalistic elements of impressionism, but the unique and innovative art of the 1870s and 1880s was all that and more.

In 1874, in Paris, the Société anonyme coopérative d'artistes, peintres, sculpteurs, graveurs, etc. held its first exhibition in Nadar's photography studio, an aptly modern locale. Thirty artists, including Claude Monet, Camille Pissarro, Auguste Renoir, Edgar Degas, and Paul Cézanne, displayed works that with their pure colors and rejection of historical, religious, and allegorical motifs, contrasted with the academic Salon paintings of the era. The shimmering sun and dissolving forms in Monet's *Impression, Sunrise*, reminiscent of J. M. W. Turner, led one critic to attack this and other "impressionistic" works in the exhibit. The label, at first derisive, has survived.

But, as one contemporary noted, impressionists did not "grow like mushrooms" overnight. Earlier in the century Barbizon artists had investigated color and light in natural settings; realists, with Gustave Courbet in the lead, had rejected the Salon and infuriated critics by filling immense canvases with scenes of workers, peasants, and petty bourgeois; and in the late 1850s and 1860s, Edouard Manet, the master and guiding force of early impressionism, had committed Baudelaire's "modern life" to paint in *The Absinthe Drinker, Déjeuner sur l'herbe*, and *Olympia*. These were the avant-garde traditions from which impressionism emerged.

Despite stylistic affinities and close friendships, Manet refused to participate in the first exhibit. By the eighth and final show in 1886, Cézanne, Pissarro, and others had begun to probe new techniques and compositional structures we now define as neoimpressionist, postimpressionist, symbolist, and so on. The boundaries are arbitrary, the distinctions blurred, but it is well to limit studies of impressionism to the artists and works of the 1870s and 1880s.

Controversy centered on the dissolution of form, the artists' daring repudiation of carefully composed, finished tableaux. Impressionists renounced the academics' refined brushwork and opted for bold, seemingly spontaneous patches of juxtaposed colors. They wished to capture ephemeral movements of light, to translate onto canvas momentary visual sensations, and, in so doing, to penetrate reality further. In this sense, impressionism was realism heightened, and, as Courbet and Manet had learned from critics, realism was unacceptable because it was revolutionary.

Subject matter—cafés, theaters, railroads, boating parties, street scenes— provided an equally important leitmotif. Impressionism has been called an urban style because it described the sudden, transitory movements of city life. Paris was undergoing massive demographic, physical, and social change in the second half of the century, and impressionists (consciously or not) chronicled those transformations. Degas' dancers, jockeys, and café habitués (*Absinthe*, 1876), Monet's *Gare St. Lazare* series of the 1870s, and Renoir's Montmartre revelers (*Moulin de la Galette*, 1876) show that while individual artists concentrated on new formalistic principles, their works provide rich documentation of urban life and suburban leisure (Degas' *Carriage at the Races*, 1873; Renoir's *Boating Party*, 1881). Meanwhile, Pissarro and others moved beyond the city to the countryside where peasant work routines served as a visual contrast to urban industry (and fit well with Pissarro's brand of anarchism inspired by Pyotr Kropotkin). To be sure, form, technique, and design were of primary importance, but both the style and text of impressionism made it a quintessentially modern art.

The term *impressionism* has also been applied to music. The shifting, unfocused melodies of Claude Debussy, the contiguous units that make a whole in Maurice Ravel's compositions, may be broadly defined as impressionist, but a common set of artistic principles binding composers and painters into a cohesive movement did not exist, and the difficulties of subsuming music or literature in the impressionist group present more problems than benefits.

By the late 1880s, impressionism was being criticized from without and within as too superficial, too obsessed with the visual and decorative. A flight began that led Pissarro, briefly, to the scientific experiments of the pointillists, Cézanne back to Provence and the study of geometric motifs in nature, and Gauguin to Brittany and then Tahiti to probe "the mysterious centers of thought" he believed impressionists had ignored. This interiorization and subjectivism would distinguish the art of the new century.

Impressionism may be seen as the final, realistic investigation of the outside world, or as the first explosion of traditional forms leading to abstraction and the ongoing deemphasis of subject matter: the last of the old or the first of the new. It is fitting that 1886 marked two symbolic moments in the history of French art: the final impressionist exhibit and the arrival of Vincent Van Gogh in Paris.

E. Duranty, *La Nouvelle Peinture* (Paris, 1876); T. Duret, *Les Peintres Impressionistes* (Paris, 1878); L. Nochlin, *Impressionism and Post-Impressionism, 1874–1904* (Englewood Cliffs, N.J., 1966); J. Rewald, *The History of Impressionism* (Greenwich, Conn., 1973); L. Venturi, *Les Archives de l'impressionisme* (Paris and New York, 1939).

M. Burns

Related entries: ART: MAJOR STYLES AND MOVEMENTS; CEZANNE; DEBUSSY; DEGAS; GAUGUIN; MONET; PHOTOGRAPHY: CULTURAL USES; PISSARRO; POSTIMPRESSIONISM; RAVEL; RENOIR; SISLEY; SYMBOLISM; VAN GOGH.

INDUSTRY. Industrial advance was the highlight of economic progress under the Third Republic. The average annual rate of growth of industrial product and investment exceeded that of all other sectors, especially between 1896 and 1913 and during the 1920s. In the 1920s, industrial growth was higher in France than in any other European country. Industry was also the leading sector in a more dynamic, qualitative sense. Between 1880 and 1900 industrial investment replaced basic investment in construction, public works, and transport as the leading component of aggregate investment and as the most dynamic element of aggregate demand. Industry was the locus of innovation as well as of capitalization, which together enhanced overall productivity. A significant shift of working population to the industrial sector, notably to factory industry, and an increasing concentration of employment, capital, and production among firms within this sector indicated, moreover, the importance of this sector in the structural transformation of the Republican economy. The major role of industry in economic growth of this period is suggested in the common designation of the economically most progressive part of the Third Republic, the years 1896 to 1931, as the era of the second industrialization.

Industrial growth occurred differently, however, in different branches of industry. These differences have been analyzed according to a variety of schemas, the most common of which are these: the quantitative indexes of aggregate growth, especially size and rate of growth of output, value-added, investment, and productivity (notably labor productivity); capitalization and mechanization; concentration of labor and capital; and innovation. These schemas have been used to differentiate leading from trailing branches within the industrial sector, as well as to assess French industrial development comparatively with other periods and countries. Each schema will be used here as a means of delineating the various forms of industrial production under the Third Republic.

The pace of industrial expansion, in terms of output and productivity growth, was most rapid between 1896 and 1931, excepting the war years. Average annual growth rates of production in industry were above 2 percent during this period and reached even 4 to 5 percent between 1906 and 1913 and between 1924 and 1929. These rates distinguished this period from the earlier decades of the Republic (1870–96), when the average annual growth rate was below 2 percent, and from the 1930s, when industrial product declined absolutely. Labor productivity increased at an especially dramatic pace during the second industrialization, from a near 1 percent annual average rate of growth of output per person-hour before 1896 to 2 percent between 1896 and 1913, 3.4 percent between 1913 and 1929 (the pre-1950 record), and 2.9 percent between 1929 and 1938 (Carré et al.) This growth of product and productivity reflected a rise in rates of increase of domestic investment from 2.4 percent annual average between 1865 and 1869 and 1890 to 1894 to 3.3 percent between 1890 and 1894 and 1910 to 1913, a trend continued in the 1920s. Largely through such investment, innovation and mechanization spread throughout industry, explaining most of the increase in labor productivity. For instance, the quantity of horsepower (hp) in industry increased dramatically during the same period, from an annual average of 21,600 hp between 1863 and 1883 to a yearly average of 141,800 hp between 1903 and 1913, while the power of primary motors, including electrical generators, increased 14 percent per year between 1906 and 1931. The pace of mechanization during this period exceeded that of the United States and Britain and equaled that of Germany, probably reflecting France's significantly lesser utilization of mechanical techniques at the beginning of the period. French industry caught up, in short, with the industry of other major national economies during the second industrialization. Given the much slower growth of the labor force during the same years because of slow population growth, such productivity-raising investment also increased significantly the degree of substitution of capital for labor in industrial process, or capitalization.

The different branches of industry grew in a more or less constant manner over the period 1896 to 1931. Metallurgy, chemical manufacture, mechanical and electrical industries, and metal-working industries were the leading branches. Their rates of growth of output, productivity, and investment were above that of the industrial sector as a whole throughout this period. Some of the newer industries, such as rubber, oil, aluminum, and automobile manufacture, belong in this group as well. Branches with significantly lower rates of product growth were textiles, clothing and leather goods manufacture, and food processing. Productivity growth in the textile-clothing-leather group was significant but not remarkable; output per person-hour grew at 2.5 percent annual average between 1896 and 1929, slightly less than the total industry average of 2.7 percent. Within this group, however, there were differences in the evolution of investment and of its relation to productivity. Within textiles the growth of investment was not spectacular, despite the significant productivity increase; in food processing a sizable growth of investment did not yield a notable improvement of productivity. In mining the growth of output, sizable but not exceptional, contrasted sharply with the near stagnation of productivity. In coal mining, for instance, production grew at an average annual rate above 2 percent between 1880 and 1913, while productivity improved at a mere 0.2 percent rate. Metallurgy, metal-working, chemicals, and mechanical-electrical industries raised their proportional contributions to the total value-added—an index best reflecting structural change in the economy—while textiles, clothing and leather goods, food processing, and wood-working industries witnessed a stagnation or decline in their respective shares, along with construction and public works. In short, the branches of industry contributing most strongly to output and productivity growth were the capital goods producers, whereas the consumer goods producers of older vintage— the grand consumption industries, like textiles, whose growth highlighted nineteenth-century development—constituted something of a brake on overall growth of industry (Crouzet). Among the former, the part of the mechanical and electrical industries that included machinery manufacture was especially important. The growth rate of the mechanical industries was the highest in the group of industries studied by Crouzet for the period 1880 through 1913—5.7 percent— while Carré et al. assessed the contribution of the mechanical and electrical industries to overall investment growth as preeminent, largely through production of capital equipment.

The apparent homogeneity of growth patterns of each branch suggested by the above schema belies, however, important differences within particular branches. This becomes clearest in an examination of degrees of capitalization and mechanization. In textile manufacture, for instance, dualism remained a feature of productive methods and performance, as labor-intensive domestic and handicraft methods persisted alongside more capitalistic mechanized factory production. The difference between textile growth of this period and that of the first three-quarters of the nineteenth century was the rising importance, and indeed final victory, of capitalistic over labor-intensive methods in all categories of textile production. Between 1870 and 1913, for instance, the number of mechanical looms finally surpassed that of handlooms in the weaving of all textile fabrics, including silks. Moreover, an increasing share of output in this branch came from the largest firms and establishments, where the ratio of capital to labor was the highest; this was especially true in the cotton industry and in woolen spinning. In short, textiles experienced an important internal structural transformation in the direction of more capitalized, mechanized production, raising productivity at a higher rate than output. This transformation in some ways put the French textile industry on a ground reached by English and Belgian industry around 1850; it did not achieve the heights of contemporary German industry, however, with its very large establishments and capital structures. A similar process affected the clothing trades during the 1920s, although that transformation was both slower and less radical.

Another instance of differential internal growth was chemical manufacture. Here the dualism was evident not so much in competing production methods as in different destinies of categories of chemical manufacture in adapting to a more innovative, internationally competitive environment. Growth in this branch was more notable in some new areas, such as electrochemistry, than in basic chemicals and dyes, where French performance had once been superior. Production of inorganic chemicals was negligible, alkali production advanced from the Leblanc to the Solvay method during the 1880s but failed to take the next step to electrolytic methods after 1900 when these became current, and dye manufacture, once a respected preserve of French industry, capitulated to foreign (especially German and Swiss) competition even within France—largely, it has been argued, because of the too-close dependence of dyeing chemistry on textile manufacture. As a consequence, French chemical production rapidly fell behind that of foreign industry. Coal mining illustrated the most unusual growth pattern, one that on the surface seemed almost contradictory. Capitalization and mechanization promoted growth of productivity at a handsome rate in this sector between the 1860s and 1890s, when coal prices and profits were falling and when coal-using industries, such as railroads, were learning to economize on their coal consumption. After 1896, however, when prices began to rise, productivity growth stagnated; the rate of growth of output fell, despite rising demand for coal to fuel industrialization, reflected in rising coal imports. Coal-mining profits nevertheless reached record levels during this period as coal miners reaped the cost advantages of earlier efficiency-raising investment in a currently inflationary market. But tariffs, cartels, and geography—especially in the Nord and the Pas-de-Calais, the strongest coal-mining regions—also gave this branch several advantages of protection, of which it readily availed itself.

The third schema of differentiation, concentration, has two main dimensions: the concentration of workers, reflected in size of establishment, and the concentration of production and capital, reflected in capital assets and output of firms (or enterprises). Between 1890 and 1930 a persistent theme in the evolution of establishment size was increased concentration along with a persistently wide dispersion of sizes and the prevalence of medium-sized establishments (100 to 500 workers). Concentration was reflected in the increase in the size of the average establishment, from a median of 45 workers in 1906 to a median of 100 workers in 1931 and in the number of establishments of large (greater than 500 workers) and even very large (greater than 1,000 workers) dimensions. Correspondingly, the place of the small craftsman with 0 to 4 employees, so prominent in industry throughout most of the nineteenth century, fell from a majority of industrial workers in 1906 (53 percent) to little more than a quarter (28 percent) in 1931 (Carré et al.). Simultaneously, the number of wage earners rose from 3.7 million to 5.4 million (an increase of 47 percent), largely as a result of absolute and relative increase of wage-labor in establishments employing more than 100, 500, and even 1,000 workers. Such growing concentration of workers correlated closely with growing utilization of mechanical power and with investment in capital equipment. In short, concentration, capitalization, and mechanization were related developments, and together these explained the significantly increased proletarianization of the work force. This concatenation of transformative processes was especially strong and observable during the interwar years.

The movement toward concentration in the workplace did not eliminate small-scale production; rather it changed the character of the latter. Throughout most of the nineteenth century, such production was characterized by labor intensity, either that of an unqualified (unskilled) type of labor for low-quality manufacture, whose advantage over more advanced capitalistic methods was its abundance and low cost, or that of skilled handicraft labor for luxury or semiluxury manufacture, where technological or institutional considerations limited the relative profitability of mechanical methods. Most commonly, this small-scale production took the form of domestic, or cottage, industry. The persistence of the latter reflected the competitive strength of traditional forms and methods of production. After 1896 such forms and methods were confined increasingly to very few industrial branches where labor exploitation was both facile and advantageous, as in the clothing industry where a largely unskilled, female work force was employed at poverty wages, and to the remnants of luxury manufacture, usually highest luxury, such as some textile weaving (woolen and silk primarily) and leather working trades, where handicraft methods still commanded a premium over the more progressive techniques. More commonly domestic industry became a marginal, near-extinct form of small-scale production in the branches where it had prevailed earlier. In its place, a variety of specialized trades for making parts and for providing repair and upkeep services were spawned by the more dynamic industrial branches, such as automobile, metal, machinery, and electrical parts manufacture. Often these small, craft-like establishments were appendages of the largest and most technologically progressive establishments and proliferated as the dimensions of the latter expanded. In short, small-scale production persisted in a different form in the era of the second industrialization, one dependent on the innovative, more capitalistic movement in industry rather than as a legacy of the past.

The various movements in size of establishment on the level of industry branch are best viewed through the censuses of 1906 and 1931. From the first census, a profile of five size categories can be discerned, where size is measured as the number of wage earners per establishment (Bouvier et al., vol. 1): (1) a coherent group of small, relatively underindustrialized branches, including food, clothing, and wood-working industries, representing 30 percent of all wage earners, 60 percent of whom worked in establishments with fewer than 10 workers; (2) a less coherent, middling group composed mainly of construction and leather workers employed in small establishments but also including a variety of other trades, such as printing and quarry work, in medium or even larger establishments, representing 18 percent of wage earners, 40 percent of whom were in establishments of 10 to 100 workers; (3) a relatively homogeneous group of so-called true industries whose medium-sized establishments (100 to 200 workers) might be considered the French norm for this period, including textiles, chemicals, paper, glassworks, and ceramics, with 30 percent of wage earners, 60 percent of whom worked in establishments with more than 100 employees; (4) the complex metal-working sector, with 15 percent of wage earners distributed among establishments of widely varying size, from the smallest forges and workshops to the largest locomotive or machinery manufacture plants; (5) the uniformly largest industries, mostly mining and metallurgy, whose 7 to 10 percent of wage earners worked in their overwhelming majority (over 80 percent) in establishments employing more than 500 workers. Thus most food, clothing, and construction industries and a portion of the metal-working branch constituted the domain of small industry, while nearly all mining and metallurgy, another portion of metal working, and some textiles formed that of large factory industry. By 1906 most textile production was concentrated in factories employing more than 100 workers. In fact the textile factory represented the normal type of French factory industry. Forty percent of wage earners employed in establishments with 100 to 1,000 workers were textile workers, while the overall median for textiles was 200 workers, very close to the median for all branches of industry in the 100 to 1,000-worker size category.

Changes in establishment size, in particular the increase in wage earners and their concentration in larger establishments, affected the metal-working, food processing, construction, and clothing industries especially. Most of the increase in the number of wage earners and in that of establishments employing more than 1,000 workers was situated in metal working. The other branches mentioned moved from the small industry group into the domain of medium-size establishments. Textiles remained in the position of the norm but in a significantly enlarged industrial population whose distribution was skewed more strongly in the direction of larger establishments. Finally, domestic industry, which still commanded an important position in 1906 with its 1.5 million isolated workers (as compared with 3.7 million wage earners), ceded this position by 1931 to the auxiliary and service industries dependent on the most dynamic and often most concentrated branches. The form of domestic industry employing the largest number of workers in 1906, clothing manufacture, was increasingly taken over by large-scale production in the general movement toward concentration between these two census years.

In contrast to this significant movement in size of establishment, concentration of capital and production was relatively weak in French industry, especially in comparison with foreign industry. This was primarily the result of the large number of small and medium capitalized firms and, during the 1920s, of the proliferation of small corporate establishments with limited liability (*anonymes*) in a more liberalized environment of company law. During the Third Republic, notably between the early 1900s and the 1930s, the aggregate statistics of this type of concentration provide little evidence of significant change in overall structure, a fact that has led some authors to describe the situation as one of crystallization. This global image, however, veils the important expansion of relative market and capital shares of some very large firms, as well as their growing power over small and medium enterprise, especially during the 1920s. The crystallization that set in subsequently was the consequence of the depression and the Second World War, both of which blocked further movement toward concentration in most branches.

A related area of conflicting assessment is industrial combination and cooperative agreements, such as cartels. These seem on the whole to have been less extensive in scope and not quite as strong in France as in other major industrial countries. The most important combinations—those merging large firms into enterprises having considerable market power—occurred primarily between 1900 and 1911 as part of the cycle of expansion of that period. The more effective cartels and cartel-like agreements, such as those in metallurgy, coal mining, and aluminum, were established also in this prewar decade. After the war, combination served merely as an auxiliary means of expansion and affected the status of small and medium firms primarily; the latter were often absorbed by larger enterprises as an alternative to liquidation. Industrial agreements declined both in number and in strength during the 1920s; they were revived in a few rare instances later in the decade—in aluminum and steel, for instance—nearly exclusively to present a common front in international product agreements, sometimes (as in the case of steel) as a result of government pressure. During the

1930s a larger number of industries attempted some form of price fixing, product quota, or equipment liquidation agreement as a means of coping with the depression, often with government inducement, but in most cases these agreements were fragile and short-lived. Both before and after the war, such agreements tended to be informal and even secretive, with little joint administration and vertical interlocking. As a consequence, they provided little occasion for rationalization of production, as they did in Germany.

Such an image of interfirm cooperation obscures the extent to which decision making was coordinated in practice, however. In some branches, such as basic chemical manufacture, the domination of one or very few large firms in a particular product area promoted a uniformity of pricing and production according to that firm's priorities. A more common type of interfirm coordination was fostered by the industrial group, a network of financial participation in the various subdivisions of a particular branch giving the participating firms a role in decision making in these several subdivisions. Most often such firms were the largest in each branch, so that this form of interlocking interests also gave the larger enterprises most influence within the branch. About a hundred firms were prominent participants in such groups during the interwar period. Indeed groups were important steps in the expansion of firms in metallurgy and chemical manufacture.

In general, concentration of capital and production became most advanced, and intraindustry cooperation most effective, in branches concerned with primary or intermediate stages of production, largely of capital goods, and least so in the manufacture of finished products, parts, and consumers' goods. Three categories of concentration have been proposed (Bouvier et al., vol. 1). The first, where concentration was weakest, included firms of varying dimension, none of which, or no small group of which, dominated the branch as a whole. This was the pattern in textiles, in prewar automobile manufacture, in steel, cycle, and aeronautical manufacture, and in some subdivisions of the machinery industry, such as the manufacture of gas motors and hydraulic turbines. The second category, where some ten to twelve firms controlled 80 percent of the capital or output of the branch, included coal mining, metallurgy, and other subdivisions of machinery and mechanics, such as steam engine and armaments manufacture. The third category, that of monopoly or oligopoly, where fewer than five firms controlled the industry, covered heavy chemicals, aluminum, and still other subdivisions of the mechanical industry, such as locomotive production. Despite some correspondence between industrial branch and level of concentration, there was no clear hierarchy of branches in this respect. The dispersion of subdivisions of the machinery and mechanical industries over several categories illustrates this best. Moreover, the quality of concentration within particular branches was more complex than this three-category schema suggests. In metallurgy, for instance, at least three overlapping layers of concentration and related intraindustry cooperation might be distinguished: (1) local or intraregional domination by a few large firms surrounded by an array of medium, small, and even very small affiliates or auxiliary trades; (2) an interregional shift in production of cast iron and steel from the north and center to the east, centered on the metallurgical enterprises of Lorraine; and (3) a network of interregional groupings (financial participations) permitting the formation of national sales counters restricting competition, without, however, creating an effective oligopoly. Despite many changes of ownership and geographic concentration, especially before the war, the overall degree of concentration in this branch was not modified significantly. The chemical industry displayed another complex form of concentration, one in which the contrasts were most striking. Production of basic chemicals was an effective monopoly for some products, such as alkali manufacture (dominated by Solvay), while oligopoly or group networking, giving one or two firms major influence, prevailed in most other basic products. In the production of finished chemical products, such as dyes, economic power was more widely distributed. Between 1900 and 1930 concentration increased to the advantage of the three chemical giants—Saint-Gobain, Alais-Froges and Camargue, and at the top, Kuhlmann. But during the 1920s some newcomers, notably Rhône-Poulenc of Lyons, the result of a powerful fusion, also entered the ranks of the grand chemical firms, with ability to compete with the giants in some products. In automobile manufacture, finally, a dispersed prewar competitive pattern of small to medium enterprises, all of more or less equal strength and equally modest in their origins, was succeeded following the war by a more differentiated hierarchy of firms dominated by the big three—Renault, Citroën and Peugeot.

Innovation, the final schema of differentiation to be discussed here, had at least two major dimensions: the development of new products (product innovation) and the development of new industrial processes (methods innovation). Both of these constituted technical change in the industry of the Third Republic; however, product innovation was the relatively more dynamic element. Among the new product areas were electricity, the cycle and automobile, aluminum (from a rare to an abundant product), rubber, and petroleum. These were all prominent in the group of industries with the most rapid growth rates, and electricity especially was central to both productivity improvement and methods innovation in a wide range of industries, especially in the machinery and mechanical industries. The decade of the 1920s was especially prolific in new products; artificial cement and synthetic textiles, notably synthetic silks, were among the creations of this period. Methods innovation was evident in the rapid substitution of the Solvay for the Leblanc soda manufacturing process, in the spread of the Thomas and Martin steel-making process in place of the Bessemer technique, in the increased application of scientific methods to metallurgy, and in the development of hydroelectric power, electrometallurgy, and electrochemistry. These methods were developed and diffused in the early Third Republic (pre-1914) and had a continuing impact through the 1920s; they were vital to the transformation and the productivity growth in several branches of capital goods industry. However, such methods innovation did not generally proceed as rapidly or as fully—that is, to the limits of the most advanced current technique—as product innovation. Methods development tended to lag or to stagnate at a certain stage of technique in some important areas. For instance, the transition to electrical methods of soda manufacture was not as rapid as that from Leblanc to Solvay, despite the significant developments in French electrochemistry.The steam turbine was slow to replace the steam engine, and the rationalizationof industrial processes and of labor management (Taylorism, or scientific management) in the mechanical and machinery industries was exceptional—as in Creusot locomotive and armaments manufacture—in contrast to the more generalized and advanced application of such techniques in contemporary German and U.S. industry. Finally, despite France's early lead and rapid growth in automobile manufacture, productive methods generally failed to move to the standardized, mass production stage, causing France to lose its dominant position internationally during the interwar years. Among the explanations offered for these several lags in methods innovation are skilled labor traditions, habits of domestic consumption oriented to quality and variety of goods, commercial over manufacturing orientation to industry, and the small size of the domestic market.

Despite these weaknesses, technology under the Third Republic displayed many features of complementarity and interaction between techniques and branches associated with the more advanced stages of the technological revolution. For instance, electricity transformed the chemical industry as well as the metallurgical, metal-working, and machinery industries, besides serving as an important market for the products of the latter. The new automobile industry was an important consumer of the products of the new aluminum industry; both benefited from improvements in the metallurgical and mechanical industries and from electricity. The effects of such interaction might be observed in the close correspondence between productivity growth and the growth of investment in the three branches of industry having the strongest indexes of expansion—metallurgy, chemical manufacture, and the mechanical industries. In short, the Third Republic might easily be called the most technologically progressive era in modern French history before 1950, even though the nature and rate of technological change were inferior to the contemporary performance of some other major industrial nations.

J. Bouvier et al., *Histoire économique et sociale de la France*, 4 vols. (Paris, 1979–80), vol. 4: *L'Ere industrielle et la société d'aujourd'hui (siècle 1880–1980)*; F. Caron, *An Economic History of Modern France*, trans. B. Bray (New York, 1979); J.-J. Carré, P. Dubois, and E. Malinvaud, *French Economic Growth*, trans. J. Hatfield (Stanford, Calif., 1975); D. S. Landes, *The Unbound Prometheus* (Cambridge, Mass., 1969); M. Lévy-Leboyer, "Capital Investment and Economic Growth in France, 1820–1930," in *The Cambridge Economic History of Europe*, vol. 7: *The Industrial Economies: Capital, Labour, and Enterprise*, ed. Peter Mathias and M. M. Postan (Cambridge, England, 1978); T. J. Markovitch, "The Dominant Sectors of French Industry" and F. Crouzet, "An Annual Index of French Industrial Production in the 19th Century," in *Essays in French Economic History*, ed. Rondo Cameron (Homewood, Ill., 1970).

G. J. Sheridan

Related entries: BUSINESS ORGANIZATION; WORKERS, INDUSTRIAL.

INDUSTRY: AUTO. Gasoline automobile production began in France in 1890. Peugeot, a provincial hardware and bicycle manufacturer, and Panhard et Levassor, a Paris maker of woodworking machinery, each built a car using engines designed by the German engineer Gottlieb Daimler. Production at these two firms gradually increased as they promoted autos by shows and races. Others entered the young industry, including Alexandre Darracq and Adolphe Clément from the bicycle trade, and new firms such as De Dion-Bouton, Renault, and Berliet were established. Steam and electric cars never found much support in France.

A boom developed by 1898 when some 1,500 cars were produced. From this period until the First World War, French output led Europe, and French exports led the world. This leadership sprang from the excellent road system, the fortuitous fact that the two earliest producers were both serious and well-established firms, and the skillful promotion of autos by French makers. From the beginning most production centered at Paris, with its large market, plentiful skilled labor, and many component suppliers. In 1913 the French produced about 45,000 autos, the British 34,000, and the Germans about 23,000. (U.S. output had surged to 485,000.) Automobile manufacturing had become the largest single segment of the metal-working industry in France, employing some 60,000 to 70,000 and acting as a major factor in the country's rapid economic growth from the late 1890s to 1914.

During World War I, French auto firms converted quickly to making shells, other munitions, and especially aircraft engines and tanks. In the 1920s André Citroën joined Renault and Peugeot as a major producer and led the way in adopting U.S. methods of production and marketing. In 1929 the French auto industry turned out 253,000 cars and trucks, slightly more than Britain and considerably more than Germany. France lost this European leadership during the depression of the 1930s as the German and, especially, the British auto industries boomed. Despite its technical innovations, the Citroën company had financial troubles, and the Michelin tire company took it over in 1934. In 1938 French output was 228,000, as the Simca firm, a Fiat subsidiary, joined the big three as a major manufacturer. The French did less than the other European producers with a small, mass market car in this decade, which helps explain the loss of production leadership.

J. M. Laux, *In First Gear: The French Automobile Industry to 1914* (Montreal, 1976); P. Fridenson, *Histoire des usines Renault* (Paris, 1972); J. Bardou et al., *The Automobile Revolution* (Chapel Hill, N.C. 1982); J. Nwafor, "L'Evolution de l'industrie automobile en France" (thesis, University of Paris, 1974).

J. M. Laux

Related entries: CITROEN; DION; INDUSTRY; RENAULT.

INDUSTRY: CHEMICAL, the first science-based, high-tech industry. The manufacture of chemicals was and remained a relatively small sector in France, comprising many firms in a number of different product lines. By 1929, chemicals accounted for about 2 percent of total output (5 percent of value added in industry). However, the industry furnishes a good case study in the ongoing debate over the degree of technological, entrepreneurial, and economic vigor of the nation. Industrial chemicals played a strategic role, akin to that of machinery, in supplying technologically sophisticated inputs to large and relatively static sectors such as agriculture and textiles. They also offered potential solutions to natural-resource problems, frequently cited as a limiting factor in French economic growth.

The chemical industry may be defined narrowly or broadly. The tight definition includes the inorganic sector, the principal products being sulfuric acid, soda ash, superphosphates, and chlorine derivatives, and the organic sector, notably synthetic dyestuffs. A wider definition would encompass the majority of process industries, from beet sugar refining and soapmaking to photographic materials, pharmaceuticals, petroleum, and synthetics.

So diverse an industrial group naturally could be found in a variety of locations, but some concentrations stand out. Large plants were often located near deposits of raw materials, salt and coal in particular. However, many chemicals were too dangerous to transport far and so were produced near the customer industries. Large urban concentrations also provided the right human milieu for entrepreneurial and scientific activity. A final locational factor was transport, with imported materials often processed in major ports. These considerations help explain why the industrial north, Paris, and Lyons were the main chemical centers, with important concentrations also around Nancy and Marseilles.

The early years of the Third Republic were inauspicious for the French chemical industry. It was in the early 1870s that the country lost its strong early position in soda ash and dyestuffs. On the one hand, the Leblanc process, elaborated in France under the First Empire, was displaced by the Belgian ammonia-soda or Solvay process. On the other hand, the first synthetic dye equivalent to a natural one came out in 1869. The head start given France by the discovery of magenta or Fuchsine in 1859 was quite obliterated, and in addition a flourishing madder crop lost its market to the new alizarin. This advance came not from Britain, heretofore the only country with a larger industry and equivalent technological credentials, but from Germany, just then moving past France as an economic power. It is in this context that the quantitative progress of the French chemical industry until 1914 must be viewed. Although sulfuric acid production, a frequently cited indicator of general industrial development, rose from 150,000 tons per year in 1877 to 1.5 million tons in 1913, the core Leblanc process disappeared after decades of low-profit retreat. In the organic area, the Compagnie des matières colorantes de St. Denis was virtually the only dyestuff maker under French control. However, innovation and growth flourished in a set of chemical and related products lines introduced during the 1880s and 1890s, including electrochemicals and metals, compressed gases, and artificial fibers.

World War I forced France to catch up quickly, to make up for the loss of industrial territories and foreign expertise, as well as to meet the unprecedented wartime demand. Great strides were made, which ironically aggravated the process of consolidation and concentration in the 1920s and 1930s, when difficult economic conditions and a rush of foreign competition made it difficult to utilize the newly created capacity.

In order of age, the principal companies in the industry were St. Gobain (also a glass maker), Kuhlmann, Pechiney (leader in aluminum), Rhône-Poulenc (fine chemicals and pharmaceuticals), and Air Liquide.

F. Braudel and E. Labrousse, eds., *Histoire économique et sociale de la France*, vols. 3, 4 (Paris, 1976, 1979, 1980); P. Hohenberg, *Chemicals in Western Europe, 1850– 1914* (Chicago, 1967); *Le Monde des affaires en France de 1830 à nos jours* (Paris, 1952).

P. M. Hohenberg

Related entries: BUSINESS ORGANIZATION; INDUSTRY.

INDUSTRY: COAL, France's basic source of energy throughout the period. By 1870 coal had already overtaken wood and water as the chief source of energy in France, and Frenchmen were already posing a question historians are still debating: whether a relatively poor endowment in coal resources significantly retarded French industrialization. But whatever the shortage of reserves and of good coking coal, the high cost of extraction stemming from difficult geological conditions, and the extreme northern frontier location of the largest field may have meant for coal users, the decades before World War I were a golden age for the industry itself.

Between 1870 and 1913 coal production tripled. Most of the growth occurred in the northern field near the Belgian frontier (35 percent of national output in 1870, 67 percent in 1913) where the new Pas-de-Calais extension (opened 1847) rapidly outstripped the older Nord pits to supply over one-half of French output by 1913. Output in the upper Loire field, once France's largest, actually declined after 1900, and output in the lesser fields around the edges of the Massif Central leveled off. Coal consumption grew even faster than production; France was the only major industrial country to import a large fraction of its energy needs (37 percent in 1913). Coal enjoyed only moderate tariff protection, and rapidly falling transport costs benefited importers as much as French producers. Belgium was the chief supplier until the 1890s when Great Britain took its place, especially along the coasts. After 1900 Germany penetrated the eastern frontier where the Lorraine steel industry depended heavily on Ruhr coking coal. On the eve of World War I, France ranked a distant fifth in world production but stood much closer to the leaders in per capita consumption.

Although some of France's largest firms were coal companies (Lens, Anzin), the industry was marked by a relatively low concentration of firms (higher than Great Britain, lower than Germany). Except in the one-company smaller fields, the government's concession system and the companies' own prized independence prevented horizontal integration by merger. Nor was there much vertical integration with other industries in the northern field, although its twenty-five companies increasingly processed their output by washing and sorting, briquetting, and coking (with gas and tar as by-products). The companies were largely owned by thousands of local stockholders and controlled by the descendants of local founders. The industry's national association, the Comité central des houillères, remained a relatively weak lobby for higher tariffs and lower transport costs, but after 1901 most of the northern firms successfully fixed prices and set production quotas through a syndicate (*entente*). While never establishing a central sales office like the rival Belgian and Ruhr coal cartels, the syndicate did set up a three-tier pricing system, selling highest near the mines and lowest in western and southern France. The syndicate, like the foreign cartels, eliminated price competition among its own members in order to pursue it vigorously against the organizations of rival fields. These stratagems worked well at a time when the major markets for coal—domestic heating, iron and steel, general industry, railroads, and thermoelectricity—were expanding. Total profits rose fairly steadily decade by decade, but, an ominous sign for the future, productivity began to decline after 1890 since steady technological improvement (such as electrification) was more than offset by increasing unit costs of extraction as the most easily and cheaply mined coal was worked out.

During World War I, the Germans occupied and heavily damaged most of the pits of the northern field. With massive state aid, the companies rapidly reconstructed and modernized their installations. Output recovered its prewar level by 1925 and soared one-third beyond by 1929, only to fall back with the onset of the depression (1913, 40 million tons; 1929, 53 million; 1938, 46 million). Four fundamental problems—labor shortages, low productivity, inefficient organization, and stagnant markets—plagued the industry throughout the interwar years. A new generation of Frenchmen refused to work in the mines; by 1927, 46 percent of the miners in the northern field were Poles and other immigrants. New extraction techniques such as coal-cutting machines were ill suited to the thin, faulted seams of the French fields; the average pit in the Ruhr, larger and more mechanized, produced two and one-half times as much coal as one in the northern field. The structure of the industry remained fragmented; few coal firms merged with each other or with firms in other industries. The long-term market forecast was bleak; some coal-using industries stagnated, some cut coal consumption by improving their fuel efficiency, and still others began to turn to new sources of energy (oil, natural gas, hydroelectricity). Although coal was still king in 1940, supplying 80 percent of France's energy, these problems left a frightening legacy for the postwar planners.

R. Gendarme, *La Région du Nord* (Paris, 1954); M. Gillet, *Les Charbonnages du Nord de la France au XIXe siècle* (Paris and The Hague, 1973); N. J. G. Pounds and W. N. Parker, *Coal and Steel in Western Europe* (London, 1957).

R. G. Geiger

Related entry: INDUSTRY.

INDUSTRY: TEXTILE. Textile manufacturing was one of France's largest industries during the Third Republic. Its five main branches, in order of size, were woolens, cotton, linen, silk, and jute (burlap). In the 1870s, wool was spun and woven mainly in the north, at Reims, Fourmies, Sedan, Elbeuf, and Roubaix-Tourcoing. Roubaix was the world's leader in mechanized wool combing. Normandy, the Nord, and the Vosges emerged as the principal areas of cotton manufacture in 1871 after the loss of Alsace, previously the foremost cotton producer of France. Linen spinning was found mainly in the Nord and jute spinning and weaving in the Somme. Lyons and its environs continued to be the center of the silk industry. At the outset of the Third Republic, silk and woolens production in France were oriented toward high-quality goods for export, whereas the cotton and linen industries produced a range of goods, from shoddy to high quality, primarily for domestic consumption.

The early decades of the Third Republic were years of depression for most of French textiles as rising competition at home and abroad eroded prices and profits even as the quantity of output held steady or increased. The value of French silk exports peaked in 1875 and then declined 50 percent in the next twenty years. The value of woolen exports from Reims and Fourmies fell in the 1880s after a peak in 1875–80. The volume of cotton production rose steadily from 1870 to 1900, but falling prices kept the value of production from rising apace. Meanwhile, the volume, as well as the value, of linen production declined as consumers switched to cotton and as traditional applications (such as sailcloth) contracted. Only the jute industry experienced rapid growth between 1871 and 1900, the result of growing demand for packing materials in an age of expanding trade.

The depression fostered retrenchment, concentration, and modernization throughout the industry. Although already mechanized, spinning remained dispersed and rural in the 1870s. By 1900, however, most cotton spinning had been concentrated in Rouen, Lille and its suburbs, and the department of the Vosges; wool spinning had been concentrated in Roubaix, and linen spinning was found exclusively in Lille and Armentières. Similar trends occurred in weaving. In the 1870s, there were still more hand looms than power looms in use in the cotton industry; by 1900, virtually all cotton weaving had been mechanized and concentrated in a few centers (Rouen, the Vosges, Roanne). Silk weaving was still an artisanal industry in the 1870s, but the 1880s and 1890s brought a rapid conversion to electrically powered looms grouped in large mills in the suburbs of Lyons.

Greater efficiency in production, increased protection of the home market and assimilation of colonial markets after the tariff reforms of 1892, and a general business upturn brought renewed growth and prosperity to most sectors of French textiles between 1900 and 1914, as indicated by T. J. Markovitch's figures for average annual production (millions of francs):

	1875–84	*1885–94*	*1895–1904*	*1905–13*
Cotton yarn and thread	291	330	521	1071
Cotton cloth	495	513	718	1092
Wool yarn	541	564	391	640
Wool cloth	780	820	633	696
Silk cloth	291	295	277	350
Linen yarn and thread	371	236	170	216
Linen cloth	438	247	181	310
Jute sacks	30	46	68	110

With fighting on the Western front engulfing its main textile centers between 1914 and 1918, France lost two-thirds of its woolens production, one-third of its cotton spinning, and its entire linen and wool combing industries for the duration of World War I. Efforts to transfer production to unoccupied areas were ineffective in part because importation of cotton, wool, and flax from overseas was disrupted by the hostilities. Thus, instead of being a net exporter of cottons and woolens, France became a net importer. Among its major textile industries, only silk continued production on a prewar scale.

After the war, the fortunes of French textiles paralleled those of the economy as a whole; recovery in 1919–24 was followed by prosperity (1925–30) and then by stagnation and decline (1930–40). Still, there were sectoral variations. With the return of Alsace and the rebuilding of the Nord, cotton and woolen production recovered quickly and exceeded prewar levels from 1925 to 1935. Linen production, however, never recovered from wartime destruction; its prewar pattern of contraction continued, with annual output falling to 21,000 tons in 1935–38 (versus 65,000 in 1905–13). Silk production also declined, with thread and cloth output falling to one-third and one-half of prewar levels, respectively, by 1938. The impact on Lyons was offset, however, by the rapid growth of synthetic fiber production. Launched in Lyons in 1903, the manufacture of artificial silk (rayon) reached 73,000 tons per year by 1939, making France the world's fourth largest producer of synthetics behind the United States, Japan, and Italy. Lyons also emerged as a center of acetate yarn production in the interwar years. The development of synthetics aside, the French textile industry as a whole played the role of a mature industry—large but slow growing and technologically static—in the final decades of the Third Republic.

A. Aftalion, *L'Industrie textile en France pendant la guerre* (Paris, 1924); L. G. Fauquet, *Histoire de la rayonne et les textiles synthétiques* (Paris, 1960); R. B. Forrester, *The Cotton Industry of France* (Manchester, 1921); J. Lambert-Dansette, *Quelques familles du patronat textile de Lille-Armentières* (Lille, 1954); E. Levasseur, *Questions ouvrières et industrielles sous la 3e République* (Paris, 1907); T. J. Markovitch, "Histoire quantitative de l'économie française," *Cahiers de l'institut de science économique appliquée*, 5–6 (1966).

M. S. Smith

Related entries: BUSINESS ORGANIZATION; COMMERCE: FOREIGN; CONFEDERATION GENERALE DU TRAVAIL; INDUSTRY; LABOR MOVEMENT; LILLE; LYONS; SOCIAL REFORM: GOVERNMENTAL POLICIES AND ACTS.

INTERNATIONAL, FIRST WORKINGMEN'S (1864–1872), a working-class organization seeking the emancipation of labor. Organized in 1864 by British and French working-class leaders, the International Workingmen's Association, better known later as the First International, was the first attempt to organize labor on local, national, and international levels simultaneously. Its creation came about from the contact established by French workers attending the London Exhibition of 1862, though the concept of an international association of workingmen had surfaced on a number of occasions in the preceding twenty years. The International was coordinated by an administrative committee, the General Council, based in London, and its ideological orientation was hammered out in annual conferences and congresses (London, 1865; Geneva, 1866; Lausanne, 1867; Brussels, 1868; Basel, 1869; London, 1871; the Hague, 1872). The essential strength of the International, however, lay with its branches in each European country. A branch was established in Paris four months after the International was created, and within three years there were several dozen in the provinces located in cities such as Lyons, Marseilles, Bordeaux, Rouen, and Vienne.

Initially the International had no ideological cast, being scarcely more than a forum for the exchange of views, but the French delegates at the Geneva Congress sought to commit the International to the emancipation of labor through Joseph Proudhon's mutualism, a cooperative association of artisan producers where individuals made reciprocal promises but were not bound by any organizational rules. Although the congress went on record as favoring producers' cooperatives, it did not adopt the limitations sought by the French. Throughout its existence the International stood by the cooperative as the agency for obliterating capitalist production. Within France the branches worked tirelessly to create or assist cooperatives, and when labor unions appeared at the end of the 1860s, they received their wholehearted support, for they were seen as elements that could evolve naturally into producers' cooperatives. At the same time, the International endorsed collectivization of agricultural property, which most of the French members accepted because they saw it as extending the cooperative idea to agriculture.

The International was twice suppressed in France, first in 1868 and again in 1870. Following the first repressions, many of the Proudhonists quit the organization and left it in the hands of a younger generation of activists—Benoît Malon and Eugène Varlin in Paris, Albert Richard in Lyons, André Bastelica in Marseilles, and Emile Aubry in Rouen. When war between France and Prussia threatened in 1870 and even after it broke out, French leaders of the International made frequent declarations of solidarity with workingmen in Germany and condemned the war as a dynastic struggle. Once the Third Republic had been proclaimed and Prussia sought to annex French territory, the testimonials of solidarity ceased, and the leaders rallied to national defense. Taking advantage of the turmoil within France and relying on the support he had cultivated within the International's Lyons branch, the Russian anarchist Mikhail Bakunin came to Lyons and carried out an ill-starred attempt to overthrow the state through a seizure of the city hall that lasted scarcely one day. In the provinces the International was effectively dead, however, though in Paris activity would continue through May 1871. In the latter, 1870–71 saw the creation of approximately sixty-five branches and the adherence of some seventy-five trade unions to the International, though this apparent growth was largely ephemeral. Immediate political and military questions occupied the members, and in a real test of strength, the National Assembly election of 8 February 1871, only five (only two of whom were workers) of the forty-three candidates proposed by the International were elected. In private it was admitted that the International in Paris was in disarray. A thorough reorganization was underway, but when the Paris Commune was created, it absorbed all the energies of the International's leadership, and the suppression of the Commune in May effectively ended the last arena of the International's existence in France. Indeed, in 1870–71, actions by individuals associated with the International rather than actions of the International itself were more significant. Nonetheless, the opponents of the Commune and the French Left considered the International to be a conspiratorial organization responsible for the revolutionary activities of 1870–71. This belief resulted in an intense persecution of the International. In France, by the law of 14 March 1872, membership in the International or even agreement with its principles was punishable by imprisonment. Similar attacks occurred in the rest of Europe, the only exceptions being Britain and Switzerland. The struggle between Karl Marx and Bakunin for control of the organization, heightened by the events of 1870–71, brought about the effective collapse of the International in 1872. During the 1880s the memory of the International inspired a number of attempts in France to create a new organization, one of which was successful in 1889. This Second International, as it came to be called, indicates by its name alone its spiritual obligation to the International of 1864–72.

J. Archer, "The Cooperative Ideal in the Socialist Thought of the First International in France," *Proceedings of the Sixth Annual Meeting of the Western Society for French History* (1979); J. Freymond, ed., *La Première Internationale*, 2 vols. (Geneva, 1962); E. E. Fribourg, *L'Association internationale des travailleurs* (Paris, 1871); J. Guillaume, *L'Internationale*, 4 vols. (Paris, 1905–10).

J.P.W. Archer

Related entries: COLLECTIVISM; COMMUNARDS; COMMUNE OF PARIS; MALON; MARXISM; MUTUALISM; TOLAIN; VARLIN.

ITALY, RELATIONS WITH, a component of the Third Republic's great power diplomacy. Italy's emergence as a European power occurred at a time when France's great power status was brought severely into question by defeat in the Franco-Prussian War (1870–71). Throughout the life of the Third Republic, the position of Germany in Europe was to be the major determinant in understanding the Quai d'Orsay's policies regarding Italy. Franco-Italian relations can be gauged largely by the magnitude of France's uncertainty about German ambitions.

Otto von Bismarck initially sought to deflect *revanchiste* sentiment west of the Rhine by encouraging French expansion in Tunisia. The establishment of the protectorate there in 1881, in an area regarded by Italian expansionists as lying within Italy's sphere of influence, engendered bitter resentment. Concern in Rome about potential conflict with France led Italy to ally with Austria-Hungary and Germany in 1882. Italy remained, however, the weak link in the Triple Alliance; only the fear of France had encouraged Italian leaders to shelve the question of the *Italia irredenta* under Habsburg control. This was the lever by which the French and English were able to disrupt the Triple Alliance during World War I. Franco-Italian relations reached their nadir during the late 1880s. But as French concern about German policy under William II began to mount, a new generation of diplomats emerged determined to breach the isolation of the Bismarckian system. The Franco-Russian alliance was established in 1894. Under the direction of Foreign Minister Théophile Delcassé and French ambassador in Rome Camille Barrère, a secret colonial understanding was achieved between Paris and Rome in 1900. This was followed in 1902 by a second exchange of notes pledging the maintenance of strict neutrality should either party be the object of aggression. Italy remained a member of the Triple Alliance, but its commitment had been shaken. Italy's stature as weakest of the great powers guaranteed its posture of seeking maximum influence by playing on the balance of power between the two alliance systems. When World War I erupted in 1914, Italian leaders had to assess whether Italian interest would best be served by neutrality or by active participation with the Triple Entente. Negotiations proceeded with both sides; the interventionists prevailed in 1915. The Treaty of London brought Italy into the war against the Central Powers in exchange for territorial compensations (the Brenner line in the north and northern Dalmatia) tantamount to making the Adriatic an Italian lake. Italy was also promised colonial compensations. When these gains failed to be fully recognized at the Paris peace negotiations of 1919–20, Italian resentment was acute. The bitterness at having won only a mutilated victory was exacerbated by the awareness that neither the French nor the British had energetically supported Italy's claims to the full Treaty of London agenda.

Relations between the two countries were anything but amicable after the war. Beyond a common desire to preserve Austrian independence, there was little apparent identity of interest. Yet the requirements of French security regarding Germany indicated that Franco-Italian tensions needed to be mitigated. Perhaps, as Barrère insisted, the Italians could be integrated into a French security system designed to counterbalance English hostility to France's German policies. Such an expectation undergirded the benevolence with which several French ministries regarded the nascent fascist movement in Italy. Documents now available in the Quai d'Orsay show that French diplomats regarded the fascists as a force of stability and Benito Mussolini as potentially favorable to French foreign policy goals in Germany. When Mussolini came to power in 1922, therefore, his accession provided the occasion for the resurrection of old clichés about the two "Latin sisters," and there was a great deal of speculation about the *duce* as a declared francophile. It is not surprising that Raymond Poincaré's efforts to flatter the new Italian leaders coincided with the intensification of Franco-German bitterness over reparations. Given the opposition of Great Britain to the French thesis on reparations, Italy's vote in the Reparations Commission and its support for the Ruhr expedition of 1923 were deemed vital. Italian interests coincided with the French at this juncture. Although Italian enthusiasm for the Ruhr occupation waned as time passed, Mussolini's cooperation was amply rewarded when France, virtually alone among world nations, refused to condemn the aggressive Italian occupation of the Greek island of Corfu. It was Poincaré, in fact, who devised the face-saving solution to the crisis in September 1923—just as the Germans appeared on the verge of capitulating in the Ruhr, and continued Italian support was regarded as essential.

Although Poincaré was inclined to pursue rapprochement with the Mussolini regime, his government remained in power only until 1924. Direction of French foreign policy passed briefly to Edouard Herriot and then to Aristide Briand, whose principal technique for guaranteeing French security lay in direct negotiation with Germany. Under Briand relations between the two countries became progressively more strained over such issues as Italian nationality rights in Tunisia and the stridently antifascist activities of Italian émigrés in France. Appeasement of Italy seemed less essential after the Dawes Plan of 1924 and the Locarno Accords of 1925 had apparently defused the German question. Briand remained in control of the Foreign Ministry until his retirement in 1932, a period when Franco-Italian relations remained a secondary issue.

The rise of Adolf Hitler in Germany, however, strengthened those who advocated a Franco-Italian entente. Under the direction of Joseph Paul-Boncour (December 1932–January 1934) and Pierre Laval (November 1934–January 1936), the Quai d'Orsay strove to recapture the policies advocated by Barrère and Raymond Poincaré in the early 1920s. These efforts climaxed in 1935. In January the Laval-Mussolini accords resolved colonial issues between the two powers, although misunderstandings about Laval's assurances to the *duce* concerning French *desintéressement* in Ethiopia were to cause difficulties later. In April, following German rearmament, the informal Stresa Front, pledging mutual consultation among France, England, and Italy, was established. This apparent reconstitution of the wartime coalition was destroyed by the outbreak of the Italian-Ethiopian War in October. The war undermined the League of Nations, strengthened ties between Italy and Germany, and weakened Laval's credibility. His resignation in January 1936 ended serious efforts at Franco-Italian conciliation. As war approached in 1939, Italy found itself in a situation analogous to that of 1914, with one major difference. In 1914 the choice was either neutrality or alliance with the Western powers. In 1939 it was neutrality or alliance with Germany.

The military collapse of the Third Republic in 1940 forced Mussolini's fateful decision.

F. Charles-Roux, *Une Grande Ambassade à Rome* (Paris, 1961); C. Lowe and F. Marzari, *Italian Foreign Policy, 1870–1914* (London, 1975); P. Milza, *L'Italie fasciste devant l'opinion française, 1920–1940* (Paris, 1967); W. Shorrock, "France and the Rise of Fascism in Italy," *Journal of Contemporary History* 10/4 (1975).

W. *I. Shorrock*

Related entries: DELCASSE; FOREIGN POLICY; HOARE-LAVAL PLAN; ITALY, SECRET TREATY WITH; LAVAL; LOCARNO ACCORDS; POINCARE, R.; RUHR OCCUPATION.

ITALY, SECRET TREATY WITH (1902), a secret accord that led Italy toward neutrality vis-à-vis France and Germany. The treaty was made possible by the resolution of Franco-Italian differences over colonies in North Africa. After France established a protectorate over Tunisia in 1881, Italy joined the Triple Alliance in 1882. Sharp tension followed, particularly when Francesco Crispi held power, but after he fell in 1896, other Italian leaders regained international maneuverability and balanced Italy between France and Germany. Meanwhile, French leaders courted Italy away from Germany. Franco-Italian rancor had developed in colonial, commercial, and international spheres; rapprochement followed the same paths. An 1896 accord stabilized the position of Italian settlers in Tunisia. An 1898 commercial pact ended a tariff war. In December 1900 French Ambassador Camille Barrère and Foreign Minister Théophile Delcassé agreed with Italian Foreign Minister Emilio Visconti-Venosta to recognize Italian interests in Libya while Italy reciprocated in Morocco.

In accordance with the provisions of the secret treaty of 1902, Barrère and Italian Foreign Minister Giulio Prinetti exchanged recognition of France's and Italy's spheres of influence in Morocco and Libya respectively; Italian leaders also promised to declare neutrality if Germany provoked war with France. At the same time Italy renewed the Triple Alliance. The Franco-Italian pact was kept secret, for a while even from the French military. From 1902 to 1914, Barrère defended the agreement despite intermittent Franco-Italian discord. Later he maintained that the treaty was responsible for Italian neutrality in 1914.

C. Andrew, *Théophile Delcassé and the Making of the Entente Cordiale* (New York, 1968); C. Barrère, "Lettres à Delcassé," *Revue de Paris*, April 18, 1937; G. Déthan, "Le Rapprochement franco-italien après la chute de Crispi jusqu'aux accords Barrère-Visconti-Venosta sur le Maroc et la Tripolitaine (1896–1900)," *Revue d' histoire diplomatique* 70 (October–December 1956); P. Milza, "La Politique étrangère française et l'Italie (1896–1902)," *Rassegna Storica Toscana* 13 (January–June 1967); E. Serra, *Camille Barrère e l' intesa italo-francese* (Milan, 1950).

J. *Blatt*

Related entries: BARRERE; DELCASSE; ITALY, RELATIONS WITH.

J

JACOBINISM, a term connoting fundamental political commitments, derived from the experience of the French revolutionary movement from 1789 to 1871 and shared by a wide spectrum of left-wing politicians independent of party during the early years of the Third Republic. The term first acquired political meaning in 1789 when a former monastery of that name became an informal meeting place for reform-minded delegates to the National Assembly. During the next few years, this Jacobin society became the hub of a network of clubs throughout France. By 1793, moreover, Jacobinism was as often identified with radical political ideas as with radical political organizations. In the quasi-religious faith in an abstract ideal of community that it inspired, Jacobinism represented a new way of thinking about politics, distinct not only from the conservatism of the Old Regime but also from the liberalism that shaped political discourse in public forums in the early years of the Revolution. Among the most important Jacobin ideals were: (1) a fierce nationalism, based on the notion of popular sovereignty but with an accent on the nation in danger (the struggle required to liberate the nation from authoritarian oppression); (2) a faith that the comradeship engendered through such struggle promotes the social bonding essential for the making of a nation; (3) a tendency to describe that struggle as a polarization of social virtue and vice; (4) a belief that the struggle against oppression, once successful, must be sustained by direct democracy (constant vigilance and if necessary popular intervention) to ensure that government remains a public trust; and (5) a sense of the responsibility of the nation to provide for the social well-being of its citizenry by redistributing wealth to eliminate the extremes of affluence and poverty.

If the Jacobin ideal was national unity, there was within Jacobin thinking an ambiguity about how that ideal was to be realized. The goal of Jacobinism was an alliance between the revolutionary elite and ordinary citizens, but the issue of leadership in promoting such an accord proved troublesome. During the French Revolution, it led to the conflict between Maximilien Robespierre of the Committee

of Public Safety (who argued for strong authority in revolutionary crises) and
Jacques Hébert (who contended that the leader's primary duty was to inspire
ordinary citizens to revolutionary action), and it endured as a critical issue in
the early nineteenth century, when the revolutionary movement was driven
underground and obliged to function through secret societies. The most famous
among nineteenth-century leaders of such societies, Auguste Blanqui, took pains
to emphasize this distinction by condemning Robespierre and praising Hébert.
But Blanqui's Jacobinism in fact represented an amalgamation of the egalitarian
ideals of Hébert and the implicitly authoritarian political strategy of Gracchus
Babeuf, the conspirator during the French Revolution who first called for a
professional vanguard of revolutionary leaders. The revolutions of 1830, 1848,
and 1871 (Paris Commune) were Jacobin upheavals in that all were made possible
by armed popular insurrections in the name of the ideals noted. But the relative
importance of direction from above vis-à-vis enthusiastic participation from below
was a divisive issue in all three.

Jacobinism was still a term in wide currency in the early Third Republic,
although it was increasingly measured against Marxism, which had the allure
of being a new and more scientific expression of revolutionary thought. Jacobinism,
once the intellectual viewpoint of the revolutionary vanguard, ironically was
seen by Marxists after 1871 as old-fashioned and naively romantic because of
its emphasis on ideological willpower rather than economic determinism. But
Marxism was never the viewpoint of the majority on the extreme Left before
the First World War, and many who called themselves socialists preferred a
Jacobin to a Marxist prefix. Moreover, the radicals, the more important political
grouping on the extreme Left, espoused what was in many ways a tamed version
of Jacobin ideology. As the politics of popular insurrection became unrealistic
in the face of the organization of mass political parties, the radicals sought to
take advantage of the democratic electoral process of the Third Republic to give
the combative posture of Jacobinism a new expression. Many of the radicals'
most celebrated electoral campaigns in the late nineteenth century (notably that
for Blanqui in 1879, for Ernest Roche in 1886, for Georges Boulanger in 1888,
and for Paul Lafargue in 1891) were demonstrations of Jacobinism in a new
style of political intransigence, staged less to win elections than to make manifest
the depth of popular discontent with governmental policy.

Jacobinism remained a motto for many of the extreme Left until the First
World War. Even after, tacitly held Jacobin conceptions may account for certain
inveterate traits of left-wing politicians, regardless of their party affiliations: a
hostility to political pluralism, a search for unity of moral purpose, and a belief
in popular intervention as the deepest expression of democracy.

C. Brinton, *The Jacobins* (New York, 1930); F. Furet, *Interpreting the French Revolution* (Cambridge, 1981); P. H. Hutton, *The Cult of the Revolutionary Tradition* (Berkeley, 1981); C. Mazauric, "Quelques vois nouvelles pour l'histoire politique de la Révolution

Française," *Annales historiques de la Révolution française* 47 (1975); A. Soboul, "Tradition et création dans le mouvement révolutionnaire français au XIXe siècle," *Le Mouvement social* no. 79 (April–June 1972).

P. H. Hutton

Related entries: BLANQUI; BLANQUISTS; BOULANGER AFFAIR; COMMUNE OF PARIS; MARXISM; NATIONALISM; POLITICS; RADICAL AND RADICAL-SOCIALIST PARTY; ROCHE, ERNEST; SOCIALISM, 1870–1914.

JARRY, ALFRED (1873–1907), writer, humorist, and journalist. His *Ubu* series announced the dadaist, surrealist, and antitheater movements of the twentieth century and paved the way for Antonin Artaud's theatrical experimentation. The inspiration for Jarry's most famous character, Père Ubu, was a teacher of physics at a school he attended in Rennes, and Jarry's was but a compilation of many satires about this M. Hébert. As early as 1888 Jarry had read a work called *Les Polonais*, which gave rise to the Polish theme in the Ubu cycle. That same year Jarry composed a first version of *Ubu cocu* (published in 1897) using Hébert as a model. Several of these early works were staged in a marionette theater, Théâtre des Phynances, in Jarry's home, and even a clay statue of Ubu was sculpted by his sister Charlotte.

In Paris, Jarry was a regular visitor to the salons of Stéphane Mallarmé and of Marguerite Eymery Vallette (called Rachilde). He contributed to several journals: *Le Livre d'art, L'Ymager, La Revue blanche,* and *Le Mercure de France.* The rumor mills of Paris also linked Jarry with Léon-Paul Fargue in a homosexual relationship. Jarry and *Ubu roi* became causes célèbres after the work was published in June 1896. Later, in his capacity as secretary to Lugné-Poe, director of the Théâtre de l'oeuvre, the five-act play was staged on 10 December 1896. Critics attacked the work for its obscene language and lack of structure. Other critics, few in number, hailed the work as a move away from stifling realism and as the anarchistic statement of a new age.

Jarry seems to have become a prisoner of his character, Ubu, and numerous accounts state that he affected a high-pitched, nasal voice, and used Ubu's colorful language profusely. This was, however, simply another aspect of Jarry's lifelong quest to shock middle-class sensitivities and to cultivate his own mythological stature. His nihilism, use of black humor and sick jokes, and personal nonconformity belie a verbal and poetic vision that has greatly changed twentieth-century theater in France and Germany and influenced the later playwrights Samuel Beckett, Arabal, Eugène Ionesco as well as Artaud. Jarry was hardly a student of politics, but his commentaries on social evils, his scorn for religion, and his contempt for the bourgeoisie served as themes which were developed by these writers.

Along with the famous Ubu cycle (*Ubu roi, Ubu cocu, Ubu enchaîné, L'Almanach du Père Ubu* and *Ubu sur la Butte*), Jarry left an impressive array of other works, the best known of which are: *Les Jours et les nuits* (1897),

L'Amour en visite and *L'Amour absolu* (1898–99), *Messaline* (1901), *Le Surmâle* (1902), *La Papesse Jeanne* (1908), and *Gestes et opinions du Docteur Faustroll* (1911). Jarry, in an advanced state of alcoholism, died in poverty.

N. Arnaud, *Alfred Jarry* (Paris, 1974); M. Arrivé, *Les Langages de Jarry* (Paris, 1972); H. Béhar, *Etude sur le théâtre Dada et surréaliste* (Paris, 1967), and *Jarry, le monstre et la marionnette* (Paris, 1973); M. LaBelle, *Alfred Jarry* (New York, 1980); R. Shattuck, *The Banquet Years* (New York, 1968).

M. Berkvam

Related entries: ARTAUD; DADAISM; SURREALISM.

JAURES, JEAN (1859–1914), philosopher, teacher, journalist, socialist orator, and theoretician. He was born in Castres (Tarn) on 3 September 1859 into a family of traders and rural smallholders. His early intellectual brilliance was noted by an *inspecteur général* who channeled him toward the Ecole normale supérieure. In 1881, he came third in the *agrégation de philosophie* and began a teaching career at the Lycée d'Albi and Toulouse University.

An outstanding orator, Jaurès' natural passion for republican politics won him a place on the republican list for the Tarn department in the 1885 elections. As the youngest deputy in the 1885–89 parliament, his gradual disillusionmentwith Jules Ferry's Opportunism and his instinctive rejection of individualistic radicalism left him ill at ease as an unattached Left-Centrist. His real political education began to take shape only after his defeat in 1889 and his return to the University of Toulouse.

There, his insatiable thirst for ideas brought him into contact with socialist theory (Louis Blanc, Joseph Proudhon, Ferdinand Lassalle, and Karl Marx) at the same time as his voracious appetite for activism drew him toward the working class, especially the Carmaux miners. After his election as municipal councillor for Toulouse (July 1890), he gradually shifted, through closer contact with the urban working classes, toward an embryonic socialist commitment.

The Carmaux mining strike of 1892 saw the birth of Jaurès the socialist, as he witnessed for the first time the horrors of class struggle. The rest of his life was to be an uninterrupted attempt to synthesize his youthful and unshakeable republican credo with his mature and equally solid socialist faith. Elected deputy for Carmaux in a by-election in 1892 and the general election in 1893, he spent the 1890s broadening and deepening his political horizons. As a seminal theoretician and the supreme orator, he soon emerged as a natural leader of the socialist parliamentary caucus. In the Chamber of Deputies, he spoke with authority on a vast range of subjects, from education to agriculture, from military affairs to fiscal reform. As a socialist militant, he learned to appreciate, through regular participation in labor disputes (especially that of the Carmaux glass workers in 1895), both the moral and spiritual strengths of working-class culture and the tragic weakness of working-class collective organization. His early repudiation of anarchosyndicalism at the international Congress of London in 1896 (which also marked his entry into the Second International) was merely the first shot in a battle he was to wage with the Confédération générale du travail (CGT) for the next ten years.

The exuberance resulting from the socialist victory of 1893 gave way by 1897 to a more circumspect approach as Jaurès came to perceive the power of the state and the complexity of the task at hand. Narrowly defeated in 1898 after an electoral campaign marked by great physical violence, he withdrew temporarily from labor politics into journalism (as editor of the Paris daily *La Petite République*), history (he planned and in large part wrote the monumental *Histoire socialiste de la Révolution française*), and establishment politics (as an ardent champion of Alfred Dreyfus). The Dreyfus campaign, and his energetic support for the entry of socialist lawyer Alexandre Millerand into the bourgeois government of René Waldeck-Rousseau in 1899, marked the prelude to a five-year battle Jaurès was to wage in favor of a reformist ministerialist socialism whose primary task was to defend and consolidate the radical republic. Breaking with Edouard Vaillant and Jules Guesde, he founded the Parti socialiste français in 1902 and devoted himself to the republican politics of the Bloc des gauches, becoming, after his reelection in 1902, one of the vice-presidents of the Chamber of Deputies.

By 1904 Jaurès decided to abandon this ministerialist approach in favor of the more traditional revolutionary line, which was to form the basis for socialist unity in 1905. The decision of the Socialist International at Amsterdam in 1904 denouncing ministerialism and revisionism and demanding socialist unity was one factor among many that persuaded Jaurès to accept unity on the terms laid down by his rivals Guesde and Vaillant.

From this moment, however, his political alliance with Vaillant became the cornerstone of the unified Socialist party (SFIO) in the ten years before World War I. Even while, as the undisputed leader of the party, he took the leading role in formulating policy on almost every subject, two problems above all henceforth occupied his mind: the need for international action to prevent war and the need for closer working unity between the CGT and the SFIO. Not only did he inject into Vaillant's twenty-year-old campaign for socialist acceptance of syndicalist autonomy a remarkable degree of rhetorical passion and political flexibility, but he also developed a theory of the working class, which historiography has only recently begun to decipher.

On the international front, Jaurès worked ceaselessly, alongside Vaillant, for socialist action against war. His major theoretical contribution to the debate on republicanization of the army—*L'Armée nouvelle* (1911)—wasonly one element of Jaurès' deepening internationalism. His trip to Latin America in 1911 and his growing familiarity with the culture of Islam modified profoundly his earlier Eurocentrism. His impassioned orations in favor of peace, at Basel (1912), Pré St. Gervais (1913), and Brussels (1914), made many feel that he alone was the last barrier to the projects of warmongers and militarists. His assassination by a right-wing fanatic on 31 July 1914 was widely seen as a green light for the coming holocaust. His ashes were transferred to the Pantheon on 23 November 1924. He remains to this day the undisputed founding father of French socialism.

H. Goldberg, *The Life of Jean Jaurès* (Madison, Wisc., 1962); M. Rebérioux, "Jean Jaurès," in J. Maitron, ed., *Dictionnaire biographique du mouvement ouvrier français*, vol. 13, (Paris, 1975); *Bulletin de la Société d'études jaurésiennes* (Paris, 1960–present); M. Rebérioux, ed., *Jaurès et la classe ouvrière* (Paris, 1981).

J. Howorth

Related entries: ANTIMILITARISM; DREYFUS AFFAIR; SOCIALISM, 1870–1914; SOCIALIST PARTY; VAILLANT.

JEWS. Throughout the Third Republic, the French Jewish community was dwarfed by the much larger concentrations in North America and in Central and Eastern Europe. Intellectual achievement in Jewish matters and political leadership in the Zionist and Jewish socialist movements all came from elsewhere. Nevertheless, Jews played a role in French society that extended considerably beyond what their small numbers would suggest.

Jewish population figures cast into relief the wild exaggerations of anti-Jewish publicists, who frequently claimed that France was swamped with Jews. After 1872 the French government considered religious affiliation to be a private matter, and so information on it was no longer collected by government statisticians. In that year the French Jewish population was officially listed at 49,439 (not including Algeria or portions of Alsace lost to the German Empire), of whom 24,319 lived in Paris. Thereafter the numbers grew slowly and unevenly, following the rhythms of Jewish immigration, and so similarly did the concentration of Jews in the capital. East European Jews began to arrive in the 1880s, followed by Jews from Greece and Turkey after 1908. At the turn of the century, there were about 80,000 Jews in France, and 50,000 in Paris. By 1914, the total reached 100,000, of whom 40,000 were foreign born. In addition, there were about 70,000 Jews in Algeria. The post–World War I immigration, the first to reach a massive scale, significantly transformed the community. By 1939 there were about 300,000 Jews in France, about half of whom were foreign born and two-thirds of whom lived in Paris. Algerian Jewry grew to over 110,000, largely due to natural increase. Throughout the 1920s and into the 1930s came Russian, Polish, Rumanian, Greek, and Turkish Jews. Beginning in 1933 came Jewish refugees from nazism. The latter often left France soon after their arrival, and the total remaining in France probably did not exceed 50,000. Finally, in 1940, with the defeat of Belgium and Holland, came more Jewish refugees from those countries, the last to reach France before its own military collapse. The Jewish population had risen significantly between the world wars but remained much less than 1 percent of the total population. During the period of Nazi occupation, there were never more than 350,000 Jews in France, over 75,000 of whom were murdered by the Nazis.

French Jewry was extremely heterogeneous. The most assimilated among them, about half of the 1939 community, came from families that had lived in France for only a few generations, coming either from the old Sephardic concentrations in the south and southwest or, in far greater numbers, from eastern

France, mainly Alsace. These Jews manned the highly centralized community structures known as *consistoires*, set up by Napoleon I, and blazed a trail of achievement in French society. During the entire period, these Jews entered all walks of French life, with noted individual successes in intellectual and artistic pursuits (Marcel Proust, Emile Durkheim, Henri Bergson, Léon Brunschwicg), business (the Rothschilds, André Citroën), and politics (Joseph Reinach, Georges Mandel, Léon Blum). But along with material success and professional attainment went a marked separation from traditional Judaism and even a significant weakening of Jewish identity. Native French Jews tended to be extremely patriotic and liberal in matters of religious belief, and they progressively defined their Jewishness in terms derived from French republican ideals.

As Wladimir Rabi has said, French Jewry would likely have gradually dissolved had it not been for successive waves of immigration that renewed its collective sensibility. Immigrant Jews created a significant Jewish working class in Paris, with its own Yiddish-language press, its own organizations, and a distinctly different religious orientation. These Jews came from a much more traditional Jewish background, and although they realized a high degree of upward mobility, they nevertheless remained apart from the established community. With a Jewish identity generally much more clearly defined and firmly rooted in Jewish experience, these Jews were active in diverse and sometimes conflicting Jewish spheres—Zionism, Jewish socialism, religious orthodoxy.

However great the differences, all Jews were affected by the changing climate of opinion toward them in France. The French revolutionary tradition prescribed a unitary society, in which all citizens were theoretically equal and in which all were supposed to submerge their ethnic or cultural identities in the national community. Having benefited from the revolutionary tradition that emancipated them during the French Revolution, established French Jews sometimes felt uncomfortable when faced with unassimilated manifestations among their fellow Jews.

The anti-Semitic movement that began in the 1880s, in the sense of reaching a mass audience, attacked Jews for their lack of loyalty, for their disposition to exploit their non-Jewish neighbors, as well as for a variety of other sins, depending on the tastes and obsessions of particular anti-Jewish writers. During the Dreyfus affair at the end of the nineteenth century, opposition to Jews became a major item of public discourse, broadly associated with the antirepublican Right—nationalist, militarist, Catholic, and socially conservative. Although anti-Jewish views continued when the affair was finally settled, popular feeling against Jews diminished with the defeat of antirepublican forces. Jews benefited from the official favoring of immigration during the 1920s, a policy designed to help repair what was perceived to be French underpopulation. Anti-Semitic voices still existed, notably the monarchist newspaper and movement Action française, but they had little echo in French society. All this was to change, however, in a France beset with depression. With hard times came a recrudescence of anti-Jewish feeling, feeding on a handful of financial scandals in which Jews seemed to be prominently involved—Albert Oustric in 1930, Serge Stavisky (alias Serge Alexandre) in 1933. In addition to their failure to assimilate, Jews were now taxed with corrupting French public life and creating unemployment through their supposedly unrestricted immigration. The riots of February 1934 and particularly the advent of the Popular Front, led by the Jewish socialist and eventual prime minister Léon Blum, witnessed an explosion of hatred. For the Right and also for many who considered themselves of the Center, Jews were held to be at the root of France's problems. The Munich crisis of 1938 brought a new fearful image: the Jews leading France into an unwanted war. Jewish refugees were especially unpopular, and the government of Edouard Daladier took stern steps to curtail their flow to France. The last years of the Third Republic saw Jews besieged in French society, with many politicians and political groups calling openly for laws to restrict their rights.

P. Aubery, *Milieux juifs de la France contemporaine* (Paris, 1957); R. F. Byrnes, *Antisemitism in Modern France*, vol. 1 (New Brunswick, N.J., 1950); P. Hyman, *From Dreyfus to Vichy* (New York, 1979); M. R. Marrus, *The Politics of Assimilation* (Oxford, 1971); W. Rabi, *Anatomie du judaisme français* (Paris, 1962); D. Weinberg, *A Community on Trial* (Chicago, 1977).

M. R. Marrus
Related entries: ANTISEMITIC LEAGUE; ANTI-SEMITISM; DREYFUS AFFAIR; JUDAISM.

JOFFRE, JOSEPH (1852–1931), career army officer; commander in chief of the French armies on the Western Front in the First World War (1914–1916); marshal of France. Born in Rivesaltes (Pyrénées-Orientales) to an artisan family, he entered the Ecole polytechnique in 1869 at the age of seventeen. He participated in the defense of Paris during the Franco-Prussian War (1870–71) with the Army Engineers. He received a commission in the army as a captain in 1876 and for several years prepared fortifications on the eastern frontier. From 1885 to 1911 he served in the colonies in Indochina, the Sudan, and Madagascar. In 1911, he was named chief of the general staff, in part because he was considered a sound republican and could be relied on to carry out the directives formulated by the Ministry of War.

Joffre was responsible for French strategic planning for the First World War and took much of the blame for the failure of Plan XVII, which devised a mass attack by the French across their common border with Germany. Because he had not foreseen the potential for a German offensive through Belgium, his strategy was ineffective in meeting the German challenge. Following the German movement through Belgium, Joffre responded by stationing a French force on the outer flank of the British Army. Faced with superior German power, however, he was compelled to order a retreat until his forces were fighting on the outskirts of Paris. Joffre's skill in managing this retreat prevented the French Army from becoming encircled, and on 6 September 1914, he ordered a counterattack, which decisively stalled the German advance at the Battle of the Marne and saved the capital. His reputation as a commander displaying calm in battle is based on this victory.

The trench warfare that followed imposed tremendous hardship on the troops, and offensive movements could be attempted only at great cost. Joffre was unable to devise any effective means of attack, and his reputation suffered along with troop morale. When the Germans attacked Verdun early in 1916, Joffre persisted in pursuing a previously arranged plan and thereby delayed the effort to relieve that city. The costs of the defense of Verdun and the Battle of the Somme, which followed in July 1916, so thoroughly tarnished his reputation that he was removed from power on 13 December 1916 and relegated to a post as technical adviser to the government. On 26 December Joffre resigned his post and was named marshal of France, but his active military career was over. He continued to serve France as head of a mission to the United States in 1917, and to Japan after the war. In 1918 he was elected to the Académie française.

G. Arnoux, *Histoire populaire du Maréchal Joffre* (Paris, 1918); J. Badin and J. Tallez, *Joffre le catalan ou le maréchal en espadrilles* (Paris, 1935); H. Bordeaux, *Joffre ou l'art du commander* (Paris, 1933); R. Cahisa, *Joffre, Foch, Gallieni, fils des Pyrénées* (Villeneuve-de-Rivière, Haute-Garonne, 1943); F. Canonge, *Cinq épées glorieuses: Joffre, Pétain, Franchet d'Esperez, Fayolle, Foch* (Dijon, 1925); J. Converset, *Joffre* (Paris, 1918); M. Desmazes, *Joffre, ou la victoire du caractère* (Paris, 1955); J. d'Esme, *Joffre* (Paris, 1953), and, *Joffre le Père* (Paris, 1962); J. Fabry, *Joffre et son destin* (Paris, 1931); G. Hanotaux and J. Fabry, *Joffre le vainqueur de la Marne* (Paris, 1929); J. Isaac, *Joffre et Lanvezac, étude critique des témoignages sur le rôle de la V° Armée (août, 1914)* (Paris, 1922); J. Joffre, *Discours de réception à l'Académie française* (Paris, 1919), and *La Préparation de la guerre et la conduite des opérations (1914–1915)* (Paris, 1920); P. Lyet, *Joffre et Gallieni á la Marne* (Paris, 1938); G. Mermeix, *Joffre, la première crise du commandement (novembre 1915–décembre 1916)* (Paris, 1919); C. Muller, *Joffre et la Marne* (Paris, 1931); R. Recouly, *Joffre* (Paris, 1931); P. Varillon, *Joffre* (Paris, 1956).

J. K. Whiting

Related entries: MARNE, BATTLE OF THE; SOMME, BATTLE OF THE; VERDUN, BATTLE OF; WORLD WAR I.

JOFFRIN, JULES (1849–1890), militant of the post-Commune working-class movement in Paris; socialist municipal councillor and deputy. He was born in Vendeuvre-sur-Barse (Aube) and at age eighteen moved to Paris where he became a mechanic. He helped establish the mechanics' trade union in 1868 and was involved politically against the Second Empire. A member of the First International, he was involved in a minor way with the Commune and fled to England in May 1871. He played only a small role in exile politics in London and returned after the amnesty to Paris. He became an active member of the socialist movement and won the first major electoral victory for the socialists when he was elected a municipal councillor in 1882. He remained on the Paris municipal council until his death, with a brief interruption in 1884–86, and was elected to the Chamber of Deputies in 1885. A pragmatist, as well as a popular speaker, he played an important part in seeking modifications in the Parti ouvrier's minimum program and was in the forefront of opposition to Jules Guesde and Paul Lafargue. He thus joined with Paul Brousse and Jean Allemane in the intraparty dispute and following the split at the St. Etienne Congress in 1882 became one of the most militant activists of the Possibilist party in Paris. As a municipal councillor he fought for the municipalization of essential public services, and as a defender of the Republic he actively opposed Boulangism. He was identified with the Brousse faction during the conflicts that led to the departure of the Allemanists in 1890. His death of cancer in 1890 was a factor in weakening the position of the Possibilists in Paris in the 1890s.

G. Lefranc, *Le Mouvement socialiste sous la Troisième République, 1875–1940* (Paris, 1963); J. Maitron, ed., *Dictionnaire biographique du mouvement ouvrier*, vols. 6, 13 (Paris, 1964); D. Stafford, *From Anarchism to Reformism* (Toronto, 1971).

D. A. Stafford

Related entries: ALLEMANE; BROUSSE; POSSIBILISTS; SOCIALISM, MUNICIPAL.

JOUHAUX, LEON (1878–1954), syndicalist militant, long-term president of the Confédération générale du travail (CGT), winner of the Nobel Peace Prize. Born in Paris, he abandoned his studies and went to work in a safety match factory at Aubervilliers in 1895. He became an activist in his trade union and in 1905 was named a member of the national committee of the CGT. In 1909, he was elected secretary-general of that organization, a post he held until 1947.

Although he was committed to the syndicalist doctrine that the labor movement should remain free of political influence, Jouhaux's approach to syndicalism was pragmatic. His emphasis was on short-term economic gains for workers rather than the long-range goal of revolution. He was also willing to cooperate with the government when it seemed advisable. On the outbreak of World War I, he supported the *Union sacrée* and prevailed on a majority of the CGT's directors to cooperate with the government's war policies.

After the war, Jouhaux continued to champion reformist policies for the CGT. His minimum program, adopted by that body in December 1918, called for a shorter work day, better working conditions, and a role for workers in industrial management and in national economic planning. His suspicion of bolshevism and his refusal to align the CGT with the international Communist movement led to the exodus of some labor leaders, who in 1921 formed the rival Confédération générale du travail unitaire (CGTU). But the CGT continued to flourish under Jouhaux's leadership. Its membership increased, many of its policies won governmental approval, and in 1936 the CGTU rejoined the CGT. Jouhaux supported Léon Blum's Popular Front government in 1936 and played a role in the formulation of the Matignon Accords.

Although opposed to the Vichy regime (1940–44), Jouhaux remained in France. He was arrested in 1942 and imprisoned until the Liberation. Following World

War II, he returned to a leadership role in the labor movement. He was awarded the Nobel Peace Prize in 1951. He died on 28 April 1954.

B. Georges et al., *Léon Jouhaux*, 2 vols. (Paris, 1962–79); N. Papayanis, "Collaboration and Pacifism in France during World War I," *Francia* 5 (1977).

N. Papayanis

Related entries: CONFEDERATION GENERALE DU TRAVAIL; CONFEDERATION GENERALE DU TRAVAIL UNITAIRE; GRIFFUELHES; LABOR MOVEMENT; MATIGNON AGREEMENTS; MERRHEIM; SYNDICALISM; TRADE UNION MOVEMENT; *UNION SACREE*.

JOURDAIN, FRANTZ (1847–1935), Art Nouveau architect, propagandist for avant-garde art. He was born in Antwerp, Belgium, in 1847. His father was a singer and his mother a recognized poet. He was educated in Paris lycées and studied architecture at the Ecole des beaux-arts between 1867 and 1870. In 1870 he obtained French nationality and served as a volunteer in the Franco-Prussian War, being wounded and receiving the Military Medal. Starting in the 1880s, he began participating widely in the various artistic Salons and became an outspoken and influential critic of the academic system. He received the Legion of Honor in 1894 and became an officer in 1900.

As an architect, Jourdain restored chateaux and built villas, factories, shops, and modest houses, making inventive use of iron and concrete, the new materials of his time, in a generally simple, conservative version of Art Nouveau, quite the reverse of his virulent rhetoric. He is best known as the architect of the Samaritaine Department Store in Paris, having built the original store in an iron-framed, colorfully decorated Art Nouveau style between 1891 and 1907, and having later collaborated with Henri Sauvage on the store's Art Deco stone building along the Seine (1926–28).

Jourdain was a polemicist for modernity and for the avant-garde in the arts. In an autobiographical novel published in 1893, *L'Atelier Chantorel*, he castigated the narrow-minded, traditional teaching of the Ecole des beaux-arts. He campaigned against the conservatism of the Salons and was a cofounder and the first president of the avant-garde Salon d'automne in 1903. He was an anarchist and applied his libertarian political beliefs to a quest for free expression in the arts. He defended and aided many younger architects and artists, including Hector Guimard, Henri Sauvage, Le Corbusier, and Robert Mallet-Stevens. His son, Francis Jourdain, was a noted interior designer during the 1920s.

F. Borsi and E. Godoli, *Paris 1900* (New York, 1977); *Henri Sauvage, 1873–1932* (Brussels, 1976).

T. Shapiro

Related entries: ARCHITECTURE AND URBAN PLANNING; GUIMARD; LE CORBUSIER; MALLET-STEVENS; SAUVAGE.

JOUVENEL, BERTRAND DE (1903–), journalist, economist, and political philosopher. Born in Paris, the son of Henry de Jouvenel, senator for the Corrèze and editor of *Le Matin*, and Clair Boas, of a Jewish industrialist family, Bertrand de Jouvenel studied law, mathematics, and biology at the Sorbonne. His political education came with short periods as a secretary to the Czech foreign minister, Éduard Beneš, and as an assistant to Albert Thomas at the International Labor Office in Geneva. His career in journalism began with the position of editor-in-chief of the Radical weekly *La Voix* (1928–30), followed by four years as the economic specialist of the Radical daily *La République* (1930–34). Having joined the Radical party in 1928, he quickly became the leading theoretician of the left-wing "young Turks" within the party. His first two programmatic works, *L'Economie dirigée* (Paris, 1928) and *Vers les Etats-Unis d'Europe* (Paris, 1930), captured the central themes of his young associates.

Disillusioned by the Radicals' inability to implement reforms following their 1932 victory, he resigned from the party during the February 1934 crisis. Jouvenel then placed his hopes in the possibility of a coalition of youth disenchanted with the movements of both the Right and the Left but able to unite in support of an anticapitalist program. To this end he founded the short-lived *La Lutte des jeunes* (1934) and helped organize the Etats-généraux de la jeunesse. When this too failed, he turned to journalism of a different sort, as a special correspondent for two of the largest French dailies, *Le Petit Journal* and *Paris-Soir*. Frequently outside France, he scored his greatest journalistic coups in 1936 interviews with both Adolf Hitler and Benito Mussolini. In that same year, Jouvenel ran unsuccessfully for the neo-Socialist party in Bordeaux, did an enthusiastic tour of rebel frontlines in the first month of the Spanish Civil War, and returned to join the Parti populaire français of Jacques Doriot. He saw in Doriot the leader whom the youth movement had so sadly lacked, and for the next two years his energies went largely to writing for the party press, *L'Emancipation nationale* and *La Liberté*. Jouvenel broke with the party following the Munich crisis for, having strong ties to Czechoslovakia, he could not tolerate Doriot's support for appeasement.

He resumed the vagabond existence of an international reporter, touring Central and Eastern Europe for *Gringoire, Candide, Le Journal*, and *Paris-Soir*, but also sending reports to French military intelligence. His work for the army's Service de renseignements continued through the first year of the Occupation, at which time he withdrew from active political involvement to pursue the philosophical studies on which his current reputation is based. Works such as *Du pouvoir* (1945), *De la souveraineté* (1955), *The Pure Theory of Politics* (1963), *L'Art de la conjecture* (1964), *Arcadie* (1968), and *La Civilisation de puissance* (1976) differ radically in tone from his prewar writings but nevertheless reflect the wisdom gained through years of wandering in the political wilderness. His other writings include: *La Crise du capitalisme américain* (Paris, 1933); *Le Reveil de l'Europe* (Paris, 1938); *D'une guerre à l'autre* (Paris, 1940–42); *Après la défaite* (Paris, 1941); *La Dernier Année. Choses vues de Munich à la guerre* (Geneva, 1947); and *Un Voyageur dans le siècle* (Paris, 1980).

S. Berstein, *Histoire du parti radical* (Paris, 1980–81); J. R. Braun, "*Une Fidélité difficile*: The Early Life and Ideas of Bertrand de Jouvenel" (Ph.D. dissertation, University of Waterloo); R. Pierce, *Contemporary French Political Thought* (London, 1966); C.

Slevin, "Social Change and Human Values: A Study of the Thought of Bertrand de Jouvenel," *Political Studies* 19 (1971).

J. R. Braun

Related entries: BERGERY; CZECHOSLOVAKIA, ALLIANCE WITH; DEAT; DORIOT; LUCHAIRE; RADICAL AND RADICAL-SOCIALIST PARTY; ROCHE, EMILE; THOMAS.

JUDAISM. French Judaism was relatively uniform and assimilationist under the early Third Republic, but it became much more complex and diverse in the twentieth century under the influence of Jewish immigrants to France. The French Jewish community of the early Third Republic was socially, economically, and politically quite homogeneous. French Jews had been integrating themselves into the mainstream of society since their emancipation during the French Revolution; they defined their Judaism only in religious terms, they had great faith in republican institutions, and in times of crisis such as the Dreyfus affair, they tended to pursue a policy of official silence on political matters. The homogeneity of French Jewry was all the greater because the populous and tradition-minded Jewish communities of Alsace and Lorraine had been severed from France in the Franco-Prussian War.

Both the structure and the religious ideology of French Judaism in the final decades of the nineteenth century reflected the relative homogeneity and the general acculturation of the Jewish community. French Judaism was governed under a consistorial system at both the local and the national levels. Each of France's individual Jewish communities was directed by a board of rabbis and lay leaders, and a Central Consistory in Paris dominated the entire consistorial structure. The chief rabbi of France was a member of the Central Consistory, and that body directed the French rabbinical seminary. The government recognized consistorial authority as exclusive and absolute in Jewish affairs, it provided financial support for religious functions, and it paid the salaries of French rabbis. The consistories defined specifically Jewish interests rather narrowly and became involved only in purely religious, philanthropic, and educational affairs.

Although no Jewish Reform movement took root in nineteenth-century France, the leadership of French Jewry by 1870 had accepted an extensive liberalization of traditional practice in order to accommodate it to its French environment. In the late nineteenth century, shorter and more structured worship services incorporating a greater use of the French language were widely accepted, as were innovative services for newborns, for confirmands, and for the dead, all of which were influenced by the dominant Catholic idiom. Nonetheless, large numbers of French Jews had ceased the practice of even this modified Judaism by the end of the century.

Beginning around the turn of the twentieth century and culminating in the interwar years, a tremendous diversification occurred in French Judaism. The chief cause of this diversification was the arrival in France of thousands of Jewish immigrants, primarily from Eastern Europe. These immigrants came from societies in which their Judaism had always been viewed not only as a religious identity but as an ethnic and cultural identity as well, and they brought this broadly defined Judaism to France, where it had been largely abandoned by native Jews since their emancipation. One segment of the immigrant community also brought with it a religious orthodoxy that had not been altered by the nineteenth-century trend toward secularization. The immigrants found the existing French Jewish institutions at the turn of the century both unfamiliar and inadequate, and they soon began to organize their own philanthropic organizations, establish their own educational facilities, and appoint their own rabbis. As early as 1911 several of the small Orthodox congregations serving the immigrant community in Paris banded together in their own federation. The immigrants also initiated a wide variety of cultural activities and supported an active Yiddish press and theater; no fewer than 133 Yiddish periodicals appeared in France between 1918 and 1939. The religious and ethnocultural distinctions between the established Jewish community and that of the newcomers were reinforced by the general socioeconomic differences that divided a largely middle-class and liberal native Jewry from a largely working-class and often socialist immigrant Jewry.

The ability of the immigrant Jews to establish their own institutions outside the structure of the established Jewish community was enhanced by the separation of church and state that took effect in France in 1906, ending the consistories' near monopoly on organized Jewish life and opening the way for a proliferation of religious, cultural, and social organization. After 1906, state participation in religious expenses ceased, and the power of the consistorial system came to rest solely on the willingness of individual Jews to accept its authority. A state-supported consistorial system survived only in Alsace and Lorraine, which had been under German rule in 1906 and retained their system of religious organization when they were returned to France.

Initially relations between the established Jewish community and the immigrant community were dominated by the feeling of the native Jews that although they had a paternalistic obligation to aid the newcomers, they could expect the immigrants to accept their leadership and quickly conform to their image of Judaism. Although the consistorial leadership never abandoned its desire to integrate the immigrants into the narrowly defined Judaism, some younger members of the native community and some intellectuals for whom religious practice meant little did come to recognize the greater vitality of the ethnocultural Judaism of the newcomers. Seeking a way to redefine and revitalize French Judaism, some native Jews were attracted to the vigor of the immigrant community and also to elements of the Zionist ideology that many of the immigrants espoused. Thus, while young immigrant Jews were adapting more and more to the French culture around them, young native Jews were moving increasingly toward an accommodation of their French identity with an intensified Jewish identity. Although at some levels the two communities were beginning to grow closer together in the interwar years, a basic distinction between the ideology of the native Jewish leadership and that of the immigrants persisted. The difference in ideology was most clearly manifested in the responses of the two communities to the growing anti-Semitism of the 1930s; while the native Jews resorted to their traditional policy of quiet diplomacy and faith in the Republic, the immigrant community embarked on a variety of aggressive self-defense programs. The French Judaism that existed in 1940 was a far more complex and diverse one than that which had existed at the inception of the Republic some seventy years earlier, but the full development of the new French Judaism that was emerging in the early twentieth century under the influence of the newest French Jews was abruptly interrupted by the fall of the Republic and the decimation of the French Jewish community during the Holocaust.

P. Hyman, *From Dreyfus to Vichy* (New York, 1979); D. Weinberg, *A Community on Trial* (Chicago, 1977).

L. S. Weissbach

Related entries: JEWS; KAHN.

JUDICIAL SYSTEM: COURTS, civil, criminal, and administrative tribunals. There were four levels of civil courts: the justice of the peace (in each canton), the tribunal of first instance (in each arrondissement), the appeals court (in each of twenty-six jurisdictions—twenty-seven after 1919), and the court of cassation (Paris). In 1926, a law reduced to one per department the tribunals of first instance, but the former system was restored in 1930.

The justice of the peace heard cases involving fewer than 300 francs; cases involving larger sums had original jurisdiction in the tribunals of first instance. The decisions of the latter could be brought to the appeals court only to determine if the judges had decided a point of law correctly. If the appeals court reversed the original verdict, the case was sent down to another tribunal of first instance. If the second verdict agreed with the first, it could be brought to a second appeals court, the decision of which was final. The court of cassation could receive from the appeals courts, or initiate itself, questions about legal procedure, but it never reviewed a complete case from a lower court. It could not, therefore, be considered a French supreme court. The court of cassation was organized in three chambers, one each for civil cases, for criminal cases, and for the decision of which cases to accept for review. Once, in 1899 by parliamentary fiat, the three chambers sat together to order the retrial of Alfred Dreyfus.

There were three levels of criminal courts above the justice of the peace, who could impose small fines and brief imprisonments in trivial matters. Each arrondissement convened a correctional court to hear misdemeanors (*délits*) before a panel of judges drawn from the tribunal of first instance. The verdict of the judges could be appealed to the appeals court of the jurisdiction. For felonies (*crimes*), each department convened an assizes court, where alone among French courts a jury decided the verdict. The panel of judges was drawn from the appeals court of the jurisdiction and the tribunals of first instance of the department. There could be no appeal from the assizes court except on a point of law to the court of cassation.

A parallel set of administrative courts heard suits against the state or state officials. For each department, there was the prefect's council. Above them in Paris, with appellate authority, stood the Council of State (Conseil d'état).

R. C. K. Ensor, *Courts and Judges in France, Germany, and England* (London, 1933); R. David and H. P. de Vries, *The French Legal System: An Introduction to Civil Law Systems* (New York, 1958); R. de La Grasserie, *De la justice en France et à l'étranger au XXe siècle*, 3 vols. (Paris, 1914); B. F. Martin, *The Hypocrisy of Justice: Politics and the Courts in France in the Belle Epoque* (Baton Rouge, La., 1984).

J. M. Rife, Jr., and B. F. Martin

Related entries: GOVERNMENT: CONSEIL D'ETAT; JUDICIAL SYSTEM: JUDGES.

JUDICIAL SYSTEM: JUDGES, qualification, appointment, and ranks of magistrates; *avocats* and *avoués*. The French system of justice created a great distinction between the bar and the magistrature. Law students decided by the age of twenty-five which direction their careers were to take; crossovers were few.

A candidate for the magistrature had to complete his *licence en droit*, serve a twelve-month clerkship (*stage d'avocat*), pass a relatively easy *examen d'aptitude*, and win recommendation to the Ministry of Justice from a chief judge or justice. After 1908, there was a second, and no more difficult, examination. A successful candidate was appointed to a post in the Ministry of Justice, on the bench (as a judge), or on the parquet (as a prosecutor). In the ministry, the positions advanced from copying clerk (*expéditionnaire*) to clerk (*commis*) to head clerk (*rédacteur*) to deputy bureau chief (*sous-chef*) to bureau chief (*chef du bureau*). On the bench, the ranking was from substitute judge (*juge suppléant*) to judge (*juge*) to examining magistrate (*juge d'instruction*) to vice-president (*vice-président*) to chief judge (*président*) on the tribunals of first instance; for the appeals courts and the court of cassation, from associate justice (*conseiller*) to presiding justice (*président de la chambre*) to chief justice (*premier président*). For the parquet of a tribunal, there were assistant district attorneys (*substituts*) and a single district attorney (*procureur de la République*); for the parquets of the appeals courts and the court of cassation, there were assistant attorneys general (*substituts généraux*), solicitors-general (*avocats-généraux*), and, for each court, an attorney general (*procureur général*). Judges could not be removed; members of the parquet could be dismissed, as could ministry bureaucracy.

Promotions could be from any one of the three categories to the other two or within the original. As salaries and prestige at the lower ranks were minimal, there was great competition for promotion. The result was an inevitable politicization of the magistrature. Magistrates had to curry favor with the chief judges and justices, who recommended promotion of their subordinates, and with members of the Senate and the Chamber of Deputies, whose political power was respected by the minister of justice. Many politicians were members of the bar, and their influence over the minister of justice made magistrates, whether judges or prosecutors, leery of aggravating them in important cases.

Members of the bar practiced as either *avocats* or *avoués*. Each department was assigned a specific number of *avoués*, the attorneys who drew up the written briefs in cases before the tribunals of first instance and the appeals courts. In a species of venality, the office was purchased from the state. The conditions of candidature were almost identical to those for the post of magistrate. *Avocats*, independent professionals, could make oral arguments before the tribunals and appeals courts and were most effective in the assizes court before juries. A special group of sixty *avocats* was allowed to make both written and oral arguments before the court of cassation.

The justices of the peace were neither attorneys nor true magistrates. They were appointed by the president of the Republic on the recommendation of the minister of justice. They either held a certificate of *capacitaire en droit* or, more often, had completed ten years of public service.

R. C. K. Ensor, *Courts and Judges in France, Germany, and England* (London, 1933); R. David and H. P. de Vries, *The French Legal System: An Introduction to Civil Law Systems* (New York, 1958); R. de La Grasserie, *De la justice en France et à l'étranger au XXe siècle*, 3 vols. (Paris, 1914); B. F. Martin, "The Courts, the Magistrature, and Promotions in Third Republic France, 1871–1914," *American Historical Review* 87 (1982).

J. M. Rife, Jr., and B. F. Martin

Related entry: JUDICIAL SYSTEM: COURTS.

K

KAHN, ZADOC (1839–1905), chief Rabbi of France, 1889–1905. He was born in the Alsatian town of Mommenheim on 18 February 1839. He studied for the rabbinate in Metz and Paris and upon ordination became head of the preparatory school of the Paris rabbinical seminary. He became chief rabbi of Paris in 1868 and in 1889 was elected chief rabbi of France as well. He remained in his dual positions until his death on 8 February 1905. Throughout his career, Kahn was a great conciliator, working for the unity of the various elements within the French Jewish community. The implementation of the separation of church and state in 1906 meant that he was the last chief rabbi of France whose position was officially sanctioned by the government, and toward the end of his career he helped prepare for the transition to a communal organization based on the voluntary acceptance of consistorial authority.

Although Kahn's ability to become politically active was restricted by his sensitive public position and by his need to work closely with a largely conservative Jewish lay leadership, he nonetheless took an interest in virtually all the major political developments of his day which touched French Jewry. He was an early supporter of Alfred Dreyfus, the first leader of the Zionist Hibbat Zion movement in France, and a quiet supporter of Theodor Herzl's political Zionism. As chief rabbi, Kahn was concerned with the fate of persecuted Russian Jews and with the welfare of Jewish immigrants to the West. He was a principal organizer of the Société des études juives, and was instrumental in the establishment of its scholarly journal, the *Revue des études juives*.

M. R. Marrus, *The Politics of Assimilation* (Oxford, 1971); J. Weill, *Zadoc Kahn* (Paris, 1912).

L. S. Weissbach

Related entries: JEWS; JUDAISM.

KAYSER, JACQUES (1900–1963), radical journalist and historian of the press. Born in Paris, Kayser began his long career as a political militant by joining the Radical party in 1920 while still a law student. He was also active in the Internationale démocratique des jeunes, a short-lived attempt at a European coalition of non-Marxist but leftist youth groups, for which he undertook an organizing tour of the Balkans in 1922. A year later he was elected to the national bureau of the Radical party at a young age, beginning the first of many terms as a vice-president of the party. And quite naturally for a nephew of Alfred Dreyfus, he was also active in the Ligue des droits de l'homme. In 1924, he became a member of Edouard Herriot's cabinet at the Foreign Ministry. For the 1928 elections, he served as a full-time Radical organizer, giving speeches and, together with Jean Montigny, writing the main programmatic pamphlet for the party's oppositionist executive: *Le Drame financier: Les responsables*. Kayser's loyalty to Edouard Daladier was rewarded by appointment as the first administrative secretary of the Radical parliamentary group and, in 1929, as the first editor-in-chief of the new Radical daily, *La République*. With this Kayser began an active career in journalism, contributing regular articles to a host of Radical and leftist papers, including *La Voix, La Concorde, Le Monde, La Lumière*, and *La France de Bordeaux*, and later, *L'Oeuvre, Marianne, Vu, Vendredi* and *L'Europe nouvelle*.

The overriding themes of his writings were *paix* and *liberté*—a pacifist call for international accommodation and understanding and a leftist appreciation of the reforms necessary for the survival of democratic freedoms. Though Kayser is usually considered a leading member of the "Young Turks" movement within the Radical party, his concerns were often as close to the traditional republicanism of the party as to the more pragmatic reformism that typified the movement. Always on the left of the party, he was disconcerted enough with Radical inertia to resign as secretary of the parliamentary group during the February 1934 crisis, but he nevertheless remained in the party and played a leading role in the creation of the Popular Front as a Radical representative on the organizing committee. With the success of that coalition, he became Jean Zay's first *directeur du cabinet* at the Ministry of Education. Having already given courses at the Ecole des hautes études internationales, he turned to education as a career and, after the war, devoted himself primarily to lecturing and writing about the press. His writings include: *L'Europe et la Turquie nouvelle* (Paris, 1923); *Les Etats-Unis d'Europe* (Paris, 1926); *La Paix en péril* (Paris, 1931); *La Presse de province sous la IIIe République* (Paris, 1958); "Souvenirs d'un militant (1934–1939)," *Cahiers de la République* 12 (1958).

P. Larmour, *The Radical Party in the 1930's* (Stanford, 1964); M. Schlesinger, "The Development of the Radical Party in the Third Republic: The New Radical Movement, 1926–32," *Journal of Modern History* 46 (1974); P. Steinfels, "French Left-Wing Intellectuals and Foreign Policy: The Ligue des droits de l'homme" (Ph.D dissertation, Columbia University, 1976).

                                                                                J. R. Braun
Related entries: DALADIER; DREYFUS; HERRIOT; POPULAR FRONT; RADICAL AND RADICAL-SOCIALIST PARTY; ROCHE, EMILE.

KLEE, PAUL (1879–1940), Swiss painter, printmaker, and educator. His art, rooted in a variety of artistic traditions, defies precise categorization. He has been grouped with both expressionism and surrealism. Klee spent his youth and adolescence in Berne, Switzerland, where his father was a music teacher. Though equally given to art, music, and poetry, he decided to become a painter. At age nineteen he went to study in Munich, where he remained through World War I. During these years he traveled frequently, both inside Germany and abroad. Especially important for Klee's artistic development were his trips to France, Italy, and Tunisia. The last greatly influenced his use of color.

In 1920 Klee became a professor at the newly founded Bauhaus, where he was to teach until 1931, first in Weimar, then in Dessau. These years, during which he was in close contact with such artists as Wassily Kandinsky, Lyonel Feininger, Alexej von Jawlensky, and Oskar Schlemmer, were probably Klee's most fertile period. Heavily criticized by the emerging Nazi regime, Klee in 1933 returned to Berne, where he spent the remainder of his life.

Klee's work, mostly small scale, displays a variety of media and techniques. His imagery, inspired by such diverse sources as nature, architecture, children's drawings, non-Western calligraphy, and primitive art, is apparently playful yet highly sophisticated, combining automatism or psychic improvisation with a profound understanding of art theory and tradition. Whether representational, abstract, or semiabstract, Klee's work stands out through its poetic fantasy and subtle humor.

W. Grohmann, *Paul Klee* (New York, 1954); P. Klee, *Notebooks* (New York, 1978), and *Pedagogical Sketch Book* (New York, 1953).

P. t-D. Chu

Related entries: ART: MAJOR STYLES AND MOVEMENTS; EXPRESSIONISM; SURREALISM.

KUPKA, FRANK (1871–1957), Czechoslovakian painter, one of the founders of abstract and nonobjective art. Born in Opocno, Bohemia, on 23 September 1871, he worked from 1881 to 1886 as an apprentice to the village saddle maker. He attended the Prague School of Fine Arts from 1887 to 1891 and the Vienna Academy of Fine Arts from 1891 to 1893. During the late 1880s, he became deeply involved in spiritualism and became a medium. Around 1894 he moved to Paris, where he supported himself by drawing posters and illustrating books, as well as drawing for socialist and anarchist publications. He moved in 1904 to Puteaux, a working-class suburb of Paris, which remained his residence for many years.

The turning point in Kupka's career came in 1911 when he began research and experimentation studies that led him to paint his first abstract works. He was a member of the Salon d'automne and in 1912 exhibited paintings there that showed bright colors and fauvist cubist tendencies. Kupka volunteered for the French army in World War I and then returned to Czechoslovakia, where he was named professor at the Prague Academy of Fine Arts in 1918.

Although one of the founders of abstract art, his work received little attention until the late 1930s when his accomplishments were finally recognized. He was honored by exhibitions at the Jeu de Paume (1936) and in Czechoslovakia (1946), where a museum was founded in his name. After the Liberation he found new energy to overcome the bitterness and isolation he had encountered during the previous decade and worked strenuously until his death in June 1957. A major retrospective exhibition was held posthumously in 1958 at the National Museum of Modern Art (Paris), to which Kupka's second wife donated fifty of his paintings.

J. Cassau and D. Fedit, *Kupka* (New York, 1964); D. Fedit, *L'Oeuvre de Kupka* (Paris, 1966); Guggenheim Museum, *Frantisek Kupka, 1871–1957: A Retrospective* (New York, 1975); B. Meyers, *McGraw-Hill Dictionary of Art*, vol. 3 (New York, 1969); T. Shapiro, *Painters and Politics* (New York, 1976).

A. J. Staples

Related entries: ART: MAJOR STYLES AND MOVEMENTS; ART NOU-VEAU; CUBISM; SYMBOLISM.

L

LA ROCQUE, FRANCOIS DE (1886–1946), right-wing activist and leader of the Croix de feu. A cavalry officer who attained the rank of colonel and who saw active service in World War I and in North Africa, he entered politics on his retirement in 1929 when he joined the Croix de feu, theretofore a modest, apolitical veterans' organization. La Rocque soon became a dominant force in the Croix de feu, becoming president in 1931. The league expanded dramatically in the next several years, and La Rocque became a major force on the extraparliamentary Right. A handsome and imposing figure, he was an attractive symbol for those who were disgusted with the decadence of the Republic and sought a more authoritarian alternative. In fact, however, La Rocque was a singularly mediocre politician, lacking any clear ideological stance beyond vague and muddled rhetorical effusions. Although he boasted that he was above politics and independent of politicians, for several years he received subsidies from the conservative prime minister, André Tardieu. Despite his repeated calls for decisive action, he disappointed many by his vacillation and inaction on 6 February 1934 and during the sit-in strikes of May–June 1936. His denunciations of deputies and parliamentary politics sounded hollow when, after the dissolution of the leagues in June 1936, he founded the Parti social français (PSF), which actively sought to elect deputies. By the late 1930s the contradictions in his policies and the revelations of his relations with Tardieu prompted some major resignations from the PSF. He rallied to Philippe Pétain in 1940 but was awarded only an insignificant post.

W. D. Irvine, *French Conservatism in Crisis* (Baton Rouge, 1979); E. and G. de La Rocque, *La Rocque tel qu'il était* (Paris, 1962); P. Machefer, "Les Croix de Feu, 1927–1936." *L'Information Historique* (January–February 1972); P. Rudaux, *Les Croix de Feu et le PSF* (Paris, 1967).

W. D. Irvine

Related entries: CROIX DE FEU; FASCISM.

LA TOUR DU PIN CHAMBLY, RENE, COMTE DE (1834–1924), marquis de la Charce, monarchist and social Catholic theorist. Born 1 April 1834 in Arrancy-en-Laonnois (Meuse) to an ancient noble family of military and royalist tradition, La Tour du Pin was educated at St.-Cyr and the Staff School. He made a notable career in the Imperial Army in the Crimean War, the Italo-Austrian War, and the Franco-Prussian War. Taken prisoner at Metz in 1870, he met Albert de Mun and the following year joined with him to found the Oeuvre des cercles catholiques d'ouvriers. La Tour du Pin viewed social Catholicism as an extension of his family's paternalistic *noblesse oblige* and as a means of restoring a medieval corporatist society. In *L'Association catholique*, the journal of the Oeuvre des cercles, he developed a social Catholic theory that criticized economic and political liberalism and insisted that only a traditional monarchy could restore corporatism. In 1881, he futilely urged a military coup d'état in favor of the comte de Chambord, leading him to resign from the army, and in 1888–89, he organized a counter-centenary to the celebration of the 1789 Revolution. He refused to accept Pope Leo XIII's call for a *ralliement* in 1892 and broke with de Mun over it. After 1900, he turned to Charles Maurras and the Action française. He collected his writings in *Vers un ordre social chrétien; jalons de route, 1882–1907* (1907) and *Aphorismes de politique sociale* (1909). In March 1918, he was taken prisoner by the Germans for a second time when the family lands were occupied. He died in retirement at Lausanne, Switzerland, on 4 December 1924.

M. H. Elbow, *French Corporative Theory, 1789–1948* (New York, 1948); R. Talmy, *Aux sources du catholicisme social* (Tournai, 1963).

B. F. Martin

Related entries: ACTION FRANCAISE; CHAMBORD; CONSERVATISM; FRANCO-PRUSSIAN WAR; MAURRAS; MUN; *RALLIEMENT*.

LABOR MOVEMENT, efforts to advance the interests of workers, especially through trade-union activities. Any assessment of the labor movement under the Third Republic must take into account three basic variables: the socioprofessional composition of the French work force, mirroring the evolution of technology and industrial organization; of fundamental importance, the role and impact of ideology; and the political tensions and struggles within the French Left as a whole.

Alongside the traditional, militant, revolutionary labor movement, there existed two other labor movements, one based on Christian precepts of social morality and the other a right-wing instrument of the employers' pleasure. The former, the Confédération française des travailleurs Chrétiens (CFTC) (founded in 1919) was, in 1964, as the Confédération française démocratique du travail (CFDT), to merge into and become a vital part of the mainstream labor movement. The latter, the so-called *Jaunes*, cannot be counted as an integral part of the autonomous militant labor movement in France.

Until 1914 French labor remained essentially nonindustrial. As late as 1911 not only did agriculture still account for well over 40 percent of the working population, but also the tertiary sector, with 29.1 percent of the work force, was approximately the same size as the secondary (29.7 percent). As for the latter, it remained profoundly artisanal. On the eve of World War I, 60 percent of all industrial workers were employed in small shops of fewer than ten employees, and perhaps as many as 50 percent of these small shop workers were self-employed, independent artisans.

The persistence among these laboring people of a preindustrial mentality and culture was the predominant feature of the syndicalist movement during the *belle époque*, and the ideology generated at the time has had a lasting impact on the French labor movement right down to the present day, despite vast changes in technology and industrial organisation ever since. The values of *liberté, savoir-faire*, and *travail bien fait* combined with the rejection of collectivist socialism to perpetuate an individualistic, self-sufficient, pseudo-anarchist ideology that was the theoretical bedrock of what is often called revolutionary syndicalism or anarchosyndicalism. Bernard Moss prefers the term "socialism of skilled workers," and Jacques Julliard favors "direct action syndicalism" to designate this trend, but behind the diversity of label, most historians are agreed on the basic contours of this early labor ideology.

The first point to note is the almost total absence of anything approaching the trade union mentality that characterizes most Anglo-Saxon countries. The universalist rhetoric of the Jacobin tradition, coupled with the pluralist libertarianism of the Proudhonian ethos and an assertion of the primacy of the social as opposed to the political revolution, produced that unique blend of theory and practice, of rhetoric and reality, of utopia and science that was encapsulated in the Amiens Charter of 1906. To this day all labor organizations in France consider (or claim to consider) the Amiens Charter as the cornerstone of French syndicalism. In that seminal text, quantitative demands for immediate improvements in conditions are carefully balanced by qualitative aspirations toward the revolutionary new social order in which the *syndicats* (worker-controlled autonomous production units) would become the focal point of all social, economic, and political relations. Article 1 of the statutes of every French labor confederation has always included some reference to the ideological objective of replacing capitalism with a new social order.

But the Amiens Charter was also a product of the bitter infighting that characterized the entire French Left in the early Third Republic and, in particular, the violent tensions that marked relations between the labor and socialist movements. The revolutionary tradition charioted two potentially contradictory messages through the nineteenth century. It was the centralizing, statist, universalist political absolutes of Maximilien Robespierre that, taking a detour via Auguste Blanqui and Karl Marx, most attracted the socialists and, later, the communists. But it was the tradition inaugurated by the particularist, quasi-corporatist, decentralizing, direct social aspirations of the *sans-culottes*, updated and given new theoretical impetus by Pierre-Joseph Proudhon, that most appealed to the skilled workers. In the political context of the early Third Republic, this secular clash led to an extreme polarization, in which both sides exaggerated their claims, some socialists (especially the Guesdists) concentrating exclusively on the political conquest of the central state by a disciplined party and denigrating any other form of action, while many syndicalists going to the other extreme by claiming that it was possible to bypass political action altogether in favor of direct industrial action at shop-floor level.

Alongside the typographers, hatmakers, pottery workers, skilled builders, leather craftsmen, and other representatives of the artisanal world, who dominated the early Confédération générale du travail (CGT) because of a voting system that gave equal weighting to each trade irrespective of membership, new categories of industrial worker created by changing technology were beginning to emerge: textile workers, metal workers in light and heavy engineering, extraction workers, railwaymen. Some of these, especially the more unskilled, uprooted operatives of the vast textile factories of the north or the impersonal metal transforming plants of the center of France, could be persuaded by socialist orators to opt for a collectivist political solution to their problems. They were to provide the embryonic model for latter communist attempts to organize the labor movement. Other workers, either because their leader happened to be a moderate man or for more complex psychopolitical reasons, took their distance from the insurrectionary rhetoric of the revolutionary syndicalist majority and even before 1914 stressed the quantitative element of the Amiens Charter rather more than the qualitative.

Some historians have drawn attention to these internal divisions within the CGT to question the reality of the revolutionary commitment of the early labor movement. Others, poring over membership figures, have seen a cause without rebels. Both approaches ignore the fundamental role of ideology as the heart of a political culture in which the revolutionary objective was always taken for granted. The debate was not so much between revolutionaries and reformists as between two conflicting strategies for arriving at the social revolution all believed in (even if it was only at the level of myth). The structure of the CGT in terms of vast multiprofessional industrial federations rather than along trade or corporatist lines was a conscious attempt to foster ideological awareness at the expense of corporate or sectional interest. When the basic objective was not financial provision for a long strike aimed at increasing wages (as in trade unionism) but ideological and political training for a new society, paid-up members were less important than genuine widespread, if latent, support and comprehension in quiet times, followed by a serious commitment to militant action when *le Grand Soir* was felt to be nigh.

It was the illusions spread by the revolutionaries as to the imminence or simplicity of *le Grand Soir* (rather than the event itself) that were the main target of the reformists' critiques. They felt that, while awaiting the event that all of French history since 1789 had taught them to be inevitable, much more could be done through various institutional channels to alleviate immediate problems.

Nevertheless, from 1896 when the CGT was founded, until 1909, when it began to tone down some of its more radical rhetoric, it was the ideological faith of the revolutionaries that drew most attention.

That ideological faith was profoundly rocked (but never destroyed) by developments in the early twentieth century. Politically the years 1906 to 1920 saw a series of grave defeats for the tactics of revolutionary syndicalism. The abysmal failure of the 1906 general strike, the increasingly bloody confrontation with troops on the strike field, the humiliating collapse of syndicalist antimilitarism in 1914, the success of the Bolshevik model in 1917, and the total failure of the second attempt (if such it was) to activate a revolutionary general strike in 1920 combined to transfer the patents for revolutionary action from the pre-1914 CGT to two new pretenders: communism and a peculiarly French form of democratic statist unionism developed by Léon Jouhaux.

These political developments were assisted by major shifts in the work experience after 1918. Although by 1939 the statistical composition of the work force had not changed dramatically from its 1906 configuration (see table), vast shifts in the pattern of wage labor had produced important changes in the attitudes and methods of the labor movement.

Work Force Statistics, 1872–1936 (in millions)

	1872	1911	1936
Total population	36.1	39.6	41.9
Working population	14.6	20.9	20.5
	(40.4%)	(52.8%)	(48.9%)
Primary	7.2	8.6	7.2
	(49%)	(41.2%)	(35.1%)
Secondary	3.8	6.2	6.2
	(26%)	(29.7%)	(30.5%)
Tertiary	3.5	6.1	6.9
	(24%)	(29.1%)	(33.9%)

Source: J.-C. Toutain, "La Population de la France de 1700 à 1959," cahiers de l'ISEA, Série AF, no. 3 (January 1963).

The advent of Taylorism in the mass production industries, and even in extractive industries such as mining, rapidly broke down the predominance of the individualistic or local political cultures that had characterized the pre-1914 labor movement. Combined with the aforementioned political defeats, this gave much of the syndicalist movement a sense, first, of despair and, later, of salvation through collective action either of the communist or of the democratic statist variety. Both were derivatives of the Robespierre ethos. For the moment, the libertarian tradition was to be put on ice.

Communism, combining the insurrectionary energy of *Hébertisme* with the elitist *dirigisme* of Auguste Blanqui and Vladimir Lenin, sought the fulfillment of the universals first mooted in 1792 through the political action of a new party, to which the social aspirations of the labor movement (in conformity with condition 9 of the Twenty-one Conditions for membership of the Comintern) were to be strictly subordinated. The CGTU (Confédération générale du travail unitaire), founded in 1922 as a direct consequence of the splitting of the world Left on Bolshevik orders, attracted initial support from the huge, increasingly proletarian industrial federations whose members had either been subjected to Taylorist disqualification (automobile workers and other metallurgical trades, miners) or had suffered most directly from the defeat of anarchosyndicalism in 1920 (railway workers, builders). However, their numbers were to oscillate wildly as the political battles on the Left and bolshevization of the Parti communiste français (PCF) were to take their toll on workers' faith in any form of action.

Jouhaux's interwar CGT, mindful of the failure of the confrontational tactics of the anarchosyndicalists, elaborated a new ideological and political approach, which was a combination of prudence, realism, and vision. Reversing totally the pre-1914 antistatist approach, Jouhaux pleaded in favor of a "politics of presence," which advocated the participation of CGT functionaries at every level where negotiations were taking place. The ideological objective now became a new, tripartite form of industrial control, in which representatives of the workers, the consumers, and the state would share power in a series of vast nationalized industries. In this way, the aspirations of the skilled workers could be ideologically married both to the developments of industry and to the requirements of a transformed social, economic, and political world. The new CGT appealed to both the continuing remnants of the old artisan trades (tailors, typographers, leather workers, glassmakers) and the growing ranks of public-sector workers, for whom negotiations with, and even a place in, the state seemed quite natural.

These two contending organizations succeeded in splitting the French labor movement more deeply than even the architects of the Amiens Charter in their worst nightmares could have feared. In the context of the bitter polemics between socialists and communists throughout the 1920s and early 1930s, French workers, already defeated and demoralized professionally and politically, now became a prey to the rival organizational and ideological ambitions of CGTU and CGT. Not surprisingly, membership in both organizations plummeted. It must be borne in mind, however, that the strategy and forms of action of both wings of the labor movement tended to downplay membership in favor of support. Jouhaux's emphasis on presence in the negotiating chamber depended less on the ability of the labor movement to impose itself by force of numbers than on the emergence of an ideological and political climate in France in which the role of labor as an equal social partner would be recognized by the state, the political class, and, if possible, the employers. The CGTU's strategy, predicated as it was on a communist takeover of power through the central state, relied more on syndicalist cadres than on members. Those cadres were to prove invaluable in orienting and directing the masses when they began to flood into the reunified movement in the heady days of the Popular Front after 1936, especially in the wake of the great strikes of that year.

The 1936 strikes have been the subject of endless historiographical controversy. Neither entirely spontaneous nor evidence of a Moscow-controlled conspiracy, the strikes were probably a complex reaction to a combination of pent-up frustration, long-term oppression, illusions created by the election of the left-wing government and by the sempiternal myth of *le Grand Soir*. Recent case studies have established a clear communist influence in the outbreak of the strike at some of the largest plants (Renault and the coal mines), but elsewhere workers struck with no clear sense of what they were aiming at or of what to do next. Moreover, while the PCF and the CGTU may have aimed to take advantage of the new social explosion to increase their influence and control, the evidence suggests that they never really succeeded in doing more than help organize the day-to-day management of the strikes. However, their clear-sighted and energetic approach to this task did facilitate their renewal of contact with the mass labor movement. The result was that communist influence within the CGT began to increase dramatically even before the Second World War. The communists' ability to give a sense of meaning and direction to what was in 1936 a highly amorphous movement won them the mass support that the distant and increasingly remote Jouhaux was neither particularly able nor particularly concerned to secure. The increasing proletarianization of French labor, coupled with the heroic role played from 1941 to 1945 by communists in the Resistance and by the Soviet Union, combined to complete a process begun in 1935. The takeover of the French labor movement by communism after 1945 in many ways was a logical development of the events of the interwar and war years. But the spirit that presided over the birth of French labor—the pluralistic libertarianism of the anarchosyndicalists—had roots that were too deep in French social and political culture to die away altogether. They were to be revived in a new form, in large part as a reaction to communist influence over the labor movement, in the post-1964 CFDT.

The two strands of political culture (Jacobin centralism and *sans-culotte* direct action) have acquired unshakeable credentials within the French labor movements over the centuries. History has given priority first to the one and then to the other. Neither is likely to disappear overnight. The French labor movement cannot escape the heritage of its past.

J. Bron, *Histoire du mouvement ouvrier français*, 3 vols. (Paris, 1968–74); E. Dolléans, *Histoire du mouvement ouvrier*, 3 vols, (Paris, 1936–53); H. Dubief, *Le Syndicalisme révolutionnaire* (Paris, 1969); J. Julliard, *Fernand Pelloutier et les origines du syndicalisme d'action directe* (Paris, 1971); M. Labi, *La Grande Division des travailleurs: première scission de la CGT* (Paris, 1964); G. Lefranc, *Le Mouvement syndical sous la Troisième République* (Paris, 1967); V. Lorwin, *The French Labor Movement* (Cambridge, Mass., 1954); J. Maitron, *Histoire du mouvement anarchiste en France* (Paris, 1951); P. Monatte, *La Lutte syndicale* (Paris, 1978); B. Moss, *The Origins of the French Labor Movement: The Socialism of Skilled Workers* (Berkeley, 1976); F. Ridley, *Rev-*

olutionary Syndicalism in France: The Direct Action of Its Time (Cambridge, England, 1971); P. Stearns, *Revolutionary Syndicalism and French Labor, a Cause without Rebels* (New Brunswick, N.J., 1971).

J. Howorth

Related entries: AMIENS, CHARTER OF; ANARCHISM; BOURSE DU TRAVAIL; CONFEDERATION GENERALE DU TRAVAIL; CONFEDERATION GENERALE DU TRAVAIL UNITAIRE; GRIFFUELHES; INDUSTRY; JACOBINISM; JOUHAUX; STRIKES: TYPES AND PATTERNS; SYNDICALISM; TRADE UNION MOVEMENT; WORKERS, INDUSTRIAL.

LAFARGUE, LAURA (1846–1911), daughter of Karl Marx and wife of socialist Paul Lafargue. Born in Brussels, she was reared and educated in England. In 1868 she married Paul Lafargue, a frequent visitor in the Marx home. The couple had three children, all of whom died young. Always poor, the Lafargues became financially secure only with an inheritance from Friedrich Engels upon his death in 1895. With her husband, she committed suicide in 1911.

F. Engels and P. and L. Lafargue, *Correspondance* (Moscow, 1960); D. McClellan, *Karl Marx* (New York, 1974); C. Willard, *Les Guesdistes* (Paris, 1965).

C. S. Doty

Related entries: GUESDE; GUESDISTS; LAFARGUE, P.; MARXISM; SOCIALISM, 1870–1914.

LAFARGUE, PAUL (1842–1911), socialist politician, Marxist theoretician, medical doctor. Of mixed French Jewish, Carib Indian, and mulatto ancestry, he was born in Santiago, Cuba, the son of a Bordeaux businessman with property holdings in Cuba. He spent his early childhood in Cuba, but returned to France at the age of nine to further his education first at the lycée in Bordeaux, then in Toulouse. He moved to Paris in the early 1860s, where he studied pharmacy and worked briefly as a pharmacist before enrolling in the School of Medicine of the University of Paris. During these years he also became involved in the radical student opposition to the political and educational policies of Emperor Napoleon III and wrote for *La Rive gauche* and other ephemeral republican newspapers. In 1865 he journeyed to London, where he met Karl Marx, and in October of the same year helped to organize an international student congress in Liège, Belgium, whose proceedings were marked by inflammatory speeches critical of higher education in France. Expelled from the University of Paris for his role in the congress, he went to London in 1866 to continue his medical studies. A frequent visitor at the home of Marx, he courted and in 1868 married Marx's daughter, Laura. He earned his medical degree in the same year.

While in London, Lafargue was drawn into the activities of the First Workingmen's International, of which Marx was president. From 1866 he served as Spain's representative on the International's general council. Gradually he discarded his eclectic radicalism for Marxist collectivism, and he became close to Friedrich Engels, with whom he maintained an extensive correspondence for more than twenty-five years. Returning to France in 1870, Lafargue remained deeply involved in the work of the International, briefly in Paris, then in Bordeaux where he served as corresponding secretary for the local section. Fearing prosecution for his participation in a campaign of April 1871 to establish a revolutionary municipal government in Bordeaux modeled on the Commune of Paris, Lafargue and his family fled to Spain. As delegate of the general council of the International, he spent a year in Madrid seeking unsuccessfully to advance the cause of the Marxists against the rival Bakuninists within the Spanish section.

During these years in France and Spain, the Lafargues suffered the loss of three children. Sustained by their close personal and working relationship, they returned to London in 1872, where they remained for a decade. Despondent over the character of the medical profession, Lafargue abandoned his medical practice during this period. Working only occasionally at modest commercial pursuits, he and Laura lived on subsidies from Engels and other benefactors while they devoted themselves more exclusively to the socialist cause.

In 1882 Lafargue returned to France, where over the following thirty years he played an instrumental role in the organization and growth of the socialist movement. Together with Jules Guesde, he transformed the Workers party (*Parti ouvrier*) during the 1880s and 1890s from a small sect with scattered constituencies into a well-organized national party. Lafargue contributed to all aspects of the party's endeavor: the planning of party congresses, journalism, the formulation of party platforms and doctrine, the translation of the basic works of Marx and of Engels into French, and speaking tours throughout the country. He was a better writer than speaker, and he soon acquired a reputation as one of the party's leading Marxist theoreticians, although the depth of his thought is a topic that continues to be debated among historians.

Lafargue was elected to the Chamber of Deputies in 1891, thanks in large measure to a campaign launched by the Workers party to advance his candidacy in protest over his arrest, conviction, and imprisonment for having incited riots among workers at Fourmies on May Day 1891. He had delivered speeches in that town a few days before. Gaining an upset victory in the first electoral district of Lille in October, he was immediately released from prison and took his seat in the Chamber. Unable to win reelection in 1893, he continued to work for the unification of the various socialist factions into a single party, a goal accomplished in 1905 with the founding of the Socialist party (SFIO). An active leader in this party until his death six years later, he was suspicious of proposals for collaboration with non-socialist parties, as he was of the revisionist tendencies among many Marxist theoreticians.

Unwilling to face the ravages of old age, the Lafargues committed suicide together on 25 November 1911, just short of Paul's seventieth and Laura's sixty-sixth birthday.

E. Bottigelli, ed., *Friedrich Engels, Paul and Laura Lafargue: Correspondance*, 3 vols. (Paris, 1956–59); J. Bruhat, "Paul Lafargue et la tradition du socialisme révolutionnaire français," *Cahiers internationaux* 6 (1949); J. Girault, *La Commune et Bordeaux*

(Paris, 1971); L. Kolakowski, *Main Currents of Marxism*, vol. 2 (New York, 1981); G. Lichtheim, *Marxism in Modern France* (New York, 1966); N. McInnes, "Les Débuts du marxisme théorique en France et en Italie, 1880–1897," *Cahiers de l'institut de science économique appliquée*, series S, 102 (June 1960); J. Maitron, ed., *Dictionnaire du mouvement ouvrier*, vol. 6 (1969); C. Willard, *Les Guesdistes* (Paris, 1965), and "Paul Lafargue et la critique de la société bourgeoise," in D. Grisoni, ed., *Histoire du marxisme contemporain*, vol. 3 (Paris, 1977).

P. H. Hutton

Related entries: COLLECTIVISM; COMMUNES IN PROVINCIAL CITIES; DEVILLE; GUESDE; GUESDISTS; INTERNATIONAL, FIRST WORKING-MEN'S; LAFARGUE, L.; MARXISM; SOCIALISM, 1870–1914; SOCIALIST PARTY.

LAGUERRE, GEORGES (1858–1912), eloquent radical politician, stalwart of the Boulangist movement, celebrated trial lawyer. He was born in Paris, the son of a notary's clerk. He studied at the lycée Condorcet in Paris, then entered the military academy at Saint-Cyr, but left to study law. He was admitted to the bar in Paris in 1879. He became interested in politics at an early age, serving as secretary to the social theorist Louis Blanc in 1878 and as a reporter for Georges Clemenceau's newspaper, *La Justice*, during the early 1880s. But it was as a trial lawyer that Laguerre established his reputation during these years, gaining wide publicity for his defense of notorious criminals, as well as social revolutionaries (Blanquist demonstrators), anarchists (Pyotr Kropotkin, Louise Michel), and striking workers (in Montceau-les-mines, Decazeville, Lyons, and Saint-Etienne). He married feminist leader Marguerite Durand.

Laguerre was elected to serve the Vaucluse in the Chamber of Deputies in 1883 and was reelected in 1885. Associating himself with the radical faction of Georges Clemenceau, he used his forensic skill to promote such causes as revision of the constitutional laws, tax and judicial reform. From 1887 he lent energetic support to General Georges Boulanger, and during the Boulangist electoral campaigns of 1888–89 he served as editor of *La Presse*, the official Boulangist newspaper, and as a member of both the Republican Committee of National Protest (the Boulangist campaign headquarters) and the directorate of the League of Patriots. He was easily elected to the Chamber of Deputies as the Boulangist candidate for the fifteenth arrondissement of Paris in 1889.

But the demise of the Boulangist movement permanently damaged Laguerre's political career. He was defeated in his bid for reelection in Paris in 1893, and three times more (1898, 1902, and 1906) in his attempt to regain his old seat in the electoral district of Apt in the Vaucluse before finally being elected a senator for the Vaucluse in 1910. During these many years of political inactivity, he returned to the practice of law. He died suddenly at Gournay-sur-Marne (Seine-et-Oise) at the age of fifty-four.

A. Bertrand, *La Chambre de 1889* (Paris, 1890); C. d'Eschevannes, *Laguerre et ses amis* (Vaison, Vaucluse, 1924); J. Jolly, ed., *Dictionnaire des parlementaires français*, vol. 6 (1970); J. Néré, *Le Boulangisme et la presse* (Paris, 1964); A. Robert et al., eds.,

Dictionnaire des parlementaires français, vol. 3 (1891); F. H. Seager, *The Boulanger Affair* (Ithaca, N.Y., 1969).

P. H. Hutton

Related entries: BOULANGER; BOULANGER AFFAIR; DURAND; LAISANT; LAUR; NAQUET.

LAISANT, CHARLES-ANGE (1841–1920), radical politician, ardent supporter of General Georges Boulanger, journalist and pamphleteer, engineer and mathematician. He was born at La Basse-Indre (Loire-Inférieure) on 1 November 1841. A student at the Ecole polytechnique from 1861 to 1863, he was commissioned an engineering officer in the army upon graduation and served as a captain during the Franco-Prussian War (1870–71). Resigning from the army in 1875, he earned the *doctorat ès sciences* in mathematics in 1877.

Laisant was actively involved in politics from the outset of the Third Republic. He was elected to the general council of the department of the Loire-Inférieure in 1871 and to the Chamber of Deputies in 1876, where he served continuously until 1893, representing the Loire-Inférieure until 1885 and the department of the Seine thereafter. In the Chamber, he sat with the extreme left wing of the republicans and supported such proposals as amnesty for the Communards, the separation of church and state, the termination of colonization abroad, and democratic reform of the constitutional laws. Among the most vigorous radical critics of the moderate republican (Opportunist) leaders of government, he was the author of several political pamphlets and served as political director or as editor of a number of newspapers, among them *Le Petit Parisien* (1879) and *La République radicale* (1881). His political philosophy is most completely expressed in his book, *L'Anarchie bourgeoise* (1887).

Laisant is best known for his leading role in the electoral campaign in behalf of General Boulanger from 1887 to 1889. He was a member of both the Republican Committee of National Protest (the Boulangist headquarters) and the League of Patriots during these years, and he successfully ran for the Chamber of Deputies as a Boulangist candidate in Paris' eighteenth arrondissement in 1889.

Retiring from politics in 1893, Laisant turned to teaching and scholarship in his later years. He participated actively in learned societies, was keenly interested in pedagogy and wrote a number of papers on mathematics. He died at Asnières (Seine) on 5 May 1920.

A. Bertrand, *La Chamber de 1889* (Paris, 1890); P. H. Hutton, "Popular Boulangism and the Advent of Mass Politics in France, 1886–90," *Journal of Contemporary History* 11 (1976); J. Jolly, ed., *Dictionnaire des parlementaires français*, vol. 6 (1970); J. Néré, *Le Boulangisme et la presse* (Paris, 1964); A. Robert et al., eds., *Dictionnaire des parlementaires français*, vol. 3 (1891).

P. H. Hutton

Related entries: BOULANGER; BOULANGER AFFAIR; LAGUERRE; LAUR; NAQUET.

LAMY, ETIENNE (1846–1919), a leader of the *ralliement*. Elected to the Chamber of Deputies as a republican in 1871, Lamy voted with the republican majority in the *seize mai* crisis. His continued support for the regime despite the fact that he was a devout Catholic caused Pope Leo XIII to choose him as leader of the *rallié* forces in preparation for the legislative elections of 1898. Lamy believed that the *ralliement* would succeed if Catholic candidates made clear their support for the Republic and their willingness to cooperate with the Opportunist majority. His hopes were dashed by the poor showing of *rallié* candidates in the elections. His policy failed because he was unable to persuade Catholic politicians to adhere to the regime without reservations or republicans that the *ralliement* had effectively put an end to conservative opposition to the existing form of government.

A. Sedgwick, *The Ralliement in French Politics, 1890–98* (Cambridge, Mass., 1965).

A. Sedgwick

Related entries: RALLIEMENT; ROMAN CATHOLICISM: CHURCH–STATE RELATIONS.

LANGE, ROBERT (1903–), the most active French propagandist for the League of Nations. Few men have devoted their formative years to the cause of a single institution as did Lange. In January 1923, while still a student in the Law Faculty in Paris, he organized the Groupement universitaire pour la Société des Nations and later in the same year was the key instigator of the Comité d'action pour la Société des Nations, a coalition of adult and youth groups for the League of Nations and the sympathetic Union fédérale veterans' group. In April 1924, he went to Prague to found the Fédération universitaire internationale pour la Société des Nations. In 1925 he founded the Tribune internationale, a debating forum for foreign students studying in Paris. All four ventures were relatively successful, gaining wide publicity, attracting talented members, and sustaining activity well into the 1930s. Several of Lange's key activists in the youth group went on to stellar careers: Pierre Cot, Bertrand de Jouvenel, Pierre Brossolette, René Pleven, and even the very young Georges Pompidou. Lange devoted much of his time in the 1920s to propagating the idea of the league in meetings, speeches, and brochures. Even his doctoral dissertation in law dealt with the league: "Vers un gouvernement international? La Société des Nations et la composition du conseil" (Paris, 1928).

Upon its completion, Lange took up journalism, becoming editor in chief first of *La Renaissance* (1928–31) and then of *La République* (1933–34), followed in turn by a year as assistant director of Jean Luchaire's *Notre temps* (1934–35). Long active in the Radical party, he achieved prominence within its ranks in the mid-1930s with election to the national bureau, also serving as a party delegate on the Popular Front committee and running unsuccessfully in the 1936 elections. His active support for the Popular Front coincided with a reversal of his earlier foreign policy emphasis on the need for a Franco-German understanding. The turning point appears to have been a 1935 trip to Germany as an impartial witness to Georges Scapini's private interview with Adolf Hitler. Being Jewish, Lange had developed a natural distaste for the Nazi regime from the beginning, but only in 1935 did he conclude that a diplomatic understanding with that regime was no longer possible. Lange is currently engaged in writing his memoirs.

G. Lefranc, *Histoire du front populaire* (Paris, 1974).

J. R. Braun

Related entries: COT; JOUVENEL; LUCHAIRE; POPULAR FRONT; RADICAL AND RADICAL-SOCIALIST PARTY; ROCHE, EMILE.

LANGLOIS, CHARLES-VICTOR (1863–1929), one of the most influential proponents of the new type of historical scholarship introduced in the French university system toward the end of the nineteenth century. He became the beloved patron of an entire generation of medievalists in France who rejected the anecdotal, impressionistic approach to historical research and writing in favor of the critical methods of scholarship developed in the seminars of the German universities. He was the object of harsh criticism from defenders of the literary and philosophical tradition of historical writing, such as Charles Péguy, who accused him of undermining that tradition and poisoning the minds of France's future historians with the pseudoscientific canons of monographic scholarship borrowed from across the Rhine.

Langlois received his professional training at the Ecole des chartes under the German-trained scholar Paul Meyer and then at the Sorbonne, where he completed his doctorate under Ernest Lavisse in 1887. A year later he received an appointment at the Sorbonne, where he codirected with Charles Seignobos the renowned historiography course that resulted in the publication of their influential primer on historical methodology, *Introduction aux études historiques*, in 1898. In addition to his methodological writings, Langlois produced a number of groundbreaking monographic studies in French medieval history as well as the synthetic work *La Vie en France du moyen age* (1908).

W. R. Keylor, *Academy and Community: The Foundation of the French Historical Profession* (Cambridge, Mass., 1975), and "Charles Péguy as Historical Critic," in D. B. Weiner and W. R. Keylor, eds., *From Parnassus: Essays in Honor of Jacques Barzun* (New York, 1976); M. Siegel, "Science and the Historical Imagination: Patterns of French Historiographical Thought, 1866–1914" (Ph.D dissertation, Columbia University, 1966).

W. R. Keylor

Related entries: LAVISSE; SEIGNOBOS.

LANGUAGES OF FRANCE. Among the languages spoken in France in the Third Republic, only French itself registered any real gains in the percentage of the population able to deal in that language. This was largely the result of the laws of June 1881 mandating free primary state education in French. A concomitant result was an increase in bilingualism, as many people, though conversant with the official language, maintained their native language in unofficial surroundings.

The percentage conversant with another language declined also, but this process has been much slower, as the romantic interest in folklore and dialects counterbalanced the centralizing forces to maintain secondary languages in vigor.

Standard French underwent few changes in the course of its natural development: the velarization of the *r*, introduced in the late eighteenth century, was standard pronunciation by 1940, as was the pronunciation [wa] for *oi*, which eliminated [we] after centuries of hesitation. Distinctions of vowel by length disappeared, and [j] became the general pronunciation of *ill*.

There were few syntactical changes, of which the emergence of the *passé surcomposé* is the most notable. Vocabulary changes were considerable and consonant with evolving technology and mores; the major sources for borrowings were the classical languages and English. The publication of Emile Littré's *Dictionnaire de la langue française* (1863–73) marked a new sense of concern for correctness and standardization, and its success and that of its imitators indicate the increasing literacy of the period. The many dialect dictionaries— Jules Gilliéron and Edmond Edmont's *Atlas linguistique de la France* (1902– 10), as well as Frédéric Godefroy's *Dictionnaire de l'ancien français*—are further evidence of keen awareness of linguistic and cultural heritage.

The dialects of French are the following: Norman, Maine, Wallon, Picard, Champenois, Burgundian, Franche-Comté, Lorrain, Poitevin, Saintongeais, Angevin, Orléanais, Tourain, and Francien. This last, the dialect of Paris, had been the dialect of prestige for centuries, but in the twentieth century most French have come to regard Tourain as the model of fine pronunciation and syntax.

Occitan, whose earliest attestations date from the tenth century, is a Romance language comprised of the dialects Auvergnat, Limousin, Quercinol, Rouergat, Languedocien, Bas-Languedocien, Provençal, and Dauphinois. Phonetically and morphologically distinct from French, Occitan flourished as a poetic language in the Middle Ages but had declined in prestige to the status of regionalism before Frédéric Mistral and the Félibrige (1854) reclaimed it. The artistic achievement of this group, particularly that of Mistral and Théodore Aubanel, won renewed literary and cultural status; their successful efforts at standardization of grammar and spelling increased its audience and augmented its prestige, which probably reached its apex at the turn of the century. Its speakers, numbering in the millions, represented a considerable cultural and ethnic force.

Other Romance languages continued to flourish in France: Franco-Provençal in the Rhône basin and Savoy, with its many dialects; Gascon in Gascony south of the Garonne, in particular the literary dialect of Béarnais; Corsican, a language more closely allied to Italian than to French; and Catalán, whose population center lies across the border in Catalonia but is linked to Occitan by historical and cultural ties in the Roussillon.

Armorican Breton (or Brezoneg), spoken by 500,000 to 750,000 people, is largely confined to Finistère but is also spoken in Côtes-du-Nord, Morbihan, Ille-et-Vilaine, and Loire-Atlantique. It is a Celtic language of the Brythonic branch, as are Welsh and Cornish; Irish, Scottish, and Manx form the Gaedilic (or Gaelic) branch. The Celtic settlers of prehistoric times were displaced by the Romans to the British Isles, whence many returned after the Saxon victories of the sixth and seventh centuries; ties with Wales and Cornwall seem to have remained strong through the Middle Ages, but Celtic languages have since suffered, as minority tongues do before a strong centralized national language. But in the nineteeth century, interest in folklore and the development of philology spurred a new regionalism and a new interest in Breton as a cultural medium. The useful efforts by Jean-François Le Gonidec and René Leroux to standardize the language notwithstanding, the Breton movement remained limited in its success, for it leaned toward overambitious literary goals and a purging of French loan words, which restricted its audience. Among its noted authors are short story writer Yves le Moal, novelist Jacques Riou, and dramatist Tanguy Malmanche.

The Germanic languages are Flemish (especially in the Artois), with roughly 100,000 speakers, and German in the Bas-Rhin, Haut-Rhin, Moselle (Alsace-Lorraine). After Alsace and Lorraine were returned to France in 1919, there were nearly 1 million German speakers in France.

The only language not belonging to the Indo-European group is Basque, spoken by perhaps 50,000 people in the Pyrénées. (Like Catalán, its center is across the Spanish border.) It has not been proved to be related to any other known language.

P. Bec, *Manuel pratique de philologie romane*, 2 vols. (Paris, 1971); F. Gourvil, *Langue et littérature bretonnes* (Paris, 1968); P. Rickard, *A History of the French Language* (London, 1974).

S. M. Whitebook

Related entries: LITTRE; MISTRAL.

LANSON, GUSTAVE (1857–1934), literary historian whose methods recast the way French literature was taught in the early twentieth century. Born in Orléans (Loiret), he studied in Paris at the Lycée Charlemagne and the Ecole normale supérieure. After teaching for several years in lycées, he assumed positions at the Ecole normale in 1894 and at the Sorbonne in 1900. He became *professeur d'éloquence française* at the Ecole normale at the end of 1903, assuming the directorship of the institution in 1919, a post he held until his retirement in 1927.

Lanson was a literary historian in the tradition of Hippolyte Taine, Ernest Renan, and Ferdinand Brunetière, although he criticized the narrowness of their application of scientific principles to literary study. "Let us remember," he wrote at the end of his career, "that all the procedures which are *real* in the case of laboratory sciences can only be metaphorical or ideal so far as literary history is concerned, and that the analysis of a poetic genius has nothing in common with the analysis of sugar. Our only means of participating in scientific discovery is to develop a scientific attitude of mind" ("Méthodes de l'histoire littéraire," 1925, a passage translated by Eugène Vinaver). The experience of literature involves our aesthetic sensibility, but the study of literature must be historical; positivistic methods lead to the discovery of differences—to the ability to distinguish between the individual and the collective, the original and the traditional; to group authors and works by schools, movements, and genres; to relate such groupings to the intellectual and social life of France and of Europe. (See also "L'Esprit scientifique et la méthode de l'histoire littéraire," 1909, and "La Méthode de l'histoire littéraire," 1910.)

Thus Lanson emphasized bibliographical studies, the establishment of authentic texts, the conditions of the genesis of particular works, and the subsequent influence of these works. His most important book was *Histoire de la littérature française* (1894), a manual that was constantly reissued and was called "le Lanson" by generations of students. In the preface to the first edition, Lanson rejected Renan's claim in *Avenir de la science* that the study of literary history was destined to replace in large part the reading of specific works. Rather, the goal of literary history is to describe individualities, to discover a Corneille or a Hugo, not a type. The works themselves can never be lost from sight.

Lanson also directed the publication of the *Manuel bibliographique de la littérature française* (four vols., 1909–12), a project that laid the foundation for modern French studies. His books include studies of the great writers of the classical tradition, (for example of Corneille, Boileau, and Voltaire) for the pedagogical Collection des grands écrivains, published by Hachette.

For many twentieth-century critics, *le lansonisme* became a pejorative synonym for historical methods that often never came directly to grips with the ambiguities and complexities of actual literary texts. (For decades, many university theses in literature were historically oriented.) In the years before World War I a series of attacks was launched against university and *normalien* professors by professional critics, among them Charles Péguy. Later, in the 1960s, when the methods of *la nouvelle critique* began to revolutionize textual studies, academic literary history was again attacked and eventually dislodged from its preeminent position in university circles.

A. François-Poncet et al., *Gustave Lanson, 1857–1934* (Paris, 1958); H. Peyre, "Présentation" to G. Lanson, *Essais de méthode de critique et d'histoire littéraire* (Paris, 1965); R. Wellek, "Gustave Lanson (1857–1934)," in *A History of Modern Criticism: 1750–1950*, vol. 4 (New Haven, 1965).

P. A. Ward

Related entries: BRUNETIERE; LITERARY CRITICS AND CRITICISM; RENAN; TAINE.

LAUR, FRANCIS (1844–1934), radical politician, leading supporter of General Georges Boulanger, and mining engineer. He was born at Nevers (Nièvre) on 5 September 1844. A graduate of the Ecole des mines de Saint-Etienne, he worked as a civil engineer and wrote professionally on topics dealing with the mining and metallurgical industries during the early years of the Third Republic. Simultaneously he made his way from local to national political office. He was elected to the municipal council of Saint-Etienne in 1881, was chosen to be an assistant mayor of that city in 1884, and was elected to the Chamber of Deputies from the department of the Loire on the republican ticket in 1885.

In the Chamber, Laur became a prominent figure in the left-wing faction that backed the campaign of General Boulanger for political reform. Laur also used the campaign to further projects for labor reform, especially his proposal to establish mining cooperatives, which he publicized in a book, *Essais de socialisme expérimental: La Mine aux mineurs* (1887). As a Boulangist candidate for the Chamber of Deputies in 1889, he was elected in the third district of Saint-Denis (Neuilly). When his election was invalidated, he stood for election again in early 1890 and won by a large majority, in part because of the support of polemicists of the Antisemitic League who used his campaign as one of their first forays into national politics. During his second term in the Chamber (1889–93), Laur worked actively to promote labor reform, especially measures to ameliorate the working conditions of miners. He was an advocate of the nationalization of the railroads, an income tax, and improvements in public transportation. Because he was impetuous and tended to overstate his views, he was not always taken seriously by his colleagues.

Retiring from politics in 1893, he continued to write extensively about the mining industry. Late in life, he wrote a book on the Boulanger Affair, *L'Epoque boulangiste* (1912–14). His political ideas are most completely expressed in *De l'accaparement* (1900–07). He died at the age of ninety.

C. S. Doty, "Parliamentary Boulangism after 1889," *Historian* 32 (1970); J. Jolly, ed., *Dictionnaire des parlementaires français*, vol. 6 (1970); J. Néré, *Le Boulangisme et la presse* (Paris, 1964); A. Robert et al., eds., *Dictionnaire des parlementaires français* vol. 3 (1891); Z. Sternhell, *La Droite révolutionnaire* (Paris, 1978); G. Terrail (Mermeix, pseud.), *Les Antisémites en France* (Paris, 1892).

P. H. Hutton

Related entries: ANTISEMITIC LEAGUE; BOULANGER; BOULANGER AFFAIR; LAGUERRE; LAISANT; NAQUET.

LAURENS, HENRI (1885–1954), cubist sculptor. He came from a Parisian working-class family. He studied with an ornamental sculptor, took night classes with an academic sculptor, and worked as a stonecutter on construction sites (1899–1904). He was briefly influenced by Auguste Rodin, then more profoundly by Georges Braque, whom he met in 1911 and who introduced him to cubism. Beginning in 1912 Laurens produced the idiosyncratic cubist sculptures for which he is famous, made of stone, terracotta, and often mixtures of wood, plaster, iron, and stone, frequently colored. Usually depicting still lifes or human figures, his works are extraordinarily refined. In the 1920s he moved somewhat away from cubism to more rounded, less geometric volumes. In the 1920s and 1930s, Laurens illustrated books and did decorative work (including sets for the Ballets russes production of Darius Milhaud's *Le Train bleu*). He exhibited numerous works in the 1937 Paris Exposition universelle.

Henri Laurens: Exposition de la donation aux musées nationaux (Paris, 1967); W. Hofmann, *The Sculpture of Henri Laurens* (New York, 1970).

T. Shapiro

Related entries: ART: MAJOR STYLES AND MOVEMENTS; BRAQUE; CUBISM; RODIN.

LAVAL, PIERRE (1883–1945), politician, prime minister, foreign minister, who acquired greatest notoriety as second in command to Marshall Philippe Pétain at Vichy. Born at Châteldon in the Auvergne, Laval was first elected to the Chamber of Deputies in 1914 as a left-wing socialist and pacifist. His peace-at-any-price pacifism remained constant throughout a career of political shifts and eventually led him to defeatist collaborationism during the Vichy era. Following the Socialist party split in 1920, Laval became a nonparty moderate. He drifted steadily toward the Right but maintained a political base in staunchly working-class Aubervilliers. From 1925 to 1931, Laval served in the cabinets of Paul Painlevé, Aristide Briand, and André Tardieu and acquired a reputation as an unprincipled parliamentary manipulator. His political career peaked during the early 1930s; he was premier in three successive conservative governments from January 1931 to February 1932 and again headed the government (and also held the post of foreign minister) from November 1934 to January 1936.

It is impossible to determine if any consistent philosophy underpinned his conduct of foreign policy. But in retrospect, as he awaited trial in 1945, Laval wrote: "*Les régimes se succèdent, les révolutions s'accomplissent, mais la géographie subsiste toujours*" ["governments rise and fall, revolutions take place, but geography always remains the same."—editor's translation]. A powerful Germany on France's border represented a permanent geographical fact to be faced realistically without regard for governmental forms or ideological persuasions. France must either get along with Germany (Laval had supported Briand's efforts at rapprochement), or if that were impossible, it must pursue a policy capable of containing German ambitions. From 1934 to 1936, Laval followed the second alternative. He continued negotiations begun by Louis Barthou for a Franco-Soviet mutual assistance pact and at the same time sought a Franco-Italian understanding. The latter reached fruition in the Laval-Mussolini Accords of January 1935, a series of agreements resolving colonial differences. These paved the way for general staff talks designed to coordinate military and naval policies in the event of German aggression. Laval went to his grave denying that he had promised the fascist leader anything more than French economic *désintéressement* in Ethiopia. Circumstantial evidence exists, however, to suggest that Laval had offered Italy a free hand there, thus eliminating a major obstacle to Benito Mussolini's African imperial ambitions. The outbreak of the Italo-Ethiopian War in October 1935 ended Laval's efforts to construct a political encirclement of Germany. He did work to soften the impact of League of Nations sanctions and attempted to appease the Italians with the Hoare-Laval Plan of December 1936. These failed to save the keystone of his foreign policy. Following his resignation in January 1936, he remained an embittered outcast, isolated from the mainstream of French politics. He sought his revenge on the political system following France's defeat in 1940. Some observers have concluded that the fact that such an unprincipled man could reach the pinnacle of French politics is symptomatic of the ills plaguing the Third Republic in its final years.

F. Kupferman, *Pierre Laval* (Paris, 1976); P. Laval, *Laval parle* (Paris, 1948); G. Warner, *Pierre Laval and the Eclipse of France* (London, 1968).

W. I. Shorrock

Related entries: HOARE-LAVAL PLAN; ITALY, RELATIONS WITH.

LAVIGERIE, CHARLES (1825–1892), cardinal, archbishop of Algiers, missionary activist, and leader of the *ralliement*. Born near Bayonne (Basses-Pyrénées), ordained in 1849, Lavigerie devoted much of his life to missionary activities in Lebanon and in North Africa. He was named bishop of Nancy in 1863 and archbishop of Algiers four years later. Lavigerie was acutely conscious of the ancient Christian tradition in North Africa and hoped to revive it by effective missionary work that would appeal to the Muslim population. To this end he founded the White Fathers, an order that continues to be active in Africa, and he devoted much of his time to the suppression of slavery in the region. Lavigerie favored a policy of assimilation by which the indigenous population would eventually become Europeanized and Christianized, a policy that met with resistance from French colonial authorities at the time. His missionary zeal caused Pope Leo XIII to name him a cardinal in 1881 and primate of North Africa in 1884.

Lavigerie was a royalist who went so far as to encourage the comte de Chambord to risk a coup d'état in 1874 in order to restore the monarchy. Although he never had much enthusiasm for the Republic, he believed as Pope Leo XIII did that the interests of the church in France would best be served by Catholics accepting the republican form of government. At a dinner given in honor of a French naval squadron visiting Algiers in 1890, Lavigerie proposed in a toast that conservatives adhere "without reservations" to the regime in the interests of social order. Lavigerie's toast formally launched the *ralliement*.

L. Baunard, *Le Cardinal Lavigerie* (Paris, 1912); X. de Montclos, *Lavigerie, le Saint-Siège et l'église* (Rome, 1965); J. Tournier, *Le Cardinal Lavigerie et son action politique* (Paris, 1913).

A. Sedgwick

Related entries: CHAMBORD; *RALLIEMENT*; ROMAN CATHOLICISM: OVERSEAS MISSIONS.

LAVIGNE, RAYMOND (1851–1930), socialist and syndicalist militant; disciple of Jules Guesde. A native of Bordeaux, he made a living as an accountant in the retail wine business. He was thirty years old when he was converted to Marxist socialism by the oratory of Jules Guesde and entered politics energetically by becoming secretary-general of the Parti ouvrier français (POF) in the Gironde, a post he held from 1882 until 1902.

Ineligible for public office after he declared bankruptcy in 1888, he regarded his situation less as an impediment to his ambitions than as a mark of his selfless commitment to the socialist cause. A dedicated organizer, he built a local political party around a nucleus of social studies groups and an allied trade union federation. In the latter group, he gave special attention to the creation of a worker-sponsored *bourse du travail*, which opened in 1890. A frequent participant in socialist and syndicalist congresses in the 1880s and 1890s, he served as secretary-general of the French trade union federation from 1886 to 1888 and with Jean Dormoy was responsible for the inauguration of the May Day movement in France in 1890.

Despite his personal and ideological loyalty to Guesde, Lavigne employed unorthodox tactics to advance the socialist cause. In 1889 he committed the Bordeaux section of the POF to the Boulangist campaign and in 1896 to the Pact of Bordeaux, in both cases coalitions of left- and right-wing parties designed to oust the Opportunist republicans from power. At the same time, he had little use for ideological abstraction, and in the face of the doctrinal quarrels on the Left at the turn of the century, he retreated from his positions of leadership in both the trade union and the socialist movements: from the former in 1894 after denouncing Aristide Briand's notion of a general strike, from the latter in 1902 in opposition to the revisionism of Alexandre Millerand and Jean Jaurès. An apostle of socialist unity, Lavigne maintained membership in the Socialist party until its schism at the Tours Congress of 1920.

Lavigne's extensive correspondence with Guesde is found in the Guesde Collection, International Institute for Social History, Amsterdam, the Netherlands.

M. Dommanget, *Histoire du Première Mai* (Paris, 1953); P. H. Hutton, "The Impact of the Boulangist Crisis upon the Guesdist Party at Bordeaux," *French Historical Studies* 7 (1971); J. Maitron, ed, *Dictionnaire biographique du mouvement ouvrier français*, vol. 13 (Paris, 1975); L. Osmin, *Figures de jadis* (Paris, 1934); C. Willard, *Les Guesdistes* (Paris, 1965).

P. H. Hutton

Related entries: BORDEAUX; BOULANGER AFFAIR; BOURSE DU TRAVAIL; FESTIVALS: POLITICAL; GUESDE; GUESDISTS; LABOR MOVEMENT; MARXISM; SOCIALISM, 1870–1914; SOCIALIST PARTY.

LAVISSE, ERNEST (1842–1922), noted historian and educational reformer. Although trained in the traditional methods of literary history at the elite Ecole normale supérieure, Lavisse became an early convert to the scientific school of historical writing that emerged in France in the last quarter of the nineteenth century. Greatly impressed by the example of historical scholarship and teaching set by the German universities and alarmed at the absence of a similar tradition in French higher education, Lavisse spearheaded the movement to institutionalize the study of history in the French university system. In 1883 he became director of historical studies at the Sorbonne, a position that enabled him to train a generation of historians in the modern methods of critical historical scholarship.

As a historian, Lavisse is remembered less for his ground-breaking contributions to specialized scholarship than for his general synthetic histories and textbooks. In the latter genre, his monumental *Histoire de France depuis les origines jusqu'à la Révolution* (9 vols., 1900–11) represented one of the first collaborative efforts to summarize the results of monographic scholarship in a multivolume synthesis. His textbooks on French history became the familiar companions of millions of children in France during the first four decades of the Third Republic. They were widely used as primers of citizenship training in the primary and secondary schools, serving to inculcate democratic values and patriotic sentiments in the nation's youth.

Lavisse was a prominent participant in the campaign to reform French higher education between 1880 and 1900. A founding member of the Société de l'enseignment supérieure, a pressure group established in 1880 to promote the cause of educational reform at the university level, Lavisse worked tirelessly for the creation of a modern university system in France. This goal was achieved at the end of the nineteenth century with the amalgamation of the diverse faculties of letters and science and the establishment of centralized authority in Paris. When the Ecole normale supriéeure was absorbed by the University of Paris to complete this process in 1903, Lavisse was rewarded for his efforts on behalf of educational centralization with the directorship of the elite teacher training school.

Throughout his career, Lavisse was active in political affairs. He served as adviser to several governments of the Third Republic and remained on intimate terms with a number of leading republican statesmen. The apex of his political influence came at the end of the First World War, when he was appointed director of a committee of experts charged with the task of determining the extent of German responsibility in the war and recommending appropriate territorial and reparation claims for France. A dyed-in-the-wool French patriot, Lavisse revealed in his historical writings and political activities an antipathy for Germany and a preoccupation with strengthening the military power of his own country. This attitude earned him the enmity of internationalists and pacifists, as well as the respect of French nationalists, both republican and royalist.

W. R. Keylor, *Academy and Community: The Foundation of the French Historical Profession* (Cambridge, Mass., 1975); P. Nora, "Ernest Lavisse: son rôle dans la formation du sentiment national," *Revue historique* 228 (July 1962); B. Schmitt, ed., *Some Historians of Modern Europe* (Port Washington, 1966).

W. R. Keylor

Related entries: NATIONALISM; MONOD; SEIGNOBOS.

LAZARE, BERNARD (1865–1903), an anarchist journalist and *littérateur*, best known for his efforts on behalf of Alfred Dreyfus during the Dreyfus affair. Born Lazare Bernard in Nîmes (Gard) and coming from a well-assimilated Jewish family, he went to Paris as an aspiring writer in 1886. Lazare became part of the literary avant-garde of his day, the symbolist circle about Stéphane Mallarmé. He contributed stories and essays on a variety of themes to literary journals and to daily newspapers, attacking the current literary vogue of Parnassian poetry and the realism of Emile Zola. An independent and pugnacious critic, he won further notoriety as an outspoken defender of anarchists, notably at the celebrated Procès des trente, which followed the assassination of the president of the Republic, Sadi Carnot, in 1894.

Convinced by relatives of Dreyfus in early 1895 that the Jewish captain had been unjustly convicted of selling military secrets to the Germans, Lazare wrote a stinging pamphlet on the case, which was finally published in November 1896. This was the opening salvo in the campaign to overturn the judgment against Dreyfus; with it the Dreyfus affair may be said to have begun. Lazare participated actively in the early phase of the affair. But following the publication of a second brochure in 1897, Dreyfus' brother, Mathieu, persuaded Lazare to restrict his role; henceforth the cause was to be guided by republican notables, who found the flamboyant anarchist publicist something of an embarrassment.

During the course of the affair, Lazare turned his efforts increasingly to Jewish matters. Having previously absorbed some of the anti-Jewish mood of his culture during the 1880s, particularly the negative view of unassimilated East European Jews, he had been reassessing this position even before Dreyfus' arrest as a result of work on a major study of anti-Semitism that he published in 1894. With the affair itself came a ferocious outburst of anti-Semitism, against which Lazare leveled some blistering ripostes. In 1896 he fought a duel with Edouard Drumont, editor of the anti-Jewish *La Libre Parole*. In the latter half of the 1890s Lazare became a Jewish nationalist; he championed the Jewish proletariat, which he saw as victimized all over the world; he attacked the assimilatory politics of the Jewish establishment; and he deepened the pursuit of his own Jewish identity. Lazare's Judaism was far from rabbinic orthodoxy; his quest led him to a Jewish tradition founded on reason and social justice, exemplified in the writings of the Hebrew prophets. Lazare's answer for the Jews was Zionism, the mobilization of the Jewish masses for the re-creation of a Jewish nation.

Lazare collaborated in several Zionist periodicals and was briefly associated with the East European Zionist organization Hoveve Zion. He attended the Second Zionist Congress in Basel in 1898 and worked closely with top Zionist leaders. But in the following year he broke with the head of the movement, Theodor Herzl, denouncing the latter's autocratic methods and bourgeois outlook. Lazare retained the anarchist's idealism and populist optimism. He remained in sympathy with the Zionist enterprise but eschewed diplomatic or financial negotiations. Simultaneously, Lazare took up the cause of the Armenians and was a prominent member of the Armenian Congress held in Brussels in July 1902. This was his last public campaign. He died in September 1903 at the age of thirty-eight.

M. R. Marrus, *The Politics of Assimilation* (Oxford, 1971), and "Bernard Lazare—An Anarchist's Zionism," *Midstream* 23 (June–July 1977); N. Wilson, *Bernard Lazare* (Cambridge, England, 1978).

M. R. Marrus

Related entries: ANTI-SEMITISM; DREYFUS AFFAIR; JEWS; JUDAISM; MALLARME; SYMBOLISM.

LE CHATELIER, HENRY LOUIS (1850–1936), chemist, engineer, and advocate of scientific management. Born in Paris, he was the son of a republican engineer who directed the construction of much of the French railway system. He entered the Ecole polytechnique in 1869, served in the army during the Franco-Prussian War, and graduated in 1873 from the Ecole des mines. Until 1877 Le Châtelier worked as an engineer, when he became professor of general chemistry at the Ecole des mines. From 1887 until his retirement in 1919, his title was professor of industrial chemistry and metallurgy. While teaching at the Ecole des mines, he also held the chair of chemistry at the Collège de France (1887–1908) and the chair of general chemistry at the Sorbonne (1907–25). He became a member of the Académie des sciences in 1907.

Le Châtelier is best known for his work in thermodynamics on problems of chemical equilibria in homogeneous reversible systems (*Loi de stabilité de l'équilibre chimique*, 1888). A fundamental chemical principle bears his name: that any strain placed on a system in equilibrium, such as a change in temperature or pressure, occasions a readjustment in the direction that will most effectively relieve the strain. An important illustration of this principle is the catalytic synthesis of ammonia from a mixture of hydrogen and nitrogen gases. The German chemist Fritz Haber demonstrated in 1905 the practical feasibility of this process, a few years after Le Châtelier stopped work on the problem following a laboratory explosion. The Haber process took on more importance during the First World War as a crucial step in the artificial manufacture of nitric acid for explosives.

Le Châtelier's earliest researches dealt with the chemical properties of cements, ceramics, and glass. His studies of combustible gases resulted in the development of the oxyacetylene torch for welding, as well as improvements in industrial furnaces. In work on alloys, Le Châtelier demonstrated the existence of intermetallic compounds, and his data from studies of the chemistry and metallurgy of iron and steel were used in the first application of the phase rule to the iron-carbon system. He founded and edited the specialized journal *Revue de metallurgie*.

Le Châtelier was equally motivated by interests in theoretical results and practical applications. He was sympathetic to the Comtian positivist program for science and society. In epistemology, this view inclined him to eliminate abstract entities like force from scientific discussions and to avoid the use of atomistic models or descriptions. In the Comtian and St.-Simonian tradition, he served on many governmental commissions and boards, and he staunchly advocated the application to French industry of F. W. Taylor's system of scientific management, a system based on the notion that sound management is the result of organizing industry according to laws and principles rather than policies.

"À la mémoire de Henry Le Châtelier, 1850–1936," *Revue de métallurgie* 34 (1937); C. H. Desch, "The Le Châtelier Memorial Lecture," *Journal of the Chemical Society* (1938); F. Le Châtelier, *Henry Le Châtelier, un grand savant d'hier, un précurseur: Sa vie, son oeuvre, son temps* (Paris, 1968); R. E. Oesper, "The Scientific Career of Henry Louis Le Châtelier," *Journal of Chemical Education* 8 (1931).

M. J. Nye

Related entries: INDUSTRY: CHEMICAL; POSITIVISM; SCIENCE AND TECHNOLOGY.

LE CORBUSIER (1887–1965), leading modernist architect and urban planner, painter, polemicist. Le Corbusier was born Charles-Edouard Jeanneret in La Chaux-de-Fonds, the Swiss watchmaking capital, in 1887, and adopted his famous pseudonym around 1920. His family was middle class, but he was profoundly influenced by both the precision of the watchmaker's craft and the socialism of its milieu. He studied engraving at the School of Fine Arts in La Chaux-de-Fonds (1900–1905) and built his first house, a private villa in the arts-and-crafts style, when only nineteen. Between 1907 and 1910 he traveled extensively in Europe, getting apprenticeship training in architecture in the offices of Josef Hoffman in Vienna, Auguste Perret in Paris, and Peter Behrens in Berlin (there encountering two other future architectural giants, Walter Gropius and Ludwig Mies van der Rohe). He also came under the influence of Tony Garnier in Lyons. A visit to a Carthusian monastery in Italy influenced him toward his later stylistic asceticism and gave him the idea of the *unité d'habitation*, a building combining individual dwellings with communal services.

Le Corbusier developed as a painter as well as an architect, and his personal familiarity with the plastic arts accounts for the individuality and sculptural quality of his buildings. As he developed his personal architectural ideas during and after World War I—which he publicized in a series of polemical books beginning with *Vers une architecture* of 1923—he tried to wed the simplicity and repetition of the assembly-line product with a utopian socialist dream of providing salubrious surroundings for the urban masses by increasing the proximity of home and workplace and the availability of green space. He first applied these ideas in projects for mass-produced housing (the Dom-Ino house, 1914; the Citrohan house, 1920–22) and in a workers' development he built in Pessac, near Bordeaux, in 1925–26. Fully accepting the high density of the metropolis, he developed urban plans, most notably several for Paris, that suggested the replacement of the haphazard street networks of old cities by Cartesian alignments of high- and medium-rise buildings occupied by enormous numbers of apartments and offices and interspersed with generous green spaces. In the Voisin plan for Paris (1925), he suggested razing a large area of the historic Right Bank and replacing the accretion of medieval and early modern streets and buildings with eighteen 200 meter office buildings aligned in an immense grid pattern within a park. While this and similar projects, and Le Corbusier's virulent rhetoric and unbending conviction, provoked violent reactions in their time, they have had a tremendous influence on the work of post–World War II epigoni in the *grands ensembles* surrounding major French cities.

As an architect Le Corbusier had a practice in Paris from 1917 until his death in 1965, from 1922 to 1940 in partnership with his cousin Pierre Jeanneret. He became a French citizen in 1930. He produced some of the most brilliant constructions of the international style, an architecture that emphasizes functionalism and simple volumes and opposes historical or national-regional decoration. Most impressive during the interwar period were his private houses in and around Paris, constructed in concrete and featuring various levels of rooms and terraces: the temporary Pavillon de l'esprit nouveau at the 1925 Exposition des arts décoratifs; the Stein villa at Garches (1927), built for Gertrude Stein's brother; the Villa Savoie in Poissy (1929–31); and many others. As a painter he was an adherent of the purist movement of the early 1920s, and with the painter Amédée Ozenfant and the poet Paul Dermée he edited the modern art review *L'Esprit nouveau* (1919–25). Although he built several public buildings between 1925 and 1940—for instance, the Swiss dormitory at the Paris Cité universitaire (1930–32) and a Salvation Army hostel in Paris (1929–33)—he was virtually ignored by the Third Republic leaders, who preferred the more traditional, classicizing architecture of Auguste Perret and others. Le Corbusier was a cofounder of the International Congress of Modern Architecture in 1928, which defended the international principles of the modernists against growing nationalist attacks by government leaders and architects. He was one of the drafters of the Athens Charter (1932), in which the congress tried to formulate a common definition of the international style.

After the Second World War, Le Corbusier came to worldwide prominence, receiving numerous public commissions for buildings and urban plans in France and abroad.

W. Boesiger, *Le Corbusier* (Zurich, 1972); Le Corbusier, *Vers une architecture* (Paris, 1923), *Urbanisme* (Paris, 1925), *La Ville radieuse* (Paris, 1935), and *La Charte d'Athènes* (Paris, 1943).

T. Shapiro

Related entries: ARCHITECTURE AND URBAN PLANNING; ART: MAJOR STYLES AND MOVEMENTS; GARNIER; PERRET.

LE PLAY, FREDERIC (1806–1882), sociologist and theoretician of management. An early experience of estrangement from family and village seems to have engendered an unhappiness in Le Play, which convinced him that *bonheur* is not to be found in a mobile, urban, industrial way of life. Although trained as an engineer, Le Play did not believe in engineering humanity or in using technology as a model for social planning. Instead, he sought to reconcile technological change with social tradition, the need for daily bread with the equally imperative need (in his mind) for unchanging moral law.

In 1855 Le Play published the family monographs he had been collecting for a quarter-century under the title *Les Ouvriers européens* and then turned his attention to propagandizing the causes his data supposedly supported: family cohesion, religious faith based on obedience to the Ten Commandments, and *patronage* (socially responsible management). With the advent of the Third Republic, Le Play devoted his energies to establishing Unions de la paix sociale, small, local, largely autonomous groups that distributed Le Play's writings, studied local social problems, and tried to apply Le Play's teachings to them in a practical way.

Le Play was most influential as a teacher and theoretician of management. He stressed that industry has social purposes as well as monetary ones and claimed that technological change did not necessarily conflict with older social forms. He brought up the important issue of how modern industry can promote social welfare in the broadest sense rather than merely creating wealth.

J. R. Pitts, "Frédéric Le Play," in *International Encyclopedia of the Social Sciences*, ed. D. L. Sills, vol. 9 (New York, 1968); M. Z. Brooke, *Le Play: Engineer and Social Scientist* (London, 1970).

R. H. Williams

LE ROY, EUGENE (1836–1907), rustic novelist. Born into a humble family, he was strongly influenced by the works of Joseph Proudhon. He published several works on the history of Périgord. A self-confessed free-thinker and republican, he was dismissed from his position as tax collector in the wave of reaction following the *seize mai* crisis (16 May 1877). His novels are noted for their detailed and sympathetic portraits of humble peasants. In 1895 he published *Le Moulin du Frau*, his first major regionalist novel which was regarded as a masterpiece by Alphonse Daudet. His fame rests chiefly on the publication in 1899 of *Jacquou le croquant* for which he was offered the Légion d'honneur in 1905. His other works included *Nicette et Milou* (1901), *Le Pays des pierres* (1906), and *Les Gens d'Abéroque* (1907).

M. Ballot, *Eugène Le Roy, écrivain rustique* (Bordeaux, 1949); *Eugène Le Roy*, no. spécial d'*Europe* 35 (Paris, 1957); G. Guillaumie, *Eugène Le Roy* (Bordeaux, 1929); M. Shaw, *L'Histoire du Périgord dans l'oeuvre d'Eugène Le Roy* (Dijon, 1946).

R. E. Sandstrom

LEAGUE OF PATRIOTS (1882–1906), a political organization designed to provide patriotic education in the wake of the French defeat in 1870–71. In actuality it functioned as a political action group in the Boulangist movement (1887–90) and the Dreyfus affair (1894–99). Its founding in 1882 was a response to the political and economic conditions surrounding the fall of Léon Gambetta's ministry that same year. In its rhetorical claim to a position above politics, the league stood for the military strength, patriotic education, and *revanchard* nationalism advocated by its chief animator, Paul Déroulède. Its initial adherence to a program of domestic political reform, specifically revision of the Constitution of 1875, and its opposition to Opportunist practice of imperialism and reconciliation with Germany, reveal its strong radical republican origins. Building on existing gymnastic and shooting clubs, appropriating the journal *Le Drapeau*, and using the slogan *Qui Vive?-France!* the league appealed to anti-Opportunist republican opinion to revive France, internally and externally, in the face of domestic and international crisis.

Between 1882 and 1887, the league's apolitical rhetoric masked its anti-Opportunist program. But in late 1887 and early 1888 Déroulède maneuvered the league into a clearly pro-Boulangist position. Joining forces with the republican Committee of National Protest, the Boulangist headquarters' organization, the league provided the bulk of Boulanger's popular support in the electoral campaign of 1888–89. Calling for restitution of the "Lost Provinces," for *revanche* (revenge against Germany), and for revision of the constitutional arrangement of 1875 that favored parliamentary over presidential powers, Déroulède and the league supported Boulanger as Gambetta's heir. Nevertheless, in the wake of the Opportunist counterattack in 1889, the league was fined and then dissolved for failure to register according to the 1834 Law of Associations. Although Déroulède remained active in Boulangist circles for several years, he made no attempt to revive the league until 1898.

The leaders of the league during the Boulangist crisis (1888–89) were men whose political consciousness had been forged in the experience of the Franco-Prussian War and the Paris Commune (1870–71). Boulangism was their last political act, and, when the league was revived almost a decade later, their place was taken by a younger, less prosperous generation. Similarly the rank and file of the league in 1889 was composed of middle-class Frenchmen (at its height, membership was judged to be above 100,000), with a particularly strong representation of veterans.

Despite its official dissolution, a skeletal league survived the Boulangist episode. Yearly between 1890 and 1897 a handful of Parisian *ligueurs* demonstrated for the "Lost Provinces" and occasionally protested at performances of German operas in Paris. It was not, however, until the reopening of the Dreyfus affair in mid-1898 that the league was reconstituted by Déroulède and his closest colleague, Marcel Habert, to exercise public and political pressure for the anti-Dreyfusard cause. Paralleling efforts by newly emergent anti-Semitic groups, particularly the Antisemitic League of Jules Guérin, the league emerged from August 1898 to February 1899 in the forefront of the anti-Dreyfusard street leagues. In contrast with its Boulangist activities, which were electoral and national, the new league was *manifestant* and Parisian. Its new membership was young, distinctly lower middle class, and responsive to the covert racial nationalism that had entered the league's rhetoric. In September, October, and November 1898, the league conducted meetings and torchlight parades. Demonstrations doubled and redoubled as the process of revision in favor of Alfred Dreyfus gained momentum.

By January 1899, with a membership of more than 20,000, the League of

Patriots constituted a considerable force in the street politics of the capital. Such success did not go unnoticed by its right-wing rivals, royalists and anti-Semites, each of whom planned to subvert the league's popularity or at least to use it when the time came. The famous coup of 23 February 1899 was such an incident. Its failure sent the league into eclipse, gave encouragement to its rivals, and forced Déroulède to redefine the league's position. It became apparent by June 1899 that the anti-Semites in particular were drawing successfully on the league's membership, which was as responsive to economic and cultural conditions as to political events. The Parisian lower middle class was buffeted not only by industrial change but also by the appearance in its *quartiers* of recently arrived Eastern European Jews. The appeal of racial anti-Semitism was successful in this setting. Consequently, in the summer of 1899, just before the new Dreyfus trial at Rennes, Déroulède reorganized the league into three paramilitary battalions, which were prepared to go underground. At the same time the league modified its ideology to embrace racist anti-Semitism. Calling for "France of the French," the league had completed the social, political, and ideological transformation that made it a precursor of twentieth-century totalitarian movements. The arrest, trial, and banishment of Déroulède and Habert in August 1899 prevented the organization from expanding in the last months of the nineteenth century. From 1900 to 1906 the league took advantage of the revival of nationalism to gain control of municipal government in Paris, and under the directorship of Maurice Barrès the weekly *Drapeau* became a nationalist daily.

By 1906 the league's militant members had joined Action française, and the police closed its books on an organization it had been following since 1886. Although the League of Patriots continued to exist through World War I and the remainder of the Third Republic, its historic period belongs to the years 1882–1900. Déroulède, its founder-president, died weeks before the outbreak of World War I. His funeral, it is said, was the largest since the passing of Victor Hugo.

C. S. Doty, "Parliamentary Boulangism after 1889," *Historian* (October, 1971); R. Girardet, "Notes sur l'esprit d'un fascisme française" *Revue française de science politique* 5 (July 1955), and "Pour une introduction à l'histoire du nationalisme français," *Revue française de science politique* 3 (1958); P. Rutkoff, "The Ligue des Patriotes: The Nature of the Radical Right and the Dreyfus Affair," *French Historical Studies* (Fall 1974); Z. Sternhell, *La Droite révolutionaire* (Paris, 1978).

P. M. Rutkoff

Related entries: ACTION FRANÇAISE; ANTISEMITIC LEAGUE; BOULANGER AFFAIR; DEROULEDE; DREYFUS AFFAIR; FASCISM; NATIONALISM; RIGHT, THE.

LEBON, GUSTAVE (1841–1931), social theorist, amateur physicist, and scientific vulgarizer. Born in Nogent-le-Rotrou (Eure-et-Loir) on 7 May 1841 of stock with a long history of bureaucratic service in local government, he attended lycée at Tours and obtained a medical degree at Paris in 1866. He never practiced medicine, preferring to use his scientific education in a series of publishing projects that included chemistry, human physiology, and ethnography. These early works were in the mainstream of European positivism and scientific materialism and in general endeavored to illustrate the physicochemical foundations of life and the evolutionary influences on human biology and social development. *L'Homme et les sociétés* (1881) is a kind of encyclopedia of the progressive scientific anthropology of the day, containing in germ all the work of his mature years.

Although maintaining the scientific pretensions of his earlier work, LeBon adopted an increasingly popular and political tone after 1894. He employed a pungent and aphoristic style and sought a mass audience for his work. LeBon supported a variety of causes throughout the remainder of his career that were typical of the nonmonarchist Right, including economic liberalism, nationalism, and the modernization of French educational institutions. He was best known for what he opposed. LeBon was a vigorous and effective critic of socialism, which he regarded as a virulent species of statist anti-individualism. In *La Psychologie du socialisme* (1898) and many other works, LeBon exposed the religious appeal and the psychopathological elements in modern socialism. His ideas were regularly employed by conservative political figures in the Third Republic, many of whom—Raymond Poincaré, Denys Cochin, Aristide Briand—cultivated LeBon's friendship and advice. In this connection LeBon played an important role in popularizing many of the themes of the prewar national revival.

LeBon is best known as the chief figure in the elaboration of a theory of collective behavior. Although he built on the work of Hippolyte Taine and the Italian Scipio Sighele, hypnotic theory, and French psychiatry, LeBon was the first to present a theory of the group mind to the general public with a sufficient quantity of anecdote and political content that it could take permanent root. *La Psychologie des foules* (1895), now in its forty-sixth French edition, has become one of the best-selling scientific books in history, influencing the later development of elite theory, psychoanalysis, and radical social theories of direct action.

LeBon died in 1931, more celebrated by the Center-Right political establishment than by the Parisian intellectual elite, which regarded his political and social writings, and his brief foray into experimental physics, as hopelessly unscientific. There are clear signs that since World War II, the French Right, in its search for the native origins of antidemocratic ideology, has rediscovered LeBon and is making an effort to revive interest in his work.

R. L. Geiger, "Democracy and the Crowd: The Social History of an Idea in France and Italy," *Societas* 8 (1977); M. J. Nye, "Gustave LeBon's Black Light," *Historical Studies in the Physical Sciences* 4 (1974); R. A. Nye, "Two Paths to a Psychology of Social Action: Gustave LeBon and Georges Sorel," *Journal of Modern History* 45 (1973), and *The Origins of Crowd Psychology* (London and Beverly Hills, 1975).

R. A. Nye

Related entries: NATIONALISM; POSITIVISM; SOCIALISM, 1870–1914; SOREL; TAINE; TARDE.

LEBRUN, ALBERT (1871–1950), colorless politician who was the last constitutional president of the Republic. From Lorraine, he graduated first in his class at the Ecole polytechnique and later from the Ecole nationale des mines. As a mining and civil engineer, he expressed the belief that the regeneration of France after 1870 depended on the efficient use of scientific knowledge by an educated elite. Elected in 1900 to the Chamber of Deputies from Meurthe-et-Moselle as a moderate republican, he soon gained a reputation for hard work and intelligence. Lebrun served as minister of colonies in the Joseph Caillaux government of 1911, where he opposed making concessions to the Germans in the Congo. Damning the Caillaux agreement with faint praise secured him the post of minister of war in the Raymond Poincaré government of 1912–13. Serving as an artillery major in the First World War, he was recalled by Georges Clemenceau to serve as minister of the blockade and minister of invaded regions. A speech concerning the 1917 mutinies solidified his reputation. He was, however, dismissed from his post by allowing his name to appear on a ballot with those who opposed the Treaty of Versailles. In 1920, he was elected senator from Lorraine and served for nine years as the chairman of the Senate Army Committee. He was also appointed by Poincaré to head the Caisse d'amortissement (or debt commission, 1926–31).

His mild manner and compromising tendencies led to his election as Senate president in 1931. He withdrew his name from the 1931 race for president of the Republic but was elected on 10 May 1932 following the assassination of Paul Doumer. Lebrun successfully restored domestic stability in the wake of street demonstrations of right-wing groups by persuading Gaston Doumergue to assume the premiership of a coalition government in 1933. Although personally opposed to the Popular Front, he supported Léon Blum's policies designed to end the strikes of 1936. A strong supporter of Edouard Daladier, who was named premier in 1938, Lebrun himself on 8 April 1939 became the second person to be reelected president (the first being Jules Grévy). His inaction, however, played a pivotal role in the fall of France in 1940. Characteristically weeping and wringing his hands, Lebrun made feeble attempts to support Paul Reynaud's policy of continuing the war overseas, but he sealed the fate of the Republic by asking Marshal Philippe Pétain on 16 June 1940 to form a government dedicated to seeking an armistice. Unwilling to support the government proposed by Pétain and Pierre Laval, which ended the Republic on 10 July, and unwilling to oppose it, Lebrun retired. He was arrested by the Gestapo and was detained for several months until released because of ill health.

L. Derfler, *President and Parliament* (Boca Raton, 1983); A. Lebrun, *Témoignage* (Paris, 1945).

M. L. Mickelsen

Related entries: ARMISTICE OF 1940; BLUM; CAILLAUX; CHAUTEMPS; CLEMENCEAU; DALADIER; DEPRESSION OF THE 1930S; DOUMER; DOUMERGUE; FALL OF FRANCE, 1940; FEBRUARY RIOTS; HERRIOT; PETAIN; POINCARE, R.; POPULAR FRONT; REYNAUD.

LEFEBVRE, GEORGES (1874–1959), eminent economic and social historian of the French Revolution. He was born to a modest family in Flanders, grandson of a wool carder and son of a bookkeeper. Scholarships enabled him to study at the communal school, lycée, and faculty of letters of Lille. While an undergraduate at the university, he came under the influence of the medievalist Charles Petit-Dutaillis, under whose direction he later translated William Stubbs' *Constitutional History of England* into French. Lefebvre began his teaching career as a tutor and became an *agrégé d'histoire* in 1899. After fulfilling his military service, he taught at secondary schools in Cherbourg, Tourcoing, Lille, and St. Omer. During World War I, he was forced to leave his native region for Paris and was named to a post at Orléans, where he remained during the conflict.

Even before 1914 Lefebvre had begun work on the social and economic history of the Revolution. Influenced by the studies done by Russian economic historians and by the *Histoire socialiste* of Jean Jaurès, he published a two-volume collection of documents on food supply in the Nord department during the Revolution (1914–22). This work served as a preliminary to his doctoral dissertation, "Les Paysans du Nord pendant la Révolution française" (1924), which he defended at the Sorbonne. His thesis analyzed agrarian conditions and the situation of the peasantry in northern France before and after 1789, meticulously examining property holdings, manorial dues and services, and changes in land ownership as a result of the political upheaval. He followed this study with two other works on agrarian history: *La Grande Peur de 1789* (1932), which described the peasant uprising that swept France during the early months of the Revolution, and *Questions agraires au temps de la Terreur* (1932), which investigated peasant conditions during the 1790s.

His ability to synthesize quantities of information into readable form was evident in the chapters he contributed to *La Révolution française* (1930), as well as his *Napoléon* (1935), *Les Thermidoriens* (1937), and *Quatre-vingt-neuf* (1939), the last written to mark the sesquicentennial of the Revolution. By 1935 he had moved from teaching posts at Clermont-Ferrand and Strasbourg to the Sorbonne, where he held the chair in the history of the French Revolution from 1937 until his retirement in 1945. He succeeded to the presidency of the Société des études Robespierristes and the editorship of the *Annales historiques de la Révolution française* in 1932 after the death of Albert Mathiez, contributing numerous articles and reviews.

Early a socialist who admired both Jules Guesde and Jean Jaurès, Lefebvre became a Marxist during the mid-1930s. He nonetheless subordinated ideology to the patient gathering and interpretation of facts about material economic problems in the history of the Revolution. He paid special attention to psychological problems, particularly popular mentality (mass panic and violence resulting from insecurity and food shortages).

During World War II Lefebvre's output was sharply reduced, but after the Liberation he resumed his writing, producing his *Directoire* (1946) and a general history of the Revolution (1951). Lefebvre also supervised publication of the multivolume edition of the speeches of Robespierre, as well as documents on the Estates General of 1789. The postwar period saw him win international recognition for his work since many of his books and articles were translated into foreign languages. His influence continued even after his death with the publication of a two-volume study of Orléans during the Revolution (1962–63), one on Cherbourg at the end of the Old Regime (1965), a work on historiography (1971), and a detailed history of the Directory (1978).

Annales historiques de la Révolution française (memorial issues: 1960, 1969, 1979); J. Friguglietti, *Bibliographie de Georges Lefebvre* (Paris, 1972); J. Godechot, *Un Jury pour la Révolution* (Paris, 1974); R. R. Palmer, ''Georges Lefebvre: The Peasants and the French Revolution,'' *Journal of Modern History* 31 (1959).

J. Friguglietti

Related entries: AULARD; JAURES; MARXISM; MATHIEZ.

LEFT, THE, portion of the political spectrum comprising reformist and revolutionary socialists, syndicalists, and communists. The notion of the Left was born in France during the Revolution of 1789 and has preserved its favorable connotation in modern French politics. Even moderate and center parties in France have placed themselves on the Left, to the extent that *left* reflects the enlightenment ideals of progress, the perfectibility of humanity, and freedom. As a result these attributes no longer provide a precise definition of the term's meaning as a form of political classification. Nor can one define the Left by its social constituency or its regional base, although both have been tried. The term is often identified with the working class, but more than a third of French workers have always manifested a commitment to the Right, while the Left has enjoyed a long attachment among sectors of the land-owning peasantry and has been most successful among the liberal professions and intellectuals. A truism about the French is that their hearts are on the Left but their pocketbooks on the Right, which is another way of expressing their practical conservatism.

In the Third Republic the term *Left* is best used to denote political parties and organizations advocating the socialization or public ownership of the means of production and exchange. By this definition the Radical party, despite its occasional use of the title Radical-*Socialist* and its alliance with the Socialist and Communist parties for precise political objectives (whether anticlerical, broadly democratic, or Keynesian), must be classified as centrist if not to the right. The Left under the Third Republic was socialist in the sense that it wished to dispense with capitalism. But socialism was conceived broadly enough to encompass a bewildering variety of organizations, principles, and strategic outlooks. Consequently the Left in France has been known more for its division than its unity, although the eventual achievement of unity has remained its most cherished ideal.

Three competing visions of the socialist future have stubbornly persisted in France, at times coinciding with, but more often diverging from, the political strategies designed to achieve the socialist goal. Anarchosyndicalism arose among skilled workers jealously seeking to retain autonomy over their crafts in the face of the devaluation of their skills by industrialization and the factory system. The anarchosyndicalist vision was a federalist utopia based on worker self-management of enterprises, with the trade union as the basic governing unit of society. Following Joseph Proudhon, the anarchosyndicalists condemned the state as the source of social evil and forswore political action, bringing the scene of struggle for social change to the workplace itself. The anarchosyndicalist legacy ran deep; even after the socialists achieved a precarious political unity in 1905, they were obliged to recognize the independence of the trade unions through the Charter of Amiens (1906), and the Confédération générale de travail (CGT) retained its independence through the interwar period, relinquishing it only when it fell under Communist domination between 1936 and 1945. The Marxist socialism of Jules Guesde was statist and collectivist, its obsessive concern for organization a consequence of the narrow perception of the hierarchical and disciplined factory system of the unskilled as the all-embracing social model. Although Guesdism made compromises with reformism and tried to defend peasant interests for electoral reasons, its pessimistic statist social vision was bequeathed to French Communists, who subsequently rallied to the defense of East European "people's democracies" as the incarnation of the society they hoped to achieve. The reformist socialism of Paul Brousse, Jean Jaurès, and Léon Blum is the most difficult to define. Jaurès, the most extraordinary figure of the Second International, was eclectic in doctrine, seeking to balance syndicalism and statism, idealism and materialism, and patriotism and internationalism. Considering bourgeois democracy a moral absolute rather than a tactical phase of sociopolitical evolution (like the Guesdists and Communists after them), Jaurès' vision was of a mixed society evolving naturally from specific French cultural and historical traditions.

The reformist-revolutionary stategic split, common to socialists everywhere, always involved a mix of ideological, circumstantial, and temperamental elements. Karl Marx himself was ambiguous on the issue, and the problem was particularly acute in France, a vibrant parliamentary democracy endowed with a rich revolutionary tradition. The necessity of championing the Paris Commune (1871), in which federalist, statist, and mixed socialist visions briefly coexisted within a revolutionary framework, endowed French socialism with a Jacobin-insurrectionary legacy to which even reformists had to give lip-service. Revolutionaries were in turn divided between Blanquists, who stressed willpower and disciplined organization and technique, and more orthodox Marxists, who stressed political education of the masses and counseled patience until the revolutionary situation presented itself. Edouard Vaillant, Blanqui's successor, tried to reconcile these divergent strategies but without much success. Blum recognized in the enthusiasm for Leninism after World War I the revival of a form of Blanquism, and the Communists, while criticizing the great conspirator's alleged lack of scientific social vision, have just as frequently praised his revolutionary capacities and social ends.

Anarchosyndicalism fell into a kind of hibernation between the wars, its energies exhausted by the failure of the 1919–20 strike movements and its belief in Russian soviets as the fulfillment of the federalist dream dispelled. The Communist party, which captured a majority of the socialist delegates in December 1920 at Tours, was bolshevized in 1924–25 and then Stalinized in 1929–36. The first process gave the party its distinctively proletarian character: factory cells and working-class leaders. The second brought rigid centralization, a cult of personality, obsessive concern for the correct line, purges, and paranoia. The Socialist party, valiantly rebuilt under the guidance of Blum, uneasily combined reformist and revolutionary elements in an unstable mixture. An important segment of the Left, including Trotskyists and anarchosyndicalist splinter groups, remained outside Socialist organizations. Nevertheless, the Socialists managed to provide leadership for a substantial amount of social reform in 1936–37, taking a serious step toward a society that mixed capitalist and collectivist enterprises. At the same time, they displayed remarkable naiveté about the realities of political power, prematurely surrendering it in a dispute with the conservative Senate and opening the way for a return of right-wing government and appeasement.

D. N. Baker, "Seven Perspectives on the Socialist Movement of the Third Republic," *Historical Reflections* 1 (Winter 1974); D. Caute, *The Left in Europe since 1789* (New York, 1966); J. Colton, *Léon Blum, Humanist in Politics* (New York, 1966); H. Goldberg, *The Life of Jean Jaurès* (Madison, Wisc., 1962); G. Lefranc, *Le Mouvement Socialiste sous la Troisième République, 1875–40* (Paris, 1963); G. Lichtheim, *Marxism in Modern France* (New York, 1966); B. Moss, *The Origins of the French Labor Movement* (Berkeley, 1979).

I. M. Wall

Related entries: BLANQUISTS; COMMUNIST PARTY; GUESDISTS; MARXISM; POLITICS; RIGHT, THE; SOCIALIST PARTY; SYNDICALISM.

LEGER, ALEXIS SAINT-LEGER (1887–1975), diplomat and Nobel Prize poet. Born on a family-owned island, Saint-Léger les Feuilles, near Guadeloupe in the French West Indies on 31 May 1887, he was educated by the bishop of Guadeloupe and his nurse, a Hindu priestess of Shiva. He attended the lycée at Point-à-Pitre, finishing at Pau (Basses-Pyrénées). He studied at the University of Bordeaux and completed his *licence en droit* at Paris.

He joined the foreign service in 1914 and was secretary to the French embassy in Peking, China, from 1916 until 1921. Aristide Briand brought him to the Washington Disarmament Conference (1922) as an expert on the Far East and was so impressed with him that he was assigned to the Foreign Office (Quai d'Orsay) in Paris. He remained there, eventually becoming secretary-generalof the Ministry of Foreign Affairs (with the rank of ambassador) in 1932, the highest permanent Foreign Office post. He was active and influential in the formulation of Briand's diplomacy, but after Briand's retirement in 1932, he became disillusioned with his successors, for he believed that only Louis Barthou among foreign ministers had the will and vision to carry out French policies. He expressed concern about the prospect of German resurgence as early as 1930 and was exiled in 1940 after refusing to serve as Vichy's ambassador to the United States. He sought refuge in the United States, where Archibald MacLeish obtained for him a consultantship in French poetry at the Library of Congress. He was stripped of his honors, citizenship, and pension by the Vichy government, but these were restored by the Fourth Republic.

He wrote poetry under the pseudonym of St.-Jean Perse, an avocation he never admitted to his Foreign Office colleagues Briand and Barthou. His published works are: *Eloges* (1911), *Anabase* (1924), *Exil* (1942), *Vents* (1946), *Amers* (1957), *Chronique* (1959), and *Oiseaux* (1962). In 1965 Gallimard published *Honneur à Saint-Jean Perse*. His poems are noted for imagery and symbolism and the power of life to overcome disaster. His works have been translated into 17 languages. MacLeish, T. S. Eliot, and Louise Varèse are among poets influenced by him.

His honors include the grand officer of the Legion of Honor; commander of the Order of Bath; grand cross of the British Empire; Charles Elliot Norton Chair of Poetry, Harvard University, 1947; honorary doctorate, Yale University, 1959; Nobel Prize in Literature, 1960. He married Dorothy Milburn Russell of Washington D.C., in 1958. His later years were spent in Georgetown and then Giens, France, where he died on 20 September 1975.

E. R. Cameron, "Alexis Saint-Léger Léger," in G. A. Craig and F. Gilbert, eds., *The Diplomats* (Princeton, 1953); A. St.-L. Léger, *Briand* (Aurora, N.Y., 1943).

J. M. Rife, Jr.

Related entries: BARTHOU; BRIAND; FOREIGN POLICY; GERMANY, RE-LATIONS WITH (1914–1940).

LEGER, FERNAND (1881–1955), cubist and abstract painter. He was born in Argentan, the son of a livestock breeder of modest means. After an apprenticeship with an architect in Caen (1897–99), Léger settled in Paris, worked for architects and a photographer (1900–1905), and studied at the Ecole des arts décoratifs and the Ecole des beaux-arts. In 1908–9 he lived at the Ruche, an artist colony in Montparnasse, among many Eastern European artists, and also became friendly with the Montmartre group who were then developing cubism. Influenced by Paul Cézanne and by industrial modernity, Léger's variant of cubism, dubbed "Tubism" by a critic, was characterized by the juxtaposition of curved and angular robot-like forms at the verge of abstraction and by an interest in landscape and the modern cityscape. He participated in the Section d'or movement (1912).

His service in the engineers during World War I was to shape his subsequent career through his perception of beauty in the machinery of war (divorced from its purpose) and of the intelligence and humanity of the common man in the trenches. His work during the interwar period would greatly vary in direction— verging on the abstract at times, tending toward the classical at others—but predominating his art would be a humanist and populist emphasis and a love of machinery and the modern metropolis.

In the early 1920s, Léger collaborated with rationalist abstract painters, both the purists (Ozenfant, Jeanneret [Le Corbusier]) and the De Stijl group (Mondrian, Van Doesburg), and also maintained contact with the Russian constructivists and the Bauhaus in Germany. These movements inspired him to paint large public murals to bring his art into contact with the masses. For the 1925 Exposition des arts décoratifs he decorated with Robert Delaunay the entrance hall of Mallet-Stevens' French Embassy pavilion and did another mural for Le Corbusier's Pavillon de l'esprit nouveau. He was active in theater and film, designing sets and costumes for Blaise Cendrars' and Darius Milhaud's *La création du monde* (1923) and a short, plotless film, *Ballet mécanique* (1924), in which common objects create dance rhythms while humans behave mechanically.

After 1930 his works became simpler and more direct. The Popular Front influenced him toward a more realist depiction of everyday themes, but in the debate over communism's insistence on realism, Léger staunchly defended modernism as the appropriate vehicle for a truly popular art. He painted murals for the 1935 Brussels World's Fair and one glorifying science for the Palais de la découverte at the 1937 Paris Exposition universelle. In 1940 he left for voluntary exile in New York until 1945.

C. Green, *Léger and the Avant-Garde* (New Haven, 1976); R. Herbert, *Léger's "Le Grand Déjeuner"* (Minneapolis, 1980); F. Léger, *Functions of Painting* (New York, 1973); *Léger and Purist Paris* (London, 1970).

T. Shapiro

Related entries: ART: MAJOR STYLES AND MOVEMENTS; CEZANNE; DELAUNAY, R.; LE CORBUSIER; MALLET-STEVENS; MONDRIAN; OZENFANT; POPULAR FRONT.

LEGION OF HONOR, the national order of France and most prestigious system of honors and decorations of the Third Republic. It was created by Napoleon Bonaparte by decree of 29 Floreal Year X (19 May 1802) over the objections of those who feared it was a regression to the old monarchical orders of chivalry abolished by the Convention. The remark attributed to Napoleon, "that it is by these baubles one leads men," is well known and prophetic, for the order with its five-pointed star (subsequently known as a cross) survived successive changes in regime with suitable alterations in details of the insignia. Bonaparte also decreed it to be a reward for civil, as well as military, service, and this too has survived, although in September 1870 the Government of National Defense restricted the order to reward for military service. This was revoked in 1873, although in practical terms in both world wars virtually all nominations were for military service. The Legion of Honor became and remained solidly established as a French tradition with precedence over all other French decorations.

The head of the order, the *grand-maître*, is the chief of state or president of the Republic, who receives the collar on his election. The *grand chancelier*, traditionally a distinguished soldier or sailor, directs the actual administration of the order and presides over the Council of the Order, which consists of fourteen members who assist in the examination of candidates. There are three grades (in order of importance)—*chevalier, officier, commandeur*—and two dignities—*grand-officier* and *grand-croix*. The insignia varies according to grade, but the most common form of displaying membership was by means of a red ribbon in the buttonhole of civil dress, a simple ribbon for *chevalier*, and rosette for higher grades.

Frenchmen were admitted to the order after having rendered eminent service to the nation for twenty years in civil or military office or twenty-five years in private functions, but exceptions could be made in time of peace for exceptional services or in time of war for outstanding bravery, subject to the approval of the *grand chancelier* and council. There were usually two promotions per year, in January and July. Ministers, who were given a quota, would draw up lists of their subordinates who were eligible or those private individuals whose activities related to their departments, and these would be sent to the *grand chancelier* and council for examination. After acceptance and announcement in the *Journal officiel*, there would be a formal reception of new members or those promoted within the order. This ceremony was essential (except for foreigners). According to the rules of the order, a legionnaire of at least equal rank received the new member "in the name of the president of the Republic," bestowing the insignia and traditional accolade. Women members were rare before the turn of the century. The first was admitted in 1851, but there were few (Queen Victoria was one) until the First World War. There were around 110 women in 1914 and 3,000 in 1939.

Frenchmen entered the order as *chevalier* and could advance to the higher ranks only after passing through the intervening grades. Promotion in the order was in theory for new services, not for services already rewarded, and required a minimum period of seniority. Eight years were required for promotion from *chevalier* to *officier*, five for *officier* to *commandeur*, three for *commandeur* to *grand-officier*, and three for *grand-officier* to *grand-croix*. The order could also be awarded posthumously, a common practice in the world wars when entire promotions might fall in this category.

The system gave great power to the ministers and their advisers, and the question of what constituted eminent service to the nation was open to interpretation, particularly for those in private life. It is easy to see how politics or money could enter into the nominations, and there was the unfortunate example of the Wilson scandal (1887), in which the president of the Republic, Jules Grévy, was obliged to resign when his son-in-law was inculpated for trafficking in the Legion's decorations. The number of legionnaires varied between 30,000 and 78,000 throughout the nineteenth century. The great majority were military nominations. There were approximately 50,000 in May 1914, but the number multiplied as a result of the First World War. These were 94,000 in 1921 and 196,000 in 1937, plus 25,000 foreigners. The inflation in membership continued after the Second World War, and in 1956 there were almost 252,700 members. There were other orders of merit in the Republic, notably Mérite agricole (1883),

Mérite maritime (1930), Mérite sociale (1936), Santé publique (1938), and Mérite commerciale (1939), as well as the traditional Palmes académiques, but it was the Legion of Honor that retained its great prestige.

J. Daniel, *La Légion d'honneur* (Paris, 1957); C. Ducourtial, *Ordres et décorations*, 2d ed. (Paris, 1968); H. de Regnier, R. Anchel, and P.-F. Caillé, *Histoire des décorations françaises contemporaines* (Paris, 1933).

P. G. Halpern

Related entry: WILSON SCANDAL.

LEGITIMISM, the political viewpoint espoused by supporters of the eldest line of royalty in the house of France, the Bourbons, who had last reigned during the Restoration of 1814–30. In the early 1870s, they were still a powerful force, with their main goal being the restoration of the monarchy by their pretender to the throne, Henri, comte de Chambord (Henri V, 1820–83), who had lived in exile since 1830 in Frohsdorf, Austria. During the Third Republic, the Legitimists were obliged to act in concert with the Orleanists, supporters of the collateral line descended from Louis-Philippe, who had reigned from 1830 until 1848.

Together, the Legitimists and Orleanists had a majority in the National Assembly, convened at Bordeaux in 1871. There the Legitimists were led mainly by the *chevaux légers*, the extreme Right-wing faction of about eighty deputies who remained staunch supporters of Chambord and his policies until his death. Outside the Assembly, they were backed by many diehard Legitimist notables and by the Catholic hierarchy. Communications with Chambord were carried out by the Paris Bureau du roi, a central executive committee of twelve members who held weekly meetings and were Chambord's only contact with France. The party also had an official newspaper, *L'Union*.

Fidelity is the best word to describe the Legitimists. Always loyal to Chambord and to the principles of the monarchy, they showed considerable hostility toward the ideals of the Revolution of 1789. As they saw it, the Revolution had dissolved the ties to the Catholic Church and, more important, had ruined the traditional relationship between the aristocracy and the peasantry. Nostalgic for these lost days, they dreamed of a return to a hierarchical society, where all were loyal to the Church and everyone knew his social rank and function and where the socially superior notables could assume responsibility for the peasants. This society would be based on personal ties, as it was during the *ancien régime*. The Legitimists saw in Chambord the embodiment of these principles.

The summer of 1873 provided the Legitimists with their best opportunity for a restoration. By that date, the head of state, Adolphe Thiers, an Orleanist leader, became too oppressive and was forced to resign on 24 May 1873. This political vacuum paved the way for Chambord's return, but he demanded conditions unacceptable to most Frenchmen. For Chambord, the white flag of his ancestors was the incarnation of the monarchical principle, a matter of honor and political integrity. He thus stated in his manifesto, published 7 July 1873 in the *Union*, that there could be no compromise, that he would not accept the tricolor flag: "Henri V cannot abandon the white flag of Henri IV." Indeed Chambord would not compromise, and after final rejection of his conditions in mid-October, Maurice de MacMahon, an Orleanist politician, was elected president (19–20 November 1873).

Even as late as 1879, Chambord expressed his desire to return to rule France. Until this date, the Legitimists were still a considerable political force, though they realized that a restoration was no longer possible. When Chambord died on 24 August 1883, Legitimism as an independent cause died along with him, although many Legitimists, in concert with Orleanists and Bonapartists, constituted an important conservative coalition until the end of the century.

F. Brabant, *The Beginning of the Third Republic* (New York, 1972); J. Chastenet, *Histoire de la Troisième République* (Paris, 1970); R. Locke, *French Legitimists and the Politics of Moral Order in the Early Third Republic* (Princeton, 1974); S. Osgood, *French Royalism since 1870* (The Hague, 1970); R. Rémond, *La Droite en France de 1815 à nos jours* (Paris, 1954); J. Rothney, *Bonapartism after Sedan* (Ithaca, 1969); T. Zeldin, *France 1848–1945*, vol. 1 (Oxford, 1973).

A. J. Staples

Related entries: CHAMBORD; CONSERVATISM; NOTABLES; ORLEAN-ISM; PARIS, PHILIPPE D'ORLEANS.

LEMAIGRE DUBREUIL, JACQUES (1894–1955), industrialist, organizer of taxpayer protest in the 1930s. He combined a career in business with taxpayer politics and protest in the interwar period. From the Paris offices of Georges Lesieur et Ses Fils (Huile Lesieur), he spoke out against waste and corruption in government, the parliamentary game and the political Left, high taxes, and the financial squeeze on the middle class. As president (1935–39) of the Fédération nationale des contribuables, a group involved in the 6 February 1934 march on parliament, he built a national organization for public pressure on economic issues. For a time it was the preserve of well-heeled businessmen, professionals, and academics concerned about reform—reinforcing executive authority in government, stripping parliament of its right to initiate budget legislation, creating labor corporations, establishing a plan of regional economic development. Later it appealed to the more pinched and cramped of the middle class—storekeepers and small entrepreneurs hurt by the economic depression and terrified by the progress of socialism and communism—who were ready for revolt against the Popular Front government. Now the federation adopted more aggressive tactics: the tax strike, the mass meeting, the protest march, the shop closing. Not surprisingly, in the leftist press Lemaigre Dubreuil was linked to all sorts of plots against republican institutions, the federation dismissed as a front organization for big business. Dissolved at the outbreak of war in 1939, the federation was never reconstituted, yet some of its ideas and many of its tactics were adopted by the followers of Pierre Poujade in the 1950s.

During the Second World War Lemaigre Dubreuil expanded Lesieur operations in French Africa and conspired with U.S. diplomats to return France to the war; he recruited General Henri Giraud to the conspiracy and aided in the negotiation of the Murphy-Giraud agreements, the diplomatic prelude to the Allied landings of November 1942. After the war he was associated with a policy of Franco-Moroccan understanding and cooperation, which earned him credentials as a political liberal. He was assassinated at Casablanca in 1955.

W. A. Hoisington, Jr., *Taxpayer Revolt in France* (Stanford, 1973).

W. A. Hoisington, Jr.

Related entries: BUSINESSMEN; FEBRUARY RIOTS; LEFT, THE; POPULAR FRONT; TAXATION: GOVERNMENTAL POLICIES CONCERNING.

LEON, XAVIER (1868–1935), philosopher, editor, and publisher. Scion of a prosperous Parisian Jewish family, he founded the Société française de philosophie (1901) and the Revue de métaphysique et de morale (1893), two of the most influential institutions of philosophical inquiry in the Republic. They were intended by Léon and cofounder Elie Halévy to be vital organs of national resurgence and rationalist, idealist philosophy, and they became the forum for the major intellectual movements from 1893 to the mid-1930s. The catholicity of subjects, points of view, and personalities represented in both indicate Léon's exceptional talents and organizational ability.

Léon's studies of Johann Fichte (*Fichte et ses rapports avec la conscience contemporaine*, 1902, and *Fichte et son temps*, 3 vols., 1922–27) stress the idealist's incessant efforts in the cause of human liberty. Fichte's commitment to rationalist, secular education, liberty and the rule of law, and belief in the progressive elevation of humanity to the fullest exercise of its powers was Léon's theme in the three-volume study, which remains a classic inquiry into the milieu of Georg Hegel, Friedrich von Schelling, and Fichte.

M. Geroult, "Xavier Léon: vingt-cinq ans après" *Revue de métaphysique et de morale* 65 (1960); D. Parodi, *La Philosophie contemporaine en France* (Paris, 1919).

M. Chase

Related entries: BOUTROUX; DURKHEIM; HALEVY, E; POSITIVISM.

LEROY-BEAULIEU, PAUL (1843–1916), economist and journalist. Born of upper-middle-class parents in a family whose ascension began with the Revolution of 1789—both his father and grandfather were deputies—he specialized in political economy from the beginning of his career. In 1873, he founded the influential *Economiste français*, which was modeled after its English namesake and became the organ for high finance. He served as its editor and contributed a weekly column until his death. In 1880, he replaced his father-in-law, Michel Chevalier, as holder of the chair of political economy at the Collège de France. He was a member of the ultra-liberal Société d'économie politique of Paris. A prolific writer, his early works dealt with the condition of the working class, including *Le Travail des femmes au XIXe siècle* (1873). He penned standard works on public finance (*Traité de la science des finances*, 2 vols., 1877) and political economy (*Traité théorique et pratique d'économie politique*, 4 vols., 1895). Deeply concerned with the growth of socialism, he attacked its doctrines and defended those of laissez-faire liberalism. His *L'Etat moderne et ses fonctions* (1890) was a classic statement of the liberal position on the proper limits of state authority and an attack on the government's invasion of the domain of individual liberty. He contended in *Essai sur la répartition des richesses* (1880) that the distribution of wealth and income was becoming more equal. As a prominent exponent of French colonial expansion, he argued in the many editions of his *De la colonisation chez les peuples modernes* (2 vols., 1874) that the colonies were economically beneficial and could provide a fruitful area for capital investment.

R. Stourm, "Paul Leroy-Beaulieu," *Revue des deux mondes* 38, sixth ser. (1917).

C. E. Freedeman

Related entry: LIBERALISM.

LESSEPS, FERDINAND DE (1805–1894), one of France's leading entrepreneurs and diplomats of the nineteenth century. Lesseps' long and extraordinary career culminated with the opening of the Suez Canal in 1869. His bold, industrious character caused Léon Gambetta to proclaim him *le grand français*, and his reputation earned him the universal respect and admiration of his contemporaries.

He was born 19 November 1805 at Versailles (Seine-et-Oise) into a family committed to public service. At the age of twenty he entered the consular service and served in Lisbon, Tunis, and Cairo. This last post inspired his dream of building a canal at Suez. In 1869 he stood for election in Marseilles but was defeated by Léon Gambetta.

After 1870 he refused other political campaigns but maintained an interest in public affairs. In 1873 he considered plans for linking Europe and Asia by rail, and he encouraged Pierre de Brazza's expedition in Africa. In 1879 his great popularity and reputation caused him to head the committee charged with building a canal across Panama. Despite his advanced age, he accepted the task, which ultimately would jeopardize his image as a successful innovator.

The Panama Canal project was plagued by difficulties from the outset. By 1888 the company Lesseps headed was in serious trouble. Lesseps stubbornly insisted on building a canal without locks. Because the project was touted as an achievement of the Third Republic, opponents of the regime sought to discredit the undertaking. Because of questionable financial practices, those implicated in the enterprise (politicians, builders, and journalists) were condemned by an outraged public; and the government was severely shaken. In fairness to Lesseps, it should be noted that it was his son Charles who was in charge of the actual operation and who received most of the public censure. Ferdinand's reputation saved him from opprobrium.

Lesseps died on 7 December 1894. In spite of the controversy of his final years, he was to be remembered by most as the incarnation of the French enterprising spirit.

552

LEVASSEUR, EMILE

C. Beatty, *Ferdinand de Lesseps* (London, 1956); G. Edgar-Bonnet, *Ferdinand de Lesseps* (Paris, 1951); G. B. Smith, *The Life and Enterprises of Ferdinand de Lesseps* (London, 1893).

F. Busi

Related entries: BRAZZA; BUSINESSMEN; DRUMONT; CLEMENCEAU; PANAMA SCANDAL.

LEVASSEUR, EMILE (1828–1911), liberal academic, economic historian, and pioneer of social history. A disciple of Jean-Baptiste Say and Frédéric Bastiat, he completed one of the first French doctoral theses in economics in 1854. He became a respected academic in the liberal, moderate republican circles around René Waldeck-Rousseau. In 1871, with fellow free-trade and free-market economists and politicians, Levasseur participated in the establishment of the Ecole libre des sciences politiques, a training ground for the higher levels of government administration. In addition to his courses on political economy, economic history, geography, and the new field of social economy at "Sciences Po," Levasseur was an administrator and lecturer at the prestigious Collège de France.

Levasseur's most important scholarly contribution was his multivolume study of the working classes from the pre-Revolutionary era to 1900. This work brought together an enormous collection of data on a wide range of issues rarely considered by the same (or any) scholar. Levasseur analyzed the growth of industry, changes in technology, wage levels, cost of living indexes, labor relations, workers' organizations, strike frequencies, legislation, and ideologies. Levasseur had begun to indicate areas of central concern to social historians. While defending the virtues of the free market, he also demonstrated that neither the historian, economist, nor politician could ignore the social and economic realities of the enfranchised worker.

E. Levasseur, *Questions ouvrières et industrielles en France* (Paris, 1907).

J. F. Stone

Related entries: LEROY-BEAULIEU; LIBERALISM; SCHOOLS, HIGHER EDUCATION: ECOLE LIBRE DES SCIENCES POLITIQUES; WALDECK-ROUSSEAU.

LEYGUES, GEORGES (1857–1933), politician and eleven times minister of marine. Born in Villeneuve-sur-Lot (Lot-et-Garonne), he entered the Chamber of Deputies from Lot-et-Garonne in 1885 and represented it without interruption until his death. He was associated with the Gauche démocratique and became minister of instruction and beaux arts in the Charles Dupuy and René Waldeck-Rousseau cabinets (May 1894–January 1895 and November 1898–June 1902), with an interval as minister of the interior in the Alexandre Ribot cabinet (January–November 1895). Leygues was minister of colonies in the Ferdinand Sarrien cabinet from March to October 1906 and in 1909 inherited a large sum of money from the founder of the Louvre department store, Alfred Chauchard. This cast a shadow over his career for a number of years. He served early in the First World War as a captain in the infantry and was also one of the leaders of the group that favored acquiring a protectorate over Syria. He was eventually called by Georges Clemenceau to be minister of marine from November 1917 to January 1920. This was the beginning of a long association between Leygues and the navy; he would hold the portfolio over seven years.

Leygues experienced a relatively short and unhappy period as premier and minister of foreign affairs from September 1920 to January 1921. His predecessor, Alexandre Millerand, had been elected president of the Republic but wanted to increase the powers of the presidency. He therefore continued to direct affairs, and Leygues, who had left the members of Millerand's cabinet in place, was regarded as a figurehead lacking real authority. He spent an interval as minister of the interior (December 1930–January 1931), but it was as minister of marine that he made his reputation. He held the portfolio in successive cabinets from November 1925 to January 1930 and from June 1932 until his death in September 1933.

During Leygues' term in office, there was a rejuvenation of the French fleet. He is credited with signing orders for laying down 120 ships, including 9 cruisers, 27 destroyers, and 55 submarines for a total of 300,000 tons. He was responsible for the decree of 22 April 1927 reorganizing the services of the navy and the cadre law of 5 March 1929 improving conditions of recruitment and advancement, and he laid the cornerstone for the new Ecole navale in 1929. He liked to style himself the Colbert of the Third Republic and wrote a study, *Colbert et son oeuvre*, as well as short brochures, *La Marine française pendant la grande guerre* and *Marins de France*. Shortly after his death he was honored by having one of the light cruisers named after him. This tradition is maintained in the French Navy with a guided missile destroyer launched in 1975. He is, with the obvious exception of Georges Clemenceau, the only political figure of the Third Republic to be so honored.

R. de Belot and A. Reussner, *La Puissance navale dans l'histoire*, vol. 3 (Paris, 1960); J. Jolly, ed., *Dictionnaire des parlementaires français*, vol. 6 (Paris, 1970); E. du Ravay, *Vingt ans de politique navale (1919–1939)* (Grenoble, 1941); H. Le Masson, *The French Navy*, 2 vols. (London, 1969); E. Taillermite, *Dictionnaire de la marine* (Paris, 1962).

P. G. Halpern

Related entries: CLEMENCEAU; NAVY; NAVY: GOVERNMENTAL POLICY ON NAVAL WARFARE; MILLERAND; WORLD WAR I, FRANCE'S ROLE IN.

LIARD, LOUIS (1846–1917), administrator and philosopher who as director of higher education and vice-rector of the Academy of Paris helped bring French higher education into the modern world. A Norman raised by a widow's high standard of duty, Liard graduated first in philosophy from the Ecole normale supérieure in 1869 where under the influence of the Kantian philosophers Jules Lachelier and Charles Renouvier he found in the categorical imperative a reinforcement of earlier values. An indefatigable worker and devotee of science, Liard, while teaching at the lycées of Mont de Marsans (1869) and Poitiers (1871), prepared both his *licence ès sciences* and *docteur ès lettres*. Transferred to Poitiers because of political activities, Liard never hid his republicanism. Appointed to the Faculty of Letters at Bordeaux (1874) after the brilliant defense of his theses, Liard won election to the city's municipal council (1878) where he served as deputy mayor and delegate for public education. Bordeaux's city hall provided, he said, his schooling in administration.

Jules Ferry, impressed by Liard's administrative abilities and republican allegiance, secured his appointment first as rector of the University of Caen (1880) and later, on the death of Albert Dumont, as director of higher education (1884). Liard thus joined that group of reformers who, after France's defeat in 1870, devoted themselves to the modernization of public education. If frustrated in his more ambitious goals, Liard, through perseverance and a systematic approach that he attributed to his philosophical training, secured numerous reforms highlighted by the decree of 1885, which strengthened the legal status of the faculties, and finally by the law of 1896, which united the scattered faculties into fifteen university centers. During his term as director, higher education doubled its enrollment from 15,000 in 1885 to 30,000 by 1902. That year Liard became vice-rector of the Paris Academy, and the Sorbonne under his aegis increased its faculty from 756 to 950 and its student body from 12,414 to 17,606. As vice-rector he also introduced and successfully pursued a policy that encouraged private benefactors to add to the Sorbonne's endowment.

The public mood, the work of predecessors, the skill of his staff, and the long terms of his major offices aided Liard in his task, but the Republic still remained heavily indebted to the personal qualities of an exemplary administrator who maintained a fruitful relationship with many ministers and whose dedication and intelligence found further confirmation in philosophical and scholarly works published throughout his career.

P. Gerbod, "Un Directeur de l'enseignement supérieur: Louis Liard," *Centre de recherche d'histoire et de philologie de l'école pratique des hautes études* 5 (1976); E. Lavisse, "Louis Liard," *La Revue de Paris* 25 (1918); L. Liard, *L'Enseignement supérieur en France* (Paris, 1888–94).

L. M. Greenberg
Related entries: EDUCATION: ACADEMIC DEGREES; EDUCATION: ADMINISTRATION OF; EDUCATION: GOVERNMENTAL POLICIES CONCERNING; LAVISSE; RENOUVIER; UNIVERSITIES.

LIBERALISM, a significant viewpoint in French thought and politics during the Third Republic. It was identified with a variety of intellectual movements, sometimes overlapping, sometimes distinct. This diversity was a product of French history, with each current having its origin in a particular phase of that history. The most important for the Third Republic were the Jacobin, Orleanist, economist, libertarian, and neoliberal currents. They differed not only in origin but also in social foundation and political orientation. Yet they all deserve to be called liberal because of a common commitment—however variously interpreted—to human rights, individual freedom, and responsible government.

All French liberals thought of themselves as heirs of the 1789 Revolution; the Jacobins took this more literally than most others. Not only did they derive their program from the Declaration of the Rights of Man and the Citizen, they tended to think of themselves as representatives of the Third Estate, defending the people against the machinations of the clergy, the *ci-devants*, and the foreign enemy. Their vision of politics as a life-and-death struggle—confirmed by the birth pangs of the Third Republic—led them to favor authoritarian methods of government so long as these were directed against the enemies of the people. No one political party completely encompassed any of the currents of liberalism, but most of the Jacobins would find a home in the Radical and Radical-Socialist party. That hybrid title was symptomatic of their problems under the Third Republic. Accustomed to thinking of themselves as the only party of the Left, the Jacobins were divided in their response to the rise of socialism. Some saw the socialists as the new enemies of the people, more insidious because they disguised servitude as popular welfare, while others saw them as the modern Jacobins, erring only in their tendency toward economic collectivization. The evolution of republican political life would place the Radicals in the center of the political spectrum, giving them an importance, especially after 1900, exceeding their numbers. They would furnish a major part of the ministerial personnel of the Republic, but their liberalism suffered increasingly from arrested intellectual development.

The Orleanist current was the least democratic branch of French liberalism; it did promote representative government and individual rights but tended in practice to interpret them too narrowly in the interests of the propertied classes. Having emerged from the 1830 revolution, they remained popularly associated with the July Monarchy, the era of the *grande bourgeoisie*. There was even, at the beginning of the Third Republic, a continuity of personnel; Adolphe Thiers, first president of the Republic, had been a premier under the July Monarchy. Most Orleanists continued to prefer a parliamentary Monarchy, perhaps even with a restricted suffrage, but accepted Thiers' conviction that a democratic republic was the only viable regime in the 1870s. While striving to make that regime safe for the interests of private property, they played a vital role in the Republic's foundation and furnished much of its early leadership.

Neither the Jacobins nor the Orleanists were strict adherents to the doctrine of laissez-faire, which never had the importance in French that it did in English liberalism. Only the sect of the economists, who carried into the Third Republic the tradition of Jean-Baptiste Say, continued to preach the virtues of laissez-faire and, especially, of free trade. Their influence was largely confined to the law schools, where economics was taught, and did not penetrate the business community. Some liberals promoted economic modernization and the interests of big business, and others favored the small entrepreneur and traditional French practices, but both groups appealed to the government and not the free market to advance their positions.

Like the economists, the libertarians were a small intellectual community without much practical influence. They served mainly to demonstrate the French penchant for pushing logic to the point of irrationality and the affinity of liberalism, when coupled with a belief in the innate goodness of humanity, for anarchism. Their main influence was in the internationalist and pacifist movements, which often carried liberalism to the point of caricature.

The emergence of a new liberalism around the turn of the century demonstrated that French liberalism possessed a capacity for change and adaptation despite its strong attachment to historical doctrines. This new liberalism was a conscious effort to democratize liberalism by adapting it to changing social realities. An effort to make liberalism of more practical benefit to all strata of society, it was inspired both by the emergence of democratic socialism and by intellectual doubts about the old liberalism. The intellectual inspiration for the new liberalism came primarily from neo-Kantian philosophy and Comtean positivism.

Charles Renouvier led the effort to reestablish liberalism on a neo-Kantian foundation; many other liberals sought a more scientific and less rationalistic base. They turned toward sociology in the hope of establishing a liberal science of society. Both the neo-Kantians and the sociologists, Emile Durkheim foremost, sought to separate liberalism from a narrow individualism and to show that the individual could be integrated into society more firmly without the loss of individual rights. This socialized liberalism paved the way for a more extended concept of the role of the state and helped prepare the French middle classes for the mixed economy and welfare state of the later twentieth century.

While there was little new in French liberal ideas after the 1914–18 war, the growing practical significance of the new liberalism is visible in the struggle of French political leaders against the polarization of politics that might have destroyed the Republic. This influence can be seen most clearly in the Popular Front program, which was radically reformist without being socialist. Despite the short-term failure of the Popular Front, it demonstrated that liberalism remained a vital force throughout the Third Republic.

A. Brecht, *Political Theory* (Princeton, 1959); W. H. Logue, *From Philosophy to Sociology: The Evolution of French Liberalism, 1870–1914* (Dekalb, Illinois, 1983); H. Michel, *L'Idée de l'état* (Paris,1895).

W. H. Logue

Related entries: ALAIN; ANTICLERICALISM; ANTIMILITARISM; BERT; BOURGEOIS; BROGLIE; BUISSON; CARTEL DES GAUCHES; DUR-KHEIM; FERRY; HERRIOT; JACOBINISM; LEFT, THE; ORLEANISM; RADICAL AND RADICAL-SOCIALIST PARTY; RENOUVIER; SIMON; SOLIDARISM; TARDE; THIERS.

LILLE, capital city of the department of the Nord (from 1804) and part of the urban agglomeration Lille-Roubaix-Tourcoing. The city grew rapidly in the nineteenth century both in size by annexing adjoining communes and in population, reaching a peak of 220,000 inhabitants in the first decade of the twentieth century.

For the rest of the Third Republic, population dispersed to the suburbs as a result of an interurban tramway (the Mongy).

An administrative, military, and university center, Lille had long been important for its production of textiles and, especially in the nineteenth century, of cotton and linen thread and household linens. These businesses had the reputation of being secretive, familial enterprises, often resistant to modernization until the early twentieth century when economic survival demanded mergers and other modifications in production. Alongside textiles was a large garment-making industry and heavy metallurgical firms, the largest of which, Fives-Lille, specialized in locomotives, machinery for textile production, and bridges. Chemicals, sugar refining, brewing, and other food processing also contributed to the urban economy.

The misery of the heavily Belgian working class, along with the paucity of embellishments such as historical monuments, made Lille a synonym for urban dreariness. Living in dank cellars, crowded into *courettes*, the working class had a particularly high rate of fertility and of infant mortality. Street and café life, fêtes such as the Broquelet, and the *patois* songs of Alexandre Desrousseaux served to liven existence in the short run, while socialists worked so eagerly for long-run solutions that Gustave Delory became mayor in the municipal elections in 1896.

In part socialists succeeded for a brief time because of sharp hostilities between republican and Catholic factions in the city during the first decades of the Third Republic. Laicization of the schools, struggle for control of municipal welfare projects, and health services made for bitter political disputes culminating in the socialist victory and ending officially with the election of centrist Charles Delesalle to the mayor's office in 1904. Prominent among Catholic laymen was Paul Feron-Vrau, textile manufacturer and publisher of *La Croix*.

Lille endured severe German occupations in both world wars. The occupation from 1914 to 1918 caused extreme hardship because of the physical damage, systematic dismantling of many factories by the enemy, and the number of prominent politicians, religious leaders, and businessmen deported to Germany as hostages. This dislocation in part accounts for the difficult interwar period of massive unemployment, inflation, strikes, and business depression. Union leaders and socialists saw a dramatic upsurge in membership, Gustave Delory followed by the militant Roger Salengro held the mayor's office until 1936, and socialists virtually monopolized the city council. Lille businessmen did not follow the path of their neighbors in Roubaix-Tourcoing in organizing a consortium of *patrons* to control wages and benefits, but they did complain, especially to the central government, about an urgent need to restore the proper relationship between capital and labor.

Lille in the Third Republic also experienced continued "haussmannization" of the city, the development of an outstanding Musée des beaux-arts, the creation of scientific and technical institutes and learned societies, a renaissance in northern poetry, and the birth of Charles de Gaulle.

F.-P. Codaccioni, *De l'inégalité sociale dans une grande ville industrielle. Le drame de Lille, 1850–1914* (Lille, 1976); J. Lambert-Dansette, *Quelques familles du patronat textile de Lille-Armentières (1789–1914)* (Lille, 1954); P. Pierrard, *Lille et les lillois* (Paris, 1967) and *La Vie quotidienne dans le Nord au XIX siècle* (Paris, 1976); B. Smith, *Ladies of the Leisure Class* (Princeton, 1981); L. Trenard, ed., *Histoire d'une métropole. Lille, Roubaix, Tourcoing* (Toulouse, 1977).

B. G. Smith

Related entries: DESROUSSEAUX; URBANIZATION AND THE GROWTH OF CITIES.

LIMOGES. During the nineteenth century it emerged as a center of industry and one of the fastest-growing cities in France. It also earned a reputation as *la ville rouge*, a center of class conflict and radicalism. Bourgeois liberals had vigorously opposed the alliance of altar and throne in the late 1820s. The 1830s saw the first strikes in the city, by skilled workers in Limoges' most important industry, the manufacture of porcelain. Many workers were influenced by utopian socialism and radical bourgeois republicans. Following disappointment in the legislative elections of April 1848, Limoges' workers briefly seized power, disarming the bourgeois National Guard. By May 1849, the workers of Limoges and their radical bourgeois allies seemed to have converted most of the department to democratic socialism; in the elections of May 1849, the department of Haute-Vienne returned only socialists. After the coup d'état of 2 December 1851, what was left of the Montagnard organization attempted an insurrection in Limoges' hinterland, which the army easily crushed. Yet during the Second Empire, Limoges' republicans and socialists gradually rebuilt their forces. In 1864, workers greeted the legalization of strikes with a wave of work stoppages, led by the porcelain workers. The months before the Franco-Prussian War saw a wave of organization and working-class militancy. Early in April 1871, workers prevented troops from leaving the city to aid the Versailles government and attempted to proclaim the Commune.

The concentration of capital and industry in Limoges characterized the first decades of the Third Republic. The Havilands led the way with technological advances in the porcelain industry (David Haviland first began exporting Limoges porcelain in the 1840s and was the first to combine production and decoration in the same factory), expanded production, and increased standardization while retaining the reputation of Limoges porcelain. The shift from wood to coal as fuel for the kilns, the gradual replacement of hand-painted decoration by decals, and improvements in the kilns and their increased size expanded production and enhanced standardization. The railway, which reached Limoges in 1856, aided the product's distribution. By 1905, there were approximately 13,000 porcelain workers in Limoges, some 40 percent of the city's 32,000 workers. Limoges' second industry, shoemaking, expanded rapidly in the 1880s and 1890s, employing 4,000 people in 1905. Although relatively small units of production and decoration remained in the porcelain industry and a good deal of shoemaking continued to be done by home workers, the large factories of Theodore Haviland and of

Charles Haviland (the latter employing over 2,000 workers) and the Monteux shoe manufacture reflected the concentration of industry in Limoges. Both industries also employed an increasing number of unskilled or semiskilled female workers.

Limoges' population grew from about 55,000 in 1872 to over 84,000 at the turn of the century. Its largely industrial faubourgs pushed the periphery of the city to the north and northwest, most notably the route de Paris and the faubourgs Montmailler and the Montjovis. The majority of workers moving to Limoges were drawn from a narrow range of migration, principally from the Haute-Vienne's southern half. Life and work in the faubourgs contrasted with that of the city's groups of traditional workers, particularly the clans of butchers living on the rue de la Boucherie and the washerwomen of L'Abbessaille, along the Vienne River.

Politically Limoges remained on the left, staunchly republican and anticlerical in the days of Adolphe Thiers and Maurice de MacMahon, radical republican in the heyday of the Opportunists, and republican-socialist and then socialist in the era of the Radical Republic. Political clubs brought ideology and organization to Limoges' socialists. In 1895, Limoges became a socialist municipality, led by Mayor Emile Labussière, a public works entrepreneur from the Creuse, who became a reform socialist in the spirit of Jean Jaurès. Nineteen of Limoges's thirty-six municipal councilmen in 1904 were workers. In 1898, Labussière was elected to the Chamber of Deputies, and the Haute-Vienne moved to the forefront of France's left. 1895 inaugurated the *belle époque* of popular political life in the city, what one might call the banquet years of class conflict, characterized by political meetings, *punches populaires*, and *conférences contradictoires*, political debates that brought a variety of ideological alternatives to ordinary people. The socialist Catholics abbé Desgranges and abbé Marévéry, despite little popular following, were among the most active participants, while the Opportunists-Progressists of Dr. François Chénieux, Labussière's archenemy, stayed away from such plebeian encounters. Limoges, once known for its religious fervor and processions (particularly the septennial Ostensions), became known for political *manifestations* and a lively municipal political life. Limoges' Guesdist minority, despite major differences with the reform socialists that were accentuated by the Alexandre Millerand crisis of 1899, participated in the electoral alliance with the Allemanists and reform socialists against the combined forces of the bourgeois moderates and the clerical and monarchist faction. The Guesdists and Allemanists had little success when they ran their own candidates.

One of the first acts of the socialist municipality had been to establish the Bourse du travail, previously refused by the Opportunist municipality. The period from 1895 to 1900 was characterized by close ties between the Bourse—run by the moderate Guesdist Edouard Treich, in whose café some of the planning had occurred for the Seventh Corporative Congress of 1895 that gave birth to the General Confederation of Labor (CGT)—and the socialist municipality. By 1905, 6,500 of the city's workers were organized. Not surprisingly, 1895 also marked the beginning of a wave of strikes that lasted two years; fifty-three strikes occurred during the next ten years as porcelain workers, the most organized workers, and shoemakers resisted industrial discipline. The foreman, enforcing the rules of the *patron*, was a frequent target of strikes. Following Treich's departure in the wake of a scandal over a *pot-du-vin*, the Bourse fell gradually under the influence of more radical Guesdists. Yet Limoges remained dominated by reform socialists, who contributed much to the improvement of the city, while changing the names of streets to reflect the socialist heritage of the Limousin's capital. The dilapidated old quarters of Verdurier and Viraclaud were transformed. Limoges' reform socialists emphasized the possibilities of decentralization and communal autonomy, in contrast to the centralization of the existing bourgeois state and of the Guesdist socialism.

A second major wave of strikes in 1904 and 1905 culminated in the violence of April. Troops fired at porcelain workers after the second of two days of marches and barricades, killing a young porcelain worker, Camille Vardelle. The army's action reaffirmed the city's antimilitary tradition but frightened many bourgeois allies of the socialists and, following the end of the strikes, brought the resignation of Labussière at the end of the year and the subsequent return to power of Chénieux and the Opportunists-Progressists, who received the support of the small clerical and monarchist faction. The Bourse du travail lost most of its municipal funding and declined in influence. Strikes in Limoges thereafter tended to focus on specific issues that seemed to suggest a grudging acceptance of the power of the *patronat*. Demonstrations lost much of their aggressive character and focused on winning public support and the goodwill of the government rather than confronting their bosses and the army. An era ended in Limoges.

In 1912, the socialists returned to municipal power, led by Léon Betoulle who would, except during the Vichy years and the immediate post–World War II period, remain mayor until his death in 1956. In 1914, the department returned five socialist deputies in the legislative elections, and the world slipped toward war. In 1915, these deputies of Haute-Vienne signed the first call for peace of World War I.

In the 1920s, shoemaking replaced the production of porcelain as Limoges' major industry. The Congress of Tours brought a deep split within the socialist camp in the Haute-Vienne, as elsewhere in France. Limoges' labor movement remained moderate, with close ties to reform socialism during these years. During World War II, the Communists dominated the resistance in the region, which saw two of the worst atrocities committed in Western Europe, the hangings in Tulle (Corrèze) and the massacre at Oradour-sur-Glane, the old town which still stands as it did that day in June 1944, when the Germans shot the men of the commune and burned the women and children in the church. Limoges remains an industrial city of the Left, one still identified in much of the world with its porcelain despite that industry's diminished share in the city's economy.

K. E. Amdur, "Unity and Schism in French Labor Politics: Limoges and Saint-Etienne,

1914–1922'' (Ph.D. dissertation, Stanford University, 1978); G. E. Clancier, *La Vie quotidienne en Limousin au XIX siècle* (Paris, 1976); A. Corbin, *Archaïsme et modernité en Limousin, 1845–1880*, 2 vols. (Paris, 1975); G. Désiré-Vuillemin,''Une Grève fevolutionnaire: Les Porcelainiers de Limoges en avril 1905,'' *Annales du Midi* 83 (January–March 1971); J. M. Merriman, ''Incident at the Statue of the Virgin Mary: The Conflict of Old and New in Nineteenth-Century Limoges,'' in J. M. Merriman, ed., *Consciousness and Class Experience in Nineteenth-Century Europe* (New York, 1979), and *The Last Revolution: Limoges and the French Nineteenth Century* (New York, 1985).

J. Merriman

Related entries: BETOULLE; PRESSEMANE; URBANIZATION AND THE GROWTH OF CITIES.

LIPCHITZ, JACQUES (1891–1973), Lithuanian-born modernist sculptor. The son of a Lithuanian-Jewish building contractor from a wealthy banking family, he was early drawn to sculpture. His father wanted him to be an engineer or architect, but in 1909 his mother helped him leave for Paris without telling his father. He studied academic sculpture at the Ecole des beaux-arts (1909–10) and also attended more liberal art schools. He settled in Montparnasse, along with other Eastern European artists and many sculptors. In 1912–13 he became friendly with Pablo Picasso, Amedeo Modigliani, Chaim Soutine, and the Mexican artist Diego Rivera and came under the cubist influence, which became a major aspect of his work up to 1930.

Lipchitz' enormous output varied from austere cubist works to highly expressive ones, the extremes sometimes produced contemporaneously. He worked frequently on a monumental scale in bronze but also made smaller works in stone, clay, and wax, and sometimes he incorporated found objects. He was strongly drawn to classical and Judeo-Christian themes and to universal experiences such as motherhood, communication by music, the sexual embrace—all rendered in highly abstract terms.

In 1924 Lipchitz became a French citizen. During the interwar period he received numerous commissions, notably from Vicomte Charles de Noailles in 1927 for *La Joie de vivre*, one of his most famous works, and from the French government for *Prometheus Strangling the Vulture*, which was placed atop the Grand Palais during the Exposition universelle of 1937. In 1941 he emigrated to the United States.

A. M. Hammacher, *Jacques Lipchitz* (New York, 1975); J. Lipchitz with H. H. Arnason, *My Life in Sculpture* (New York, 1972); I. Patai, *Encounters* (New York, 1961).

T. Shapiro

Related entries: ART: MAJOR STYLES AND MOVEMENTS; MODIGLIANI; PICASSO; SOUTINE.

LISSAGARAY, PROSPER-OLIVIER (1838–1901), Communard, journalist, revolutionary, historian. Lissagaray is an essential source for understanding the Commune. By the time he arrived in Paris in 1860, the young Basque had performed admirably in his studies and had traveled to the United States. He was steadily drawn into the ranks of republican and socialist activists and by 1870 had a long police record. During the Franco-Prussian War he served in Toulouse and in the army of General Antoine Chanzy. At the beginning of the insurrection of the Paris Commune in 1871, Lissagaray chose not to participate in the government but rather to remain on the barricades as a soldier.

During the Commune he founded two newspapers, both short-lived: *L'Action* (4–9 April) and *Le Tribun du peuple* (17–24 May). He participated in the last skirmishes of the insurrection and escaped to Belgium on 28 May. In Brussels, Lissagaray began to write his eye-witness accounts of the Commune, first publishing *Les Huit Journées de mai derrière les barricades* (1871), which was essentially an outline for his most important work, the *Histoire de la Commune de 1871* (1876). This book was first printed in Belgium and finally in France in 1896. (The most recent edition was published by François Maspero in 1967.) Lissagaray's other work, *La Vision de Versailles* (1873), was not based on his own experience but recounted in a literary fiction the lives of those members of the Commune who were imprisoned, judged, and condemned during the trials in Versailles.

After the amnesty of 1880 Lissagaray returned to Paris and founded another journal, *La Bataille* (1881–83 and 1888–93), through which he especially attacked the Boulangist movement.

As Jacques Rougerie pointed out, Lissagaray's works on the Commune have not been dated by the passage of time. Historians continue to value and admire his accounts for their authenticity, wealth of information, and ability to recapture the emotional quality of the insurrection.

M. Dommanget, *La Commune et les Communards* (Paris, 1947); J. Rougerie, *Procès des Communards* (Paris, 1964); G. Soria, *Grande Histoire de la Commune* (Paris, 1970–71).

M. Berkvam

Related entries: COMMUNARDS; COMMUNE OF PARIS; FRANCO-PRUSSIAN WAR.

LITERARY CRITICS AND CRITICISM. During the Third Republic, literary criticism was practiced by professional critics who usually wrote for reviews, journals, or literary magazines, by university scholar-critics, and by creative writers who were also essayists and polemicists. Criticism thus included practical, or applied, criticism (the evaluation and interpretation of particular works or writers) and theoretical essays that set forth the aesthetic principles of a particular writer or literary movement.

In the last years of the nineteenth century and the period before the outbreak of World War I, criticism reflected the broader currents of French intellectual life: nineteenth-century positivism and historical theory, the social and political crisis posed by the Dreyfus affair, and various avant-garde movements. In addition, many critics continued the tradition of impressionism or dilettantism—of writing essays based on the refined and educated taste of the individual critic.

Hippolyte Taine and Ernest Renan, who attempted to integrate the methods and spirit of science into the humanistic disciplines, were influential figures in the early years of the Third Republic. In his famous preface to his *Histoire de la littérature anglaise* (1864), Taine had set forth the analogy between literature and a natural organism that has a dynamic relationship with its environment. The literary work is not the product of an isolated genius, according to Taine, but is affected by race (the national tradition to which it belongs), milieu (its social and political environment), and moment (its place within the historical process). Taine viewed literature more as a social document, in contrast to the romantics who had emphasized the creative genius of the individual writer. Along with Charles Sainte-Beuve, Taine was a major reason that the teaching of literature and the writing of literary history for several decades emphasized the factors in the author's life and times that lay behind a text while saying little about the qualities of a text as literature.

Renan, on the other hand, retained an exegetical understanding of criticism as the "seizing of the physiognomy of each portion of humanity" (*L'Avenir de la science*, written in 1848, published in 1890). The critic does not find fault or judge; he accepts the work as it is, subjecting it to scrutiny in order to find the truth within it. Although Renan's position was indebted to recent developments in science, his influence on criticism was to encourage impressionism; Taine, however, demanded that criticism use a methodology like that of science.

The tendency to argue by means of analogy in extending to literature the methodology of the natural sciences is evident in Emile Zola's *Le Roman expérimental* (1880), a major manifesto of naturalism, the movement in prose fiction and the theater that viewed literature as a slice of life. Naturalist characters are subject to the laws of heredity and environment. Zola claimed that the writer, although showing his genius in the hypothesis at the heart of his novel, is nothing more than an experimental scientist who sets his characters in motion and then sits back to observe what happens to them during his aesthetic experiment.

A far different spirit dominated the criticism surrounding the symbolist movement; in many respects the aesthetics of the symbolists was post-romantic. A number of papers and magazines were linked to the symbolist poets and to the composer Richard Wagner, including the *Revue Wagnerienne, Revue indépendante, Mercure de France, Vogue, Symboliste,* and *Revue blanche.* Among the critics writing for such outlets were Edouard Dujardin, Gustave Kahn, Paul Léautaud, and Remy de Gourmont. Gourmont was the leading critic for the *Mercure*; his *Livres des masques* (2 volumes, 1896–98) collect his essays on the symbolists. He saw the critic as the creator of art by helping his own age to overcome its prejudices so that it could recognize beauty, no matter what its aesthetic form might be. Paul Verlaine's *Poètes maudits* (1884) is an introduction to the new poetry; it was Verlaine who recognized that Stéphane Mallarmé was both a poet and a critic. The latter wrote a series of articles for the *Revue blanche* in 1895–96 called "Variations sur un sujet." These spell out many of his mature aesthetic ideas; two of the most influential are "Le Livre, instrument spirituel" and "Le Mystère dans les lettres."

Many critical essays written before World War I continued to be impressionistic, based primarily on the taste of the critic. The two most famous critics to which this label is attached were Jules Lemaître and Anatole France. During the 1890s their opponents labeled their critical position as *dilettantisme*. Gourmont's *Promenades littéraires* (1904–7) are also impressionistic, but Gourmont's impressionism constitutes a process of dissociation, an analysis of the ideas within a text.

Ferdinand Brunetière, leading critic among the *normaliens* (writers linked to the Ecole normale supérieure), was an enemy of both impressionistic criticism and naturalism. As director of the *Revue des deux mondes*, he also revealed little sympathy for most contemporary literature. A classicist by taste, Brunetière nevertheless was influenced by the new theories of evolution, which he applied to a theory of literary genres: genres rise, evolve, and change like species. His many books include *Le Roman naturaliste* (1883), *L'Evolution de la poésie lyrique en France* (1894), *Etudes critiques* (1880–1925), and *Balzac* (1906). A decisive audience with Pope Leo XIII in 1894 turned Brunetière toward a form of social catholicism as the answer to the issues of his day. Brunetière came to speak of the bankruptcy of science because of its failure to fulfill its promises of social progress.

Brunetière's dual role as literary and social critic is representative of the response of many writers to the problems of *la belle époque*, most notably the Dreyfus affair. Critics and their papers and journals became *engagés* in the controversy. For instance, *La Revue blanche*, founded in 1891, included writers like Léon Blum who were labeled as belonging to the party of the intellectuals because of their leftist, pro-Dreyfus position. On the other hand, the linking of nationalism, traditionalism, and royalism in the Action française movement also touched literary criticism. Charles Maurras, although primarily a political writer, also wrote literary essays that reflect his conservative ideology—for example *Trois idées politiques* (1898) on Chateaubriand, Michelet, and Sainte-Beuve.

The leading university figure before World War I was Gustave Lanson. Basing his essays on meticulous research focused on the factors affecting the genesis of a work, Lanson claimed that literary interpretation must be based on historical research. He thus directed the teaching and criticism of literature in the university milieu toward a science of literary history; this historical orientation, an extension of the ideas of Taine, remained dominant within universities through the rest of the Third Republic. One of Lanson's mature works that demonstrates his historical method is the two-volume collection, *Mélanges d'histoire littéraire* (1906).

The writer Charles Péguy (who had sided with Dreyfus) vehemently opposed the influence of Taine and of Lanson because they kept criticism from focusing its attention on the text itself. Péguy presented his position both in the journal *Cahiers de la Quinzaine*, which he founded (with which figures such as Romain Rolland and Daniel Halévy were connected), and in his study of Hugo, *Victor-*

Marie comte Hugo (1910). Péguy claimed a superiority of insight for any creative writer over a professional critic in interpreting the life and work of the great writers of the past.

A turning point in the history of modern French criticism occurred when the journal, *La Nouvelle Revue française* (*NRF*), was founded in 1909 with André Gide as its guiding spirit. Gide's own stance was that of an enlightened classicist who wished to turn criticism toward vital aesthetic issues and away from moral dogmatism. Many of the critics and writers connected with the *NRF*, like Gide himself, had been influenced by the symbolist movement. Under the direction of Jacques Rivière (secretary-general in 1911 and editor from 1919 until his death in 1925), the *NRF* fostered the publication of new works by new authors and of essays by an outstanding group of critics. Whereas critics in the early years of the Third Republic had failed to do justice to their contemporaries (one thinks of Brunetière), Rivière wrote major essays on such figures as Paul Claudel, Gide, Marcel Proust, and Igor Stravinsky and on the dada movement. Rivière approaches each work or author without preconceived moral judgments, combining intellectual analysis of the inner world of the work with an awareness of its emotional impact. After Rivière's untimely death, Jean Paulhan succeeded him as editor of the *NRF* in 1925.

Albert Thibaudet became the leading French critic between the two world wars, primarily through the essays he wrote for the *NRF*. (Thibaudet taught at the University of Geneva from 1924 until his death in 1936.) Influenced by the symbolists and by Henri Bergson, Thibaudet first gained attention for his book-length study of Mallarmé, published in 1912. Thibaudet believed that the greatest critics are the creative critics (such as Paul Valéry) who have imaginative powers themselves. The critic reconstructs or recreates the work through both sympathetic identification with the creative genius of the writer in question and through such analytic concepts as genre, tradition, generation, and geography.

In fact, a number of authors of imaginative literature engaged in literary criticism during the first decades of the twentieth century. In addition to Gide, whose early essays were collected in two volumes, *Prétextes* (1908) and *Nouveaux prétextes* (1911), only a few examples can be cited. In his posthumous volume, *Contre Sainte-Beuve*, Proust rejects his own early allegiance to Ruskin and reflects on Sainte-Beuve; Proust postulates the complete originality of the creative artist and the origin of the work deep within a self that is not the social self of the artist. Valéry published a series of extremely important essays during his career, beginning with "Introduction à la méthode de Léonard de Vinci" (1894). (Valéry was silent as a critic between 1895 and 1917.) He is almost always concerned with identifying the central attitude and operating method of consciousness of an author. For Valéry, the aesthetic object is a complex formal equivalent of a mental construct. After 1917, Valéry began to write a steady series of critical essays, collected in the five-volume *Variété*, published through 1945.

The 1920s saw two major developments in literary criticism and theory. In

1925, the abbé Henri Bremond read a paper on pure poetry at a meeting of the five academies. Using the analogy with religious mysticism and prayer, Bremond maintained that poetry conveys an emotion to the reader born of a spiritual element mysteriously present in the words of the text (apart from their meaning). The publication of Bremond's paper set off a series of replies and rejoinders; a debate about pure poetry ensued that touched on the issues of form, content, and language in modern poetry. Over two hundred articles on the subject appeared in the next five years, including an essay by Valéry.

The second development in the 1920s was crucial in directing the attention of both creative writers and critics to the creative process itself. The surrealist movement, particularly in the manifestos of André Breton in 1924 and 1930, reflected not only the discoveries of Sigmund Freud but also the practice of the poets and artists themselves in emphasizing that the imagination expresses the images and themes of the subconscious.

While not followers of the surrealists, a group of critics began to emerge in the 1930s who have been called critics of consciousness. Marcel Raymond's *De Baudelaire au surréalisme* (1933) and Albert Béguin's *L'Ame romantique et le rêve* (1937) were studies of immense influence, tracing the roots of romantic, post-romantic, and surrealist poetry in the dreams and preoccupations of the subconscious. Later critics, like Georges Poulet, who came to see the act of reading as an encounter with the consciousness of an author were influenced by Raymond, Béguin, Thibaudet, and the far-ranging essayist Charles Du Bos (who died in 1939). The essays of Du Bos (published in seven volumes, entitled *Approximations*) reveal the influence of Henri Bergson and an antirational stance. Literature for Du Bos constitutes the full expression of life and of the soul of the genius; in the act of writing, an author of genius can express both the essence of a Bergsonian *durée* and of his own consciousness.

In the later 1930s two major figures appeared on the critical scene. Jean-Paul Sartre's first critical essays were published by the *NRF* between 1936 and 1940. In these pieces Sartre examines novels by writers like William Faulkner, John Dos Passos, and François Mauriac; his analysis reflects his own philosophical concerns based on a post-Hegelian, Husserlian set of categories.

The philosopher-physician Gaston Bachelard published his first major studies, *La Psychanalyse du feu* (1937) and *L'Eau et les rêves* (1940). He analyzed the imagery of literature as a starting point in order to discover the structures of the imagination. Building on the ideas of Carl Jung and the surrealists, Bachelard shows an alchemy of the basic elements of material existence in the images of the poetic imagination.

Within the Third Republic, there was a movement toward an ever-richer and more complex approach to the criticism of literature, an approach amply illustrated by the criticism appearing after World War I. Both theoretical and practical criticism also evolved toward more narrowly aesthetic concerns (that is, toward the description of the nature of creativity and of formal qualities in the art object) while drawing on the insights and analytical vocabulary of other disciplines such as psychology and philosophy.

R. Fayolle, *La Critique littéraire en France du XVIe siècle à nos jours* (Paris, 1964); W. Fowlie, *The French Critic, 1549–1967* (Carbondale, Ill., 1968); S. Lawall, *Critics of Consciousness, the Existential Structures of Literature* (Cambridge, Mass., 1968); W. Martins, *Les Théories critiques dans l'histoire de la littérature française* (Curitiba, 1952); P. Moreau, *La Critique littéraire en France* (Paris, 1960); J. K. Simon, ed., *Modern French Criticism from Proust and Valéry to Structuralism* (Chicago, 1972); A. Thibaudet, *Physiologie de la critique* (Paris, 1930); R. Wellek, *History of Modern Criticism*, vol. 4: *The Later Nineteenth Century* (New Haven, 1965).

P. A. Ward

Related entries: BACHELARD; BREMOND; BRETON; BRUNETIERE; DREYFUS AFFAIR; GIDE; FAGUET; LANSON; LITERATURE; MALLARME; MAURRAS; PEGUY; PROUST; RENAN; SARTRE; SURREALISM; TAINE; THIBAUDET; THOUGHT AND INTELLECTUAL LIFE; VALERY; ZOLA.

LITERATURE. The literature of the Third Republic breaks conveniently into two periods. Prior to World War I, writers were occupied with challenging the conventions of their art forms with more or less radical experiments. Thereafter, perhaps because of the horrors of modern warfare, a didactic tone predominates.

On the surface, the turmoil that accompanied the establishment of the Third Republic was not reflected in letters. While Victor Hugo, whose rant against Napoleon "le petit" had amused and shocked his public, returned from self-imposed exile, prepared to remain center stage until his death in 1885, most of the great romantics had already passed away, and there was little to impede the triumphant march of positivism's allies. Gustave Flaubert had just finished *L'Education sentimentale* (1869), which, though considerably less pathological than the Goncourt brothers' efforts, presented a decidedly pessimistic view of middle-class France. Emile Zola was about to begin publishing his enormously successful masterpiece in twenty volumes, *Les Rougon-Macquart* (1871–92). Little seemed to have changed.

There is some question whether Zola really believed his frequently trumpeted claims that as a novelist he was a scientific investigator searching for truth. He was a master of public relations, and he knew that the controversy he aroused would sell books. More than anything else, his pseudoscientific naturalism provided him with a loose framework to study the influence of heredity, environment, and circumstances on the two families, which he followed into all levels of the Second Empire. The results prove him to be a first-class storyteller who excelled at thematic development and at animating the inanimate, whether the still of *L'Assommoir* (1877) or the locomotive of *La Bête humaine* (1890). His skill at making crowds come alive, as he did, for example, in *Germinal* (1885) and *L'Oeuvre* (1886), is particularly notable. But when the rotting body of Nana (1880) and the dramatic defeat of *La Débâcle* (1892) finally announce the fictional death of the Second Empire, in fact Napoleon III had long ago left the scene, and Zola was being pushed to the wings.

Poets like Arthur Rimbaud (1854–91), Tristan Corbière (1845–75), and Lautréamont (1846–70) foreshadow the literary world until the cataclysm of World War I. Their cynicism marks the end of the century's blind faith in science, progress, and the individual. More important, they felt free to experiment with the poetic conventions and devices that had dominated poetry for several hundred years. Paul Verlaine (1844–96) provided a model. In the pursuit of musicality, he developed the *vers impair*, surely aware that *impair* can mean either the uneven number of syllables that characterized his verses or "blunder." His internal rhymes, accentual rhythms, and sonorities weakened the traditional building block of French poetry, the alexandrine, to the point where it never fully recovered. Rimbaud and other poets seemingly turned disdainful backs on the world as they found it. Their attempts to remake the world by placing images in strange and shocking relationships led directly to surrealism.

Perhaps only Stéphane Mallarmé (1842–98) was completely aware of the extent of his revolutionary activities. The young symbolist school claimed him as master, and through the Tuesday gatherings at his home on Rome Street, he had significant, formative impact on such major artists as Henri de Régnier (1864–1936), Paul Claudel (1868–1955), André Gide (1869–1951), Joris-Karl Huysmans (1848–1907), and Paul Valéry (1871–1945). Following in the footsteps of Baudelaire, Mallarmé exploited the use of familiar objects and qualities like windows, mirrors, eyes, and the color azure to express symbolically his feeling of alienation and desire for perfection. The poetic results of his aspiration for the Ideal are considerably less accessible than the poems of Baudelaire, however. Mallarmé explicitly sought an audience of elite readers capable of going beyond the perceptible level of appearances to the ideal essence of things. He typifies the first thirty or forty years of the Third Republic in his revolts against the prevailing techniques and conventions of poetry.

The frustration apparent in Lautréamont is particularly noticeable during Mallarmé's day. Artists manifested their growing dissatisfaction with the old ways of making aesthetic objects. They proclaimed an important quest for new subjects, techniques, and forms, perhaps even for a new vision. Writers increasingly refused to cater to the public's expectations of neatly rhymed verse, clearly delineated plots, and well-defined characters. It was as though these artists felt blocked in their efforts to create meaningful aesthetic experiences. There was nothing unconscious in their revolt. Few writers show such a mastery of their genre as Huysmans, Gide, Mallarmé, and Valéry. Nor did they expect a great popular following. Huysmans, in fact, was dumbfounded when his *Là-Bas* (1891) turned out to be a success.

Long a disciple of Zola, Huysmans announced his independence with the publication of *A rebours* (1884). Though the book sold few copies, sales were apparently to the most influential writers, for its impact was enormous, both in the realm of its subject matter—the main character, Des Esseintes, came to typify the Decadents—and in the realm of technique—its virtually nonexistent plot is widely believed to contain interchangeable chapters. He justified his interest in dreams, hallucinations, and outright madness by having one of his characters announce a turn away from naturalism toward a "spiritualistic naturalism." His later efforts push the novel to the limits of the genre. In *En rade* (1887), three hallucinatory dreams interrupt a weak plot to serve as major structuring devices. *Là-Bas* intersperses the story of the main character's investigation of the occult with parallel chapters from the history he is writing on Bluebeard. *La Cathédrale* (1898) and *L'Oblat* (1903) seemingly attempt to make plot of description.

Henry Becque's *Les Corbeaux* (1882) and *La Parisienne* (1885) brought naturalistic drama to an end almost before it began, though it had an important legacy in the belief that theater could directly touch the life of its day. In a theater that had become openly moralizing, Octave Mirbeau (1850–1917) comments bitterly on the viciousness of the wealthy and the powerful. François de Curel (1854–1929), Paul Hervieu (1857–1915), and Eugène Brieux (1858–1922) deal with the conflict of the classes, with marriage and divorce, and with the problems of an institutionalized bureaucracy, castigating injustice wherever they found it.

Most theater, however, was far less serious. If romanticism had really died with the failure of Hugo's *Les Burgraves* (1843), it experienced rebirth in the last few years of the century. There were a few notable plays, like Edmond Rostand's *Cyrano de Bergerac* (1897) and Georges de Porto-Riche's *Amoureuse* (1891), but for the most part the Parisian public was so preoccupied in an orgy of self-indulgent sex, food, and ostentation that it wanted a more facile entertainment. It was richly satisfied by the vaudeville of Georges Feydeau (1862–1921) and perhaps almost as well by the long-forgotten authors of the Théâtre du boulevard. The themes of these plays were as old as melodrama—love and marriage, duty and death, crisis and reprieve—relieved by more topical concerns like divorce or feminism.

Although symbolism encouraged all too many poets to indulge in vapid verse describing wan youths wandering through enchanted, often bejeweled, forests, there were notable practitioners of the movement in both theater and poetry. Maurice Maeterlinck's *Pelléas et Mélisande* (1892) and *L'Oiseau bleu* (1909) succeed in presenting man in the midst of eternity, mystery, and poetry. Valéry struggled to come to grips with the workings of the human mind. The precision of his verse as he plays with several levels of meaning constantly suggests the existence of something living behind the fluttery edge of perception. The actual number of his poems is limited, but like those of his even more unproductive spiritual father, Mallarmé, they have had considerable impact. *Charmes* (1922), which includes the widely anthologized "Cimetière Marin," brought his poetic career to a virtual close. His influence remained and remains active, however, through his essay-meditations on poetry, creation, and consciousness. These writings reveal his constant preoccupation with awareness and labor in the effort to attain perfection.

The aesthetic confusion prior to the First World War also produced three major figures, whose work may go in and out of fashion but whose basic value is seldom questioned: Claudel, Marcel Proust, and Gide. In Claudel's own rhythmical verse form influenced by classical and biblical poetry, his *Grandes Odes* (1904–8) and, especially, his theater received inspiration largely from the Bible. The results frequently disconcerted, if not horrified, the Catholic church of which he considered himself a part. The interest in such plays as *Partage du midi* (1906), *L'Annonce faite à Marie* (1910), and *Le Soulier de Satin* (1924) continued, however, to grow through his long life, making him—along with Valéry and Gide—a major literary figure, with all the public attention that that implies in France.

Proust had a relatively short life. Born almost with the Third Republic in 1871, he died in 1922. Still, if, as he believed, his real life is incorporated in his 3,000 page novel, *A la recherche du temps perdu* (1913–27), he has already lived long, with no end in sight. Proust's obvious preoccupation with aesthetics places the origin of his masterpiece in the period prior to the First World War where the author was formed. Its other themes—love, death, sickness, time, memory, change—make it timeless. Scholars used to bemoan the apparent fact that the long war years encouraged the asthmatic author to closet himself with potions and pen and double the length of an already extensive novel. Several tried to suggest passages that because "unwisely" added, could be safely cut. More recent readers have appreciated the loosely connected narrative blocks as an indication that the novel's unity depends not on narration but rather on thematic development. The work's young narrator can make little sense of his life and is consequently unable to write the masterpiece he dreams about until well into a sated but discouraged middle age. Suddenly, because of an almost miraculous moment of involuntary memory, he then understands that he himself provides the unity for his life. At that point, near the end of the novel, as the reader sees the hidden organization, the narrator decides to begin to write his work of art. *A la recherche du temps perdu* provides a picture of the period's high society, governed by an idle aristocracy still hanging onto life though its usefulness had long since ended. And it serves as a capstone for the nineteenth-century novel. But more important, its innovative structure makes it a reference point in France's literature.

While Gide has considerable importance as an autobiographer, his major contribution was made in fiction, especially as a master stylist whose technical innovations continue to challenge modern writers and readers. To a large degree, it was Gide who, with Mallarmé and Proust, established the grounds for the aesthetic experimentation that has occupied recent novelists. By his own definitions, he wrote only one novel—he reserved the term for the most complex of fictions—but he composed several satirical works, a volume of verse, and numerous *récits* or narrations. The ironic *récits* include the highly regarded *L'Immoraliste* (1902), *La Porte étroite* (1909), and *La Symphonie pastorale* (1919). Making use of unreliable narrators, these works reveal a Gide who proposed a clear-headed individualism devoted to a search for freedom, purity, and pleasure. The satirical *Les Caves du Vatican* (1914) marks his frustration with the novel, his awareness of well-worn aesthetic conventions, and his mastery of the techniques of the art form as it existed then. At the end of the work, one has a clear conception of the limitations of plot, character, themes, and symbols—in short, of most of the prevailing devices. His later attempt to go beyond such limited possibilities in *Les Faux Monnayeurs* (1925) has dated rapidly, though it has done nothing to downgrade his significance as a stimulating, aesthetic gadfly.

World War I left in its wake village after village with no living adult males, thousands of invalids incapable of taking an active part in society, and, in most writers, a sense of mission. They realized long before the atomic bomb that humanity is capable of destroying itself, and they felt called to see that it did not do so. The surrealists may constitute an exception. Under the direction of the theorist and poet André Breton (1896–1966), they combined exploration of psychic phenomena with continuing technical experimentation inspired by such writers as Guillaume Apollinaire (1880–1918). But even the surrealists, despite their nihilistic beginnings in dada, could not effectively combat the trend of the times. By the mid-1930s, the group had virtually dissolved, and Louis Aragon (1897–) and Paul Eluard (1895–1952) had evolved toward political activism. They devoted their poetry to effecting significant change within society.

François Mauriac and Georges Bernanos propose a life of obedience to the Catholic church and commitment to Jesus Christ. While Mauriac contented himself for the most part with painting the troubled misery of godless men—in such novels as *Thérèse Desqueyroux* (1927) or *Le Noeud de vipères* (1932)—Bernanos attempted to represent man grappling, like Jacob, with God. His masterpiece, *Journal d'un curé de campagne* (1936), illuminates the mystical adventure of a priest's becoming the very communion sacrifice and joining with God.

Most writers did not raise their eyes so high in their quest for solutions to the century's problems. Though with differing specific answers, the majority looked to man. Jules Romains believed that the inherent goodwill of humanity would eventually win out over evil, a belief that wavered only occasionally through the twenty-seven volumes of *Les Hommes de bonne volonté* (1932–47). Romains' cycle of novels attempts to portray the advance of humanity not through a representative family or reappearing characters, as with his predecessors, Zola and Balzac, but by means of a diversity of individuals united only because of their belief in and progress toward a better world. Georges Duhamel had joined Romains as an early supporter of unanimism—a literary movement that rejected symbolism for the portrayal of a unifying thrust in the diverse lives of humanity. In his two cycles, that turning on the character Louis Salavin (1920–32) and that concerned with the Pasquier family (1933–45), his hope-filled humanism is slowly colored by the widespread disillusionment born from the tragic events of the late 1930s and early 1940s. This growing skepticism also mars the enlightened humanism of Roger Martin du Gard and his masterpiece, *Les Thibault* (1922–40). As with all of these novelists who looked optimistically to their own kind to prevent the kind of tragedies that marked the first quarter of the century, Martin du Gard's idealism and lucid self-control soon turn into an anguished contemplation of humanism's bankruptcy as World War II became a reality.

A similar pattern is apparent in the theater of the period's playwright, Jean Giraudoux (1882–1944). He devoted a rich, elegant style that charmed several generations to portraying the glory of being a human being, satisfied to be a man, and firmly convinced of being in control of his destiny. As his characters succeed in finding, if not preserving, a romantic love that delighted audiences, the didacticism so apparent in contemporary authors was muted by wit and poetry. Still, little by little, the optimistic pacifism and gay fantasy depart, heroism appears less possible, and one begins to make out the silhouette of anguished helplessness before humanity's apparently self-destructive nature. His late plays seem to lead into those of Jean Anouilh (1910–), who typically creates characters in the throes of irreconcilable needs or demands.

Over against those who believed to a greater or lesser degree in communal man, a significant number of writers proclaimed the efficacy of the individual. Henry de Montherlant (1896–1972) cast his characters in a decidedly heroic mode. In his novels, but especially in his theater, he creates a series of personages apparently incapable of bending before the ravages of life. Malraux had a short career as a novelist. The first novel, *Les Conquérants*, appeared in 1928, the last, *Les Noyers de l'Altenburg,* in 1943, after which he devoted himself to art criticism and public service. In all his creative work, he sets the adventures in moments of crisis, where heroic men and women rise above themselves, glorifying fraternity, integrity, and courage. *La Condition humaine* (1933), his best-known novel, takes place against the backdrop of the Communist revolution in China. A multinational and multiracial cast respond in differing ways to insult, degradation, torture, and death to leave the reader with a fairly clear sense of what it means to be human. But as he and such other writers as Antoine de Saint-Exupéry (1900–44) probe man's limits and glories, readers progressively have the sense of human weakness and incapacity before a world gone out of control. Early existentialistic works, like Jean-Paul Sartre's *La Nausée* (1938) and *Le Mur* (1939) merely emphasize the writers' frustration at their inability to make significant changes while sensing that they would nonetheless pay in the apparently unavoidable menace of the Second World War.

A. Balakian, *Surrealism: The Road to the Absolute* (New York, 1959); G. Brée and M. Guiton, *The French Novel from Gide to Camus* (New York, 1962); R. Dumesnil, *Le Réalisme et le naturalisme* (Paris, 1962); M. A. Caws, *The Eye in the Text: Essays on Perception, Mannerist to Modern* (Princeton, 1981); R. Lalou, *Le Théâtre en France depuis 1900* (Paris, 1951); M. Nadeau, *The History of Surrealism* (New York, 1965); H. Peyre, *French Novelists of Today* (New York, 1967); M. Raimond, *La Crise du roman, des lendemains du naturalisme aux années vingt* (Paris, 1966); M. Raymond, *De*

Baudelaire au surréalisme (Paris, 1940); R. Shattuck, *The Banquet Years: The Arts in France—1885–1918—Alfred Jarry, Henri Rousseau, Erik Satie, Guillaume Apollinaire* (New York, 1958).

A. H. Pasco

Related entries: ALAIN-FOURNIER; APOLLINAIRE; ARAGON; ARTAUD; AYME; BARBUSSE; BARRES; BERNANOS; BOURGET; BRETON; CATHOLIC LITERARY RENAISSANCE; CELINE; CLAUDEL; COCTEAU; COLETTE; DADAISM; DAUDET, A.; DAUDET, L.; DUHAMEL; EXISTENTIALISM; FRANCE; GIDE; HUGO; JARRY; LITERATURE, PROLETARIAN; LITERARY CRITICS AND CRITICISM; MALLARME; MALRAUX; MARTIN DU GARD; MAUPASSANT; MAURIAC; MAUROIS; MONTHERLANT; PEGUY; NOVEL, POLITICS AND THE; PROUST; RIMBAUD; ROMAINS; SAND; SARTRE; SURREALISM; THOUGHT AND INTELLECTUAL LIFE; VALERY; VERLAINE; VERNE; ZOLA.

LITERATURE, PROLETARIAN (1921–1940), a term used to describe both a literary program occasionally advocated by the French Communist party (PCF) and a literary school, outside the party, dominated by Henry Poulaille (1896–). For the Communists, taking their cue from the U.S.S.R., proletarian literature would be the class counterpart of the bourgeois literature then dominant. Communist interest was limited by doubts over whether a proletarian literature did or could exist and by PCF preference for established writers. Although some attempts to sponsor a working-class literature were made earlier, the PCF supported this doctrine most actively from 1926 to 1929 when Henri Barbusse (1873–1935), author of the antiwar novel *Le Feu*, controlled the literary page of *L'Humanité*. His goal was to create a new literature by fusing intellectual and manual labor. From 1928 to 1935, Barbusse carried on his campaign in the fellow-traveling journal *Monde* where he made overtures to Poulaille and his group.

In 1930, an international Communist writers' congress at Kharkov (U.S.S.R.) condemned Barbusse's line as insufficiently worker oriented, but the Kharkov decision was not publicized in France until early 1932. For a short time the PCF backed the Kharkov version of proletarian literature based on "Rabcors," workers assigned to write about their factories. The Kharkov program was soon abandoned by the PCF under the influence of two factors. The first was the movement for unity on the Left, which began with the intellectuals in the Amsterdam-Pleyel antiwar movement in 1932, before being extended into the Popular Front in 1935. The second factor was the replacement of proletarian literature by the doctrine of socialist realism in the U.S.S.R. in 1932, which gradually spread to the PCF.

While the PCF was experimenting with and finally rejecting proletarian literature, Poulaille was building a literary movement around this concept. For Poulaille, proletarian literature (also referred to as literature of popular expression) meant literature that was proletarian in origin, reflected the lives of those who worked with their hands, and was intended for popular consumption.

Born in a working-class family in Paris, Poulaille was an autodidact who worked at a variety of trades, finally receiving a white-collar position with the editor Grasset. In the early 1920s, a few of his short stories appeared in *L'Humanité*, and in 1926 Poulaille took over the literary page of the Confédération générale du travail (CGT) daily, *Le Peuple*. To advocate and publish proletarian literature, he edited a series of short-lived journals: *Nouvel age* (1931), *Prolétariat* (1933), and *A contre courant* (1935–36). Poulaille further defined his school through polemics with two other groups, the populists and the Communists. The populists were bourgeois authors who took the people as their subject. Poulaille, himself an anarchist, disliked the Communist tendency to politicize literature.

While in theory proletarian literature should be the work of manual laborers, the school also included autodidacts no longer forced to work with their hands and, more rarely, *boursiers* (scholarship students) who still felt part of the people and described the class from which they sprang. Thus, the ancestry of proletarian literature included not only genuinely popular literature from the troubadours to the worker poets of the nineteenth century but also spiritual progenitors like the autodidact Rousseau and the *boursier* Charles Péguy. The true literary founders of the school, however, were Charles-Louis Philippe (1874–1909) and Lucien Jean (1870–1908). Philippe was a *boursier* and Jean an autodidact forced to break off his education. Good friends, both traveled in anarchist circles associated with the journal *L'Art social*, both worked for the Paris municipal administration, and both painted naturalistic but sentimental pictures of urban poverty; Charles-Louis Philippe's *Bubu de Montparnasse* had a pimp as a hero. The two proletarian writers who achieved most fame in their lifetimes were Emile Guillaumin (1873–1951) and Marguerite Audoux (1863–1937). Guillaumin was a self-educated peasant and agricultural syndicalist whose novel (patronized by Philippe) gave a peasant's view of country life. A similar success greeted Audoux's *Marie-Claire*, an autobiographical novel describing the author's life as a seamstress.

While Philippe, Jean, Guillaumin, and Audoux acted as models, Poulaille worked in close collaboration with Tristan Rémy (1897–). Rémy was also an autodidact and had worked for thirty years for the railroad companies. He published many novels set in working-class districts and poems through which breathes a great respect for manual labor. The heroes of the movement for proletarian literature were those workers, devoid of education, who managed to write, like the printing worker Lucien Bourgeois and the miner Constant Malva. Their works, like those of so many other proletarian writers, tended to autobiography and even simple testimony.

The ideals of the proletarian school, thus, were sincerity and authenticity. Saluting a story by Philippe that described the battle of a mother for her own and her child's bread, Poulaille declared that the struggle around the daily bread offered a better focus for literature than the psychological conflicts and problems of bourgeois heroes. He gave expression to this ideal through a series of autobiographical novels that began with *Le Pain quotidien (Daily bread)* and continued with *Pain de soldat (Soldier's bread)*.

Although only a few of their authors achieved national prominence, the movement for proletarian literature was important as a literary option for branches of the French Left and as a monument to the distance these writers, mostly graduates of the primary schools, felt from the intellectuals of the Left or Right who had gone to the parallel lycée system.

J.-P. A. Bernard, *Le Parti Communiste français et la question littéraire* (Grenoble, 1972); H. Poulaille, *Nouvel age littéraire* (Paris, 1930); M. Ragon, *Histoire de la littérature prolétarienne* (Paris, 1974).

A. Douglas

Related entries: ANARCHISM; BARBUSSE; COMMUNIST PARTY; CONFEDERATION GENERALE DU TRAVAIL; GUILLAUMIN; LITERATURE; PEGUY; POPULAR FRONT.

LITTLE ENTENTE, THE (1921–1938), a coalition of three Eastern European countries (Czechoslovakia, Rumania, and Yugoslavia) created in 1921 in response to the threat of a Habsburg restoration. During 1921 there were two attempts to restore Karl von Habsburg in Hungary. As a reaction to this, these countries drew up three similarly worded bilateral treaties (Rumania-Czechoslovakia, Rumania-Yugoslavia, Czechoslovakia-Yugoslavia), dedicated principally to averting a restoration and preventing changes in the June 1920 Treaty of Trianon (between the three countries and Hungary).

France acted as a sponsor to the Little Entente, mainly providing loans and military advice. France saw these small republics as barriers to a Habsburg restoration and bolshevism alike and created mutual alliance treaties with each of the countries (Czechoslovakia 1922, Yugoslavia 1927, Rumania 1926). While this gave the smaller countries security and protection, France got little in return. As a result, the Little Entente came to be more of a burden than a support for France and hindered its relations with Italy and Russia.

In February 1933, the Little Entente was reorganized because of the potential dangers of Nazi Germany. The three countries vigorously opposed Benito Mussolini's Four Power Pact in the spring of that year. With Adolf Hitler's victories in the 30 September 1928 Munich Agreement, the Little Entente ceased to be an important factor in international relations.

R. Albrecht-Carrié, *France, Europe and The Two World Wars* (New York, 1961); A. Komjathy, *The Crises of France's Eastern Central European Diplomacy* (New York, 1976); J. Néré, *The Foreign Policy of France from 1914 to 1945* (London, 1973); F. L. Schuman, *War and Diplomacy in the French Republic* (New York, 1931).

A. J. Staples

Related entries: FOREIGN POLICY; GERMANY, RELATIONS WITH (1914–1940); RUSSIA, RELATIONS WITH.

LITTRE, EMILE (1801–1881), philologist, positivist, and lexicographer. He was born in Paris. His avid interest in foreign languages prepared his later work in philology. In addition to being a brilliant linguist, he spent eight years studying medicine. Although he never became a doctor, his interest in medicine endured throughout his life. He produced articles of historical interest on medical topics, as well as a translation of the works of Hippocrates (10 vols., 1839–61), which he counted among his most important achievements.

Littré was elected to the French Academy in 1871, although he had been denied admission in 1863 because of his identification with the atheism and materialism of the positivists. As a student and defender of Auguste Comte, he helped popularize Comte's doctrines in articles and such books as *Analyse raisonnée du cours de philosophie positive* (1852) and *Conservation, révolution et positivisme* (1852). In a critical biography, *Auguste Comte et la philosophie positive* (1863), Littré remained a faithful disciple of Comte's earlier works and ideas but declined to follow him into the religious phase of his philosophy, feeling that Comte had forsaken experimental method for metaphysics.

Littré is best known for his four-volume *Dictionnaire de la langue française* (1863–72). In *Etudes et glanures pour faire suite à l'histoire de la langue française* (1880), he traces the history of the enormous task. The originality of the project rests in two complementary aspects. Each entry is discussed first in its relationship to contemporary usage and illustrated where possible with examples drawn from writers of the seventeenth, eighteenth, and nineteenth centuries. Second, the history of each word is examined for its relation to dialects and to other Romance languages. Examples of the word in context from the earliest time through the sixteenth century are arranged in chronological order. Finally, the etymology of the word is given. Certainly one of the most impressive dictionaries complied by one individual, it is still of great service to scholars and is considered one of the finest examples of a dictionary that traces the changing usage and meaning of language.

S. Aquarone, *The Life and Works of Emile Littré* (Leyden, 1958); A. Rey, *Littré: L'humaniste et les mots* (Paris, 1970); J.-F. Six, *Littré devant Dieu* (Paris, 1962).

R. F. O'Reilly

Related entries: LITERARY CRITICS AND CRITICISM; POSITIVISM.

LOCARNO ACCORDS (October 1925), diplomatic initiatives promoted by German foreign minister Gustav Stresemann to reassure European nations (notably France) about Germany's intention to abide by the territorial provisions of the Treaty of Versailles (1919). The conference took place 5–16 October 1925 in Locarno, Switzerland. The ensuing accords (negotiated by Stresemann of Germany, Aristide Briand of France, and Austen Chamberlain of Great Britain) consisted of the Treaty of Mutual Guarantee ("the Rhineland Pact"), which guaranteed the status quo of the German frontiers of France and Belgium (as set by the Versailles Treaty), the demilitarization of the Rhineland zone, and an agreement not to attack each other; four nonagression pacts between Germany and its neighbors (Belgium, France, Poland, and Czechoslovakia); and two treaties of mutual assistance (between France and Poland, France and Czechoslovakia) in case of attack by Germany. These accords were signed by seven countries (Germany, Belgium, France, Great Britain, Italy, Poland and Czechoslovakia), which thereby committed themselves to the first overt peace policy since the war.

The immediate result of the Locarno Conference was the entry of Germany into the League of Nations (8 September 1926). For the first time in diplomatic history, the great powers surrendered their historic right to make war and turned instead toward a policy of pacifism and goodwill. The importance of the Locarno Accords lies more in their profound psychological effect than in the details of the treaties themselves. They constituted the end of the psychological aftermath of World War I, and the spirit of Locarno marked a brief era of security after decades of tension between France and Germany.

The years 1925 through 1929 are known as the Locarno era when this newfound possibility for peace prospered. The end of the 1920s, however, saw a decline of this spirit and of relations between Germany and its neighbors. Because of the economic depression, German reparations were no longer being paid after 1931 and in October 1933, Germany withdrew from the League of Nations. In 1936, Adolf Hitler dealt the Locarno Accords its final blow when he defied the treaties and remilitarized the Rhineland. The Locarno Accords were thus a sincere, if short-lived, attempt at peace but were unable to erase the fundamental rivalries and ideological differences between Germany and its neighbors.

A. Fabre-Luce, *Locarno: The Reality* (New York, 1928); G. Glasgow, *From Dawes to Locarno* (New York, 1925); J. Jacobson, *Locarno Diplomacy: Germany and the West 1925–29* (Princeton, 1972).

A. J. Staples

Related entries: BELGIUM, RELATIONS WITH; BRIAND; DISARMA-MENT CONFERENCE; GERMANY, RELATIONS WITH (1914–1940); RE-PARATIONS POLICY.

LOCKROY, EDOUARD (1840–1913), republican politician, deputy from the Eleventh Arrondissement of Paris (1876–1906); minister of commerce under Charles de Freycinet (1886-1887); minister of the marine under Léon Bourgeois (1895–1896) and Henri Brisson (1898) and Charles Dupuy (1898-9). Lockroy belonged to the same Masonic lodge as Jules Ferry, Emile Littré, and Louis Blanc. An ardent patriot and admirer of modern engineering, he used his talent for debate, biting wit, and organizational skills to promote a practical approach to the domestic and international problems that industrialization posed for the Republic.

Like many others of his generation, Lockroy saw culture and politics as closely intertwined. He had studied art as a youth, joined Giuseppe Garibaldi in Sicily (1860), acted as secretary and illustrator for Ernest Renan in the Near East, and then worked as a journalist for *Le Rappel*. During the Franco-Prussian War he was a battalion leader and mayor of the Eighth Arrondissement during the Commune. In 1873 he married Charles Hugo's widow and thus became an important figure in the circle around Victor Hugo, although the two men were not on good terms. Three years later he was elected to the Chamber of Deputies. Here he argued (1876) that amnesty for the Communards would return to France the skilled workers needed to reestablish its position as a leading producer of consumer goods. He supported the legalization of trade unions (1884) for similar reasons.

An acute awareness of the growing competition among industrializing nations colored all his policies. This is apparent in programs he designed to benefit skilled workers, small manufacturers, and large-scale industrialists, which reflect his belief that the interests of all three were inseparable from those of the nation. He adopted the pragmatic outlook characteristic of engineers like Gustave Eiffel, and as minister of commerce and minister of the marine he attempted to modernize the bureaucracy and encourage cooperation between government and private enterprise. His major achievements were the organization of the 1889 Universal Exposition, including contractual arrangements for the Eiffel Tower; the creation of the Ecole supérieure de la Marine; the reform of the Ministry of the Marine; and the introduction of a program intended to give the French navy an edge in the naval war with Germany he felt was inevitable.

"Nécrologie: Edouard Lockroy," *Le Temps,* (23 November 1913); E. Lockroy, *Au hazard de la vie* (Paris, 1913).

M. R. Levin

Related entries: BOURGEOIS; EIFFEL TOWER; FREYCINET; HUGO.

LOISY, ALFRED (1857–1940), Catholic priest and biblical scholar, key figure in the Catholic modernist movement of 1890–1910. He was born into a peasant family at Ambières (Marne) 28 February 1857. His poor health made it impossible for him to farm, and his intellectual promise and personal piety led him to the Catholic seminary at Châlons-sur-Marne in 1874. He studied at the Catholic University of Paris (later known as the Institut catholique) in 1878 and was ordained a priest the following year. Following a brief assignment in a country parish, Loisy was called back to the Institut, where he taught elementary Hebrew and worked toward a doctoral degree, which he received in 1890. While at the Institut in the 1880s Loisy was influenced by Monsignor Louis Duchesne, a professor of ecclesiastical history whose critical treatment of church history was regarded with suspicion by church officials. Loisy also attended Ernest Renan's lectures on the Old Testament at the Collège de France and studied Assyriology and Egyptology at the Ecole des hautes études of the Sorbonne.

Named professor of sacred scripture at the Institut in 1890, Loisy held this position until 1893 when the French bishops forced his resignation because of his unorthodox views on the issue of divine inspiration of the Scriptures. According to Loisy, belief in divine inspiration was a theological doctrine that should have no effect on the study of Scriptures, which should proceed according to the same critical techniques applied to other historical documents. From 1894 until 1899 Loisy served as chaplain at a Dominican convent at Neuilly. While there he continued to write and publish, and in 1900 he was appointed a lecturer in the religious sciences at the Ecole des hautes études. Loisy was already a figure of some controversy when he published *L'Evangile et l'église* in 1902, a major work in the history of the Catholic modernist movement. In this work, a response to Adolf von Harnack's classical treatment of liberal Protestantism in *Das Wesen des Christenthums* (1900), Loisy described a church whose essence was not fixed but changed over time according to altered historical circumstances. Loisy argued that the church should accept and welcome such evolution since "the adaptation of the gospel to the changing circumstances of humanity is as pressing a need today as it ever was and ever will be." Loisy's argument included the controversial assertion that church doctrine and the sacramental system were the creation of the institutional church and not the direct result of Christ's teachings.

Loisy's book was formally condemned by Cardinal François Richard, archbishop of Paris, in January 1903. Encouraged by supporters such as Archbishop Edouard Mignot of Albi, Loisy responded with a defense of *L'Evangile, Autour d'un petit livre* (1903), in which he defended the independence of biblical criticism from theology and proposed a clear distinction between the historical Jesus and the mythic figure of Christ. With the election of the conservative Pius X to the papacy in 1903, such positions became even less acceptable to church officials, and *L'Evangile* and several other of Loisy's books were placed on the Church's Index of Forbidden Books in that year. Forced to suspend his teaching in 1904, Loisy continued to say Mass and work as a scholar and polemicist. In 1907 the encyclical *Pascendi dominici gregis* condemned the modernists as heretics, and in 1908 Loisy was formally excommunicated. These actions of the papacy effectively ended the attempt by the modernists to adjust Catholic positions on the Scriptures and church history to the findings of modern historical scholarship. Loisy remained an active scholar for the rest of his life, at the Collège de France (1909–26) and the Ecole des hautes études (1924–27). In his retirement Loisy published his *Mémoires pour servir à l'histoire religieuse de notre temps* (3 vols., 1930–31). He died in Paris in 1940.

A. Houtin and F. Sartiaux, *Alfred Loisy; sa vie—son oeuvre; manuscrit annoté et publié avec une bibliographie Loisy . . . par Emile Poulat* (Paris, 1960); E. Poulat, *Histoire, dogme et critique dans la crise moderniste,* 2d ed. rev. (Paris, 1979); B. M. G. Reardon, ed., *Roman Catholic Modernism* (Stanford, Calif., 1970).

T. A. Kselman

Related entries: BRUNETIERE; CATHOLIC LITERARY RENAISSANCE; RENAN.

LOUBET, EMILE (1838–1929), seventh president of the Republic (1899–1906), noted for his support of the Russian alliance and his efforts to seal an understanding with Great Britain. Born into a rural, republican family, he became a mayor, general councillor, deputy, senator, minister, prime minister, speaker of the Senate, and finally chief of state. Loubet sat with moderate elements in the Senate, to which he was elected in 1885. He formed a government in 1892, was caught up in the turmoil of the Panama scandal, and was accused (unjustly) of corruption. Supported by Georges Clemenceau, he was elected as Félix Faure's successor in the Elysée.

Loubet was perceived as a Dreyfusard and insulted by nationalist mobs on his return from Versailles (site of the presidential election) on 16 February 1899. After France's highest court reopened the Dreyfus case in June 1899, he was assaulted by a nationalist nobleman at the Auteuil racetrack. Yet the president's position throughout could more precisely be identified with that of seeking an end to the affair rather than of supporting one side or another. Although personally opposed to the anticlericalism that emerged in the wake of the Dreyfusard victory and to the separation of church and state, Loubet named the vigorously anticlerical Emile Combes to form a government in 1902, recognizing that he best reflected the Radical majority in the Chamber. He had similarly accepted legislation initiated by René Waldeck-Rousseau to repress the most politicized religious orders. Moreover, it was Loubet's reception of and visit to the Italian king that led to the break between France and the Vatican.

The president reinforced the now-traditional role of the Elysée by taking an active part in foreign policy making. He supported a pro-English policy and kept its leading spokesman, Théophile Delcassé, in office. He received, visited, and reassured Nicholas II of France's faithfulness to the Russian alliance, and his exchange of visits with Edward VII prepared the way for the Entente cordiale. Like his recent predecessors, however, he easily accepted a subordinate role to parliament. Loubet became the first president to refuse to seek reelection after completing a term of office.

A. Combarieu, *Sept ans à l'Elysée avec le président Emile Loubet* (Paris, 1932); A. Dansette, *Histoire des présidents de la République* (Paris, 1960); L. Derfler, *President and Parliament* (Boca Raton, 1983).

L. Derfler

Related entries: ANTICLERICALISM; CLEMENCEAU; COMBES; DELCASSE; DREYFUS AFFAIR; ENTENTE CORDIALE; PANAMA SCANDAL; PRESIDENT OF THE REPUBLIC, OFFICE OF; RUSSIA, ENTENTE WITH; WALDECK-ROUSSEAU.

LOUCHEUR, LOUIS (1872–1931), engineer and businessman who turned to government service and politics. A self-made man, he attended a lycée in Lille and entered the Ecole polytechnique as a scholarship student. After graduation and military service (his superior was Captain Ferdinand Foch), he took a job with the Chemins de Fer du Nord, where his organizing skills and engineering talent won him rapid promotion. In 1899 he left the railway to enter a business partnership with a former schoolmate.

The new company of Giros and Loucheur prospered and expanded rapidly, winning contracts for hydroelectric projects, electrification, and transportation construction in France, the colonies, the Ottoman Empire, and Russia. By 1914 Loucheur had become a leading industrialist, known for his innovation and willingness to take risks that invariably paid off.

When war was declared, Loucheur was mobilized as a lieutenant in the artillery, but he soon returned to the home front where he began construction of badly needed munitions factories. Loucheur's abilities gained the notice of political leaders. Aristide Briand brought him into the government as undersecretary for munitions. In 1917 he succeeded Albert Thomas at the munitions ministry, and he served as Georges Clemenceau's minister for industrial reconstruction. He was also a member of Clemenceau's war council, where he supported Foch's appointment as supreme commander for allied forces.

Loucheur was one of the first technocrats to enter government service. He had access to the highest circles of government although he had never been elected to office. After the war, he turned fully to politics, entering the Chamber of Deputies from the Nord. He participated in several cabinets during the 1920s, devoting his energies to problems of reconstruction, subsidized housing, and social questions. He was a champion of European cooperation and reconciliation who participated in several international conferences, notably the Locarno (1925) and The Hague (1929) meetings. He represented France for two years at the League of Nations in the 1920s.

L. Loucheur, *Carnets secrets* (Brussels, 1962).

J. K. Munholland

Related entries: BRIAND; BUSINESSMEN; CLEMENCEAU; FOCH; THOMAS; WORLD WAR I, FRANCE'S ROLE IN.

LUCHAIRE, JEAN (1901–1946), diplomatic journalist, youth leader, and director of *Notre temps* and *Les Nouveaux Temps*. Born and raised in Italy where his father, Julien, a distinguished professor of Italian literature, spent many years establishing French institutes, Jean Luchaire came to internationalism as naturally as to journalism. At the age of 12 he launched the first of several youth journals to promote Franco-Italian friendship and, later, European unity. He took up professional journalism in 1921 to support a growing family. In the early 1920s, Luchaire wrote for *L'Ere nouvelle, Le Matin, Le Petit Parisien* and *L'Homme libre*, before serving as secretary-general of *La Volonté* and editor of *Le Carnet de la semaine*, both owned by the notoriously corrupt Albert Dubarry. For all these papers, Luchaire was primarily a commentator on foreign affairs.

Close to the Radical party, active in the Jeunesse laïques et républicaines, and a member of Richard Coudenhove-Kalergi's Pan-Europa movement, Luchaire held views on diplomatic questions typical of the more pacifist elements on the Left. His regular beat, the Quai d'Orsay and Geneva, brought him into frequent contact with Aristide Briand, whose friendship he cemented by providing the foreign minister with detective novels. The favor was returned in 1928 when Briand initiated a Quai subsidy for the last and only successful of Luchaire's youth journals, *Notre temps*. Founded as a monthly in 1927 and appearing weekly from 1930, *Notre temps* was arguably the most important outlet for the thought of the generation born in the first decade of the Twentieth Century. Loosely identified with the Radical party, its contributors included not only such young Radicals as Bertrand de Jouvenel, Pierre Mendès-France, Jacques Kayser, and Jean Montigny, but also such Socialists as Pierre Brossolette, Paul Marion, and Marcel Déat.

Luchaire saw himself as a guardian of the idealistic realism of his generation, which he defined in his *Une Génération réaliste* (Paris, 1929). What such realism entailed on an international level, always his prime concern, was European unity and especially a Franco-German understanding. To further this goal, Luchaire, together with a young German art teacher, Otto Abetz, initiated a series of yearly camps to bring together politically active youth from their respective countries. The series, begun at Sohlberg in 1930, enjoyed considerable success until Adolf Hitler's victory broke its momentum, and a January 1934 meeting in Berlin proved to be the last. Luchaire, meanwhile, used an ever-increasing governmental subsidy to transform *Notre temps* into a daily in 1933, which lasted until Louis Barthou ended the subsidy a year later. Although Laval restored a small subsidy in 1935, *Notre temps* appeared only irregularly until the war.

Luchaire continued to advocate a Franco-German understanding, but his association with Abetz, Joachim von Ribbentrop's agent in France, increasingly tarnished his reputation. By the late 1930s, Luchaire was embittered enough that one can give credence to reports that he was being subsidized by the German embassy in Paris. There is no doubt that it was massive German support, directed his way by Abetz, Hitler's ambassador to occupied France, that enabled Luchaire to become director of a major collaborationist daily, *Les Nouveaux Temps,* and to become head of the press corporation in German-controlled Paris, activities for which he was executed in 1946. The cloud over his final years, however, has unjustly led to the neglect of his important role in promoting internationalism earlier in his career.

C. Lévy, *Les Nouveaux Temps et l'idéologie de la collaboration* (Paris, 1974); Julien Luchaire, *Confession d'un français moyen,* vol. 2 (Florence, 1965).

J. R. Braun

Related entries: BRIAND; DEAT; GERMANY, RELATIONS WITH (1914–1940); ITALY, RELATIONS WITH; JOUVENEL; MARION; MENDES-FRANCE; NEWSPAPERS, ROLE OF; ROCHE, EMILE.

LYAUTEY, HUBERT (1854–1934), marshal of France, colonial administrator, and man of letters. He has been described as a royalist who served the Republic and built an empire. The description captures the complexity of Lyautey's contribution to French history. Born into an aristocratic family of royalist and Catholic views, Lyautey followed a family tradition of service to France when he entered St.-Cyr in 1873, despite a childhood injury that had nearly paralyzed him. Under the influence of the Catholic social reformer, Albert de Mun, Lyautey became concerned with the social cleavages between soldiers and officers in the French Army. He urged that officers become concerned with the social and spiritual welfare of draftees in the mass army, and he embodied such ideas in an article "On the Social Role of the Officer in Universal Military Service," published anonymously in 1891. His views proved unpopular with his superiors, who decided to send the young officer to distant Tonkin as a reprimand.

The Tonkin assignment was a turning point in Lyautey's career. Having become bored with the sterile routines of garrison life and tired of the refinements of the aristocratic literary salons of Paris, Lyautey welcomed an opportunity to satisfy his taste for action and adventure. Under the guidance of his mentor, Joseph Gallieni, first in Indochina and then in Madagascar, Lyautey became an advocate of the officer's mission as builder of the French empire. In Lyautey's phrase, the colonial army was "an organization that marches," combining conquest with responsibility for the construction of roads, schools, and hospitals that would benefit and win the gratitude of France's newly acquired colonial subjects. During his apprenticeship Lyautey became convinced that only officers on the spot understood the needs of empire, while the politicians in Paris hesitated.

Promoted to colonel in 1900, Lyautey soon had occasion to demonstrate his ideas and his taste for independent action along the Algerian-Moroccan border. In 1904 his aggressive action led to the occupation of Moroccan villages and embarrassed the foreign minister, Théophile Delcassé, who had embarked on a delicate maneuver to gain French ascendancy in that region. He continued to press for military intervention in Morocco, and after a tour of duty in France he returned to Africa in 1912, this time to subjugate Morocco, which had been declared a French protectorate. Through a combination of force and the exploitation of Moroccan customs, Lyautey gradually pacified much of the mountainous country. Despite the depletion of his forces and the government's order that he withdraw to the coast, Lyautey pressed his campaigns into the interior throughout the First World War.

Lyautey briefly served as war minister (December 1916–March 1917) under Aristide Briand, but his imperious manner led to conflict with the deputies, and his resignation brought down the Briand cabinet. He returned to Morocco to pursue his pacification policies in the 1920s while simultaneously promoting the commercial development of Morocco. In 1921 he was made a marshal of France for his services. The intractable resistance of Abd-el-Krim in the Rif region caused Lyautey considerable difficulty, however, and led to his replacement by Marshal Philippe Petain in repressing Abd-el-Krim's rebellion in 1925-26. Lyautey returned to France, his retirement clouded by this Rif war. He returned to public life as the organizer of a massive colonial exposition in 1931, which enjoyed a certain popular success. It was rumored that the aged Lyautey would have become part of an authoritarian government if the right-wing leagues had succeeded in toppling the Third Republic at the time of the 6 February 1934 riot in Paris.

Y. de Boisboissel, *Dans l'ombre de Lyautey* (Paris, 1954); G. Hardy, *Portrait de Lyautey* (Mayenne, 1949); S. E. Howe, *Lyautey of Morocco* (London, 1931); A. Maurois, *Lyautey* (Paris, 1931); A. Scham, *Lyautey in Morocco* (Berkeley, 1970).

                                                                    J. K. Munholland

Related entries: ARMY: POLITICAL ROLE; BRIAND; FEBRUARY RIOTS; GALLIENI; MOROCCAN CRISES; MUN; OVERSEAS EMPIRE: FRENCH IMPERIALISM; OVERSEAS EMPIRE: MOROCCO; PETAIN; RIF REBELLION.

LYONS, autonomy seeking, republican, and left-of-center third city of France that was also the industrial heart of the south. Situated at the confluence of the Rhône and the Saône rivers, Lyons has been an important urban center since Roman times. The republican sentiments of a majority of the populace and the thwarting of municipal autonomy by governmental centralization under the Second Empire made for a revolutionary potential in Lyons in 1870. When the news of Napoleon III's surrender reached the city, crowds early on the morning of 4 September invaded the city hall and proclaimed France a Republic for the third time, an overthrow that occurred many hours before the one in Paris. Governed first by a self-appointed Committee of Public Safety and subsequently by an elected municipal council, Lyons pursued a policy of municipal autonomy. Feeling that Lyons still was bursting with revolutionary potential, the Russian anarchist Michael Bakunin hurried there and on 28 September tried to overthrow the state in a seizure of the city hall that lasted scarcely a few hours. The city's energies were principally directed, however, to repulsing the German invasion, and Lyons distinguished itself through recruitment of volunteers, subscription to war loans, and provisionment of the army. After the election of a pro-monarchist, centralist National Assembly and the conclusion of a peace treaty with Germany, the earlier concerns of republicanism and autonomy came to the fore again. The appearance of the Paris Commune prompted the creation of a commune in Lyons (22–25 March 1871) that evoked minimal support and was dissolved without bloodshed. A second attempt (30 April 1871) to support the Commune, an uprising in the area of La Guillotière, resulted in twenty-one persons being killed. As earnestly as the majority of the Lyonnais might support the Republic and municipal liberties, they sought to achieve them without resort to civil war.

The central government quickly stripped Lyons of its autonomy, and it was not until 1884 that a number of municipal liberties were regained. Radical Socialists predominated in the municipal council, a situation typified by the mayor's office being occupied by Edouard Herriot from 1905 until 1955, though the council in the twentieth century did include a significant number of Socialist and later Communist members. While conservatives never gained a majority in Lyons, they were a constant force in the city, especially through the strong Catholic education system.

During the Third Republic, the city limits of Lyons were not expanded, though surrounding towns experienced enormous population growth. The old Lyons of the peninsula—the slopes of La Croix-Rousse and the hill of Fourvière, plus the left bank of the Rhône—became the hub of what was and is still called the Lyonnaise agglomeration, where suburbs (principally on the plain to the east of the city) collectively came to surpass the city proper in population.

The city planning efforts of the Second Empire were not carried on by the Third Republic, so the urban growth lacked adequate thoroughfares and public parks. The shift of the population center reflected an economic realignment for Lyons. Once the focus of European silk weaving—which, surprisingly, even in the latter half of the nineteenth century was done on hand looms (120,000 in 1866)—Lyons' economy turned to chemicals, metallurgy, electrical machinery, and automobiles. These plants established themselves on the left bank of the Rhône and after the First World War dominated the city's economic life. Despite a mechanization of looms, the shift of the public's preference for cheaper and artificial materials doomed Lyons' silk industry to extinction. The cosmopolitan nature of the silk industry did leave its imprint on the entire Lyons commercial scene, though, for the city became a center of support for free trade and colonial expansion. And the establishment of Western Europe's first international trade fair in Lyons was a testimony to the city's worldwide commercial interests. The city's dedication to republicanism led it to acquire the title during the Second World War of Capital of the Resistance.

J. Archer, "La Naissance de la IIIe République à Lyon," *Cahiers d'histoire* 16 (1971); A. Kleinclausz, *Histoire de Lyon*, vol. 3 (Lyons, 1952); A. Latreille ed., *Histoire de Lyon et du Lyonnais* (Toulouse, 1975).

J. P. W. Archer

Related entries: COMMUNES IN PROVINCIAL CITIES; FRANCO-PRUSSIAN WAR; HERRIOT; SEPTEMBER 4, 1870; URBANIZATION AND THE GROWTH OF CITIES.